People's
Plants

A guide to useful plants of
southern Africa

THE CARL & EMILY FUCHS
FOUNDATION

The Carl & Emily Fuchs Foundation is a co-sponsor of the Teachers Without Borders project of the Research Focus Area, Self-Directed Learning at the North West University.

The Foundation is a private grantmaking organisation, operating nationally within South Africa. It was established on 1 August 1969 by the late Dr Carl and Mrs Emily Fuchs, with an endowment from the CJ Fuchs (Pty) Ltd group of companies, which was founded in 1929. The Foundation's reserves have subsequently been further augmented by the proceeds from the personal estates of Dr and Mrs Fuchs.

The Foundation is registered both as a non-profit organisation (NPO) and a public benefit organisation (PBO) and its funding focuses mainly on the areas of child care, health services and educational programmes.

On 1 August 2019, the Carl & Emily Fuchs Foundation will celebrate its 50th Anniversary. To mark the occasion, the Foundation introduced a national flagship project entitled "FUCHS – The Golden Years" which will run from 2016 to 2019. The project funding is structured into the four main strategic areas of the Foundation's grantmaking practice, namely:

- Childcare & Youth Development
- Health Services
- Higher Education
- Technology Development, Innovation & Entrepreneurship.

The NWU's Teachers Without Borders project, which aims to create indigenous knowledge science laboratories in rural schools, was awarded one of these national flagship grants in the Higher Education category.

People's Plants – A guide to useful plants of southern Africa will be used as a classroom resource by Life Sciences teachers and learners while engaging in ethnobotanical research. Schools are encouraged to participate in ethnobotanical surveys, using the Matrix Method. The NWU's Self-Directed Learning Research Focus Area aims to promote self-directed learning in our schools through this ethnobotanical research. *People's Plants* is a valuable resource in this regard and this informative and beautiful book will hopefully inspire a new generation of learners to consider a career in botany or ethnobotany.

Teachers Without Borders project: https://youtube/hrA3_MpsA2Q

REVISED EDITION

People's
Plants

A guide to useful plants of
southern Africa

Ben-Erik van Wyk ■ Nigel Gericke

BRIZA

Published by
BRIZA PUBLICATIONS
CK 90/11690/23
PO Box 11050, Queenswood 0121
Pretoria, South Africa
www.briza.co.za

First published in 2000, reprinted in 2003 and 2007
Second edition, revised and expanded, first impression 2018
Second edition, second impression 2022

ISBN 978-1-920217-71-6

This publication has been peer-reviewed by two international experts.

Authors' addresses:
Prof Dr Ben-Erik van Wyk
DST-NRF SARChI National Research Chair in Indigenous Plant Use
Department of Botany and Plant Biotechnology
University of Johannesburg
PO Box 524, Auckland Park 2006, Johannesburg, South Africa

Dr Nigel Peter Gericke
3 Loquat Place, 5 Loquat Walk, Constantia 7806, Cape Town, South Africa

Citing this publication
Van Wyk, B.-E. & Gericke, N. 2017. People's plants – a guide to useful plants of
    southern Africa. 2nd ed. Briza Publications, Pretoria.

Categories
Plants; Botany; Ethnobotany; South Africa; General Interest; South African Culture

Cover and inside design: Ronelle Oosthuizen
Typesetting: Melinda Bosch, Lebone Publishing Services
Reproduction: Resolution Colour, Cape Town
Printed in China by Guangzhou Timi Printing Co., Ltd

Contents

General introduction

SOUTHERN AFRICA IS exceptionally rich in plant diversity with some 30 000 species of flowering plants, accounting for almost 10 per cent of the world's higher plants. The region also has great cultural diversity, with many people still using a wide variety of plants in their daily lives for food, water, shelter, fuel, medicine and other necessities of life. This book gives a broad overview of indigenous plant use and is the first fully illustrated ethnobotanical guide for southern Africa.

In the last few decades the region has seen great changes in access to modern health care and education, shifts of populations from rural to urban areas, changes from subsistence farming to cash-crop production, migrant labour, and unprecedented environmental degradation. These changes in the sociocultural and environmental landscapes have severely eroded the indigenous knowledge base. The study of the use of plants by local people, or ethnobotany, is still a relatively underdeveloped discipline in southern Africa, and knowledge of indigenous plant use in the region needs urgent scientific documentation before it is irretrievably lost to future generations.

The intention of this book is primarily to raise awareness of the role plants play in people's daily lives by illustrating some of the most common and interesting traditional uses of plants, and highlighting selected categories of use for the first time. The book is not intended to be encyclopaedic in scope, and interested readers are encouraged to consult the primary references listed in each chapter. We hope to stimulate ongoing scientific documentation of indigenous knowledge for future generations, and most importantly, the application and beneficiation of this knowledge as instruments for sustainable development in the region. Innovative mechanisms need to be created to ensure that impoverished rural communities can share directly in the benefits arising from the commercialisation of this profound knowledge base.

A new era has already dawned in southern Africa. Unique collaborations are being forged between government departments, science councils, universities, local communities, traditional healers, farmers and entrepreneurs. The first natural products are already appearing on local and international markets.

REFERENCES ON SOUTHERN AFRICAN ETHNOBOTANY (only general ethnobotanical references are given here; publications on medicinal, food and craft plants are listed at the end of each relevant chapter): **Craven, P. & Sullivan, S. 2002.** *Inventory and review of ethnobotanical research in Namibia.* Occasional Contribution 3. National Botanical Research Institute, Windhoek. **Cunningham, A.B. 1989.** Indigenous plant use: balancing human needs and resources. In: Huntley, B.J. (ed.), *Biotic diversity in southern Africa*, Oxford University Press, pp. 93–106. **Cunningham, A.B., De Jager, P.J. & Hansen, L.C.B. 1992.** *The Indigenous Plant Use Forum Programme.* Foundation for Research Development, Pretoria. **Dold, T. & Cocks, M. 2012.** *Voices from the forest.* Jacana Media, Johannesburg. **Liengme, C.A. 1983.** A survey of ethnobotanical research in southern Africa. *Bothalia* 14: 621–629. **Marloth, R. 1913–1932.** *The Flora of South Africa* (6 vols). William Wesley, London. **Moffett, R. 2010.** *Sesotho plant and animal names and plants used by the Basotho.* Sun Media, Stellenbosch. **Ngwenya, M.A., Koopman, A. & Williams, R. 2003.** *Zulu botanical knowledge: an introduction.* National Botanical Institute, Durban. **Skead, C.J. 2009.** *Historical plant incidence in southern Africa: a collection of early travel records in southern Africa.* South African National Biodiversity Institute, Pretoria. **Smith, C.A. 1966.** Common names of South African plants. *Memoirs of the Botanical Survey of South Africa* 35. **Van der Stel, S. 1685.** *Simon van der Stel's journey to Namaqualand in 1685.* Facsimile edition, 1979. Human & Rousseau, Cape Town. **Van Wyk, B.-E. 2002.** A review of ethnobotanical research in southern Africa. *S. Afr. J. Bot.* 68: 1–13. **Van Wyk, B.-E., Gericke, N. 2000.** *People's plants – a guide to useful plants of southern Africa.* 1st ed. Briza Publications, Pretoria. **Williamson, J. 1975.** *Useful plants of Malawi* (revised and extended edition). University of Malawi, Zomba.

LEFT: Jan September of Dysselsdorp with an example of the flower pots that he makes from hollowed-out agave stems

Some popular cereals: oats, pearl millet, barley, sorghum, bread wheat, white maize, durum wheat and yellow maize

Winnowing basket with maize

Stamping maize

CHAPTER 1

Cereals

SINCE ANCIENT TIMES, cereals and products derived from cereals have formed the staple diets of practically all people. The annual cycle of sowing and harvesting has introduced cultural rituals that became an integral part of human existence since the dawn of agriculture, some 10 000 years ago. One of the most ancient forms of cereal use still exists in southern Africa – in the Kalahari the seeds of wild grasses that are harvested and stored by ants are collected and boiled into a nutritious porridge.

Cereals belong to the grass family, the Poaceae or Gramineae. What is usually called the grass grain or grass seed is actually a one-seeded dry fruit (caryopsis). The grain can be naked, as in wheat or maize, or it can have persistent husks or chaff, as in barley and oats. The husks are the fibrous remains of the grass flower or inflorescence. The major part of the grain or caryopsis is made up of endosperm, a storage tissue with starch-filled cells. The outer covering of the grain consists of two layers fused into one: the seed coat (testa) on the inside, fused to the fruit wall (pericarp) on the outside. Just inside this outer wall is a layer of protein or oil-rich cells known as the aleurone layer, which has an important contribution to the quality of cereal products. Inside the grain is also the embryo with its plumule, which will develop into the above-ground parts of the plant, and the radicle, which will form the root system.

Sorghum, finger millet and pearl millet are examples of indigenous grains which have remained in common use in southern Africa. Sorghum is the only indigenous cereal of commercial importance, with an annual harvest of about 74 000 tons. Pearl millet is commonly cultivated in rural areas and some wild grasses are locally valued, while others have been used in times of famine. Indigenous cereals as staple foods have gradually been replaced by exotics. Maize has been grown since early times and nowadays more than 7.5 million tons are produced each year. Wheat is a later arrival but it has become an important staple food, with an annual consumption of several million tons. Of lesser importance are barley and oats. There are large fluctuations in the annual yields as a result of erratic rainfall, resulting in surplus becoming available for export in some years, or a need for imports in other years. In former times, wild grasses often served as famine food during drought. Some examples are *Echinochloa stagnina, E. crus-pavonis, Miscanthus capensis, Sporobolus fimbriatus* and *Stenotaphrum secundatum.*

Apart from their direct use as food, cereal grains are very often converted to malt, which is used mainly to brew beer. Malting is a process of controlled germination followed by rapid drying. During germination, the carbohydrate storage tissue (endosperm) is partially converted, through enzymatic action, to simple sugars. The processes of malting and beer making are described in more detail in relation to beverages (see Chapter 6). In rural areas, pearl millet, finger millet and sorghum are most often grown for beer making, while maize has replaced other cereals as the main staple food. There are, however, many traditional dishes in which both the grains and the malt of indigenous cereals are used.

It is essential to preserve the genetic diversity of indigenous cereal crops by promoting the planting of these crops by subsistence farmers, and by maintaining the germplasm under controlled conditions. These crops have been selected for millennia for their vigour, drought-resistance and disease-resistance, and have a decreased requirement for water, fertilisers and pesticides. Although they generally give lower yields than maize, they provide fundamental food security to remote rural communities in times of drought.

Avena sativa | Poaceae | **OATS** ■ Oats is an exotic cereal, widely cultivated in southern Africa for human and animal food.

Coix lacryma-jobi | Poaceae | **JOB'S TEARS** ■ The plant is an exotic grass, occasionally cultivated in rural areas to obtain the swollen shiny beads (false fruits) within the flower heads, which are usually grey but vary from white to black. These are used to make necklaces. The plant is grown as a cereal crop in some parts of the world and is said to produce a useful beer.

Eleusine coracana | Poaceae | **AFRICAN FINGER MILLET**; *Afrika-manna, osgras* (Afrikaans); *uphoko* (Zulu); *mpogo* (Pedi); *majolothi* (Ndebele); *mufhoho* (Venda) ■ There are two types of African finger millet, namely a wild form, known as subsp. *africana*, and a cultivated form derived from it, known as subsp. *coracana*. Both are relatively small, tufted grasses (rarely up to one metre tall) with characteristic finger-like spikes bearing small, rounded grains. African finger millet is similar to Indian goosegrass (*Eleusine indica* subsp. *indica*) but the latter has smaller spikelets and oblong, not rounded grains.

This plant is an ancient African crop. The cultivated form (subsp. *coracana*) has been found in 5 000-year-old archaeological sites in Ethiopia. It is an important staple crop in many parts of Africa and has been cultivated throughout eastern and southern Africa since the beginning of the Iron Age. This millet is much hardier and less susceptible to pests and diseases than other grain crops and can be grown in almost any soil, as long as the rainfall is above 800 millimetres per year. Yields are not much affected by bird damage and vary tremendously, from 600 to 5 000 kilograms per hectare. What counts most in rural areas is not so much yield per hectare, as yield per unit labour, and at least some yield during drought.

The crop is harvested by hand, using a knife, and it is stored in the head until needed for porridge or beer. The heads are then threshed and winnowed, and the grains ground between stones or germinated to make a sweet malt. The flour may be baked or cooked with other ingredients. Finger millet is generally produced for own consumption, but trading is known to occur in Malawi. In southern Africa, finger millet is particularly popular (and more so in the past) as a source of malt for beer brewing, the popularity being ascribed to the sweetness of the malt. It is not a major food source except in Zambia and Malawi.

Eragrostis chloromelas, E. cilianensis, E. curvula and ***E. plana*** | Poaceae | ■ These indigenous grasses have sometimes been used as famine foods, to make bread and beer.

Fagopyrum esculentum | Polygonaceae | **BUCKWHEAT**; *bokwiet* (Afrikaans) ■ This introduced crop plant has heart-shaped leaves and small white flowers, followed by small triangular fruits and seeds. It is one of very few cereals which are not from the grass family. Buckwheat is grown in Europe and Asia for the seeds, which are traditionally used as a cereal to produce pancakes (e.g. the Russian *blini*), breakfast cereals, noodles, pastas and biscuits. In southern Africa it is mainly considered to be a fodder crop, although it is nowadays becoming popular as a health food.

Hordeum vulgare | Poaceae | **BARLEY**; *gars* (Afrikaans) ■ An important exotic cereal, widely grown for food and especially for malting to produce beer. As food, the hulled grain (groats, *gort*) is often eaten boiled or as soup. Naked forms of barley (*kaalgars*) are sometimes preferred.

Oryza sativa | Poaceae | **RICE** ■ An exotic plant and staple food in southern Africa, rice is reported to have been cultivated in some parts of Mozambique since the early 1800s.

Panicum miliaceum | Poaceae | **COMMON MILLET**, proso millet ■ This is an exotic plant, cultivated to a limited extent. The grains of *P. subalbidum* are eaten in Mozambique.

Indian finger millet (*Eleusine indica*, left) and cultivated African finger millet (*Eleusine coracana*, right)

Millets: African finger millet (left), Indian finger millet (middle) and common millet (right)

Flowers of buckwheat (*Fagopyrum esculentum*)

Buckwheat seeds

Pennisetum glaucum | Poaceae | **PEARL MILLET**, bulrush millet (English); *babala, manna* (Afrikaans); *leotsa* (Pedi); *nyalothi* (Sotho); *inyouti* (Ndebele); *mhuga, mhungu* (Shangaan); *unyaluthi, unyawoti, unyawothi* (Zulu) ■ Pearl millet is a large perennial grass of one to five metres in height (usually about three metres) with several culms, each ending in a dense, cylindrical false spike. The spikes are bristly, pale to dark brown or purplish and vary in length from 150 millimetres to more than a metre. The grains are white to grey, about four millimetres long, pointed at the base and rounded at the tip.

Pearl millet is indigenous to Africa and is an ancient crop plant that has been selected and cultivated in many parts of Africa for about 4 000 years. Millions of hectares are cultivated in Africa and also in India, where the plant was introduced at least 3 000 years ago. It is widely grown in West Africa (Senegal to Sudan), East Africa and southwards to Malawi, Angola, Namibia, Botswana and South Africa. It is a staple cereal in northern Namibia, the Okavango and the adjoining parts of Angola. Cultivated pearl millet is a remarkably heat and drought tolerant plant, producing a reliable but variable crop. Yields vary from 250 to 3 000 kilograms per hectare under dryland (rainfed) conditions. As a result, modern breeding has focused on yield improvement and disease resistance under commercial irrigation systems. There are many wild and weedy forms of pearl millet in Africa, so that the exact origin of the domesticated form, known correctly as *Pennisetum glaucum*, is not clear.

The heads or ears ripen over a period of several weeks, so that the crop has to be protected from birds. The mature ears are cut off, allowed to dry and then stored on the heads before use. Unlike most other grain crops, the grains are not readily attacked by weevils, so that the winnowed grain is not usually treated with the traditional aloe ash insect repellent. To produce flour, the grain is pounded twice: first with a little water to produce a sticky mass which is then dried, and then the final pounding (or grinding) to produce a fine flour. Pearl millet is not of any commercial importance outside Africa and India. In southern Africa it is produced in rural areas for own use and is rarely traded.

Pearl millet is eaten as a porridge or may also be mixed with other ingredients (and other grains) in a wide variety of traditional dishes, including porridges and gruels prepared from fresh, fermented or malted grains (Quin 1959). It is an important source of malt for traditional intoxicating beers. The grains are soaked in cold water for 24 hours, after which they start to sprout. When the plumules have reached a length of about 25 millimetres, the sprouted grain is spread out to dry in the sun, after which it is pounded or ground to a coarse flour. Malted millet flour is fermented and used to brew traditional beers, such as *bjalwa bja leotsa* ("beer from millet").

Under dryland conditions, no other cereal crop can provide better food security than pearl millet. It is likely to replace sorghum and maize as staple food in some drought-prone parts of southern Africa. The species was previously known by numerous different names, most commonly *Pennisetum americanum* and *P. typhoides*.

Setaria italica | Poaceae | **FOXTAIL MILLET**; *boermanna, mannakoring, giers* (Afrikaans); *lebelebele* (Sotho) ■ This cereal of Eurasian origin (Prasada Rao *et al.* 1987) was an important grain crop in Europe until classical times. It is grown on a small scale for human consumption and commercially on the Springbok flats for bird food. Several cultivars are known, differing in the colour of the grain, namely white, yellow and red millet (respectively *wit, geel* and *rooi giers* in Afrikaans).

Setaria sphacelata* var. *sphacelata | Poaceae | **COMMON BRISTLE GRASS** ■ When used as a famine food in KwaZulu-Natal, the grains are reported to be boiled before grinding, apparently to get rid of some toxic substances. The Topnaar people of Namibia grind the seeds of *S. verticillata* (bur-bristle grass or ‡*areb* in Nama) to make a porridge with water, milk or fat, and in South Africa a beer is brewed from the seeds. Hats are woven from the grass (Van den Eynden *et al.* 1992).

Pearl millet plants (*Pennisetum glaucum*)

Heads of pearl millet (*Pennisetum glaucum*)

Heads of foxtail millet (*Setaria italica*)

Pearl millet (*Pennisetum glaucum*)

Foxtail millet (*Setaria italica*)

Sorghum bicolor |Poaceae| **SORGHUM**, grain sorghum (English); *graansorghum* (Afrikaans); *mabele* (Pedi, Sotho, Ndebele); *amazimba* (Xhosa); *amabele* (Zulu) ■ This important traditional source of food and beer is a robust grass of up to three metres in height, with large, much-branched clusters of grains. The grain or caryopsis is small, about three to four millimetres in diameter, more or less rounded, pale yellowish to reddish brown or dark brown and partly covered by two hairy bracts (glumes). There are numerous cultivated forms which are nowadays all included under subsp. *bicolor*, while the wild form is known as subsp. *arundinaceum*. The most commonly cultivated type in southern Africa (previously known as *Sorghum caffrorum*) has compact elongated heads. Another robust type with more open and sparse heads, previously known as *S. dochna*, is still a staple crop in Malawi. Sweet-stemmed forms of this type are widely grown in southern Africa for chewing like sugar cane (see notes under *Saccharum officinarum* in Chapter 6). A third cultivated type (the so-called guinea type), with gaping glumes that reveal part of the grain at maturity, is found from Malawi to Swaziland.

Sorghum is an indigenous staple food and source of beer that has been cultivated in sub-Saharan Africa for at least 3 000 years. The greatest variety of sorghum types is found in northeastern Africa and the crop was perhaps originally developed in Ethiopia. It was introduced into India at least 3 000 years ago but only became an important crop in the New World in the last century. The main advantage of sorghum is its ability to produce at least some grain, even under drought conditions, when a maize crop would fail totally.

Grain is traditionally stored in the head and only pounded, ground and boiled when needed. In addition to beer brewing, it may be used for unleavened or leavened bread, gruel, porridge or boiled whole grain. Ground malted grain is popular for porridge, and is well known in southern Africa as "malted *mabele*" or "*maltebele*". Malted sorghum is used commercially to brew sorghum beer, a popular consumer product. However, the traditional methods of beer brewing (malting and fermenting) are still widely practised in rural areas.

Maize has largely replaced sorghum as a staple food, but more than 200 000 tons of the annual commercial harvest are still used for human consumption. By far the largest proportion is used in stock feed. The nutritional value is inferior to other grains but the price is significantly lower. Crop residues may be used as hay, thatching, basketry or as fuel. "Broomcorn" refers to cultivars specially grown for the stiff heads, which are used as brooms. Cultivars with low levels of hydrocyanic acid are important fodder and silage crops. Sorghum is prone to bird damage and bird-resistant strains with high tannin levels have been developed. The tannin content of the grain adversely affects brewing quality and nutritional value, however.

Stipagrostis uniplumis |Poaceae| **LARGE BUSHMANGRASS** ■ See Chapter 20. The seeds are reported to be eaten by the San. Early travellers also reported that the San people used the grains of *Stipagrostis brevifolia* (*twagras* or *boesmangras* in Afrikaans) as food. The common name *twagras* appears to be derived from "*umTwa*" the name given when the San spoke of himself (Smith 1966).

Triticum aestivum |Poaceae| **BREAD WHEAT** ■ It is a cultivated crop plant, used mainly for bread, one of the staple foods in southern Africa. Sprouted grain is sometimes used to make beer. Another introduced grain, *Triticum durum* (durum wheat) is cultivated for the manufacturing of pasta.

Urochloa mosambicensis |Poaceae| **BUSHVELD SIGNAL GRASS** ■ This is an indigenous grass that is commonly used as a cereal in rural areas. The heads are picked when still slightly green and then spread out in the sun to dry. Once dry, the spikelets are easily rubbed from the stalks, and they are ground into a meal and used for making porridge.

Heads of sorghum being dried before storage

Sorghum beer for sale at the roadside (Botswana)

Wild grass (bushveld signal grass, *Urochloa mosambicensis*) harvested for use as cereal

Seeds of bushveld signal grass (*Urochloa mosambicensis*)

Zea mays | Poaceae | **MAIZE**, mealies, Indian corn (English); *mielies* (Afrikaans); *lefela* (Pedi); *chibahwe, poone* (Sotho); *godi* (Shona); *mavhele* (Venda); *ummbila* (Zulu) ■ Several types of maize are distinguished, depending on the size and colour of the grains, as well as the presence of soft floury tissue near the centre of the kernel. Flint maize differs from popcorn in the presence of this opaque, floury endosperm which is surrounded by the normal hard endosperm, as in popcorn. Soft maize (flour maize) has a large soft centre with a layer of hard endosperm around, but it does not shrink. Dent corn has a central core of soft endosperm which causes shrinking and hence results in a dent at the end of each mature kernel. The type with white or yellow grains is most commonly grown in South Africa, together with soft maize types. Sweetcorn has more free sugars and less starch than other maize types so that the kernels shrink upon drying. Maize with reddish-brown or purplish grains is sometimes cultivated for decoration and to be used in dry flower arrangements.

Maize is said to have been introduced to Africa by early explorers and traders and it has been in cultivation in southern Africa perhaps since AD 1500. The plant originated in Central America, but the exact relationship between the cultivated crop and putative ancestral species is not clear. It is believed that the first maize was a popcorn. Maize is less drought-resistant than finger millet, pearl millet and sorghum but under favourable conditions will produce much larger crops. It is not prone to bird damage, so that harvesting can be done at any time, once the crop is ripe. Yields of eight tons or more per hectare can be expected under optimum conditions of moisture and nutrition.

"Maize is for food, *amabele* is for beer." The grains are pounded or ground and then cooked or boiled. It is used for porridge or numerous other dishes. For human use in South Africa, white maize is preferred to yellow maize. Unripe cobs (or sweetcorn) are delicious when boiled or roasted and are commonly sold along roadsides, in both green (fresh) or roasted form. Maize is similar to other cereals in energy value but is somewhat less nutritious because of lower levels of essential amino acids, particularly lysine and tryptophan.

REFERENCES AND FURTHER READING: Anon. 1989. *Agriculture in South Africa*, 4th ed. Chris van Rensburg Publikasies, Johannesburg. **Ashton, E.H. 1939.** A sociological sketch of Sotho diet. *Trans. R. Soc. S. Afr.* 27: 147–214. **Brink, M. & Belay, G. (eds), 2006.** *Plant resources of tropical Africa 1. Cereals and pulses.* PROTA Foundation, Wageningen, Netherlands. **Brunken, J.N. et al. 1977.** The morphology and domestication of pearl millet. *Econ. Bot.* 31: 163–174. **Clayton, W.D. & Renvoize, S.A. 1982.** Gramineae. In: Polhill, R.M. (ed.), *Flora of tropical East Africa*, Part 3, Rotterdam. **De Wet, J.M.J. 1976.** Domestication of *Eleusine coracana. Econ. Bot.* 30: 194–208. **De Wet, J.M.J. 1978.** Systematics and evolution of *Sorghum* sect. *Sorghum* (Gramineae). *Amer. J. Bot.* 65: 477–482. **De Wet, J.M.J., et al. 1984.** Systematics and evolution of *Eleusine coracana* (Gramineae). *Amer. J. Bot.* 71: 550. **De Wet, J.M.J. 1995.** Pearl millet. In: Smartt, J. & Simmonds, N.W. (eds), *Evolution of crop plants*, 2nd ed., pp. 156–159. Longman, London. **Doggett, H. 1988.** *Sorghum,* 2nd ed. Longman, Harlow. **Doggett, H. & Prasada Rao, K.E. 1995.** *Sorghum.* In: Smartt, J. & Simmonds, N.W. (eds), *Evolution of crop plants,* 2nd ed., pp. 173–1180. Longman, London. **Fox, F.W. 1938.** Some Bantu recipes from the Eastern Cape Province. *Bantu Studies* 13: 65–74. **Fox, F.W. & Norwood Young, M.E. 1982.** *Food from the veld.* Delta Books, Johannesburg. **Gibbon, D. & Pain, A. 1985.** *Crops for the drier regions of the tropics.* Longman, Harlow. **Gibbs Russell, G.E. et al. 1990.** *Grasses of southern Africa.* National Botanical Institute, Pretoria. **Goodman, M.M. 1995.** Maize. In: Smartt, J. & Simmonds, N.W. (eds), *Evolution of crop plants,* 2nd ed., pp. 192–201. Longman, London. **Harlan, J.R. & de Wet, J.M.J. 1972.** A simplified classification of cultivated *Sorghum. Crop Sci.* 12: 172–176. **Hilu, K.W. et al. 1979.** Archaeobotanical studies of *Eleusine coracana* ssp. *coracana* (finger millet). *Am. J. Bot.* 66: 330–333. **Jacot Guillarmot, A. 1966.** A contribution towards the economic botany of Basutoland. *Bot. Notiser* 119(2): 109–212. **Junod, H.A. 1913.** *The life of a South African tribe.* Vol. 2. Neuchatel, Switzerland. **Moffett, R. 1997.** *Grasses of the eastern Free State.* Uniqwa, Phuthaditjhaba. **Moffett, R. 2010.** *Sesotho plant and animal names, and plants used by the Basotho.* Sun Press, Bloemfontein. **Peters, C.R. et al. 1992.** *Edible wild plants of sub-Saharan Africa.* Royal Botanic Gardens, Kew. **Prasada, K.E. et al. 1985.** Infraspecific variation and systematics of cultivated *Setaria italica*, foxtail millet (Poaceae). *Econ. Bot.* 41: 108–116. **Quin, P.J. 1959.** *Foods and feeding habits of the Pedi.* Witwatersrand University Press, Johannesburg. **Rose, E.F. & Jacot Guillarmod, A. 1974.** Plants gathered as foodstuffs by the Transkeian peoples. *S.A. Med. J.* 48: 1688–1690. **Smith, C.A. 1966.** Common names of South African plants. *Mem. Bot. Surv. S. Afr.* 35. **Snowden, J.D. 1936.** *The cultivated races of* Sorghum. Adlard & Son, London. **Van den Eynden, V., Vernemmen, P. & Van Damme, P. 1992.** *The ethnobotany of the Topnaar.* Universiteit Gent, Gent. **Van Oudtshoorn, F. 2012.** *Guide to the grasses of southern Africa.* 3rd ed. Briza Publications, Pretoria. **Watt, J.M. & Breyer-Brandwijk, M.G. 1962.** *The medicinal and poisonous plants of southern and eastern Africa,* 2nd ed. Livingstone, London. **Williamson, J. 1972.** *Useful plants of Malawi.* Government Printer, Zomba. **Zeven, A.C. & De Wet, J.M.J. 1982.** *Dictionary of cultivated plants and their regions of diversity.* Centre for Agricultural Publishing and Documentation, Wageningen. **Zohary, D. & Hopf, M. 1994.** *Domestication of plants in the Old World,* 2nd ed. Clarendon Press, Oxford.

Coceka Cezulu selling maize

Heads of maize

Ornamental maize

Some popular nuts and seeds: marula pips, cowpea, mung bean, jugo bean, jack bean and pigeon pea

Manketti nut shells (*Schinziophyton rautanenii*)

Fruits and seeds of the groundnut plant (*Arachis hypogea*)

Cone and nuts of stone pine (*Pinus pinea*)

Seeds of the castor oil plant (*Ricinus communis*)

CHAPTER 2
Seeds & nuts

SEEDS AND NUTS form an important part of the human diet and are almost as important as cereal crops. Botanically, a nut is defined as a single-seeded indehiscent fruit with a leathery or bony fruit wall. Nuts often have a high oil content and are rich in proteins and amino acids.

Many different members of the legume family have seeds that are also directly consumed as food. The main advantage of legumes is that they fix atmospheric nitrogen by means of their root nodules. Nitrogen-fixing bacteria live inside the root nodules and allow the plants to grow on nitrogen-poor soils, where grasses and other herbs will hardly survive. The edible dry seeds of legumes are called "peas and beans" or "pulses", and include dry beans, dry peas, dry broad beans, chickpeas, lentils, jack bean, lablab bean, mung bean, cowpea, pigeon pea, jugo bean and many more. Soya beans and groundnuts are also legumes, but they are mainly grown for oil, although soya bean is of major importance as a food in the Far East and is fast becoming equally important as a protein source in the rest of the world. Other oily seeds that are commonly grown for human consumption include sunflower, sesame, linseed and rapeseed. The oil from these crops is used directly as cooking oil or salad oil, or it is converted into margarine. Some of the vegetable oils are processed and used in industrial applications such as paints, varnishes and lubricants. Others are used in hair and skin care products (see Chapter 14).

Fats and oils are important in the human diet as a source of energy. They also serve as carriers of vitamin A, D, E and K because these vitamins are not soluble in water. Dietary fats and oils mostly occur in nature as triglycerides (a combination of glycerol with three fatty acids). Fatty acids without double bonds in the carbon chain are called saturated fatty acid, while those with double bonds are unsaturated. Monounsaturated fatty acids have a single double bond. An example is oleic acid from olive oil. They are further distinguished by the position of the double bond. Omega-3 fatty acids have the double bond on the third carbon; omega-6 fatty acids on the sixth carbon. Polyunsaturated fatty acids have two or more double bonds. Examples are linoleic acid and linolenic acid, both of which are found in many plant oils. These two are called essential fatty acids because they cannot be made in the human body but have to be obtained directly from food. Natural fats and oils with a high level of monounsaturated fatty acids, as is found in olive oil for example, are healthier than margarine.

Important African plants used for commercial oil production include the West African oil palm (*Elaeis guineensis*), the vegetable tallow tree (*Allanblackia floribunda*) and the shea butter tree (*Vitelluria paradoxa*). Ethiopians use oils from two native Ethiopian plants every day: noug (the oil from niger seed, *Guizotia abyssinica*) is their main cooking oil, and castor oil (from *Ricinus communis*) is used to oil the *mitad* – the traditional clay pan for making *injera* (tef bread), the local staple food.

There are some interesting indigenous nuts and seeds that have been used in southern Africa for a very long time. Manketti nuts, for example, have been used as a staple food in the Kalahari Desert for at least 7 000 years (Robbins & Campbell 1990). The seeds of marula (*Sclerocarya birrea*), marama bean (*Tylosema esculentum*) and baobab (*Adansonia digitata*) have a long history of use by local people and are all very tasty and highly nutritious. These are important food resources collected in the wild that have not yet been cultivated to any significant extent, yet they are of considerable interest as potential crop plants for the dry regions of the world (Bostid 1979; Arnold *et al.* 1995). Many of these nuts and seeds are highly nutritious and detailed analyses of nutrient compositions are available (Arnold *et al.* 1995; Van der Vossen & Mkamilo 2007). Africa is rich in genetic resources (Attere *et al.* 1991; Ng *et al.* 1991; Peters *et al.* 1992) and there is much scope for crop development, crop improvement and germplasm conservation.

Acanthosicyos horridus | Cucurbitaceae | **!NARA** (Nama); *nara* ■ See Chapter 3. The seeds (*botterpitte* in Afrikaans) are delicious edible nuts.

Adansonia digitata | Malvaceae | **BAOBAB** ■ See Chapters 3 and 19. The seeds are roasted and eaten as nuts; they are highly nutritious. The dried fruit pulp has become popular as a commercial functional food and beverage ingredient.

Anacardium occidentale | Anacardiaceae | **CASHEW NUT**; *caja* (Portuguese) ■ The cashew nut is a scraggly evergreen tree of about 10 metres in height, with large simple leaves. Flowers are red and only form the fruits after two or three months (Gibbon & Pain 1985; Williams *et al.* 1980). The flower stalk and flower base develop and swell to form a large fleshy structure, the so-called cashew apple. Attached to the fleshy part is the actual fruit, with the nut inside. The fruit is hard and kidney-shaped, with a tough grey-green skin.

Cashew nuts come from the northern part of South America and were distributed to many parts of the world by early Portuguese explorers (Cundall 1995). Trees are cultivated in tropical parts of southern Africa, mainly in northern KwaZulu-Natal, Mozambique and Malawi. A long dry period is required for successful flowering and seed set.

Both the fleshy cashew apple and the actual fruits are utilised. The former is eaten when ripe or is fermented (in southern Mozambique and Malawi) to produce alcoholic drinks. The fruit skin contains a poisonous and irritating oil, which makes the extraction of the nuts an unpleasant activity. Fortunately, mechanical methods have been developed. Before the nuts can be eaten, the oil has to be driven off by roasting. Commercial developments in the cashew nut industry in Mozambique are aimed at increasing the annual exports from about 80 000 to 200 000 tons per year. The nuts are delicious to eat and form an important part of the diet in parts of Mozambique. They are very nutritious and contain high-quality proteins of up to 25 per cent (Cundall 1995). In Malawi, the nuts are pounded and added to other foods.

Arachis hypogea | Fabaceae | **PEANUT**, groundnut ■ See notes under *Vigna subterranea*.

Bauhinia petersiana | Fabaceae | **WILD COFFEE BEAN** ■ This is an upright woody shrub with white flowers and many-seeded flat and edible pods. It occurs in Angola, Zambia, Namibia, Zimbabwe, Botswana and South Africa. The roasted seeds are eaten as nuts in rural areas or may be pounded into a nourishing meal which is said to be a staple food. Roasted nuts are also ground and used as a coffee substitute, hence the common name.

Brabejum stellatifolium | Proteaceae | **WILD ALMOND**; *wilde amandel* (Afrikaans); *ghoo* (Khoi) ■ This is a robust shrub or small tree (up to 8 metres in height) with thick branches and characteristic leaves, which are borne in distinct groups of four to nine along the stems. The clusters of small cream-coloured flowers are followed by brown, velvety, almond-like nuts. Toxic substances (cyanogenic glucosides) are present in the nuts, so that a lengthy leaching process is called for to make them edible. The nuts are said to have been a popular food item of the early Cape people but are also known to have caused fatalities. The first Dutch settler at the Cape, Jan van Riebeeck, planted a famous hedge in 1660, parts of which are still visible at the National Botanical Garden at Kirstenbosch. It has been declared a national monument. The first recorded death "from eating too many wild almonds" was reported in 1655. *Brabejum stellatifolium* has no close relatives amongst the southern African members of the Proteaceae family but has its closest relatives (such as *Macadamia*) in Australia. Extensive leaching in sacks placed in running water render the seeds edible. The seeds were used as a coffee substitute (called *ghoo* coffee) after soaking, boiling, and then roasting. The wood was used for ornamental woodworking, and the bark for tanning in earlier times.

Fruit pulp and seeds of baobab (*Adansonia digitata*)

Propagation of cashew nuts (*Anacardium occidentale*) by cuttings

Leaves and flowers of wild coffee bean (*Bauhinia petersiana*)

Roasted seeds of wild coffee bean (*Bauhinia petersiana*)

Fruits of the wild almond (*Brabejum stellatifolium*)

Wild almond nuts (*Brabejum stellatifolium*)

Flowers of the wild almond (*Brabejum stellatifolium*)

Macadamia nuts (*Macadamia integrifolia*)

Cajanus cajan | Fabaceae | **PIGEON PEA**; *duifert* (Afrikaans); *udali* (Zulu) ■ The pigeon pea is a short-lived perennial shrub, up to four metres in height, with hairy stems and spirally arranged leaves on long stalks. Each leaf is divided into three smaller leaflets. The flowers are usually yellow but are often streaked with red, particularly on the back of the standard petal. The pods are green, dark purple or mottled and contain from two to eight seeds each. They are borne scattered amongst the branch tips, but may also form dense clusters in some cultivars. The seeds are exceptionally variable in size and surface colour (uniform or mottled) and vary from red or brown to white and grey (see also the photograph on page 18).

There is now good evidence that the pigeon pea originated in India, from where it was introduced to East Africa around 2000 BC (Van der Maesen 1995). From here it has spread through most parts of Africa. The crop requires high temperatures for optimal growth and seed set. It has become a very important crop plant in rural areas and is used not only for the seeds, but also as a green vegetable.

Pigeon peas are grown almost exclusively for domestic consumption and only small quantities reach the local and international markets. Annual yield worldwide is about two million tons, most of it being produced in India, with some minor production areas in East Africa and the Caribbean (Van der Maesen 1995). The yield of dry seeds per hectare rarely exceeds one ton.

The seeds require several hours of soaking before they are pounded and then fried or steamed. Ripe seeds may also be germinated and eaten as sprouts. Immature pods may be boiled and eaten as a vegetable. The whole plant, the plant remains or the seeds are used as animal fodder. Dry stalks may be used for thatching and for fuel. Dahl (split peas) is prepared by softening and removing the seed coat and splitting the seed to separate the two cotyledons. The nutritional value of the seeds was evaluated at Roodeplaat (see Venter & Coertze 1997). Although the protein content is quite high at 17 per cent, the seeds are relatively low in essential amino acids, particularly tryptophan.

Canavalia ensiformis | Fabaceae | **JACK BEAN** ■ This robust creeper is occasionally culti-vated in rural areas in southern Africa. The ripe seeds are pale grey or white in colour and are only palatable after extensive cooking and removal of the seed coat, but they are frequently used as a coffee substitute (Erika van den Heever, pers. comm.) – see Chapter 6. Leaves and young pods are used as tasty green vegetables. It is sometimes confused with the velvet bean (*Mucuna pruriens* var. *utilis*), which is also cultivated in southern Africa for its edible seeds.

Guibourtia coleosperma | Fabaceae | **COPALWOOD**; *bastermopanie* (Afrikaans); */gwi* (San) ■ The copalwood is a large evergreen bushveld tree which occurs on deep Kalahari sands in northern Namibia and northern Botswana. The leaves resemble those of the mopane but they are less triangular and have short but distinct stalks. The small, white flowers are followed by small, dark brown, oval pods, which break open to reveal brown seeds covered in bright red arils. This is a food of primary importance to the !Khu Bushmen of northeastern Namibia. After removal of the seed coat, the seeds are eaten raw or they are roasted and pounded. The oily arils are used as a famine food and various parts of the plant are used for traditional medicine.

Helianthus annuus | Asteraceae | **SUNFLOWER**; *sonneblom* (Afrikaans) ■ The sunflower was first domesticated as a crop by native North Americans. It is an important commercial seed crop in southern Africa, and is particularly popular because of its drought resistance. Cooking oil in southern Africa is to a large extent derived from this source.

Leucadendron pubescens | Proteaceae | ***KNOKKERS*** (Afrikaans) ■ Female plants of this common fynbos shrub bear typical cone-like structures with numerous seeds about the size of peas. These small nuts are delicious and are eaten as a veld food in the Clanwilliam area in the Cape, where the common name was recorded (Chris de Wet, pers. comm.).

Leaves, flowers and young pods of pigeon pea (*Cajanus cajan*)

Ripe fruits (pods) of the pigeon pea (*Cajanus cajan*)

Pigeon peas (*Cajanus cajan*)

Flowers and young pods of the velvet bean (*Mucuna pruriens* var. *utilis*)

Pods and seeds of copalwood (*Guibourtia coleosperma*) – note the bright red arils around the seeds

Female cones of *knokkers* (*Leucadendron pubescens*)

Edible nuts of *Leucadendron pubescens*, known as *knokkers*

Macadamia integrifolia | Proteaceae | **MACADAMIA NUT** ■ This is an important edible nut from Australia, related to the wild almond (*Brabejum stellatifolium*). It is grown as a commercial crop in the subtropical parts of southern Africa.

Phaseolus vulgaris | Fabaceae | **COMMON BEAN**, French bean ■ This exotic plant is an important food source in rural areas and is widely cultivated in southern Africa. The leaves and young pods are used as green vegetables or the ripe seeds (dry beans) are harvested.

Pinus pinea | Pinaceae | **STONE PINE**; *kroonden* (Afrikaans) ■ See photograph on page 18. The stone pine is a large tree from the Mediterranean region of Europe that has been imported to South Africa as a garden tree. It has a characteristic umbrella-shaped crown, robust, round cones and large edible nuts. The cones are picked when ripe (but before they open) and are dried in an oven to release the seeds (pine nuts). Children in Cape Town collect the seeds, known locally as *dennepitjies*, from under the trees. Pine nuts are an important ingredient in Middle Eastern cooking. *Pinus cembroides* (Mexican stone pine) is a garden tree in southern Africa which also produces edible nuts similar to those of the stone pine.

Ricinodendron rautanenii – see *Schinziophyton rautanenii*.

Ricinus communis | Euphorbiaceae | **CASTOR OIL**; *kasterolie* (Afrikaans) ■ See photo on page 18. The castor oil plant is a naturalised weed in many parts of the world but archaeological excavations show that it has been in South Africa for thousands of years. The origin is almost certainly Ethiopia, where the greatest diversity of seed types (and genotypes) can be found. The seeds are highly toxic due to the content of ricin, which is not present in the oil. The oil is commonly used as a purgative and as an emollient, and is used in creams, ointments, clear soaps and lipstick.

Schinziophyton rautanenii | Euphorbiaceae | **MANKETTI, MONGONGO** (English, Afrikaans); *mongongo* (Herero, !Kung San) ■ Manketti trees are either male or female. They have large, rounded crowns and hand-shaped leaves, with five to seven large stalked leaflets. The yellowish flowers are followed by egg-shaped velvety fruits which ripen and fall from the tree from the end of March to April or May (Lee 1973). Each fruit has a thin fleshy layer around the very thick, hard, pitted shell that covers the nutritious nut.

The manketti or mongongo is indigenous to northern Botswana, northern Namibia, southeastern Angola, western Zimbabwe and northern Mozambique. A few trees occur along the border between Botswana and South Africa. Archaeological studies have shown that the nuts have been utilised in the western Kalahari for at least 7 000 years (Robbins & Campbell 1990).

The main reason why this is such an important food source is because the fruits and nuts remain edible for a large part of the year. Dry fruits are first steamed to soften the skins. The peeled fruits are then cooked in water until the maroon-coloured fruit flesh separates from the hard inner nuts (Lee 1973). The pulp is eaten, and the nuts are saved to be roasted later. During roasting, direct contact with the fire is avoided by using sand to distribute the heat evenly. The thick and hard outer shell dries out and becomes easier to crack. The roasted nuts are tasty and up to 300 may be eaten in a day, with or without removal of the softer inner shell (Lee 1973). Some shelled nuts are processed further by pounding them with roots and leaves to make a variety of dishes. Analyses of the nutrient content of the fruits and nuts have shown that they compare well with some of the world's most nutritious foods. The main fatty acids are linoleic acid (38%), oleic acid (15%) and α-eleostearic acid (29%) (Van der Vossen & Mkamilo 2007). The oil from the nuts is used as a body rub in the dry winter months (Lee 1973), to clean and moisten the skin. The hard shells of the nut are popular as divining "bones" (see photograph on page 18).

Manketti trees (*Schinziophyton rautanenii*)

Cracking manketti nuts

Mankotti fruits

Manketti nuts

Schotia afra | Fabaceae | **KAROO BOERBEAN**; *Karoo boerboon* (Afrikaans) ■ The seeds are reported to be edible, raw when green or cooked and pounded when ripe. The seeds of *Schotia brachypetala* – weeping boerbean (*huilboerboon* in Afrikaans) are edible after roasting. The seeds and young pods of *Schotia latifolia* – bush boerbean (*bosboerboon* in Afrikaans) are reported to be edible.

Sclerocarya birrea | Anacardiaceae | **MARULA**; *maroela* (Afrikaans) ■ See Chapter 6. The hard stones of the marula fruit contain three small nuts which are much sought after as a food item. Each nut is covered with a hard, bony "lid" that has to be removed to extract the nut. The photograph on page 18 shows marula pips on the far left, most of them with the "lids" removed to reveal the nuts below. These nuts are highly nutritious and contain a valuable oil. Considerable skill is required to crack open the hard shells to extract the nuts. The Tsonga people of South Africa and Mozambique use the oil for cooking and as a moisturiser for women and as a baby oil (Patrick Ndlovu, pers. comm.).

Sesamum indicum | Pedaliaceae | **SESAME**; *oliebossie* (Afrikaans) ■ This important commercial oil seed is an ancient crop, possibly of East African or Indian origin. It is a weedy annual with large, lobed leaves and pale pink to purple flowers. The small egg-shaped and highly nutritious seeds are borne in small capsules. The plant is grown on a small scale in rural areas in southern Africa. There are several indigenous species with seeds that are said to be edible. They are used in the same way as sesame (eaten with boiled maize, for example). These include *Sesamum capense* – *aprilbaadjie, brandogie* or *seeroogblaar* (Afrikaans) and *S. triphyllum* – wild sesame (*oliebossie* – Afrikaans).

Strelitzia nicolai | Strelitziaceae | **NATAL WILD BANANA**; *kuswildepiesang* (Afrikaans) ■ The wild banana is a robust leafy tree that occurs along the east coast of South Africa. The large attractive flowers develop into large seed capsules, which burst open to release black seeds that have decorative bright orange, oily arils. The seeds are ground into flour. The flour is mixed with water, formed into a patty and the oily seed arils are embedded on both sides. It is then baked over coals to make a dense, filling meal although the taste is somewhat bland (Ben Dekker, pers. comm.).

Trichilia dregeana | Meliaceae | **FOREST NATAL-MAHOGANY**; *bosrooiessenhout* (Afrikaans); *mmaba* (Northern Sotho); *umkhuhlu* (Xhosa, Zulu) ■ The two common species of *Trichilia* are very similar and can easily be confused with one another. Mature fruits provide an easy means of identification. They are without a distinct stalk (stipe) in *T. dregeana*, while a stipe of up to 10 millimetres is present in *T. emetica*. The seeds of *T. dregeana* contain 55 to 65 per cent oil, dominated by palmitic and oleic acids. It is used to make candles, cosmetics and soaps (Van der Vossen & Mkamilo 2007). The seed arils are eaten but the seed coat is said to be poisonous. For oil production, *T. emetica* is usually preferred.

Trichilia emetica | Meliaceae | **BUSHVELD NATAL-MAHOGANY**; *bosveldrooiessenhout* (Afrikaans); *mmaba* (Northern Sotho); *umkhuhlu* (Xhosa, Zulu) ■ The seeds of this widely distributed bushveld tree are pounded in a mortar and then boiled in water to extract the oil, which is used to moisturise the skin, and sometimes to manufacture soap. The oil is taken orally for rheumatism, and is applied topically as a dressing to cuts and to the site of a fractured bone to facilitate healing. The arils, separated from the seeds, are soaked and cooked together with sweet potatoes or squash. The seeds yield mafura oil (obtained from the fleshy seed coat, ca. 35 to 60% yield) and mafura butter (obtained from the seed kernel, ca. 60 to 65% yield). Annual amounts of up to 300 tons of mafura butter have been exported from Mozambique (Van der Vossen & Mkamilo 2007). An average annual yield of seeds is about 45 to 65 kilograms per tree.

Flowers of Karoo boerbean (*Schotia afra*)

Roasted seeds of weeping boerbean (*Schotia brachypetala*)

Sesame (*Sesamum indicum*)

Wild sesame (*Sesamum triphyllum*)

Cake made from the seed flour of wild banana (*Strelitzia nicolai*)

Fruit capsule and seeds of wild banana (note the orange seed arils)

Fruits and seeds of forest Natal-mahogany (*Trichilia dregeana*)

Fruits of bushveld Natal-mahogany (*Trichilia emetica*)

Tylosema esculentum │Fabaceae│ **MARAMA BEAN**, gemsbok bean (English); *marama-boontjie, elandsboontjie, braaiboontjie* (Afrikaans); *marama, morama* (Tswana); *marumama* (Tsonga); *tsi, tsin* (!Kung San); *gami* (Khoi); *ombanui* (Herero) ■ The marama bean is a robust plant with creeping stems of up to three metres in length which spread from an enormous woody tuber below the ground. Tubers have a reddish-brown bark and usually taper to a thinner neck-like structure near the soil surface, from where the annual branches grow during the rainy season. Forked tendrils are found along the stems, but the plant is not really a creeper (vine) and the branches merely spread out along the ground. The characteristic leaves are deeply two-lobed, hairless and firm in texture. Attractive bright yellow flowers are borne along the stems, each with erect petals and stamens, and are followed by large woody pods. The pod contains between two and six large brown seeds of about 20 millimetres in diameter, weighing about 20 to 30 grams each. The seed coat is about two millimetres thick, and encloses the delicious white nut inside.

There are two closely related species of *Tylosema* in southern Africa (Coetzer & Ross 1977). The common plant from the Kalahari (*T. esculentum*) has deeply lobed leaves (the notch is usually more than halfway down the leaf) and the leaf stalks are short (up to 35 millimetres long). The other species, *T. fassoglense*, has shallowly lobed leaves (the notch is usually less than a third of the total leaf length) and the leaf stalks are longer. *Tylosema fassoglense* is a bushveld creeper (vine) that climbs into trees with the aid of well-developed tendrils. *Tylosema esculentum* is the only legume that shows heterostyly – there are two or three flower types on the same plant that differ in the length of the pistil and anthers. This mechanism prevents self-pollination and promotes outcrossing, thus leading to genetic diversity (Hartley *et al.* 2002).

The fibrous but watery underground tuber of *T. esculentum* can attain an enormous size (Bergström & Skarpe 1981), as tall as a man and weighing more than 250 kilograms. Specimens weighing between 150 and 250 kilograms are quite common, showing that the size of marama tubers was underestimated in the past. A specimen that was accurately weighed tipped the scale at 277 kilograms. It was calculated by Bergström & Skarpe (1981) that the 81 per cent moisture content of this specimen meant that it contained about 224 litres of pure water!

Tylosema esculentum is restricted to southern Africa, and occurs in South Africa, Botswana and northern Namibia. The closely related *T. fassoglense* occurs in South Africa, Swaziland, Namibia and Angola, northwards through tropical Africa to Sudan (Coetzer & Ross 1977). Marama bean has considerable potential as a crop plant for arid regions (Bostid 1979; Keegan & Van Staden 1981; Powell 1987; Monaghan & Halloran 1996) and is being developed in Texas, Australia and Israel. It has already been successfully cultivated in these parts of the world and programmes are underway to do selection and breeding work.

The marama forms an important part of the diet of rural people in the Kalahari, the Kaokoveld and in Mozambique. It is regarded as a staple diet in many parts. Young pods are said to be edible as a vegetable, but the main attraction is the large seeds. These beans are not eaten raw but are delicious when roasted. Roasting is usually done by placing the seeds in a container of sand. The container is then put on the fire or in the oven. This method ensures that the heat is evenly distributed and that the seed coats do not rupture. The seeds may be eaten as nuts – the taste is considered to be superior to that of groundnuts – or they may be ground to make coffee or porridge. Roasted nuts have been sold locally but only on a small scale. The young tubers are roasted and eaten, while the larger ones may provide water in an emergency.

Marama beans are highly nutritious and compare favourably with many existing legume crops (Wehmeyer *et al.* 1967; Bower *et al.* 1988; Maruatona *et al.* 2010). The protein content is about 30 to 35 per cent and the oil content varies from 35 to 42 per cent. Experiments have shown that the seeds can be processed into marama flour and marama milk. These products have potential as new functional food ingredients.

Flowers and pod of marama bean (*Tylosema esculentum*)

Seeds of marama bean (*Tylosema esculentum*)

Edible root of a young marama bean plant (*Tylosema esculentum*)

Large tuber of a marama bean plant (*Tylosema esculentum*)

Vigna subterranea | Fabaceae| **JUGO BEAN**, Bambara groundnut (English); *jugoboon* (Afrikaans); *ditloo-marapo* (Sotho); *izidlubu* (Zulu) ■ This truly African crop plant is an annual herb with small pale yellow flowers that curl down after fertilisation and grow downwards into the ground, so that the fruit develops below the ground. The fruit is a rounded, single-seeded or two-seeded pod. There are several cultivars in southern Africa, differing mainly in the colour of the seed: black, spotted, yellow-brown, red or cream. The black variety matures quickly and is most commonly grown (Venter & Coertze 1996) but the red one is a prolific bearer and is also popular.

The jugo bean is indigenous to Africa and is widely cultivated all over the tropical parts of the continent. Nowadays there is a renewed interest in jugo beans because of their ability to produce reasonably well, even under extreme conditions (drought and poor soil). It is considered to be one of the most underestimated and underdeveloped crop plants of the world.

The beans are often intercropped with maize and pumpkin – a nutritional triad. Young plants are mounded to reduce attack by insects and perhaps also to improve the yields. Harvesting starts about four months after sowing and the plants are simply pulled out of the ground. Yields of about 1 000 kilograms per hectare can be expected (Gibbon & Pain 1985). The crop is grown exclusively as a protein source and is not used for oil production. Seeds are commercially canned in Zimbabwe (Venter & Coertze 1996), but the largest part of the annual production is for own consumption in rural areas, so that only limited quantities reach local markets and practically nothing enters the international market.

Immature beans are eaten raw or cooked, while the ripe ones are often pounded into a flour, or soaked and then cooked or roasted in oil. There are many different traditional recipes for preparing dishes from the cooked, pounded or crushed beans (Junod 1913; Quin 1959). In the Limpopo Province of South Africa, the ripe beans are cooked in the pod, in heavily salted water and the soft beans eaten as a nutritious snack. The Venda people hold a harvest ritual only for this crop and for finger millet (Fox & Norwood Young 1982). It is considered to be a substitute for meat, and analyses have shown that the ripe beans are remarkably nutritious (Venter & Coertze 1996). It contains about 16 per cent protein, six per cent fat and relatively high levels of amino acids. The plant was previously known as *Voandzeia subterranea*. There is much confusion about the names that have been applied to this crop, because different colour forms and even different dishes may have specific vernacular names.

Simple selection may result in dramatic improvements of up to 300 per cent in terms of seed size within a single rotation (At Kruger, pers. comm.). It is thought that large seeds have traditionally been selected for eating, while small seeds have been kept as seed for the next year's sowing, so that there may well have been a form of selection against seed size. Some seed lots are remarkably variable in terms of seed size and seed colour – note the extreme variability in the commercial sample shown in the top photograph on page 18. It is not hard to imagine that crop development may lead to rapid improvement in seed size, uniformity and disease resistance. The jugo bean is starting to regain its former prominence as a staple food, and there has been a steady increase in commercial plantings in recent years.

Arachis hypogea, the groundnut (*grondboontjie* in Afrikaans), is an exotic nut closely similar to the jugo bean, which it has replaced in many rural parts of Africa. The plant has bright yellow flowers which curiously start to grow down into the ground as soon as they have been pollinated. As a result, the fruits are formed below the ground, well hidden from birds and other seed-eaters. Groundnut is sometimes confused with the jugo bean, but the two species are not particularly closely related and the resemblance is only superficial. The groundnut is an important commercial crop and is cultivated on a large scale in many parts of southern Africa. When harvested, the plants are piled up into stacks for drying, a familiar sight in some parts of the Kalahari where irrigation is possible. The leaf remains make a valuable fodder for animals.

Jugo bean plant (*Vigna subterranea*)

Jugo bean plant showing underground pods

Leaves and flowers of the groundnut plant (*Arachis hypogea*)

Pods ot jugo bean (*Vigna subterranea*)

Seeds of jugo bean (*Vigna subterranea*)

Vigna unguiculata |Fabaceae| **COWPEA**; *akkerbone* (Afrikaans); *dinawa* (Sotho, Tswana); *munawa* (Venda) ■ This indigenous African legume is an important commercial pulse (grain legume), usually cultivated for its seeds. In southern Africa, the dry beans are a favourite foodstuff and commonly form part of other dishes. The leaves and young pods are very popular as green vegetables, used fresh or dried.

Vigna radiata |Fabaceae| **MUNG BEAN** ■ The mung bean is an important food plant in rural southern Africa, grown not only for its dry beans, but also as a green vegetable. The beans are small and usually olive green in colour. It is not indigenous but an introduced crop plant from India.

Vigna vexillata |Fabaceae| **WILD SWEETPEA** ■ The plant is indigenous to southern Africa and is said to be cultivated on a small scale in the region.

Ximenia caffra |Olacaceae| **SOURPLUM**; *suurpruim* (Afrikaans) ■ See Chapter 3. The fleshy fruits contain a hard-shelled nut which is delicious to eat and which was once much in demand as a lubricant for leather (Vaughan-Kirby 1918). *Ximenia americana* (blue sourplum) has oily nuts similar to those of *X. caffra* and are used in the same way.

REFERENCES AND FURTHER READING: Attere, F., Zedan, H., Ng, N.Q. & Perrino, P. (eds) 1991. *Crop genetic resources of Africa.* Vol. 1. IBPGR, Rome. **Arnold, T.H. *et al.* 1985.** Khoisan food plants: taxa with potential for future economic exploitation. Chapter 6 in: *Plants for arid lands*, Royal Botanic Gardens, Kew. **Bergström, R. & Skarpe, C. 1981.** The tuber of morama (*Tylosema esculentum*). *Botswana Notes & Records* 13: 156–157. **Borget, M. 1992.** *Food legumes.* Macmillan, London. **Bostid, A. 1979.** *Tropical legumes: Resources for the future.* National Academy of Sciences, Washington, DC, USA. **Bower, N., Hertel, K., Oh, J. & Storey, R. 1988.** Nutritional evaluation of marama bean (*Tylosema esculentum*, Fabaceae): Analysis of the seed. *Econ. Bot.* 42: 533–540. **Brink, M. & Belay, G. (eds) 2006.** *Plant resources of tropical Africa 1. Cereals and pulses.* PROTA Foundation, Wageningen, Netherlands. **Coates Palgrave, K. 1977.** *Trees of Southern Africa.* Struik, Cape Town. **Coetzer, L.A. & Ross, J.H. 1977.** Subfamily 2. Caesalpinioideae. *Flora of southern Africa* 16(2): 61–64. Botanical Research Institute, Pretoria. **Cundall, E.P. 1995.** Cashew. In: Smartt, J. & Simmonds, N.W. (eds), *Evolution of crop plants*, 2nd ed., pp. 11–13. Longman, London. **Engelter, C. & Wehmeyer, A.S. 1970.** Fatty acid composition of oils of some edible seeds of wild plants. *J. Agric. Food Chem.* 18, 1: 25–26. **Fox, F.W. & Norwood Young, M.E. 1982.** *Food from the veld.* Delta Books, Johannesburg. **Gibbon, D. & Pain, A. 1985.** *Crops for the drier regions of the tropics.* Longman, Harlow. **Hartley, M.L., Tshamekeng, E. & Thomas, S.M. 2002.** Functional heterostyly in *Tylosema esculentum* (Caesalpinioideae). *Ann. Bot.* 89: 67–76. **Junod, H.A. 1913.** *The life of a South African tribe.* Vol. 2. Neuchatel, Switzerland. **Keegan, A.B. & Van Staden, J. 1981.** Marama bean, *Tylosema esculentum*, a plant worthy of cultivation. *S. Afr. J. Sci.* 77: 387. **Lee, R.B. 1973.** Mongongo: the ethnography of a major wild food resource. *Ecology of food and nutrition* 2: 307–321. **Maguire, B. 1978.** *The food plants of the !Khu Bushmen of north-eastern South West Africa.* M.Sc. thesis, University of the Witwatersrand. **Malan, J.S. & Owen-Smith, G.L. 1974.** The ethnobotany of Kaokoland. *Cimbebasia* Ser. B 2,5: 131–178. **Maruatona, G.N., Duodu, K.G. & Minnaar, A. 2010.** Physicochemical, nutritional and functional properties of marama bean flour. *Food Chem.* 121: 400–405. **Monaghan, B.G. & Halloran, G.M. 1996.** RAPD variation within and between natural populations of morama [*Tylosema esculentum* (Burchell) Schreiber] in southern Africa. *S. Afr. J. Bot.* 62: 287–291. **Ng, N.Q. *et al.* (eds) 1991.** *Crop genetic resources of Africa.* Vol. 2. IBPGR, Rome. **Palmer, E. & Pitman, N. 1972.** *Trees of Southern Africa.* (3 vols). Balkema, Cape Town. **Peters, C.R. 1987.** *Ricinodendron rautanenii* (Euphorbiaceae): Zambezian wild food plant for all seasons. *Econ. Bot.* 41: 494–502. **Peters, C.R. *et al.* 1992.** *Edible wild plants of sub-Saharan Africa.* Royal Botanic Gardens, Kew. **Powell, A.M. 1987.** Marama bean (*Tylosema esculentum*, Fabaceae) seed crop in Texas. *Econ. Bot.* 41: 216–220. **Quin, P.J. 1959.** *Foods and feeding habits of the Pedi.* Witwatersrand University Press, Johannesburg. **Robbins, L.H. & Campbell, A.C. 1990.** Prehistory of mongongo nut exploitation in the western Kalahari Desert, Botswana. *Botswana Notes & Records* 22: 37–42. **Smith, C.A. 1966.** Common names of South African plants. *Mem. Bot. Surv. S. Afr.* 35. **Steyn, H.P. 1981.** Nharo plant utilization. An overview. *Khoisis* 1: 1–30. **Story, R. 1959.** Some plants used by the Bushmen in obtaining food and water. *Mem. Bot. Surv. S. Afr.* 30. **Van den Eynden, V., Vernemmen, P. & Van Damme, P. 1992.** *The ethnobotany of the Topnaar.* Universiteit Gent, Gent. **Van der Maesen, L.J.G. 1995.** Pigeonpea. In: Smartt, J. & Simmonds, (eds), *Evolution of crop plants*, 2nd ed., pp. 251–254. Longman, London. **Van der Vossen, H.A.M. & Mkamilo, G.S. (eds) 2007.** *Plant resources of tropical Africa. 14. Vegetable oils.* PROTA Foundation, Wageningen / Backhuys Publishers, Leiden. **Van Wyk, B.-E. 2005.** *Food plants of the world.* Briza Publications, Pretoria. **Vaughan-Kirby, F. 1918.** Skin dressing: a description of the process of converting the raw hides of game or domestic cattle into articles of native wearing apparel. *Man* 18, 23: 36–40. **Venter, S. & Coertze, A.F. 1996.** *Bambara groundnut.* Information leaflet A.1. Vegetable and Ornamental Plant Institute, Pretoria. **Venter, S. & Coertze, A.F. 1997.** *Pigeon peas.* Information leaflet A.2. Vegetable and Ornamental Plant Institute, Pretoria. **Watt, J.M. & Breyer-Brandwijk, M.G. 1962.** *The medicinal and poisonous plants of southern and eastern Africa*, 2nd ed. Livingstone, London. **Williams, C.N., Chew, W.Y. & Rajaratnam, J.A. 1980.** *Tree and field crops of the wetter regions of the tropics.* Longman, Harlow. **Wehmeyer, A.S., Lee, R.B. & Whiting, M. 1969.** Nutrient composition and dietary importance of some vegetable foods eaten by the !Kung Bushmen. *S. Afr. Med. J.* 43: 1529–1530. **Zohary, D. & Hopf, M. 1994.** *Domestication of plants in the Old World*, 2nd ed. Clarendon Press, Oxford.

Flowers and pods of cowpea (*Vigna unguiculata*)

Field of cowpeas (*Vigna unguiculata*)

Cowpeas (seeds of *Vigna unguiculata*)

Pods of mung bean (*Vigna radiata*)

Flowers of wild sweetpea (*Vigna vexillata*)

Mung beans (seeds of *Vigna radiata*)

Roadside stall with granadilla fruits ("guavadilla"), *Passiflora edulis*

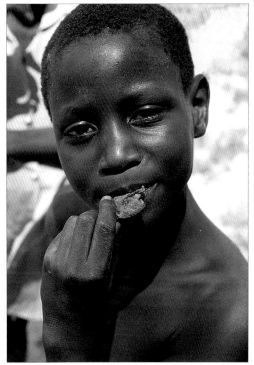

Eating wild sycamore figs (*Ficus sycomorus*)

Selling sour figs (*Carpobrotus edulis*)

CHAPTER 3

Fruits & berries

RURAL CHILDREN IN particular snack extensively on a remarkable diversity of wild fruits across the seasons, which provide an important source of vitamins, minerals, amino acids, and trace elements. The contribution that these wild resources make to maintaining health and preventing disease is generally unrecognised, but may well be of survival value among impoverished people subsisting mainly on maize, and during seasons when other food is scarce. In some cases a single species of fruit is of vital importance for the survival of the local community, such as tsamma (*Citrillus lanatus*) in the Kalahari, nara (*Acanthosicyos horridus*) in Namibia and the mongongo (*Schinziophyton rautanenii*) in northern Botswana. Another fruit of special significance is the calabash (*Lagenaria siceraria*). It is used as vegetable but the main value lies in the mature dry fruits which play an important role inside and outside the house, as unique and versatile containers.

Few people realise that there is already a significant trade in wild fruits in southern Africa. In Zimbabwe, for example, wild fruits can be found on most markets, with *mahobohobo* (*Uapaca kirkiana*) particularly prominent, and snot-apple (*Azanza garckeana*), ber or desert apple from India (*Ziziphus mauritiana*), corky monkey-apple (*Strychnos cocculoides*) and green or spiny monkey-apple (*S. spinosa*) also popular in some areas. Some fruits are sold on local markets or by roadside vendors and they are of considerable importance as a source of income for local communities. These include *mahobohobo* in Malawi and Zimbabwe, *suurvye* (*Carpobrotus edulis*) in the Cape and *umsoba* (*Solanum nigrum*) in the eastern parts of South Africa. One can regularly buy prickly pear (*Opuntia ficus-indica*), Kei-apple (*Dovyalis caffra*), stamvrug (*Englerophytum magalismontanum*), sourplum (*Ximenia caffra*), blue sourplum (*X. americana*), red-milkwood (*Mimusops* species) and passion fruit (*Passiflora edulis*), also known as granadilla.

There are many southern African fruits with considerable potential as new commercial crops and some progress has already been made towards ennobling the marula (*Sclerocarya birrea*) and a few others. Trial plantings of southern African fruit trees in the Negev Desert in Israel include marula, wild medlar (*Vangueria infausta*), wild plum (*Harpephyllum caffrum*), jackalberry (*Diospyros mespiliformis*), velvet raisin bush (*Grewia flava*) and Kei-apple (*Dovyalis caffra*). Marula showed particularly promising results; 12-year-old trees flourish despite the desert conditions and saline irrigation water, producing some 500 kilograms of fruit per tree. In Malawi, at least 22 different indigenous fruit trees from miombo woodland have potential for cultivation by small-scale farmers (Maghembe 1994).

On the basis of fruit size, palatability, yield, abundance and nutritional value, the following fruits have exceptional potential (Ackhurst 1996): marula, sourplum, blue sourplum, jacketplum (*Pappea capensis*), baobab (*Adansonia digitata*), mobola plum (*Parinari curatellifolia*), African mangosteen (*Garcinia livingstonei*), forest milkberry (*Manilkara discolor*), the common cluster fig (*Ficus sycomorus*), green monkey-apple and black monkey-apple (*Strychnos madagascariensis*), wild custard apple (*Annona senegalensis*) and wild date palm (*Phoenix reclinata*). The dry fruit pulp of baobab has indeed become an important commercial product (Kamatou *et al.* 2011). Analyses of the nutritional value of wild fruits (Wehmeyer 1966, 1976; see tables in Fox & Norwood Young 1982 and in Arnold *et al.* 1995) have shown that many of them have very high vitamin C levels.

Much has been written about the delicious indigenous fruits of southern Africa. A popular overview by Swart (1988–91), for example, has contributed to a greater awareness of their value and potential. More attention is already being given to the domestication and cultivation of some of our wild fruits and berries (Ham *et al.* 2008; Van Wyk 2011; Du Preez & De Jager, pers. comm.). Most of the well-known and commonly used edible fruits are described and illustrated here.

Acanthosicyos horridus | Cucurbitaceae | **NARA**; *naras, botterpitte* (Afrikaans); *!nara* (Nama) ■
Nara is a large spiky bush of up to 10 metres in diameter and a metre tall. The branches are completely leafless and very thorny. Plants are either male or female (i.e. male and female flowers occur on separate plants). The small yellow flowers appear in summer, followed (in female plants) by large, rounded, thorny fruits weighing up to a kilogram or more. The fruit surface is greenish yellow and becomes orange when ripe. Inside is a yellowish-orange flesh with numerous pips. The plant is a close relative of the pumpkin and tsamma but it is unlike any other member of the Cucurbitaceae family.

This species is restricted to the sand dunes of the Namib Desert and always grows in areas where subterranean water can be reached by the roots. It is said that they go down more than 15 metres to reach the water supply. A more widely distributed species, which is common in the Kalahari region, is the *gemsbokkomkommer* or Herero melon (see *Acanthosicyos naudiana*).

Seed coat fragments of the *nara* have been found in an archaeological site far removed from the present day distribution of the plant, and were dated at about 8 000 years (Dentlinger 1977). It therefore seems likely that the *nara* has played an important role in the food ecology of the Namib Desert for a very long time. The fruit is important in the lives of the Nama-speaking Topnaar people, said to be an offshoot of the *Rooi Nasie*, one of the five main Nama tribes of the region. Another name for the Topnaar is the *!Naranin* (derived from *!nara*), showing the importance of the plant in this culture (Dentlinger 1977; Van den Eynden *et al.* 1992).

Nara fruits are eaten fresh and are also processed to produce nuts (*botterpitte*, "butter pips") and a special dried fruit roll, which lasts for several months (Van den Eynden *et al.* 1992). The fruits are prodded with the sharp end of the digging stick to test their ripeness. Ripe or near-ripe fruits are cut off with the sharp end of the digging stick and are then scooped up and thrown clear of the thorny branches of the *nara* shrubs, so that they can be picked up on the dune slope below the bush. The load is carried to the homestead where the fruits are buried in a shallow hole to ripen for a few days. Unripe fruit may cause a burning sensation in the mouth. After about four days, the ripe fruits are removed, cut in half and the flesh segments cut out and boiled in a drum over a fire. No water is added, but the natural juices, helped along by regular stirring, soon turns the fruit mass into a thin soup. The soup is used directly with mealie meal to make a sweet porridge, or it is carefully strained to remove all the pips, after which it is poured over the sand in a thin layer, which solidifies to a thin, pancake-like lump. After removal of the sand, the lump is sliced into sections and stored for later use. It is said to last up to a year (Van den Eynden *et al.* 1992). The seeds are carefully dried and used as nuts (known as "*botterpitte*", because the interior of the seed is soft as butter).

The Topnaar people crack the pips between their teeth to open them. Oil from *nara* seeds has cosmetic uses (see Chapter 14). According to Smith (1966), the trade in "butterpips" started in 1877 and they were exported to Cape Town until recently where they were sold as nuts on the Grand Parade.

Acanthosicyos naudiniana | Cucurbitaceae | **GEMSBOK CUCUMBER**, Herero melon ■ This perennial herb is easily recognised by the tsamma-like growth form, with trailing stems, five-lobed leaves, typical yellow flowers and the thick, fleshy rootstock. Unlike the *nara*, this species has male and female flowers on the same plant. The fruits are similar to those of the *nara* – they also have the prominent prickles on the surface and cause the same burning sensation of the tongue and lips if an unripe fruit is eaten. The burning effect is also present in ripe fruits but they are nevertheless eaten by humans at times. The plant is considered to be a candidate for domestication as a high-yielding, dryland crop. Selection and breeding work to produce larger and more palatable fruits will be possible (Grubben & Denton 2004).

The *nara* plant (*Acanthosicyos horridus*)

Cooking the fruit pulp of *nara* (*Acanthosicyos horridus*)

Dried fruit pulp of *nara* (*Acanthosicyos horridus*)

Fruits of gemsbok cucumber (*Acanthosicyos naudiana*)

Flower and thorny branches of the *nara* plant (*Acanthosicyos horridus*)

Adansonia digitata | Malvaceae | **BAOBAB**; *kremetartboom* (Afrikaans); *muvhuyu* (Venda); *movana* (Tswana) ■ This tree is one of the most recognisable trees in the subtropical parts of southern Africa, with its relatively massive trunk, smooth grey bark, glossy green leaves and large woody fruits (Wickens 1982; Kamatou *et al.* 2011; Stutchbury 2013). It has a wide distribution throughout the African continent and is considered to be an indicator of ancient trade routes and villages, where seeds have been dispersed by people over centuries. Large specimens are up to 15 metres tall and more than 20 metres in circumference. During the dry (winter) season, the trees are leafless. The stems are sometimes hollow and collect water, so that they serve as natural water reservoirs in arid regions. The hollow stems are used as shelters by animals (e.g. bats, bees, birds) and humans.

Large pendulous white flowers in early summer are followed by egg-shaped to oblong, calabash-like fruits with velvety outer surfaces. The numerous seeds are each surrounded by a powdery white pulp ("cream-of-tartar") that has traditionally been used to treat fevers, diarrhoea and haemoptysis.

A simple refreshing drink is commonly made by mixing the powdered fruit pulp with cold water, with or without added sugar. In 2008 the European Commission authorised marketing of the baobab dried fruit pulp as a novel food ingredient. This was followed in 2009 with baobab fruit pulp being granted Generally Recognized As Safe (GRAS) status in the USA, allowing for baobab fruit pulp to be used as an ingredient making up 10 per cent of the content of blended fruit drinks and 15 per cent of the content of fruit cereal bars respectively. Subsequent to these approvals, baobab pulp has increasingly been used as an ingredient in diverse foods, beverages, confections, sauces and sorbet ice-creams. It is used for its pleasant tart lemony taste, vitamin and mineral content, and its thickening properties.

Ancylobotrys capensis (=*Landolphia capensis*) | Apocynaceae | **WILD APRICOT**, wild peach; *wilde appelkoos* (Afrikaans); *marapa* (Sotho); *mompudu* (Tswana) ■ The plant is a climbing shrub with milky latex, forming an untidy clump of up to two metres in diameter. Attractive, fragrant, white or pinkish flowers are followed by round, apricot-like fruits of up to 40 millimetres in diameter. They have a tough skin with sweet and tasty fruit pulp surrounding several seeds. The fruits are eaten raw or may be used to make jam. *Ancylobotrys kirkii* and *A. petersiana* also bear edible fruits which are important to local people.

Annona senegalensis | Annonaceae | **WILD CUSTARD APPLE**; *wildesuikerappel* (Afrikaans); *motlepe* (Sotho); *muembe* (Venda); *isiphofu* (Zulu) ■ The tree bears delicious segmented fruits of up to 40 millimetres in diameter, not unlike those of the true custard apple (*A. cherimola*) from South and Central America. They are best picked when green and are then ripened in a dark, warm place until they turn yellow or orange.

Azanza garckeana | Malvaceae | **AZANZA**, slime-apple, snot-apple; *slymappel, snotappel* (Afrikaans); *morojwa* (Tswana); *mutogwe* (Venda) ■ The fruits of this tree are edible while still young. They have a sweet, slimy flesh inside but the fruit wall and pips are not eaten. When the dried fruit pulp is chewed, it gradually absorbs moisture and becomes slimy, hence the vernacular names.

Berchemia discolor | Rhamnaceae | **BROWN IVORY**; *bruinivoor* (Afrikaans); *mogokgomo* (Northern Sotho); *nyiyi* (Tsonga); *muṇie* (Venda); *nmumu* (Zulu) ■ See Chapter 16. The small drupes of this tree turn yellow to orange when ripe, and have a delicious sweet taste. They are not only a popular snack food for rural children, but are also used for brewing beer and for flavouring porridge. Brown ivory is also an important dye plant (see Chapter 16). In the Limpopo Province, the fruits of *Berchemia zeyheri* (red ivory – see Chapter 17) are stored in baskets until they form a sticky mass, which is enjoyed as a sweetmeat.

Fruits of baobab (*Adansonia digitata*)

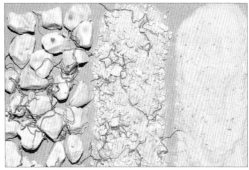

Fruit pulp of baobab (*Adansonia digitata*)

Fruits of wild custard apple (*Annona senegalensis*)

Fruit of wild apricot (*Ancylobotrys capensis*)

Leaves and fruit of wild custard apple (*Annona senegalensis*)

Fruits of the slime-apple (*Azanza garckeana*)

Fruits of brown ivory (*Berchemia discolor*)

Bridelia mollis | Phyllanthaceae, formerly part of Euphorbiaceae | **VELVET SWEETBERRY**; *fluweelsoetbessie* (Afrikaans); *mokokonala* (Tswana); *mukumba-kumbane* (Venda) ■ This is a shrub or small tree of up to seven metres high that occurs mainly in the northern parts of South Africa and in Zimbabwe. It has distinctive velvety leaves with prominent parallel veins extending to the leaf margin. The edible berries are almost spherical, about 10 millimetres in diameter and black when mature. They make a useful jam.

Another valuable fruit tree with potential for domestication is *Bridelia micrantha* (mitzeeri). The tree is known as *mitseeri* in Afrikaans, *motsêrê* in Northern Sotho and *munzere* in Venda. The fruit is an edible oval berry which turns black when it ripens. *Bridelia cathartica* (blue sweetberry) has small, round berries which also turn black when ripe and are used medicinally.

Carissa macrocarpa | Apocynaceae | **AMATUNGULU**, big num-num, Natal plum; *grootnoem-noem* (Afrikaans); *umthungulu* (Zulu) ■ The plant is a spiny shrub or small tree with bright green glossy leaves and forked thorns. The large, bright red fruit (up to 50 millimetres long) is edible (skin, pips, milky juice and all!). Ripe fruits are highly nutritious and make an excellent jelly.

Carissa bispinosa (forest num-num) is known by the forked spines and small (five millimetres in diameter), red edible berries. *Carissa edulis* (simple-spined num-num) differs in its unbranched spines and the delicious fruits which are slightly larger than those of *C. bispinosa* and are purplish black. They are used to make jam and jelly. *Carissa haematocarpa* (Karoo num-num) has small black edible berries.

Carpobrotus edulis | Aizoaceae | **SOUR FIG**; *suurvy* (Afrikaans); *ghaukum* (Khoi) ■ This well-known Cape plant is a robust creeping succulent with large yellow flowers and conical, reddish-brown, fleshy fruit capsules. The plant is easily distinguished from all other species (which may also be harvested to some extent) by the markedly dissimilar size of the large, fleshy sepals (still visible in the fruiting stage) and by the yellow flowers that turn orange-purple with age (the flowers are purple in other similar species such as *Carpobrotus deliciosus* and *C. acinaciformis*). Seven *Carpobrotus* species are found in the Cape coastal region and from there along the east coast to southern Mozambique.

Carpobrotus edulis has become a weed of sandy places in many parts of the world. This species and *C. acinaciformis* are commonly cultivated to stabilise sand dunes and sandy banks, or simply as an attractive and drought-hardy groundcover. The leaves of all the species are astringent and have been used for medicinal purposes (see Chapters 7 and 11).

The fruit contains an edible slimy pulp with shiny brown seeds. The base of the ripe fruit (when it becomes yellow but is still soft) is simply bitten off and the sweet-sour pulp is sucked out – a popular snack amongst Cape children. The dry fruits (brown and shrivelled) are regularly sold on local markets in and around Cape Town, mainly to be processed as jam, but also as an important ingredient of oriental cooking.

Ceratonia siliqua | Fabaceae | **CAROB**; *Johannesbroodboom* (Afrikaans) ■ This evergreen and highly drought-resistant exotic tree, commonly planted in southern Africa, is believed to be of Arabian origin but has been widely cultivated in the Mediterranean region since ancient times. It is a member of the legume family and produces sweet, edible pods that are sold as sweets and are used in confectionery.

Another exotic legume with edible pods is the tamarind (*Tamarindus indica*). The tart, sweet fruit pulp is a popular additive to curry dishes in South Africa, and mixed with water, is a mild purgative. In Zimbabwe, an infusion of the fruit is taken orally to treat venereal disease, and the burned root, mixed with salt is taken in porridge to treat sore throats. Antibacterial, antifungal, antiviral and anthelmintic activities have been found in studies on extracts of the plant (Ponglux *et al.* 1987).

Fruits of the velvet sweetberry (*Bridelia mollis*)

Flowers and fruits of amatungulu (*Carissa macrocarpa*)

Fruits of the forest num-num (*Carissa bispinosa*)

Flowers and fruit of Karoo num-num (*Carissa haematocarpa*)

Leaves and flower of sour fig (*Carpobrotus edulis*)

Sour figs and sour fig jam

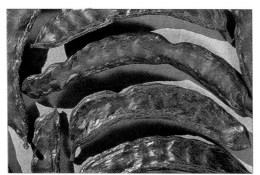

Edible pods of carob (*Ceratonia siliqua*)

Leaves and flowers of *perdevy* (*Carpobrotus acinaciformis*)

Citrillus lanatus | Cucurbitaceae | **TSAMMA**, tsamma melon, wild watermelon; *karkoer, bitter-waatlemoen* (Afrikaans); *t'sama* (Khoisan); *makataan* (Tswana) ∎ This important vegetable and source of water is a creeping annual herb with hairy stems, forked tendrils and three-lobed hairy leaves. Male and female flowers are borne on the same plant and they are bright yellow. The fruits vary considerably, from small and round in the tsamma melon (the wild Kalahari form) to large and oblong in some cultivated forms, such as the *makataan*. The surface of the fruit is smooth, pale green or greyish green with irregular mottled bands of dark green radiating from the stalk. The flesh is pale greenish yellow to reddish pink in modern cultivars. Numerous seeds are embedded in the fruit pulp. They are usually brown to black.

The wild watermelon is widely distributed in Africa and Asia but in southern Africa is best known as the famous tsamma of the Kalahari. The early history of the watermelon can be traced back to at least 4 000 years and the plant was grown as a crop in the Nile valley (Bates & Robinson 1995). Several regional forms have been recorded from various parts of southern Africa, where it is usually cultivated with other crops such as sorghum and maize. It is one of the most popular summer fruits in southern Africa.

Tsamma fruits are the most important water source in the Kalahari during the nine dry months of the year when no surface water is available. It is said that early travellers did not dare cross the Kalahari except in the fruiting time of the tsamma, to ensure a readily available food and moisture supply. According to MacCrone (1937) a person can survive for six weeks on an exclusive diet of tsamma. The fruit is cut open on the one end and the first piece of flesh is eaten. Using a stick, the content is then pounded to a pulp, which is eaten and drunk. The fruits ripen during the winter months and they are said to last for many months without deteriorating. In the Kalahari, the fruits were traditionally gathered in a net bag made from animal sinew (MacCrone 1937). The seeds are considered to be a delicacy and are extracted from the fruits, roasted in the fire, and then sieved and winnowed to separate them from the sand and ash. The seeds are then ground on a flat stone and the white tsamma meal is gathered on a tanned animal skin. This meal is said to be nutritious and has a pleasant nutty taste (it is also used for cosmetic purposes – see Chapter 14).

The large-fruited forms, which have been traditionally cultivated in rural areas since precolonial times, are known by the original Tswana name *makataan*. The leaves and young fruits are utilised as green vegetables, while the fruit flesh may be cooked as a porridge with mealie meal. It is also a useful stock feed in times of drought. Bitter fruits (known as *karkoer* or *bitterwaatlemoen*) are occasionally encountered and these are believed to be poisonous, but have been used as purgatives and for other medicinal applications (Smith 1966). The normal sweet form, especially the large *makataan*, is an old favourite for making jam. Pieces of the fruit from just below the rind are cut into neat squares and used to make what is known in Afrikaans as "*waatlemoenstukkekonfyt*". Recipes for this product and for *makataan* pickles are given by Rood (1994).

Cocos nucifera | Arecaceae | **COCONUT**; *klapperboom* (Afrikaans) ∎ This distinctive and useful palm is a conspicuous feature of the Mozambique coast, but it is not indigenous to southern Africa. The fruits yield coconut milk and the dried fruit flesh, known as copra, is a rich source of oil. The fibre from the husks, called coir, is used for padding and for rope.

Cordyla africana | Fabaceae | **WILD-MANGO**; *wildemango* (Afrikaans); *igowane-lehlati* (Zulu) ∎ Wild-mango is a tree from the eastern subtropical and tropical parts of southern Africa. It bears large oval fruits containing large pips and an edible (but not very tasty) fruit pulp rich in vitamin C.

Cryptocarya wyliei | Lauraceae | **RED QUINCE**; *rooikweper* (Afrikaans); *umngcabe* (Zulu) ∎ The tree occurs along the east coast of South Africa. The round red drupes are edible but have large pips and are not particularly tasty.

The tsamma plant (*Citrillus lanatus*)

Tsamma seeds (*Citrillus lanatus*)

Fruits of the tsamma plant (*Citrillus lanatus*)

The large-fruited *makataan*, a form of *Citrillus lanatus* popular for making preserves

Cucumis anguria | Cucurbitaceae | **GHERKIN**; West Indian gherkin; *agurkie* (Afrikaans) ■ The plant is an annual creeping herb without a woody rootstock and no tubers. It is the only wild cucumber with prickly (aculeate) stems and leaf stalks, and is therefore easy to distinguish from all similar-looking species (Kirkbride 1993). Male and female flowers occur on different plants. The small yellow female flowers are followed by prickly (aculeate) fruits. There are two varieties of this well-known relative of the cucumber. The typical variety, var. *anguria*, is the popular gherkin or *agurkie*, widely cultivated in southern Africa, particularly for pickles and jam (*agurkiekonfyt*). The var. *longipes* is a wild plant with much longer and denser spikes on the fruit and is not suitable for jam because it is bitter. The gherkin may be confused with two other species, *Cucumis africanus* (*doringkomkommer* in Afrikaans) and *C. zeyheri* (wild cucumber; *wildekomkommer* in Afrikaans). Both these species are perennial herbs with woody rootstocks and they both lack fleshy tubers (unlike *C. kalahariensis*, see Chapter 5). They also differ from *C. anguria* and *C. kalahariensis* in being monoecious (i.e., male and female flowers occur on the same plant). *Cucumis africanus* is widely distributed in Angola, Botswana, Namibia, South Africa and Zimbabwe (Kirkbride 1993). The fruits are very variable but are mostly large and oblong, with yellow-brown longitudinal stripes on a green background. The oblong fruit type is usually non-bitter and occurs only in South Africa, Namibia and Angola. It has been used as a source of water. In contrast, the smaller ellipsoid fruit type of *C. africanus* is bitter, poisonous and therefore not suitable for human use. *Cucumis zeyheri* is similar to *C. africana* but the prickles on the fruits are rounded in cross-section, not flattened near their bases as in the latter. Some fruits are said to be bitter while others are edible. *Cucumis zeyheri* is more restricted in its distribution and occurs only in the eastern part of the region (Lesotho, South Africa, Swaziland, Mozambique, Zimbabwe and Zambia). The name "gherkin" is somewhat confusing, because it is also applied to young fruits of the ordinary cucumber (*C. sativus*) which are used for pickles.

Cucumis metuliferus | Cucurbitaceae | **JELLY MELON**, African horned cucumber ■ The plant is an annual with creeping stems radiating from a woody rootstock. Fleshy tubers are absent. Male and female flowers are borne on the same plant. The large fruits are uniformly yellow, orange or red. They are very distinctive because of the widely spaced, very large conical protuberances (aculei) on their surfaces. These prickles are blunt, about 10 millimetres long and two to five millimetres in diameter. The fruit flesh is greenish and translucent. Commercial cultivation for export is known from Kenya and from New Zealand (Bates & Robinson 1995). In New Zealand, the jelly melon is known as "Kiwano", a registered trademark (Morton 1987).

Cucurbita pepo | Cucurbitaceae | **PUMPKIN**; *pampoen* (Afrikaans) ■ The pumpkin, with its characteristic white-skinned fruit is a familiar sight in rural southern Africa, often stored for months in the sun on rooftops after harvesting. The large, yellow flowers are somewhat bitter, but are boiled into a colourful relish to be eaten with maize meal. The seeds are roasted and eaten as a snack. Leaves are boiled and applied to the chest as a hot compress in cases of pneumonia. Root infusions are taken orally for rheumatism, and the ground seeds are eaten to treat tapeworm. Some cultivars of *C. pepo* are grown as ornamental gourds (*sierkalbassie* or *stopkalbassie* in Afrikaans). These are cultivars of squash that closely resemble the ordinary vegetable squash in growth form, leaves and flowers, but differ in their ornate fruits. They are often confused with the bottle gourd (*Lagenaria siceraria*) because the fruits are somewhat similar and they are also used as gourds and small containers. However, these ornamental gourds are easily distinguished from *Lagenaria*. They have smaller, more coarsely hairy leaves, yellow flowers (not white as in *Lagenaria*) and small, smooth seeds (not angular and winged as in *Lagenaria*). The fruits resemble calabashes. They are small, hard-shelled and variously shaped, often with decorative warty protuberances. These fruits are usually bitter and not edible, but are used for ornamental purposes and traditionally as a form on which to darn stockings.

Fruits of wild gherkin (*Cucumis anguria* var. *longipes*), together with leaves of wild cucumber (*Cucumis zeyheri*)

Flowers and fruits of the gherkin (*Cucumis anguria*)

Preserves made from gherkin (*Cucumis anguria* var. *anguria*)

Flower and fruit of wild cucumber (*Cucumis zeyheri*)

Preserves made from wild cucumber (*Cucumis zeyheri*)

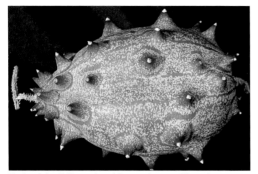

Fruit of the jelly melon (*Cucumis metuliferus*)

Flower and fruit of ornamental gourd (*Cucurbita pepo*)

Diospyros mespiliformis | Ebenaceae | **JACKALBERRY**; *jakkalsbessie* (Afrikaans); *umtoma* (Swazi); *ntoma* (Tsonga); *musuma* (Venda) ■ The plant is a large bushveld tree, occurring in Angola, the extreme northern part of Namibia, Botswana, Zimbabwe, Mozambique and the lowveld region of South Africa. The fruits are about 20 millimetres in diameter, and turn yellow or purplish when they ripen. They are delicious when eaten fresh, but are also popular for brewing beer and to store as a preserve for later use. *Diospyros ramulosa* (*koenoekam* in Khoi) is a Karoo shrub which yields small edible fruits, considered to be the best of all locally available wild fruits (Willem Steenkamp, pers. comm.). The jackalberry and *koenoekam* are closely related to persimmon (*Diospyros kaki*), which has similar but much larger fruits. *Diospyros* means "pear of the gods".

Dovyalis caffra | Flacourtiaceae | **KEI-APPLE**; *Keiappel* (Afrikaans); *mohlono* (Northern Sotho); *umqokolo* (Xhosa, Zulu) ■ The Kei-apple is a shrub or small tree with long, sharp thorns and leathery, glossy leaves clustered along the branches. Male and female flowers occur on separate trees. The rounded, yellow fruits are up to 40 millimetres in diameter. They are sour but very tasty, and have become popular for making jellies and jams. Rosemary du Preez and Karen de Jager of the Agricultural Research Council have already made selections of superior clones. The edible but sour fruits of *Dovyalis rhamnoides* (common sourberry) and *D. zeyheri* (wild apricot) are both also popular for making jelly and jam. All three species of *Dovyalis* occur in the eastern parts of South Africa, and the distributions of *D. caffra* and *D. zeyheri* also extends northwards to Zimbabwe.

Englerophytum magalismontanum | Sapotaceae | **STEMFRUIT**, stamvrug, Transvaal milk-plum; *stamvrug* (Afrikaans); *mohlatswa* (Northern Sotho); *umnumbela* (Swazi, Zulu) ■ This small to medium-sized tree, previously known as *Bequertiodendron magalismontanum*, occurs mainly in South Africa and Zimbabwe. It has characteristic brown hairy stems, dark green glossy leaves with silver hairs on the lower surfaces and dense clusters of flowers (and fruits) along the stems. The edible and tasty red berries are about 25 millimetres in diameter, with a single seed inside. They are sometimes sold on the roadsides and are popular not only for eating fresh, but also for making jam, jelly and wine. Related plants such as Natal milkplum (*Englerophytum natalensis*), fluted milkwood (*Chrysophyllum viridifolium*) and the milkberries (see *Manilkara mochisia* on page 52) all have tasty edible fruits.

Ficus sycomorus | Moraceae | **SYCAMORE FIG**, common cluster fig; *trosvy* (Afrikaans); *mogo-bôya* (Northern Sotho); *umncongo* (Zulu) ■ This fig is a large tree with a wide spreading crown and heart-shaped, hairy leaves. The fruits (figs or so-called syconia) are 20 to 50 millimetres in diameter and are much sought after, especially by rural children. They are eaten fresh or may be dried for storage. The tree occurs from the tropical parts of southern Africa northwards to the Mediterranean region and particularly Egypt, where it has been cultivated for its syconia and timber since at least 3000 BC (Zohary & Hopf 1994). *Ficus sur* and *F. vallis-choudae* are two other wild figs with edible syconia. The former has irregularly toothed leaves and fruits borne in large clusters on the main trunk, while the latter is similar to *F. sycomorus* but can be distinguished by the more or less hairless leaves and the figs which are borne on young stems. The common fig in gardens is *Ficus carica*, originally from the Mediterranean region.

Flacourtia indica | Flacourtiaceae | **GOVERNOR'S PLUM** ■ The dark red to purplish berries of this shrub or small tree are sour but edible and have been used for making jam.

Garcinia livingstonei | Clusiaceae | **AFRICAN MANGOSTEEN**; *Afrikageelmelkhout* (Afrikaans); *mokongono* (Northern Sotho); *muphiphi* (Venda); *umphimbi* (Zulu) ■ The tree has a characteristic rigid branching pattern and large leathery leaves. The delicious, bright orange-red berries are about 30 millimetres in diameter and are widely used for eating and for brewing beer. As a fruit tree with possible commercial potential, the African mangosteen deserves more attention.

Fruits of the jackalberry (*Diospyros mespiliformis*)

Flower and fruit of the *koenoekam* (*Diospyros ramulosa*)

Fruits of the Kei-apple (*Dovyalis caffra*)

Leaves and fruit of *stamvrug* (*Englerophytum magalismontanum*)

Fruits (figs) of the sycamore fig (*Ficus sycomorus*)

Fruits (figs) of the wild fig (*Ficus sur*)

Fruits of the governor's plum (*Flacourtia indica*)

Fruits of African mangosteen (*Garcinia livingstonei*)

Grewia flava | Malvaceae | **VELVET RAISIN**, bushman raisin bush; *rosyntjiebos* (Afrikaans); *morêtlwa* (Tswana) ■ The plant is a multi-stemmed shrub or small tree with a very wide distribution in the central parts of southern Africa. The leaves are characteristically greyish green and densely hairy. The attractive small, yellow flowers have numerous stamens arranged in a group in the centre. They are followed by rounded or somewhat lobed drupes of less than 10 millimetres in diameter. Most of the volume of the fruit is made up of the pips, with only a thin layer of sweet flesh. Despite their small size and thin flesh layer, these fruits are an important food item, particularly in the Kalahari region.

Few other plants are more useful to the Kalahari people than the velvet raisin. The stems were traditionally used for making hunting bows and arrows, and the fibrous bark serves as a useful rope for tying things together (see photograph of fire-drill on page 347). The fruits are much sought after as a food and as a basis for brewing beer. They may also be dried and stored for later use.

The stems of several other *Grewia* species are used in southern Africa for spear handles, hut poles and fish traps. Edible fruits are obtained from several other species such as *Grewia microthyrsa*, *G. monticola*, *G. retinervis* and *G. villosa*. In Kaokoland, the berries of *G. flavescens* (*omuhe* in Herero) are soaked in water for two or three days to make a refreshing drink. In this region, edible berries are also obtained from *Grewia schinzii*, *G. tenax* and *G. villosa* (Malan & Owen-Smith 1974). The former two species are used for bows and arrow shafts.

Harpephyllum caffrum | Anacardiaceae | **WILD PLUM**; *wildepruim, suurpruim* (Afrikaans); *umgwenya* (Xhosa, Zulu) ■ The wild plum is a large tree, mainly from the forests along the east coast of South Africa. Dark green, glossy leaves, robust stems and ornamental red berries (drupes) make this an attractive and popular garden tree. The edible fruits are commonly used for eating and for making jams and jellies. The tree has some potential as a commercial fruit crop but preliminary trial plantings in Israel were rather disappointing. Several other uses are known – the bark is a popular traditional medicine and cosmetic for facial saunas, and the timber has been used for furniture and carvery.

Hexalobus monopetalus | Annonaceae | **SHAKAMA-PLUM**; *xakama* (Tsonga); *shakama-pruim* (Afrikaans); *muhuhuma* (Venda) ■ This relative of the custard apple is a deciduous shrub or small tree from bushveld areas in the northern parts of southern Africa. Cylindrical or oval berries of about 30 millimetres long, often constricted between the seeds, are borne in late summer. They turn orange to red when ripe and are much sought after for eating and for making jam because of their delicious taste.

Hydnora africana | Hydnoraceae | ***JAKKALSKOS*** (Afrikaans); *kanni(e), kannip* (Khoi) ■ This unusual leafless plant is a parasite that grows only on the roots of *Euphorbia mauritanica* plants. It only becomes visible when the flowers appear above the ground. The fruit superficially resembles a pomegranate and is a traditional Khoi food item, first recorded by Thunberg in 1774 from the Agter-Hantam (De Beer & Van Wyk 2011). The over-ripe fruits are delicious when eaten raw or baked on a fire – the white fruit pulp has a sweetish mealy taste. *Jakkalskos* is used for several Cape dishes (recipes are given by Rood 1994). One way of preparing the fruit is to scoop out the flesh with a spoon and then to push it through a sieve to remove the numerous seeds. The fruit pulp may be whipped with cream, a little sherry, sugar and cinnamon, and served like ice-cream (Rood 1994). Leipoldt's recipe for *jakkalskos* soufflé calls for the white of three eggs instead of cream. The mixture is baked in the oven, and served as a warm pudding (Rood 1994). The fruit wall (pericarp) is extremely astringent and has been used for tanning and to preserve fishing nets. Infusions and decoctions of the plant are used to treat diarrhoea, dysentery, and kidney and bladder complaints, and are gargled for sore throats. Infusions are used as face washes and are taken orally for acne (Sylvia Malinga, pers. comm.).

Flower of the velvet raisin (*Grewia flava*)

Fruits of the velvet raisin (*Grewia flava*)

Flowers of Kalahari sand raisin (*Grewia retinervis*)

Fruits of the Kalahari sand raisin (*Grewia retinervis*)

Fruits of the wild plum (*Harpephyllum caffrum*)

Fruit of the shakama-plum (*Hexalobus monopetalus*)

Flowers of the *kanni* or *jakkalskos* (*Hydnora africana*)

Ripe fruit of the *kanni* or *jakkalskos* (*Hydnora africana*)

Lagenaria siceraria | Cucurbitaceae | **CALABASH, BOTTLE GOURD**; *kalbas* (Afrikaans); *iselwa* (Xhosa, Zulu); *segwana* (Tswana); *moraka* (Northern Sotho) ∎ The plant is a close relative of pumpkins and squashes. It is a creeping and climbing annual herb with the stems supported by many tendrils. The large, rounded leaves are somewhat toothed along the margins and are hairy below. Hairs are also present on the leaf stalks and young fruits. The flowers resemble those of pumpkins but they are white (not yellow) and open at night. White flowers are unique in the family as a whole, and are therefore an easy way to distinguish *Lagenaria* from all other gourds and pumpkins. The wild cucumber (*Coccinia rehmannii* – see Chapter 5) has small cream-coloured flowers but this plant is unlikely to be confused with gourds and pumpkins.

The fruit is green at first, but becomes pale brown when it ripens and dries, leaving a thick, hard, hollow shell with practically nothing inside except the seeds (the fruit flesh dries out completely). *Lagenaria* seeds are easily distinguished from those of other cucurbits. They are angular in shape, with ridges and wings along the surface. The fruits are remarkably variable in size and shape.

Lagenaria is one of the most ancient of all crop plants and is considered to be indigenous to Africa. There are many enigmatic questions around the origin of the bottle gourd, however. Did it really originate in Africa, as is usually supposed? Was it domesticated as a food plant or as a source of gourds? Why are all the other five wild species of *Lagenaria* perennial and *L. siceraria* the only annual? Archaeological remains in Africa date back a mere 2 000 years, while Central and South American sites have seeds dating back about 9 000 years. No-one can say with certainty if the seemingly spontaneous populations in Africa are truly wild. It is possible that early wild forms were dispersed along the sea currents to tropical America, Asia and Papua New Guinea. The fruits are known to float in the sea for many months without the seeds losing their viability. A study using fruit rind thickness and radiocarbon dating (Erickson *et al.* 2005) came to the conclusion that the domesticated form of the calabash was already present in the Americas 10 000 years ago and that it was introduced from Asia to the Americas by ancient humans who colonised the New World. These authors suggested that the calabash was domesticated long before any other food crop.

In southern Africa, the leaves are commonly eaten as a vegetable and are added fresh to maize porridge, or they are made into a relish, mixed with other plants. Dried leaves are stored for use in the dry season. The young shoots seem to be an important vegetable, unlike the young fruits, which are considered by some to be an emergency food. Leaves are also used as traditional medicine in several African countries (Neuwinger 2000).

Immature fruits are nevertheless used as vegetables in many parts of the world, including southern Africa. One cultivar with a slender fruit shape is particularly popular in Chinese cooking. In some parts of southern Africa, the fruit is a popular cooked vegetable when it is young, sweet and green (Gift Kafundo, pers. comm.), but bitter fruits are not eaten, and may be poisonous.

A form of small gourd with a coarse skin is commonly available and is especially popular as a vegetable (known as *maranka*), but this is actually a true squash (see *Cucurbita pepo*). Numerous recipes are available for bottle gourd and *maranka* (see Rood 1994). These include stews, cakes, curries and even fish dishes. One popular dish is to slice the young calabash into small discs, which are then layered with white bread torn into small pieces, followed by sugar, cinnamon and butter. The mixture is finally topped with a thin cornflour batter. The dish is baked slowly until done, and is then grilled for a short time before serving (Rood 1994).

Bottle gourds are widely used in rural southern Africa for bowls, cups, ladles, bottles, floats, pipes and musical instruments. Non-bitter types are used for water, milk and beer containers. Dry fruits are popularly known as calabashes, and these calabashes and products made from them are frequently offered for sale at roadside stalls and curio markets. They are mostly used as ornaments, often in flower arrangements. As attractive natural containers, calabashes are put to many practical or decorative uses in and around the house.

Calabash or bottle gourd (*Lagenaria siceraria*)

The characteristic white flower of calabash
(*Lagenaria siceraria*)

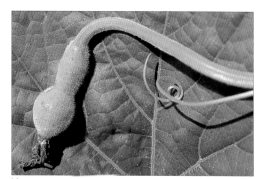
Young fruit of calabash (*Lagenaria siceraria*)

Calabashes are commonly cultivated in rural areas in southern Africa

Himba milk bottle made from a calabash fruit
(*Lagenaria siceraria*)

Lannea edulis | Anacardiaceae | **WILD GRAPE**; *wildedruif* (Afrikaans); *pheho* (Tswana); *muporotso* (Venda) ■ The wild grape is a dwarf shrub with enormous woody branches below ground level, giving rise to short flowering and fruiting branches, usually less than a metre tall. The fruit is about 10 millimetres in diameter and characteristically have a few little points at the tip, in common with other *Lannea* species. Marula fruit, when very young, also has these small points at the tip. Although there is only a thin layer of flesh around the stone, the fruit of wild grape is popular for eating, the taste being reminiscent of grapes. The tough skin and pips are discarded. The underground rhizomes are said to be edible when cooked but they are also popular for making infusions or decoctions to treat diarrhoea. Two related species, the live-long (*Lannea discolor*) and the false marula (*Lannea schweinfurthii* var. *stuhlmannii*) also have edible fruits similar to those of the wild grape, but both these species are deciduous bushveld trees. The bark of the live-long is sometimes used for medicine and for tanning and rope making. Split roots are used in basketry and the timber may be used for carving bowls and spoons. Leaf poultices of the wild grape and the live-long are applied to sore eyes, boils and abscesses. The bark of the false marula (so named because the trees closely resemble marula trees) is used for dyeing and tanning. Root surfaces are covered with a velvety layer of yellowish brown hairs, which have interesting uses (see Chapter 9). For medicinal uses of *Lannea edulis* see Chapter 10.

Luffa cylindrica | Cucurbitaceae | **SPONGE GOURD**, vegetable sponge ■ This interesting pumpkin-like plant is thought to be of Asian origin, but has been cultivated since early times. The young fruit is eaten as a vegetable, but the main interest for cultivating the plant in southern Africa is for the mature fruit. When it dries out, the inside yields a dense network of tough fibres which are sold as natural bath sponges and as scrubbing utensils.

Manilkara mochisia | Sapotaceae | **LOWVELD MILKBERRY**; *laeveldmelkbessie* (Afrikaans); *n'wambu* (Tsonga); *muṇamba* (Venda); *umnquambo* (Zulu) ■ This useful plant is a shrub or small tree from low-lying bushveld areas in the northern parts of southern Africa. The leaves are oblong, hairless, often notched at the tip and occur in terminal clusters. Delicious edible berries are produced in large numbers. They are oval in shape, with a yellow skin and red fruit pulp surrounding the one to three pips. The lowveld milkberry is considered to have commercial potential as a fruit tree. Two other species of *Manilkara* with delicious edible fruits are worth mentioning: the Zulu milkberry (*M. concolor*) and the forest milkberry (*M. discolor*). They all have milky latex, hence the common name milkberry (*melkbessie* in Afrikaans). The roots of all three species are used in traditional medicine and the wood is used for various purposes, such as xylophone keys in the case of *M. discolor* and fencing poles in the case of *M. mochisia*.

Mimusops zeyheri | Sapotaceae | **COMMON RED-MILKWOOD**; *moepel* (Afrikaans); *mmupudu* (Northern Sotho, Tswana); *mububulu* (Venda); *umphushane* (Swazi, Zulu) ■ This milkwood is a shrub or medium-sized tree of bushveld areas in northern South Africa, Zimbabwe and parts of Botswana. The branches and leathery leaves have reddish-brown hairs and contain milky latex. The attractive orange fruits are egg-shaped and about 25 millimetres long. The fruit pulp, rich in vitamin C, is very sweet and tasty and has a mealy texture. Large trees are found in the temple of Great Zimbabwe, suggesting that this milkberry has been an important food source since early times.

Two other red-milkwoods are commonly encountered along the east coast of southern Africa: a forest species, the bush red-milkwood (*Mimusops obovata*) and a dune specialist, the coastal red-milkwood (*M. caffra*). Both have tasty edible fruits similar to those of *Mimusops zeyheri*. Both produce useful timber and the bark is used in traditional medicine. Another member of the family with edible berries is the Natal bush-milkwood (*Vitellariopsis marginata*), which is also restricted to the east coast (Eastern Cape to Mozambique).

Fruits of the wild grape (*Lannea edulis*)

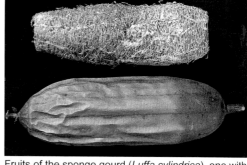
Fruits of the sponge gourd (*Luffa cylindrica*), one with the fruit skin removed

Fruits of the lowveld milkberry (*Manilkara mochisia*)

Fruits of the Zulu milkberry (*Manilkara concolor*)

Flowers of the common red-milkwood (*Mimusops zeyheri*)

Fruits of the common red-milkwood (*Mimusops zeyheri*)

Fruits of the bush red-milkwood (*Mimusops obovata*)

Fruits of the coastal red-milkwood (*Mimusops caffra*)

Monanthotaxis caffra | Annonaceae | **DWABA BERRY**; *dwababessie* (Afrikaans); *isidwaba* (Xhosa) ■ The plant is a woody climber or shrub with aromatic leaves, cream-coloured flowers and clusters of attractive, orange-red, edible berries. The stems are used for tying in hut construction and in making rafts from *Raphia* palm leaf stalks.

Muraltia spinosa (=*Nylandtia spinosa*) | Polygalaceae | **TORTOISE BERRY**; *skilpadbessie* (Afrikaans) ■ The tortoise berry is a spiny shrub (up to one metre in height) from the Western Cape, with small pink flowers and attractive orange to red berries. This plant, called *cargoe* by the locals, was illustrated in Simon van der Stel's expedition to Namaqualand in 1685, and the fruit was reported to be thirst-quenching. The fruit is still a popular snack, and an infusion of the leaves and stems, mixed with those of *Calobota angustifolia* (=*Lebeckia multiflora*), is taken for colds, influenza and bronchitis (Mrs Bester, pers. comm.). Infusions of the leaves and stems have been taken as a general tonic and for tuberculosis, abdominal pain and as a bitter digestive. The fruit of the closely related but taller (up to 2.5 metres) *Muraltia scoparia* (*duinebessie* or *bokbessie* in Afrikaans) is almost identical to those of *M. spinosa* and is used in the same way.

Opuntia ficus-indica | Cactaceae | **PRICKLY PEAR**; *turksvy* (Afrikaans) ■ The plant is a robust, spiny succulent from central America that has become an integral part of the southern African flora. The thick, fleshy stems are leaf-like and perform the function of leaves (so-called cladodes). Flowers are usually orange and they are followed by delicious orange-green or red fruits with a tasty fruit pulp in which numerous black seeds are embedded.

Prickly pear has become a troublesome weed in the subtropical parts of southern Africa, but the introduction of biological control measures has alleviated the problem to some extent. Despite their weedy nature, prickly pears have played an important role in the rural economy of southern Africa since early times and have become an important commercial fruit crop. Three types of cultivars can be distinguished (Wessels 1988): the "blue-leaved type", with rounded, bluish-grey cladodes and red fruits of inferior quality, grown mainly as livestock fodder in dry areas; the "long-leaved or tree types" with erect stems, relatively small thorns and green, yellowish-green or white fruits; and the "bushy types" with a small, spreading habit and variable leaves and fruits (green, red, pink or even mottled). The "bushy types" are highly productive and include several modern cultivars. Innovative work to develop prickly pears for livestock fodder and fruit production has been done over the last 50 years in South Africa and Israel. A useful overview of the industry in southern Africa is given by Wessels (1988). Yields of up to 60 tons per hectare have been recorded, but commercial harvests of modern cultivars are in the region of 20 to 30 tons per hectare. Fruit size varies from 80 to more than 150 grams and the nutritional value is comparable to that of other commercial fruits.

The prickly pear is best known as a source of livestock fodder and delicious fruits, but there are numerous other products that may be derived from this versatile plant. The young cladodes are eaten as a vegetable and salad. The mature cladodes are processed into useable soap, the immature fruit is pickled as mock gherkins, and the mature fruit turned into jams, syrups, crystallised fruit, alcoholic drinks, and used as a flavouring agent for yogurt, ice-cream and liqueurs. The fruit has long been fermented and used to make wine (amongst others by the Pedi people). The red fruit type is said to be most suitable for wine making. Dried flowers are used in Italy as a treatment for prostate hypertrophy.

Osteospermum moniliferum (=*Chrysanthemoides monilifera*) | Asteraceae | **BIETOU** (Khoi, Afrikaans); bush tickberry ■ *Bietou* is a common shrub or small tree with somewhat fleshy leaves, attractive yellow flower heads and small, black or orange-brown, fleshy, edible drupes. The fruits are nowadays mainly eaten by children, but are said to have been an important Khoi food. As a snack food, the orange-brown fruits of the Western Cape form of the species are particularly tasty. The name *bietou* has been applied to several different species.

FRUITS & BERRIES

Fruits of the dwaba berry (*Monanthotaxis caffra*)

Fruits of the *duinebessie* (*Muraltia scoparia*)

Flowers and fruit of tortoise berry or *skilpadbessie* (*Muraltia spinosa*)

Flowers of the *duinebessie* (*Muraltia scoparia*)

Prickly pear fruits (*Opuntia ficus-indica*)

Flowers and fruits of *bietou* (*Osteospermum moniliferum*) – widespread form with black drupes

Fruits of *bietou* (*Osteospermum moniliferum*) – Western Cape form with orange drupes

Pappea capensis │Sapindaceae│ **JACKETPLUM**; *doppruim* (Afrikaans); *mopsinyugane* (Northern Sotho); *umgqogqo* (Zulu) ■ The plant is a small to medium-sized tree, often with an umbrella-shaped growth form resulting from the removal of lower branches by goats and other browsers. It occurs over large parts of southern Africa and is absent only from the western Kalahari and northern Namibia. Male and female flowers occur on separate trees. In the late summer, the round capsules split open to reveal shiny black seeds surrounded by a brightly coloured red or brown fleshy aril. An aril is a fleshy layer attached to a seed, as is also found in the related litchi "fruit". The latter is translucent and jelly-like, with a delicious sweet-sour flavour. It can be collected to make jelly and jam. The seed oil is edible and has been used to oil guns and to make soap.

Parinari curatellifolia │Chrysobalanaceae│ **MOBOLA PLUM**; *grysappel* (Afrikaans); *mmola* (Northern Sotho); *muchakata* (Shona); *amabulwa* (Zulu) ■ The mobola plum is a medium-sized to large tree of four to 20 metres tall, restricted to bushveld areas in the northeastern parts of southern Africa (mainly Zimbabwe) and the lowveld region in South Africa. The tree is variable but can be recognised by the felted leaves with their prominent parallel side veins and the relatively large, yellowish brown, scaly fruits of about 40 millimetres long. Because of the value of the fruit, the trees are not felled when new agricultural land is being cleared. The fruit is very tasty when ripe and is also used to make beer. The two large seeds (nuts) inside the bony endocarp are eaten or may be used as an ingredient of other dishes. Dry fruits may be kept as an emergency foodstuff. The timber and bark have many uses. Bark is harvested for medicine, for dyeing in basketry and for tanning leather. The mobola plum has a close relative, the dwarf mobola plum (*Parinari capensis*), which occurs over large parts of tropical and subtropical southern Africa, including Namibia, Angola, Zambia, Zimbabwe, Mozambique, South Africa and Botswana. This plant is a small shrub (usually less than 0.3 metres tall but rarely up to two metres) with thick woody underground rhizomes and short flowering and fruiting branches emerging seasonally above the ground. Apart from the difference in growth form, the two species are almost identical. The fruit of the dwarf mobola is equally popular to those of *Parinari curatellifolia* for eating and for brewing beer.

Passiflora edulis │Passifloraceae│ **GRANADILLA**; passion fruit ■ This South American creeper is frequently cultivated in South Africa for its tasty fruit. There are two forms of the species: var. *edulis*, with dark purple fruit (the most commonly cultivated form) and var. *flava*, with yellow fruit. These fruits are sometimes called "guavadillas", presumably because their appearance is reminiscent of both guavas and granadillas, but there is obviously no real relation with guava. The yellow granadilla has become naturalised in parts of KwaZulu-Natal and fruit is often sold along roadsides. It has a delicious sweet-sour taste and a very tasty cold drink may be prepared from the fruit pulp. Several other species of *Passiflora* have become weeds in southern Africa.

Phoenix reclinata │Arecaceae or Palmae│ **WILD DATE PALM**; *wildedadelboom* (Afrikaans); *isundu* (Xhosa, Zulu); *ankindu* (Tsonga) ■ The wild date palm is a clump-forming palm, easily recognised by the multi-stemmed appearance and slender leaning stems. The closely related real date palm from North Africa and Arabia (*Phoenix dactylifera*) is similar, but has a thick, single stem and distinctly grey leaves. Male and female flowers occur on separate trees. The orange-brown fruit is about 15 millimetres long and date-like in appearance. Wild date palms are found in the subtropical and tropical regions of southern Africa, from the eastern Cape northwards to Mozambique, Zimbabwe, northern Botswana, northern Namibia, Angola, Zambia and Malawi.

The wild date palm is a valuable resource to rural people in southern Africa. The fruit, although small and with only a thin layer of flesh, is edible and highly nutritious. Stems are turned into hand brooms by separating the fibres. The young stem tips (palm hearts) are harvested as food in some parts. The leaf segments are important for making baskets and mats, while the midribs are used in hut construction and for making fish kraals. Perhaps the most important use of the plant is for sap tapping, to produce palm wine. The wild date palm is not as important as the ilala palm and mokola

Male flowers of the jacketplum (*Pappea capensis*)

Fruits of the jacketplum (*Pappea capensis*) showing arils

Dwarf mobola plum (*Parinari capensis*)

Fruits of mobola plum (*Parinari curatellifolia*)

Flower of granadilla (*Passiflora edulis*)

Fruits of yellow granadilla or "guavadilla" (*Passiflora edulis* var. *flava*)

palm as a source of palm wine, but it nevertheless contributes significantly to the palm wine industry (see *Hyphaene petersiana* in Chapter 6).

The roots of *Phoenix reclinata*, used in a mixture with other plants, are taken orally by apprentice healers to facilitate learning the healing arts (Ncindani, Maswanganyi, pers. comm.). The fruit of the real date palm have GABA activity. It is produced on a small scale in southern Africa and is regularly available at farm stalls nowadays. The first date palms in the northern Cape and southern Namibia are said to have originated from pips discarded by English and German soldiers.

Physalis peruviana | Solanaceae | **CAPE(D) GOOSEBERRY**; *appelliefie* (Afrikaans); *iguzi* (Xhosa); *murungudane* (Venda) ■ This South American plant is an erect herb of about a metre tall with heart-shaped, velvety leaves, yellow flowers and characteristic bladdery fruits. It occurs as wild or semi-wild plants in many parts of South Africa, Lesotho and Namibia. The fruit is actually a bright orange, many-seeded berry, which is enclosed by the persistent papery calyx. The berries fall down when they ripen and are not picked but collected from under the plants. They are widely eaten fresh by rural children but their main use is to make a delicious jam. The leaves are commonly eaten raw or cooked as a pot herb. Infusions of the leaves have been administered as enemas in children for upset stomachs, and have been applied as warm poultices to swellings. Root infusions have many uses, not unlike those of *Withania somnifera* (see Chapter 8).

Piliostigma thonningii | Fabaceae | **CAMEL'S FOOT**; *kameelspoor* (Afrikaans); *nkolokotso* (Tsonga); *mokgataba* (Tswana) ■ The mealy fruit pulp is eaten by children in Zimbabwe.

Pollichia campestris | Caryophyllaceae | ***TEESUIKERKAROO*** (Afrikaans) ■ The plant is a herb or small shrub with slender branches, numerous small leaves and small white berries, which are actually the bracts of the flowers that become fleshy as the small black seeds ripen inside. These small berries have a sweet but bland taste and are eaten by rural children. *Pollichia* is an excellent grazing plant and occurs over most parts of southern Africa.

Prosopis glandulosa | Fabaceae | **MESQUITE**; *muskietboom* (Afrikaans) ■ This North American tree has become a serious invader, especially in the Northern Cape Province of South Africa. The ripe pods have a sweet taste and are commonly eaten by rural children as a snack.

Rhoicissus tomentosa | Vitaceae | **WILD GRAPE**; *bosdruif* (Afrikaans); *isaqoni* (Xhosa); *isinwazi* (Zulu) ■ This woody climber has large velvety leaves, tendrils for climbing and purple, grape-like berries that turn red to dark purple or black when they ripen. The fruit is eaten by children and it has few equals for making good-quality jam, jelly and vinegar. Recipes can be found in Rood (1994). Wild grape jelly is made by boiling the fruit in just enough water to almost cover the fruit in the pot. When soft, the fruit flesh is separated from the skins and pips, to obtain a thin, juicy pulp. About 200 grams of sugar are added for every 250 millilitres of fruit pulp, and the mixture is then boiled slowly, stirring to dissolve the sugar. Ten minutes after adding the sugar, the consistency of the mixture is tested by slowly pouring a small quantity from a spoon after a brief period of cooling. Boiling continues until the mixture runs down the spoon as a single blob, indicating that the desired jelly consistency has been reached. The hot jelly is transferred to sterilised jars and sealed.

The berries of other species such as *Rhoicissus digitata* and *R. tridentata* are also said to be edible. The tuberous rootstock of the latter species, also known as *isinwazi* in Zulu, is an important traditional medicine (see Chapter 10).

Romulea rosea | Iridaceae | **FRUTANG**; *froetang, knikkers* (Afrikaans) ■ This is a small bulbous plant from the Cape, with narrow leaves arising from a small corm under the ground. The small, pink, star-shaped flowers are followed by green, fleshy fruits which are eaten by children before the fruits ripen and dry out.

Fruits of the wild date palm (*Phoenix reclinata*)

Fruits of the real date palm (*Phoenix dactylifera*)

Flower and fruits of Cape(d) gooseberry (*Physalis peruviana*)

Fleshy "berries" of *teesuikerkaroo* (*Pollichia campestris*)

Fruits of wild grape (*Rhoicissus tomentosa*)

Flowers and fruit of the *frutang* (*Romulea rosea*)

Rubus rigidus | Rosaceae | **WILD BRAMBLE**; *wildebraam* (Afrikaans); *ijingijolo* (Zulu) ■ The plant is a sprawling shrub with sharp, hooked prickles on long trailing branches. The leaves are characteristically white-hairy below and the relatively large flowers are pink, followed by red berries that become purple when they mature. This species is similar to *Rubus pinnatus* (bramble; *braambos* in Afrikaans; *munambala* in Venda), but the leaves of the latter lack the dense white hairs of *R. rigidus* and the flowers are smaller. Both species are widely distributed in the eastern parts of southern Africa, from the Cape to East Africa. A third well-known species is *R. cuneifolius* (sand bramble), a troublesome weed from North America. This plant has white flowers and tends to hybridise with indigenous brambles. It forms dense stands in many parts of southern Africa and is difficult to eradicate. Bramble fruits are delicious to eat and they are an important food source in some rural areas. The fruits are popular for making jam, jelly and cold drinks (Rood 1994). Wild bramble is closely related to the commercial raspberries and blackberries from Europe and North America, all of which are derived from *Rubus* species.

Salacia kraussii | Celastraceae | ***IBONTSI*** (Zulu) ■ The plant occurs in KwaZulu-Natal and in Mozambique. It is a small shrub with yellowish flowers and large, orange fruits. The fruit pulp of this and several other species (*Salacia gerrardii*, *S. luebbertii* and *S. rehmannii*) are edible and are eaten when fresh, but the plants and their uses are poorly recorded. The roots of *Salacia* species are important Zulu aphrodisiacs, known as *bangalala*. Although there are many different plants sold as *bangalala*, *Salacia* species are the most important and they warrant further research into the mechanism of action, as well as their conservation status.

Schinziophyton rautanenii (=*Ricinodendron rautanenii*) | Euphorbiaceae | **MONGONGO** ■ See Chapter 2. This tree provides the staple diet for people in northern Botswana. The fruit dries out and remains edible for many months. It is eaten fresh or once dried out, is boiled to soften the red, fleshy pulp. The hard-shelled manketti nuts or mongongo nuts form an important part of the people's diet.

Sclerocarya birrea | Anacardiaceae | **MARULA** ■ See Chapter 6. This is perhaps the most important of all southern African fruit trees. The delicious fruit is eaten fresh or is commonly fermented to produce marula beer. Valuable and tasty nuts are extracted (with difficulty!) from the hard pips.

Searsia undulata (=*Rhus undulata*) | Anacardiaceae | **KAREE**; *taaibos, njarabessie, rosyntjie-bos* (Afrikaans); *kuni, t'garra* (Khoi) ■ The plant is a shrub or tree with resinous bark and distinctive leaves that are divided into three small leaflets. Inconspicuous flowers are followed by tiny mango-shaped fruits. It is widely distributed in the dry interior of southern Africa. Several *Searsia* species have edible, thinly fleshy, sour fruits that were traditionally used to flavour mead (honey beer). The common name for these plants, *karee*, is claimed to be derived from the original Khoi name for mead or honey beer, still commonly used in names such as *kareemoer* or *kirriemoer* (see Chapter 6). In Namaqualand, the fruits of *Searsia undulata* or *S. burchellii* (*smalblaartaaibos* in Afrikaans) are rubbed between the palms of the hands to remove the tough skins. They are then eaten fresh or soaked overnight in milk to form a kind of curd (Archer 1982). The fruits of *Searsia pendulina* are mixed with the gum of *Vachellia karroo* (locally known as *hyra*) to make a sticky sweet with a taste reminiscent of dates (Archer 1990). Several other species of *Searsia* have edible fruits that are traditionally used as a food source and as an ingredient of honey beer. In various parts of southern Africa, the fruits of *Searsia lancea* and numerous other species are recorded to be edible, and most of them have been used for beer brewing. They are usually rubbed between the hands as described above before they are eaten as a snack, or they are soaked in milk or mixed with sour milk before eating (see Chapter 6).

Wild bramble (*Rubus rigidus*)

Fruit of the *ibontsi* (*Salacia kraussii*)

Fruits of karee (*Searsia lancea*)

Fruits of *smalblaartaaibos* (*Searsia burchellii*)

Fruits of the *taaibos* or *t'garra* (*Searsia undulata*)

Sechium edule | Cucurbitaceae| **SHU-SHU** (Afrikaans); chayote ■ This creeping pumpkin-like vine has edible fruits that are used in stews and other dishes. It is very popular in Malaysia and is thought to have been brought to the Cape by Malay people many years ago.

Solanum retroflexum | Solanaceae| **UMSOBA**, *msoba* (Zulu); nightshade (English); *nastergal* (Afrikaans) ■ The plant is a common indigenous herb with sparsely hairy, toothed leaves, white flowers and small black berries with numerous tiny brown seeds inside. This species occurs in practically all parts of southern Africa and is by far the most common of the small-fruited solanums. The berries are said to be poisonous when green, but when they ripen and turn black, they are popular for eating and for making jam. Although the berries are most commonly harvested from the wild, they are cultivated on a small scale for the production of jam nowadays. Several other species, such as *Solanum nigrum*, *S. chenopodioides* and *S. melanocerasum*, are similar to *S. retroflexum* and are used in the same way, both for their fruit and for the young leaves, used as pot herbs.

Strychnos spinosa | Strychnaceae, formerly Loganiaceae| **GREEN MONKEY-APPLE**, spiny monkey-apple; *groenklapper* (Afrikaans); *muramba* (Venda); *umhlala* (Zulu) ■ The plant is a spiny shrub or small tree with a somewhat corky bark, straight and curved spines and large fruits of up to 120 millimetres in diameter. Like several other *Strychnos* species, it occurs in the bushveld regions of southern Africa, from the Eastern Cape to the Limpopo Province, Mozambique, Zimbabwe, Botswana, Namibia and further north into tropical Africa. Species of *Strychnos* are easily recognised by the simple opposite leaves that have three to five prominent veins arising from their bases.

Fruits of all the large-fruited species are considered to be edible, but only the ripe fruit pulp is eaten, as the seeds contain strychnine and related alkaloids and may be very poisonous. Fruits of *Strychnos spinosa* and *S. cocculoides* (corky monkey-apple) are delicious and are considered to be the tastiest of all, but fruits of *S. madagascariensis* (black monkey-orange) and *S. pungens* (spine-leaved monkey-orange) are also used. Fruit pulp is sometimes dried and stored for later use.

The shells of dried fruits are used in craftwork and as sounding-boxes for musical instruments. The timber of several species is used for implement handles, fighting sticks, hut poles, carvery and carpentry, while the bark and roots of species such as *Strychnos decussata*, *S. henningsii*, *S. pungens* and *S. spinosa* are used in traditional medicine.

The unripe fruits and seeds of *Strychnos* species are eaten throughout southern Africa by victims of snakebite, until vomiting occurs. It is widely held that this will enable a person to survive a cobra or mamba bite and there may well be a scientific rationale behind this practice. It is possible that the stimulation of the central nervous system by strychnine or strychnine-type alkaloids may overcome the respiratory depression that causes death in cobra and mamba bites.

Syzygium cordatum | Myrtaceae| **UMDONI**, waterberry; *umdoni* (Zulu); *waterbessie* (Afrikaans); *umswi* (Xhosa); *muthwa* (Tsonga; *muṭu* (Venda) ■ An evergreen tree with opposite leaves, fluffy white flowers and oblong, edible berries. Waterberry (*S. cordatum*), forest waterberry (*S. gerrardii*) and water pear (*S. guineense*) all grow in moist places or near water and they all have edible but rather bland-tasting fruit. The bark of all three species is used in traditional medicine and the timber is strong and durable. According to Palmer & Pitman (1972), umdoni logs are traditionally used to make the jetties and slipways around the swamps in the Kosi Bay area.

Several species of *Syzygium* are of commercial importance in Asia, not only as fruit trees, but also as the source of cloves (cloves are the dried flower buds of *S. aromaticum*). Other indigenous members of the family that bear edible fruit include *Eugenia albanensis* and several other *Eugenia* species (wild myrtles). Two naturalised exotics from tropical America, the guava (*Psidium guajava*) and cherry guava or strawberry guava (*P. littorale* var. *longipes*, previously known as *P. cattleianum*) bear delicious fruits that are much sought after in rural areas.

FRUITS & BERRIES

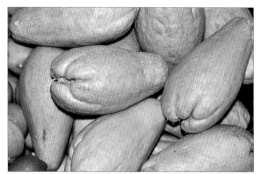

Fruits of the *shu-shu* (*Sechium edule*)

Fruits of *msoba* (*Solanum retroflexum*)

Msoba jam, made from *Solanum* berries

Green monkey-apple (*Strychnos spinosa*)

Decorative container made from a dry *Strychnos* fruit

Fruits of spine-leaved monkey-orange (*Strychnos pungens*)

Fruits from umdoni (*Syzygium cordatum*)

Uapaca kirkiana │Phyllanthaceae, formerly Euphorbiaceae│ ***MAHOBOHOBO*** ■ The tree is called *muzhanje* and the fruits are known as *mahobohobo*. The spherical yellow-brown fruits of this tree are suitable for making jam and are very popular for making a fermented wine. They can be picked and ripened in the dark for several days and are traditionally processed in many different ways. It has potential as a commercial fruit tree and is an important food source in Zimbabwe, Zambia, Malawi and Mozambique.

Vangueria infausta │Rubiaceae│ **WILD MEDLAR**; *wildemispel* (Afrikaans); *mmilo* (Northern Sotho); *mpfilwa* (Tsonga); *mmilô* (Tswana); *muzwilu* (Venda); *umvilo* (Xhosa); *umviyo* (Zulu) ■ The wild medlar is widely distributed in all southern African countries (except Lesotho). It is a shrub or small tree with hairy opposite leaves and pale brown fruits of about 30 millimetres in diameter. They have a mealy texture and a characteristic sweet-sour taste. Fruits of cultivated trees may be up to ten times larger than those of trees in the wild. Yields of between 2.5 and 5 kilograms per tree were attained in trial plantings of a *Vangueria* species in Malawi (Maghembe 1994). Favourable results have also been achieved in trials in Israel. The fruits of the related mountain medlar (*Tapiphyllum parvifolium*) are similar and also edible, but much smaller.

Ximenia americana │Olacaceae│ **BLUE SOURPLUM**; *kleinsuurpruim* (Afrikaans); *mutanzwa* (Venda); *ukolotshane* (Zulu) ■ See photographs on page 67. The plants are about four metres tall and slightly smaller than *Ximenia caffra*, which grows six metres tall. They have a wide distribution in southern Africa but also occur in the rest of Africa, Asia and tropical America, hence the scientific name. Two varieties are distinguished: var. *americana* has leaves that are not particularly blue-green and occurs in Namibia and Botswana; var. *microphylla* has much smaller, typically blue-green leaves and occurs throughout the rest of the distribution area (to the north and east). The fruits are uniformly orange and about 25 millimetres in diameter and tend to be somewhat bitter. Apparently there is a difference in taste between the fruits of the two varieties (Coates Palgrave 2002). In southeastern Botswana, people refer to the more pleasantly tasting fruit of var. *microphylla* as *moretologana*, while the less tasty fruit of var. *americana* is called *moretologa wa pudi*. The fruit is often eaten in such a way as to avoid the skin and also the extremely sour flesh around the kernel. This is done by sucking out the juice or by squeezing the fruit so that the fruit flesh and juice is ejected into the mouth. In Namibia, the fruits have been used to prepare a delicious cool drink concentrate. In the Limpopo Province, a fruit wine (beer) is traditionally made from the ripe fruits. In KwaZulu-Natal, the fruit juice was boiled and mixed with sorghum meal to make a delicious sour porridge (Fox & Norwood-Young 1982). It was part of the Pedi food culture to dry the fruit and store it for future use in various porridges (Quin 1959). The fruit formed an important component of the diet of the San people in various parts of Namibia and Botswana. The seed oil is also used as cosmetic oil and to soften leather.

Ximenia caffra │Olacaceae│ **SOURPLUM**, large sourplum; *grootsuurpruim* (Afrikaans); *omumbeke* (Herero); *gui* (!Kung); *motshidi* (Pedi, Sotho); *umthunduluka* (Zulu) ■ See photograph on page 67. Both this species and *Ximenia americana* are spiny shrubs or small trees, partly parasitic on other bushveld plants. They are widely distributed throughout the bushveld regions of southern Africa. Male and female flowers occur on different plants. The tufted leaves are dark green in this species but bluish grey in *X. americana*. They are characteristically folded lengthwise. Fruits of both species are sweet-sour and are commonly eaten in rural areas. The fruit of *Ximenia caffra* is bright red, white-spotted and larger (about 40 millimetres in diameter) than that of *X. americana*. It is often very sour near the seed but makes an excellent tart jelly. Both species have potential as fruit crops (Schweikerdt 1937) and for making fruit nectars. The seeds contain a valuable oil which has traditionally been used to soften leather (Vaughan-Kirby 1918) and as a cosmetic and skin ointment. It is rubbed into animal hides and bowstrings.

Mahobohobo tree (*Uapaca kirkiana*)

Mahobohobo fruits (*Uapaca kirkiana*)

Cultivated tree of the wild medlar (*Vangueria infausta*)

Leaves and fruits of the wild medlar (*Vangueria infausta*)

Ripe fruits of the wild medlar (*Vangueria infausta*)

Ziziphus mucronata |Rhamnaceae| **BUFFALO-THORN**; *blinkblaar wag-'n-bietjie* (Afrikaans); *mokgalwa* (Northern Sotho); *umphafa* (Xhosa, Zulu) ■ See Chapter 8, and photographs on page 183. This common tree has edible but not very tasty fruit. The related ber or desert apple from India (*Ziziphus mauritiana*), however, has delicious crunchy fruit and it has much potential as a fruit tree in dry parts of Africa. The fruits are sold in rural markets in Zimbabwe. The leaves of *Ziziphus abyssinica* (*jujube*) are used medicinally.

REFERENCES AND FURTHER READING: Ackhurst, A.A. 1996. *Interactive data base on all edible fruits in southern Africa.* Unpublished honours project, Department of Botany, Rand Afrikaans University. **Archer, F.M. 1982.** 'n Voorstudie in verband met die eetbare plante van die Kamiesberge. *J. S. Afr. Bot.* 48: 433–449. **Arnold, T.H. *et al.* 1985.** Khoisan food plants: taxa with potential for future economic exploitation. Chapter 6 in: *Plants for arid lands,* Royal Botanic Gardens, Kew. **Bates, D.M., Robinson, R.W. & Jeffrey, C. (eds) 1990.** *Biology and utilization of the Cucurbitaceae.* Ithaca, New York **Bates, D.M. & Robinson, R.W. 1995.** Cucumbers, melons and water-melons. In: Smartt, J. & Simmonds, N.W. (eds), *Evolution of crop plants,* 2nd ed., pp. 89–96. Longman, London. **Bates, D.M., Merrick, L.C. & Robinson, R.W. 1995.** Minor cucurbits. In: Smartt, J. & Simmonds, N.W. (eds), *Evolution of crop plants,* 2nd ed., pp. 105–111. Longman, London. **Bohme, H.E. 1976.** Some Nguni crafts. Part 1, Calabashes. *Ann. S. Afr. Mus.* 70,1: 1–78. **Campbell, B.M. 1987.** The use of wild fruits in Zimbabwe. *Econ. Bot.* 41: 375–385. **Coates Palgrave, K. 1977.** *Trees of Southern Africa.* Struik, Cape Town. **De Beer, J.J.J. & Van Wyk, B.-E. 2011.** An ethnobotanical survey of the Agter-Hantam, Northern Cape Province, South Africa. *S. Afr. J. Bot.* 77: 741–754. **Dentlinger, U. 1977.** The !Nara plant in the Topnaar Hottentot Culture of Namibia. *Munger Africana Library Notes,* No 38. California Institute of Technology, Pasadena. **Dzerefos, C.M. *et al.* 1995.** *Use of edible herbs and fruits in the Bushbuckridge region of the eastern Transvaal lowveld.* Wits Rural Facility, Acornhoek (unpublished). **Engelke, R. 1993.** Research update. *The Indigenous Plant Use Newsletter* 1(2): 7. **Erickson, D.L., Smith, B.D., Clarke, A.C., Sandweiss, D.H. & Tuross, N. 2005.** An Asian origin for a 10,000-year-old domesticated plant in the Americas. *Proceedings of the National Academy of Sciences* 102: 18315–18320. **Fox, F.W. & Norwood Young, M.E. 1982.** *Food from the veld.* Delta Books, Johannesburg. **Grubben, G.J.H. & Denton, O.A. (eds) 2004.** *Plant resources of tropical Africa 2. Vegetables.* PROTA Foundation, Wageningen, Netherlands. **Ham, C. *et al.* 2008.** Opportunities for commercialization and enterprise development of indigenous fruits in Southern Africa. In: Akinnifesi, F.K. *et al.* (eds), *Indigenous fruit trees in the tropics: Domestication, utilization and commercialization.* CAB International, Oxfordshire, pp. 254–272. **Human & Rousseau Publishers. 1979.** *Simon van der Stel's Journey to Namaqualand in 1685.* Human & Rousseau, Cape Town. **Kamatou, G.P.P., Vermaak, I. & Viljoen, A.M. 2011.** An updated review of *Adansonia digitata*: a commercially important African tree. *S. Afr. J. Bot.* 77: 908–919. **Kirkbride, J.H. 1993.** *Biosystematic monograph of the genus* Cucumis *(Cucurbitaceae).* Parkway Publishers, Boone, North Carolina. **Liengme, C.A. 1981.** Plants used by the Tsonga people of Gazankulu. *Bothalia* 13, 3&4: 501–518. **MacCrone, I.D. 1937.** A note on the Tsamma and its uses among the Bushmen. *Bantu Stud.* 11: 251–252. **Maghembe, J. 1994.** Research update from ICRAF ... fruits of the forest. *The Indigenous Plant Use Newsletter* 2(3): 6–7. **Maguire, B. 1978.** *The food plants of the !Khu Bushmen of north-eastern South West Africa.* M.Sc. thesis, University of the Witwatersrand. **Malan, J.S. & Owen-Smith, G.L. 1974.** The ethnobotany of Kaokoland. *Cimbebasia* Ser. B 2,5: 131–178. **Morton, J.F. 1987.** The horned cucumber, alias "Kiwano" (*Cucumis metuliferus,* Cucurbitaceae). *Econ. Bot.* 41: 325–327. **Neuwinger, H.D. 2000.** African traditional medicine. Medpharm, Stuttgart. **Palmer, E. & Pitman, N. 1972.** *Trees of Southern Africa.* (3 vols). Balkema, Cape Town. **Peters, C.R., O'Brien, E.M. & Drummond, R.B. 1992.** *Edible wild plants of sub-Saharan Africa.* Royal Botanic Gardens, Kew. **Ponglux, D. *et al.* (eds) 1987.** *Medicinal plants.* The first Princess Chulabhorn Science Congress, Bangkok, Thailand. **Pooley, E. 1993.** *The complete field guide to trees of Natal, Zululand & Transkei.* Natal Flora Trust, Durban. **Pooley, E. 1998.** *A field guide to wild flowers of KwaZulu-Natal and the eastern region.* Natal Flora Trust, Durban. **Rood, B. 1994.** *Kos uit die veldkombuis.* Tafelberg, Cape Town. **Renew, A. 1968.** Some edible wild cucumbers of Botswana. *Botswana Notes and Records* 1: 5–8. **Schweikerdt, H.G. 1937.** A note on the South African species of *Ximenia* L., and their possible economic uses. *Bothalia* 3,2: 179–182. **Smith, C.A. 1966.** Common names of South African plants. *Mem. Bot. Surv. S. Afr.* 35. **Steyn, H.P. 1981.** Nharo plant utilization. An overview. *Khoisis* 1: 1–30. **Story, R. 1959.** Some plants used by the Bushmen in obtaining food and water. *Mem. Bot. Surv. S. Afr.* 30. **Stutchbury, R. 2013.** *Baobab.* Camera Africa, Zimbabwe. **Swart, W.J. 1988–1991.** Survival off the veld (parts 1 to 12). *Trees in South Africa,* April 1988 to March 1991. (A twelve-part series of articles, originally published in *Farmer's Weekly*). **Van den Eynden, V., Vernemmen, P. & Van Damme, P. 1992.** *The ethnobotany of the Topnaar.* Universiteit Gent, Gent. **Van Wyk, B.-E. 2011.** The potential of South African plants in the development of new food and beverage products. *S. Afr. J. Bot.* 77: 857–868. **Van Wyk, B. & Van Wyk, P. 1997.** *Field guide to trees of southern Africa.* Struik, Cape Town. **Vaughan-Kirby, F. 1918.** Skin dressing: a description of the process of converting the raw hides of game or domestic cattle into articles of native wearing apparel. *Man* 18,23: 36–40. **Venter, F. & Venter, J.-A. 1996.** *Making the most of indigenous trees.* Briza Publications, Pretoria. **Verdoorn, I.C. 1938.** Edible wild fruits of the Transvaal. *Bull. Dep. Agric. For. Un. S. Afr.* 185. **Von Koenen, E. 2001.** *Medicinal, poisonous and edible plants in Namibia.* Klaus Hess Publishers, Windhoek and Göttingen. **Watt, J.M. & Breyer-Brandwijk, M.G. 1962.** *The medicinal and poisonous plants of southern and eastern Africa,* 2nd ed. Livingstone, London. **Wehmeyer, A.S. 1966.** The nutrient composition of some edible wild fruits found in the Transvaal. *S. Afr. med. J.* 40: 1102. **Wehmeyer, A.S. 1976.** Food from the veld. *Scientiae* 17,4: 2–11. **Wessels, A.B. 1988.** *Spineless prickly pears.* Perskor Publishers, Johannesburg. **Wickens, G.E. 1982.** The baobab – Africa's upside down tree. *Kew Bull.* 37(2): 173–209. **Zeven, A.C. & De Wet, J.M.J. 1982.** *Dictionary of cultivated plants and their regions of diversity.* Centre for Agricultural Publishing and Documentation, Wageningen. **Zohary, D. & Hopf, M. 1994.** *Domestication of plants in the Old World,* 2nd ed. Clarendon Press, Oxford.

Leaves of large sourplum (*Ximenia caffra*)

Leaves and fruit of blue sourplum (*Ximenia americana*)

Fruits of blue sourplum (*Ximenia americana*)

Seeds and nuts of blue sourplum (*Ximenia americana*)

Harvesting *waterblommetjies* (*Aponogeton distachyos*)

CHAPTER 4

Vegetables

GREEN VEGETABLES ARE not far behind the cereals in terms of their importance as food sources in southern Africa. They may be eaten fresh or are more often used as pot herbs. Leaves of various plants are traditionally cooked and eaten with porridge as a relish (the terms spinach, *morogo* or *imfino* are used for the leaves of any species, or mixture of species, cooked in this way).

Green leaves add important nutrients to the diet. Analyses of the most popular sources of *morogo* have shown that they are rich in minerals (iron, calcium, magnesium), amino acids (especially thiamine, riboflavin and nicotinic acid) and vitamins A and C. Nutrient compositions of indigenous leaf vegetables are given by Fox & Norwood Young (1982; see table on page 376) and by Arnold *et al.* (1985). Several other studies on the nutritional value of indigenous vegetables are given in the reference list.

Leaves are most often cooked fresh, but those of *Amaranthus, Vigna, Cleome* and *Chenopodium* and *Corchorus* are also sun-dried and stored for winter use. Dried leaves are often sold on local markets. Some leaf vegetables are considered to be as valuable as meat in terms of their flavour and popularity. In former times, green leaves were considered to be "women's food" but nowadays this preference seems to be diminishing. Popular traditional spinach plants are *Amaranthus hybridus* (and other *Amaranthus* species), *Cleome gynandra, Chenopodium album, Bidens pilosa, Sonchus oleraceus, Portulaca oleracea, Solanum nigrum, Urtica dioica,* and pumpkin and calabash leaves.

Leafy greens are usually boiled with other pot herbs to form a relish that is served with maize porridge. They can also be cooked into a porridge together with maize meal. This is the traditional way in which leaves are prepared, especially in the eastern and northern parts of southern Africa. The Venda people are especially well known for the diversity of leaves that are used as vegetables (Khathu Magwede, pers. comm.), harvested from many different herbs, shrubs and trees. Some are considered to be exceptionally tasty and are preferred, while others are regarded as famine food and only utilised in case of emergency. Leaves that are very fibrous may be cooked and softened in specially prepared cooking ash or soda ash (called *mukango* in Venda). *Mukango* is commonly sold at local markets and is simply ash obtained after burning plant materials such as the fruits of the toadtree (*Tabernaemontana elegans*) or the dry fruit pods of the pod-mahogany (*Afzelia quanzensis*).

One of the truly indigenous vegetables that has captured the imagination of many people in recent years is the Cape *waterblommetjie* (*Aponogeton distachyos*), which forms the basis of a delicious traditional Cape dish called *waterblommetjiebredie*. This is a tasty stew that is an old-time favourite amongst people in the Cape. It is also becoming increasingly popular in other parts of southern Africa and even amongst tourists to the Cape, who enjoy sampling typical examples of the local cuisine. The fact that the product has become readily available throughout the year in canned form, will no doubt contribute to it becoming even more popular and well known.

People sometimes snack on fresh leaves and plants in the raw state. Historically, however, fresh leaves have been a major component of the diet of Khoi and San people. While roots and bulbs were carried home to be baked in the fire for the evening meal, leaves were eaten fresh as part of the daily foraging activity. Foraging is still encountered in parts of the Kalahari and sporadically also in the Cape region, and has been witnessed by the authors. Popular plants for this use are *Hoodia* species, *Kedrostis foetidissima, Oxalis pes-caprae, Oxygonum alatum, Pelargonium* species, *Portulacaria afra, Quaqua mammillaris* and *Talinum* species.

Abelmoschus esculentus │Malvaceae│ **OKRA,** lady's fingers ■ This is a popular vegetable of Asian origin which has become naturalised in many parts of Africa, to the extent that it is often mistaken for an indigenous plant. It is sometimes grown in rural areas for the green, finger-like young fruits that have a slimy texture when cooked. The fruit is popular as an ingredient in Asian and West African cooking.

Acmella oleracea (=*Spilanthes acmella, S. oleracea*) │Asteraceae│ **PARA-CRESS,** spilanthes ■ The plant is an annual weed and is found throughout the tropical parts of Africa. It is believed to have been introduced to the Indian Ocean Islands from Brazil by the Portuguese, from where it spread to East Africa. The leaves are used as a steamed vegetable but can also be used in soups. Fresh leaves can be added to salads. The fresh herb, and especially the flower head, causes a powerful tingling sensation in the mouth due to the presence of spilanthol (an isobutylamide). Experimental plantings have been made in the North West Province of South Africa. Isobutylamides are also found in the original Chinese pepper and Japanese pepper (the small ripe fruits of *Zanthoxylum simulans* and *Z. piperitum*, respectively). They cause the same tingling or buzzing sensation in the mouth (called *ma* or *málà* in Chinese and *hiri-hiri* in Japanese).

Adansonia digitata │Malvaceae│ **BAOBAB** ■ See Chapter 2. The distinctive, digitately compound leaves are used fresh as a cooked vegetable. They may also be sun-dried and powdered for storage and later use in sauces and soups. The flowers can be eaten fresh. The roots and shoots of young seedlings are reported to be eaten as vegetables.

Afrosciadium magalismontanum │Apiaceae│ **WILD CARROT** ■ The leaves of this carrot-like plant are eaten as a pot herb or relish (Fox & Norwood Young 1982), and whole plants (with leaves and roots) are commonly sold on muthi markets in South Africa (Van Wyk *et al.* 2013). The wild carrot was previously known as *Peucedanum magalismontanum*.

Alepidea peduncularis (=*Alepidea longifolia*) │Apiaceae│ **LIKHOKHWANE** (Swazi); *ikhokhwane* (Zulu) ■ The plant is a member of the carrot family and has a resinous flavour somewhat reminiscent of carrots or parsnips. It is a perennial grassland species with underground rhizomes. Rosettes of leaves emerge in spring and flowering stalks are formed in summer. The young leaves are used as a popular spinach (*marogo*).

Allium dregeanum │Alliaceae│ **WILD LEEK**; *wildeprei, wildelook* (Afrikaans) ■ This is the only wild onion in southern Africa. It resembles garlic (*Allium sativum*) and especially leek (*A. ameloprasum*) because the leaves are flat and not tubular as in onions (*A. cepa*). The bulb is small, hardly wider in diameter than the elongated, sheathing leaf bases, and therefore also similar to leek in overall appearance (but not in size – it is much smaller). The dense cluster of white or purple flowers, however, is very similar to that of onions. The leaves of wild leek are sometimes used as a spinach or added to stews.

    A close relative, wild garlic (*Tulbaghia violacea*), is also known to be utilised as a vegetable and relish. (See photographs of *Tulbaghia* species on page 161.) It is commonly cultivated in gardens and has attractive pale violet or rarely white flowers. The leaves are harvested and boiled with other ingredients. The orange-flowered *Tulbaghia alliacea* (also known as wild garlic) is less common but can be used in the same way. In the Western Cape, another wild garlic (*Tulbaghia capensis*) is sometimes used as a garlic substitute. It can be distinguished from *T. alliacea* by the deeply lobed orange corona (i.e., the central outgrowth in the flower), the much broader leaves and relatively large bulb (the other species have branched rhizomes). The leaves and bulb of this species have a powerful garlic taste that can easily overpower a dish if it is not used sparingly. Unfortunately this species has become scarce and endangered because it is over-harvested for the trade in traditional medicine.

Flower and fruits of okra (*Abelmoschus esculentus*)

Brazilian cress or spilanthes (*Acmella oleracea*)

Leaves of wild carrot (*Afrosciadium magalismontanum*)

Flowers of wild carrot (*Afrosciadium magalismontanum*)

Leaves of *ikhokhwane* (*Alepidea peduncularis*)

Flower heads of *ikhokhwane* (*Alepidea peduncularis*)

Bulbs and leaves of wild onion or *wildeprei* (*Allium dregeanum*)

Flower head of wild onion or *wildeprei* (*Allium dregeanum*)

Amaranthus hybridus | Amaranthaceae | **MAROG**; common pigweed, Cape pigweed; *marog, gewone misbredie* (Afrikaans); *marogo, tepe* (Sotho); *umfino* (Zulu) ■ *Amaranthus* species are erect, annual herbs of up to two metres in height. The leaves are variable in size, green or purple, and with slender stalks. Tiny green flowers are borne in dense elongated clusters, usually on the tips of the branches. The small seeds are usually shiny black in colour and there are up to 3 000 seeds per gram. More than 20 indigenous species of *Amaranthus* occur in southern Africa, several of which are of commercial importance as food plants and also as weeds. Some exotic species are grown as ornamental plants, especially *A. caudatus* (*hanekam* in Afrikaans) and ornamental forms of *A. tricolor*.

In terms of food, *Amaranthus* species are either grown for their seeds (the so-called grain amaranths of the New World), known as *kiwicha* or Inca wheat, or they are grown as spinach (*marog*). The best-known grain amaranths are *A. cruentus* of southern Mexico, *A. hypochondriacus* of northern Mexico and *A. caudatus* of the Andes.

Although *A. hybridus* is the most commonly cultivated marog, several others are also widely used as green vegetables (Grubben & Denton 2004). These include *A. thunbergii, A. spinosus, A. deflexus* and *A. hypochondriacus*, all except the last-mentioned grow as weeds in southern Africa.

Amaranthus species are easily cultivated. They tolerate high temperatures but do not withstand frost. Most species and cultivars are adapted to short day lengths. They are grown from seeds sown early in the season, as soon as day temperatures start rising. Plants are spaced in rows about a metre apart when they are to be repeatedly harvested by regular cutting (usually every 10 days). High levels of soil nitrogen are required for optimal yields.

The leaves of all *Amaranthus* species are edible, and yields of up to an astounding 30 to 60 tons per hectare can be achieved. The high productivity can be ascribed to the fact that amaranths are C4 plants (like maize and sugar cane, they follow the 4-carbon photosynthetic pathway), making very effective use of sunlight with a relatively low water consumption.

The small grey or white seeds of grain amaranths differ markedly from the black or brown seeds of the wild forms. The seeds are highly nutritious, mainly as a result of the high levels of lysine (so they are a useful supplement to other cereals such as maize and wheat). Ironically, most of the annual production is not used to alleviate malnutrition, but to supply health food shops in developed countries.

In southern Africa, amaranths are widely used as spinach. The fact that the name *marog* is also used for other relishes, testifies to the popularity of the plant in rural diets. Commercial scale farming has become popular in recent years, and nowadays the leaves are also processed and canned.

The leaves are a valuable source of protein and vitamin A, particularly in semi-arid rural areas where other leaf vegetables are difficult to grow. Analyses of the nutritional value of various *Amaranthus* species performed by the Vegetable and Ornamental Research Institute at Roodeplaat, north of Pretoria, have shown that these plants are truly exceptional in terms of their food value. *Amaranthus* is more valuable than all other leaf vegetables. The protein content varies between 26 and 30 per cent, so that practically half the recommended daily allowance can be obtained from a single 100 gram portion (Erika van den Heever, pers. comm.). The iron content may be as high as five times the recommended daily allowance, the calcium content at least double, and the vitamin A content no less than 20 times the recommended daily allowance! The results indicate that a suitable species or cultivar must be chosen, depending on the specific product requirements.

Amaranthus is clearly a crop with much potential, especially as a source of high-quality food. The trials done at Roodeplaat have shown that it can easily be grown by small farmers and that the cultivation of the crop in rural areas can contribute significantly to a reduction in the incidence of malnutrition amongst young children.

Marog (*Amaranthus hybridus*)

Purple grain amaranth (*Amaranthus cruentus*)

Grain amaranth (*Amaranthus hypochondriacus*)

Canned *marog*

Aponogeton distachyos │Aponogetonaceae│ ***WATERBLOMMETJIES***, Cape pondweed; *wateruintjies* (Afrikaans) ■ These attractive aquatic plants grow in standing or slow-flowing water. They have characteristic oblong leaves on slender stalks that float horizontally on the surface of water. In winter and early spring, the attractive fragrant white flowers appear in masses, protruding above the surface of the water. Each flower cluster is forked in two parts, each with a double row of showy white bracts protecting the small and inconspicuous flowers. The edible part is not really the flower, but actually the whole flower cluster with bracts.

The plants are found over large parts of southern Africa, but are mainly popular as a vegetable in the Cape. They are being domesticated in the south of France and in Peru, according to Fox & Norwood Young (1982). The plant is becoming increasingly popular as an ornamental aquatic plant in southern Africa and can be successfully grown in a fish pond. The lovely fragrance of the flowers is an added attraction and is especially noticeable in the evenings. If the pond is large enough, a valuable and almost continuous supply of fresh *waterblommetjies* can be produced for home use.

On a commercial scale, the plants are usually harvested twice a day by workers in waders towing small rafts. Newly opened flowers, and some flowers with young immature fruits, are harvested together with stems and put onto the rafts. The stems are twisted off when the rafts are brought to the dam's edge. The stems may be used as feed for goats and pigs. A system of rotational harvesting between dams is followed, so that a continuous supply of *waterblommetjies* can be obtained for four to five months of the year, and sometimes longer. July is generally considered the best season. The flowers from later months are not regarded as having as fine a flavour.

There are differences of opinion as to the correct age at which the flowers should be harvested. If they are too young, they tend to be watery, while old fruits may become fibrous. Rood (1994) prefers young fruits which have already formed seeds inside. The flowers are packed into clear plastic bags for sale at roadside stalls. They are increasingly appearing in supermarkets in urban areas throughout South Africa, neatly packaged in plastic punnets. Some canned products are also appearing on the market, and most experts agree that there is no discernible difference in taste between canned and fresh *waterblommetjies* when they are used in a stew. Harvesting is time-consuming and labour-intensive, and certainly contributes to job creation on a small scale in the Cape.

These flowers were undoubtedly a Khoi and San food in early times, and the starchy rhizomes were also eaten. The most popular present use of the fresh flowers is in a *bredie* or stew that usually includes onions and potatoes, and sometimes lamb. The *waterblommetjies* are usually cooked to a pulp with the other ingredients, imparting a distinctive fine flavour and thick sauce to the dish. There are many traditional recipes (see Coetzee 1977; Leipoldt 1976; Rood 1994), most of which call for the inclusion of sorrel leaves (*Oxalis pes-caprae*) as an indispensable ingredient, as the tart taste complements the subtle *waterblommetjie* flavour. Typical recipes for *waterblommetjiebredie* include one kilogram lamb for every kilogram of *waterblommetjies*, two onions, about half a kilogram of young potatoes, a cup of dry white wine, a pinch of sugar, and salt and pepper according to taste. One should remember that *waterblommetjies* have an own distinctive taste so that too much pepper or spice may spoil the dish. Some cooks add a few pieces of pork or bacon to improve the flavour, while others insist that this goes against tradition. Many people appreciate the availability of canned *waterblommetjies*. Keeping a few cans in the pantry is certainly very convenient, as unexpected visitors can be treated to a truly South African culinary experience at relatively short notice.

In addition to the famous stew or *bredie*, *waterblommetjies* may also be used for pickles, salads and soups. The fresh young flowers can also be eaten on their own, steamed until tender, and dressed with lemon butter. The taste is reminiscent of asparagus.

The juice pressed from fresh stems can be used to dress burns, abrasions and sunburn, and the fresh leaves can be applied as a poultice to sores and burns (Roberts 1990).

Commercial harvesting of *waterblommetjies* (*Aponogeton distachyos*)

Leaves and flower clusters of *waterblommetjies*
(*Aponogeton distachyos*)

Canned *waterblommetjies*

Asparagus laricinus | Asparagaceae | **WILD ASPARAGUS**; *katdoring* (Afrikaans) ■ There are several indigenous *Asparagus* species in southern Africa and many of them are known to be edible. The young shoots are harvested and used in the same way as the real asparagus (*Asparagus officinalis*). Some of the species known to be used as vegetables include *A. aethiopicus, A. capensis, A. setaceus, A. africanus* and *A. suaveolens*. There is an old belief, in the Karoo and in Sekhukhuneland (Mahlatse Mogale, pers. comm.), that storms and rainy weather can be driven away by burning the stems of wild asparagus plants.

Astephanus triflorus | Apocynaceae | **VISSIES** (Afrikaans) ■ The plant is a hairy climber of about one metre high with opposite leaves and small white flowers. The young fruits are eaten fresh (De Vynck *et al.* 2016).

Bidens pilosa | Asteraceae | **BLACK-JACK**; *knapsakkerwel* (Afrikaans); *mokolonyane* (Sotho); *umhlabangubo* (Xhosa) ■ This annual herb with its well-known black fruits which cling tenaciously to clothing, is a cosmopolitan weed and grows in all parts of southern Africa. The young shoots are one of the most popular pot herbs and are used by people from many different regions. It may also be sun-dried and stored for later use. A closely related species, *Bidens bipinnata*, with finely dissected leaves, is used in the same way.

Carpanthea pomeridiana | Aizoaceae | **VETKOUSIE** (Afrikaans) ■ This annual succulent from sandy places along the west coast of the Cape is a popular green vegetable for stews. Young plants were formerly also used as a fresh salad. According to Smith (1966) the vernacular name is partly a corruption and partly a translation of the original Khoi name.

Centella asiatica | Apiaceae | **PENNYWORT**; *inyongwane* (Xhosa) ■ This common creeping herb from moist places has round leaves that are cooked as spinach (Million Matonsi, pers. comm.). It is also an important medicinal and tonic plant (see Chapters 8 and 11).

Chenopodium album | Amaranthaceae | **MISBREDIE** (Afrikaans); goosefoot; *imbilikicane* (Xhosa, Zulu) ■ This cosmopolitan weed is widely distributed in southern Africa and it is one of the most important and popular wild spinach (*marog*) plants. The young twigs are boiled and eaten as spinach on their own or with other foods. It may be dried and stored for later use. *Chenopodium murale* and *C. glaucum* are also used.

Cleome gynandra | Capparaceae | **AFRICAN CABBAGE**; *oorpeultjie* (Afrikaans); *lerotho* (Pedi) ■ *Cleome* is a large genus of annual or perennial herbs and shrubs. The compound leaves have several leaflets which radiate from the tip of the leaf stalk. Erect clusters of spider-like, white to purple flowers are followed by elongated fruit capsules. *Cleome gynandra* is the only species which has a fruit stalk attached directly on the fruit (inside the flower), a so-called gynophore (visible in the photograph). Other species such as *Cleome monophylla* are used in the same way as *C. gynandra*. The two species are the most popular ones used as vegetables and they are widely distributed in southern Africa. *Cleome gynandra* and *C. monophylla* are cultivated on a small scale in warm parts of southern Africa nowadays, and yields of two tons or more per hectare can be expected (Van den Heever & Coertze 1997). The young plants and all young parts (stems, leaves and young fruits) are cooked as vegetables and the young leaves are used as spinach. The leaves may also be dried after cooking and stored for later use, usually as a relish with porridge. As a food, *C. gynandra* is particularly rich in magnesium and iron, and also has relatively high levels of nicotinic acid (Arnold *et al.* 1985).

Conicosia pugioniformis | Aizoaceae | **VARKSLAAI**, *varkwortel, snotwortel* (Afrikaans) ■ This succulent plant grows in sandy places in the western parts of the Cape. The slimy roots are edible and the young fruit capsules are included in stews.

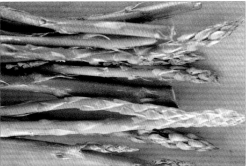

Young stems of wild asparagus (*Asparagus capensis*)

Plants of *vetkousie* (*Carpanthea pomeridiana*)

Picking *misbredie* (*Chenopodium album*) in Johannesburg

Flowering plant of *misbredie* (*Chenopodium album*)

Flowering plant of African cabbage (*Cleome gynandra*)

Harvesting African cabbage (*Cleome gynandra*) near Maun

Corchorus tridens | Malvaceae | ***LIGUSHA*** (Sotho); wild jute ■ This erect annual herb is easily recognised by the hair-like teeth at the base of the leaf blades, the serrated leaf margin and the small yellow flowers. The cooked leaves are eaten with porridge, and are mucilaginous, giving a pleasant smooth consistency to the food. Several other species are eaten as food, including *C. asplenifolius*, *C. trilocularis* and *C. olitorius*.

Dolichos lablab | Fabaceae | **LABLAB BEAN**, hyacinth bean ■ This bean is of Asian origin but is widely grown in southern Africa as a food plant. The leaves and young pods may be boiled as a vegetable and the ripe seeds, which have narrow white arils, are edible after prolonged boiling.

Gasteria* species** | Asphodelaceae | ***OUKOSSIES (Afrikaans) ■ Gasterias are close relatives of aloes and are easily distinguished from them by the keeled leaves and swollen base of the tubular flowers. Plants are usually found in the shade of bushes. Flowers are stripped from the flowering stalks and cooked as vegetables. They are full of nectar and may also be eaten raw.

Hoodia currorii | Apocynaceae | ***GHAAP***, !khobab, *ghôwa* (Khoi) ■ *Hoodia* plants are leafless succulents with thick, fleshy, finger-like stems which branch near the ground. Rows of small thorns are usually present along the stems, which bear fascinating flesh-coloured flowers resembling small radar antennas. The flowers smell strongly of decaying meat, so that they attract flies and blowflies. By laying their eggs inside the flowers, they pollinate them. There is a fascinating diversity of these fly-pollinated succulents, so-called carrion-flowers or stapeliads, in southern Africa (Bruyns 2005).

Two basic types of *ghaap* were previously recognised, namely true *ghaap* (*Trichocaulon* species) and *bobbejaanghaap* (*Hoodia* species), the former considered to be edible, the latter mostly inedible. The plants previously known as *Trichocaulon* have smaller and more rounded, almost thornless stems, and usually tiny flowers, while true *Hoodia* species have long, narrow and thorny stems and large showy flowers. Bruyns (1993) has shown that there is considerable overlap between the two groups. He therefore united all the *ghaap* and *bobbejaanghaap* species under a single genus, *Hoodia*. At risk of adding to the confusion, it should be mentioned that several other members of the stapeliad group have numerous different regional vernacular names, and that several are also loosely called *ghaap* (see *Pectinaria maughamii*, for example).

Several species of *Hoodia* are eaten fresh as a raw food. They are used by shepherds as appetite and thirst suppressants. *Hoodia* species form a convenient emergency food and moisture source in harsh arid environments. As a food, the spines are scraped off the succulent stems with a stone, and the stem is then eaten, rather like a cucumber. The taste is bitter and the texture somewhat mucilaginous. Stems are preferred after recent rains when they have swelled and are more moist. They are also sometimes taken home to be soaked in water before being eaten. An interesting liquorice-like aftertaste results which apparently gives tobacco smoke a particularly pleasant taste.

Hoodia currorii is eaten as a food. It is also used as an appetite suppressant (Andries Kotze, pers. comm.), and to treat indigestion, hypertension, diabetes and stomach-ache.

Hoodia gordonii (*bitterghaap, ghôwa*) is eaten fresh as a food, and is used as an appetite suppressant by shepherds; paradoxically it can also be used as an appetite stimulant, and it is also eaten for abdominal pain suggestive of peptic ulceration (Gert Dirkse, John Cloete, pers. comm.).

Hoodia flava (yellow-flowered *ghaap*) is eaten fresh as a food, and it is also used as an appetite- and thirst-suppressant (Stephanus Cloete, Sophie Basson, pers. comm.).

Hoodia officinalis subsp. *officinalis* has been used to treat pulmonary tuberculosis, and was once imported to the United States as a remedy for haemorrhoids (Bruyns 1993, 2005).

Marloth originally reported the use of *H. pilifera* to suppress hunger and thirst (Smith 1966). It is known to be edible. Stems of the plant have been used in brandy tinctures as a stomachic and to treat haemorrhoids. It was also used to treat pulmonary tuberculosis.

Characteristic leaf of *ligusha* (*Corchorus tridens*)

Flower of *ligusha* (*Corchorus tridens*)

Flowering plant of *bitterghaap* (*Hoodia gordonii*)

Fruiting plant of *bitterghaap* (*Hoodia gordonii*)

Jan Baadjies with flowering stems of *bitterghaap*

Thorny stem and flower of yellow *ghaap* (*Hoodia flava*)

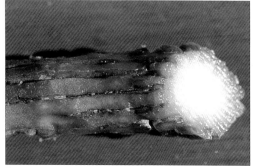

Peeled stem of *bitterghaap*

Kedrostis foetidissima | Cucurbitaceae | ■ This cucumber-like creeper is an important food source in the Kalahari. The heart-shaped leaves have coarse hairs and an unpleasant sulphurous smell but are nevertheless eaten fresh.

Lepidium schinzii | Brassicaceae | ***LEROTHO*** (Sotho); pepperwort, pepperweed; *peperbossie* (Afrikaans) ■ *Lepidium* species are erect herbaceous weeds that occur over many parts of southern Africa. Several species are used as vegetables or as relishes to be eaten with porridge, including *L. capense* and *L. myriocarpum*.

Microloma sagittatum | Apocynaceae | ***BOKHORINKIES***, *kannetjies* (Afrikaans) ■ This plant is a twining creeping herb with opposite leaves, small red flowers and milky latex in the stems. The young fruit capsules are paired and erect (hence *bokhorinkies*, the diminutive form of the Afrikaans for "antelope horns") and are eaten fresh or cooked as a vegetable. The flowers are also edible and are eaten fresh. *Orthanthera jasminiflora* (Apocynaceae) is similar to *Microloma* species and the paired young fruits are used as food in northern Botswana. Similarly, the young fruits of *Cynanchum obtusifolium* (called *pok-pôk*, *kapôke*, *pa-pôk* or *papie*) are eaten fresh along the Cape south coast (De Vynck *et al.* 2016).

Momordica balsamina | Cucurbitaceae | **BALSAM PEAR**, African cucumber; *mohodu* (Sotho); *nkaka* (Tsonga) ■ Balsam pear is a creeping herb with slender stems, lobed leaves and tendrils for climbing. The yellow flowers are followed by pointed fruits which turn orange to red when they mature. The edible seeds have bright red arils, which are also considered to be edible. Leaves and young fruits are cooked and used as vegetables. Another species, *M. foetida* (*inshungu*), is used as a spinach in Malawi and in South Africa. *Momordica balsamina* is said to be effective in treating diabetes.

Nymphaea nouchali | Nymphaeaceae | **BLUE WATER LILY**; *blouwaterlelie* (Afrikaans); *tswii, modidima* (Tswana) ■ This is a well-known water plant with round, floating leaves and attractive yellowish or blue flowers. The stem tubers are peeled (leaving characteristic leaf scars) and are eaten fresh or mostly cooked like potatoes. The tubers are of particular importance in parts of Zimbabwe and in the Okavango, where they are considered to be a staple food. Dried tubers can be stored for later use. The boiled tuber is soft, with a spongy consistency and no particular flavour. The flower heads and seeds are also considered edible, and the powdered root taken in porridge, has been used to treat asthma.

Oxalis pes-caprae | Oxalidaceae | **SORREL**; *suring* (Afrikaans) ■ *Oxalis* is a large genus of herbs with small bulb-like structures below the ground and characteristic lobed, clover-like leaves. *Oxalis pes-caprae* is well known in the Cape, where its sour leaves are an essential ingredient of *waterblommetjie* stew and other stews. Vinegar simply will not do as substitute. The leaves and roots are eaten raw, especially by children. The leaves of several species are used all over southern Africa as pot herbs and the roots or corms are eaten fresh or cooked, often with milk. *Suringpap* (literally "sorrel porridge") is a traditional Cape dish or dessert made by mixing and boiling goat's milk with sorrel leaves. It resembles yogurt in appearance and taste. *Oxalis copiosa* (*skaapsuring*) is used as a vegetable in Namaqualand and the corms of at least two other species are eaten raw, grilled or cooked in milk (Archer 1982).

Oxygonum alatum | Polygonaceae | **SALT OF THE TORTOISE** ■ This is an erect, fleshy herb with oblong, somewhat toothed, fleshy leaves and small white flowers. It is commonly found in the Kalahari and appears to be very variable, with some forms having bright green leaves, while others are bluish grey in colour. The whole young plant is eaten raw, not only for the refreshing acid taste but also for the moisture which it contains.

VEGETABLES

Fresh leaves of *Kedrostis foetidissima* are eaten in the Kalahari

Flowers and fruit of *bokhorinkies* (*Microloma sagittatum*)

Stems (rhizomes) of the blue water lily (*Nymphaea nouchali*) on a street market in Maun

Sorrel (*Oxalis pes-caprae*), an important ingredient of *waterblommetjie* stew

Leaves of *Oxygonum alatum* are eaten fresh in the Kalahari

Pectinaria maughamii | Apocynaceae | ***GHAAP, GHAPIE*** ■ This succulent only grows in the so-called northern Bokkeveld of the Cape (from Clanwilliam northwards to Nieuwoudtville and Calvinia). It has the same vernacular name – *ghaap* – as *Hoodia* species but is more often referred to by the diminutive form *ghapie* because of its much smaller size. Interestingly, it can be eaten as a fresh vegetable and also has appetite-suppressant activity. After eating two or three small pieces of this plant, Willem ("Blikkies") Steenkamp reports that he can "walk behind sheep all day without getting hungry".

Pelargonium fulgidum | Geraniaceae | ***ROOIMALVA*** (Afrikaans) ■ The fresh leaves are snacked on as a wild food, as are those of *dikbeen malva*, *Pelargonium gibbosum* (Dawid Bester, pers. comm.). The taste is slightly tart and astringent but palatable. In the Agter-Hantam, the stems of *Pelargonium carnosum* (called *aree* or *oupa aree*) are baked in the fire and eaten, while the fresh leaves provide a sweet-sour snack enjoyed mainly by children (De Beer & Van Wyk 2011).

Pentarrhinum insipidum | Apocynaceae | ***LESWA*** (Sotho) ■ The plant is a twining creeper with milky latex in the stems. The leaves and young fruits (which resemble small cucumbers) are important vegetables in southern Africa and are used in many parts as a valuable component of the diet. The leaves are rich in calcium, iron and riboflavin (Arnold *et al.* 1985) and the young fruits, which may be eaten raw or cooked, have high levels of magnesium and copper. The plant is considered to have some potential for development as a commercial vegetable.

Portulaca oleracea | Portulacaceae | **PURSLANE**, pigweed; *porselein* (Afrikaans) ■ This succulent weed is a favourite vegetable in all parts of southern Africa. Children eat the leaves raw.

Portulacaria afra | Didiereaceae | ***SPEKBOOM*** (Afrikaans) ■ The plant is a robust succulent shrub with round, fleshy leaves, often with distinctive reddish margins. Small pink flowers are borne in profusion on the stems and they develop into small winged fruits. The fleshy leaves are eaten raw. The plant is also a valuable stock feed but some forms appear to be unpalatable. This species is endemic to southern Africa and is the dominant component of *spekboomveld*, a vegetation type characteristic of some parts of the Little Karoo and Great Karoo in South Africa. It is also typical of the Subtropical Thickets in the Eastern Cape Province. In recent years, large numbers of *spekboom* plants have been used in veld restoration projects in the Little Karoo (with the added benefits of job creation and the fixing of atmospheric carbon). The genus *Portulacaria* includes seven species and was shown (on the basis of DNA evidence) to belong to the family Didiereaceae (and not Portulacaceae, where it was formerly placed).

Prionium serratum | Thurniaceae or Prioniaceae | ***PALMIET*** (Afrikaans) ■ The plant is a robust perennial (palm-like) shrub of up to two metres in height with thick branches and long, greyish leaves borne in rosettes. It is endemic to the Cape region, from the Gifberg near Vanrhynsdorp to the Cape Peninsula and eastwards to southern KwaZulu-Natal. Plants typically grow in dense stands in streams and rivers. Until recently, the food uses of *palmiet* were poorly recorded, with Pappe (1862) stating that the roots were used as food. Recent ethnobotanical field studies, however, have shown that the young stems (meristems) are not only edible but a popular food item in rural parts of the Western Cape (the Cederberg region and along the Berg River). This use was also recorded and described from the southern Cape (Still Bay area) by De Vynck *et al.* (2016). The fleshy edible parts of the stems are easily harvested by firmly grasping the young leaves around the growth tips and twisting them. They are eaten fresh and have a pleasant albeit somewhat bland taste. The presence of *palmiet* leaf fibres at some archaeological sites indicates that this abundant resource may have been an important source of carbohydrates in pre-colonial times. Unlike corms and tubers, which are typically only edible at the end of the growing season, the aquatic habitat of *palmiet* ensures that edible stems are available all year round.

Willem Steenkamp with flowering stem of small *ghaap* (*Pectinaria maughamii*)

Edible stem of *aree* (*Pelargonium carnosum*)

Leaves, flowers and fruit of *leswa* (*Pentarrhinum insipidum*)

Leaves and flowers of purslane (*Portulaca oleracea*)

Palmiet plants (*Prionium serratum*)

Edible young stem of *palmiet* (*Prionium serratum*)

Quaqua mammillaris | Apocynaceae | **AROENA** (Khoi) ■ This inconspicuous plant grows in the shade of bushes and is very difficult to locate, even if you are in the right vicinity. Species of *Quaqua* are similar to *Hoodia* species but are generally smaller plants with fewer (four to five) ridges on the stems, more widely spaced, thorny tubercles and smaller flowers. *Quaqua mammillaris* is perhaps the best known of all the species. The plant has a single main stem and grows as an upright shrublet with large spines and intriguing black flowers. It is very similar to the black-flowered *Q. armata* but the latter is a spreading plant, with side branches forming roots. The stems are still widely eaten as a veld food and regarded as an appetite suppressant (Gert Dirkse, pers. comm.).

The name *qua-qua* (or *gwa-gwa*) is still used today and is believed to be a Khoi name for *Quaqua incarnata* (previously known as *Quaqua hottentorum* or *Caralluma incarnata*), a favourite Khoi food item first reported by Thunberg in 1772. This species usually has yellow flowers and is almost indistinguishable from *Q. aurea*. The latter is found on the Bokkeveld plateau at Nieuwoudtville and southwards to the Cederberg region. Two 100 millimetre lengths of stem are sufficient to suppress thirst and hunger for a day, and the plant can be eaten in larger quantities as a food, but it should not be eaten by pregnant women. It is also eaten for peptic ulceration, and to treat a hangover or to reverse drunkenness (Willem Steenkamp, pers. comm.). Both *Q. mammillaris* and *Q. incarnata* were first collected by Simon van der Stel during his expedition to Namaqualand in 1685.

Rumex lanceolatus | Polygonaceae | **DOCK**; *tongblaar* (Afrikaans); *idololenkonyane* (Zulu) ■ This is a weed of seasonally wet places and occurs in many parts of southern Africa. The leaves are cooked and mixed with porridge. It is said to be a minor crop plant in the Eastern Cape Province of South Africa. Several other species of *Rumex* are used as pot herbs, including *R. crispus, R. saggitatus* and *R. nepalensis*. The popularity is no doubt due in part to the presence of oxalic acid, which makes these plants similar to culinary sorrel. Several medicinal uses have been recorded.

Sarcocornia littorea | Amaranthaceae | **SEA CORAL**; *seekoraal* (Afrikaans) ■ This widely distributed and characteristic leafless succulent shrub with erect, jointed stems grows in saline marshes and in moist sand close to the sea. It is a so-called halophyte, adapted to withstand high levels of salt. Thunberg reported in 1773 that it was eaten fresh for scurvy, as a salad dressed with vinegar and olive oil. *Sarcocornia littorea* and *S. natalensis* (also called *seekoraal*) have potential as commercial crops using seawater irrigation.

Sisymbrium capense | Brassicaceae | **WILD MUSTARD** ■ The plant is a weedy herb with erect stems, hairy leaves, small yellow flowers and oblong seed capsules. It is a popular vegetable in rural areas in southern Africa. Some other species are also known to be used as pot herbs, including *Sisymbrium thellungii* and *S. turczaninowii*.

Symphytum officinale | Boraginaceae | **COMFREY**; *smeerwortel* (Afrikaans) ■ This European plant was once grown as a pot herb but it contains poisonous alkaloids which have a cumulative effect. Comfrey root is used for wound healing, as are the leaves of the related but indigenous *Lobostemon fruticosus* (see Chapter 11).

Talinum caffrum | Talinaceae, formerly Portulacaceae | **KGALAHETE** (Tswana); *fasi, //kasi* (San); *khutsana* (Sotho); *ondindina* (Herero); *osbossie, ystervarkwortel* (Afrikaans) ■ The plant has fleshy stems and leaves arising from a carrot-like rootstock. The small star-shaped flowers are bright yellow and they tend to be closed in the daytime, opening only at dawn. Species are similar and are sometimes difficult to tell apart. The leaves of most species are edible when fresh or are used as a spinach in many parts of southern Africa. The leaves of *Talinum crispatulum* (*xlabe* or *xlare* in San) can be recognised by their wavy margins. They are eaten raw by women in the Kalahari, both as a source of nourishment and for the high water content. *Talinum arnotii* (also *kgalahete* in Tswana) is used as a vegetable in northern Botswana.

Aroena (Quaqua mammillaris)

Yellow *aroena* or *qua-qua* (*Quaqua aurea*)

Succulent stems of the edible *seekoraal* (*Sarcocornia littorea*)

Leaves of *xlabe* (*Talinum crispatulum*) are eaten raw in the Kalahari

Tetragonia decumbens | Aizoaceae | **DUNE SPINACH**; *duinespinasie* (Afrikaans) ■ The plant is a spreading shrub with dark green leaves and small yellow flowers, commonly found on sand dunes close to the sea. It is an early coloniser of moist sand dunes and helps to stabilise the sand, generate organic matter and act as a seed-trap. It has broad succulent leaves covered with small shiny bladder cells that give the plant a distinctive appearance, similar to, but less pronounced than in *Mesembryanthemum* species, to which it is distantly related. The flowers are small and yellow, with five petals and numerous stamens. The fruits are four-winged and superficially very similar to those of *Combretum* species. These winged fruits are adapted to be blown around by the wind, thereby adding to the dispersal of the plants.

Leafy stems and tops are harvested, and the new growth during the rainy season is best. The plant material must be washed thoroughly as the sea sand is tenacious. It is boiled as for spinach. The resulting texture is somewhat granular, and the taste rather bland. The addition of butter and the Cape favourite *Oxalis pes-caprae* results in a rather satisfying dish.

This plant could certainly be domesticated, and with some selection would be as palatable as its close relative, *Tetragonia tetragonoides* – New Zealand spinach. *Tetragonia tetragonoides* is commercially cultivated as a spinach, and it has been reported to grow on the beaches of KwaZulu-Natal. Zulus living at Richards Bay used to load their canoes at Spinach Point (Fox & Norwood Young 1982).

Trachyandra falcata | Asphodelaceae | **WILD CABBAGE**; *veldkool* (Afrikaans) ■ This onion-like plant is widely distributed in the Cape and southern Namibia. It has fleshy, strap-shaped, somewhat sickle-shaped leaves and a dense cluster of white flowers on a thick stalk. There are several different species of *Trachyandra* which are all used in the same way as *T. falcata,* including *strandkool* (*T. divaricata*), hairy *veldkool* (*T. hispida* and *T. hirsuta*) and *T. ciliata* (also known as *veldkool*). These plants are exceptionally common and are not cultivated. The young inflorescences (clusters of buds) are harvested before the flowers open. These are traditionally used to cook a delicious stew (Leipoldt 1976, 1978; Rood 1994). To promote indigenous Cape cuisine, a few recipes are given here.

According to Leipoldt (1978), *veldkool* can be prepared in many different ways. The flowering tops are thoroughly washed, dried and then finely chopped.

To make *veldkoolbredie* (*veldkool* stew), the chopped vegetable is braised in a little butter or fat in a pot with a tight-fitting lid. Discard the liquid that forms and remove the lid to allow the moisture to evaporate. Braise a chopped onion with small cubes of mutton until the meat is tender. Add the *veldkool*, stir well and season with salt and pepper. Let the dish simmer until the meat and *veldkool* are well integrated.

"Boiled *veldkool* with cream" is made by boiling *veldkool* in salted water until soft. Stir in some butter, season to taste with pepper and salt and let the dish simmer uncovered until the liquid has evaporated. Mash the *veldkool* with a wooden spoon (nowadays one would use a blender) and add a cup of cream. A white sauce may be used instead of cream. Finely chopped *suring* leaves (*Oxalis pes-caprae*) can also be added.

Another version is "*veldkool* with onion". Sautee chopped onion until pale brown. Add some garlic, salt and pepper to taste, and then the chopped *veldkool*. Braise (while stirring regularly) until the liquid has evaporated. Serve on a bed of mashed potato.

"*Veldkool* with tomatoes" is prepared by placing alternate layers of tomato slices and *veldkool* in a pot. Add a cup of beef stock or beef soup and allow it to simmer slowly. Season with a teaspoon of sugar, a pinch of salt and a little white pepper. When the sauce has thickened, serve in the centre of a plate surrounded by pieces of white bread.

"*Veldkool* with cheese" calls for boiled and pureed *veldkool* to which some salt, pepper and finely ground coriander have been added. A few anchovies will impart extra flavour. Beat a few eggs into the mixture and pour into a flat earthenware dish. Sprinkle with a few knobs of butter, followed by a generous topping of grated cheese and bake slowly in the oven until done.

Leaves and flowers of dune spinach (*Tetragonia decumbens*)

Large plant of dune spinach (*Tetragonia decumbens*)

Flowering plant of *veldkool* (*Trachyandra falcata*)

Young flower cluster of *duinekool* (*Trachyandra divaricata*)

Flowers of hairy *veldkool* (*Trachyandra hirsuta*)

Harvested flower clusters of *veldkool* (*Trachyandra ciliata*)

Vigna unguiculata | Fabaceae | **COWPEA** ■ See Chapter 2. The dried leaves (actually the young shoots) are commonly sold on street markets in southern Africa.

REFERENCES AND FURTHER READING: Archer, F.M. 1982. 'n Voorstudie in verband met die eetbare plante van die Kamiesberge. *J. S. Afr. Bot.* 48: 433–449. **Archer, F.M. 1990.** Planning with people – ethnobotany and African uses of plants in Namaqualand (South Africa). *Mitt. Inst. Allg. Bot. Hamburg* 23: 959–972. **Arnold, T.H.** *et al.* **1985.** Khoisan food plants: taxa with potential for future economic exploitation. Chapter 6 in *Plants for arid lands*, Royal Botanic Gardens, Kew. **Bruyns, P. 1993.** A revision of *Hoodia* and *Lavranea. Bot. Jahrb. Syst.* 115: 145–207. **Bruyns P.V. 2005.** Stapeliads of South Africa and Madagascar. 2 Vols. Umdaus Press, Hatfield. **Coetzee, R. 1977.** *The South African culinary tradition.* Struik, Cape Town. **Coetzee, R. & Miros, V. 2009.** *Koekemakranka. Khoi-khoin-kultuurgoed en kom-kuier-kos.* Lapa Publishers, Pretoria. **De Beer, J.J.J. & Van Wyk, B.-E. 2011.** An ethnobotanical survey of the Agter-Hantam, Northern Cape Province, South Africa. *S. Afr. J. Bot.* 77(3): 741–754. **De Vynck, J.C., Van Wyk, B.-E. & Cowling, R.M. 2016.** Indigenous edible plant use by contemporary Khoe-San descendants of South Africa's Cape South Coast. *S. Afr. J. Bot.* 102: 60–69. **Dzerefos, C.M.** *et al.* **1995.** *Use of edible herbs and fruits in the Bushbuckridge region of the eastern Transvaal lowveld.* Wits Rural Facility, Acornhoek (unpublished). **Fox, F.W. 1938.** Some Bantu recipes from the Eastern Cape. *Bantu Stud.* 13: 65–74. **Fox, F.W. & Norwood Young, M.E. 1982.** *Food from the veld.* Delta Books, Johannesburg. (Note table of nutritional analyses by Wehmeyer & Rose on page 376.) **Franz, H.C. 1971.** Traditional diet of the Bantu of the Pietersburg district. *S. Afr. Med. J.* 45: 1323–1325. **Giess, W. 1966.** *The 'Veldkost' of South West Africa.* South West Africa-Yearbook. 1966. **Giess, W. 1966.** 'Veldkost' in Südwestafrika. *J. S. W. Africa Scient. Soc.* 20: 59–68. **Grivetti, L.E. 1979.** Kalahari agro-pastoral-hunter-gatherers: the Tswana example. *Ecology of Food and Nutrition* 7: 235–256. **Grubben, G.J.H. & Denton, O.A. (eds) 2004.** *Plant resources of tropical Africa 2. Vegetables.* PROTA Foundation, Wageningen, Netherlands. **Heinz, H.J. & Maguire, B. no date.** *The ethnobiology of the !Ko Bushmen – their botanical knowledge and plant lore.* Occasional Paper No 1, Botswana Society, Gaborone. **Hennesey, E.F. & Lewis, O.A.M. 1971.** Anti-pellagragenic properties of wild plants used as dietary supplements in Natal (South Africa). *Plant Foods for Human Nutrition* 2: 75–78. **Jacot Guillarmot, A. 1966.** A contribution towards the economic botany of Basutoland. *Botaniska Notiser* 119(2): 209–212. **Keith, M.E. & Renew, A. 1975.** Notes on some edible wild plants found in the Kalahari. *Koedoe* 18: 1–12. **Lee, R.B. 1979.** *The !Kung San: Men, women and work in a foraging society.* Cambridge University Press, Cambridge. **Leipoldt, C.L. 1976.** *Leipoldt's Cape Cookery.* W.J. Flesch & partners, Cape Town. **Leipoldt, C.L. 1978.** *Kos vir die Kenner.* 2nd ed. Tafelberg, Cape Town. **Leistner, O.A. no date.** *Some edible plants of the Kimberley area* (N. Cape). Unpublished. **Levy, L.F.** *et al.* **1936.** The food value of some common edible leaves. *S. Afr. med. J.* 10, 20: 699–707. **Lewis, O.A.M.** *et al.* **1971.** The leaf protein nutritional value of four wild plants used as dietary supplements by the Zulu. In: *Proteins and food supply in the Republic of South Africa.* Symposium held at the University of the Orange Free State, 8–11 April 1968. Balkema, Cape Town. **Liengme, C.A. 1981.** Plants used by the Tsonga people of Gazankulu. *Bothalia* 13, 3&4: 501–518. **Maguire, B. 1978.** *The food plants of the !Khu Bushmen of north-eastern South West Africa.* M.Sc. thesis, University of the Witwatersrand. **Malan, J.S. & Owen-Smith, G.L. 1974.** The ethnobotany of Kaokoland. *Cimbebasia* Ser. B 2,5: 131–178. **Marloth, R. 1917–1930.** *The Flora of South Africa* (3 vols). William Wesley, London. **Ogle, B.M. & Gravetti, L.E. 1985.** Legacy of the cameleon: edible wild plants in the kingdom of Swaziland, southern Africa: a cultural, nutritional study; part IV, nutritional analysis and conclusions. *Ecology of Food and Nutrition* 17: 41–64. **Pappe, C.W.L. 1862.** *Silva capensis, or a description of South African forest-trees and arborescent shrubs used for technical and economical purposes by the colonists of the Cape of Good Hope,* 2nd ed. Van de Sandt de Villiers, Cape Town. **Peters, C.R.** *et al.* **1992.** *Edible wild plants of sub-Saharan Africa.* Royal Botanic Gardens, Kew. **Phillips, E.P. 1917.** A contribution to the flora of the Leribe plateau and environs. *Ann. S. Afr. Mus.* 16. **Quin, P.J. 1959.** *Food and feeding habits of the Pedi.* Witwatersrand University Press, Johannesburg. **Renew, A. 1968.** Some edible wild cucumbers of Botswana. *Botswana Notes and Records* 1: 5–8. **Roberts, M. 1990.** *Indigenous healing plants.* Southern Book Publishers, Halfway House. **Rood, B. 1994.** *Kos uit die veldkombuis.* Tafelberg, Cape Town. **Rose, E.F. 1972.** *Senecio* species: toxic plans used as food and medicine in the Transkei. *S. Afr. Med. J.* 46: 1039–1043. **Rose, E.F. 1972.** Some observations on the diet and farming practices of the people of the Transkei. *S. Afr. Med. J.* 46: 1353–1358. **Rose, E.F. & Jacot Guillarmod, A. 1974.** Plants gathered as foodstuffs by the Transkeian peoples. *S. Afr. Med. J.* 48: 1688–1690. **Santos Oliveira, J. & Fidalgo de Carvalho, M. 1975.** Nutritional value of some edible leaves used in Moçambique. *Econ. Bot.* 29(3): 355–263. **Shanley, B.M. & Lewis, O.A.M. 1969.** The protein nutritional value of wild plants as dietary supplements in Natal. *Plant Foods for Human Nutrition* 1. **Smith, C.A. 1966.** Common names of South African plants. *Mem. Bot. Surv. S. Afr.* 35. **Steyn, H.P. 1981.** Nharo plant utilization. An overview. *Khoisis* 1. **Story, R. 1959.** Some plants used by the Bushmen in obtaining food and water. *Mem. Bot. Surv. S. Afr.* 30. **Van den Eynden, V.** *et al.* **1992.** *The ethnobotany of the Topnaar.* Universiteit Gent, Gent. **Van den Heever, E. & Coertze, A.F. 1997.** *Cleome.* Information leaflet A.2. Vegetable and Ornamental Plant Institute, Pretoria. **Van Wyk, B.-E. 2005.** *Food plants of the world.* Briza Publications, Pretoria. **Van Wyk, B.-E. 2011.** The potential of South African plants in the development of new food and beverage products. *S. Afr. J. Bot.* 77(4), 857–868. **Van Wyk, B.-E., Tilney P.M. & Magee, A.R. 2013.** *African Apiaceae.* Briza Academic Books, Pretoria. **Von Koenen, E. 2001.** *Medicinal, poisonous and edible plants in Namibia.* Klaus Hess Publishers, Windhoek and Göttingen. **Watt, J.M. & Breyer-Brandwijk, M.G. 1962.** *The medicinal and poisonous plants of southern and eastern Africa,* 2nd ed. Livingstone, London. **Williamson, J. 1975.** *Useful plants of Malawi* (revised and extended ed.). University of Malawi, Zomba. **Zinyama, L.M.** *et al.* **1990.** The use of wild foods during periods of food shortage in rural Zimbabwe. *Ecology of Food and Nutrition* 24: 251–265.

Cowpea plant (*Vigna unguiculata*)

Flowers of cowpea (*Vigna unguiculata*)

Cooked and dried cowpea leaves (tips) on a street market

The traditional *uintjiesak* ("*uintjie* bag"), used for carrying bulbs and roots

The edible root of wild cucumber (*Coccinia rehmannii*)

In the Kalahari, children eat *Ledebouria revoluta* bulbs as snacks

Eating *kambro* (*Fockea angustifolia*)

CHAPTER 5

Roots, bulbs & tubers

IN EARLY DAYS, underground organs of wild plants (roots, bulbs, tubers and stems or rhizomes) were widely used as sources of starch foods, often after some form of processing, including baking (in hot ash) or boiling. The best-known examples are the stems of the bread palm or African cycad (*Encephalartos* species), the roots of cassava (*Manihot esculenta*) and the rhizomes of bulrush (*Typha capensis*). Some other important root and tuber foods include the Livingstone potato (*Plectranthus esculentus*), the Zulu round potato (*Plectranthus rotundifolius*) and the *indumbe* (*Colocasia esculenta*). Indigenous tubers as starch sources have largely been replaced by the exotic potato (*Solanum tuberosum*) and the sweet potato (*Ipomoea batatas*). These two South American crops have become popular in many parts of the world and often serve as non-traditional staple foods. While some underground storage organs can be eaten raw, the starch-rich roots and tubers are far more digestible after they have been baked or boiled.

Various bulbs and corms, collectively known as *uintjies*, were once important food items but nowadays they are often eaten merely as snacks or to supplement the diet. In Namaqualand, the Kalahari and in northern Namibia, *uintjies* still form part of the economic and social life of people, just as it was in the olden days when time and the seasons were determined by the appearance of *uintjies*, and when everyone carried a special bag, the *uintjiesak*, when moving about to collect food. The term *uintjies* is an early Afrikaans word derived from the original Dutch *ajuin*, literally "onion" – particularly the more common diminutive form *ajuintjie*. The popularity and cultural importance of *uintjies* is reflected in numerous common names such as *klipuintjie, berguintjie, bobbejaanuintjie, boesmanuintjie, raapuintjie, vlei-uintjie, wateruintjie* and many more (Archer 1982, 1990; Rood 1994). Most *uintjies* belong to one of four important "*uintjie*" families, the Cyperaceae, Iridaceae, Tecophilaeaceae and Oxalidaceae. *Uintjies* from the Iridaceae should be harvested with care, as some extremely poisonous species have corms that superficially resemble those of edible species.

Roots and tubers are also important sources of moisture, particularly in the dry parts of southern Africa. In the Kalahari region, surface water is only available for about three months of the year, so that the water stored in plant roots and tubers contributes significantly to survival during the nine dry months of the year. Well-known examples of such water sources include *kambro* (*Fockea* species), *baroe* (*Cyphia* species), *bi* (*Raphionacme burkei*) and *dza* (*Commiphora angolensis*).

Bulbs, corms and tubers (often referred to by the general term "geophytes") are believed to have played an important role in the development and survival of the first modern humans along the southern Cape coast. The Cape flora is exceptionally rich in geophytes and these may have been an important source of carbohydrates for early humans, who relied on the abundant, protein-rich seafood resources along the Cape coast (Proches *et al.* 2005). It is believed that geophytes played a critical role in the diet and hence in the survival of our species during an extremely cold period (some 140 000 years ago), when humans were threatened with extinction.

Although *baroe* (*Cyphia* species) and other *uintjies* are still eaten in the Cape region, they have lost their importance as a primary food source (De Vynck *et al.* 2016). The knowledge about *uintjies* is generally poorly recorded and it is often not clear exactly which species of a particular genus have been traditionally used. Examples include *Babiana, Ferraria, Gladiolus, Hexaglottis, Ledebouria, Moraea, Oxalis* and *Pelargonium*. In some areas, the wire fences that are erected in the interest of nature conservation are preventing the transfer of knowledge to the next generation because rural children and their parents are no longer able to roam freely in the veld as they used to.

Annesorhiza macrocarpa | Apiaceae | **ANISE ROOT**; *anyswortel* (Afrikaans) ■ This carrot-like plant grows in sandy places in the Cape. It is often confused with other members of the carrot family, such as *Glia* and *Cynorrhiza* (formerly *Peucedanum*). A distinctive feature of *Annesorhiza* species is that they are summer-deciduous and that leaves and flowers are formed at different times of the year (Van Wyk *et al.* 2013). The leaves of these plants emerge in early winter (at the start of the rainy season) after the plants have flowered in summer and produced ripe fruits in autumn (the leaves are heisteranthous, i.e. produced after flowering). As a result, it is often difficult to identify the species, because both the leaves and the fruits are usually needed for a positive identification. *Cynorrhiza* species differ from *Annesorhiza* in their flat and markedly winged fruits (*Annesorhiza* has ·more rounded fruits, usually with several short wings or ridges). *Glia gummifera*, which was once used as a source of yeast to brew beer, is superficially very similar to *Annesorhiza* but the leaves and flowers or fruits are simultaneously present on the plants and the leaves have coarse hairs, mainly along the lower midribs.

Annesorhiza macrocarpa has numerous fleshy roots that have a distinctive anise-like flavour, hence the common name *anyswortel*. The name was probably first applied to the roots of *Annesorhiza nuda* (previously known as *A. capensis*), that have a particularly strong anise scent. These roots were likely to have been used as a vegetable by the Khoi and San from the earliest times, although the earliest documented use may date back to 1652. In 1772 Thunberg recorded that "the *anyswortel* was eaten roasted in the embers and boiled in milk, or else stewed with meat and tasted well" (Smith 1966). This anecdote of Thunberg applies to *Annesorhiza grandiflora*, which produces a bunch of thick white roots resembling medium-sized carrots in shape. Pappe also reported that anise root was used as a food by all people in the Cape, and that on cultivation it loses its acrid taste and becomes a palatable vegetable. The authors tried *A. macrocarpa* cooked in milk, but the taste was bitter and resinous, although the texture was soft and pleasing. There may be a commercial opportunity to domesticate *A. macrocarpa, A. nuda* or *A. grandiflora* again for specialty restaurants catering for the tourist trade.

Babiana dregei | Iridaceae | ***KLIPUINTJIE*** (Afrikaans) ■ *Babiana* species are bulbous plants mainly from the Cape, and are easily recognised by their leaves, which are pleated (folded lengthwise) and their distinctive flowers, which are usually blue, rarely red. The fibrous covering of the corms are removed and they are then eaten fresh or may be cooked in milk. The corms may also be baked in hot ash or coals. The fibrous sheaths are left for protection until they are eaten.

Four different *Babiana* species are reported to be utilised in the Kamiesberg in Namaqualand (Archer 1982), of which the *klipuintjie* was considered to be a local staple food. The low moisture content and relatively high nutrient levels (Archer 1990) support the local view that the species is a nutritious food. Several other species are used, including *B. ambigua* (*poepuintjie*), *B. hypogea* (*perde-uintjie*) and *B. namaquensis* (*draai-uintjie*).

Babiania hypogea corms are baked and eaten by the San people of the western Kalahari, where the plant is called *g//orosa* (Steyn 1981). In Namibia, the plant is known as *bobbejaanuintjie* in Afrikaans, *‡gunus* in Nama (Damara) and *otjitore* in Herero (Von Koenen 2001). The small corms are eaten raw or may be roasted. *Babiana sambucina* (known locally as *bloublomsamuel* or *middeldeurklas*) is eaten by children in the Nieuwoudtville district (Willem Steenkamp, pers. comm.). In the southern Cape region, all blue-flowered species are considered to be edible (De Vynck *et al.* 2016).

Babiana species are harvested in the wet season and are not considered to be edible during the dry summer months. The genus name *Babiana* is derived from the Dutch *baviaan*, meaning baboon, as baboons are also fond of the corms. This is also reflected in *bobbejaantjie*, the Afrikaans common name for all *Babiana* species.

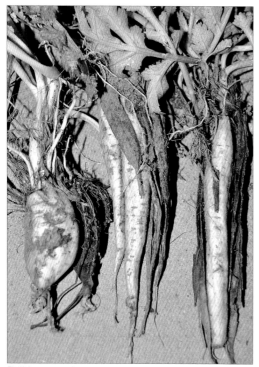

Edible roots of Cape anise root or *anyswortel* (*Annesorhiza nuda*)

Edible roots of *duine-anyswortel* (*Annesorhiza macrocarpa*)

Edible roots of *anyswortel* (*Annesorhiza grandiflora*)

Nico Steenkamp with flowering plants of *bloublomsamuel* (*Babiana sambucina*)

Flowering plant of the *klipuintjie* (*Babiana dregei*)

Edible corm of the *klipuintjie* (*Babiana dregei*)

Ceropegia rendalii │Apocynaceae│ ***SEROWE*** (San) ■ The plant has a whitish, round tuber under the ground and a thin twining stem with fleshy edible leaves. This species and *C. multiflora* subsp. *tentaculata* are important sources of food and water in the Kalahari.

Chamarea capensis │Apiaceae│ ***VINKELWORTEL*** (Afrikaans); *chamare, gammare* (Khoi) ■ This is a small plant with feathery leaves and a pencil-like root which was once an important food of the people at the Cape. The generic name was derived from the original Khoi name that was first recorded by Simon van der Stel in the account of his journey to Namaqualand in 1685.

The plants are similar to *Annesorhiza* species in that they are also summer-deciduous and have hysteranthous leaves (i.e. the leaves emerge in early winter, after flowering and fruiting which take place in summer and autumn). Another similarity is that the fleshy roots of both are replaced every year, with the newly formed root(s) replacing the old one(s).

Recent studies have shown that there are several *Chamarea* species not previously recognised as distinct from *C. capensis* (Van Wyk *et al.* 2013), and that all or most of them are still popular food items in rural parts of the Cape. The species differ in the size, shape and number of roots (in addition to differences in the leaves and fruits). The roots of *Chamarea longipedicellata* and *C. snijmaniae* are eaten at Nieuwoudtville, while the roots of an as yet undescribed *Chamarea* species are eaten in the Agter-Hantam (De Beer & Van Wyk 2011). These watery roots are typically eaten fresh as a snack food during spring and early summer, when the newly formed roots have reached maturity.

Coccinia rehmannii │Cucurbitaceae│ **WILD CUCUMBER** ■ See photograph on page 90. The plant is a perennial herb with hand-shaped leaves and cream-coloured flowers. The strongly tapered, carrot-like root is an important food item in the Kalahari, both as a source of water and starch. The roots are usually roasted before eating. Another species, *Coccinia sessilifolia*, has a much wider distribution in southern Africa and is also used for its fleshy tuber. This common plant is known as *bobbejaankomkommer* or *wildekarkoer* in Afrikaans and *borobahlolo* in Sotho. The tuber is eaten raw for the moisture or boiled or roasted as food. The bright red fruits are said to be edible, both raw and baked.

Colocasia esculenta │Araceae│ **AMADUMBE** (Zulu); elephant's ear, taro potato, cocoyam; *ama-doembie* (Afrikaans) ■ The plant is a robust herb with very large heart-shaped leaves borne on thick stalks, superficially similar to the common arum lily (*Zantedeschia aethiopica*). The cylindrical rhizomes or corms are harvested and boiled, baked, roasted or fried like potatoes. Many people consider sliced and fried *amadumbe* to be superior in taste to fried potato chips.

Amadumbe originated in Southeast Asia and is now grown as a crop in many tropical and subtropical parts of the world. It has been widely cultivated in southern Africa since early times, and was probably introduced by Portuguese traders before 1500. The starch-rich corms are a staple diet in many parts of southern Africa. *Amadumbe* corms are particularly popular in KwaZulu-Natal and are a common sight at street markets in Durban. The leaves and stalks are used as pot herbs, and are often mixed with other ingredients. Leaves of a purple-veined form are used in Asian cooking in South Africa, and are known as *pateria*. The leaf veins are removed carefully, otherwise the sharp crystals (raphides) may cause severe irritation of the mouth. For the same reason, the corms of some types have to be cooked repeatedly in fresh water. *Amadumbe* grows well in moist, heavy soils and matures after five to 10 months. Yields of 20 to 40 tons per hectare can be expected.

The tuberous rootstock of the arum lily (*Zantedeschia aethiopica*) is said to have been used as a food source in early days at the Cape, after extensive boiling to counteract the burning effect of the raphide crystals.

Plant of *serowe* (*Ceropegia rendalii*)

Edible roots of *vinkelwortel* (*Chamarea capensis*)

Plants of *amadumbe* (*Colocasia esculenta*)

Edible rhizomes of *amadumbe* (*Colocasia esculenta*)

Commiphora angolensis │ Burseraceae│ ***DZA*** (San); sand corkwood (English); *sandkanniedood* (Afrikaans) ■ This species is a multi-stemmed shrub or small tree with a papery bark, velvety stems and compound leaves, each with three to nine toothed leaflets. It occurs in the dry interior of southern Africa, mainly in the Kalahari, northern Namibia, Angola and western Zimbabwe. The tree is an important source of water in the Kalahari. It can easily be confused with *C. africana*, the host of the poison grub (see Chapter 15). Long lengths of root are easily dug up out of the sand in the Kalahari using digging sticks. The thick roots are peeled to remove the astringent red bark, after which it is chewed and sucked to separate the tasty fresh water from the fibrous pith, which is discarded. It is rather like chewing on sugar cane. The roots of *Commiphora africana*, *C. pyracanthoides* and *C. neglecta* have been similarly used. The roots of *C. mollis* and *C. mossambicencis* are reported to be eaten in Zimbabwe, probably for the moisture.

Several species of *Commiphora* are popular for their soft timbers, which are used to carve ornaments and household items. Species such as *Commiphora pyracanthoides* and *C. giessii* are used as a source of fire-sticks. The soft wood is used for both the "male" and "female" fire-sticks (see Chapter 18).

Cucumis kalahariensis │ Cucurbitaceae│ **KALAHARI CUCUMBER**, wild potato ■ This is a perennial creeper with male and female flowers on separate plants. The small prickly fruit is not edible. The fleshy roots are a favourite source of water (when eaten raw) or starch food (when baked in the fire). It is an important food plant in the central Kalahari.

Cussonia paniculata │ Araliaceae│ **HIGHVELD CABBAGE TREE**; *bergkiepersol* (Afrikaans); *motsetse* (Sotho, Tswana) ■ The tree has a thick stem and attractive, drooping grey leaves. The thick tuberous roots are peeled and eaten raw as an emergency food or as a source of water (Fox & Norwood Young 1982). The roots of the lowveld cabbage tree (*Cussonia spicata*) were once commonly eaten raw in the northern parts of South Africa, with about 125 grams of fresh root consumed at a time. The Cape cabbage tree (*C. thyrsiflora*) was used in the same way. Care should be taken, as the roots of *C. spicata* have been reported to be poisonous.

Cyanella hyacinthoides │ Tecophilaeaceae│ ***RAAPUINTJIE***, *raaptol, raap* (Afrikaans) ■ This bulbous plant has several slender leaves arising from a characteristic rounded corm. The scented flowers are usually blue or mauve but may also be white. Each one has a cluster of five small stamens above and one large stamen below. This unusual arrangement of the stamens is characteristic for *Cyanella*. The species is widely distributed, from Namaqualand to the southern Cape. There are seven other species of *Cyanella* (Scott 1991), of which the *raaptol* or *waterraap* (*C. orchidiformis*), the *toe-toe uintjie* (*C. alba*) and the *geelraaptol* (*C. lutea*) are perhaps the best-known ones. *Cyanella orchidiformis* can easily be distinguished from *C. hyacinthoides* by the shape of the flowers (see photographs). The flower colour of *Cyanella alba* (white) and *C. lutea* (yellow) is an easy way to distinguish these two species.

In Namaqualand, *C. hyacinthoides* is one of the most important *uintjies* and is considered to be a high-quality staple food. The corms are nutritious, with a relatively low moisture content and a high protein content. After cleaning, they weigh about 14 grams each (Archer 1982). Harvesting occurs in the wet season (July to October) and the corms are eaten raw or are roasted or boiled in milk. In the Cederberg, *raaptol* (also known locally as *dolraap, raapdol, tolraap* or *wilderaap*) is one of the most popular veld foods. In this case, the name refers to both *C. hyacinthoides* and *C. orchidiformis*. Some old-timers of the Cederberg remember how they used to boil *raaptol* in an old jam tin over an open fire when they were out in the veld looking after the household's sheep and goats. The extent to which other *raapuintjies* such as *Cyanella alba* (*toe-toe uintjie*) and *C. lutea* (*geelraaptol*) are utilised is poorly recorded.

Chewing and sucking the watery roots of *dza* (*Commiphora angolensis*)

Root of *dza* (*Commiphora angolensis*), showing the astringent red bark

Leaves and fleshy edible roots of the Kalahari cucumber (*Cucumis kalahariensis*)

Edible corms of *raapuintjie* (*Cyanella hyacinthoides*)

Flowering plant of *raapuintjie* (*Cyanella hyacinthoides*)

Flowering plant of *raaptol* or *waterraap* (*Cyanella orchidiformis*)

Flowering plant of *geelraaptol* (*Cyanella lutea*)

Cyperus esculentus | Cyperaceae | **TIGERNUT**, yellow nutsedge; *indawo* (Zulu); *ofio* (Yoruba); *akiausa* (Igbo); *habb el'-aziz, habb el-zalam* (Arabic); *chufa* (Spanish); *souchet comestible, almond de terre* (French) ■ The cultivated form of *Cyperus esculentus* has not been recorded in southern Africa, but it is an important African crop plant, cultivated since ancient times in Egypt (De Vries 1991; Negbi 1992) and still cultivated commercially in Ghana, Nigeria, and the Mediterranean region. The tuberous rhizomes may be eaten fresh as a snack, or the dry "tubers" are soaked and then roasted and eaten, or they may be ground to a meal and mixed with honey to make a simple confection. Tigernut flour is used to make biscuits, cakes, and ice-cream.

The cultivar Chufa (also known as cv. *sativa* or var. *sativa*) rarely flowers and the tubers contain more oil and less fibre than the weedy yellow form. A refreshing, sweetish milky beverage is prepared from the crushed fresh tigernuts, or from dry tigernuts macerated in water. This drink is known as *atadwe* in Ghana. A similar drink is prepared in Spain, where it is known as *horchata de chufa*. This popular, milk-like beverage has a delicious almond-like flavour and is typically served ice-cold in a *hortacheria*.

The tigernut or yellow nutsedge is sometimes confused with the red nutsedge (*Cyperus rotundus*) which is also a troublesome weed though less widely distributed in southern Africa. It is not edible and can be recognised by the swollen stem bases, the horizontally spreading rhizomes and the reddish-brown glumes. The red nutsedge is an ancient perfume plant that was used since 2000 BC for making perfume. It is still sold in rural markets in North Africa and Arabia for medicinal use.

Cyperus fulgens | Cyperaceae | ***UINTJIE***, *boesmanuintjie* (Afrikaans); *n!ani, !gewu* (San); *oseu* (Herero) ■ This species is by far the most important local *uintjie* of the Cyperaceae family and has a very wide distribution in southern Africa, particularly in the Kalahari and other dry parts. The plant has erect, shiny, bright green leaves with a loose cluster of spikelets. The flower bracts (glumes) are characteristically reddish brown in colour. The bulbs (corms) are about 12 millimetres in diameter, rounded and pointed at the tip, with brown papery scales which are removed to reveal the reddish or yellowish nut-like central part.

The corms are edible and were once collected in large quantities as a staple food in many parts of southern Africa. They are still important in the Kalahari and in Kaokoland. The corms are easily gathered, since they are borne directly below the flowering stalks of the plants at a relatively shallow depth. Furthermore, they are gregarious and usually occur in very large numbers of individuals. The fresh corms are sweetish and somewhat astringent, but roasting in hot ash is said to improve the sweetish nutty taste, as does boiling in milk.

Although of lesser importance, two other sedges are occasionally gathered and eaten in southern Africa. The one is *Cyperus usitatus* (also called *boesmanuintjie*), which is often confused with *C. fulgens*. It has a similar corm, but the spikelets are more densely arranged, and the bracts (glumes) are chestnut brown in colour, not reddish brown (Claire Read, pers. comm.). The other is *Cyperus esculentus*, the well-known yellow nutsedge (*geeluintjie* in Afrikaans). The weedy form of this species is widely distributed in southern Africa, especially in cultivated lands, where it may rapidly multiply and cause severe problems. It differs from the two edible species discussed above by the bright yellow flower clusters and the absence of corms. The edible part in this species is a thickened section of stem (tuber), which is borne on a horizontally spreading thin rhizome. This is a fundamental difference between the two corm-bearing species (*C. fulgens* and *C. usitatus*), which actually belong to the genus *Mariscus*, and two well-known rhizome-bearing weedy plants (*C. esculentus* and *C. rotundus*, see above), which are true *Cyperus* species. The important Kalahari food *uintjie* recorded by Story (1959) as *Mariscus congestus* was incorrectly identified and is actually *Cyperus fulgens*.

Digging *uintjies* (*Cyperus fulgens*)

Plants of *uintjie* (*Cyperus fulgens*)

The edible corms of *uintjie* (*Cyperus fulgens*)

Tigernuts or *chufa* (rhizomes of *Cyperus esculentus*)

Eating *uintjies* (*Cyperus fulgens*)

Cyphia volubilis | Lobeliaceae | ***BAROE****, bouroe* (Khoi); *waterbaroe* (Afrikaans, Khoi) ◼ The plant is an inconspicuous herb with slender, twining stems arising from a potato-like fleshy tuber. It is easily located in the spring by the distinctive small white flowers. Various species of *baroe* were once popular and important wild foods in the Cape but their uses are poorly recorded. They are still amongst the most popular snack foods in rural areas. Species such as *Cyphia sylvatica* (*melkbaroe*) is considered to be particularly tasty, and this species together with *Cyphia undulata* (*baroe*) are reported to be locally important in Namaqualand (Archer 1982). The tubers are peeled and eaten raw, or may be baked or fried. *Melkbaroe* is said to have a milky juice, while *waterbaroe* has a watery juice. Both species are considered to be staple foods which also have a thirst-quenching function because of their high water content (Archer 1982). In the southern Cape, both *C. digitata* (*baroe, bruin baroe*) and *C. undulata* (*baroe, wit baroe*) are commonly used veld foods, especially amongst children (De Vynck *et al.* 2016). A nutritional analysis of *Cyphia volubilis* is given by Archer (1990).

Dioscorea elephantipes | Dioscoreaceae | ***HOTTENTOTSBROOD****, olifantsvoet* (Afrikaans); *naka, !nakaa, t'nakaa* (Khoi); wild yam (English) ◼ This peculiar yam with its trailing stems and large, scaly, above-ground tubers is said to be edible after leaching. The tuber was reported by Patterson in 1889 to be an important food item of the Khoi people, hence the vernacular name (Smith 1966). Practically no information on its traditional food use seems to have survived. Other yams such as *Dioscorea dumetorum* and *D. rupicola* are said to be emergency foods.

Dioscorea elephantipes has become relatively rare because many large tubers were once harvested for chemical analysis to determine their content of steroidal compounds. Fortunately it is relatively easy to cultivate from seeds and has become a popular collector's item amongst succulent plant enthusiasts. *Dioscorea* species are still important sources of diosgenin, used as an intermediate for the synthesis of many steroid hormones, including the anti-inflammatory cortisone, and progestogens used in oral contraceptives.

In West Africa, the white yam (*Dioscorea cayenensis*) is an important staple food, used to prepare the traditional food item known as *fufu*. This yam can be used in the same way as potatoes or sweet potatoes. Various yams are also popular food items in China and Japan.

Encephalartos longifolius | Zamiaceae | **BREAD PALM**; Suurberg cycad; *broodboom* (Afrikaans) ◼ In early times, the thick stems were processed into a starch food after a period of fermentation below the ground. Exact details of the way in which the fermented stem pulp was converted into a bread no longer seem to be available.

The red, date-like seeds are known to be poisonous and human fatalities have been recorded. The fleshy layer around the seed is said to be non-toxic (or at least contains lower levels of poison), while the seed itself is rich in toxic glycosides. A famous case of poisoning occurred during the South African War (1899–1902), when General Jan Smuts and his commando ate seeds of *Encephalartos longifolius* (Watt & Breyer-Brandwijk 1962).

Various species are used in traditional medicine and many of them have become critically rare or endangered as a result of unscrupulous collectors and cycad enthusiasts who remove large plants from nature.

Eulophia hereroensis | Orchidaceae | **WILD MANGO**; *kauguna, tuo* (San); *mufondo, mutodo* (Shona) ◼ The fleshy corms of this ground orchid are an important food source of the Kalahari, Kung and Jul'hoansi San. They are either eaten raw on the spot or are taken home and prepared in several different ways (Fox & Norwood Young 1982; Leffers 2003). Corms of *Eulophia speciosa* are used in the same way.

Flowers of *baroe* (*Cyphia volubilis*)

Edible tubers of baroe (*Cyphia volubilis*)

Melkbaroe (*Cyphia sylvatica*)

Elephant's foot (*Dioscorea elephantipes*)

Tuber of elephant's foot (*Dioscorea elephantipes*)

Fockea angustifolia | Apocynaceae | ***KAMBRO*** (Khoi) ■ This important source of moisture in the dry parts of southern Africa has a huge fleshy tuber below the ground, from which slender twining and creeping branches emerge in the wet season. The stems have a milky juice and bear opposite leaves with wavy margins; narrow in the case of *Fockea angustifolia* and somewhat broader in *F. edulis*. These two species are the most frequently used. They are easily identified: the tuber of *F. angustifolia* is quite smooth, while that of *F. edulis* has a warty surface. Two other species, *F. comaru* and *F. crispa* are occasionally used. *Fockea comaru* can be distinguished by the smaller size of the plant, both below and above the ground, and by the small, very narrow leaves. *Fockea crispa* is also a relatively small plant but it has bright green, broad leaves with wavy margins. The flowers of *Fockea* species are rarely seen. They are small, greenish yellow and resemble those of other members of the family.

Fockea species are restricted to southern Africa and the exact distribution ranges are now well recorded (Bruyns & Klak 2006). The most frequently used species, *Fockea angustifolia*, occurs in the Kalahari regions and the Northern Cape, while the other popular food species, *F. edulis*, has a more southern distribution in parts of the Western and Eastern Cape provinces.

The abundant water in large *Fockea* tubers was of fundamental survival value to San in the Kalahari, enabling them to survive a period of a few months between the end of the tsamma melon supply, and the start of a new rainy season. Water stored in ostrich egg shells, baobab trunks, and other water plants such as *Coccinia rehmannii, Raphionacme burkei, Ceropegia rendalii* and *Commiphora angolensis*, also played an important role.

Tubers are dug out with a digging stick. It is often necessary to dig down to a depth of one metre or more to ensure that the tuber is recovered intact. The smooth bark is easily scraped off with the sharp end of the digging stick and the tuber is simply cut into chunks and eaten. Large quantities of the watery, white flesh are consumed in a short time.

A good illustration of a *Fockea* tuber with stem and opposite leaves is given in Simon van der Stel's diary of his expedition to Namaqualand in 1685 (Gericke 2014). The accompanying note in Dutch can be translated as follows: "This root is generally found in damp and sandy soil, mostly between the Oliphants and Doornbosch Rivers, and is called *Camerebi* by the Namaquaas and *Camoa* by the Griquas, who esteem it greatly. They eat it to relieve themselves of water, and on that account was taken by us to be a kind of *Brionia*." The suggestion that the plant is taken as a diuretic is probably based on the observation that diuresis follows consumption of a reasonable portion because of the high water content of the tuber.

In South Africa, *kambro* species are occasionally eaten but they are better known as sources of jam. The roots are treated in much the same way as wild watermelon, to produce a chunky jam. For detailed recipes see Rood (1994). Kambro may also be eaten as a side dish and for this purpose is prepared in much the same way as sweet potatoes – either baked whole in the oven or sliced and baked in butter with sugar or honey and cinnamon.

Fockea angustifolia tubers are important as sources of water, and have no doubt contributed over many ages to human survival during the nine dry months in the Kalahari, when no surface water is available. Other species found in the Karoo are eaten fresh as an occasional veld food. Tubers of some species (*Fockea edulis, F. comaru*) are still used to cook jam, but the plants have become scarce and the practice is nowadays little more than a mere curiosity.

Several common names have been recorded (Smith 1966). *Fockea angustifolia* is also known as *bergkambroo, gameroo*(n), *gameru*(n), *hottentotswaatlemoen, kamb*(e)*roe, kambroo, kampbaroo* and *kombroo*; *F. comaru* as *comaru, kamaroo, komaroo, komaru, kombroo* and *kombru*(a); *F. capensis* and *F. crispa* as *bergbar*(r)*oe, bergkombroo, bergkoe, bergkoo, bergku, ghwarriekoe* and *kamb*(a)*roo*; *F. edulis* as *bergkambro, hottentotswaatlemoen, kamkoo, kon, koo, ku*(u) and *!ku*. The diversity of recorded Khoi names testifies to the traditional importance of these plants in the Cape and Kalahari regions.

Ernst van Jaarsveld with a large tuber of *kambro* (*Fockea edulis*)

Leaves and flower of *kambro* (*Fockea edulis*)

Leaves of the narrow-leaved *kambro* (*Fockea angustifolia*)

Large tuber of the narrow-leaved *kambro* (*Fockea angustifolia*)

Foeniculum vulgare │Apiaceae│ **FENNEL**; *vinkel* (Afrikaans) ■ Fennel is a robust perennial herb with shiny, bright green, feathery leaves borne on sturdy, hollow stems. It is a naturalised weed that is commonly found along road verges and other disturbed places. Roots are said to be edible. The plant is better known for its small dry fruits (commonly referred to as "seeds"), which contain a valuable essential oil. They are sometimes added as ingredient to sweetmeats and confectionery (breads, buns and rusks). Leaves are often used as a culinary herb with fish, in the same way as dill (the latter has dull, greyish-green leaves). Children often nibble on the fresh leaves and leaf stalks for their sweet, liquorice-like taste.

Grielum humifusum │Neuradaceae│ ***PIET SNOT***, *duikerwortel* (Afrikaans) ■ This is a common herb in Namaqualand, with somewhat fleshy stems and leaves arising from a thick, edible root. The bright yellow flowers are followed by characteristic horned fruits. The root is eaten fresh as a source of moisture (confirmed by Willem Steenkamp, pers. comm.), but according to a study by Archer (1982, 1990) has a high protein content, so that it is also nutritious. It is extremely mucilaginous (hence the common name), and it would make a good substitute for marshmallow root, which is obtained from the European *Althaea officinalis*.

***Ipomoea* species** │Convolvulaceae│ **WILD POTATOES**, *veldpatats* ■ These plants resemble the well-known morning glory (*I. purpurea*) except that they are perennial herbs with fleshy tubers below the ground. Several species are known to be used as emergency sources of water in the Kalahari, or as emergency foods in times of famine. The well-known sweet potato (*Ipomoea batatas*) is widely cultivated in southern Africa as a starch food and forms an important part of several dishes in Malawi. It is an important food plant of the Tsonga people (Liengme 1981).

Kohautia amatymbica │Rubiaceae│ ■ The plant has slender, wiry stems and small tubular white flowers. It is a common plant from grassland areas in southern Africa but is so inconspicuous that it is often overlooked. No vernacular names seem to be recorded. The fleshy roots are said to be edible.

Manihot esculenta │Euphorbiaceae│ **CASSAVA**, tapioca (English); *kassava* (Afrikaans); *ntjumbulu* (Tsonga); *mutumbula* (Venda); *umbumbulu* (Zulu) ■ Cassava is a woody shrub with large, hand-shaped leaves, and leaf lobes varying from narrow to broad, and from bright green to dark purple. Male and female flowers appear on the same plant, but some cultivars rarely flower. The edible parts are the large cylindrical tuberous roots, which may be up to a metre in length and thicker than a man's arm. Cassava originated in central America, from where it was introduced as a crop plant to most tropical parts of the world. From West Africa it gradually spread eastwards and southwards. The plant only reached southern Africa perhaps a few hundred years ago. It has not become as popular as it is in tropical Africa. Cassava has not replaced maize as the staple diet, but is nevertheless grown on a small scale by rural farmers in Namibia, Angola, Zambia, Zimbabwe and Mozambique. The advantage of cassava is that it provides food security in times of drought. It is therefore largely considered to be a famine food. Stem cuttings are planted at the beginning of the rainy season and the roots are usually harvested after a year or more. The roots are dug up by hand and are used fresh, since they deteriorate very rapidly. Sliced and dried roots may be kept indefinitely.

Two types of cassava, sweet and bitter, are found. Bitter cassava contains high levels of a cyanogenic glucoside known as linamarin, which releases toxic hydrogen cyanide when the tissue is damaged. For this reason, special processing is necessary to allow bitter cassava to be utilised as food. Sweet cassava has been selected for low levels of the glucoside so that it can be directly boiled and eaten. The roots are prepared for eating in a variety of ways. They may be baked, boiled, fried, or pounded into a meal. Cassava root is an important industrial source of starch and is used to manufacture tapioca and other starch foods. The leaves are relatively rich in protein and are sometimes mixed with nuts and eaten as a vegetable dish, known as *mutapa*. In contrast, the tubers are low in protein and are mainly a source of starch.

Fennel plants (*Foeniculum vulgare*)

Fennel leaf and flowers (*Foeniculum vulgare*)

Flowering plant of *duikerwortel* (*Grielum humifusum*)

Fleshy roots of *duikerwortel* (*Grielum humifusum*)

Roots of cassava (*Manihot esculenta*)

Leaves of cassava (*Manihot esculenta*)

Moraea fugax (=*Moraea edulis*) │Iridaceae│ **WITUINTJIE**, *soetuintjie, hottentotsuintjie* (Afrikaans) ■ This species is one of the most important of all *uintjies* and its use by early Cape people was recorded in Van der Stel's journal. It occurs from Namaqualand southwards along the west coast and eastwards to the Eastern Cape. The plant has one or two slender leaves arising from the short stem below the flower stalk. Flowers may be white, yellow or bluish, with yellow spots on the lower petals. Each corm is small, oblong and covered in a fibrous sheath. They are usually tied in bundles when harvested. As with most other *uintjies*, the *wituintjie* is roasted in hot ash or it is boiled in milk. Several traditional recipes for *wituintjies* are given by Rood (1994). When prepared in milk, the corms are said to be delicious, the taste reminiscent of sweet potatoes. Another *Moraea* species with an edible corm is *M. viscari* (*uintjie, teeruintjie*), which has to be boiled to remove the dark liquid inside (Archer 1982; Smith 1966).

Several other members of the family are (or were) of local importance as food sources, including *patrysuintjie* (*Gladiolus permeabilis* subsp. *edulis*), *spinnekopblom* or *parara-uintjie* (*Ferraria crispa* and *F. divaricata*) and *swartuintjie* or *volstruisuintjie* (*Hexaglottis longifolia*). The latter is an important food source in Namaqualand. Unfortunately, we do not know much about the harvesting and use of these *uintjies* except for some information recorded by Smith (1966) and Archer (1982). For other *uintjies* see *Babiana dregei, Cyanella hyacinthoides, Cyperus fulgens, Oxalis* species and *Pelargonium incrassatum*.

***Oxalis* species** │Oxalidaceae│ **SURINGS** (Afrikaans) ■ *Oxalis* species are interesting because they are the only known dicotyledonous plants to produce corms. The plants have characteristically lobed and long-stalked leaves that have sleep movements – they fold up at night and unfold again in the daytime. The flowers of all the species vary considerably in colour, but they are all rather similar in general appearance. The best-known species is perhaps the large *geelsuring* (*Oxalis pes-caprae*), a weedy leaf vegetable from the Cape (see Chapter 4). This species not only produces a small edible corm but also a slender white, fleshy and watery root or underground stem that is eaten raw after brushing off the sand. There are many other species with a wide distribution in southern Africa, with a high concentration of species diversity in the Cape and in Namaqualand. The corm of *Oxalis* cf. *tricolor* is considered to be an important food source in Namaqualand (Archer 1982). In the Suid-Bokkeveld south of Nieuwoudtville, the large and gummy corms of the *t'goeiuintjie* (*O. luteola*) are eaten raw (Koos Paulse, pers. comm.). Several other species are also used for their *uintjies*, including *O. convexula, O. semiloba* and *O. smithiana* (Fox & Norwood Young 1982).

Pelargonium incrassatum │Geraniaceae│ **'NYTJIE**, *n/eitjie* (Nama) ■ This tuberous wild pelargonium has distinctive compound leaves and attractive pink or mauve flowers. It is very common in the Khamiesberg in Namaqualand, where the tubers are collected in large numbers as staple food, between June and October (Archer 1982). It is comparable to *Cyanella* in terms of its local importance as readily available food source. The tubers are reddish or purplish inside and are used in the same way as *uintjies* – they are eaten raw, boiled in milk or roasted in the ash of the fire.

Pelargonium rapaceum │Geraniaceae│ **NORRA**, */oertjie* (Nama) ■ This species has large tuberous roots which are very popular as a staple food in Namaqualand. The root superficially resembles a medium-sized beetroot in size and shape but it is covered in a parchment-like outer layer that can easily be peeled off to reveal the fleshy but firm edible part. They are said to be delicious when roasted and have a high caloric value (Archer 1982). Several other species have thick tubers or stems which are used as food and medicine. Examples are *Pelargonium pulchellum* (*n/pita*), another food source in Namaqualand, *P. triste* (*wit n/eitjie*), more important for tanning than as a food, *P. antidysentericum*, a species with large woody tubers, which, as the name implies, has been important as medicine, and *P. carnosum* (*aree*) the fleshy twigs of which are eaten as a snack.

Flowers of *wituintjie* (*Moraea fugax*)

A handful of *wituintjies* (*Moraea fugax*)

Corms of the *spinnekopblom* (*Ferraria crispa*)

Edible tubers of the *'nytjie* (*Pelargonium incrassatum*)

Flowers of the *'nytjie* (*Pelargonium incrassatum*)

Edible tubers of the *norra* or */oertjie* (*Pelargonium rapaceum*)

Phragmites australis | Poaceae | ***FLUITJIESRIET*** (Afrikaans); common reed (English) ■ See Chapter 20. The rhizomes are said to have been a traditional source of starch, and the hollow reeds were used as tobacco pipe-stems, flutes and as parts of musical instruments. The seeds were ground and made into an ointment for burns. The rhizomes are diuretic and diaphoretic, and Rood (1994) reports that a sweet liquid can be obtained by piercing the stem and shaking out the resulting sap. The liquid is used as a sweetener, and also to treat pneumonia, as it is expectorant and relieves pain.

Plectranthus esculentus | Lamiaceae | **LIVINGSTONE POTATO**, wild potato (English); *wilde aartappel* (Afrikaans); *itapile* (Xhosa); *tsenza* (Shona); *mutada* (Venda); *ulujilo, umbondive* (Zulu) ■ The plant is a perennial herb, more than one metre in height, with square hairy stems and pairs of opposite, broad, almost stalkless, toothed leaves. Attractive yellow flowers appear in erect clusters early in the season, before the leaves have emerged. The edible parts of the plants are stem tubers, which grow in clusters from those parts of the branches in contact with the soil. They are oblong, white or yellowish in colour and covered with minute hairs.

This interesting crop plant is of African origin, and appears to have two centres of origin, namely in southern Africa (Malawi and Zambia) and Ethiopia (Alleman & Coertze 1996). As a crop plant, the Livingstone potato is highly adaptable and can be grown in almost any climatic zone, provided that rainfall is evenly distributed over the growing season and that the soil is well drained. Propagation is usually from sections of stem tubers, and a harvest of up to six tons or more per hectare can be expected after about five to seven months.

The tubers are used as a substitute for potato or sweet potato and are mostly boiled before being eaten. They have a unique taste said to resemble that of turnips or parsnip. The use of the tubers as food has been reported from many parts of southern Africa, but the plant's popularity seems to have decreased, perhaps as a result of the introduction of potatoes and sweet potatoes.

The nutritional value is nevertheless exceptionally high and the crop has the added advantage that it will produce tubers even under very unfavourable climatic conditions, thereby adding to food security in remote rural areas. Tubers may be briefly dried and then successfully stored for winter use. Numerous forms of the plant are known, to which several vernacular names have been applied.

Plectranthus rotundifolius (=*Solenostemon rotundifolius*) | Lamiaceae | **ZULU ROUND POTATO**, Hausa potato (English); *Zulu ronde aartappel* (Afrikaans); *amadada, amatambane* (Zulu); *amatabhane* (Sotho) ■ The plant is a small herbaceous perennial of about 300 millimetres in height, with angular stems bearing oval-shaped, aromatic leaves. Pale violet or bluish flowers are borne in elongated clusters. The edible parts are rounded or oblong, dark brown tubers formed on the lower parts of the stems (Grubben & Denton 2004).

The Zulu round potato is a poorly known African crop and the exact centre of origin is not clear. It may possibly have originated from Malawi or Zambia, but it is also found in other parts of eastern and southern Africa, particularly in warm, wet regions. The plant is said to have been cultivated in KwaZulu-Natal long before the arrival of Europeans.

To produce well as a crop, the plant requires a regular supply of water and well-drained soil. It can tolerate low temperatures and will produce some tubers, even under drought conditions. Cultivation is from the small tubers of the previous harvest, which are planted at the beginning of the growing season. Tubers form directly below the surface and may be harvested by hand after five to seven months. Yields of between five and 15 tons per hectare can be expected, with a potential for higher yields under favourable conditions (Alleman, pers. comm.).

The nutritional value of the tubers is quite outstanding, and superior to that of potatoes and sweet potatoes in some respects. Analyses by Alleman (pers. comm.) showed protein levels of around five per cent, with significant quantities of calcium, iron and most of the essential amino acids. It seems strange that this potentially valuable crop has remained poorly known for so long.

Fluitjiesriet or common reed (*Phragmites australis*)

Livingstone potato (*Plectranthus esculentus*)

Tubers of Livingstone potato (*Plectranthus esculentus*)

Flowers of the Zulu round potato (*Plectranthus rotundifolius*)

Tubers of the Zulu round potato (*Plectranthus rotundifolius*)

Raphionacme burkei | Apocynaceae | ***BI*** (San) ■ This plant has a thick, round tuber from which the erect trailing stems emerge in the growing season. The stem produces milky latex. Clusters of small, green, hairy flowers are borne amongst the leaves, followed by a pair of long, thin fruit capsules.

The plant is an important traditional source of water in the Kalahari. It is commonly used despite the bitter taste. The San of the central Kalahari insist that the liquid expressed from the tubers is fatally poisonous to dogs. This could be a taboo which would prevent people in extreme situations of water shortage from having to share their precious water supply with their hunting dogs.

The traditional way in which the tubers are utilised is illustrated here. The bulbous root is held firmly between the feet, stabilised against a digging stick that is stuck into the ground. The sharp edge of a stick is used to scrape shavings of the root, which are collected on top of leaves or grass. The shavings are squeezed in the hand with the thumb pointing downwards, so that the watery juice trickles down into the mouth. After drinking the water, the wet shavings are rubbed over the face and neck, just as airline passengers nowadays use a special wet cloth to refresh themselves. The milky liquid is bitter to the taste and the pounded leaves of *Terminalia sericea* are sometimes added to make it more palatable.

Raphionacme velutina is used exactly in the same way by the Jul'hoansi San, as described in detail by Leffers (2003). The tubers do not grow very deep and are easily dug up. He also states that the gratings can be thrown towards the sun as a symbolic gesture to ask for rain. Hunters use these plants (including *R. lanceolata*) to add moisture to arrow poison and in former times children used to carve toys from the tubers.

Similar-looking tubers of the related plants of the genera *Brachystelma* and *Ceropegia* are not used primarily as sources of moisture but are used as food. They are either eaten raw on the spot or are more often carried home to be baked in hot ash. According to Fox & Norwood Young (1982), the peeled tubers of *Brachystelma foetidum* are eaten throughout the year. The plant is known as *t'kalcuni* in Khoi and *seru* in Ndebele, Pedi and Swati. Leffers (2003) lists six species of edible *Brachystelma* that are used by the Jul'hoansi San: *B. arnotii, B. circinatum, B. cupulatum, B. dinteri, B. discoideum* and *B. gymnopodum*. The outer skin is often removed because it is bitter but the tubers are said to resemble potatoes in texture, appearance and taste. The tubers of *Ceropegia* species are similarly used (often pounded and mixed with other ingredients such as *Eulophia* tubers). The remarkable diversity of edible plants from the family Apocynaceae in southern Africa (Welcome & Van Wyk, unpublished data) is noteworthy.

Solanum tuberosum | Solanaceae | **POTATO**; *aartappel* (Afrikaans); *tapole* (Sotho); *izambane* (Zulu) ■ This important and well-known exotic crop plant of South American origin has replaced many indigenous food plants as a source of starch. It forms the basis of a large agricultural industry in southern Africa, but is also widely grown in rural areas to supplement the diet. The edible part is not a root but a swollen, tuberous, underground stem.

Stenostelma capense | Apocynaceae | **BUSH CARROT** ■ This is an inconspicuous Kalahari plant (growing up to 300 mm in height) with slender, somewhat hairy leaves and tiny flowers borne in clusters. According to Leffers (2003), the carrot-like roots are eaten after they have been baked in hot ash.

Trochomeria macrocarpa | Cucurbitaceae | **BABOON CUCUMBER** ■ The plant is a perennial creeper with deeply lobed leaves, characteristic toothed bracts, small yellowish-green flowers and small, pointed, orange-red fruits. The large tubers, 300 mm or more in length, are roasted in hot ash and eaten (Leffers 2003). It is not a very popular food source and only partly edible, as the core of the tuber is said to be bitter.

ROOTS, BULBS & TUBERS

Fruiting plant of *bi* (*Raphionacme burkei*)

Fleshy tubers of *bi* (*Raphionacme burkei*)

Scraping shavings off a *bi* tuber (onto grass)

Squeezing *bi* shavings to obtain water

Typha capensis | Typhaceae| **BULRUSH** (English); *papkuil* (Afrikaans); *ibhuma* (Swazi, Zulu); *ingcongolo* (Xhosa); *motsitla* (Sotho) ■ The bulrush is a well-known plant of wet places, with ribbon-like leaves and characteristic flower heads. The plant occurs over large parts of southern Africa and has many traditional uses. The fleshy, spongy rhizomes are dug up and may be pounded to a meal and used as a source of starch. The pollen may also be used as a high-protein food. Rhizomes are widely used in traditional medicine, mainly to enhance fertility and potency, to improve circulation and to ensure an easy delivery. Leaves are used to make hand brooms and are also used to some extent in weaving and thatching. The fruiting stalks have been used as torches and the dry seed fluff for stuffing pillows.

Vigna vexillata **subsp.** ***lobatifolia*** | Fabaceae| **CÀ** (San) ■ The plant is a perennial climber with lobed leaves and typical asymmetrical pink flowers. The large clusters of thread-like tubers are reported to be one of the most important food sources of the Jul'hoansi people. It is used in winter when few other foods are available (Leffers 2003). The tubers are a staple food and are usually eaten raw, but may also be baked in hot ash or cooked like potatoes.

The typical form of the species, known as the wild sweetpea (*Vigna vexillata* subsp. *vexillata* – see Chapter 2) does not produce the typical tubers that are found in the subspecies *lobatifolia*. It is occasionally cultivated in southern Africa as a vegetable (for the leaves) and also as a pulse (for the edible seeds).

Walleria nutans | Tecophilaeaceae| **DCHÙN** (San); bush potato ■ The plant is widely distributed in southern and central Africa. It is a small perennial herb with slender leaves resembling those of grasses – they are not only keeled but also clasp the stems as they do in grasses. The pale purple flowers point downwards and have a central staminal column. The small, rounded tubers (resembling small potatoes) are usually baked in hot ash and pounded with other ingredients (Leffers 2003).

REFERENCES AND FURTHER READING: Alleman, J. & Coertze, A.F. 1996. *Plectranthus*. Information leaflet A2. Vegetable and Ornamental Plant Institute, Pretoria. **Archer, F.M. 1982**. 'n Voorstudie in verband met die eetbare plante van die Kamiesberge. *J. S. Afr. Bot.* 48: 433–449. **Archer, F.M. 1990**. Planning with people – ethnobotany and African uses of plants in Namaqualand (South Africa). *Mitt. Inst. Allg. Bot. Hamburg* 23: 959–972. **Arnold, T.H.** *et al.* **1985**. Khoisan food plants: taxa with potential for future economic exploitation. Chapter 6 in: *Plants for arid lands*, Royal Botanic Gardens, Kew. **Bruyns, P.V. & Klak, C. 2006**. A systematic study of the Old World genus *Fockea* (Apocynaceae–Asclepiadoideae). *Ann. Missouri Bot. Gard.* 93: 535–564. **De Vries, F.T. 1991**. Chufa (*Cyperus esculentus*, Cyperaceae): a weedy cultivar or a cultivated weed? *Econ. Bot.* 45(1): 27–37. **De Vynck, J.C., Van Wyk, B.-E. & Cowling, R.M. 2016**. Indigenous edible plant use by contemporary Khoe-San descendants of South Africa's Cape South Coast. *S. Afr. J. Bot.* 102: 60–69. **Gericke, N. 2014**. Ethnobotanical records from a corporate expedition in South Africa in 1685. *Herbalgram* 102: 48–61. **Grubben, G.J.H. & Denton, O.A. (eds) 2004**. *Plant resources of tropical Africa 2. Vegetables*. PROTA Foundation, Wageningen, Netherlands. **Fox, F.W. & Norwood Young, M.E. 1982**. *Food from the veld*. Delta Books, Johannesburg. (Note table of nutritional analyses of common foods on page 64, and analyses of leaf vegetables by Wehmeyer & Rose on page 376). **Leffers, A. 2003**. *Gemsbok bean and Kalahari truffle. Traditional plant use by Jul'hoansi in north-eastern Namibia*. Macmillan Education Namibia Publishers, Windhoek. **Liengme, C.A. 1981**. Plants used by the Tsonga people of Gazankulu. *Bothalia* 13, 3&4: 501–518. **Maguire, B. 1978**. *The food plants of the !Khu Bushmen of north-eastern South West Africa*. M.Sc. thesis, University of the Witwatersrand. **Malan, J.S. & Owen-Smith, G.L. 1974**. The ethnobotany of Kaokoland. *Cimbebasia* Ser. B 2,5: 131–178. **Marloth, R. 1917–1932**. *The Flora of South Africa* (4 vols). William Wesley, London. **Negbi, M. 1992**. A sweetmeat plant, a perfume plant and their weedy relatives: a chapter in the history of *Cyperus esculentus* L. and *C. rotundus* L. *Econ. Bot.* 46(1): 64–71. **Peters, C.R., O'Brien, E.M. & Drummond, R.B. 1992**. *Edible wild plants of sub-Saharan Africa*. Royal Botanic Gardens, Kew. **Procheş, S., Cowling, R.M. & Du Preez, D.R. 2005**. Patterns of geophyte diversity and storage organ size in the winter-rainfall region of southern Africa. *Diversity and Distributions* 11, 101–109. **Rood, B. 1994**. *Kos uit die veldkombuis*. Tafelberg, Cape Town. **Rose, E.F. & Jacot Guillarmod, A. 1974**. Plants gathered as foodstuffs by the Transkeian peoples. *S. Afr. Med. J.* 48: 1688–1690. **Smith, C.A. 1966**. Common names of South African plants. *Mem. Bot. Surv. S. Afr.* 35. **Steyn, H.P. 1981**. Nharo plant utilization. An overview. *Khoisis* 1. **Story, R. 1959**. Some plants used by the Bushmen in obtaining food and water. *Mem. Bot. Surv. S. Afr.* 30. **Van der Stel, S. 1685**. *Simon van der Stel's journey to Namaqualand in 1685*. Facsimile edition, 1979. Human & Rousseau, Cape Town. **Van Wyk, B.-E., Tilney, P.M. & Magee, A.R. 2013**. *African Apiaceae*. Briza Academic Books, Pretoria. **Von Koenen, E. 1996**. *Heil-, Gift- und Essbare Pflanzen in Namibia*. Klaus Hess Verlag, Göttingen. **Von Koenen, E. 2001**. *Medicinal, poisonous and edible plants in Namibia*. Klaus Hess Publishers, Windhoek and Göttingen. **Watt, J.M. & Breyer-Brandwijk, M.G. 1962**. *The medicinal and poisonous plants of southern and eastern Africa*, 2nd ed. Livingstone, London.

Bulrush plants (*Typha capensis*)

Flower cluster of bulrush (*Typha capensis*), showing pollen

Pancake made from flour and bulrush pollen

Starchy rhizomes of bulrush (*Typha capensis*)

Basotho traditional healer Sera Khamokha drinking *joala* (sorghum beer) from a *mopotjoana* (small beer pot). Note the *mosetla* (a hat made from *Merxmuellera* grass), worn only by women in former times

Flowering plant of commercial tea (*Thea sinensis*)

Traditional method of distilling *witblits*, a potent alcoholic liquor (Kleinplasie Farm Museum)

Flower and fruits of the coffee plant (*Coffea arabica*)

Witblits trickling from the still (note the funnel made from a lemon tree leaf)

CHAPTER 6

Beverages

SOUTHERN AFRICA HAS a diverse and interesting indigenous tea, wine and beer culture. The terms tea, wine and beer may be misleading, because they imply a relation with the three main beverage plants of the modern world (*Thea sinensis* – tea, *Vitis vinifera* – wine, *Hordeum vulgare* – barley malt used for beer). Traditional drinks are often highly nutritious and form an important component of the diet. The diversity of alcoholic and non-alcoholic beverages is highlighted below.

One of the most widely used beverages in southern Africa is sorghum beer, produced from *Sorghum bicolor* malt. Beer making has become commercialised and standardised, so that the rural recipes and special ingredients are no longer used except in isolated places. The most important "beer plants" such as pearl millet (*Pennisetum glaucum*) and marula (*Sclerocarya birrea*) are no longer as widely used as in former times. Malted beers are traditionally used daily as an item of diet. Marula and other fruit brews, however, are strictly seasonal, and are used mainly for their alcohol content, to lift the spirit. A glimpse of the diversity can be seen in the study of Quin (1959) who recorded the main traditional beers (*bjalwa*) of the Pedi culture. With increasing awareness and appreciation for the value of diversity, there will hopefully be a revival of the traditional art of brewing. The traditional malting and brewing methods for *bjalwa* were recorded in detail by Quin (1959). Malting procedures are the same for sorghum, pearl millet and even non-traditional mealies: the grain is placed in a clay pot and submerged in cold water. After 24 hours, when the grain starts to sprout, it is drained and transferred to a grass basket and left until the roots are about 25 millimetres long. The mass of germinated grain is spread out and allowed to dry in the sun. The dry product is ground on a grinding stone to make a coarse meal. To brew traditional sorghum beer (Quin 1959) lukewarm water is added to the malted meal in a special clay pot; the content is stirred well and then covered with a small basket as a lid. After a day of fermentation, the supernatant liquor is transferred to an open cooking pot, brought to the boil (to reduce acidity) and the fermented mash, thinned with water, is returned to the liquor, while stirring continuously. After boiling for half an hour, the pot is left to simmer for another hour. The original clay pot is rinsed with cold water and the cooked gruel is transferred back into the pot and stored in a cool place. After 12 hours, the brew forms a gelatinous mass without any fermentation. More malted meal is added and the whole brew is stirred and left to ferment for 10 hours at room temperate. The brew is now ladled into a grass strainer and the beer is wrung into a clay pot, ready for serving.

Another important beverage is palm wine, prepared from the sap of the ilala palm (*Hyphaene coriacea*) and the mokola palm (*H. petersiana*), and to a lesser extend also the wild date palm (*Phoenix reclinata*). Details are given below.

In the dry parts of southern Africa, *karrie* or mead (honey beer) was once an important beverage. Interesting regional differences in the source materials and in the methods used have been recorded. This is certainly a dying art, perhaps because inexpensive commercial beers, wine and other alcoholic beverages have become readily available as alternatives to the traditional brews.

Rooibos tea (*Aspalathus linearis*) and honeybush tea (*Cyclopia* species) are the two best-known indigenous teas, and have become increasingly popular as health beverages, because they are devoid of caffeine but rich in phenolic compounds which have antioxidant activity and other health benefits. A Special Edition of the *South African Journal of Botany* (vol. 110), published in 2017, included important papers on the health benefits and flavour profiles of rooibos tea and honeybush tea. Several other Cape herbal teas are known (Van Wyk & Gorelik 2017), but the distinction between a tea, a tonic tea and a medicinal tea (i.e., a medicinal infusion) is somewhat blurred.

***Aloe* species** | Asphodelaceae | **ALOES** ■ Children suck nectar from the flowers of several species. The closely related *Gasteria* is also a rich source of nectar for children, and was reported to be cooked by the early Khoi as rice, hence the vernacular name *hottentotsrys* (Smith 1966).

Anacampseros ustulata (=*Avonia ustulata*) | Anacampserotaceae | *MOERPLANTJIE*, *kirriemoer, moerbossie* (Afrikaans) ■ The dried and pulverised roots and stems were once used as yeast for baking bread and to brew mead (honey beer). It is said to be an original Khoi yeast source.

Anacampseros papyracea | Anacampserotaceae | *KAREEMOERWORTEL*, *moerplantjie*, *gansmis* ■ The true leaves of this strange little plant are hidden by white papery scales. It is an early yeast plant used in the same way as *Anacampseros ustulata*. Other species reportedly used as yeast include *A. quinaria* and *A. rhodesiaca*. It is interesting to note that these plants may contain psychoactive substances (see Chapter 9), so that their use may not only have been as yeast, but to improve the "kick" of the brew.

Aspalathus linearis | Fabaceae | **ROOIBOS TEA**; *rooibostee, bossietee* (Afrikaans) ■ This plant is a shrub of up to two metres in height, with bright green needle-shaped leaves that turn reddish brown after processing. The small, yellow flowers are produced in early summer, followed by small, single-seeded pods.

Rooibos tea is a traditional beverage of the Khoi-descended people of the Cederberg region in the Cape (Van Wyk & Gorelik 2017) and is one of only a few indigenous plants that have become an important commercial crop (Joubert *et al.* 2008; Joubert & De Beer 2011; Van Wyk 2011). Production is still centred in its natural distribution area (the districts of Nieuwoudtville, Clanwilliam, Citrusdal and Piquetberg). Seeds have to be treated with sulphuric acid to break the impermeable seed coat and seedlings are transplanted to deep acid sandy soils. The production area has cold wet winters and hot dry summers, with a mere 300 to 350 millimetres of rain per year. Some wild types of rooibos tea are harvested on a small scale (e.g. the Heiveld and Cederberg types), but only one form, the so-called red type or Rocklands type, is commercially cultivated.

Annual yields vary from about four to nine million kilograms or more, depending on the rainfall. The plants are mostly harvested with sickles and tied into bundles. They are then chopped into short segments, moistened, bruised and left in heaps to "sweat" or "ferment" for several hours until a sweet smell develops. So-called "fermentation" is actually an oxidation process, during which the phenolic compounds in the plant are enzymatically oxidised. When the tea-maker is satisfied with the colour and aroma, the tea is spread out thinly to sun-dry.

Marketing started in 1904, through the efforts of Benjamin Ginsberg, who bought wild tea from local people. During the early 1930s, Dr P. le Fras Nortier helped to develop rooibos as a crop plant and Mr James van Putten played a major role in later years. The Rooibos Tea Control Board was established in 1954 to stabilise producer prices through orderly marketing and quality control. This Board was subsequently turned into a private company. Through imaginative marketing, rooibos tea has become an important commercial product, with retail and export earnings running into many millions of rands per year. Since 2003, export volumes to Germany alone have exceeded the volumes consumed locally.

Rooibos is popular as a health beverage, prepared and used in much the same way as black tea. However, it contains no harmful stimulants and is totally devoid of caffeine. It has gained popularity as an excellent iced tea. Nowadays one can also get green rooibos, red cappuccino and red espresso. The health properties are ascribed mainly to the low tannin content, the presence of minerals and the antispasmodic and free-radical capturing properties of several unique flavonoid *C*-glycosides, such as aspalathin and nothofagin. The product is also used as an ingredient in cosmetics, in slimming products, as a flavouring agent in baking, cooking, cocktails and even as a milk substitute for infants who are prone to colic.

Twigs of the *moerplantjie* (*Anacampseros ustulata*)

The scaly stems of *kareemoerwortel* (*Anacampseros papyracea*)

Plantation of rooibos tea (*Aspalathus linearis*)

Flowering plant of rooibos tea (*Aspalathus linearis*)

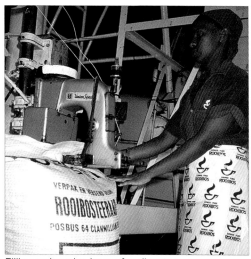

Filling and sewing bags of rooibos tea

Athrixia phylicoides | Asteraceae | **MOUNTAIN TEA**, bush tea; *tee ya thaba* (Sotho) ■ The plant is an erect shrub with silvery leaves and attractive purple flower heads. The tea prepared from this traditional tea plant was considered by some to be better than low-quality real tea (Smith 1966). The plant is suitable for domestication and development as a commercial health tea (Joubert *et al.* 2008; Lerotholi *et al.* 2017). In Venda it is believed to have aphrodisiac properties. It is sometimes called bushman's tea, but should not be confused with *Catha edulis*. A beverage known as *wildetee* or daisy tea (*tee* in Sotho) is prepared from the leaves and twigs of a related species, *Athrixia elata*.

Bauhinia petersiana | Fabaceae | **WILD COFFEE BEANS**; *koffiebeesklou* (Afrikaans); *mogotswe* (Tswana) ■ The seeds are roasted as a coffee substitute. Seeds of the related *Tylosema esculentum* (marama bean – see Chapter 2) are used in the same way.

Boscia albitrunca | Capparaceae | ***WITGATBOOM***, *witgat, gaat* (Afrikaans); shepherd's tree; *motlopi* (Tswana) ■ This is a shrub or small tree with an attractive umbrella-shaped crown and characteristic pale grey to white bark. The leaves are usually borne in clusters and are greyish green in colour. Small, yellowish flowers are followed by yellow or pink, edible berries.

The shepherd's tree is one of the most common and widely distributed of all southern African trees. It occurs over practically all of the interior of southern Africa, even in extremely dry parts. Many parts of the tree are used. Leaves are nutritious and are heavily browsed by cattle and game. The roots are edible and are sometimes pounded and used to make porridge. The fruit is used to prepare traditional dishes. Flower buds are pickled in vinegar and are used as a substitute for capers. The most well-known use of the tree, however, is as a coffee substitute.

The thick, fleshy roots are cut into short sections and the hard inner cores are pushed out. These ring-like sections are now pounded and spread in the sun to dry. When dry, the roots are burnt in an iron pot or pan until they turn brown and start to smoke. A little brown sugar and some fat are usually added. The product is mixed with coffee beans (in various ratios, depending on taste and on the availability of the latter), ground, and used as coffee. A beer is made with pounded fresh root. Water and sugar are added and the brew is left to ferment overnight. The resulting liquid is pungent and intoxicating. *Witgat* coffee or just *witgat* or *gaat* (as the beverage is widely known in rural areas) was once popular as substitute or partial substitute for coffee and chicory. The taste is an acquired one.

Canavalia ensiformis | Fabaceae | **JACK BEAN** ■ The large white seeds or beans (see photograph on page 18) are popular as a coffee substitute in the northern parts of South Africa (Erika van den Heever, pers. comm.).

Catha edulis | Celastraceae | **BUSHMAN'S TEA**, khat ■ This well-known African masticatory has been used in the Eastern Cape as a stimulant tea (see Chapter 9). The English explorer, naturalist, artist and author William Burchell recorded the name *bushman's tea* for *Catha edulis* on the herbarium specimen he collected in 1814 in the vicinity of the Zwarte Kei River. In Ethiopia, tea of *Catha edulis* is used as an aid in concentration by students in Addis Ababa, and is given to teenagers with attention deficit disorder as a substitute for the stimulant pharmaceutical methylphenidate (Ermias Dagne, pers. comm.).

Cichorium intybus | Asteraceae | **CHICORY**; *sigorei* (Afrikaans) ■ This plant is a robust herb with large, soft leaves and attractive blue flower heads. It is an exotic crop plant that has become a weed over large parts of southern Africa. The roots are processed into a commercial product known as chicory, which is sold as a coffee additive or coffee substitute. The root has a high concentration of inulin, and has tonic, sedative and mild laxative activities. *Ghoo* coffee is another coffee substitute traditionally made from the leached and roasted seeds (nuts) of wild almond or *ghoo, Brabejum stellatifolium* (see Chapter 2). Other coffee substitutes include the roasted seeds of *Vachellia karroo* (sweet thorn) and *V. erioloba* (camel thorn).

Flowering plant of mountain tea (*Athrixia phylicoides*)

Flowering plant of *tee* or daisy tea (*Athrixia elata*)

A stunted specimen of the shepherd's tree or *witgat* (*Boscia albitrunca*)

Roots of the shepherd's tree, which are processed for use as a coffee substitute

Coffea arabica | Rubiaceae | **COFFEE** ■ The beans of the coffee plant are the commercial source of coffee, and the plant is grown to a limited extent as a crop in the tropical parts of southern Africa. *Coffea arabica* yields the highest quality of coffee, but *C. robusta* (sometimes called *C. canephora*) is commonly grown, especially in humid tropical areas. The latter is mainly used to manufacture instant coffee. Several local substitutes for coffee have been developed (see *Cichorium intybus*).

Combretum apiculatum | Combretaceae | **RED BUSHWILLOW**; *rooibos* (Afrikaans) ■ The leaves are commonly used to make tea. *Combretum micranthum* leaves are used in West Africa to make a tonic tea known commercially as *kinkeliba* (Van Wyk 2015).

Cyclopia intermedia | Fabaceae | **HONEYBUSH TEA**; *heuningbostee* (Afrikaans) ■ Honeybush tea is a name that applies to herbal tea made from several different species of *Cyclopia*. These plants are all fynbos shrubs with golden yellow stems and stalkless, hairless leaves, each of which is divided into three smaller leaflets.

The original honeybush tea was made from *Cyclopia genistoides*, a small shrub with distinctive narrow leaflets, restricted to the mountains near the Cape Peninsula. The plant has become quite scarce in nature but is now one of the main species used to establish plantations. The main production area first moved to the Langkloof area near Port Elizabeth, where substantial quantities of tea are produced from *Cyclopia intermedia* (so-called *bergtee*, a resprouter after fire) and *C. subternata* (so-called *vleitee*, a reseeder after fire) (Schutte *et al.* 1995; Schutte 1997). Nowadays, tea is also produced in the western and southern Cape areas, where *Cyclopia genistoides* (the original *honigthee / heuningtee* or honeybush tea) has become an important crop. *Cyclopia sessilifolia* (so-called Heidelberg tea) is harvested on a small scale in the Heidelberg district of the Cape, while *C. maculata* is traditionally produced at Genadendal near Caledon. Cultivation methods have been developed by Kirstenbosch Botanical Garden (De Lange 1997), resulting in a lively interest among Cape farmers to grow and produce honeybush tea.

Traditionally, honeybush plants were harvested in spring (October and the first half of November), as the flowers were considered important in adding flavour and aroma to the tea (Fanie Wagenaar, pers. comm.). Nowadays, plants are harvested over a much longer period. Branches are harvested in bundles and often have to be carried over long distances in mountainous terrain. The stems and leaves are chopped into small sections using a modified silage cutter, after which the material is bruised and moistened. The heaps of material are left to oxidise spontaneously, or the material is heated in an oven to about 60 degrees to enhance the process. Oxidation turns the chopped material into a rich brown colour and enhances the characteristic sweet smell of the herb. After a few hours, when the teamaker decides that the desired quality and aroma has been achieved, the tea is spread out in the sun to dry. Honeybush tea is freely available at roadside stalls and health shops, and as a packed product in supermarkets. The industry is still relatively small compared to rooibos tea, but it is likely to expand as the demand increases. Research and development activities have accelerated in recent years, as highlighted in a Special Edition of the *South African Journal of Botany* (vol. 110), published in 2017.

Honeybush tea is a traditional substitute for ordinary tea, but is enjoyed as a health tea nowadays for its own delicious taste and aroma. It is used in much the same way as ordinary tea, except that prolonged boiling at low heat enhances the flavour. For this reason, a special kettle used to be kept permanently on the coal stove in the old farmhouse kitchens. The caffeine-free brew was conveniently at hand any time of the day. The kettle was occasionally topped up with water and new tea added to maintain the required strength.

Honeybush tea contains various phenolic compounds such as flavonoids and xanthone *C*-glycosides which are considered to be healthy because of their antioxidant properties (Joubert *et al.* 2008). The tea has a natural sweet taste and is said to stimulate milk flow in lactating mothers.

Honeybush tea or *bergtee* (*Cyclopia intermedia*)

The original, narrow-leaved honeybush tea or *heuningtee* (*Cyclopia genistoides*)

Honeybush tea or *vleitee* (*Cyclopia subternata*)

Heidelberg tea (*Cyclopia sessilifolia*)

Honeybush tea processed in the modern (above) and traditional way (below)

Cynorhiza typica (=*Peucedanum sulcatum*) │Apiaceae│ **BIERWORTEL** (Afrikaans); beer root ■ The root of this wild relative of the carrot, which grows along the Cape West coast, was once popular for brewing mead (honey beer). See also *Glia gummifera*.

The large tap root of *Cynorhiza typica* is dug up, cleaned of sand and cut into 10 millimetre thick sections which are left to dry in the sun. The root has a sweetish smell, and tastes rather like turnip. As the material dries it becomes distinctly orange-yellow, and the outer cortex shrinks, leaving the middle section prominent. The hard and fibrous middle portion is easily removed and discarded. When the remaining material is thoroughly dry, it is finely ground and added to water with honeycomb. It is important to include honeycomb that contains bee embryos.

The mixture ferments, turning the liquid yellow. Once it has stopped bubbling, usually after one day, the granules sink to the bottom. The granules are strained, dried and retained as a "yeast" for future beer making. The remaining liquid is allowed to ferment for another half day before drinking. The traditional mead is highly intoxicating, and can cause a bad hangover. In the West Coast area of the Cape the common name for this beer is *karri* and locals say this is because the yellow colour resembles curry. We believe that *karri* is in fact a corruption of the original Khoi word *karee*, meaning mead (see *Searsia lancea*; formerly known as *Rhus lancea*). The late Dawid Bester (pers. comm.) is acknowledged for providing the only detailed information known on making this authentic mead.

Datura stramonium │Solanaceae│ **COMMON THORN APPLE** ■ See Chapter 9. Leaves of this potentially poisonous plant are sometimes added to beer in Zimbabwe to make it more intoxicating (Gift Kafundo, pers. comm.).

Ficus sycomorus │Moraceae│ **SYCAMORE FIG**; *grootvrugtrosvy* (Afrikaans) ■ See Chapter 3. A spirit is distilled from the fermented fruits in northern Namibia and in Zambia (Van den Eynden *et al.* 1992).

Geranium incanum │Geraniaceae│ **VROUEBOSSIE**, *bergtee* (Afrikaans) ■ See Chapter 10. This species is a source of traditional herbal tea in the Cape (apart from its medicinal uses).

Glia gummifera │Apiaceae│ **GLI** (Khoi); *moerwortel, dronkwortel* (Afrikaans) ■ This is another member of the Apiaceae family that was once used as a ferment (*moer*) in beer brewing (see *Cynorhiza typica*). Thunberg recorded the vernacular name (*gli*) and described the use of the plant in 1774. This is one of very few examples where an early ethnobotanical anecdote, complete with the vernacular name, is supported by an herbarium specimen (preserved in the Thunberg Herbarium). The Khoi people mixed two handfuls of the dried and powdered root with honey and cold water to produce an intoxicating drink. It is possible that the edible tuber of the related *gatagaai* (*Glia decidua*) was similarly used.

Glycyrrhiza glabra │Fabaceae│ **LIQUORICE**, licorice ■ See Chapter 8. This exotic legume is an important commercial source of sweetener, especially popular in hiding the unpleasant taste of medicines. Extracts are used to flavour food and beverages and to make liquorice sweets (also known as licorice or *drop*).

Helichrysum imbricatum (=*H. auriculatum*) │Asteraceae│ **DUINETEE** (Afrikaans) ■ Leaves were traditionally infused as a tea, said to be popular amongst the Khoi population of the Cape. It was also used for medicinal purposes against chest ailments, and as demulcent and emollient.

Helichrysum nudifolium │Asteraceae│ **VAALTEE**, *hottentotstee* (Afrikaans) ■ See Chapter 11. Leaf infusions were not only used as traditional medicine at the Cape (against chest ailments and colds) but also as a substitute for Chinese tea.

Root and leaves of the *bierwortel* (*Cynorhiza typica*)

Beer prepared from *bierwortel* (*Cynorhiza typica*)

Root and leaves of the *bierwortel* (*Cynorrhiza typica*)

Dried root segments of the *bierwortel* (*Cynorhiza typica*)

Leaves and flowers of liquorice (*Glycyrrhiza glabra*)

Liquorice root (*Glycyrrhiza glabra*)

Hyphaene coriacea | Arecaceae | **ILALA PALM** ■ An important source of palm wine in South Africa and Mozambique – see *Hyphaene petersiana*.

Hyphaene petersiana | Arecaceae | **MOKOLA PALM**, real fan palm, vegetable ivory palm (English); *opregte waaierpalm* (Afrikaans); *omurungu* (Herero); *omulunga* (Ovambo) ■ The mokola palm is an erect, single-stemmed, clump-forming tree of up to 16 metres in height. The bluish-grey, fan-shaped leaves are large, up to two metres long, with black thorns along the stalks. Female trees bear round, dark brown, single-seeded fruit of about 50 millimetres in diameter. Underneath the fibrous outer husk is a hard, white layer of bony material, the so-called vegetable ivory. Inside the seed is a small quantity of sweet liquid, similar to coconut milk. Differences between the various useful palms are given under *Hyphaene coriacea* in Chapter 19. The mokola palm occurs in the northern tropical parts of southern Africa (further details are given under *Hyphaene coriacea* – see Chapter 19).

Both the mokola palm and the ilala palm are important sources of palm wine and contribute significantly to the rural economies of Maputaland (Cunningham 1990a, 1990b) and the Okavango–Zambezi regions. The wild date palm (*Phoenix reclinata*) is also used for palm wine but to a limited extent. The process of tapping has been described in detail by Meredith (1948) and Cunningham (1990a). Stem clumps are burnt to make the stems accessible and to remove the leaf spines. The stem tips are trimmed with a sharp knife to initiate sap flow. The apical meristem and leaf bases are cut at an angle to direct the sap flow to a piece of leaf which functions as a spout above the collection container (a calabash, ox horn or clay container was traditionally used). The prepared stems are covered with a woven palm leaf hood to protect them against the elements (sun and rain), to keep dust and insects out and to prevent birds from settling on the exposed part. During the tapping period, which lasts about five to seven weeks, the sap flow is initially slow but gradually increases to a peak and then decreases again. Each stem yields between three and eight litres of palm sap (Cunningham 1990a) but large trees are said to produce an average of more than 60 litres (Meredith 1948). To keep the sap flowing, the cut surfaces have to be "opened up" on each collecting round (usually three visits per day). A few millimetres of the hardened stem tip and leaf bases are trimmed away, thus also removing the crust of solidified sap which forms on the surface. Palm wine is normally consumed about 36 hours after collection, when the sap has been sufficiently fermented by natural yeasts. The wine is normally used in undiluted form, but it may also be diluted (with sugar added) to increase profit. In Zimbabwe, the wine is home-distilled to a potent spirit known as *skokiaan* (see notes on sugar cane, *Saccharum officinale* later in this chapter). In tropical Africa and particularly in Nigeria (Mmegwa *et al.* 1985), local enterprises are now bottling both natural and formulated palm wine on a commercial scale.

Palm wine is delicious and refreshing. It tastes like good-quality ginger beer to which a touch of hops beer has been added. Unlike marula wine, palm wine is not seasonal and is consumed in large quantities throughout the year. Analyses of the wine (Nash & Bornman 1973; Cunningham & Wehmeyer 1988) have shown that palm wine is an important dietary supplement, especially to rural men, adding substantial quantities of nicotinic acid, vitamin C and potassium to the normal starchy diet. The latter authors found that the alcohol content was about 3.6 per cent in undiluted wine samples from both ilala palm and wild date palm.

The mokola palm is a versatile and valuable natural resource in rural areas. In addition to palm wine, it supplies fibrous leaves for weaving (see Chapter 19) and food in the form of the edible fruits and the pith of young stems and young leaves. The fibrous outer layer of the fruit is sweet and edible, and the fluid within the seed is similar to coconut milk in taste and appearance. The white and bony seed coat is known as vegetable ivory and is used for carving small objects and for decorating wooden ornaments.

Tapping the mokola palm (*Hyphaene petersiana*)

Collecting mokola palm sap for brewing palm wine

Vegetable ivory, the seeds of mokola palm (*Hyphaene petersiana*)

Palm wine prepared from mokola palm sap

Khadia acutipetala │Aizoaceae│ **KHADI ROOT**; *khadiwortel* (Afrikaans) ■ The fleshy rootstock of this mesemb is reported to have been an important fermentation agent in beer brewing. *Khadi* is said to be the original name for a kind of beer in which the root was used as a source of yeast. The fermenting ability of *khadi* root has been ascribed to the presence of fungi. There may possibly be mesembrine-type alkaloids in the root, which may contribute to the intoxicating properties. *Khadia alticola* has apparently also been used as yeast, and the name *khadi* has been extended to several other plants with fleshy rootstocks used in a similar way, such as *Raphionacme hirsuta*.

Leysera gnaphalodes │Asteraceae│ ***HONGERTEE**, duinetee, teringtee* (Afrikaans) ■ This common species is a perennial shrublet with needle-shaped leaves and yellow flower heads. An infusion of the above-ground portions of the plant can be enjoyed as a general health tea. It has an aromatic fragrance, and is popular in the Cape, especially along the west coast and in the Cederberg region, where it was once the most popular of all herbal teas (Van Wyk & Gorelik 2017). The tea can be taken two to three times daily as an appetite stimulant in thin, wasted individuals. It has also been used to treat rheumatic fever (Dawid and Mrs. Bester, pers. comm.). The plant has been used for coughs, bronchitis and tuberculosis, and has potential for new crop development.

Mesembryanthemum tortuosum │Aizoaceae│ **SCELETIUM**; *kougoed* (Afrikaans) ■ See Chapter 9. This traditional masticatory has become a popular health tea. It is often mixed with other herbal teas such as rooibos tea or honeybush tea.

Myrothamnus flabellifolius │Myrothamnaceae│ **RESURRECTION PLANT**; *bergboegoe* (Afrikaans); *uvukwabafile* (Zulu) ■ The leaves of this interesting plant shrink and appear to be dead in the dry season, but miraculously turn green within a few hours after exposure to water (the English and the Zulu names refer to this remarkable property). For this reason the plant has been traditionally used as a symbol of hope, to treat depression and bereavement (Credo Mutwa, pers. comm.). Young plants are cultivated on a commercial scale as a novelty horticultural product. Extracts have shown powerful antimicrobial activity. The leaves contain essential oil (see Chapter 13) and have been used as a medicinal tea. A few twigs may be used to flavour regular tea (Rood 1994). The plant is used by the Topnaar people of Namibia (Van den Eynden *et al.* 1992). Leaves and stems are added to tea to flavour it, and are also used as a spice.

Phoenix reclinata │Arecaceae│ **WILD DATE PALM** ■ See Chapter 3. This palm is also tapped for palm wine, but it is of secondary importance to *Hyphaene coriacea* and *H. petersiana*. Many other uses are known; the fruits are edible, the leaves are used for weaving and the stems for making hand brooms.

Plecostachys serpyllifolia │Asteraceae│ **HOTTENTOTSTEE** (Afrikaans) ■ This is a shrublet with small silvery leaves and very small flower heads arranged in flat-topped clusters. Leafy twigs can be used to brew a tasty tea, or as a medicine for hypertension and heart failure. It has a diuretic effect (Dawid and Mrs Bester, pers. comm.).

Protea repens │Proteaceae│ ***SUIKERBOS*** (Afrikaans); sugar bush ■ This attractive protea is widely distributed over most of the fynbos region of the Cape. The plant is an erect shrub of up to three metres high, with narrow, hairless leaves. The flower heads are usually yellow, but pink and red forms are also commonly found, particularly towards the eastern part of the distribution range. The plant is grown commercially for the cut flower industry and several new cultivars have been developed. The head has a sticky exudate on the outer surface and a large supply of nectar inside. Until recently this nectar was collected by shaking the flower heads into buckets. The nectar was then strained and boiled to a syrupy consistency. The product, known as *bossiestroop*, was once a popular syrup for eating and for medicinal use, mainly as an ingredient of cough syrups.

Flowering plant of *khadi* root (*Khadia acutipetala*)

Hongertee or *teringtee* (*Lysera gnaphalodes*)

Resurrection plant (*Myrothamnus flabellifolius*)

Shrunken and expanded leaves of the resurrection plant (*Myrothamnus flabellifolius*)

Flower head of *suikerbos* (*Protea repens*)

Bossiestroop, a syrup prepared from the nectar of *Protea repens*

Pterodiscus speciosus │Pedaliaceae│ **SANDKAMBRO**, *moerwortel* (Afrikaans) ■ The plant is a succulent with a thick, fleshy stem tuber and simple, lobed leaves. The flowers vary from dark purple to yellowish pink and closely resemble those of devil's claw (*Harpagophytum procumbens*). Fruits are four-winged structures resembling those of *Combretum* and *Tetragonia*. The fleshy stem tubers were once used as a source of yeast or fermentation for beer brewing, especially by the Korana people (Smith 1966), but no details seem to have been recorded.

Rafnia amplexicaulis │Fabaceae│ **SOETHOUTBOSSIE**, *veldtee, waboomtee* (Afrikaans) ■ *Rafnia* species are fynbos shrubs with simple, hairless leaves and attractive yellow flowers. The yellowish roots of two species (*R. amplexicaulis* and *R. acuminata*) have a strong bitter-sweet taste and were once considered to be good substitutes for liquorice. These two species are closely similar and both have rounded leaves that encircle the stems. *Rafnia amplexicaulis* is an erect shrub of more than a metre high, while *R. acuminata* is a spreading shrub about half a metre high but up to two metres in diameter. The latter was previously known as *R. perfoliata*, and has the same vernacular name, *soethoutbossie*, as *R. amplexicaulis*. The leaves of both species are used to brew a tasty traditional tea (Kinfe *et al.* 2015; Van Wyk & Gorelik 2017). The tea is said to be an excellent remedy against chest ailments and is known in the Cederberg region (Ben Zimri, pers. comm.) by the Afrikaans vernacular name *borskwaal* (i.e., "chest ailment"). The extent to which other species of *Rafnia* are suitable for making herbal tea is not known but a dark brown to black and tannin-rich tea can be brewed from the leaves of *Rafnia angulata*. It is interesting to note that the fresh young leaves of *Rafnia amplexicaulis* are edible and that they provide a tasty snack. According to Koos Paulse (pers. comm.), the young leaves of what they call *appelbos* are also eaten as a preventative medicine to fight off colds and influenza, and are especially popular amongst women.

The main chemical compound responsible for the intense bitter-sweet liquorice taste of *Rafnia amplexicaulis* roots and leaves has been isolated and identified as genistein 8-*C*-β-*D*-glucoside (Kinfe *et al.* 2015). This isoflavone has demonstrated antioxidant and radio-protective activity and may be at least partly responsible for the traditional uses of *Rafnia* tea in treating asthma, influenza, back problems, infertility, catarrh and wasting. *Rafnia amplexicaulis* therefore seems to have considerable potential as new ingredient for herbal teas and functional foods.

Raphionacme purpurea │Apocynaceae│ **FALSE GENTIAN**; *khadiwortel* (Afrikaans) ■ The plant has a fleshy underground tuber, pointed leaves and small purple flowers. Tubers were reportedly used as yeast and as additive for brewing *skokiaan* (see notes under sugar cane on page 130). Experiments by Watt (1926) have shown that the fresh tuber is indeed capable of producing fermentation, and that a narcotic effect is likely to be achieved when it is added to beer. *Raphionacme hirsuta* is also a traditional beer additive (Smith 1966).

Ruta graveolens │Rutaceae│ **RUE**; *wynruit* (Afrikaans) ■ The highly aromatic leaves are commonly added to herbal mixtures that are used as medicinal teas, especially in the Cape region. It seems that rue is used as flavouring and masking agent in addition to being an active medicinal ingredient. It contains methylnonyl ketone (2-undecanone) as a major compound in the essential oil, which is used commercially in perfumery and flavouring. In Ethiopia, a leaf of *Ruta chalepensis* is commonly dipped into black coffee (*buna*) to improve the flavour.

Both *R. graveolens* and *R. chalepensis* are cultivated in herb gardens in South Africa and are used interchangeably (both are called *wynruit*). The former occurs naturally in southern Europe, while the latter is from the Mediterranean region. *Ruta chalepensis* (Aleppo rue or fringed rue) can easily be distinguished by the grey leaves and fringed petal margins, hence the vernacular name. In *R. graveolens* the leaves are bright green and the petal entire (i.e., with smooth margins).

Plant of the *sandkambro* (*Pterodiscus speciosus*)

Leaves and flowers of *soethoutbossie* or *waboomtee* (*Rafnia amplexicaulis*)

Leaves and flowers of *soethoutbossie* (*Rafnia acuminata*)

Roots of the *soethoutbossie* (*Rafnia amplexicaulis*), an early liquorice substitute

Flowering plant of Aleppo rue or fringed rue (*Ruta chalepensis*)

Flowers of rue (*Ruta graveolens*)

Flowers of Aleppo rue (*Ruta chalepensis*)

Saccharum officinarum │Poaceae│ **SUGAR CANE**; *suikerriet* (Afrikaans) ■ Sugar cane is a large, robust grass with thick, juicy stems of about three metres high. Pinkish plumes of small flowers are sometimes produced at the tips of the stems. The original cultivated forms of sugar cane are varieties of *Saccharum officinarum*, and are generally known as "noble canes". Stem colour in noble canes ranges from green to yellow, red or even glossy black.

The crop has a complicated history of domestication. It is the end result of a long process of natural and artificial hybridisation between several wild species (Roach 1995). The original cultivated form of *Saccharum officinarum* is thought to have originated by human selection in New Guinea, where people have selected plants with a sweet juice and low fibre content for chewing. From here various forms of the species spread to Southeast Asia, China and India, where they are still grown in rural areas as a backyard crop.

Sugar cane probably reached Africa and Madagascar around AD 400 to 600 and quickly became an important plantation crop in tropical areas. Many of the early plantations relied on noble canes, such as the cultivar Bourbon, which is also thought to be the first sugar cane that was planted in southern Africa. Modern commercial hybrid sugar canes are superior to the noble canes in terms of sugar content, productivity and disease resistance. They were derived through a complicated process of crossing and backcrossing between a wild species, *Saccharum spontaneum*, and various noble canes.

Plants are cultivated from stem cuttings, first producing several buds and shoots (tillers) which then lengthen to a leafy canopy. The stems continue to grow for about a year to 18 months until they are harvested. Modern cultivars have narrow, erect leaves and were developed for their productivity under high planting densities.

Sugar cane is usually harvested after a short dry spell in the weather to maximise the sugar yield. The crop is burnt to reduce the amount of leaf waste. Cutting is done by hand or sometimes mechanically, and the cane is delivered by truck or tractor-drawn trailers to industrial plants where it is milled, the juice extracted and sugar (sucrose) recovered by crystallisation. An important by-product is molasses, a dark brown syrup which contains a mixture of sucrose and reducing sugars. Molasses is used as an additive in stock feeds and silage. The fibrous residue of sugar manufacture, commonly known as *bagasse*, is used to produce paper, fibre board and other industrial products. More than two million tons of sugar is produced in southern Africa, of which about a half is consumed locally.

Sucrose is a valuable source of energy, not only in the human diet, but also as a fuel source when it is fermented to produce alcohol (ethanol). Sugar is also much used to enhance the potency of various traditional wines and beers. It is often added to palm wine and wine produced from marula, prickly pear and other fruits. Sugar cane chewing is commonly seen in southern Africa, and is no doubt an important way in which rural children supplement their diet. Before the introduction of sugar cane, sweet-stemmed forms of sorghum (*Sorghum bicolor*) were used, and are still widely grown in southern Africa. They are called *ntsoe* in Sotho, *mpshe* in Tswana, *nyoba* in Pedi, *mpye* in Venda and *imfe* in Zulu.

Sugar is added when palm wine and other brews are distilled to produce a strong alcoholic drink known in Zimbabwe and Maputaland by the Zulu name *skokiaan*. Even in the early years, people of Mozambique and the adjoining parts of South Africa developed crude presses to crush and extract juice from sugar cane, which was then used to distil a drink known as *shiwayawaya*. Golden syrup, a sugar cane product, was said to be the main ingredient for brewing and distilling the original *shikokiyane* or *skokiaan* (Junod 1913). *Skokiaan* gave its name to a well-known jazz music number. The tune is said to have originated in Zimbabwe, where it was first popularised by a group called the Bulawayo Sweet Rhythms Band. This piece of Africana became an international hit when it was performed by the famous American jazz artist, Louis Armstrong.

Field of flowering sugar cane (*Saccharum officinarum*)

Purple cultivar of sugar cane (*Saccharum officinarum*)

Sugar cane for sale on the roadside

Sclerocarya birrea | Anacardiaceae | **MARULA**; *maroela* (Afrikaans); *morula* (Northern Sotho, Tswana); *momungongo* (Herero); *munogo* (Tonga); *mushomo* (Shona); *nkanyi* (Tsonga); *mufula* (Venda); *umganu* (Swazi, Zulu) ■ Various names are used for different parts of the tree and for products derived from it.

The marula is an erect tree of up to 15 metres tall, with a rounded crown and a rough, flaky, mottled bark. The leaves are divided into 10 or more pairs of sharply pointed leaflets. The flowers are borne in small oblong clusters. Male and female flowers occur separately, usually but not always on separate trees. Large, rounded, slightly flattened fruit of about 30 millimetres in diameter are borne in profusion in late summer to midwinter, but mainly between January and March. The fruit is much sought after for its delicious pulp, high vitamin C content and tasty, edible nuts. The pip contains three oblong nuts, each protected with a small bony "lid" which becomes detached when the pip is cracked between stones.

The tree is widely distributed throughout the African continent. In southern Africa, only the subspecies *caffra* is found, and it occurs over practically all of the subtropical regions. In the extreme northern part of South Africa, the tree forms an integral part of the culture and survival of the Phalaborwa people, who use the fruit in the lean time of the year when other food is scarce. In this area, a traditional instrument specially designed to extract marula nuts from the stones, used to be worn as a pendant around the neck of every women. The instrument is known in the local language as *modukulo* and such instruments have been found in ancient archaeological sites (Krige 1937). Another feature of the "*morula* culture" of the Phalaborwa is a hammock-like container made from bark fibres and suspended between four poles, which is used to store large quantities of marula pips. Trees are usually retained when land is cleared for crops.

Experimental plantings in southern Africa and in Israel indicate that the tree has considerable potential as a cultivated fruit tree. In the Negev Desert in Israel, 12-year-old trees produced around 500 kilograms of fruit (Yosef Mizrahi, pers. comm.), despite being irrigated with 20 per cent sea water. Yields of up to three tons per tree have been recorded (Holzhausen 1993), and superior wild variants have been identified that produce large fruits of up to 98 grams each.

The fruits fall down and accumulate under the trees in large numbers. They ripen to a pale yellow colour, and are collected by many different people as an important foodstuff and to brew traditional marula beer, also known as *mokhope* (Krige 1937) or *ubuganu* (Cunningham 1990b). The methods of brewing beer are described by Quin (1959) and Junod (1962). Rood (1994) also gives numerous traditional recipes for making beer, syrup, liqueur, vinegar, jelly, preserves and sweets. The high pectin content makes it ideal for jelly and considerable quantities are already bottled and marketed.

Marula fruit pulp is used to flavour commercial marula beer and the well-known Amarula liqueur. The cream liqueur has become popular throughout the world (especially in Brazil) and is one of the biggest marketing success stories of plant-related products in South Africa. It was first marketed in September 1989.

Marula fruit pulp is not only delicious, but also highly nutritious, with a vitamin C content of between two and four times that of orange juice – around 200 milligrams per gram (Holzhausen 1993). The tasty nuts, which are an important food item in rural areas, are difficult to extract from the stony pips. They have been used to preserve meat for up to six months without refrigeration and the oil is considered to be suitable for glazing dried fruit (Holzhausen 1993) but may tend to go rancid. It has become an important product in the cosmetics industry (see Chapter 14). The marula is without a doubt one of the most important of all indigenous African trees and shows great potential as a cultivated, multi-purpose fruit crop of the future.

The bark, roots and leaves are used for a wide range of medicinal purposes, including heartburn, diarrhoea, diabetes, fever and malaria (see Chapter 7).

Twelve-year-old marula trees in Israel, yielding 500 kilograms of fruits per tree

Flowering branch of a male marula tree (*Sclerocarya birrea*)

Marula jelly

Fruits of marula (*Sclerocarya birrea*)

Sclerochiton ilicifolius | Acanthaceae | ***MOLOMO MONATE*** ■ This shrubby plant occurs mainly in the western part of the Waterberg in South Africa, where it grows in rocky places. It is a shrub of up to three metres in height, with toothed leaves and white or pale mauve flowers (Vollesen 1991). The roots contain the high-intensity sweetener monatin, which has commercial potential as an artificial sweetener (Vleggaar *et al.* 1992). The compound monatin is named after the indigenous name *molomo monate*, which literally translates as "mouth nice" meaning sweet mouth, alluding to the pleasant sweet taste of the root bark (Vahrmeijer 2010). Monatin is a sweet-tasting alpha amino acid, and the relative sweetness has been found to be about 1 200 times that of a 10 per cent sucrose solution (Holzapfel *et al.* 1993); a number of synthetic pathways for the commercial production of monatin have been published.

Searsia lancea | Anacardiaceae | ***KAREE*** ■ The small dry fruits of several species (*Searsia lancea, S. burchellii, S. undulata, S. viminalis* and *S. pendulina*) are edible and were once used as an important ingredient of mead or honey beer. The vernacular name *karee* is said to be the original Khoi word for honey beer and the word *karri* is still used in some parts of the Cape for mead. There are several traditional sources of yeast for brewing. The fleshy roots and stems of two members of the Aizoaceae, *Mestoklema tuberosum* (*donkievygie*) and *Trichodiadema stellatum* (*kareemoervygie*) are reported to have formerly been used as a yeast source for brewing mead (Smith 1966). *Euphorbia rhombifolia* (=*E. decussata*) is known as *soetmelkbos* (because the stems are edible) but also as *kareemoer* or *kirriemoer* because they are a traditional source of yeast for beer brewing. See also *Cynorhiza, Glia, Khadia, Raphionacme* and *Pterodiscus*.

The fruits of a number of *Searsia* species are used to make curdled milk. Rood (1994) gives a method as described by J.H. Cornellisen, M. van Zyl and J. Coetzee. The dry skins of the fruits are removed by winnowing. About 750 millilitres of the fruits are gradually added to 500 millilitres of milk that has been brought to the boil and then removed from the stove. The mixture is stirred continuously until it is as thick as buttermilk. The fruit pips are removed by pouring through a sieve. The curdled milk can be eaten hot or cold.

Thesium macrostachyum | Santalaceae | ***LIDJIESTEE*** (Afrikaans); reed tea ■ The leafless stems of this semi-parasitic shrub are still a popular source of tea in the Cederberg (Van Wyk & Gorelik 2017). Local people consider the taste to be better than that of rooibos tea. Another Cederberg species, *Thesium carinatum*, is known as *jakkalstee* and is similarly used (Ben Zimri, pers. comm.). Marloth (1917) and Smith (1966) recorded the name *lidjiestee* for *Thesium spicatum* but no other details were given.

Viscum capense | Viscaceae | **CAPE MISTLETOE**; *voëlenttee, lidjiestee* (Afrikaans) ■ See photographs on page 137. This parasitic plant is up to 0.5 metres in diameter and grows on a wide range of host plants. The leafless stems are widely used to prepare a herbal tonic and general health tea. Taken as a powder or decoction, the stems have also been used to treat epilepsy in children and young women, and were recommended for asthma and St Vitus's dance. In the Little Karoo and southern parts of the Great Karoo, the closely similar *Viscum continuum* is used in the same way. This species is only found on *Vachellia karroo* and can be distinguished by the shortly stalked (not sessile) fruits. It is also a much larger plant of up to one metre in diameter. Jan Schoeman, the legendary *Lappiesman* of Prince Albert in the Great Karoo (Oberholzer 2002; Van Wyk 2011), enjoyed a cup of tea made from this species every morning, and ascribed his exceptional fitness to this practice (Jan Schoeman, pers. comm.). Another *voëlent* is *Viscum rotundifolium*, also known to be used to make tea (Anonymous 1998). *Viscum anceps* has been used internally in the Eastern Cape to treat hysteria, and overdose reportedly causes drowsiness. The "woodrose" where *Viscum capense* attaches to the host plant, *Searsia burchellii*, was used to make a pipe in Namaqualand (Gert Dirkse, pers. comm.).

Leaves and flowers of *molomo monate* (*Sclerochiton ilicifolius*

Ripe fruits of *karee* (*Searsia lancea*)

Tuber of *donkievygie* (*Mestoklema tuberosum*)

Leaves of *kareemoervygie* (*Trichodiadema barbatum*)

Lidjiestee or reed tea (*Thesium macrostachyum*)

Jakkalstee (*Thesium carinatum*)

Ziziphus mucronata |Rhamnaceae| **BUFFALO-THORN** ■ See Chapters 8 and 11. The Ovambo people of Namibia brew a beer from the fruit (Van den Eynden *et al.* 1992).

REFERENCES AND FURTHER READING: Anonymous, 1998. Herbal remedies of Montagu Museum, 2nd ed. Montagu Museum, Montagu, South Africa. **Ashton, E. 1939.** A sociological sketch of Sotho diet. *Trans. R. Soc. S. Afr.* 27, 2: 147–214. **Beemer, H. 1939.** Notes on the diet of the Swazi in the Protectorates. *Bantu Stud.* 13, 3: 199–236. **Cunningham, A.B. 1988.** Collection of wild plant foods in Tembe Thonga society: a guide to Iron Age activities? *Ann. Natal Mus.* 29(2): 433–446. **Cunningham, A.B. 1989.** Indigenous plant use: balancing human needs and resources. In: Huntley, B.J. (ed.), *Biotic diversity in southern Africa,* Oxford University Press, pp. 93–106. **Cunningham, A.B. 1990a.** Income, sap yield and effects of sap tapping on palms in south-eastern Africa. *S. Afr. J. Bot.* 56(2): 137–144. **Cunningham, A.B. 1990b.** The regional distribution, marketing and economic value of the palm wine trade in the Ingwavuma district, Natal, South Africa. *S. Afr. J. Bot.* 56(2): 191–198. **Cunningham, A.B. & Wehmeyer, A.S. 1988.** Nutritional value of palm wine from *Hyphaene coriacea* and *Phoenix reclinata* (Arecaceae). *Econ. Bot.* 42(3): 301–306. **Dahlgren, R. 1968.** Revision of the genus *Aspalathus* II. The species with ericoid and pinoid leaflets. Subgenus Nortieria. With remarks on Rooibos Tea Cultivation. *Bot. Notiser* 121: 165–208. **Dahlgren, R. 1988.** Crotalarieae (*Aspalathus*). In: *Flora of southern Africa* 16, 3(6): 1–430. Botanical Research Institute, Pretoria. **De Lange, H. 1997.** *Heuningbostee Inligtingstuk,* 19 Mei 1997. National Botanical Institute, Claremont (unpublished). **De Nysschen, A.M. *et al.* 1996.** The major phenolic compounds in the leaves of *Cyclopia* species (honeybush tea). *Biochem. Syst. Ecol.* 24: 243–246. **Dzerefos, C.M. *et al.* 1995.** *Use of edible herbs and fruits in the Bushbuckridge region of the eastern Transvaal lowveld.* Wits Rural Facility, Acornhoek (unpublished). **Fanshawe, D.B. 1967.** The vegetable ivory palm – *Hyphaene ventricosa* Kirk – its ecology, silviculture & utilisation. *Kirkia* 6: 105–116. **Fox, F.W. no date.** Some Bantu recipes from the Eastern Cape. *Bantu Stud.* 13: 65–74. **Fox, F.W. 1938.** Notes on the methods of preparation, composition and nutritional value of certain beers. *J. S. Afr. Chem. Inst.* 21: 39–54. **Fox, F.W. & Norwood Young, M.E. 1982.** *Food from the veld.* Delta Books, Johannesburg. **Holzapfel, C.W. *et al.* 1993.** The synthesis of y-keto-alpha-amino acid, a key intermediate in the synthesis of monatin, a new natural sweetener. *Synth. Comm.* 23(18): 2511–2526. **Holzhausen, L.C. 1993.** Ennobling and domestication of the indigenous African marula. *The Indigenous Plant Use Newsletter* 1(2): 1, 3. **Joubert, E. 1996.** HPLC quantification of the dihydrochalcones, aspalathin and nothofagin in rooibos tea (*Aspalathus linearis*) as affected by processing. *Food Chemistry* 55: 403–411. **Joubert, E. & De Beer, D. 2011.** Rooibos (*Aspalathus linearis*) beyond the farm gate: from herbal tea to potential phytopharmaceutical. *S. Afr. J. Bot.* 77: 869–886. **Joubert, E. *et al.* 2008.** South African herbal teas: *Aspalathus linearis, Cyclopia* spp. and *Athrixia phylicoides* – a review. *J. Ethnopharmacol.* 119, 376–412. **Junod, H.A. 1962.** *The life of a South African tribe,* 2nd ed. (two volumes). University Books, New York. **Kinfe, H., Long, H.S., Stander, M. & Van Wyk, B.-E. 2015.** The ethnobotany and major flavonoid of *Rafnia amplexicaulis,* a poorly known Cape herbal tea and liquorice substitute. *S. Afr. J. Bot.* 100: 75–79. **Krige, E.J. 1937.** Note on the Phalaborwa and their morula complex. *Bantu Stud.* 11: 357–366. **Lerotholi, L., Chaudhary, S., Combrinck, S. & Viljoen, A.M. 2017.** Bush tea (*Athrixia phylicoides*): A review of the traditional uses, bioactivity and phytochemistry. *S. Afr. J. Bot.* 110: 4–17. **Malan, J.S. & Owen-Smith, G.L. 1974.** The ethnobotany of Kaokoland. *Cimbebasia* Ser. B 2, 5: 131–178. **Maguire, B. 1978.** *The food plants of the !Khu Bushmen of north-eastern South West Africa.* M.Sc. thesis, University of the Witwatersrand. **Marloth, R. 1915–1932.** *The flora of South Africa.* William Wesley, London. **Marloth, R. 1917.** *Dictionary of common names of South African plants.* The Speciality Press, Cape Town. **Marloth, R. 1925.** *The flora of Southern Africa,* Vol 2(1). Darter, Cape Town. **Meredith, C.C. 1948.** Notes on the collection of the sap of the vegetable ivory palm (*Hyphoene ventricosa*) and manufacture of palm wine spirit. *Rhodesia Agricultural Journal* 45: 414–417. **Moll, E. 1972.** The distribution, abundance and utilization of the lala palm, *Hyphaene natalensis,* in Tongaland, Natal. *Bothalia* 10: 627–636. **Nash, L.J. & Bornman, C.H. 1973.** Constituents of ilala wine. *S. Afr. J. Sci.* 69: 89–90. **Oberholzer, O. 2002.** *The Hotazel Years.* Double Storey Books, Cape Town. **Peters, C.R. *et al.* 1992.** *Edible wild plants of sub-Saharan Africa.* Royal Botanic Gardens, Kew. **Quin, P.J. 1959.** *Food and feeding habits of the Pedi.* Witwatersrand University Press, Johannesburg. **Rabe, C. *et al.* 1994.** Phenolic metabolites from Rooibos Tea (*Aspalathus linearis*). *Phytochem.* 35: 1559–1565. **Rood, B. 1994.** *Kos uit die veldkombuis.* Tafelberg, Cape Town. **Rooi Tea Control Board. 1973.** *Eighty Rooi Tea Wonders.* Muller & Retief, Cape Town. **Schutte, A.L. *et al.* 1995.** Fire-survival strategy – a character of taxonomic, ecological and evolutionary importance in fynbos legumes. *Pl. Syst. Evol.* 195: 243–259. **Schutte, A.L. 1997.** Systematics of the genus *Cyclopia* Vent. (Fabaceae, Podalyrieae). *Edinb. J. Bot.* 54: 125–170. **Smit, P. 1982.** 'n Teugie vars natuur ... heuningtee word kits. *Landbouweekblad,* 4 June 1982: 24–25, 27. **Smith, C.A. 1966.** Common names of South African plants. *Mem. Bot. Surv. S. Afr.* 35. **Steyn, H.P. 1981.** Nharo plant utilization. An overview. *Khoisis* 1: 1–30. **Story, R. 1959.** Some plants used by the Bushmen in obtaining food and water. *Mem. Bot. Surv. S. Afr.* 30. **Van der Walt, A. & Machado, R. 1992.** *New marketing success stories.* Southern Book Publishers, Halfway House. **Van Tonder, K. 1981.** Heuningblomtee: treksel met 'n toekoms. *Landbouweekblad,* 1 May 1981: 20–21, 24. **Van Wyk, B.-E. 2011.** The potential of South African plants in the development of new food and beverage products. *S. Afr. J. Bot.* 77, 857–868. **Van Wyk, B.-E. 2015.** A review of commercially important African medicinal plants. *J. Ethnopharmacol.* 176: 118–134. **Van Wyk, B.-E. & Gorelik, B. 2017.** The history and ethnobotany of Cape herbal teas. *S. Afr. J. Bot.* 110: 18–38. **Vahrmeijer, H. 2010.** The historical and present uses of Molomo Monate (*Sclerochiton ilicifolius* A. Meeuse) in the Republic of South Africa. Unpublished Report Conducted for Cargill, Incorporated. **Vleggaar, R., Ackerman, L.G.J. & Steyn, P.S. 1992.** Structure elucidation of monatin, a high-intensity sweetener isolated from the plant *Sclerochiton ilicifolius. J. Chem. Soc., Perkin Trans.* 1, 3095–3098. **Vollesen, K. 1991.** A revision of the African genus *Sclerochiton* (Acanthaceae, Acantheae). *Kew Bull.* 46: 1–50. **Von Koenen, E. 2001.** *Medicinal, poisonous and edible plants in Namibia.* Klaus Hess Publishers, Windhoek and Göttingen. **Watt, J.M. 1926.** A note on *Raphionacme purpurea. Bantu Stud.* 2: 333–334. **Watt, J.M. & Breyer-Brandwijk, M.G. 1962.** *The medicinal and poisonous plants of southern and eastern Africa,* 2nd ed. Livingstone, London. **Wehmeyer, A.S. 1966.** The nutrient composition of some edible wild fruits found in the Transvaal. *S. Afr. Med. J.* 40: 1102. **Wehmeyer, A.S. 1976.** Food from the veld. *Scientiae* 17,4: 2–11.

Plant of Cape mistletoe (*Viscum capense*)

Plant of Karoo mistletoe (*Viscum continuum*)

Flowers and translucent fruits of Cape mistletoe (*Viscum capense*)

Fruits of the Karoo mistletoe (*Viscum continuum*)

Round leaf mistletoe (*Viscum rotundifolium*)

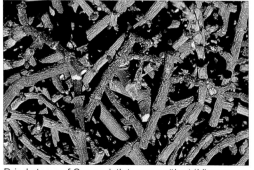

Dried stems of Cape mistletoe or *voëlent* (*Viscum capense*)

Woodrose formed by Cape mistletoe, used as a pipe

Herbal medicines

Press used for making herbal tinctures

Preparing herbs for further processing

PART 2: HEALTH & BEAUTY

CHAPTER 7

General medicines

SOMEWHERE IN THE region of 4 000 species of plants are used as medicines in southern Africa. This general chapter describes in outline some of the diverse traditional uses of a limited selection of medicinal plants. This sets the tone for Chapters 8 through 12, each of which highlights a specific therapeutic category. Readers are referred to *Medicinal Plants of South Africa* by Van Wyk *et al.* (1997, 2009) for reviews of most of the species listed in this chapter. Several other critical references are also listed and should be consulted for a more comprehensive overview of medicinal plant use in southern Africa. The importance of African and southern African medicinal plants in a continental and global context has been reviewed by Van Wyk (2008, 2015a).

In southern Africa, indigenous African medicine coexists with Western allopathic medicine, Western herbalism, homoeopathy, Ayurvedic medicine from India, and Traditional Chinese Medicine. Not all medicinal plant use can be explained from the reductionist perspective of Western science, and energetic, spiritual, ritual and symbolic aspects are fundamentally important from the perspective of other healing traditions and the world view and expectation of the patient. It is possible that unifying therapeutic principles will ultimately be found, probably based on subtle energies acting along the body–mind continuum that will unite healing systems which superficially appear to be quite distinct from each other. Some southern African herbal medicines, for example, are clearly applied homoeopathically in terms of the principle that ingestion of high doses of the remedy causes the same symptoms as the disease being treated (i.e., like cures like).

Indigenous knowledge systems are dynamic and adaptive, and over the last few hundred years many introduced plants have been incorporated into African medicine in southern Africa, including the extensive use of calamus (*Acorus calamus*), camphor (*Cinnamomum camphora*), bluegum (*Eucalyptus globulus*), liquorice (*Glycyrrhiza glabra*), guava (*Psidium guajava*), pomegranate (*Punica granatum*), rosemary (*Rosmarinus officinalis*), rue (*Ruta graveolens*), ginger (*Zingiber officinalis*) and several others (Van Wyk *et al.* 2009; Roberts & Roberts 2017).

A single plant can be viewed from a purely scientific perspective as a biosynthetic facility, manufacturing a large number of molecules from simple nutrients, water, carbon dioxide and solar energy. The resulting chemistry is astonishingly complex, and includes not only the "final" molecules in the biosynthetic pathway, but also their precursors. Molecules that are not directly involved in photosynthesis and respiration are known as secondary metabolites, and some are believed to have evolved to form part of the defence mechanism of plants. Many secondary metabolites have biological activities that can be assayed in the laboratory, such as antiviral, antifungal, antibacterial and anticancer activities, providing a scientific rationale for the use of a particular plant. In some cases isolated active compounds are commercialised in the development of drugs, and it has been estimated that about a quarter of modern drugs were originally derived from higher plants (Kinghorn & Balandrin 1993). To date no pure isolated southern African plant compound has been developed into a marketed drug, but a few phytopharmaceuticals (pharmaceuticals made from plant extracts standardised to active compounds) have been developed or are in the process of being developed (Diederichs 2006; Gericke 2011; Van Wyk 2011, 2015a; Van Wyk & Wink 2015, 2017). Many southern African plants have potential for commercialisation, especially as functional foods and nutraceuticals. Recent examples include *Hoodia gordonii* and *Adansonia digitata*. There has been a strong recent interest in research on African medicinal plants, with about 60 per cent of all scientific papers ever published on African medicinal plants appearing in the last decade (Van Wyk 2015a).

Acorus calamus |Acoraceae| ***IKALAMUZI*** (Zulu); calamus, sweet-flag; *kalmoes* (Afrikaans) ■ This reed-like perennial aquatic plant is well known and has been used as a digestive, carminative, emetic, antispasmodic, stimulant and anthelmintic since biblical times. *Acorus* is no longer used in modern medicines because of the possible toxic effect of β-asarone, a component of the essential oil from the plants. The asarone content of medicine intended for internal use should be controlled, as the compound is associated with some forms of cancer. The plant originates from Asia, but has been introduced to Europe and North America. It has been cultivated in South Africa since colonial times and is growing as a garden escape along rivers at several localities.

Kalmoes is a popular component of Zulu medicine. It retards ejaculation in men, and is used for this purpose in aphrodisiac mixtures (Solomon Mahlaba, pers. comm.). The rhizome is chewed fresh or dry, or infusions and decoctions are taken for the sedative and analgesic activity. Pieces of the rhizome are chewed to combat fatigue and hunger when walking long distances (Herman van Wyk, pers. comm.). The rhizome was used by Native Americans as an inebriant, and in Traditional Chinese Medicine it is used for the treatment of epilepsy. Asarones are believed to be the psychoactive components. Anticonvulsant, sedative and hypotensive activities have been found in animal studies of rhizome extracts.

Adansonia digitata |Malvaceae| **BAOBAB**; *kremetartboom* (Afrikaans) ■ See Chapters 3 and 19. The tart fruit pulp is traditionally taken mixed with water as a refreshing drink, and to treat fever, diarrhoea and haemoptysis. The fruit pulp is high in vitamin C (Fox & Norwood Young 1982) and has become a commercial functional food product in recent years. The bark has been used for fever, and the leaves and fruit pulp have been used to treat malaria.

Albizia adianthifolia |Fabaceae| ***UMGADANKAWU*** (Zulu); flatcrown; *platkroon* (Afrikaans) ■ The bark has been used to treat bronchitis, and the leaves and roots have been used to treat dysentery and haemorrhoids, and as purgatives. Powdered bark is used as a snuff for headache and sinusitis (Pujol 1990). Infusions of the bark are important in the topical treatment of eczema.

The bark of *Albizia anthelmintica* is commonly used as an effective anthelmintic for tapeworm and other worms in humans and stock animals, and the root and stem bark are used to treat numerous conditions, including fever, venereal disease and rheumatism.

Anacardium occidentale |Anacardiaceae| **CASHEW NUT** ■ See Chapter 2. Infusions and tinctures of the bark have been used to treat diabetes in Mozambique, and bark infusions have been used to treat dysentery and aphthous ulcers. Leaf infusions are used for coughs and are applied topically for burns and to treat skin conditions.

Aloe ferox |Asphodelaceae| **CAPE ALOES** (bitter fraction), bitter aloe; *bitteraalwyn* (Afrikaans); *umhlaba* (Xhosa, Zulu, Sotho) ■ The plant is an attractive succulent with a single erect stem and a thick rosette of fleshy, thorny leaves. The flowers are usually orange to red or less commonly yellow or white. Plants occur from near Swellendam in the Cape to central KwaZulu-Natal. Copious amounts of a thick yellow juice exude from the cut leaf surface. This yellow juice is collected by an age-old traditional method and concentrated by boiling. It forms a dark brown, lumpy product (purgative) known commercially as Cape aloes. The laxative effect is due to anthraquinones, of which aloin is the main ingredient. Good-quality Cape aloes should have at least 18 per cent aloin (Van Wyk *et al.* 1995; Chen *et al.* 2002; Standards South Africa 2007; Grace *et al.* 2008, 2009).

Cape aloes is still an important export commodity and is used as an ingredient in several medicines, including the famous "Lewensessens" and "Schweden bitters". Mixed with petroleum jelly (e.g. Vaseline), powdered Cape aloes is applied topically to herpes and shingles, and the fresh bitter fraction is applied directly to the conjunctiva for conjunctivitis and sinusitis.

GENERAL MEDICINES

Dried rhizomes of *kalmoes* (*Acorus calamus*)

Kalmoes plants (*Acorus calamus*)

Aloe bitters, also known as aloe lump or Cape aloes

Aloe bitters are produced on a sustainable basis, using an age-old method of tapping the leaf juice

Artemisia absinthium │Asteraceae│ **WORMWOOD**; *groenamara* (Afrikaans) ■ The leaves of this garden plant of European and North African origin are widely used in the Cape to treat stomach ailments.

Artemisia afra │Asteraceae│ **AFRICAN WORMWOOD**; *wildeals* (Afrikaans); *umhlonyane* (Zulu); *lengana* (Tswana) ■ This is probably the most popular and most commonly cultivated medicinal plant of South Africa. It is used for a wide range of ailments (see Chapter 8).

Asclepias crispa │Apocynaceae│ ***BITTERWORTEL***, *witvergeet* (Afrikaans) ■ Root decoctions or infusions have been used since early times in the Karoo as a diuretic and purgative medicine.

***Asparagus* species** │Asparagaceae│ **WILD ASPARAGUS**; *katdoring* (Afrikaans) ■ Rhizomes and roots of several species, including *Asparagus capensis, A. racemosus* and *A. suaveolens*, are used in traditional medicine, mainly to treat tuberculosis, rheumatism and kidney ailments. The common edible asparagus (*Asparagus officinalis*) is traditionally used as a diuretic medicine in Europe.

Aster bakeranus │Asteraceae│ ***UNDLUTSHANA*** (Zulu) ■ The powdered roots are used to treat headache and decoctions are used as emetics and purgatives, and as enemas for stomach-ache and internal parasites. It is an important traditional medicine.

Athrixia phylicoides │Asteraceae│ **MOUNTAIN TEA** ■ See Chapter 6. The roots and leaves are used for a wide range of ailments, including coughs, vomiting, hypertension, diabetes, diarrhoea and skin complaints. The plant is best known as a source of bush tea.

Ballota africana │Lamiaceae│ ***KATTEKRUID*** (Afrikaans) ■ This famous Khoi remedy is used as an infusion or tincture for a wide variety of ailments, including fever, influenza, measles, asthma, tension headache, haemorrhoids, stress, and for thrush. It is also taken as an expectorant, and for kidney and bladder infections (Dawid Bester, pers. comm.). It is sometimes applied directly, tied to the head for headache, or to the knee for joint pain (Jan Muller, pers. comm.).

Bersama lucens │Melianthaceae│ **GLOSSY BERSAMA**; *isidiyandiya* (Zulu) ■ Bark or root decoctions or tinctures of this important Zulu medicine are used to treat menstrual pain, headache, stroke and nervous disorders.

Bowiea volubilis │Hyacinthaceae│ **CLIMBING POTATO**; *rankbol* (Afrikaans); *umagaqana* (Xhosa); *igibisila* (Zulu) ■ The climbing potato is a practically leafless plant that has green or white fleshy bulbs with no vegetative branches. An unusual feature is the climbing and creeping, much-branched inflorescence (flowering stem) bearing small greenish flowers. The plant is highly toxic but is nevertheless used for a wide range of ailments, including headache, oedema, infertility, sore eyes, bladder complaints and venereal diseases. It is a powerful emetic, acting rapidly in small doses, and is also used as a purgative. Fatalities are known to have occurred from its use.

Bulbine natalensis │Asphodelaceae│ ***ROOIWORTEL*** (Afrikaans); *ibhucu* (Zulu) ■ Infusions or decoctions of the rhizomes and roots are used for vomiting, diarrhoea, convulsions, venereal disease, diabetes, rheumatism and bladder complaints, but one of the main uses is external application (see Chapter 11).

Capparis tomentosa │Capparaceae│ **WOOLLY CAPER BUSH** ■ See Chapter 10. Roots and stems are very popular in traditional medicine in southern Africa, and are used for a wide variety of conditions, including malaria, rheumatism, insanity, snakebite, jaundice, headache, coughs, pneumonia, tuberculosis and leprosy. Indole alkaloids occur in the roots, which may explain the use for insanity and for rheumatism.

GENERAL MEDICINES

Leaves and flowers of the *bitterwortel* or *witvergeet* (*Asclepias crispa*)

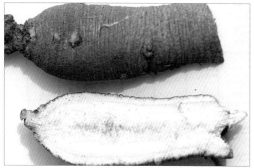

Tuberous root of the *bitterwortel* or *witvergeet* (*Asclepias crispa*)

Flowering branch of *kattekruid* (*Ballota africana*)

Bulb and fleshy, twining, flowering stalk of the *igibisila* (*Bowiea volubilis*)

Leaves and fruits of the woolly caper bush (*Capparis tomentosa*)

Carica papaya |Caricaceae| **PAWPAW**; *papaja* (Afrikaans) ■ In Mozambique, root infusions are taken for gonorrhoea, and the root is given in porridge to dehydrated infants. The fresh seeds are taken as a vermifuge, and are abortifacient in larger doses.

Carpobrotus edulis |Aizoaceae| **SOUR FIG** ■ See Chapters 3 and 11. The leaves of all the species are astringent and the leaf juice has been gargled as a popular and highly effective old Cape remedy for throat infections. It is also used for skin and eye infections. The fresh leaf juice is excellent for acute diarrhoea and for giardiasis. Small amounts of fresh leaf juice are used to rinse a baby's mouth three times daily for oral thrush (Dawid Bester, pers. comm.). The yellow-flowered *C. edulis* is the most widely distributed and best-known species, but along the coastal regions of South Africa, several purple-flowered species are also used. These are *C. acinaciformis* and *C. quadrifidus* (west coast)*, C. deliciosus* and *C. muirii* (south coast), and *C. dimidiatus* (east coast).

Cassia species – see *Senna*.

Catharanthus roseus |Apocynaceae| **MADAGASCAR PERIWINKLE**; *isisushlungu* (Zulu) ■ The plant is an attractive but weedy herb with pink or white flowers. The roots are traditionally used against diabetes and the leaves yield important binary indole alkaloids such as vincristine and vinblastine which have become important in the fight against breast cancer, uterine cancer and Hodgkin's and non-Hodgkin's lymphoma.

Catophractes alexandri |Bignoniaceae| ***SWARTDORING*** (Afrikaans) ■ In Namibia, the root is chewed for stomach problems, and the root, mixed with that of *Polygala leptophylla*, is taken as a decoction for abdominal pain, particularly in children. Infusions and decoctions of the leaves, roots or bark are used for colds, while milk decoctions of the leaves are taken for coughs.

Centella glabrata |Apiaceae| ***PERSIEGRAS****, persgras, sweetkruie* (Afrikaans) ■ This Cape plant was an early remedy for diarrhoea and dysentery. It is said to produce perspiration (Smith 1966). *Persie* is the old Cape Dutch word for diarrhoea.

Cinnamomum camphora |Lauraceae| **CAMPHOR TREE** ■ See Chapter 13. The bark is a popular medicine in South Africa, used for fever, colds, influenza and abdominal discomfort, and the leaves have been used as a ritual emetic. Wood from the tree is a source of natural camphor, which has antiseptic, rubefacient and mild analgesic activity. Antibacterial and antifungal activities have been demonstrated (Ponglux *et al.* 1987; Chen *et al.* 2013).

Cissampelos capensis |Menispermaceae| ***DAWIDJIES****, dawidjiewortel* (Afrikaans) ■ See Chapter 8. This common climber from the western parts of South Africa and the southern parts of Namibia has slender, twining stems and heart-shaped leaves growing from a woody rootstock below the ground. Pieces of the "root" are commonly used as protective charms. These "roots" are actually woody underground stems (rhizomes), easily identified in cross-section by the star-shaped pattern created by the ray cells. The rhizomes are rich in alkaloids of the bisbenzylisoquinoline type. The dry rhizome is burned, and the smoke inhaled through the nostrils to treat headache (Levit Taferaai, pers. comm.). Small portions of rhizome seem to be sedative when chewed, and infusions are used to treat pain. The fresh or dry rhizomes are very popular, chewed directly or taken as infusions or tinctures, as blood purifiers and purgatives, and are also taken for diabetes, tuberculosis and stomach and skin cancers (Dawid Bester, pers. comm.). The rhizomes are also used for dysentery, urinary stones and glandular swellings. Pulped fresh leaves are applied to snakebite, sores and boils. *Cissampelos mucronata* is also an important medicinal plant, and is used similarly, and also for fever, infertility, menstrual cramps, headache, backache, bilharzia and as a sexual stimulant. Leaf decoctions of *Cissampelos torulosa* have been administered as an enema to treat hallucinations (De Wet & Van Wyk 2008).

Leaves and flowers of the *swartdoring* (*Catophractes alexandri*)

Leaves and fruits of *dawidjies* (*Cissampelos capensis*)

Piece of rhizome of *Cissampelos mucronata*, used as lucky charm on a key ring

The characteristic rhizomes of *dawidjies* (*Cissampelos capensis*)

Conyza scabrida (=*Nidorella ivifolia*) │Asteraceae│ ***BAKBOS***, *oondbos* (Afrikaans); *isavu* (Xhosa) ■ Twigs and leaves are widely used against stomach ailments, inflammation, fever, pain, diabetes and other ailments (Van Wyk *et al.* 2009).

Cotyledon orbiculata │Crassulaceae│ **PIG'S EARS**; *plakkie* (Afrikaans); *kouterie* (Khoi); *imphewula* (Xhosa); *seredile* (Sotho) ■ See Chapter 9. The juice from a fresh leaf is swallowed once a day for sore throat, and a single leaf is eaten daily to expel worms (Dawid Bester, pers. comm.). The warmed leaf is applied to boils and abscesses, and the cut leaf surface to nappy rash.

Crinum macowanii │Amaryllidaceae│ ***UMDUZE*** (Zulu) ■ Decoctions of the bulb are taken orally by the Zulu for tuberculosis, rheumatic fever, and kidney and bladder diseases. In Zimbabwe, the boiled bulb is applied as a compress for backache, and infusions of the bulb are used as emetics. Powdered bulb is taken in porridge for venereal diseases. *Crinum bulbispermum* is used by the Southern Sotho for colds and scrofula.

Curtisia dentata │Curtisiaceae│ ***UMLAHLENI*** (Xhosa, Zulu); *amagunda* (Zulu); assegai (English); *assegaai* (Afrikaans) ■ The bark is a popular Zulu medicine and is used for stomach ailments, diarrhoea and as blood purifier and aphrodisiac.

Dichrostachys cinerea │Fabaceae│ **SICKLE BUSH**; *sekelbos* (Afrikaans) ■ The plant is a thorny shrub or small tree that often forms impenetrable thickets as a result of over-grazing. The attractive fluffy, pink and yellow flower clusters are followed by woody pods. The plant is widely distributed in southern Africa and has been divided into several subspecies and varieties. This is an important medicinal plant in southern Africa. The fresh leaves are chewed by the Haikum Bushmen in Namibia for diarrhoea, and the leaves are used for toothache and earache, and are applied directly to snakebite. Extracts of leaves and bark, and powdered bark are used to heal wounds (Von Koenen 2001). In Zimbabwe, root infusions are used for abdominal pain, coughs and pneumonia, and the powdered root is sniffed for nose bleeds. The plant has also been used for epilepsy, and leaves and roots have been smoked for head-colds and tuberculosis.

Dicoma anomala │Asteraceae│ ***HLOENYA*** (Sotho) ■ Roots and above-ground parts are very important in Basotho traditional medicine (Moffett 2016). See Chapter 8.

Dicoma capensis │Asteraceae│ ***WILDE KARMEDIK***, *koorsbossie* (Afrikaans) ■ This traditional medicine of the dry interior of South Africa is one of the most popular remedies for fever, stomach upsets, influenza, high blood pressure and diarrhoea. See Chapter 8.

Dioscorea sylvatica │Dioscoreaceae│ **WILD YAM** ■ The plant has a fleshy tuber with climbing branches and heart-shaped leaves. Root decoctions are taken for chest conditions, including bronchiectasis, and as blood purifiers and ritual emetics. Infusions of the tuber, and crushed tuber, are applied topically to swellings and rashes. The tubers contain diosgenin, which can be readily extracted and converted into a medicinal steroid. Diosgenin from the tubers was used to produce oral contraceptive compounds in the 1950s (Hutchings 1996).

Dodonaea viscosa (=*D. angustifolia*) │Sapindaceae│ **SAND OLIVE**; *ysterhout, sandolien* (Afrikaans); *t'koubi* (Nama) ■ The plant is a shrub or small tree with yellowish green leaves and small, winged fruits resembling those of *Combretum* species. Surface flavonoids on young growing tips (*toppe*) give them a sticky, shiny appearance. The tips (*ysterhouttoppe*) are a traditional remedy for fever, colds, throat infections, oral thrush, influenza, stomach trouble, pneumonia, tuberculosis and arthritis. It may be considered as one of the most important traditional medicines of southern Africa and is often used in combination with other medicinal plants, including *Viscum capense* (Willem Steenkamp, pers. comm.).

Bakbos (Conyza scabrida or *Nidorella ivifolia)*

Flowering twig of sickle bush (*Dichrostachys cinerea*)

Plant of wild yam (*Dioscorea sylvatica*)

Leaves and winged fruits of *Dodonaea viscosa*

Dodonaea tips (*toppe*) are sometimes mixed with stems of *Viscum capense*

Drimia elata (=*D. robusta*) | Hyacinthaceae | ***INDONGANA-ZIMBOMVANA*** (Zulu) ■ Bulbs are used as expectorants, emetics, diuretics and heart tonics. The plant is sometimes called *Urginea robusta* by those who consider *Drimia* and *Urginea* to belong to a single genus. In the Western Cape Province, similar uses have been recorded for the so-called *maerman* or *slangkop* (*Drimia capensis*).

Drimia sanguinea (=*Urginea sanguinea*) | Hyacinthaceae | ***SEKANAMA*** (Sotho, Tswana) ■ The bulbs are poisonous but are used as expectorants, emetics, diuretics and heart tonics. The flesh from the bulb is dark purplish red in colour and resembles meat, hence the Sotho and Tswana vernacular name (directly translated, it means "false meat").

Elaeodendron transvaalense (=*Cassine transvaalensis*) | Celastraceae | ***INGWAVUMA*** (Zulu); bushveld saffronwood ■ Bark infusions of this tree are important traditional medicines to treat general body pain, stomach-ache, fever, cramps, diarrhoea, heavy menstruation, skin rashes and infections.

Elytropappus rhinocerotis | Asteraceae | ***RENOSTERBOS***, *anosterbos* (Afrikaans) ■ The plant is an old Cape medicine for influenza, indigestion, lack of appetite, ulcers and stomach cancer, and the powdered tops (*toppe* in Afrikaans) are used for diarrhoea in children. Fresh leafy twigs are inserted into shoes to prevent or treat smelly feet.

Eucalyptus globulus | Myrtaceae | **BLUEGUM TREE** ■ See Chapter 13. Leaves are rich in essential oil, containing 1,8-cineole (eucalyptol) as main ingredient. The leaves and oil are useful as decongestant medicines to treat colds and influenza.

Eucomis autumnalis | Hyacinthaceae | ***AMATHUNGA*** (Zulu); common pineapple flower; *wildepynappel* (Afrikaans) ■ Decoctions of the bulb are commonly used as enemas for backache, to assist in post-operative recovery, and to assist in healing fractures. They are taken as emetics, and to treat fever, hangover and syphilis.

Foeniculum vulgare | Apiaceae | **FENNEL** ■ See Chapter 13. The fruits ("seeds") of this European weed are traditionally used to treat flatulence and indigestion, and as a diuretic.

Gethyllis **species** | Amaryllidaceae | **KUKUMAKRANKA**; *koekemakranka* (Khoi, Afrikaans) ■ The highly aromatic fruits are steeped in brandy and the infusion (*koekemakranka* brandy) is an old Cape remedy for colic and indigestion. Some antimicrobial and antioxidant activity have been demonstrated. The are about 33 species of *Gethyllis*, all of them endemic to southern Africa (South Africa, Botswana and Namibia), with the highest diversity in the Western Cape and Namaqualand (Duncan *et al.* 2016). *Gethyllis afra* (*koekemakranka* or *bramakranka*) is perhaps the best-known member of the genus but several other species and vernacular names are listed in Chapter 13.

Gymnospora senegalensis (=*Maytenus senegalensis*) | Celastraceae | **RED SPIKETHORN** ■ This well-known tree is widely distributed in the northern parts of southern Africa. The root is taken in Zimbabwe as a powder or as an infusion for coughs, bronchitis, pneumonia and tuberculosis. Root infusions are taken for heavy menstruation and uterine cramps, and to prevent an incipient abortion. The plant is also used for sore throats, headache, earache, fever, measles, abdominal pain, venereal disease and epilepsy. Root infusions are taken orally as an aphrodisiac, and the powdered root is rubbed onto cuts on the temple for headache.

Heteromorpha arborescens | Apiaceae | ***UMBANGANDLALA*** (Xhosa, Zulu); common parsley-tree; *gewone pietersielieboom* (Afrikaans) ■ See Chapter 13. This shrub or tree has a characteristic smooth bark and variable compound leaves. The roots are used to treat nervous disorders, headaches, fever, asthma, coughs, dysentery, infertility, weakness and intestinal worms.

Sekanama (*Drimia sanguinea*)

Maerman (*Drimia capensis*)

Matambo with a large bulb of *Drimia elata*

Renosterbos (*Elytropappus rhinocerotis*)

Amathunga (*Eucomis autumnalis*)

Umbangandlala (*Heteromorpha arborescens*)

Umbangandlala as it is sold on muthi markets

Kedrostis nana | Cucurbitaceae | **YSTERVARKPATATS** (Afrikaans) ■ The tuber is used as a cleansing emetic, and as a laxative. An infusion mixed with honey is taken for haemorrhoids. Infusions are used for diabetes and cancer, and used in low doses for diarrhoea. A decoction of the baked tuber, combined with leafy stems of *Elytropappus rhinocerotis* is taken as a contraceptive (Rood 1994), and it may have an abortifacient action since *K. gijef* has been reported to cause abortion in goats (Hutchings 1996). Another species, *K. africana*, is known as the Cape bryoni (*basterdawidjiewortel* in Afrikaans).

Jatropha curcas | Euphorbiaceae | **PURGING NUT**; *purgeerboontjie* (Afrikaans); *mathlapametse* (Tswana) ■ The seeds of this tropical American shrub are toxic but one or two are taken to treat constipation and stomach ailments. Leaf and bark extracts may be used for the same purpose.

Leonotis leonurus | Lamiaceae | ***WILDE DAGGA*** (Afrikaans) ■ Leaf infusions and decoctions are taken for a wide range of ailments, including colds, influenza, coughs, bronchitis, asthma, high blood pressure and headaches (Nsuala *et al.* 2015, 2017). In the Western Cape, it is a popular medicine for donkeys. The plant contains the same diterpenoid lactones as the European white horehound (*Marrubium vulgare*), which is traditionally used as a cough medicine.

Leonotis ocymifolia | Lamiaceae | ***KLIPDAGGA*** (Afrikaans) ■ The plant is similar to *L. leonurus* but the leaves are smaller and broader, with wavy margins. Leaf infusions have been used to treat stomach ailments, diabetes, high blood pressure, stroke and cancer.

Lippia javanica | Lamiaceae | **FEVER TEA** ■ See Chapter 13. *Lippia* species (*L. javanica* and *L. scaberrima* – respectively *musukudu* and *musukujane* in Tswana) are indigenous shrubs with aromatic, opposite leaves and small white flowers. Leaves are steeped as medicinal teas, mainly to treat coughs, colds, fever and bronchitis. Weak infusions are taken as a general health tea.

Mentha longifolia | Lamiaceae | **WILD MINT**; *ballerja, kruisement* (Afrikaans); *ufuthane lomhlange* (Zulu); *koena-ya-thaba* (Sotho); *inixina* (Xhosa) ■ The plant is a creeping indigenous herb of wet places and closely resembles some of the exotic mints that are cultivated in herb gardens. Wild mint has many medicinal uses in various parts of southern Africa. The most important uses are for respiratory ailments, headaches, fever, indigestion and urinary tract infections. The volatile oil (see Chapter 13) is likely to be partly responsible for the decongestant, antispasmodic and antibiotic effects. An infusion was used in the Cape for hysteria and insomnia, and the dry roots are taken as an infusion for epilepsy.

Mondia whitei | Apocynaceae | ***UMONDI*** (Zulu); White's ginger, tonic root; *mungurawu* (Shona) ■ The plant is a robust, woody creeper with opposite leaves, distinctive frilly stipules and attractive purplish-red (rarely yellow) flowers. It is widely distributed in sub-Saharan Africa but has become rare in southern Africa as a result of wild-harvesting for the muthi trade. Root infusions are used in Zimbabwe for constipation, anorexia, bilharzia, and as aphrodisiacs. Root infusions have been used for fits in children, and to treat stress and tension in adults. The bitter-tasting roots have a vanilla-like odour and a sweet aftertaste, and have been used to make a beer. Because of the vanilla-like odour it was thought to have potential as a novel African spice. The seeds are believed to have once been used as arrow poisons (Hutchings 1966). In Kenya, fresh roots are sold by street vendors, and powdered roots are sold in plastic bags in many markets. Quality-controlled powdered root with approval from the Pharmacy and Poisons Board of Kenya, and the Kenya Bureau of Standards, is sold in some supermarkets under the brand "Mondia Tonic". Laboratory research has shown antidepressant activity, aphrodisiac activity, anticonvulsant activity and ergogenic activity, thus supporting some of the indigenous uses (Aremu *et al.* 2011; Dohbobga *et al.* 2016). The plant is easy to grow from seeds or cuttings and is an attractive garden climber (vine) for warm regions.

Dawid Bester with a plant of *Kedrostis nana*

Cynthia Arendse with a large tuber of *Kedrostis nana* (Parade, Cape Town)

Purging nut or *mathlapametse* (*Jatropha curcas*)

Fruits and seeds (nuts) of *Jatropha curcas*

Flowers of *umondi* (*Mondia whitei*)

Dried root and powdered root of *umondi* (*Mondia whitei*)

Notobubon galbanum (=*Peucedanum galbanum*) │Apiaceae│ **BLISTER BUSH**; *bergseldery* (Afrikaans) ■ The distinctive leaves of this fynbos shrub contain phototoxic coumarins and are traditionally used as a diuretic for kidney and bladder conditions, for colds, arthritis and gout, and as a slimming remedy.

Ocotea bullata │Lauraceae│ **BLACK STINKWOOD**; *unukani* (Zulu); *stinkhout* (Afrikaans) ■ The bark of this famous timber tree is an important traditional medicine, used for headache, urinary and nervous disorders, and for treating diarrhoea in children (Solomon Mahlaba, pers. comm.).

Olea europaea **subsp.** ***africana*** │Oleaceae│ **WILD OLIVE**; *olienhout* (Afrikaans); *motholoari* (Sotho); *umquma* (Xhosa, Zulu) ■ Leaves are used to lower blood pressure and numerous other medicinal uses have been recorded (see Van Wyk *et al.* 1997, 2009). The antihypertensive activity of olive leaves is mainly due to the presence of oleuropein, a bitter-tasting secoiridoid that also gives olives their bitter taste. High levels are found in wild olive leaves (Long *et al.* 2010).

Oncosiphon suffruticosum │Asteraceae│ ***STINKKRUID*** (Afrikaans) ■ *Stinkkruid* is an exceptionally common herb of up to one metre in height. The feathery leaves and small yellow flower heads are distinctive. This partly forgotten Khoi remedy is still an important medicine in some areas. It is used as a diaphoretic for fever, and is also diuretic. Asthma and pneumonia are treated with infusions of the plant. A few drops of juice expressed from the fresh leaves are added to mother's milk as a gripe-water for infants with winds and cramps (Mrs. Bester, pers. comm.). Fresh plant material is crushed with *Exomis microphylla* and *Carpobrotus edulis*, or *Ruta graveolens* to treat infantile convulsions (Dawid Bester & Mrs Bester, pers. comm.). In the Agter-Hantam, Jan Baadjies recommended the use of the fresh herb, placed in the shoes, to counteract foot odour (De Beer & Van Wyk 2011).

Parmelia **species** │Parmeliaceae│ ***KLIPBLOM*** (Afrikaans); rock lichens ■ See also Chapter 13. A number of species of lichens are still used as medicines in rural areas in the Cape, and were originally used by the Khoi. Infusions of *klipblom* (literally meaning "rock-flower") are used for coughs, sore throats, infertility, oral thrush in infants, abdominal pain, backache, and kidney and bladder diseases. The genus *Parmelia* has been split into several separate genera, and the correct name for the common *klipblom* is now *Xanthoparmelia hottentotta* (see Chapter 13). These lichens are likely to have significant antimicrobial and anti-inflammatory activity.

Another unusual ancient Cape medicine is the dried concretion of hyrax urine, known as *hyraceum* (*dassiepis* in Afrikaans), which is still sold on the Parade market in Cape Town. *Hyraceum* is used in infusions and tinctures as an emmenagogue and abortifacient, and has also been used for hysteria, epilepsy, and as an antispasmodic. It is an export item and is used in the fragrance industry. *Klipsweet*, literally "rock-sweat", is a dark secretion that is often confused with *dassiepis*, but is the excreta of midges (found as a thin, tar-like layer on the roofs of shallow caves) that is used as a general tonic for many conditions (Gert Dirkse, pers. comm.).

Pelargonium sidoides │Geraniaceae│ ***RABAS***, *rooirabas* (Afrikaans); *kgwara e nyenyane* (Sotho); *Umckaloabo* (German) ■ The plant is a perennial herb with round, velvety leaves, dark purple to almost black flowers and swollen tubers below the ground. It is distinguished from the closely related *P. reniforme* by the pink flower colour of the latter. *Umckaloabo* is a medicine prepared from this indigenous South African plant by the German company Schwabe to treat bronchitis in children. The activity is ascribed to coumarins such as umckalin. *Pelargonium luridum* (*ishaqa* in Zulu) tubers are used to treat diarrhoea and dysentery. The leaves of *Pelargonium cucculatum* (*wildemalva* in Afrikaans), an attractive fynbos shrub, are a traditional remedy for chest ailments and coughs. The closely related *Pelargonium betulinum* (*kanferblaar* or *maagpynbossie* in Afrikaans) has also been used to heal wounds and to treat stomach-ache.

GENERAL MEDICINES

Blister bush or *bergseldery* (*Notobubon galbanum*)

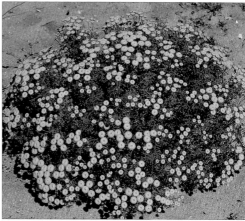

Flowering plant of *stinkkruid* (*Oncosiphon suffruticosum*)

Rock lichens or *klipblom* (*Xanthoparmelia hottentotta*)

Hyraceum or *dassiepis*, the dried concretion of hyrax urine, is a traditional Khoi medicine

Flowers of *rabas* (*Pelargonium sidoides*)

Roots of *rabas* (*Pelargonium sidoides*)

Pellaea calomelanos |Adiantaceae| **HARD FERN**; *lehorometso* (Sotho); *inkomankomo* (Zulu) ■ The leaves of several ferns are smoked for headaches and chest colds and to treat asthma.

Peltophorum africanum |Fabaceae| **WEEPING WATTLE**; *huilboom* (Afrikaans); *mosehla* (Northern Sotho); *mujiza, muzeze* (Shona); *musese* (Venda); *umsehle* (Zulu) ■ Bark and root decoctions are taken in Zimbabwe as a panacea. Root decoctions and infusions are taken for ascites, abdominal pain, nausea, venereal disease, sore throats, chest pain, and blood purification.

Pentanisia prunelloides |Rubiaceae| ***ISIMAMLILO*** (Zulu); wild verbena; *sooibrandbossie* (Afrikaans) ■ The fleshy roots of this grassland plant are commonly used to treat heartburn, and are also used in infusions for fever, coughs, diarrhoea and menstrual cramps. Infusions of the root are given as enemas for abdominal pain and haemorrhoids.

Pergularia daemia |Apocynaceae| ***ERIKO*** (Herero); *mogwapa* (Northern Sotho) ■ In Namibia and Botswana, root decoctions are taken for venereal diseases, arthritis, muscular pain, asthma and rheumatism. The leaves are eaten cooked as a spinach (Van den Eynden *et al.* 1992).

Pittosporum viridiflorum |Pittosporaceae| **CHEESEWOOD**; *umkhwenkhwe* (Xhosa, Zulu); *kgalagangwe* (Northern Sotho); *kasuur* (Afrikaans) ■ The bark of this tree is a popular remedy for stomach complaints, pain and fever.

Plumbago auriculata |Plumbaginaceae| ***UMABOPHE*** (Xhosa); *utshilitshili* (Zulu); *syselbos* (Afrikaans) ■ Powdered roots and leaves are snuffed to treat headache.

Prunus africana |Rosaceae| ***INYAZANGOMA-ELIMNYANA*** (Zulu); *umkakase* (Xhosa); *rooistinkhout* (Afrikaans); red stinkwood ■ The bark of this tree, previously known as *Pygeum africanum*, is exploited on a large scale in other parts of tropical Africa and is exported to Europe, America and Japan for the manufacture of medicine to treat prostate hypertrophy. There is concern about conservation: figures given by Cunningham *et al.* (1997) showed that some 3 200 to 4 900 tons of bark are used every year at an estimated retail value of about $220 000 000. In Zulu traditional medicine it is used to treat chest pain (Pujol 1990).

Psidium guajava |Myrtaceae| **GUAVA**; *koejawel* (Afrikaans); *ugwava* (Zulu) ■ Leaf infusions are taken to treat fever, coughs, boils and diabetes. The leaves are used in many countries to treat diarrhoea, and are also used to treat dysentery. Powdered root is used to treat scabies. The leaves have been found to have significant antibacterial properties, and also show hypoglycaemic activity (Ponglux *et al.* 1987).

Ptaeroxylon obliquum |Rutaceae| ***UMTHATHE*** (Xhosa); sneezewood; *nieshout* (Afrikaans) ■ The bark of this tree is used as a snuff to relieve headache. Infusions are said to be useful against rheumatism and arthritis.

Punica granatum |Lythraceae| **POMEGRANATE**; *granaat* (Afrikaans) ■ This Mediterranean and Middle Eastern fruit tree is widely cultivated in southern Africa. The dried fruit rind (*granaatskille* in Afrikaans) is a traditional Cape remedy for diarrhoea and stomach-ache, while the root bark is widely used as a tapeworm remedy.

Rumex lanceolatus |Polygonaceae| ***INDOLOLENKONYANE*** (Xhosa, Zulu); common dock ■ The roots are a traditional remedy for tapeworm and roundworm.

Ruta graveolens |Rutaceae| **RUE**; *wynruit* (Afrikaans) ■ The strongly aromatic leaves of this old Cape remedy is used for a wide range of ailments (see Van Wyk *et al.* 1997, 2009). The closely related *Ruta chalepensis* (Aleppo rue or fringed rue) is used in the same way.

Flowering plant of *Pergularia daemia*

Fruit of *Pergularia daemia*

Leaves and fruits of red stinkwood (*Prunus africana*)

Bark of *Prunus africana*

Guava leaves and flowers (*Psidium guajava*)

Pomegranate fruits and seeds (*Punica granatum*)

Salix mucronata | Salicaceae | **WILD WILLOW**; *wilde wilger, rivierwilger* (Afrikaans) ■ The branch tips and leaves of the tree are widely used in rural areas to treat rheumatism and fever. It has also been used to treat diseases in domestic animals. The anti-inflammatory property of willows is ascribed to salicin, which is converted into salicylic acid in the intestinal tract.

Salvia africana-caerulea | Lamiaceae | **BLOUBLOMSALIE** (Afrikaans) ■ This *salie* and other indigenous *Salvia* species such as *S. chamelaeagnea* and *S. dentata* (both also known locally as *bloublomsalie*, but the latter more often as *bergsalie*) are extensively used as traditional medicines (Van Wyk *et al.* 2009). Infusions are used for colds, influenza and bronchitis, and also for abdominal cramps and indigestion. *Salvia africana-lutea* (the brown-flowered *strandsalie*) and *S. lanceolata* (*sandsalie*) are used in the same way. These plants are rich in essential oil (Kamatou *et al.* 2006) and are known to have antimicrobial, anti-inflammatory, antipyretic and anti-tuberculosis activities, amongst others. The antimicrobial activity is ascribed to diterpenes and triterpenes. *Salvia officinalis* (sage or *maksalie*) is a well-known European culinary herb that is commonly cultivated in southern Africa. It is an old Cape remedy for indigestion and sore throat.

***Sansevieria* species** | Asparagaceae, formerly Dracaenaceae | **PILES ROOT** ■ See Chapter 19. The rhizomes and leaves of *Sansevieria aethiopica* and *S. hyacinthoides* are widely used in southern Africa for earache, haemorrhoids, stomach-ache, ulcers, diarrhoea and internal parasites. *Sansevieria* is sometimes included in the genus *Dracaena*.

Scabiosa columbaria | Caprifoliaceae | **IBHEKA** (Zulu); *selomi sa mamokgale, hlaku ya pitsi, mohudungwane* (Sotho); wild scabious; *meerjarige skurfkruid* (Afrikaans) ■ Leaves or fleshy roots are a traditional colic and heartburn remedy and powdered roots are used as a baby powder. Basotho people use it to treat women's ailments (see Chapter 10), skin rashes and venereal sores (Moffett 2010). *Scabiosa* species have been used in Europe to treat scabies, hence the generic name.

Schotia brachypetala | Fabaceae | **IHLUZE** (Zulu); weeping boer-bean ■ The bark is used to treat heartburn, hangovers and nervous conditions.

Sclerocarya birrea | Anacardiaceae | **MARULA** ■ See Chapter 6. The leaves, bark and roots of this important African fruit tree are used for a variety of medicinal purposes, including the fresh leaves for heartburn and bark or root decoctions for diarrhoea, diabetes, fever and malaria. The bark is astringent and the antidiarrhoeal effects have been linked by Galvez *et al.* (1993) to procyanidins. The leaves are widely used in African countries to treat diabetes.

Senna italica | Fabaceae | **WILD SENNA**, eland's pea (English); *elandsertjie, swartstormbossie* (Afrikaans) ■ The plant, previously known as *Cassia italica*, is a creeping shrublet with bright yellow flowers and flat, oblong pods. It is widely distributed in the central parts of southern Africa. As is the case with the famous exotic *Cassia* or *Senna* laxatives, several indigenous species also have value as purgative medicines. A root infusion of *Senna italica* is used as a laxative (Isaac Mayeng, pers. comm.). The dried, powdered root cortex of *Cassia abbreviata* is taken as a mild, non-cramping laxative (Patrick Ndlovu, pers. comm.).

Siphonochilus aethiopicus | Zingiberaceae | **AFRICAN GINGER**, wild ginger; *isiphephetho, indungulo* (Zulu) ■ See Chapter 9. This attractive plant has erect, annual leaves arising from small, cone-shaped rhizomes, and spectacular pink flowers. The rhizomes and fleshy roots are very popular in traditional medicine in southern Africa to the extent that there is concern about regional extinction. Fresh roots or rhizomes are chewed for coughs, colds and asthma, suggesting that its unique major sesquiterpenoid (Holtzapfel *et al.* 2002) has decongestant activity. The anti-inflammatory activity (Light *et al.* 2002) may be ascribed to diarylheptanoids. Several other traditional and cultural uses have been recorded (Crouch *et al.* 2000) and the plant is propagated on a small scale.

GENERAL MEDICINES

Flower cluster of *bloublomsalie* (*Salvia africana-caerulea*)

Leaves and flowers of *bergsalie* (*Salvia dentata*)

Flowers of wild senna (*Senna italica*)

Colin Ruiters with the roots and rhizome of African ginger (*Siphonochilus aethiopicus*)

Flowering plant of African ginger (*Siphonochilus aethiopicus*)

Stachys aethiopicus | Lamiaceae | ***KLEINKATTEKRUIE*** (Afrikaans); *balao ba ditaola, bokghata* (Sotho) ■ Infusions and decoctions of this small aromatic herb are used to treat colds, influenza and fever. Sotho people use it as a snakebite remedy and as a fumigant to treat feverish delirium (Moffett 2010). *Stachys rugosus* (*jakopjong*) is used in the Western Cape to alleviate the symptoms of colds, influenza and fever.

Stangeria eriopus | Stangeriaceae | ***IMFINGO*** (Zulu); *imifingwane* (Xhosa) ■ This relative of cycads is restricted to the east coast of South Africa. The peculiar white tuberous stems are widely used as an emetic and to treat high blood pressure, headache, congestion and other ailments. The bright red seeds are very poisonous.

Syzygium cordatum | Myrtaceae | ***UMDONI*** (Zulu) ■ The bark of this tree is widely used as an emetic and to treat stomach problems and diarrhoea.

Tetradenia riparia | Lamiaceae | ***IBOZA*** (Zulu) ■ Weak fresh-leaf infusions and decoctions of this robust shrub are commonly used for fever, coughs, colds, influenza and gingivitis. According to Mr Mutwa (pers. comm.), it is more effective for a bad cough than any commercial product. There seem to be chemical varieties, as only some plants have very scented and pungent leaves while others do not.

Teucrium trifidum | Lamiaceae | ***PADDAKLOU***, *aambeiebossie* (Afrikaans) ■ Infusions and tinctures of the twigs and leaves are a traditional treatment against indigestion but have also been used as general tonics against colds, influenza and fever (Ruiters *et al.* 2015). The closely related *Teucrium africanum* (*kaatjiedrieblaar*) is a smaller plant with short, single-flowered inflorescences and is used for a wide range of ailments.

Tulbaghia violacea | Alliaceae | **WILD GARLIC** ■ See photographs on page 161. The rhizomes and leaves of this indigenous garlic relative are widely used to treat fever, asthma and constipation. Wild garlic is probably similar to real garlic in some of its medicinal activities. It is also planted as a snake-repellent (Mr Mutwa, pers. comm.), and the leaves are taken in oesophageal cancer (Caroline Ntilashe, pers. comm.).

   Tulbaghia capensis and *T. alliacea* are also popular Cape traditional medicines. The former has a limited distribution in the Western Cape Province and has become threatened as a result of over-harvesting. It can easily be recognised by the large bulbs, broad leaves, deeply lobed corona and overpowering garlic smell. The name *T. alliacea* has been applied to several similar-looking species but the true *T. alliacea* is restricted to the southwestern parts of South Africa. It has branched rhizomes and a shallowly lobed corona.

Turraea nilotica | Meliaceae | ***CHIPINDURA*** (Shona); lowveld honeysuckle-tree; *tshigombo* (Venda) ■ In Zimbabwe, root infusions are used for numerous conditions, including abdominal pain, venereal diseases, constipation, menstrual cramps, epilepsy, diarrhoea and pneumonia. In South Africa, *Turraea floribunda* (honeysuckle-tree, *umadlozane* in Zulu) is used for heart failure, rheumatism, and as an emetic.

Xysmalobium undulatum | Apocynaceae | ***ISHONGWE*** (Zulu); *Uzara* (German); *bitterwortel* (Afrikaans) ■ See Chapters 9, 10 and 11; photographs on page 163. The plant is a robust, erect, perennial herb with thick, hairy branches and large, prominently veined leaves arising from a large, branched and fleshy root system. The species is widely distributed in grassland areas in the eastern parts of southern Africa. The bitter roots are popular medicines, taken as powdered root or infusions for indigestion, fever, colds, abdominal cramps, diarrhoea, dysentery and are also used for heart failure and as emetics. The powdered root is taken as a snuff for headache and for hysteria, and it seems to have a sedative action (Solomon Mahlaba, pers. comm.).

Leaves and flowers of *kleinkattekruie* (*Stachys aethiopicus*)

Leaves and flowers of *jakopjong* (*Stachys rugosus*)

Umdoni tree (*Syzygium cordatum*)

Leaves and flowers of *umdoni* (*Syzygium cordatum*)

Leaves of *iboza* (*Tetradenia riparia*)

Flowers of *iboza* (*Tetradenia riparia*)

Aambeiebossie or *paddaklou* (*Teucrium trifidum*)

Kaatjiedrieblaar (*Teucrium africanum*)

REFERENCES AND FURTHER READING: Adeniji, K.O., Amusan, O.O.G., Dlamini, P.S. *et al.* **undated.** Contribution to ethnobotanical and floristic studies in Swaziland. Organization of African Unity/Scientific, Technical & Research Commission, Lagos. **Archer, F.M. 1990.** Planning with people – ethnobotany and African uses of plants in Namaqualand (South Africa). *Mitt. Inst. Allg. Bot. Hamburg* 23: 959–972. **Aremu, A.O., Cheesman, L., Finnie, J.F. & Van Staden, J. 2011.** *Mondia whitei* (Apocynaceae): A review of its biological activities, conservation strategies and economic potential. *S. Afr. J. Bot.* 77(4), 960–971. **Arnold, T.H., Prentice, G.A., Hawker, L.C., Snyman, E.E., Tomalin, M., Crouch, N.R. & Pottas- Bircher, C. 2002.** Medicinal and magical plants of southern Africa: an annotated checklist. *Strelitzia* 13. National Botanical Institute, Pretoria. **Bruneton, J. 1995.** *Pharmacognosy, phytochemistry, medicinal plants.* Intercept, Hampshire. **Brendler, T. & Van Wyk, B.-E. 2008.** A historical, scientific and commercial perspective on the medicinal use of *Pelargonium sidoides* (Geraniaceae). *J. Ethnopharmacol.* 119: 420–433. **Brendler, T., Eloff, J.N., Gurib-Fakim, A. & Phillips, L.D. (eds) 2010.** *African Herbal Pharmacopoeia.* Association of African Medicinal Plant Standards, Port Louis. **Bryant, A.T. 1966.** *Zulu medicine and medicine men,* rev. ed. Struik, Cape Town. **Cawston, F.G. 1933.** Native medicines of Natal. *S.A. Med. J.,* 10 June 1933: 370–371. **Chen, W., Van Wyk, B.-E., Vermaak, I. & Viljoen, A.M. 2012.** Cape aloes – A review of the phytochemistry, pharmacology and commercialization of *Aloe ferox. Phytochemistry Letters* 5: 1–12. **Chen, W., Vermaak, I. & Viljoen, A.M. 2013.** Camphor – A fumigant during the Black Death and a coveted fragrant wood in ancient Egypt and Babylon – a review. *Molecules* 18: 5434–5454. **Cillié, A.M. 1992.** *Kruie op witblits, rate, resepte en feite,* p. 43. Unpublished notes, Worcester Museum. **Corrigan, B.M., Van Wyk, B.-E., Geldenhuys, C.J. & Jardine, J.M. 2011.** Ethnobotanical plant uses in the KwaNibela Peninsula, St Lucia, South Africa. *S. Afr. J. Bot.* 77(2): 346–359. **Crouch, N.R. 2000.** *Siphonochilus aethiopicus* (Zingiberaceae), the prized indungulu of the Zulu – an overview. *Herbertia* 55: 115–129. **Cunningham, A.B. 1988.** *An investigation of the herbal medicine trade in Natal/Kwazulu.* Investigational report no 29, Institute of Natural Resources, University of Natal. **Cunningham, A.B. 1989.** Indigenous plant use: balancing human needs and resources. In: Huntley, B.J. (ed.), *Biotic diversity in southern Africa.* Oxford University Press, pp. 93–106. **Cunningham, M., Cunningham, A.B. & Schippmann, U. 1997.** Trade in *Prunus africana* and the implementation of CITES: Results of the research and development project 808 05 080. Landwirtschaftsverlag, Munster. **De Almeida, A.G. 1930.** Plantas venenosas e medicinas dos indigenos de Moçambique. *Bolm agric. pecuár. Moçamb.* 1: 9–29. **De Beer, J. & Van Wyk, B.-E. 2011.** An ethnobotanical survey of the Agter-Hantam, Northern Cape Province, South Africa. *S. Afr. J. Bot.* 77: 741–754. **De Wet, H. & Van Wyk, B.-E. 2008.** An ethnobotanical survey of southern African Menispermaceae. *S. Afr. J. Bot.* 74: 2–9. **Dohbobga, R.G.B., Nso, E., Mbofung, C.M.F. & Ngogang, J.Y. 2016.** A sport drink extracted from *Mondia whitei* roots: Impact on endurance performance. *J. Food Sci. Res.* 1(2): 061–076. **Diederichs, N. (ed.) 2006.** *Commercialising medicinal plants. A southern African guide.* Sun Press, Stellenbosch. **Dold, T. & Cocks, M. 2012.** *Voices from the forest.* Jacana Media, Johannesburg. **Duncan, G., Jeppe, B. & Voigt, L. 2016.** *The Amaryllidaceae of southern Africa.* Umdaus Press, Pretoria. **Felhaber, T. (ed.) 1997.** *South African traditional healers' primary health care handbook.* Kagiso Publishers, Pretoria. **Forbes, V.S. (ed.) 1986.** *Carl Peter Thunberg Travels at the Cape of Good Hope 1772–1775.* Van Riebeeck Society, Cape Town. **Galvez, J.** *et al.* **1993.** Pharmacological activity of a procyanidin isolated from *Sclerocarya birrea* bark: anti-diarrhoeal activity and effects on isolated guinea-pig ileum. *Phytother. Res.* 7: 25–28. **Geldenhuys, C.J. & Van Wyk, B.-E. 2002.** Indigenous biological resources of Africa. In: Baijnath, H. & Singh, Y. (eds), *Rebirth of Science in Africa.* Umdaus Press, Hatfield. **Gelfand, M., Mavi, S., Drummond, R.B. & Ndemera, B. 1985.** *The traditional medical practitioner in Zimbabwe.* Mambo Press, Gweru, Zimbabwe. **Gericke, N. 2011.** Muthi to medicine. *S. Afr. J. Bot.* 77(4): 850–856. **Grace, O.M., Simmonds, M.S.J., Smith, G.F. & Van Wyk, A.E. 2008.** Therapeutic uses of *Aloe L.* (Asphodelaceae) in southern Africa. *J. Ethnopharmacol.* 119: 604–614. **Grace, O.M., Simmonds, M.S.J., Smith, G.F. & Van Wyk, A.E. 2009.** Documented utility and biocultural value of *Aloe L.* (Asphodelaceae): a review. *Econ. Bot.* 63: 167–178. **Gurib-Fakim, A. & Schmelzer, G.H. (eds) 2008.** *The plant resources of tropical Africa* 11(2). *Medicinal plants* 2. CTA PROTA, Wageningen. **Hanekom, C. 1967.** Tradisionele geneeskunde by enkele Noord-Sothostamme. *Afr. Stud.* 26: 3742. **Hedberg, I. & Staugård, F. 1989.** *Traditional medicinal plants – traditional medicine in Botswana.* Ipelegeng Publishers, Gaborone. **Henderson, M. & Anderson, J.G. 1966.** Common weeds in South Africa. *Mem. Bot. Surv. S. Afr.* 37. **Holzapfel, C.W., Marais, W., Wessels, P.L. & Van Wyk, B.-E. 2002.** Furanoterpenoids from *Siphonochilus aethiopicus. Phytochemistry* 59: 405–407. **Hutchings, A. & Van Staden, J. 1994.** Plants used for stress-related ailments in traditional Zulu, Xhosa and Sotho medicine. Part 1: Plants used for headaches. *J. Ethnopharmacol.* 43: 89–124. **Hutchings, A., Scott, A.H., Lewis, G. & Cunningham, A. 1996.** *Zulu medicinal plants.* Natal University Press, Pietermaritzburg. **Iwu, M.M. 1993.** *Handbook of African medicinal plants.* CRC Press, Boca Raton. **Jansen, P.C.M. & Mendes, O. 1983–1991.** *Plantas Medicinais. Seu Uso Tradicional em Mocambique.* Vol.1–4. Ministerio da Sude, Gabinete de Estudos de Medicina Tradicional, Republica Poular de Moçambique. **Kamatou, G., Van Zyl, R.L., Van Vuuren, S.F., Viljoen, A.M., Figueiredo, A.C., Barroso, J.G. & Pedro, L.G. 2006.** Chemical composition, leaf trichome morphology and biological activities of the essential oils of four related *Salvia* species indigenous to southern Africa. *J. Essent. Oil Res.* 18: 72–79. **Kinghorn, A.D. & Balandrin, M.F. 1993.** Human medicinal agents from plants. ACS Symposium Series 534, American Chemical Society. **Krige, E.J. 1940.** *Medicine, magic and religion of the Lovedu.* D. Litt., University of the Witwatersrand. **Laidler, P.W. 1928.** The magic medicine of the Hottentots. *S. Afr. J. Sci.* 25: 433–447. **Lawes, M.J., Eely, H.A.C., Shackleton, C.M. & Geach, B.G.S. (eds) 2004.** *Indigenous forests and woodlands in South Africa. Part. 5. Medicinal plants.* University of KwaZulu-Natal Press, Scottsville. **Light, M.E.** *et al.* **2002.** Investigation of the biological activities of *Siphonochilus aethiopicus* and the effects of seasonal senescence. *S. Afr. J. Bot.* 68: 55–61. **Long H., Tilney, P.M. & Van Wyk, B.-E. 2010.** The ethnobotany and pharmacognosy of *Olea europaea* subsp. *africana. S. Afr. J. Bot.* 76: 324–331. **Longmore, L. 1958.** Medicine, magic and witchcraft among urban Africans on the Witwatersrand. *Cent. Afr. J. Med.* 4. **Maliehe, E. 1997.** *Medicinal plants and herbs of Lesotho.* Mafeteng Development Project, Maseru, Lesotho. **Mander, M. 1998.** *Marketing of indigenous medicinal plants in South Africa: A case study in KwaZulu-Natal.* Food and Agricultural Organization of the United Nations, Rome. **Moffett, R. 2010.** *Sesotho plant and animal names, and plants used by the Basotho.* Sun Press, Stellenbosch. **Moffett, R. 2016.** *Basotho medicinal plants – Meriana ya Dimela tsa Basotho.* Sun

Wild garlic plant (*Tulbaghia alliacea*)

Wild garlic flowers (*Tulbaghia alliacea*)

Wild garlic or Cape garlic bulbs (*Tulbaghia capensis*)

Wild garlic of Cape garlic flowers (*Tulbaghia capensis*)

Wild garlic plants (*Tulbaghia violacea*)

Wild garlic flowers (*Tulbaghia violacea*)

Plants of *Tulbaghia violacea, T. capensis* and *T. simmleri*

Fragrant wild garlic (*Tulbaghia simmleri*)

Press, Stellenbosch. **Mzamane, G.I.M. 1945.** Some medicinal, edible and magical plants used by some Bantu tribes in South Africa. *Fort Hare Pap.* 1: 29–35. **Neuwinger, H.D. 1996.** *African ethnobotany: poisons and drugs: chemistry, pharmacology, toxicology.* Chapman & Hall, Germany. **Neuwinger, H.D. 2000.** *African traditional medicine – A dictionary of plant use and applications.* Medpharm Scientific Publishers, Stuttgart. **Ngubane, H. 1977.** *Body and mind in Zulu medicine. An ethnography of health and disease in Nyuswa-Zulu thought and practice.* Academic Press, London. **Nortje, J.M. & Van Wyk, B.-E. 2015.** Medicinal ethnobotany of the Kamiesberg, Namaqualand, South Africa. *J. Ethnopharmacol.* 171: 205–222. **Nsuala, B., Enslin, G. & Viljoen, A.M. 2015.** "Wild cannabis": a review of the traditional use and phytochemistry of *Leonotis leonurus. J. Ethnopharmacol.* 174: 520–539. **Nsuala, B., Kamatou, G.P.P., Sandasi, M., Enslin, G. & Viljoen, A.M. 2017.** Variation in essential oil composition of *Leonotis leonurus,* an important medicinal plant in South Africa. *Biochem. Syst. Ecol.* 70: 155–161. **Pappe, L. 1847.** *A list of South African indigenous plants used as remedies by the colonists of the Cape of Good Hope.* O.I. Pike, Cape Town. **Pappe, L. 1850.** *Florae Capensis Medicae Prodromus.* A.S. Robertson, Cape Town. **Pappe, L. 1857.** *Florae Capensis Medicae Prodromus,* 2nd ed. W. Britain Press, Cape Town. **Pappe, L. 1868.** *Florae Capensis Medicae Prodromus,* 3rd ed. W. Britain Press, Cape Town. **Philander, L.E. 2011.** An ethnobotany of Western Cape Rasta bush medicine. *J. Ethnopharmacol.* 138: 578–594. **Philander, L.E. 2012.** Hunting knowledge and gathering herbs: Rastafari bush doctors in the Western Cape of South Africa. *J. Ethnobiol.* 32:134–156. **Pienaar, A. 2008.** *Kruidjie roer my.* Umuzi, Roggebaai. **Ponglux, D. et al. (eds) 1987.** *Medicinal plants.* The first Princess Chulabhorn Science Congress, Bangkok, Thailand. **PROTA, 2010.** *Review of 25 African plants with special potential.* Backhuys Publishers and CTA PROTA, Wageningen. **Pujol, J. 1990.** *Naturafrica – the herbalist handbook.* Jean Pujol Natural Healers Foundation, Durban. **Roberts, M. 1990.** *Indigenous healing plants.* Southern Book Publishers, Halfway House. **Roberts, M. & Roberts, S. 2017.** *Indigenous healing plants,* 2nd ed. Briza Publications, Pretoria. **Rood, B. 1994.** *Uit die veldapteek.* Tafelberg, Cape Town. **Ruiters, A.K., Tilney, P.M., Van Vuuren, S.F., Viljoen, A.M., Kamatou, G.P.P. & Van Wyk, B.-E. 2015.** The anatomy, ethnobotany, antimicrobial activity and essential oil composition of southern African species of *Teucrium* (Lamiaceae). *S. Afr. J. Bot.* 102: 175–185. **Schmelzer, G.H. & Gurib-Fakim, A. (eds) 2008.** *The plant resources of tropical Africa* 11(1). *Medicinal Plants* 1. Backhuys Publishers and CTA PROTA, Wageningen. **Seleteng Kose, L., Moteetee, A. & Van Vuuren, S. 2015.** Ethnobotanical survey of medicinal plants used in the Maseru district of Lesotho. *J. Ethnopharmacol.* 170: 184–200. **Simons, H.J. 1957.** Tribal medicine: diviners and herbalists. *Afr. Stud.* 16, 2: 85–97. **Smith, A. 1888.** *A contribution to the South African materia medica.* Lovedale, South Africa. **Smith, A. 1895.** *A contribution to the South African materia medica,* 2nd ed. Lovedale, South Africa. **Smith, C.A. 1966.** Common names of South African plants. *Mem. Bot. Surv. S. Afr.* 35. **Standards South Africa, 2007.** *South African National Standard. Aloe raw material.* SANS 368: 2007, 1st ed. Standards South Africa, Pretoria. **Van Wyk, B.-E. 2002.** A review of ethnobotanical research in southern Africa. *S. Afr. J. Bot.* 68: 1–13. **Van Wyk, B.-E. 2008a.** A broad review of commercially important southern African medicinal plants. *J. Ethnopharmacol.* 119: 342–355. **Van Wyk, B.-E. 2008b.** A review of Khoi-San and Cape Dutch medical ethnobotany. *J. Ethnopharmacol.* 119: 331–341. **Van Wyk, B.-E. 2011.** The potential of South African plants in the development of new medicinal products. *S. Afr. J. Bot.* 77: 812–829. **Van Wyk, B.-E. 2015a.** A review of commercially important African medicinal plants. *J. Ethnopharmacol.* 176: 118–134. **Van Wyk, B.-E. 2015b.** Die kulturele en praktiese waarde van inheemse kennis oor plantgebruike in die 21ste eeu. *Suid-Afrikaanse Tydskrif vir Natuurwetenskap en Tegnologie / South African Journal of Science and Technology* 34(1), Art .#1349, 11 pages. **Van Wyk, B.-E. & Albrecht, A. 2008.** A review of the taxonomy, ethnobotany, chemistry and pharmacology of *Sutherlandia frutescens* (Fabaceae). *J. Ethnopharmacol.* 119: 620–629. **Van Wyk, B.-E. & Gericke, N. 2000.** *People's plants – A guide to useful plants of southern Africa.* Briza Publications, Pretoria. **Van Wyk, B.-E. & Wink, M. 2004.** *Medicinal plants of the world.* Timber Press, USA & Briza Publications, Pretoria. **Van Wyk, B.-E. & Wink, M. 2017.** *Medicinal plants of the world.* Revised and expanded 2nd ed. CABI, UK & Briza Publications, Pretoria. **Van Wyk, B.-E. & Wink, M. 2015.** *Phytomedicines, herbal drugs and poisons.* Kew Publishers, Kew and University of Chicago Press, Chicago. **Van Wyk, B.-E., Van Rheede Van Oudtshoorn, M.C.B. & Smith, G.F. 1995.** Geographical variation in the major compounds of *Aloe ferox* leaf exudate. *Planta Med.* 61: 250–253. **Van Wyk, B.-E., Van Oudtshoorn, B. & Gericke, N. 1997.** *Medicinal plants of South Africa.* Briza Publications, Pretoria. **Van Wyk, B.-E., Van Oudtshoorn, B. & Gericke, N. 2009.** *Medicinal plants of South Africa.* Revised and expanded 2nd ed. Briza Publications, Pretoria. **Van Wyk, B.-E., De Wet, H. & Van Heerden, F.R. 2008.** An ethnobotanical survey of medicinal plants in the southeastern Karoo, South Africa. *S. Afr. J. Bot.* 74: 696–704. **Van Wyk, B.-E., Wink, C. & Wink, M. 2015.** *Handbuch der Arzneipflanzen.* Wissenschaftliche Verlagsgesellschaft, Stuttgart. **Viljoen, A.M., Demirci, B., Baser, H. & Van Wyk, B.-E. 2002.** The essential oil composition of the roots and rhizomes of *Siphonochilus aethiopicus. Afr. J. Bot.* 68: 115–116. **Von Ahlefeldt, D., Crouch, N.R., Nichols, G., Symmonds, R., McKean, S., Sibiya, H. & Cele, M.P. 2003.** *Medicinal plants traded on South Africa's eastern seaboard.* Ethekwini Parks Department and University of Natal, Durban. **Venter, F. 1997.** *Botanical survey of the medicinal plants of the Northern Sotho, Northern Province, South Africa.* Land management and rural development programme, University of the North. **Von Koenen, E. 1996.** *Heil-, Gift- und Essbare Pflanzen in Namibia.* Klaus Hess Verlag, Göttingen. **Von Koenen, E. 2001.** *Medicinal, poisonous and edible plants in Namibia.* Klaus Hess Publishers, Windhoek and Göttingen. **Watt, J.M. & Breyer-Brandwijk, M.G. 1962.** *The medicinal and poisonous plants of southern and eastern Africa,* 2nd ed. Livingstone, London. **WHO Monographs on selected medicinal plants, 1999, 2003, 2007, 2009 (Vols 1–4).** World Health Organisation, Geneva. **Williams, V.L., Balkwill, K. & Witkowski, E.T.F. 2000.** Unravelling the commercial market for medicinal plants and plant parts on the Witwatersrand, South Africa. *Econ. Bot.* 54: 310–327. **Youthed, G. (ed.) no date.** *Dictionary of South African traditional medicinal plants of the Eastern Cape.* Pharmaceutical Society of South Africa, Johannesburg (unpublished). **Zukulu, S., Dold, T., Abbott, T. & Raimondo, D. 2012.** *Medicinal and charm plants of Pondoland.* South African National Biodiversity Institute, Pretoria.

Fruiting plant of *bitterhout* (*Xysmalobium undulatum*), known in Germany as *Uzara*

Flowering stems of *bitterhout* or *ishongwe* (*Xysmalobium undulatum*)

Roots of *bitterhout* or *ishongwe* (*Xysmalobium undulatum*)

Fruits and seeds of *bitterhout* or *ishongwe* (*Xysmalobium undulatum*)

Roots of *bitterhout* (*Xysmalobium undulatum*)

Echinacea purpurea, a popular North American herbal remedy, said to improve immune function

Flowering plants of *Aloe vera*

Cultivated ginseng plant (*Panax ginseng*)

Siberian ginseng (*Eleutherococcus sentricosus*)

CHAPTER 8

Tonic plants

TONIC PLANTS HAVE multiple functions in the human body, and act in the healthy individual by maintaining and supporting general physical and mental health. When an individual is ill or convalescing, tonics can assist in restoring health and are believed to tone the body's organ systems and improve immune function. They enhance the metabolism, secretion and excretion of waste products by the liver and kidneys, and improve digestion through stimulation of the gall bladder, and sometimes have a mild purgative effect. Some tonics are profound adaptogens, significantly enhancing the body's ability to adapt to physical and emotional stress.

The use of tonics is well established in traditional medicine in southern Africa, and is perhaps exemplified by the widespread use of a large variety of "strengthening" plant combinations known as *imbizas* in South Africa, which are believed to play a significant role in maintaining health and vigour. In Basotho traditional medicine, *Lessertia frutescens* and several other plants of the legume family, are used as traditional tonics known as *'musa-pelo* (Moteetee & Van Wyk 2007). *Lessertia frutescens* (better known by its older name, *Sutherlandia frutescens*) is one of the most important adaptogens in southern Africa and is widely used. The extensive use of plant infusions or decoctions as purifying ritual emetics, known as "*ukuphalaza*" or "*ukughabha*", and cleansing enemas, known as "*ukuchatha*", are also considered to have a profound tonic effect on the body, and some of these have been described in Chapter 7. The "*isihlambezo*" tonics of pregnancy are dealt with in Chapter 10.

Bitter-tasting traditional medicines have a long history of use against disorders of the digestive tract. These remedies are often referred to as bitter tonics (*amara*) or *amara-aromatica*, when the plants or products not only have a bitter taste but also contain volatile oil. The bitter taste in the mouth stimulates the secretion of gastric juice and bile, thereby improving appetite and digestion. It is also interesting to note that bitter substances were shown to have a direct effect on the heart, resulting in a reduction of stress. Although bitter tonics have been amongst the best-selling commercial medicinal products in South Africa for many years, there is now a renewed interest in the benefits of the bitter tonic (*amarum*) effect. The majority of plants treated in this chapter have a bitter taste, which likely contributes to their medicinal value. The intensity of the taste can be quantified using a formalised procedure to determine the so-called "bitterness value". Bitterness values have been determined for most of the tonic plants included in this chapter (Olivier & Van Wyk 2013). Well-known and popular examples of commercial bitter tonics of South Africa include Lewensessens and Swedish Bitters.

The potential of natural tonics for maintaining and supporting health is starting to be appreciated by modern allopathic medicine, mainly as a result of scientific investigations into the activities, pharmacology and chemistry of some well-known adaptogenic plants, including ginseng (*Panax ginseng*), American ginseng (*Panax quinquefolium*), Siberian ginseng (*Eleutherococcus senticosus*) and Indian ginseng (*Withania somnifera*). The most profound adaptogens from South Africa are *Lessertia* species, formerly known as *Sutherlandia*.

Supported by formal clinical studies, affordable natural tonics could play an important role in improving the quality of life in patients with cancer, tuberculosis, HIV/AIDS and other serious health conditions. In spite of their common use and broad utility, tonics should be used responsibly in appropriate doses, and for a defined duration.

Agathosma betulina |Rutaceae| ***BUCHU*** (Khoi); *boegoe* (Afrikaans); *ibuchu* (Xhosa) ■ The plant is a shrub of up to two metres in height, with rounded leaves dotted with conspicuous oil glands that are prominent along the margins. The leaves have a characteristic smell when crushed. *Agathosma betulina* (round-leaf buchu) and *A. crenulata* (oval-leaf buchu) are the two main species of *Agathosma* that are commonly used for medicinal purposes and which are important sources of valuable essential oil, but several others are known to be used to some extent. Amongst these are *Agathosma serratifolia* (narrow-leaf buchu), a willow-like small tree closely related to *A. betulina* and *A. crenulata*, and *A. ovata* (false buchu, *basterboegoe*), a small, rounded shrub with attractive pink flowers. *Agathosma betulina* is very similar to *A. crenulata* but the latter has more oblong leaves that are more than twice as long as they are broad. Those of *Agathosma betulina* are characteristically more rounded and less than twice as long as they are broad.

Round-leaf buchu (*Agathosma betulina*) and oval-leaf buchu (*A. crenulata*) are both restricted to the southwestern Cape Province of South Africa and occur in the mountainous regions of the Cape. Both these species survive fire by resprouting vigorously from the base, while the related *Agathosma serratifolia* appears to be an obligate reseeding species and is killed by fire. Due to the limited supply of wild-crafted material, round-leaf and oval-leaf buchu are in the process of being developed as crop plants and are already being cultivated.

Buchu was an important part of the Khoi culture in the Cape, and still enjoys a great reputation as a general health tonic and medicine throughout South Africa. The leaves are chewed fresh or dried, or infusions are made. Brandy tinctures were introduced by the early Dutch colonists, and "*boegoebrandewyn*" is still taken for many conditions. Buchu is diuretic, and is a mild urinary antiseptic, taken to stimulate kidney function and to treat mild cystitis and prostatitis. In small doses it is an appetite stimulant, and is a good digestive, carminative and antispasmodic. The mild laxative effect (Solomon Mahlaba, pers. comm.) probably results from the high mucilage content. It is a stimulant, useful for hangovers, and is also used to treat colds and influenza, coughs, rheumatism and gout. The essential oils are probably responsible for the antispasmodic, antiseptic and diuretic activities, and isomenthone and diosphenol are the major compounds. *Agathosma crenulata* is less desirable because of potentially harmful levels of pulegone. "Buchu water" – a waste product from the distillation of the essential oil – is not a substitute for buchu. Round-leaf buchu is generally regarded as being safe in most countries in the world.

Aloe ferox |Asphodelaceae| **CAPE ALOE GEL** ■ *Aloe ferox* is one of the few recognisable plant species to be found in San rock paintings in South Africa, and early European travellers documented the use of the plant by the Khoi. Tonics from *Aloe ferox* are the juices and gel derived from the translucent, fleshy inner section of the leaf, harvested fresh and processed after the bitter fraction has been removed. The bitter fraction is known as Cape aloes (see Chapter 7).

The gel in the leaf is crisp, bound within the cellular structure, but the extracted juice or gel is similar to that of *Aloe vera*, with a high water content, the remaining material consisting of complex polysaccharides, amino acids, minerals, organic acids and enzymes. Complex polysaccharides are increasingly receiving recognition for many biological activities, including anti-inflammatory and immuno-modulatory activities. *Aloe ferox* leaf gel contains around 30 different amino acids and has a very high soluble fibre and calcium content (M.C. Botha, pers. comm.; O'Brien *et al.* 2008). At present all the gel is produced from wild plants, and the high mineral and trace element content, including selenium, reflects this. Although there are anecdotal reports of beneficial effects in patients with serious health conditions, *Aloe ferox* gel and juice products should be considered as general health tonics until clinical research has formally established efficacy. *Aloe ferox* leaf gel has a long history as a food in South Africa in the form of a *konfyt* or preserve, and is enjoyed on farms to this day.

TONIC PLANTS

Round-leaf buchu (*Agathosma betulina*)

Oval-leaf buchu (*Agathosma crenulata*)

Long-leaf buchu (*Agathosma serratifolia*)

False buchu or basterboegoe (*Agathosma ovata*)

Bitter aloe or Cape aloe (*Aloe ferox*)

Dried leaves of round-leaf buchu (*Agathosma betulina*)

Cut leaf of Cape aloe, showing the glistening leaf gel

Arctopus echinatus │Apiaceae│ ***SIEKETROOS***, *platdoring* (Afrikaans) ■ This unusual plant is immediately recognisable by the rosette of spiny leaves lying flat against the ground. Male and female flowers occur on separate plants. The male flowers are small, white, and are borne on long stalks. Female flowers are greenish yellow and are borne in dense, stalkless and thorny clusters between the leaves.

The thick tap root is the part used medicinally. *Sieketroos* or *platdoring* was a Khoi medicine that is still popularly used to this day in the Cape, and it can sometimes be found on sale on street markets in central Cape Town (Magee *et al*. 2007). The Afrikaans common name was recorded in the 1770s and is derived from the original Dutch *siekentroos* – meaning "comforts the sick".

Infusions, decoctions and tinctures of the root are traditionally used as a "blood purifier", taken orally for syphilis and gonorrhoea and applied topically to soothe inflammatory skin conditions, sores and ulcers (Dawid & Mrs Bester, pers. comm.). Willem Steenkamp (pers. comm.) knows the resin of *siekentroos* as a topical remedy for ringworm. Preparations have been used for urinary calculi, cystitis and lymphadenopathy. A piece of raw tap root is chewed, and the juice swallowed, to treat a cough productive of purulent sputum (Dawid Bester, pers. comm.), and tuberculosis (Mrs Bester, Phillip Kubukhele, pers. comm.). Decoctions of the roots are sedative, and have been used for the treatment of epilepsy.

The resinous gum from the root is chemically very similar to the resin from *Alepidea* rhizomes. These plants are called *ikhathazo* in Zulu, *lesoko* in Sotho and *iqwili* in Xhosa. They are amongst the most popular traditional medicines used by Sotho, Xhosa and Zulu people against colds, influenza and respiratory ailments. The same mixture of diterpenoids has been found, such as *ent*-16-kauren-19-oic acid and other kaurenoic acids. Both genera are also rich in medicinally relevant phenolic acids (Olivier *et al*. 2008).

Artemisia afra │Asteraceae│ ***UMHLONYANE*** (Zulu); *lengana* (Sotho); *wildeals, als, alsem* (Afrikaans); African wormwood, wild wormwood ■ The plant is a multi-stemmed perennial up to two metres in height with characteristic aromatic, grey-green feathery leaves. It is widely distributed in southern Africa and is commonly cultivated in areas where it does not occur naturally. *Umhlonyane* is one of the oldest and best-known of all the indigenous medicines in southern Africa, and has such diverse and multiple uses that it should be considered a significant tonic in its own right.

The fresh and dry leaves and young stems are usually used as infusions, decoctions and tinctures. The roots are also sometimes used. Fever, colds, influenza, sore throats, coughs, asthma, pneumonia and headache are treated with *umhlonyane*, taken orally or inhaled as a steam bath. Gastritis, indigestion, poor appetite, flatulence and colic are effectively treated with appropriate doses. It has also been used to treat intestinal worms, constipation and gout. Diabetes is sometimes treated with *umhlonyane*, but it seems as if plants from certain areas are more effective than others (Credo Mutwa, pers. comm.). The geographical variability in chemical compounds is well known to us. The volatile oil, which contains mainly 1,8-cineole (=eucalyptol), α-thujone, camphor and borneol, has definite antimicrobial and antioxidative properties (Graven *et al*. 1992). Preliminary research indicates narcotic, analgesic and antihistaminic activities (Hutchings & Van Staden 1994; Suliman *et al*. 2010).

The powdered leaf has been used as a snuff for headache. Thujones, also present in *Artemisia absinthium*, from which the liquor absinthe is made, are known to be psychoactive. In high doses, thujones can cause confusion, convulsions and coma. There is considerable controversy about the role of thujone in the neurotoxic syndrome called absinthism, which resulted in absinthe being banned in many countries. It is believed that absinthism could have been caused by the high alcohol content, or adulterants known to have been used in popular cheap versions of absinthe, including copper sulphate and antimony trichloride.

TONIC PLANTS

Female plant of *sieketroos* or *platdoring* (*Arctopus echinatus*)

Male plant of *sieketroos* or *platdoring* (*Arctopus echinatus*)

Tuberous roots of *sieketroos* or *platdoring* (*Arctopus echinatus*)

Plantation of *wildeals* or *umhlonyane* (*Artemisia afra*)

Leaves of *wildeals* or *umhlonyane* (*Artemisia afra*)

Balanites maughamii |Zygophyllaceae| **TORCHWOOD**; *groendoring* (Afrikaans); *nulu* (Tsonga); *mudulu* (Venda); *iphambo, umnulu* (Zulu) ■ The tree grows up to 20 metres in height and occurs along rivers and in open savanna. It is easily recognised by the fluted bole, smooth, grey bark, unevenly branched green spines and paired leaflets. Yellowish edible fruits are produced in summer. The bark is commonly sold on traditional medicine markets as an ingredient of ritual emetics. Watery extracts produce copious amounts of white foam (see *Silene* in Chapter 9) because of the presence of saponins (steroidal glycosides). Alkaloids may also be present, as they have been found in the tropical African *Balanites aegyptiaca*. In Mozambique, a paste of the bark of *Balanites maughamii* is cooked and taken orally as a general tonic and panacea. It is also cooked with beans for haematuria. Decoctions of the bark and roots are used as emetics, and an infusion of the bark is used to make a refreshing bath.

The fruits of *Balanites aegyptiaca* (simple-thorned torchwood, *mutambanto* in Shona) are edible when ripe and are used in Zimbabwe to treat liver and spleen conditions. In Namibia, the Himba people place the dried roots of *Balanites welwitschii* (*omumbamenye* in Himba and Herero) on coals, and expose breastfeeding mothers with mastitis to the smoke, while the ash is mixed with fat to make an ointment which is applied daily to the breast (Von Koenen 1996, 2001).

Centaurea benedicta (=*Cnicus benedictus*) |Asteraceae| ***KARMEDIK***, *tuinkarmedik* (Afrikaans); holy thistle ■ The plant is a spiny weed from Europe and Asia with toothed leaves and yellow flower heads. It is still widely cultivated as a medicinal herb in South Africa. Infusions from the above-ground parts are used as a general tonic to improve appetite and to alleviate indigestion. The plant has also been used in brandy tinctures to treat internal cancers. It is one of the well-known Cape Dutch remedies that was introduced by the Dutch in the 17th and 18th centuries.

Centella asiatica |Apiaceae| ***CENTELLA***, Indian pennywort, *Hydrocotyle asiatica*; *gotu kola, brahmi* (Hindustani); *inyongwane* (Xhosa); *varkoortjies* (Afrikaans) ■ See Chapters 9 and 11. This cosmopolitan perennial herb is found in moist areas throughout southern Africa. It is a small sprawling plant with round or kidney-shaped leaves borne on thin trailing stems. The inconspicuous flowers are typically borne in groups of three. Stems and leaves are used medicinally throughout the world, including in Ayurvedic medicine in India and in Traditional Chinese Medicine. The health potential of this common plant is only just beginning to be recognised in the Western world. It is eaten as a wild spinach in South Africa in the Limpopo Province (in the erstwhile Gazankulu area) (Patrick Ndlovu, pers. comm.), and in the Eastern Cape Province as a vegetable and as a spring tonic, and is also used medicinally.

Centella is eaten as a fresh plant, and is taken orally as an infusion and a tincture. It is also applied directly externally. Apart from extensive use to treat skin conditions, it has been used to treat fever, diarrhoea, leprosy, tuberculosis, cancer and rheumatoid arthritis. Animal and laboratory studies have demonstrated anticancer activity, probably due to triterpenoids which act as spindle poisons preventing cell division. Other activities that have been reported include antibacterial, antifungal, anti-inflammatory, anti-allergic, hypotensive and antipyretic activities, as well as peptic ulcer healing (Ponglux *et al.* 1987). In addition to the well-known triterpenoid glycosides, *Centella* species are rich in caffeoylquinic acids (Long *et al.* 2012). *Centella glabrata* (*persiegras*) is an old Cape medicine (see Chapter 7), used mainly against diarrhoea and dysentery.

Cichorium intybus |Asteraceae| **CHICORY**; *sigorei* (Afrikaans) ■ The plant is an exotic herb from Europe and Asia that has become naturalised in southern Africa. It is cultivated commercially in the Eastern Cape Province for the fleshy, carrot-like roots, used to produce the well-known coffee substitute chicory (see Chapter 6). Root infusions are taken as general tonics, to stimulate appetite and to alleviate digestive disturbances.

Torchwood tree (*Balanites maughamii*)

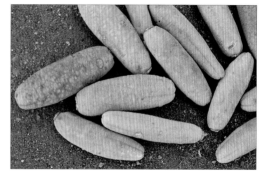

Edible fruits of the torchwood tree (*Balanites maughamii*)

Karmedik or *tuinkarmedik* (*Centaurea benedicta*)

Centella asiatica under cultivation

Leaves of *Centella asiatica*

Flower heads of the chicory plant (*Cichorium intybus*)

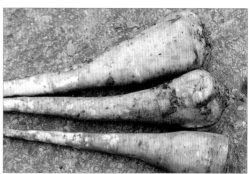

Roots of commercial chicory (*Cichorium intybus*)

Dicoma anomala | Asteraceae | **HLOENYA** (Sotho); *maagwortel, maagbitterwortel, kalwerwortel* (Afrikaans); *inyongana* (Xhosa); *isihlabamakhondlwane, umuna* (Zulu) ■ The plant is a grassland species with woody roots, dark green leaves that are typically white-hairy below and attractive mauve, thistle-like flower heads. In Zimbabwe, South Africa and Lesotho it has a great reputation as a panacea. Fresh and dry root, or root decoctions and tinctures are taken orally to treat fever, coughs, colds, sore throats, colic, abdominal pain, diarrhoea, dysentery, constipation and intestinal worms. It is used to treat gonorrhoea and other venereal diseases, and as a purgative in the treatment of haemorrhoids. Pneumonia is treated by taking the powdered root orally with porridge, and the root is believed to be a cardiac tonic and good for the circulation. A decoction of the root has been given to children for unspecified "blood diseases", and preparations are applied topically to treat toothache and ringworm (see Chapter 10).

Dicoma capensis | Asteraceae | **KOORSBOSSIE**, *wilde karmedik, vyfpondbos* (Afrikaans) ■ This common plant of the Karoo region is a short-lived perennial herb with trailing branches bearing silvery leaves and small, thistle-like flower heads. It is one of the most popular Karoo medicinal plants and is taken for fever, colds and influenza, and for hypertension, diarrhoea and cancer.

Dicoma schinzii | Asteraceae | **KALAHARI FEVER BUSH**; *Kalahari koorsbossie, vaalplatblaar* (Afrikaans) ■ The plant is closely similar to *Dicoma capensis* but has a more upright growth habit and is found mainly in the Kalahari region. The local San people use *Dicoma schinzii* to treat coughs and sore throats, and febrile convulsions in infants.

The power of mythology in perpetuating oral-traditional knowledge is vividly demonstrated in the story of "the shadow of the black-shouldered kite". According to this story, if the shadow of a black-shouldered kite falls on a baby, the baby will start behaving like the bird – arms will swing about wildly, mimicking the rapid fluttering movements of the bird as it hovers above its prey. It is also said that there will be tell-tale signs of feathers starting to develop on the baby's arms and body. *Dicoma schinzii* is used to treat this condition: a decoction is given internally to stop the arm movements, and is also applied topically to stop the feathers from growing. The full significance of the story only becomes apparent when one realises that in African mythology, fever is often associated with birds (human temperature is 37.4 degrees centigrade, while that of birds is typically between 39 and 41 degrees centigrade) so that a bird always feels warm to the touch, almost as if it has a fever. The story becomes even more interesting when one realises that other species of *Dicoma* (*D. anomala*, *D. capensis*) are commonly known as fever remedies (hence the common name *koorsbos*) in other parts of southern Africa. So the Kalahari *koorsbos* will indeed stop the arm movements (febrile convulsions) by reducing the fever, and the topical use will prevent "feather growth" (probably referring to the gooseflesh of fever).

Glycyrrhiza glabra | Fabaceae | **LIQUORICE**, *licorice*; *southoutwortel* (Afrikaans) ■ See Chapter 6. The rhizomes, usually referred to as "roots", are harvested and have been used since ancient times as sweeteners and medicine. It is included as a component in many tonic mixtures. In the Western Cape, the plant has been used since early times for tuberculosis, coughs and appendicitis. It has escaped from cultivation and become a weed in parts of the Karoo. In Zulu it is known as *mlomo-mnandi*, literally "nice mouth", due to its sweetness. In modern times, liquorice and its derivatives are used as expectorants, laxatives, and for gastritis and peptic ulcers. Glycyrrhizin, the main saponin present, has demonstrated anti-inflammatory activity, and also weak antiviral, antibacterial, antihepatotoxic and immune-stimulating activity. The roots of the Cape-endemic *soethoutbossie* (*Rafnia amplexicaulis*) taste like liquorice, and were used as a liquorice substitute by the early settlers (Pappe 1868; Kinfe *et al.* 2015). In the Suid-Bokkeveld at Nieuwoudtville, the sweet-tasting young leaves are traditionally eaten as a general tonic to prevent people (especially women) from contracting colds and influenza (Koos Paulse, pers. comm.).

Hloenya or *maagwortel* (*Dicoma anomala*)

Koorsbossie or *wilde karmedik* (*Dicoma capensis*)

Dicoma schinzii is an important medicine in the Kalahari

Harpagophytum procumbens │Pedaliaceae│ **DEVIL'S CLAW**; *sengaparile* (Tswana); *duiwels-klou, kloudoring* (Afrikaans) ■ This is a perennial plant with annual stems spreading from a central tap root. The common names are derived from the claw-like fruit. The thick, fleshy secondary roots are the parts used medicinally.

The plant is traded worldwide, and it has a reputation for efficacy in osteoarthritis, fibrositis and rheumatism, and it is particularly effective in small joint disease. Devil's claw is taken as a bitter tonic to stimulate the appetite and for indigestion. Taken in the form of infusions and decoctions, tinctures and extracts, it is used for many health conditions, including diabetes (Isaac Mayeng, pers. comm.), hypertension, gout and peptic ulcers. It is taken for fever and as an important tonic in infectious diseases, including tuberculosis (Matambo, pers. comm.). Taken on a regular daily basis, it has a subtle laxative effect. Small doses are used for menstrual cramps, and in higher doses to assist in expelling a retained placenta. It is also used post-partum as an analgesic, and to keep the uterus contracted (see Chapter 10). The dry, powdered tuber is used directly as a wound-dressing, or it is mixed with animal fat or petroleum jelly (e.g. Vaseline) to make wound-healing and burn-healing ointments. Commercial ointments and creams are applied topically for minor muscle aches and pains, and to painful joints.

The iridoids harpagoside, harpagide and procumbide have analgesic and anti-inflammatory activity, and, together with phytosterols such as β-sitosterol, may be responsible for some of the efficacy of devil's claw. Clinical studies support its use in painful joint conditions (Lecomte & Costa 1992) and low backache (Chrubasik 1996). Serum cholesterol and uric acid levels were also found to be reduced (Brady *et al*. 1981; Mncwangi *et al*. 2012).

Devil's claw has become a medicinal plant of international importance, with approximately 500 tons being traded annually, almost solely from wild-harvested material. With the increasing interest in the therapeutic potential of this plant, there is a danger of over-exploitation of wild resources. A number of private initiatives in Namibia and South Africa are successfully propagating the plant on a limited commercial scale in the interest of providing a sustainable supply of raw material, and also to control the quality of the raw material. The Agricultural Research Council of South Africa is investigating the feasibility of transferring propagation technologies to the small rural farmer in the interests of rural development.

Hypoxis hemerocallidea │Hypoxidaceae│ **INKOMFE** (Zulu); *lotsane* (Sotho); star-flower, "African potato"; *sterblom, "Afrika-aartappel"* (Afrikaans) ■ *Hypoxis* species are tuberous perennials with strap-like leaves and yellow, star-shaped flowers. The medicinal part is the tuberous rootstock (corm), which is brownish-black on the outside and yellow when freshly cut. Weak infusions and decoctions of the corm are used as convalescent and strengthening tonics in adults and children with wasting diseases (Ashley Mashigo, pers. comm.), including tuberculosis and cancer. These tonics are traditionally used three times daily for periods of up to a month. *Hypoxis* has been used traditionally for benign prostatic hypertrophy, urinary tract infections and testicular tumours (Albrecht 1996), and as a laxative and vermifuge. *Hypoxis* is also used to treat anxiety, palpitations and depression (Ashley Mashigo, pers. comm.), and there are a few anecdotal reports that fresh plant tinctures are helpful in rheumatoid arthritis. Ingestion of *Hypoxis colchicifolia* has been reported to cause delirium, and it has also been used to treat delirium (Watt & Breyer-Brandwijk 1962).

The traditional use of *Hypoxis hemerocallidea* for benign prostatic hypertrophy may be due to the sitosterols that decrease testosterone levels through inhibition of 5α-reductase, or by decreasing the binding of dihydrotestosterone within the prostate (Merck 1989; Bruneton 1995). It is interesting to note that pumpkin seed oil, high in phytosterols, is marketed in Europe for the treatment of benign prostatic hypertrophy (Bruneton 1995). Anecdotal evidence suggests that *Hypoxis* has anti-inflammatory and immune-modulatory activity, but there is as yet no convincing clinical evidence to support the use of the plant for immune stimulation or any potentially life-threatening diseases.

TONIC PLANTS

Flowers of devil's claw (*Harpagophytum procumbens*)

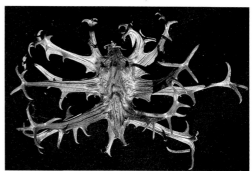

Fruit of devil's claw (*Harpagophytum procumbens*)

Devil's claw (*Harpagophytum procumbens*) under cultivation

Flowers of *inkomfe*, nowadays called "African potato" (*Hypoxis hemerocallidea*)

Flowering plant of *inkomfe* (*Hypoxis hemerocallidea*)

Tubers (corms) of *Hypoxis hemerocallidea*

Lessertia frutescens (=*Sutherlandia frutescens*) |Fabaceae| **CANCER BUSH**, sutherlandia; *kankerbos, belbos, gansies, jantjie-bêrend* (Afrikaans); *'musa-pelo* (Sotho); *pethola* (Tswana); *insiswa, unwele* (Xhosa, Zulu) ■ Cancer bush is an attractive shrub about a metre in height, with silvery leaves, red flowers and balloon-like pods. The widely distributed subsp. *frutescens* has a small, often spreading growth form and ovoid pods, while subsp. *microphylla* is a taller, erect plant with oblong pods that occurs mainly in the Great Karoo. Traditionally no distinction is made between the various subspecies or varieties of *Lessertia frutescens* for medicinal purposes, and these plants are among the most multi-purpose and useful of the medicinal plants in southern Africa. Tinctures, infusions and decoctions of the leaves and young stems of the two species have been used in the Cape from early times, the uses learned originally from the Khoi and San (Smith 1888; Van Wyk & Albrecht 2008). It is also traditionally used in Xhosa, Sotho, Tswana and Zulu herbal medicine.

Lessertia frutescens is regarded as the African adaptogen *par excellence*. Conditions that have been treated with this plant include fever, poor appetite, indigestion, gastritis, oesophagitis, peptic ulcer, dysentery, cancer (prevention and treatment), diabetes, colds and influenza, coughs, asthma, chronic bronchitis, kidney and liver conditions, rheumatism, heart failure, urinary tract infections, and stress and anxiety. Sutherlandia preparations are taken on a chronic basis when necessary, but should not be taken during pregnancy, as teratogenicity and abortions are known to have occurred (Dawid & Mrs Bester, pers. comm.).

There are a few strongly supported, recent anecdotes where cancer bush appeared to be of significant benefit in treating pancreatic and other cancers, and improved the quality of life in patients with terminal metastatic breast cancer, and for the pain and inflammation associated with rheumatoid arthritis. Ongoing research is revealing possible mechanisms of action but unfortunately no clinical studies have yet been undertaken.

A number of highly active compounds, including canavanine, pinitol and the amino acid GABA occur in high quantities in *Lessertia* species, and suggest that there is indeed a scientific basis to some of the folk uses for serious medical conditions. *L*-canavanine is a potent *L*-arginine antagonist that has documented anticancer (Swaffar *et al.* 1995; Crooks & Rosenthal 1994) and antiviral activity, including use against the influenza virus and retroviruses (Green 1988). Canavanine is an inhibitor of nitric oxide synthase, and may be beneficial in certain forms of heart failure (Liaudet *et al.* 1996). Pinitol is a known antidiabetic agent (Narayanan *et al.* 1987) that may also have an application in treating wasting in cancer and AIDS (Ostlund & Sherman 1996).

GABA is an inhibitory neurotransmitter that could account for the use of both *Lessertia frutescens* subsp. *frutescens* and *L. frutescens* subsp. *microphylla* for anxiety and stress. The seeds and leaves of *L. frutescens* have been smoked by labourers and teenagers as a *dagga* substitute in Namaqualand, and some farmers have removed it from their land as a result (Fiona Archer, Lita Cole & Dawid Bester, pers. comm.). The leaves of the Karoo form of *Lessertia frutescens* (formerly known as *Sutherlandia microphylla*) are sedative when smoked, and in several samples from different species and varieties, we found high concentrations of GABA. The first plantations were established by Mrs Winnifred Grobler and Mr Ulrich Feiter, followed in recent years by several growers in various parts of southern Africa. Suitable chemotypes have been selected (but this process is ongoing) and the first commercial products have become available in recent years.

Dawid Bester and Mrs Bester are thanked for providing detailed information on folk uses.

Muraltia heisteria |Polygalaceae| ***PERSBLOMMETJIE*** (Afrikaans) ■ The plant is a sparse, spiny, fynbos shrublet of up to one metre in height. The small pink or purple flowers are quite attractive and may be present for several months. Flowering twigs are used as an appetite stimulant in Nieuwoudtville in the Northern Cape Province of South Africa (Willem Steenkamp, pers. comm.).

TONIC PLANTS

The inflated pods of the cancer bush (*Lessertia frutescens*)

Flowers of cancer bush (*Lessertia frutescens*)

Plantation of cancer bush (*Lessertia frutescens*)

Flowering stems of the *persblommetjie* (*Muraltia heisteria*)

Vernonia amygdalina |Asteraceae| **BITTER LEAF** ■ The leaves have been reported to be eaten as a vegetable by the Pedi in South Africa (Watt & Breyer-Brandwijk 1962). In spite of its bitter taste (known locally as "bitter leaf"), it is widely appreciated as a vegetable in West Africa. In Nigeria, leaves are boiled in soups, and used as a vegetable relish, while in Cameroon the processed leaves are cooked with meat and/or prawns mixed with ground peanuts to make a famous dish called *ndole*. The production of *Vernonia amygdalina* in Cameroon in 1998 was estimated to be 21 549 tons (Smith & Eyzaguirre 2007). Laboratory studies have shown that *Vernonia amygdalina* has many functional activities of potential health application, including analgesic and antimalarial (Njan *et al.* 2008), antidiabetic (Ong *et al.* 2011), lipid-lowering (Nwanjo 2005), antihypertensive (Taiwo *et al.* 2010) and anthelmintic (Adeolu 2007) activities.

Vernonia oligocephala |Asteraceae| ***GROENAMARABOSSIE*** (Afrikaans); *mofolotsane* (Sotho) ■ The bitter leaves and flowering stems are taken as a general health tonic and appetite stimulant, and to treat general malaise, abdominal pain, diarrhoea, dysentery, rheumatism, constipation and colitis. The plant has traditionally been used for diabetes, and antidiabetic activity has been scientifically confirmed (Dr T.G. Fourie, pers. comm.). The *groenamarabossie* should not be confused with *groenamara* (*Artemisia absinthium*), a cultivated plant of European origin that has become an important part of Cape herbal medicine.

Warburgia salutaris |Canellaceae| ***ISIBHAHA*** (Zulu); *mulanga, manaka* (Venda); *shibaha* (Tsonga); pepperbark tree; *peperbasboom* (Afrikaans) ■ This tree is one of the great tonics and panaceas of southern Africa – its specific name *salutaris* means "salutary to health". The bark is generally used, and it is usually taken orally in a powdered form, or as infusions and decoctions. The inner bark is extremely pungent, hence the English common name pepperbark tree. *Warburgia* is used as a tonic for all health conditions, including fever, malaria, colds and influenza, as an expectorant in coughs, as a natural antibiotic to treat chest infections productive of purulent sputum (Solomon Mahlaba, pers. comm.), for venereal diseases, and for abdominal pain and constipation. It has been used to treat cancer (Isaac Mayeng, pers. comm.), rheumatism and stomach ulcers, is applied topically to cuts on the temples for headache, and has been used as an aphrodisiac.

Due to its popularity it has been severely over-harvested in South Africa, with most of the bark on the South African street markets now coming from Mozambique. Propagation programmes have demonstrated that the tree can be successfully mass-propagated, and extension work is being planned to enable the small-scale farmer to grow the trees for local use and as a cash-crop (Tony Balfour Cunningham, pers. comm.).

The bark contains numerous drimane sesquiterpenoids such as warburganal and polygodial, which have both shown profound anticandidal activity (Napralert database). Polygodial is potentially useful in clinical medicine as an adjunct to treatment with antibiotics and antifungals which have poor membrane permeability (Iwu 1993). *Warburgia* should never be taken during pregnancy as warburganal is a potent cytotoxic substance (Fukuyama *et al.* 1982) and *Warburgia* has been used as an abortifacient in Zimbabwe (Gelfand *et al.* 1985).

Withania somnifera |Solanaceae| ***UBUVIMBHA*** (Zulu); *ubuvuma* (Xhosa); *bofepha* (Sotho); *geneesblaarbossie* (Afrikaans); winter cherry, Indian ginseng ■ *Withania* is an adaptogenic tonic *par excellence*, with well-established and extensive use in southern Africa and in India. It is an important component of the Ayurvedic pharmacopoeia of India where it is known as *ashwaghanda*, and is regarded as the "Indian ginseng". *Withania* is rapidly becoming known and appreciated in industrialised countries. Infusions, decoctions and tinctures of the fresh and dry whole root are used, and with larger woody roots, only the soft outer cortex is used. Leaf poultices are widely used externally in southern Africa to treat wounds, open cuts, abscesses and haemorrhoids. Ointments are also made from the leaves, using fat or oil.

Bitter leaf (*Vernonia amygdalina*)

Flower heads of the bitter leaf (*Vernonia amygdalina*)

Shrub of *groenamarabossie* (*Vernonia oligocephala*)

Leaves and flower heads of the *groenamarabossie* (*Vernonia oligocephala*)

In southern Africa, *Withania* is taken for fever, colds and influenza, asthma, general ill health and debility, any infections, syphilis, abdominal discomfort, diarrhoea, typhus, typhoid, proctitis, worms, and as a sedative and hypnotic. It is also taken as an aphrodisiac; is used for women's health (see Chapter 10); applied topically for many skin conditions; and is also used for animal health. In other countries, *Withania* has folk uses as a tonic, sedative, hypnotic, amoebicide and antispasmodic; it is taken for cancer, candida, coughs, colds, bronchitis, asthma, diarrhoea, dyspepsia, general debility, inflammation, rheumatism, tuberculosis, syphilis and typhoid (Duke 1987).

The plant is chemically very complex, and more than 80 compounds are known from it (Dictionary of Natural Products 1996), including withanolides, which are of particular interest. Anti-inflammatory, antibiotic, sedative and hypnotic properties have been described. Although both immuno-suppressing and immuno-stimulating effects have been described for isolated withanolides, aqueous extracts of the actual roots have an immuno-stimulatory effect (Iwu 1993). Laboratory and clinical studies have found that *Withania* improves anxiety and mild to moderate depression, and has anticancer, anti-stress, anti-ageing and adaptogenic activity. It appears to have memory-enhancing as well as antioxidant and anti-inflammatory activity (Katiyar *et al.* 1997).

In Ayurvedic medicine, *Withania* is used for many conditions, including the treatment of fatigue, fever and asthma, and improving overall health. It is also used as a "brain tonic" in geriatric patients, and to help with learning and memory retention in the general population (Iwu 1993). A clinical study has shown that *Withania* can improve some measures of cognitive function (Pingali *et al.* 2014), and a number of human clinical studies have concluded that treatment with *Withania* resulted in greater score improvements (significantly in most cases) than placebo in outcomes on anxiety or stress scales (Pratte *et al.* 2014).

Ziziphus mucronata |Rhamnaceae| **MOKGALO** (Sotho, Tswana); buffalo-thorn ∎ This is a small to medium-sized tree with a wide-spreading crown and rough bark. Sharp thorns are present in pairs on the twigs – the one straight; the other curved. The leaves are bright green and shiny, with three main veins arising from the base. The small, yellowish-green flowers develop into reddish-brown, edible berries of about 10 millimetres in diameter, which are used in some parts to brew beer. The roots, bark and leaves of the tree are widely used in traditional medicine to treat diarrhoea, dysentery, coughs, chest problems and other ailments. Infusions and decoctions of the roots are considered to be a panacea in Zimbabwe.

REFERENCES AND FURTHER READING: Adeolu, A. 2007. Assessment of the anthelmintic efficacy of an aqueous crude extract of *Vernonia amygdalina. Pharmaceutical Biology* 45(7): 564–568. **Albrecht, C.F. 1996.** Hypoxoside as a putative nontoxic, multi-functional prodrug for the treatment of certain cancers, HIV-infection and inflammatory conditions. Lecture presented at the IOCD International Symposium, 25 to 28 February 1996, Victoria Falls, Zimbabwe. **Anonymous. 1993.** *Kruierate van die Montagu Museum.* 2nd ed. Montagu Museum, Montagu. **Anonymous. 1996.** *Centella asiatica* (Gotu kola). *American Journal of Natural Medicine* 3(6): 22–25. **Asthana, R. & Raina, M.K. 1989.** Pharmacology of *Withania somnifera* – A review. *Indian Drugs* 26(5): 199–205. **Awang, DVC. 1998.** Gotu Kola. *Canadian Pharmaceutical Pharmaceutical Journal* 1998; 131(7): 42–46. **Brady, L.R. *et al.* 1981.** *Pharmacognosy.* 8th ed. Lea & Febiger, Philadelphia. **Bruneton, J. 1995.** *Pharmacognosy, phytochemistry, medicinal plants.* Intercept, Hampshire. **Cawston, F.G. 1933.** Native Medicines in Natal. *S.A. Med. J.*, 10 June 1933: 370–371. **Chen, W., Van Wyk, B.-E., Vermaak, I. & Viljoen, A.M. 2012.** Cape aloes – A review of the phytochemistry, pharmacology and commercialization of *Aloe ferox. Phytochemistry Letters* 5(1): 1–12. **Chrubasik, S. *et al.* 1996.** Effectiveness of *Harpagophytum procumbens* in treatment of acute low back pain. *Phytomedicine* 3: 1–10. **Crooks, P.A. & Rosenthal, G.A. 1994.** Use of *L*-canavanine as a chemotherapeutic agent for the treatment of pancreatic cancer. United States Patent 5,552,440. Filed December 5, 1994. **Duke, J.A. 1987.** *Handbook of medicinal herbs.* CRC Press, Florida. **Forbes, V.S. (ed.) 1986.** *Carl Peter Thunberg: Travels at the Cape of Good Hope 1772–1775.* Van Riebeeck Society, Cape Town. **Fukuyama, Y. *et al.* 1982.** A potent cytotoxic warburganal and related drimane-type sesquiterpenoids from *Polygonum hydropiper. Phytochemistry* 21: 2895–2898. **Gelfand, M. *et al.* 1985.** *The traditional medical practitioner in Zimbabwe.* Mambo Press, Harare. **Green, M.H. 1988.** Method of treating viral infections with amino acid analogs. United States Patent 5,110,600. Filed January 25, 1988. **Hutchings, A. & Van Staden, J. 1994.** Plants used for stress-related ailments in traditional Zulu, Xhosa and Sotho medicine. Part 1: Plants used for headaches. *J. Ethnopharmacol.* 43: 89–124. **Hutchings, A., Scott, A.H., Lewis, G. & Cunningham, A. 1996.** *Zulu medicinal plants.* Natal University Press, Pietermaritzburg. **Iwu, M.M. 1993.** *Handbook of African medicinal plants.* CRC Press, Boca Raton. **Jäger, A.K. *et al.* 1996.**

Flowering branch of the pepperbark tree or *isibhaha* (*Warburgia salutaris*)

Fruiting plant of *geneesblaarbossie* or *ubuvhimba* (*Withania somnifera*)

Bark of *Warburgia salutaris*

Roots of *Withania somnifera*

Screening of Zulu medicinal plants for prostaglandin-synthesis inhibitors. *J. Ethnopharmacol*. 52: 95–100. **Katiyar, C.K.** *et al*. **1997.** Immunomodulator products from Ayurveda: Current status and future perspectives. In: Upadhyay, S.N. (ed.), *Immunomodulation*. Narosa Publishing House, New Delhi. **Kinfe, H., Long, H.S., Stander, M. & Van Wyk, B.-E. 2015.** The ethnobotany and major flavonoids of *Rafnia amplexicaulis*, a poorly known Cape herbal tea and liquorice substitute. *S. Afr. J. Bot*. 100: 75–79. **Lecomte, A. & Costa, J.P. 1992.** *Harpagophytum* dans l'arthrose: Etude en double insu contre placebo. *Le Magazine* 15: 27–30. **Leung, A.Y. & Foster, S. 1996.** *Encyclopedia of common natural ingredients used in food, drugs, and cosmetics*. John Wiley & Sons, New York. **Liaudet, L.** *et al*. **1996.** Beneficial effects of *L*-canavanine, a selective inhibitor of inducible nitric oxide synthase, during rodent endotoxaemia. *Clin. Sci*. 90(5): 369. **Long, H.S., Stander M.A. & Van Wyk, B.-E. 2012.** Notes on the occurrence and significance of triterpenoids (asiaticoside and related compounds) and caffeoylquinic acids in *Centella* species. *S. Afr. J. Bot*. 82: 53–59. **Mabogo, D.E.N. 1990.** *The ethnobotany of the Vhavenda*. Unpublished M.Sc. thesis, University of Pretoria. **Magee, A.R., Van Wyk, B.-E. & Van Vuuren, S. 2007.** The ethnobotany and anti-microbial activity of sieketroos (*Arctopus echinatus*, Apiaceae). *S. Afr. J. Bot*. 73: 159–162. **Merck 1989.** *The Merck Index*, ed. 11. Merck, Rahway. **Mncwangi, N., Chen, W., Vermaak, I., Viljoen, A.M. & Gericke, N. 2012.** Devil's claw – a review of the ethnobotany, phytochemistry and biological activity of *Harpagophytum procumbens*. *J. Ethnopharmacol*. 143: 755–771. **Moteetee, A.N. & Van Wyk, B.-E. 2007.** The concept of 'Musa-pelo and the medicinal use of shrubby legumes (Fabaceae) in Lesotho. *Bothalia* 37: 75–77. **Mzamane, G.I.M. 1945.** Some medicinal, edible and magical plants used by some Bantu tribes in South Africa. *Fort Hare Pap*. 1: 29–35. **Narayanan, R.** *et al*. **1987.** Pinitol – A new anti-diabetic compound from the leaves of *Bougainvillea spectabilis*. *Current Science* 56(3): 139–141. **Neuwinger, H.D. 1996.** *African ethnobotany: poisons and drugs: chemistry, pharmacology, toxicology*. Chapman & Hall, Germany. **Newall, C.A.** *et al*. **1996.** *Herbal medicines: a guide for health-care professionals*. The Pharmaceutical Press, London. **Njan, A.A., Adzu, B., Agaba, A.G., Byarugaba, D., Díaz-Llera, S. & Bangsberg, D.R. 2008.** The analgesic and antiplasmodial activities and toxicology of *Vernonia amygdalina*. *Journal of Medicinal Food* 11(3): 574–581. **Nwanjo, H.U. 2005.** Efficacy of aqueous leaf extract of *Vernonia amygdalina* on plasma lipoprotein and oxidative status in diabetic rat models. *Niger J. Physiol. Sci*. 20(1–2): 39–42. **O'Brien, C., Van Wyk, B.-E. & Van Heerden, F.R. 2011.** Physical and chemical characteristics of *Aloe ferox* leaf gel. *S. Afr. J. Bot*. 77(4): 988–995. **Olivier, D.K. & Van Wyk, B.-E. 2013.** Bitterness values for traditional tonic plants of southern Africa. *J. Ethnopharmacol*. 147: 676–679. **Olivier, D., Van Wyk, B.-E. & Van Heerden, F.R.** 2008. The chemotaxonomic and medicinal significance of phenolic acids in *Arctopus* and *Alepidea* (Apiaceae subfamily Saniculoideae). *Biochem. Syst. Ecol*. 36: 724–729. **Ong, K.W., Hsu, A., Song, L., Huang, D. & Tan, B.K.H. 2011.** Polyphenols-rich *Vernonia amygdalina* shows anti-diabetic effects in streptozotocin-induced diabetic rats. *J. Ethnopharmacol*. 133 (2): 598–607. **Ostlund, R.E. & Sherman, W.R. 1996.** Pinitol and derivatives thereof for the treatment of metabolic disorders. US Patent 5,8827,896 Filed March 4, 1996. **Pappe, L. 1847.** *A list of South African indigenous plants used as remedies by the colonists of the Cape of Good Hope*. O.I. Pike, Cape Town. **Pappe, L. 1850.** *Florae Capensis Medicae Prodromus*. A.S. Robertson, Cape Town. **Pappe, L. 1857.** *Florae Capensis Medicae Prodromus*, 2nd ed. W. Britain, Cape Town. **Pappe, L. 1868.** *Florae Capensis Medicae Prodromus*, 3rd ed. W. Britain, Cape Town. **Pingali, U., Pilli, R. & Fatima, N. 2014.** Effect of standardized aqueous extract of *Withania somnifera* on tests of cognitive and psychomotor performance in healthy human participants. *Pharmacognosy Research* 6(1):12–18. **Ponglux, D.** *et al*. **(eds) 1987.** *Medicinal plants*. The first Princess Chulabhorn Science Congress, Bangkok, Thailand. **Pratte, M.A., Nanavati, K.B., Young, V. & Morley, C.P. 2014.** An alternative treatment for anxiety: a systematic review of human trial results reported for the Ayurvedic herb ashwagandha (*Withania somnifera*). *The Journal of Alternative and Complementary Medicine* 20(12): 901–908. **Pujol, J. 1990.** *Naturafrica – the herbalist handbook*. Jean Pujol Natural Healers Foundation, Durban. **Smith, A. 1888.** *A contribution to the South African materia medica*, 2nd ed. Lovedale, South Africa. **Smith, C.A. 1966.** Common names of South African plants. *Mem. Bot. Surv. S. Afr*. 35. **Smith, F.I. & Eyzaguirre, P. 2007.** African leafy vegetables: their role in the WHO global fruit and vegetable initiative. *African Journal of Food Agriculture Nutrition and Development*, Vol. 7, No. 3: 1–17. **Standards South Africa, 2007.** *South African National Standard. Aloe raw material*. SANS 368: 2007, 1st ed. Standards South Africa, Pretoria. **Suliman, S., Van Vuuren, S.F. & Viljoen, A.M. 2010.** Validating the *in vitro* antimicrobial activity of *Artemisia afra* in polyherbal combinations to treat respiratory infections. *S. Afr. J. Bot*. 76: 655–661. **Swaffar, D.S.** *et al*. **1995.** Combination therapy with 5-fluorouracil and *L*-canavanine: in-vitro and in-vivo studies. *Anti-cancer Drugs* 6(4): 586–593. **Taiwo, I.A., Odeigah, P.G.C., Jaja, S. & Mojiminiyi, F. 2010.** Cardiovascular effects of *Vernonia amygdalina* in rats and the implications for treatment of hypertension in diabetes. *Researcher* 2(1): 76–79. **Van den Eynden, V.** *et al*. **1992.** *The ethnobotany of the Topnaar*. Universiteit Gent, Gent. **Van Wyk, B.-E.** *et al*. **1997.** *Medicinal plants of South Africa*. Briza Publications, Pretoria. **Van Wyk, B.-E., Van Oudtshoorn, B. & Gericke, N. 2009.** *Medicinal plants of South Africa*. Revised and expanded 2nd ed. Briza Publications, Pretoria. **Van Wyk, B.-E. & Albrecht, A. 2008.** A review of the taxonomy, ethnobotany, chemistry and pharmacology of *Sutherlandia frutescens* (Fabaceae). *J. Ethnopharmacol*. 119: 620–629. **Van Wyk, B.-E. & Gericke, N. 2000.** *People's plants – A guide to useful plants of Southern Africa*. Briza Publications, Pretoria. **Venter, F. 1997.** *Botanical survey of the medicinal plants of the Northern Sotho, Northern Province, South Africa*. Land management and rural development programme, University of the North. **Von Koenen, E. 1996.** *Heil, Gift- und Essbare Pflanzen in Namibia*. Klaus Hess Verlag, Göttingen. **Von Koenen, E. 2001.** *Medicinal, poisonous and edible plants in Namibia*. Klaus Hess Publishers, Windhoek and Göttingen. **Watt, J.M. & Breyer-Brandwijk, M.G. 1962.** *The medicinal and poisonous plants of southern and eastern Africa*, 2nd ed. Livingstone, London. **Weiss, R.F. 1988.** *Herbal medicine*. AB Arcanum, Gothenberg, Sweden. **Youthed, G. (ed.) no date.** *Dictionary of South African traditional medicinal plants of the Eastern Cape*. Pharmaceutical Society of South Africa, Johannesburg (unpublished).

Trees of buffalo-thorn (*Ziziphus mucronata*)

Leaves and fruits of buffalo-thorn (*Ziziphus mucronata*)

Smoking the bone pipe

CHAPTER 9
Mind & mood plants

IT IS LIKELY that psychotropic plants (plants with an effect on the mind) have been used by man since the earliest prehistoric times to relieve physical and psychological pain and discomfort, to treat disease, to enhance sociability and sexuality, to provide mental alertness and physical endurance for hunting, to aid in divination, to facilitate communication with ancestors and deities, and to mediate a mystical participation with Nature. Psychotropes are still used by all societies, even though some, including coffee, tea, cola, chocolate and alcohol are so much part of the modern sociocultural landscape that they are not generally considered the psychoactive drugs they indeed are.

With the development of increasingly elegant analytical techniques and biological assays, the mechanisms and sites of action of psychoactive chemicals are increasingly being elucidated. It has been found, for example, that the potent analgesic alkaloid morphine, isolated from the opium poppy (*Papaver somniferum*), acts on specific receptors in the human nervous system, and this in turn led to the remarkable discovery that the body produces its own opiate-like painkillers called endorphins. Likewise it has been found that cannabinoids, from *dagga* (*Cannabis sativa*), act on specific cannabinoid receptors in the brain, and that the body produces its own cannabinoid, called anandamide.

Psychoactive drug use and abuse is a dynamic phenomenon with potentially harmful effects resulting from use outside the social and cultural controls that evolved in the areas of original use. The social acceptance or tolerance of use of psychoactive plants, or the condemnation and prohibition of use, is often culturally determined. The customary use of the stimulant *Catha edulis* (khat, bushman's tea), for example, is an integral part of Yemeni life, but possession and trading in this plant has been prohibited in many countries. Coca leaves (*Erythroxylum coca*), the source of cocaine, were regarded as a divine gift by the indigenous people of the Peruvian Andes, who chewed the leaf for endurance and freedom from hunger in a harsh physical environment. The use of chewed coca leaves in a particular context, however, is completely unlike the urban habit of smoking or snorting pure cocaine, which is highly addictive and damaging.

The true extent of the use of psychoactive plants in southern Africa, and the context of this use, is not yet appreciated or understood. With the rapid pace of acculturation much of the original knowledge of the use of psychotropic plants has become fragmentary, with extant magical or charm uses sometimes the only remaining clue. Many African psychoactive plants undoubtedly await rediscovery, and scientific studies of these plants are likely to reveal new psychoactive molecules, novel mechanisms of action, and the potential to develop effective new drugs for the treatment of pain, migraine, epilepsy, depression, schizophrenia and other mental health conditions. Magic and ritual are associated with psychoactive plants but are poorly understood. Recent books by Dold & Cocks (2012) and Zukulu *et al.* (2012) provide fascinating glimpses into these subjects.

The first published review of southern African plants with potential for the treatment of mental health conditions dates back to Watt (1967). The topic was introduced in the previous edition of this book (Van Wyk & Gericke 2000). Some southern African species were also included in a global review of mind-altering plants by Wink & Van Wyk (2008), including monographs on *Boophone disticha*, *Catha edulis, Dioscorea dregeana, Mesembryanthemum tortuosum* and *Withania somnifera*. A more comprehensive inventory and review was that of Sobiecki (2002) who listed 306 plants, representing 94 plant families, with psychoactive uses in southern Africa. A comprehensive review of the subject was also presented by Stafford *et al.* (2008). Another paper (Sobiecki 2012) highlighted the role of the traditional category of psychoactive plants known as *ubulawu*, including *Silene undulata* (=*S. capensis*), which are used in the training and initiation of southern African diviners.

Alepidea amatymbica | Apiaceae | ***IKHATHAZO*** (Xhosa, Zulu); *iqwili* (Xhosa); *lesoko* (Sotho) ■
The plant is a perennial herb with leaves and flowering stalks emerging annually from a woody, resinous rootstock. The leaf bases are gradually tapering towards the stalks. The small, white flowers are typically encircled by a halo of bracts, so that they superficially resemble the flower heads of daisies (Asteraceae). The small, dry fruits are only a few millimetres in diameter. The related *Alepidea cordifolia* has the basal leaves heart-shaped, with an abrupt division between the leaf stalk and leaf blade. This recently described species has been confused with *A. amatymbica* for a long time and has become the most widely used and traded species. Rhizomes are almost invariably available at muthi markets. Most of the recorded uses of *Alepidea amatymbica* actually apply to *A. cordata* (Van Wyk *et al.* 2008). It is distributed from southern KwaZulu-Natal northwards throughout Lesotho and the Free State to Zimbabwe. True *Alepidea amatymbica* occurs only in the Eastern Cape and southern KwaZulu-Natal.

According to Dold & Cocks (2012), the name *ikhathazo* is derived from *inkathazo*, meaning trouble or difficulty. The implication is that the plant has the power to overcome difficulty. *Alepidea macowani* is also sometimes used, but has become quite rare. It is found only in the Eastern Cape Province and can be distinguished by the deeply serrated leaf edge – each serration has two or three large teeth.

In Lesotho and the Free State Province, *Alepidea amatymbica* and *A. cordifolia* (called *lesoko*) and *A. pilifera* and *A. setifera* (called *lesokwana*) are similarly used (Moffett 2010).

Rhizomes and roots may be chewed or decoctions are widely used to treat colds and chest complaints. The dry rhizome and roots are also smoked, or powdered and taken as a snuff by diviners and healers to assist in divination and communication with the ancestors. Smoking the roots results in mild sedation and vivid dreams. Elderly people powder the dry rhizome and take it as a snuff, or smoke the roots for headache (Patricia Hans, pers. comm.). The rhizome is carried as a lucky charm, and is commonly used for colds, influenza and asthma.

Anacampseros rhodesiaca | Anacampserotaceae, formerly Portulacaceae | ■ See Chapter 6. The plant is a beer additive, and is reported to have hallucinogenic and narcotic activity (Karin Esler, pers. comm.; Gelfand 1985).

Areca catechu | Arecaceae or Palmae | **BETEL NUT**, areca nut ■ The betel nut is a graceful palm tree of up to 30 metres in height with bright orange-red fruits, each with a single nut enclosed in a fibrous husk. The tree probably came from Malaysia or the Philippines, but its exact country of origin is not known. After the outer husk of the betel nut is removed by hand, the seed (nut) is used for chewing (as a masticatory) in raw or in processed form. The nuts may be dried in the sun before storage or they may be sliced and then boiled before drying.

The product is popularly known as *pan* and is commonly sold at oriental markets in South Africa (Cassim Petker, Salaama Ameer, pers. comm.). *Pan* is actually the Hindustani name for the fresh or processed leaf of the betel vine in which the sliced betel nuts (*supari*) are rolled, together with some lime (*chuna*), a brown spicy liquid (*catha*) and spices, often cardamom or fennel. Nowadays, sweets, syrup or even tobacco may be added.

Betel chewing is an ancient social and cultural practice in Southeast Asia, comparable to smoking or chewing tobacco. The mouth and saliva of the chewer turns dark red. The red colour results from the oxidation of polyphenols in the nut. The endosperm of betel nut seeds contains fats, carbohydrates, proteins, tannins and several alkaloids that act as stimulants. Habitual use is associated with some forms of oral cancer. The stimulant effects are ascribed to pyridine alkaloids such as arecoline, which is known to act on muscarinic and nicotinic receptors. High doses result in hypotension, vasodilation, increased salivation and numerous other symptoms.

Leaves of *Alepidea amatymbica*

Leaves of *Alepidea cordifolia*

Flowers of *Alepidea cordifolia*

Ikhathazo, the rhizomes and roots of *Alepidea cordifolia*

Betel nut palm (*Areca catechu*)

Betel nuts, betel vine leaf and *chuna*

Boophone disticha | Amaryllidaceae | **BUSHMAN POISON BULB**; *gifbol* (Afrikaans); *incwadi* (Xhosa); *incotha* (Zulu); *leshoma* (Southern Sotho, Tswana); *muwandwe* (Shona) ■ *Boophone disticha* grows as a large bulb, partially above the ground, with countless papery bulb scales and a distinctive fan-shaped crown of leaves. The pink to red flowers are borne in a typical round cluster and are usually produced before the leaves. By the time the fruits are mature, the flower stalks have lengthened, so that the whole inflorescence (infrutescence) forms a globose "wheel" that detaches from the bulb and rolls around in the wind. In this way, the seeds can be dispersed over relatively large distances. The plant has a very wide distribution in Africa and occurs throughout the central and eastern parts of southern Africa. The correct generic name is *Boophone* but the plant has been known for a long time as *Boophane disticha*.

There is a second, relatively poorly known species of *Boophone*, namely *B. haemanthifolia* (Duncan *et al.* 2016). Although it probably has properties similar to those of *B. disticha*, there appears to be no evidence that *B. haemanthifolia* has ever been used in traditional medicine. This species has a limited distribution range and occurs from southern Namibia to the Cape west coast but also the Bokkeveld plateau, the eastern Cederberg and the Roggeveld plateau. The plants have brush-like flower clusters with white, cream or yellow flowers and they usually grow in large groups, whereas *B. disticha* typically occur as scattered solitary individuals.

Boophone disticha has a long history of use in southern Africa and is one of few species depicted in ancient rock engravings (Wilman 1933). It has also been traditionally used for mummification. The discovery of a 2 000-year-old Khoisan mummy in the Eastern Cape Province that was mummified in a thick layer of *Boophone* bulb scales (Binneman 1999) shows the ancient origins of its use.

This plant has a reputation as a powerful hallucinogen, and was also previously used as an arrow poison in former times. The plant is still sometimes used as a hallucinogen in male adolescent initiation rites, and in the initiation of diviners. Some diviners administer the bulb scales orally as a decoction or as an enema to patients to induce visual hallucinations that are interpreted. This phenomenon is sometimes called "the bioscope" or "the mirror" when the patient is seated in front of a white cloth or a mirror to await the onset of visions. These visions are interpreted as being actual past and future events, and in the realm of the ancestral spirits. Since a small overdose can be fatal, meticulous care has to be taken in preparing the remedy.

A weak decoction of the bulb scales is commonly administered as a profound sedative to violent, psychotic patients, and once the drug takes effect the patient no longer needs to be restrained, and can be given milder herbal remedies. The bulb is used extensively as a medicine, including use for headache, chest pain, abdominal pain and insomnia. The dry bulb scales are applied topically as an antiseptic and pain-relieving dressing after circumcision, and to painful joints, swellings, bruises, abscesses, sores, rashes, burns and septic wounds. Similar uses by the Xhosa people have also been described by Dold & Cocks (2012), who give fascinating insights into the rite of circumcision (*ulwaluko*) and several associated rituals.

At least 11 alkaloids have been isolated from the plant, including buphanidrine, undulatine, buphanisine, buphanimine and nerbowdine. These alkaloids are mainly neurotoxins and significant analgesic activity has been demonstrated in some of them. Many deaths have been documented from the use of *Boophone disticha* in South Africa and Zimbabwe. In spite of the real danger of fatal poisoning this species is still freely available on the urban muthi markets in major centres.

Some of the information on the traditional uses of *Boophone* comes from personal communications with Nathaniel Nondeyi, David Matthe, John Molefi Sekaja, Esiah Ntamane (pers. comm. to David Matthe) and Solomon Mahlaba.

Boscia albitrunca | Capparaceae | **SHEPHERD'S TREE** ■ See Chapter 6. The unripe fruit has been used in the past as an epilepsy remedy under the name "fructus similo".

Bushman poison bulb (*Boophone disticha*) in the Kalahari

Leafless flowering plant of bushman poison bulb (*Boophone disticha*)

Bushman poison bulb (*Boophone disticha*)

Bushman poison bulbs as they are sold on muthi markets

Cannabis sativa |Cannabinaceae| ***DAGGA*** (Afrikaans); marijuana (English); *umya* (Xhosa); *matokwane* (Sotho); *nsangu* (Zulu) ■ *Dagga* is an erect annual herb of up to four metres in height with characteristic leaves divided into several leaflets with toothed margins. Male and female flowers are borne on different plants. Two groups of cultivars are grown (recognised as two different subspecies): subsp. *sativa* has negligible psychoactivity and is primarily grown for fibre, for nutritious seeds used as a health food, for edible seed oil, and for extracts rich in cannabidiol (CBD); subsp. *indica* is richer in the psychoactive Δ^9-THC and other cannabinoids, and is used both as a medicine and as a mind-altering recreational drug. The resinous female flowering tops and adjacent leaves are the parts usually used, as these have the highest concentration of psychoactive substances. The small, white or yellowish resin glands are easily visible to the naked eye (see photograph).

The earliest record of the use of *Cannabis* as a medicine is in a Chinese pharmacopoeia dated to 2737 BC. It is believed to have been introduced to Africa by Arab traders. *Dagga* is widely smoked in southern Africa to induce a feeling of relaxation, well-being, sociability and euphoria. It is also used on occasion to induce a feeling of spirituality. It is less frequently eaten in the form of cookies. The nature of the intoxication varies widely, depending on previous experience, expectations, the quality of the plant material, the setting, and the simultaneous consumption of alcohol and other drugs. The psychotropic effect can be relaxation, euphoria, sedation or acute intoxication. Although many users are generally able to achieve a desired effect, an acute toxic psychosis can result from use. Habitual smoking of *dagga* can cause bronchitis, have negative effects on learning and short-term memory, and may be associated with an increased risk of schizophrenia in adolescents. The plant has a well-established use in indigenous and folk medicine, as a weak hot water infusion, for asthma, bronchitis, headache, migraine, epilepsy, pain, colds and influenza, coughs, insomnia, labour pains, hypertension and diabetes.

The body produces its own cannabinoids, including anandamide (derived from the Sanskrit word *ananda*, meaning "bliss"), which differentially bind to the cannabinoid receptors CB_1 and CB_2. A large number of cannabinoids from cannabis, including Δ^9-THC, cannabidiol, cannabinol, cannabigerol and Δ-caryophyllene, interact with either or both of these receptors, and with other components of the endocannabinoid system. In modern medicine the crude drug, extracts of the plant, and isolated cannabinoids are used for treating migraine, glaucoma, nausea from chemotherapy and pain; to improve appetite in patients with cancer, AIDS and anorexia; and for suppressing muscular spasms in multiple sclerosis. A recent phenomenon is the rapid growth in self-medication with cannabis extracts and oils rich in cannabidiol (CBD), typically with a relatively low content of the psychoactive Δ^9-THC, for anxiety, depression, stress, pain, insomnia and inflammatory conditions.

South Africa's *dagga* crop is a significant part of the rural economy, estimated to be worth at least R10 billion a year. Although the cultivation and possession of *dagga* is still illegal in South Africa, a recent judgement of the Western Cape High Court has ruled that it is unconstitutional to prevent people from growing and using cannabis in the privacy of their own homes. Internationally, the legal status of cannabis and extracts from cannabis is complex and changing rapidly. By July 2017, Uruguay had become the first country in the world to legalise the sale and recreational use of cannabis, 25 states in the USA had legalised the medical use of marijuana, and four states (Alaska, Colorado, Oregon and Washington) had legalised the recreational use of marijuana. The regulatory developments in the USA are confounded by the fact that cannabis remains a prohibited substance under federal law.

Cassine schinoides (=*Hartogiella schinoides*) |Celastraceae| **SPOONWOOD** ■ The leaf appears to have a stimulant activity similar to *Catha edulis* when chewed. Reported activities include chewing the leaf to quench thirst (probably to suppress thirst, as the leaf is astringent rather than quenching), to prevent fatigue and to suppress appetite. Habitual users are reported to have been very thin.

MIND & MOOD PLANTS

Female *dagga* plant (*Cannabis sativa*)

Female flowers of *Cannabis sativa* showing minute white glands

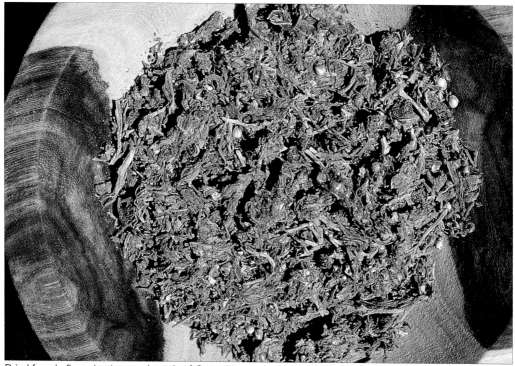

Dried female flowering tops and seeds of *Cannabis sativa*, known as *dagga*, *nsangu* or marijuana

Catha edulis | Celastraceae | ***KHAT*** (Arabic); bushman's tea; *boesmanstee* (Afrikaans); *igqwaka* (Xhosa); *mutsvahari* (Shona); *inandinandi* (Ndebele) ■ This small to medium-sized tree is widely distributed along the eastern parts of southern Africa, and further north to East Africa and south Yemen. The use of *Catha edulis* as a stimulant has been well described in East Africa and in Yemen, but it is not generally known that the plant is used in much the same way in parts of South Africa, including the Cathcart and Bolo districts in the Eastern Cape Province. The fresh, young leaves and adjacent soft stems are chewed for the energy and endurance they give the user, and for freedom from hunger and fatigue during strenuous work and walking in mountainous terrain. The slightly bitter and astringent leaves are chewed and the resulting juices swallowed. A sweet, liquorice-like aftertaste remains, accompanied by thirst. To the uninitiated, the stimulant effects are not immediately apparent, but with experience the unique psychotropic signature of the plant can be appreciated, including remarkable clarity of thought, alertness, a sense of well-being and increased sociability. Traditional uses of *Catha edulis* in the Eastern Cape Province were communicated by Manton Hirst (see also Hirst 1997). Some local users report that chewing fresh leaves was originally learned from hunter-gatherers. There is some evidence in the literature supporting this. The common English name is "bushman's tea", and tea is still occasionally brewed from the leaves but this almost certainly a colonial influence.

The fresh leaves are chewed, or an infusion of the leaves is taken orally for colds and influenza, coughs, asthma, to assist in losing weight and for menstrual cramps. Cold water infusions of the roots or bark are taken for diarrhoea and dysentery, and a root infusion is taken orally for male infertility, and to treat boils.

The stimulating effect of the fresh leaves is due to several phenethylamines, including cathinone which has amphetamine-like properties. Since cathinone is unstable, the preference for the use of fresh leaves can be understood. Prior to the isolation and identification of cathinone, it was believed that cathine [(±)-norpseudoephedrine], first isolated from *khat* in 1930, was the active principle. A synthetic salt of (±)-norpseudoephedrine is widely used as an over-the-counter appetite suppressant.

Side-effects of habitual use reported in the literature from Ethiopia, Somalia and Yemen, include the potential for the development of aggressive and paranoid behaviour, personality problems, hypertension, insomnia, constipation, low libido, emaciation and debilitating effects on family budgets. The incidence of these adverse phenomena, if indeed they occur in southern Africa, is unknown.

Cathinone has been added to the schedule of illicit drugs in the USA, and fresh *Catha edulis* itself is sold on the black market in the USA for about $30 a handful. The use of the plant in the USA is believed to be a result of the exposure of soldiers to *khat* during the US military involvement in Somalia where the plant is widely used as a stimulant.

Centella asiatica | Apiaceae | **PENNYWORT** ■ See Chapter 8. Dry, powdered leaf is taken as a snuff in South Africa. A calming, sedative effect is felt after about half an hour. *Centella asiatica* is a common ingredient in "brain tonics" in India. In laboratory studies, triterpenes from *Centella* have been demonstrated to have mild tranquillising, anti-stress and anti-anxiety action. *Centella* extracts have been found to have GABA antagonist activity.

Chenopodium ambrosioides or ***Dysphania ambrosioides*** | Amaranthaceae | ***INSUKUMBILE*** (Zulu); *rambos* (Afrikaans); *mokgankga* (Sotho) ■ Leaf infusions, a leaf rubbed on the face, and leaves burned and the smoke inhaled are used to treat insanity and convulsions. Leaf infusions are instilled into the vagina for uterine pain, and an ointment of the leaves is rubbed onto the body of an infant to treat a high fever. The plant is internationally well known as wormseed or Jesuit's tea (and as the popular culinary herb *epazote* of Mexican cuisine). It is nowadays included in the genus *Dysphania*.

Flowering tree of *Catha edulis*

Harvested leaves of *Catha edulis*

Manton Hirst (centre) with a leafy branch of *Catha edulis*

Cotyledon orbiculata |Crassulaceae| **PLAKKIE** (Afrikaans) ■ The plant is used in the treatment of epilepsy. The toxic principle, cotyledontoxin, has local anaesthetic effects, and acts as a central nervous system depressant. *Crassula arborescens*, a plant of the same family, is also used in the treatment of epilepsy.

Cullen obtusifolium |Fabaceae| **ROOIDAGGA**, *wildedagga, stinkklawer* (Afrikaans); *mojakubu* (Tswana); stink clover, wild lucerne (English); *!honab* (Nama) ■ This is a perennial herb with silvery toothed leaves and small, purple flowers. The leaves and stems are smoked in parts of the Kalahari as a tobacco and *dagga* substitute and have a sedative activity. A tea is drunk for the relief of abdominal pain.

Cussonia paniculata |Araliaceae| **HIGHVELD CABBAGE TREE** ■ A decoction of the leaf together with unspecified other plants is used to treat early mental disease. The leaves of *Schefflera umbellifera* (also Araliaceae) have been used to treat insanity.

Datura stramonium |Solanaceae| **COMMON THORN APPLE**; *gewone stinkblaar, malpitte* (Afrikaans); *ijoyi, umhlabavuthwa* (Xhosa); *iloyi, iloqi* (Zulu); *lethsowe* (Sotho); *lechoe* (Southern Sotho); *zaba-zaba* (Tsonga) ■ Species of *Datura* are robust annual herbs with large, toothed leaves, white or pale purple flowers and very characteristic thorny seed capsules. The most widely distributed species in southern Africa is *Datura stramonium*. It has white to pale purple flowers and numerous small spines on the erect fruit capsules. The other common species is *Datura ferox* (large thorn apple, *groot stinkblaar*) which has white to cream-coloured flowers and also erect but distinctive fruits, with fewer and much larger spines than *D. stramonium*. *Datura metel* and *D. innoxia* (both known as downy thorn apple) are easily recognised by their hairy leaves and stems (the latter much more densely hairy than the former) and by their nodding fruit capsules. *Datura stramonium* and the related species *D. ferox*, *D. metel* and *D. innoxia* were probably introduced into southern Africa with impure fodder or agricultural seed. *Datura stramonium* was first reported from the Cape in 1714.

Infusions and decoctions of the fresh and dried leaves are used in carefully determined doses to sedate hysterical and psychotic patients, and dried and powdered roots and leaves are sometimes used as a consciousness-altering snuff by diviners. Adequate doses of any part of the plant can cause mental confusion accompanied by vivid visual hallucinations. Weak infusions of the leaves are used for insomnia by the elderly, and as aphrodisiacs by lovers. Seeds are well known to rural children as *malpitte* (literally "mad seeds"), and are sometimes deliberately consumed to induce intoxication and hallucinations as a dangerous prank. Dried leaves can be smoked to induce euphoria, to treat headache, or to treat asthma. Preparations of the seeds, or small pellets of fresh leaf, are used topically to relieve earache. Poultices and ointments of the fresh and dried leaves are applied topically to relieve pain and inflammation, including for fractures, sprains and rheumatism, and to draw abscesses and soothe painful bruises, wounds and septic sores.

The plant contains several tropane alkaloids, of which atropine [(±)-hyoscyamine] and scopolamine [(−)-hyoscine] are the two major ones. Atropine is used in modern anaesthetics as a pre-medication to decrease bronchial and salivary secretions, and to increase heart rate. The effect on the central nervous system is firstly stimulation, then sedation. Derivatives of atropine are used in some modern asthma inhalers. Scopolamine is a potent sedative, and is used in low doses in skin patches to treat motion sickness. It has also been used successfully on its own as a general anaesthetic in China.

All parts of the plant are potentially highly toxic, and fatalities are well known to have occurred in southern Africa and elsewhere. In 1996, 52 people died in Bhiwandi, India, after eating food contaminated with *Datura stramonium*. Signs of acute poisoning include widely dilated pupils, rapid pulse, a flushed appearance, dry mouth, delirium and fever.

Leaves and flowers of *rooidagga* (*Cullen obtusifolium*)

Bone pipe, with dried *Cullen* leaves

Flower and fruit of the large thorn apple (*Datura ferox*)

Leaves and flower of the common thorn apple (*Datura stramonium*)

Dried leaves and seeds (known as "malpitte") of *Datura stramonium*

Fruit capsules of the common thorn apple (*Datura stramonium*)

Dioscorea dregeana | Dioscoreaceae | ***ISIDAKWA*** (Zulu); wild yam; *wildejam* (Afrikaans) ■
This plant is a herbaceous creeper with robust annual stems arising from a large underground tuber. The stems and characteristic leaves are usually hairy and the small flowers, which are borne in pendulous clusters, are followed by winged fruits.

Dioscorea dregeana is frequently sold on the muthi markets in South Africa. The common Zulu names *uDakwa* and *isiDakwa* respectively mean "inducing drowsiness" and "a drunkard". It is a profound sedative that is commonly used to treat epilepsy, hysteria, insomnia and acute psychosis (Nathaniel Nondeyi, Phillip Khubukhele, David Matthe, pers. comm.). This potent narcotic is used to sedate violent, psychotic patients and also used as an analgesic. In earlier times, it was used as a general anaesthetic to enable fractures of the limbs to be manipulated and stabilised by traditional bone-setters. The fresh tuber is generally taken orally as a weak decoction, with an adequate dose resulting in sleep within 20–30 minutes. Intoxication sometimes precedes sleep, and *Ascaris* roundworms may be expelled as a side-effect of the treatment. Enemas are sometimes used to administer the decoction. Hallucinations have not been reported from the use of the tuber on its own, but do occur when *Dioscorea dregeana* is combined with the known hallucinogen *Boophone disticha* for the purposes of divination (see page 188). Dried and powdered, the tuber is used in small amounts as a remedy for colic and restlessness in infants. The tuber may be hollowed out, and water heated in it is used as a lotion for cuts and sores in humans and animals. The cut surface of the tuber can be rubbed directly against the skin to treat scabies rashes.

The plant has apparently been used with criminal intent on trains, by administering it in food or drink so that the victim can be robbed while senseless. Some indigenous healers maintain that the use of this plant is behind tales of zombies and resurrection of the dead (Ashley Mashigo, pers. comm.). Since the plant is potentially highly toxic and can cause fatalities, it is only used by indigenous healers skilled in its use. Maize cobs boiled in strong decoctions of the tuber are fed to monkeys to destroy them. Tubers have been eaten as famine food after soaking them in running water for several days, a process that leaches out toxic principles. Alkaloids are most likely to be responsible for the sedative activity.

The powdered tuber, or an infusion of the tuber of *Dioscorea cochleari-apiculata* is given orally in food to immobilise a person or animal (as a tranquilliser), and an infusion of the tuber of *D. quartiniana* is instilled into the ears or nose for the same purpose. An infusion of *D. schimperiana* is also given orally as a tranquilliser. The well-known elephant's foot (*D. elephantipes*) is known as *naka* or *!nakaa* in Khoi and *olifantsvoet* or *skilpaddop* in Afrikaans. The Afrikaans common name *hottentotsbrood* and the use of the tuber as food by Khoi people (see Chapter 5) was first recorded by Patterson in 1889 (Smith 1966). Unfortunately, there are no early records of traditional medicinal uses and there appears to be only a single contemporary anecdote. According to Susan Viljoen of Britstown, a poultice of the inner flesh (mixed with flour) is applied topically to treat inflammation and blood poisoning (Rood 1994).

Some information on *Dioscorea* came from personal communications with Isaac Mayeng, Nathaniel Nondeyi, Phillip Khubukhele, Ashley Mashigo, David Matthe and John Molefi Sekaja.

Entada rheedii | Fabaceae | **SEA BEAN**; *seeboontjie* (Afrikaans); *umbhone* (Zulu) ■ The seeds of this large, woody climber are frequently washed up on the beaches of the east coast of southern Africa. The plant occurs naturally from near Durban northwards throughout tropical Africa and into India, Asia and Australia. The pods are enormous, and may be up to two metres long. The large bean-like seeds are carried or worn on necklaces and pendants as lucky charms. Tobacco smoked in a pipe made from the seed has been reported to cause vivid dreaming (Ben Dekker, pers. comm.). The seeds are commonly sold on muthi markets and have numerous medicinal uses, including topical applications in an ointment for the treatment of jaundice (Flora Ify Ilonzo, pers. comm.).

Leaf and tubers of *isidakwa* (*Dioscorea dregeana*)

Leaves and fruits of *isidakwa* (*Dioscorea dregeana*)

Tubers of *isidakwa* as they are sold on muthi markets

Pod and seeds of the sea bean (*Entada rheedii*)

Euclea divinorum |Ebenaceae| **MAGIC GUARRI**; *towerghwarrie* (Afrikaans); *mohlakola* (Northern Sotho); *umhlangula* (Zulu) ■ See Chapter 16. A root infusion given in the form of ear drops is used to treat headache, and an ointment of the root is rubbed onto the body to treat convulsions. An infusion of the root of *Euclea crispa* (blue guarri) is taken orally for epilepsy, and the root of *E. natalensis* (hairy guarri) is burned and the smoke inhaled as a hypnotic (Ashley Mashigo, pers. comm.).

Exomis microphylla |Amaranthaceae| **HONDEPISBOSSIE**, *brakbossie* (Afrikaans) ■ The plant is a much-branched perennial herb or shrublet of about 0.6 metres in height with somewhat fleshy leaves and inconspicuous flowers and fruits. The leaves have a foetid smell reminiscent of the odour of a dog's urine, hence the Afrikaans common name. Milk and water decoctions of the fresh plant have been used to treat epilepsy in South Africa. It has also been used for winds and cramps and for convulsions in infants. Usually a single dose is sufficient (Dawid and Mrs Bester, pers. comm.).

Ferraria glutinosa |Iridaceae| **GAISE** (San) ■ This plant, a geophyte with an underground corm and strap-shaped leaves, is reported to have been used at dances by San as an aid in teaching *kia* – the trance state.

Gomphocarpus fruticosus (=*Asclepias fruticosa*) |Apocynaceae| **MILKWEED**; *tontelbos* (Afrikaans); *lebejana, lereke la ntja, modimolo* (Sotho); *umsinga-lwesalukazi* (Zulu) ■ This weedy plant is commonly found along roadsides, dry river beds and other disturbed places. All parts of the plant contain milky latex. It is an erect perennial herb with narrowly oblong leaves, small yellow flowers and characteristic bladdery fruits. The small brown seeds are attached to silky seed hairs that were once used as tinder to stuff the tinder box, hence the Afrikaans name (*tontel* = tinder). A snuff of the powdered leaf is sedative, and is used to treat headache. *Gomphocarpus physocarpus* is used in the same way, and *G. decipiens* has also been used as a snuff (Solomon Mahlaba, pers. comm.). *Gomphocarpus fruticosus* root infusions and decoctions have been used as emetics and for relief of abdominal pain. Numerous Sotho vernacular names and other medicinal uses have been recorded by Moffett (2010).

Helichrysum foetidum |Asteraceae| **ISICWE** (Zulu); *muishondblaar* (Afrikaans) ■ Smoke from this strongly aromatic plant is inhaled by healers in KwaZulu-Natal to induce a trance. The smoke from *H. stenopterum* is used in the same way.

Helichrysum odoratissimum |Asteraceae| **IMPHEPHO** (Zulu); everlasting; *kooigoed* (Afrikaans); *phefo, phefo ya setlolo, towane* (Sotho) ■ The plant is a strongly aromatic, much-branched perennial herb with small, silvery leaves and small, yellow flower heads borne in groups at the tips of the branches. This species and several other species are known as *imphepho*, and are burned as ritual incenses to invoke the goodwill of the ancestors. The smoke is reportedly sedative, and helpful for insomnia. The smoke from *Helichrysum foetidum* and *H. stenopterum* are inhaled by healers in KwaZulu-Natal to induce a trance.

To this day, these plants are commonly burnt inside a house to "protect it from evil spirits" or "to keep away impurities". There is nothing sinister about these expressions. The modern term for this concept is "fumigation" – a way to get rid of harmful bacteria (and associated animals and insects that carry diseases). In the days before microscopes, people associated diseases with evil spirits, i.e., an invisible and inexplicable force that makes people ill. In addition to direct (chemical) mood-altering effects, the use of *imphepho* is therefore also likely to promote relaxation and calmness, and hence a good night's rest. Furthermore, the Afrikaans name *kooigoed* ("bedding stuff") refers to the traditional use of the plant as bedding in the form of a mattress. The highly aromatic plant material is said to repel mosquitoes, lice and other parasites.

MIND & MOOD PLANTS

Hondepisbossie (Exomis microphylla)

Flowers and fruit of the milkweed (*Gomphocarpus fruticosus*)

Bundle of *imphepho* (*Helichrysum odoratissimum*) as it is sold on the muthi market

Fruit of the milkweed (*Gomphocarpus fruticosus*)

Flowering plant of *imphepho* or *kooigoed* (*Helichrysum odoratissimum*)

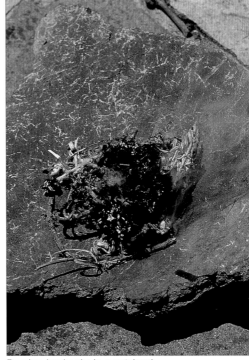

Burning *imphepho* in a potsherd

Hypericum perforatum | Hypericaceae or Clusiaceae | **ST JOHN'S WORT**; *Johanneskruid* (Afrikaans) ■ This European shrub is up to one metre high, with small glandular leaves and yellow flowers (similar to those of indigenous species). It became a troublesome weed in the Western Cape. Ironically, it was largely eradicated using an introduced insect pest, and now commercial plantations are being established to meet the growing global demand. St John's wort has enjoyed a long history of use in Europe and was used by the ancient herbalists, including Hippocrates and Dioscorides. There has been a worldwide resurgence of interest in the plant for mild to moderate depression, anxiety and sleep disorders. Originally classified as a sedative, the most common modern use is as an antidepressant and anxiolytic. Sales of St John's wort products have been reported to outsell the antidepressant drug Prozac in Germany. A number of controlled clinical studies on standardised extracts have shown that it is indeed more effective than placebo in treating depression, but long-term studies are still needed to determine whether it is as effective as other antidepressants and whether it has fewer side-effects. Possible mechanisms of action for the antidepressant effect include monoamine oxidase inhibition, selective serotonin-uptake inhibition, and modulation of interleukin-6. The antidepressant effect was originally ascribed to hypericin (modern preparations are still standardised at 0.2% hypericin) but nowadays also to hyperforin, a phloroglucinol derivative. The commercial products include teas, tinctures and formulations of soft and dry extracts, which are derived from the flowering tops. *Hypericum* is also used for fibrositis and sciatica, and the oil is used topically for healing burns, wounds and bruises and in skincare products. Antiviral activity against HIV and hepatitis C has been reported for hypericin.

Ipomoea pes-caprae | Convolvulaceae | ***STRANDPATAT*** (Afrikaans); goat's foot ■ *Ipomoea* species are well-known creepers with attractive blue, purple or white flowers that only last for one day. The seeds of *Ipomoea pes-caprae* are taken by locals at Port St John's on the Pondoland coast when catching crayfish in the surf (Ben Dekker, pers. comm.). This apparently makes movement more fluid in the sea. The tropical American *I. tricolor*, a cultivated ornamental climber, has been reported to be hallucinogenic when 200 to 500 seeds are chewed (Gelfand *et al.* 1985). It was used by the Aztecs in Mexico as part of religious ceremonies. Two to four seeds of *I. alba* (another tropical American species) crushed in water and taken at night result in vivid dreams, and the seeds of an unknown Convolvulaceae are used to induce dreams and communication with the ancestors (Solomon Mahlaba & Seth Seroka, pers. comm.). The root of *I. ommaneyi* is used as a decoction taken orally to treat convulsions, and as an infusion taken orally as an aphrodisiac. The active substances in the seeds are alkaloids such as ergine, lysergol and various clavines, which are well-described hallucinogens.

Lannea schweinfurthii* var. *stuhlmannii | Anacardiaceae | **FALSE MARULA**; *mulivhadza* (Venda) ■ The roots are covered with a dense layer of very fine, velvety hairs, which are reportedly used as a sedative snuff, and the smoke of the burned roots is inhaled as a sedative (Million Matonsi, pers. comm.). It is commonly used in the Limpopo Province as a charm to make people forget (hence the Venda name *vhulivhadza*, meaning "to forget"). The powdered root bark has been used as a snakebite remedy, by being blown into the nasal cavity of the dying victim. The leaves of *Lannea discolor* are used to treat convulsions and dizziness.

Leonotis leonurus | Lamiaceae | ***WILDE DAGGA*** (Afrikaans) ■ Leaves of this attractive plant have been smoked for epilepsy, and tinctures and decoctions of flowers, stems and leaves have been taken for headache. The earliest inhabitants of South Africa smoked it and chewed it instead of tobacco. The smoke is acrid, but smoked through a water-pipe produces a mild, sedated type of intoxication. An infusion of the root of *L. ocymifolia* is taken in Zimbabwe to drive away evil spirits, and an infusion is taken for hypertension.

St John's wort plants invading the slopes of Table Mountain

Flowers of St John's wort (*Hypericum perforatum*)

The *strandpatat* (*Ipomoea pes-caprae*)

Fruit capsules and seeds of *Ipomoea pes-caprae*

Root bark of *Lannea schweinfurthii* showing the velvety hairs

Vhulivhadza, the root bark hairs of *Lannea schweinfurthii*

Flowers of *wilde dagga* (*Leonotis leonurus*)

Klipdagga (*Leonotis ocymifolia*)

Mesembryanthemum tortuosum (=*Sceletium tortuosum*) |Aizoaceae| **SCELETIUM**; *kougoed*, (Afrikaans); *kanna* (Khoi) ■ *Kougoed* is a short-lived perennial creeping mesemb with characteristic persistent leaf veins that remain on the plant. When the leaves dry out, they become "skeletonised", hence the botanical name *Sceletium*. Fresh leaves have large, bulbous water cells on their surfaces (clearly visible to the naked eye) that give them a shiny crystalline appearance. The flowers are usually pale to bright yellow, but may also be pale orange-purple. The *Sceletium* group has eight species and is now part of the genus *Mesembryanthemum* (Gerbaulet 1996; Klak *et al.* 2007). All of them are confined to the Cape region of South Africa where they occur in dry Karoo vegetation, often in the partial shade of shrubby plants. *Mesembryanthemum tortuosum* is the best known and most widely distributed species.

This plant was likely to have been used by pastoralists and hunter-gatherers as a mood-altering substance from prehistoric times. The earliest written records of use of the plant date back to 1662 and 1685. The traditionally prepared dried plant material is chewed or smoked, or powdered and inhaled as a snuff. *Kougoed* elevates mood and decreases anxiety, stress and tension. In intoxicating doses it can cause euphoria, initially with stimulation and later with sedation. The plant is not hallucinogenic, and no severe adverse effects have been documented.

Kougoed or *kanna* was used by pastoralists to decrease thirst and hunger, and as a local anaesthetic and analgesic for extracting teeth from the lower jaw. The plant is used to this day in small quantities for colic in infants, added to a teaspoon of breast milk. A few drops of sheep-tail fat in which *kougoed* has been fried are also given to an infant with colic. It is used as a sedative in the form of a tea, decoction or a tincture and it is used effectively by indigenous healers to wean alcoholics off alcohol. To this day, the plant is sometimes called *onse droë drank* – "our dry liquor". Chronic use does not appear to result in a state of withdrawal (Dr Greg McCarthy, pers. comm.). A form of *M. tortuosum*, previously known as *M. concavum*, is used for toothache and insomnia.

Plants from particular areas are believed to be more potent, and these wild plants are harvested at the end of the growing season. The succulent plant material is crushed with a rock, and then put into closed plastic bags and left in the sun to "sweat" for a period of eight days. In earlier times leather bags were used. The macerated material is then spread out in the sun to dry, and stored for later use. *Kougoed* was once widely traded in the Cape, and trading stores in Namaqualand used to stock it until a few decades ago. Alcohol, tobacco and probably also *Cannabis* have displaced its use.

The active constituents are alkaloids, including mesembrine, mesembrenone, mesembrenol and tortuosamine. The alkaloid concentration in the dry material ranges from 0.05 to 2.3 per cent. Mesembrine has been found to be a potent serotonin-uptake inhibitor, a novel mechanism of action for this known molecule that suggests therapeutic applications for anxiety and depression, and other serious mental health conditions (Smith *et al.* 1996; Gericke & Viljoen 2008). The serotonin-uptake inhibitory activity of mesembrine is complemented by defined activities at other neuroreceptor sites, and by the activities of related alkaloids that are present. Phytopharmaceuticals from *Mesembryanthemum* have been in development, and the success of these products will depend as much on ongoing clinical studies of efficacy as on the ability to cultivate sufficient raw material of meticulously selected strains of domesticated plants. A proprietary botanical supplement based on cultivated raw material of an elite domesticated chemotype has shown promising results in clinical studies, including anti-anxiety activity and cognitive function enhancing activity (Nell *et al.* 2013; Terburg *et al.* 2013; Chiu *et al.* 2014). This product, standardised to precisely defined alkaloid content, was the first wholly South African phytopharmaceutical to reach the international market. The industrial development of a natural medicine from *kougoed* has established a product development paradigm for natural products that has profound economic and developmental implications for southern Africa.

We thank Lodewyk Morries, Gert Dirkse, Jap-Jap Klaase, Greg McCarthy, Earle Graven, Scott Perschke and staff of the Montagu Museum (see Anon. 1993) for interesting information on traditional uses and the cultivation of *kougoed*.

MIND & MOOD PLANTS

Stems of *kougoed* (*Mesembryanthemum tortuosum*), showing the skeletonised old leaves

Flowers of *kougoed* (*Mesembryanthemum tortuosum*)

Lodewyk Morries showing how *kougoed* is traditionally prepared

Selected clones of *kougoed* (*Mesembryanthemum tortuosum*) under commercial cultivation

Monadenium lugardiae |Euphorbiaceae| ***TSHISWOSWO*** (Venda) ■ The plant is a thick-stemmed succulent with irritant milky latex. Diviners swallow pieces of root to see visions and to make prophesies under its influence. Taken in sufficient quantity, the root is said to produce hallucinations and delirium. It is also used to cause an abortion, to treat stomach and chest pains and ascites, and as a remedy for worms in dogs.

Nenax microphylla |Rubiaceae| ***DAGGAPIT*** (Afrikaans); *morebakgosi, patsana* (Sotho) ■ The seeds of this Karoo shrublet were used by Khoi and Griqua people of the Karoo as a *dagga* (*Cannabis*) substitute. It is considered to be one of the most valuable of all Karoo plants – highly palatable and eaten by all types of domestic and wild animals. According to Smith (1966) the plant is also known as *daggabossie* or *granaatbossie*. The name *granaatbossie* is said to be derived from the fruits resembling miniature pomegranates (*granaatbos* is the name used for *Rhigozum obovatum*).

Boesmandagga (*Limeum aethiopicum*) is another highly palatable Karoo plant that has been used as a *dagga* substitute. It is best known as *koggelmandervoetkaroo*. This small shrublet has annual shoots with clusters of leaves resembling the small hands of the agama lizard (*koggelmander* in Afrikaans), hence the vernacular name. Explaining why it is called *boesmandagga*, several Karoo inhabitants have reported that the plant was smoked by the southern San (!Xam) people who once inhabited the Great Karoo. It is still occasionally smoked by naughty school children as a tobacco substitute, in the same way as is done with donkey droppings (*donkiedrolle* in Afrikaans). Jakop Tromp (pers. comm.) said that the plant can be used as an aphrodisiac by young men.

Nicotiana glauca |Solanaceae| ***JAN TWAK***, *wildetabak* (Afrikaans); wild tobacco; *umgqoma-gqoma* (Xhosa) ■ This is a woody shrub or small tree that has become a weed over large parts of southern Africa. The leaves contain anabasine, a highly toxic tobacco-type alkaloid similar to nicotine. Accidental deaths have been reported when young *N. glauca* plants were confused with wild spinach (*marog*). The warmed leaves are put on the head to relieve headache, on the throat to relieve pain and put in the shoes for painful, tired feet.

Nicotiana tabacum |Solanaceae| ***TOBACCO***; *tabak* (Afrikaans); *kwane* (Sotho); *ugwayi* (Zulu) ■ The plant is a robust perennial herb, grown as an annual crop. It can reach up to two metres in height and has a single thick, erect stem. The leaves are variable in size, up to 0.6 metres long. Tobacco is a native of South America, where it was cultivated and smoked long before the Spanish conquest. It was first introduced to Europe in the 16th century and is now grown in most countries in the world. Tobacco use was reportedly introduced to the Cape by Dutch sailors in 1595 (Von Bibra 1995). Tobacco use was rapidly adopted in southern Africa, and because of the potency and addictive potential of nicotine, it probably displaced the use of many local psychoactive plants. The plant is widely cultivated on a commercial scale in southern Africa, where most of the crop is cured and used for the production of cigarettes, and some for snuff. Traditionally, twist chewing tobacco (*roltwak*) was commonly made and sold throughout the country (the photographs on page 213 show how *roltwak* is traditionally made). Subsistence farmers still grow small amounts for personal use.

Tobacco is sometimes taken as a snuff by diviners at the start of a divination, and it is also sprinkled on the ground in front of an ancestral shrine as a traditional offering to the ancestors, together with sorghum beer (Ncindani Maswanganyi, pers. comm.). In Zimbabwe, ritual snuff is made by diviners and healers from tobacco by pounding sun-dried cut leaves in a mortar, and allowing it to dry again. The tobacco is then stone-ground into a powder, which is placed into a container and boiled in a clay pot with the container, before being sun-dried again. (Gelfand *et al.* 1995). Traditionally, a leaf and root infusion is taken to treat asthma, and powdered leaf is applied as a dressing to wounds. Fresh root is rubbed on warts.

MIND & MOOD PLANTS

The succulent stem of *Monadenium lugardiae*

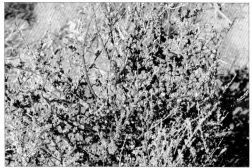

Fruiting shrub of the *daggapit* (*Nenax microphylla*)

Fruits of the *daggapit* (*Nenax microphyla*)

Boesmandagga (*Limeum aethiopicum*)

Flowers of *boesmandagga* (*Limeum aethiopicum*)

Flowers of the tobacco plant (*Nicotiana tabacum*)

Leaves and flowers of wild tobacco (*Nicotiana glauca*)

Nymphaea nouchali |Nymphaeaceae| **BLUE WATER LILY**; *blouwaterlelie* (Afrikaans); *intekwane* (Xhosa); *amazibu, izeleba, izubu, izibu* (Zulu); *tswii* (Tswana) ■ The plant is a common inhabitant of lakes and rivers in the subtropical parts of southern Africa. It has large, edible, fleshy rhizomes below the mud, with large, round, floating leaves that have toothed margins. The attractive flowers are large (about 120 millimetres in diameter) and vary from pale pink to bright blue. They are strongly scented, especially at night. The fresh or dry flowers have been used by diviners in South Africa, and tinctures of the flowers are stimulant, aphrodisiac and euphoriant in low doses, but tranquillising and anaphrodisiac in higher doses. They are thought to have had narcotic uses in ancient Egypt (Hutchings *et al.* 1996).

The leaves are reported to have been used as a grave mat in Zimbabwe. The flowers have been found to have sedative, analgesic and anti-inflammatory activity (Jahan *et al.* 2012; Sarwar *et al.* 2016). According to Tr. Dr. Credo Mutwa (pers. comm.), the blue water lily is a symbol of hope in African mythology, because it is said that "out of the darkest mud grows the most beautiful flower". Stems are used in traditional medicine to treat coughs and colds and the roots as love charms. Numerous other uses have been reported (Roodt 1998).

Pancratium tenuifolium |Amaryllidaceae| ■ The single species in southern Africa is a bulbous plant with strap-shaped leaves and attractive white flowers resembling daffodils. It is claimed that the San in Botswana induce visual hallucinations by rubbing the bulb on an incision in the head. Galanthamine, lycorine, hordenine, pacratin and trispheridine were isolated from the bulbs and roots, among other compounds. Galanthamine is a cholinesterase inhibitor and is an analgesic.

Piper betle |Piperaceae| ***PAN*** (Hindustani) ■ The betel vine is a climber with heart-shaped leaves. It is not cultivated in South Africa but fresh leaves are imported for their traditional use in wrapping betel nut and other ingredients (see betel nut – *Areca catechu*). The fibrous leaf stalk (petiole) is typically removed, and *catha* (a traditional spicy mixture in liquid form) is spread over it before it is used for wrapping the betel nut.

The raw or cooked root of *Piper capense* has been used in South Africa as a sexual stimulant, and is reported to cause sleepiness. It is likely to have a similar chemical composition to *kava-kava*, *Piper methystichum*.

Rabiea albinota |Aizoaceae, formerly Mesembryanthemaceae| ***S'KENG-KENG*** (Griqua) ■ The pulverised plant is reported to be a hallucinogenic additive to tobacco to be smoked or taken as snuff. *Gibbaeum dispar*, also known as *s'keng-keng* (*duimpiesnuif* in Afrikaans), is used as a snuff or snuff substitute. Another member of the family, *Pleiospilos bolusii* (also known as *duimpiesnuif*), is dried, powdered and used as snuff (Ernst van Jaarsveld, pers. comm.). Approximately 50 milligrams of dried plant chewed, produced a feeling of euphoria which lasted for about 20 minutes, followed by sedation. Plants of another mesemb genus, *Conophytum* (*toontjies* in Afrikaans), are believed to have sedative properties, possibly on the basis of mesembrine-type alkaloids. See sceletium or *kougoed* (*Mesembryanthemum tortuosum*).

Rauvolfia caffra |Apocynaceae| **QUININE TREE** ■ Decoctions of the bark are used in South Africa as a tranquilliser for hysteria, and for insomnia, and dried leaves are used as a snuff for headaches. A large number of indole alkaloids occur in *Rauvolfia caffra*, of which reserpine and ajmalicine (sometimes called raubasine) are of particular interest. Commercially, these alkaloids are obtained from *Rauvolfia serpentina, R. vomitaria* and *R. tetraphylla*. Reserpine, now no longer widely used, is a well-known antihypertensive, antipsychotic and sedative, although an important side-effect is depression. Ajmalicine is not used on its own. It is used in proprietary products that treat the psychological and behavioural problems associated with senility, as well as stroke and head injuries. *Rauvolfia caffra* is also used for fever, malaria, heart failure and other conditions.

Leaves and flower of the blue water lily (*Nymphaea nouchali*)

Dried flowers of the blue water lily (*Nymphaea nouchali*)

Leaves of *pan* or betel vine (*Piper betle*), with lime (*chuna*) and the traditional spice (*catha*)

Pleiospilos bolusii, one of several plants known as *duimpiesnuif*

Leaves and fruits of the quinine tree (*Rauvolfia caffra*)

Bark of the quinine tree (*Rauvolfia caffra*)

Silene undulata (=*S. capensis*) |Caryophyllaceae| **DREAM ROOT**, wild tobacco; *undlela zimhlophe* (Xhosa) ■ The plant is a perennial herb of up to 0.6 metres in height with glandular-hairy, lance-shaped leaves and distinctive white or pale pink flowers that are scented at night. Hirst (2000) reported on the use of *Silene capensis* (now included in *S. undulata*) as an *ubulawu* from personal experience as an initiate diviner. The roots of *Silene* species, including *S. bellidioides* (*gwayana* in Zulu), *S. pilosellifolia* (*popoma* in Zulu) and *S. undulata* (*undlela zimhlophe* in Xhosa), are among the plants used to make the ritual preparations classified traditionally as *ubulawu* (Sobiecki 2008). These are typically cold water infusions of one or more plants that foam readily due to the presence of saponins (see Chapter 14). The infusion is vigorously stirred or beaten with a three-pronged stick to produce a thick head of white foam. A Xhosa initiate diviner will ingest some of the foam and some of the liquid, and the body is washed with the foam. *Ubulawu* preparations have the ritual significance of purifying the initiate, facilitating meaningful vivid dreaming, and connection with the ancestral spirits. They have also been used to improve memory and develop mental faculties (Laydevant 1932), including clairvoyance. A United States patent (Jones *et al.* 2015) was granted in 2015 for the use of extracts of *S. undulata* for inhibiting craving in smokers.

Other important plants used to make *ubulawu* include *Dianthus mooiensis, Helinus integrifolius, Hippobromus pauciflorus* and *Rhoicissus tridentata* (Sobiecki 2008). These plants are also traditional sources of soap or are used as soap substitutes. *Dianthus* species are widely used in traditional medicine and are known in the Cape by their Afrikaans name *grashoutjie*. Saponins have secretolytic and antitussive activity, so that saponin-rich plants (especially roots) have been used to treat coughs and catarrh of the upper respiratory tract.

Siphonochilus aethiopicus |Zingiberaceae| **AFRICAN GINGER**, wild ginger; *isiphephetho, indungulo* (Zulu) ■ See Chapter 7. Infusions of the rhizome and roots are used to treat epilepsy and hysteria (Colin Ruiters, pers. comm.).

Stapelia gigantea |Apocynaceae| **GIANT CARRION FLOWER**; *aasblom* (Afrikaans); *ililo elikhulu, uzililo* (Zulu) ■ The plant has been used as a remedy for hysteria and to treat pain.

Synadenium cupulare |Euphorbiaceae| **DEAD-MAN'S TREE**; *umbulele* (Zulu); *gifboom* (Afrikaans) ■ This succulent tree is important in African mythology and is believed to lure people to their deaths. Leaves are used as medicine, mainly for headache, toothache and asthma. Several uses in veterinary medicine have been recorded (Mabogo 1990). The milky latex is very poisonous. Laboratory tests indicate that this plant has significant prostaglandin-synthesis inhibition (Jäger *et al.* 1996), useful in the treatment of headache and inflammatory conditions.

Synaptolepis kirkii |Thymelaeaceae| ***UVUMA-OMHLOPE*** (Zulu) ■ Root infusions have been used to treat epilepsy, and are also used as purifying ritual emetics and face and body washes to assist diviners to "see" in a metaphysical sense.

Syncolostemon bracteosus (=*Hemizygia bracteosa*) |Lamiaceae| ■ See photograph on page 258. The leaves of this aromatic herb are smoked or chewed by San in Botswana to give energy for dancing (Beza, pers. comm.).

Tarchonanthus camphoratus |Asteraceae| **WILD CAMPHOR BUSH** ■ The whole plant has a pleasant camphor-like odour, and was smoked as a narcotic by the earliest inhabitants of the Cape instead of tobacco. Several different species are now recognised, so that the early records probably refer to *T. littoralis.* Smoking the dried leaves in a pipe is sedative.

Tecomaria capensis |Bignoniaceae| **CAPE HONEYSUCKLE**; trompetters, *Kaapse kanfer-foelie* (Afrikaans); *icakatha* (Xhosa); *umunyane* (Zulu) ■ The powdered bark of this attractive indigenous garden plant is said to relieve pain and produce sleep.

Leaves of the dream root (*Silene undulata*)

Flowers of the dream root (*Silene undulata*)

Root of the dream root (*Silene undulata*)

Flowers of the *kruitbossie* (*Silene gallica*)

Roots of *Silene gallica* and foam made from them

The distinctive white roots of *uvuma-omhlope* (*Synaptolepis kirkii*)

Flowers of Cape honeysuckle (*Tecomaria capensis*)

Valeriana capensis | Valerianaceae | **CAPE VALERIAN** ■ This plant is a robust perennial herb with erect hollow stems arising from numerous long, thin rhizomes. It is widely distributed in South Africa, and further north into tropical Africa. *Valeriana capensis* is very similar to the European *V. officinalis*, but is easily distinguished by the terminal (topmost) leaflet, which is larger than those lower down, not smaller as in *V. officinalis*.

The dry roots have a peculiar, immediately recognisable odour, and in the form of infusions or tinctures are an early Cape remedy for insomnia, hysteria and epilepsy. The plant is essentially used in the same way as the European *V. officinalis*. Cape valerian was also used as a diaphoretic to treat fevers, including typhoid fever. Other uses in the past include external use as a counterirritant, and internal use to stimulate the kidneys, the circulation and the gastrointestinal tract. The essential oil from the root has been used as an antispasmodic. *Valeriana capensis* has been used combined with *Ballota africana* and *Stachys thunbergii* (both called *kattekruie* in Afrikaans) to treat asthma, bronchitis, hysteria and insomnia.

The chemical compounds of *Valeriana capensis* are likely to be similar to that of *V. officinalis*. The latter contains a number of iridoid compounds called valepotriates, such as valtrate, and sesquiterpenoid compounds, including valerenic acid and valeranone. Extracts of *Valeriana officinalis* have been demonstrated in laboratory studies to have GABA-A activity, and barbiturate receptor and benzodiazepine receptor activities, which may be the basis for the sedative effects. Spasmolytic activity has also been found. No side-effects have been reported from the use of Cape valerian, but it may have a synergistic sedative effect with alcohol and other central nervous system depressants, and may cause drowsiness if taken during the day.

REFERENCES AND FURTHER READING: Anonymous. 1993. *Kruierate van die Montagu Museum.* 2nd ed. Montagu Museum, Montagu. **Anonymous. 1996.** *Centella asiatica* (Gotu kola). *American Journal of Natural Medicine* 3(6): 22–25. **Anonymous. 1998.** Booze "far worse" than dagga. *Cape Times*, June 17, 1998. **Anonymous. 1999.** Britain researches cannabis. *Cape Times*, January 11, 1999. **Awang, D.V.C. 1998.** Gotu Kola. *Can. Pharm. J.* 131: 42–46. **Balasubrahmanyam, V.R. & Rawat, A.K.S. 1990.** Betelvine (*Piper betle* L., Piperaceae). *Econ. Bot.* 44: 540–542. **Binneman, J. 1999.** Mummified human remains from the Kouga mountains, eastern Cape. *The Digging Stick* 16: 1–2. **Bruneton, J. 1995.** *Pharmacognosy, phytochemistry, medicinal plants.* Intercept, Hampshire. **Burns, J.F. 1996.** Accident or Mass Murder? India's Food-Poisoning Mystery. *New York Times*, August 18, 1996. **Chatterjee, S.S. *et al.* 1998.** Antidepressant activity of *Hypericum perforatum* and hyperforin: the neglected possibility. *Pharmacopsychiatry* 31 (Supplement): 7–15. **Chiu, S., Gericke, N. & Farina-Woodbury, M., *et al.* 2014.** Proof-of-concept randomized controlled study of cognition effects of the proprietary extract *Sceletium tortuosum* (Zembrin) targeting phosphodiesterase-4 in cognitively healthy subjects: Implications for Alzheimer's dementia. *Evidence-based Complementary and Alternative Medicine,* 2014, art. no. 682014. **Crombie, L. *et al.* 1990.** Alkaloids of Khat (*Catha edulis*). In: Brossi, A. (ed.), *The alkaloids: chemistry and pharmacology*, vol. 39, pp. 139–164. Academic Press, San Diego. **De Smet, P.A.G.M. 1996.** Some ethnopharmacological notes on African hallucinogens. *J. Ethnopharmacol.* 50: 141–146. **De Smet, P.A.G.M. 1997.** The role of plant-derived drugs and herbal medicines in healthcare. *Drugs* 54(6): 802–840. **Dimpfel, W., Gericke, N., Suliman, S. & Dipah, G. 2017.** Effect of Zembrin® on brain electrical activity in 60 older subjects after 6 weeks of daily intake. A prospective, randomized, double-blind, placebo-controlled, 3-armed study in a parallel design. *World Journal of Neuroscience* 7: 140–171. **Dobkin De Rios, M. 1986.** Enigma of drug-induced altered states of consciousness among the !Kung bushmen of the Kalahari desert. *J. Ethnopharmacol.* 15: 297–304. **Dold, T. & Cocks, M. 2012.** *Voices from the forest.* Jacana Media, Johannesburg. **Doyle, E. & Spence, A.A. 1995.** Cannabis as a medicine? (editorial). *British Journal of Anaesthesia* 74(4): 359–361. **Dugmore, H.I. & Van Wyk, B.-E. 2008.** *Muti and myths from the African bush.* Marula Books, Pretoria [also in Afrikaans]. **Duncan, G., Jeppe, B. & Voigt, L. 2016.** *The Amaryllidaceae of southern Africa.* Umdaus Press, Pretoria. **Du Toit, M. 1974.** *Cannabis sativa* in sub-Saharan Africa. *S. Afr. J. Sci.* 70(9): 266–270. **Emboden, W. 1979.** *Narcotic plants.* Macmillan, London. **Forbes, V.S. (ed.) 1986.** *Carl Peter Thunberg Travels at the Cape of Good Hope* 1772–1775. Van Riebeeck Society, Cape Town. **Gelfand, M. *et al.* 1985.** *The traditional medical practitioner in Zimbabwe.* Mambo Press, Harare. **Gerbaulet, M. 1996.** Revision of the genus *Sceletium* N.E.Br. (Aizoaceae). *Bot. Jahrb. Syst.* 118: 9–24. **Gericke, N. & Viljoen, A.M. 2008.** *Sceletium* – A review update. *J. Ethnopharmacol.* 119: 653–663. **Getahun, A. & Krikorian, A.D. 1973.** Chat: coffee's rival from Harar, Ethiopia. *Econ. Bot.* 27: 353–389. **Gorman, P. 1994.** Marijuana and AIDS. *High Times*, December 1994, pp. 26ff. **Harvey, A.L., Young, L.C., Viljoen, A.M. & Gericke, N.P. 2011.** Pharmacological actions of the South African medicinal and functional food plant *Sceletium tortuosum* and its principal alkaloids. *J. Ethnopharmacol.* 137: 1124–1129. **Hirst, M.M. 1997.** The utilization of *Catha edulis* in the household economy of Xhosa farm inhabitants of the Bolo Reserve, Eastern Cape. *Journal of Contemporary African Studies* 15(1): 119–143. **Hirst, M. 2000.** Root, dream and myth. The use of the oneirogenic plant *Silene capensis* among the Xhosa of South Africa. *Eleusis: Journal of Psychoactive Plants and Compounds,* 4: 19–50. **Hutchings, A. & Van Staden, J. 1994.** Plants used for stress-related ailments in traditional Zulu, Xhosa and Sotho medicine. Part 1: Plants used for headaches. *J. Ethnopharmacol.* 43: 89–124.

Valeriana officinalis in cultivation

Leaf and flowers of Cape valerian (*Valeriana capensis*)

Dried roots of *Valeriana officinalis*

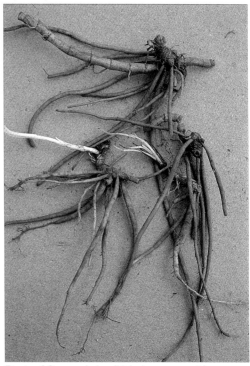

Roots of Cape valerian (*Valeriana capensis*)

Hutchings, A. *et al.* 1996. *Zulu medicinal plants.* Natal University Press, Pietermaritzburg. Iwu, M.M. 1993. *Handbook of African medicinal plants.* CRC Press, Boca Raton. Jahan, I., Mamun, M.A.A., Hossen, M.A., Sakir, J.A.M.S., Shamimuzzaman, M., Uddin, M.J. & Haque, M.E. 2012. Antioxidant, analgesic and anti-inflammatory activities of *Nymphaea nouchali* flowers. *Res. J. Pharmacol,* 6(5–6): 62–70. Jäger, A.K. *et al.* 1996. Screening of Zulu medicinal plants for prostaglandin-synthesis inhibitors. *J. Ethnopharmacol.* 52: 95–100. Jones, M.P., Benns, J.M. & Jones, D.A. 2015. *Silene capensis* for inhibiting cravings. US Patent 9198943 B2. Kalix, P. 1991. The pharmacology of psychoactive alkaloids from *Ephedra* and *Catha. J. Ethnopharmacol.* 32: 201–208. Klak, C., Bruyns, P.V. & Hedderson, T.A.J. 2007. A phylogeny and new classification for Mesembryanthemoideae. *Taxon* 56: 737–756. Koch, E. 1992. Dagga, it's the green gold of the rural poor. *The Weekly Mail,* 13 July to 6 August 1992. Leung, A.Y. & Foster, S. 1996. *Encyclopedia of common natural ingredients used in food, drugs, and cosmetics.* John Wiley & Sons, New York. Laydevant, F. 1932. Religious or sacred plants of Basutoland. *Bantu Studies* 6: 65–69. Linde, K. *et al.* 1996. St. John's wort for depression – an overview and meta-analysis of randomised clinical trials. *British Medical Journal* 313: 253–257. Mabogo, D.E.N. 1990. *The ethnobotany of the Vhavenda.* Unpublished M.Sc. thesis, University of Pretoria. Maurice, P. 1992. Grass grows on trade routes. *The Weekly Mail,* 31 July to 6 August 1992. Mennini, T. *et al.* 1993. In vitro study of extracts and pure compounds from *Valeriana officinalis* roots with GABA, benzodiazepine and barbiturate receptors in the brain. *Fitoterapia* LXIV (4): 291–300. Moffett, R. 2010. *Sesotho plant & animal names and plants used by the Basotho.* Sun Press, Bloemfontein. Müller, W.E. & Chatterjee, S.S. 1998. Hyperforin and the antidepressant activity of St. John's Wort. *Pharmacopsychiatry* 31 (Supplement 1): 1–60. Murray, M.T. 1997. Common questions about St. John's wort extract. *American Journal of Natural Medicine* 4(7): 14–19. Nell, H., Siebert, M., Chellan, P. & Gericke, N. 2013. A randomized, double-blind, parallel-group, placebo-controlled trial of extract *Sceletium tortuosum* (Zembrin) in healthy adults. *Journal of Alternative and Complementary Medicine* 19(11): 898–904. Neuwinger, H.D. 1996. *African ethnobotany: poisons and drugs: chemistry, pharmacology, toxicology.* Chapman & Hall, Germany. Neuwinger, H.D. 1997. *Boophone disticha.* Eine halluzinogene Pflanze Afrikas. *Deutsche Apotheker Zeitung* 137, Jaargang Nr. 14 (3,4): 51–56. Newall, C.A. *et al.* 1996. *Herbal medicines. A guide for health-care professionals.* The Pharmaceutical Press, London. Nevill, G. & Stephen, J. 1998. Up in Smoke. *The Big Issue,* Cape Town. Issue 14 September 1998. Volume 2. Pappe, L. 1847. *A list of South African indigenous plants used as remedies by the colonists of the Cape of Good Hope.* O.I. Pike, Cape Town. Pappe, L. 1850. *Florae Capensis Medicae Prodromus.* A.S. Robertson, Cape Town. Pappe, L. 1857. *Florae Capensis Medicae Prodromus,* 2nd ed. Cape Town. Ponglux, D. *et al.* (eds) 1987. *Medicinal plants.* The first Princess Chulabhorn Science Congress, Bangkok, Thailand. Pooley, E. 1998. *A field guide to wildflowers. KwaZulu-Natal and Eastern Region.* Natal Flora Publications Trust, Durban. Pujol, J. 1990. *Naturafrica – the herbalist handbook.* Jean Pujol Natural Healers Foundation, Durban. Ratsch, C. 1998. *Enzyklopadie der psychoactiven Pflanzen.* AT Verlag, Arau, Schweiz. Robinson, R. 1996. *The great book of hemp.* Park Street Press, Vermont. Rood, B. 1994. *Uit die veldapteek.* Tafelberg, Cape Town. Roodt, V. 1998. *Common wild flowers of the Okavango Delta.* Shell Oil, Botswana. Russo, E. 1998. Cannabis for migraine treatment: the once and future prescription? An historical and scientific review. *Pain* 76: 3–8. Sarwar, S., Khatun, A., Chowdhury, S.S., Sultana, N. & Ashikur, M. 2016. Antinociceptive and anti-depressant like activities of methanolic flower extract of *Nymphaea nouchali. Saudi J. Med. Pharm. Sci.* 2(9): 256–261. Shaw, E. M. 1938. South African native snuff boxes. *Ann. S. Afr. Mus.* 24: 221–252. Shaw, E. M. 1938. Native pipes and smoking in South Africa. *Ann. S. Afr. Mus.* 24: 277–302. Small, E. & Cronquist, A. 1976. A practical and natural taxonomy for *Cannabis. Taxon* 25: 405–435. Small, E. 1995. Hemp. In: Smartt, J. & Simmonds, N.W. (eds), *Evolution of crop plants,* 2nd ed., pp. 28–32. Longman, London. Smith, A. 1888. *A contribution to the South African materia medica,* Lovedale, South Africa. Smith, C.A. 1966. Common names of South African plants. *Mem. Bot. Surv. S. Afr.* 35. Smith, M.T. *et al.* 1996. Psychoactive constituents of the genus *Sceletium* N.E.Br. and other Mesembryanthemaceae: a review. *J. Ethnopharmacol.* 50: 119–130. Sobiecki, J.F. 2002. A preliminary inventory of plants used for psychoactive purposes in southern African healing traditions. *Trans. Roy. Soc. S. Afr.* 57: 1–24. Sobiecki, J.F. 2008. A review of plants used in divination in southern Africa and their psychoactive effects. *Southern African Humanities* 20(2): 333–351. Sobiecki, J.F. 2012. Psychoactive ubulawu spiritual medicines and healing dynamics in the initiation process of Southern Bantu diviners. *Journal of Psychoactive Drugs* 44(3): 216–223. Stafford, G.I., Pedersen, M.E., Van Staden, J. & Jäger, A.K. 2008. Review on plants with CNS-effects used in traditional South African medicine against mental diseases. *J. Ethnopharmacol.* 119(3): 513–537. Stockman, R. 1912. Stimulant narcotics, with a special account of *Catha edulis. Pharm. J.* 4th series 35. Terburg, D., Syal, S., Rosenberger, L.A., Heany, S., Phillips, N., Gericke, N., Stein, D.J. & van Honk, J. 2013. Acute effects of *Sceletium tortuosum* (Zembrin), a dual 5-HT reuptake and PDE4 inhibitor, in the human amygdala and its connection to the hypothalamus. *Neuropsychopharmacology* 38(13): 2708–2716. United States Pharmacopeia, March 1998. *Hypericum* (St. John's Wort). *Botanical Monograph Series.* Information for the Health Care Professional and Consumer. USP DI. Van den Eynden, V. *et al.* 1992. *The ethnobotany of the Topnaar.* Universiteit Gent, Gent. Van Wyk, B.-E. & Gericke, N. 2000. *People's plants – A guide to useful plants of southern Africa.* Briza Publications, Pretoria. Van Wyk, B.-E. *et al.* 1997. *Medicinal plants of South Africa.* Briza Publications, Pretoria. Van Wyk, B.-E., Van Oudtshoorn, B. & Gericke, N. 2009. *Medicinal plants of South Africa.* 2nd ed. Briza Publications, Pretoria. Van Wyk, B.-E., De Castro, A., Tilney, P.M., Winter, P.J.D. & Magee, A.R. 2008. A new species of *Alepidea* (Apiaceae, subfam. Saniculoideae). *S. Afr. J. Bot.* 74: 740–745. Von Bibra, E. 1995. *Plant intoxicants. A classic text on the use of mind-altering plants.* Healing Arts Press, Rochester, Vermont. Von Koenen, E. 2001. *Medicinal, poisonous and edible plants in Namibia.* Klaus Hess Publishers, Windhoek and Göttingen. Watt, J.M. 1967. African plants potentially useful in mental health. *Lloydia* 30: 1–22. Watt, J.M. & Breyer-Brandwijk, M.G. 1962. *The medicinal and poisonous plants of southern and eastern Africa,* 2nd ed. Livingstone, London. Wilman, M. 1933. *The rock engravings of Griqualand West and Bechuanaland.* Deighton Bell, Cambridge. Wink, M. & Van Wyk, B.-E. 2008. *Mind-altering and poisonous plants of the world.* Timber Press, USA and Briza Publications, Pretoria. Winkelman, M. & Dobkin De Rios, M. 1989. Psychoactive properties of !Kung bushmen medicine plants. *Journal of Psychoactive Drugs* 21: 51–59. Zukulu, S., Dold, T., Abbott, T. & Raimondo, D. 2012. *Medicinal and charm plants of Pondoland.* South African National Biodiversity Institute, Pretoria.

MIND & MOOD PLANTS

Flowering branch of tobacco (*Nicotiana tabacum*)

Johannes Malgas demonstrating how *roltwak* (rolled tobacco) is made (Kleinplasie Farm Museum, Worcester)

Harvested tobacco (Kleinplasie Farm Museum, Worcester)

How rolled tobacco/twist chewing tobacco (*roltwak*) is made

Rolled tobacco/twist chewing tobacco (*roltwak*)

Mrs Ndlovu explaining the role of *Xysmalobium* in women's health

CHAPTER 10

Women's health

SOMEWHERE IN THE region of two-thirds of babies born worldwide are delivered by traditional birth attendants. In the past, very little attention has been focused by ethnographers, anthropologists and medical ethnobotanists on the traditional management of women's health, and the majority of practices have not been adequately studied or documented. The chemistry, pharmacology and nutritional value of the plants used are generally unknown. The full spectrum of traditional preventive, promotive and curative interventions are still practised in remote rural areas, although these are rapidly being displaced by the increasing availability of modern health services and access to modern education. Modern obstetrics can learn a great deal from a serious study of the traditional management of labour, not least the physiologically beneficial practice of a squatting position, rather than the supine position favoured in hospitals and clinics.

Each healer or traditional midwife has a favourite *materia medica* that depends on the availability of plants in the local environment, as well as on the oral tradition training from a senior mentor in the community. A wide spectrum of plants are still used to enhance fertility, regulate the menstrual cycle, treat infection and pain, maintain pregnancy, tone the uterus, initiate and augment labour, expel a retained placenta, stimulate breast milk secretion, and ameliorate menopausal symptoms. In addition to more obvious interventions, the diet itself may be subtly changed in pregnancy, and this may reflect an increased intake of foods with higher iron, folic acid and calcium levels, not to mention other vitamins, minerals, amino acids and trace elements.

Once evaluated by a multidisciplinary team, the rationale behind traditional practices may be understood from a scientific perspective, particularly if the traditional concepts of disease and efficacy are thoroughly studied. *Isihlambezo* plant mixtures are often given in the last trimester of pregnancy. These preparations generally include plants with oxytocic action, and are used in low doses to tone and strengthen the uterine muscle in preparation for an uneventful delivery. The use of these mixtures only in the last trimester is important, because the foetus is least vulnerable to potentially harmful phytochemicals at this stage. In the first trimester the embryo is developing, and potentially toxic substances can disrupt this process, leading to abortion. In the second trimester, organ development is taking place, and potentially toxic substances can lead to congenital abnormalities.

There are many research opportunities for investigating the chemistry, pharmacology, safety, and efficacy of plants traditionally used in women's health. A valuable area of research is the laboratory screening of plant extracts and isolated plant compounds that could be used as phytoestrogens in health foods, beverages and supplements for women in menopause in order to decrease symptoms of irritability and hot flashes, decrease cardiovascular disease, and maintain bone density. Significant oestrogenic activity has recently been demonstrated in laboratory studies for extracts of two species of honeybush tea, *Cyclopia genistoides* and *C. subternata*, and for some isolated polyphenols found in these plants (Louw *et al.* 2013). Investment in human clinical research will ultimately be needed on standardised, reproducible extracts of these plants in order to demonstrate safety and efficacy in menopause, but the market potential for an evidence-based product is enormous.

Ethnobotanical surveys are continuously documenting new records of plants that have traditionally been used in various aspects of reproductive health. Recent scientific contributions and reviews on women's health and sexually transmitted diseases in southern Africa include Steenkamp (2003), Mulaudzi *et al.* (2011), De Wet *et al.* (2012) and Semenya *et al.* (2013). These studies reveal new uses of plants and provide interesting possibilities to study the scientific rationale that could explain the traditional plant use knowledge.

Acokanthera oppositifolia |Apocynaceae| **COMMON POISON BUSH** ■ See Chapter 15. Infusions of the root bark are used to treat excessive and irregular menstruation.

Adansonia digitata |Malvaceae| **BAOBAB** ■ See Chapter 19. Fruit pulp is prepared as a porridge if there is insufficient milk after delivery.

Agapanthus africanus |Agapanthaceae| ***UBANI*** (Zulu); blue lily; *leta-la-phofu* (Sotho); *bloulelie* (Afrikaans) ■ *Agapanthus africanus* can easily be recognised by the cluster of flowers on a long stalk, and by the long, strap-like leaves. The plants have thick, tuberous rhizomes, and are popular garden subjects. In addition to *A. africanus*, both *A. campanulatus* and *A. praecox* are widely used as medicines. A decoction of *A. africanus* rhizomes and roots is used on its own or in a mixture known as *isihlambezo*. This preparation is given orally or rectally as an antenatal medicine, taken from about the sixth or seventh month of pregnancy, and is mildly laxative and uterotonic. *Agapanthus* is also believed to assist in the functioning of the kidneys. In some cases, water in which the plant is grown is drunk twice a day from about the fifth month of pregnancy to ensure a healthy baby, and to ensure that the placenta is expelled normally during labour. Stronger decoctions of the rhizome are taken orally or rectally to induce labour, augment contractions in a difficult labour, and to expel a retained placenta. It is sometimes combined with *Typha capensis*, and may also be given to the baby by mouth immediately after birth, and before the first feed, or as a wash for the baby.

An infusion of the root is taken as a ritual emetic for coughs and chest and heart conditions. *Agapanthus praecox* is used as an aphrodisiac, and *A. campanulatus* is used to treat "cradle cap" in infants.

Several saponins and sapogenins have been isolated from the rhizomes of *Agapanthus* species, for example agapanthagenin, which is known only from *A. africanus* and other *Agapanthus* species. Although the identity of most phytochemicals in *Agapanthus* is not known, saponins are a highly bioactive group of molecules, and may have anti-inflammatory, immuno-regulatory, antitussive and anti-oedema activities. Laboratory studies have demonstrated definite uterotonic activity in crude decoctions of *Agapanthus* (Kaido *et al.* 1994; Veale *et al.* 1999).

Agathosma betulina |Rutaceae| **ROUND-LEAF BUCHU** ■ See Chapter 8. Infusions, decoctions and tinctures are used for menstrual cramps, and with other plants in weight-loss products, probably on the basis of its diuretic, mild laxative and stimulant effects.

Aloe zebrina |Asphodelaceae| ***KGOPALMABALAMANTSI*** (Tswana); zebra aloe; *sebra-aalwyn* (Afrikaans); *aukoreb* (Nama) ■ A decoction of powdered stems and leaf bases is taken orally twice a day after delivery to "cleanse" the system. High doses of Cape aloes (see *Aloe ferox*, Chapter 7) have been used as abortifacients, on the basis of drastic purgation induced by the anthraquinones. Leaf infusions of *Aloe chabaudii* and *A. christianii* have been taken to induce abortion, and may have fatal consequences. A decoction of the leaves of *Aloe asperifolia* (also *aukoreb* in Nama) is taken to expel the placenta, and is given to livestock for the same purpose (Van den Eynden *et al.* 1992).

Amaranthus caudatus |Amaranthaceae| **MAROG** ■ See Chapter 4. The leaf is used as an abortifacient, while an infusion of *Amaranthus thunbergii* is taken to stimulate strong contractions of the uterus in delayed onset of labour.

Annona stenophylla |Annonaceae| **DWARF CUSTARD APPLE**; *thwui* (Kung); *muroro* (Mbukushu); *dwergsuikerappel* (Afrikaans) ■ The plant is a dwarf shrublet from northern Botswana and Namibia. A root infusion is taken orally for menstrual cramps and for heavy menstruation. The root infused with *Elephantorrhiza goetzei* is taken to treat syphilis, while mixed with *Securidaca longepedunculata* it is used to treat gonorrhoea.

Flowering plants of *ubani* (*Agapanthus africanus*)

Rhizomes of *Agapanthus praecox*

Flowering plant of *Aloe chabaudii*

Aristolochia heppii |Aristolochiaceae| ***OUPA-SE-PYP*** (Afrikaans) ■ A root infusion is taken as an abortifacient, and for abdominal pain and dysentery.

Artemisia afra |Asteraceae| ***UMHLONYANE*** ■ See Chapter 8. The genitals are steamed with *Artemisia* to relieve menstrual cramps, and to relieve pain after giving birth.

Asparagus exuvialis |Asparagaceae| **WILD ASPARAGUS**; *katdoring* (Afrikaans) ■ A root decoction of *Asparagus exuvialis* is taken to expel a retained placenta but is also used for coughs, tuberculosis, abdominal pain and constipation. Other species of *Asparagus* have been used to treat pneumonia, tuberculosis, malaria and urinary tract infections, to prevent illness in children, and to treat dehydration and haemorrhoids. Use as sedatives has also been reported. An infusion of above-ground parts of *Asparagus retrofractus* is used for colds, general body aches and gout (Mrs Bester, pers. comm.). Root extracts of *Asparagus racemosus* have been demonstrated to have cardiotonic, oxytocic, galactagogue and immuno-stimulatory activities.

Aspilia pluriseta |Asteraceae| ■ In Zimbabwe, a root infusion is taken to stimulate menstruation in amenorrhoea (Gelfand *et al.* 1985). A root infusion is taken orally for pain during pregnancy, and a decoction of the roots is taken orally when labour is prolonged. Infusions of the leaves of *Aspilia natalensis* are said to cause abortion and are not prescribed during pregnancy (Watt & Breyer-Brandwijk 1962).

Barleria macrostegia |Asteraceae| ■ The plant is taken at the time of menopause. To treat infertility and prevent miscarriage, the roots and leaves of *Barleria randii* are burnt and the smoke directed into the vagina. *Barleria spinulosa* has been used to treat pneumonia.

Bauhinia galpinii |Fabaceae| **PRIDE-OF-THE-KAAP**; *vlam-van-die-vlakte* (Afrikaans); *motshiwiriri* (Northern Sotho); *mutswiriri* (Venda); *umvangatane* (Zulu) ■ A decoction of the seeds, boiled with the seeds of *Vigna unguiculata*, is taken orally to stimulate menstruation in amenorrhoea. The root infusion of the closely related *Tylosema fassoglense* is used as a drench for a retained placenta in stock animals. A decoction of the tuber is taken for pneumonia and venereal disease, and diarrhoea is treated with a porridge of the infusion. The root of the closely related *Piliostigma thonningii* (previously known as *Bauhinia thonningii*) is taken as an oral infusion for menstrual cramps and for infertility. An infusion of the leaves, or a decoction or infusion of the root of *P. thonningii* is taken for heavy menstruation, and is also given to the mother post-partum, presumably for pain and to reduce bleeding. Infusions of the leaves are used as an anti-emetic. Preparations of the plant are used for ascites, coughs, convulsions and constipation.

Boscia foetida |Capparaceae| **STINKBUSH**, nonibush; *stinkbos, noeniebos* (Afrikaans); *xaubes* (Nama); *mopipi* (Tswana) ■ In Namibia, Nama people use leaf decoctions to promote menstruation (Von Koenen 2001).

Bridelia micrantha |Phyllanthaceae| **MITZEERI**; *mitserie* (Afrikaans); *umhlahla-makhwaba* (Xhosa); *mushungunu* (Shona); *umhlalamgwababa* (Zulu) ■ In Zimbabwe, the plant is used as an abortifacient (Gelfand *et al.* 1985).

Burkea africana |Fabaceae| **WILD-SERINGA**; *wildesering* (Afrikaans); *monatô* (Tswana); *mugaranyenze* (Shona) ■ A bark infusion is taken orally for heavy menstruation. Root infusions and decoctions are taken orally for abdominal pain, dysentery and pneumonia, and are used as a gargle for toothache. The powdered bark is used as a dressing for tropical ulcers.

Capparis tomentosa |Capparaceae| **WOOLLY CAPER BUSH**; *gwambazi* (Venda); *iqwaningi* (Zulu); *wollerige kapperbos* (Afrikaans) ■ See Chapter 7. The plant has been used to prevent abortion and to treat infertility.

WOMEN'S HEALTH

Wild asparagus shrub (*Asparagus retrofractus*)

Leaf-like stems (cladodes) of *Asparagus retrofractus*

Flowers of pride-of-the-Kaap (*Bauhinia galpinii*)

Stinkbush (*Boscia foetida*)

Leaves of the stinkbush (*Boscia foetida*)

Wild-seringa tree (*Burkea africana*)

Chironia baccifera |Gentianaceae| ***BITTERBOS*** (Afrikaans) ■ This is an important medicine in South Africa, traditionally used by the Khoi. For labour, it is one of the most important Cape herbs. An infusion of fresh leaves and stems, and fruits if present, is very bitter and taken post-partum to expel a retained placenta (Dawid Bester, pers. comm.).

The plant is also used as a bitter tonic, and infusions and tinctures have been used to treat stomach ulcers, diarrhoea, syphilis, leprosy, kidney and bladder infections, diabetes and haemorrhoids, and as a "blood purifier" for skin conditions including acne, sores and boils. Side-effects that are known include a slightly loose stool, but never to the extent of causing diarrhoea (Dawid Bester, pers. comm.). The plant has been reported to be diaphoretic, and cause sleepiness. Combined with *wildeseldery* (*Notobubon galbanum*, previously known as *Peucedanum galbanum*), it is a well-known Cape remedy for arthritis (Pvt. Daniels, pers. comm.). *Chironia krebsii* and *C. palustris* have been used for colic and diarrhoea in children, and both these species are traditionally used by the Basotho people to relieve uneasiness in pregnant women (Moffett 2010).

Feeding of large quantities of *bitterbos* and *Chironia tetragona* to sheep and rabbits caused severe toxicity and death, but there are no reports of human toxicity, despite extensive use to this day in the Cape. The main secoiridoid is gentiopicroside, with small amounts of swertiamarine, chironioside and others also present. Other species of the Gentianaceae family, such as *Gentiana lutea* and *Chironia krebsii*, also contain gentiopicroside and chironioside, which are bitter substances traditionally used in the liquor industry, particularly in bitter aperitifs. Apart from some activity of *C. krebsii* extracts against the *Herpes simplex* virus, nothing seems to be known about the pharmacology of the plants.

Cissampelos mucronata |Menispermaceae| ■ Powdered root is taken with porridge for menstrual cramps, and root infusions are taken for infertility, uterine pain and heavy menstruation. Other medicinal uses of *Cissampelos* species are given in Chapter 7.

Clivia miniata |Amaryllidaceae| ***UMAYIME*** (Zulu); orange lily; *boslelie* (Afrikaans) ■ This attractive plant is a shade-loving perennial with a fleshy, tuberous rhizome and dark green, strap-shaped leaves. It is a popular garden plant and is commonly grown as a pot plant in many parts of the world. There are five species of *Clivia* and all except *C. mirabilis* are used in traditional medicine.

Preparations of the leaves and rhizome and roots are used to initiate labour when onset has been delayed, and also to facilitate delivery during labour. The rhizomes of *Clivia* species are extremely toxic due to the presence of numerous alkaloids, of which lycorine is the best-known compound, and use should be discouraged. Several structurally related alkaloids have been isolated from *C. miniata*, including clivacetine, clivonine, cliviasine and clividine. Lycorine occurs in *C. miniata* at levels of up to 0.4 per cent of the dry weight and causes salivation, vomiting and diarrhoea at low doses, and paralysis and collapse at high doses. Leaf extracts have been demonstrated to have uterotonic effects in laboratory studies.

Combretum microphyllum |Combretaceae| ***FLAMECREEPER***; *vlamklimop* (Afrikaans); *mutsiwa* (Shona); *mukopo-kopo* (Venda); *iwapha* (Zulu) ■ The plant is used to expel a retained placenta. Roots of *Combretum erythrophyllum* (river bushwillow) are used to treat venereal diseases. It is an ingredient of *isihlambezo* mixtures used to facilitate labour (Veale *et al.* 1992). In Zimbabwe, root powder is inserted into the vagina to make it tight and dry during intercourse. Fatalities have been reported from this practice. In Botswana decoctions of the roots are taken for venereal disease, and also in ointments applied topically to penile and vulval swellings (Hedberg & Staugård 1989). The Venda people use the roots of *Combretum molle* (velvet bushwillow or *mugwiti* in Venda) for infertility, and to treat post-partum bleeding.

Flowers of *bitterbos* (*Chironia baccifera*)

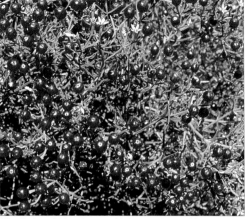

The fruits of *bitterbos* or Christmas berry (*Chironia baccifera*)

Flowers of *umayime* or orange lily (*Clivia miniata*)

Flowers of the flamecreeper (*Combretum microphyllum*)

Flowers and fruits of the river bushwillow (*Combretum erythrophyllum*)

Leaves and fruits of the velvet bushwillow (*Combretum molle*)

Commelina africana |Commelinaceae| **YELLOW COMMELINA**; *lekzotswana* (Xhosa); *idanga-bane* (Zulu); *geeleendagsblom* (Afrikaans) ■ Decoctions of the root are used for menstrual cramps. The blue-flowered *Commelina benghalensis* (Benghal commelina) is used for treating infertility in women.

Cyanotis speciosa |Commelinaceae| **DOLL'S POWDERPUFF**; *bloupoeierkwassie* (Afrikaans); *kgopo* (Sotho); *umagoswana* (Xhosa); *inkombo, udabulamafu* (Zulu) ■ Root decoctions are used for menstrual cramps and to facilitate conception.

Dicerocaryum eriocarpum |Pedaliaceae| **DEVIL'S THORN**, boot-protector, stud thorn; *bees-dubbeltjie* (Afrikaans); *tshêtlhô-êtonanyana* (Tswana) ■ See Chapter 14. The leaf infusion is clear and mucous-like. It is used to aid in the expulsion of the placenta in women and animals. An infusion of the whole plant is instilled into the vagina, and also taken orally to dilate and lubricate the birth canal. In Botswana, a decoction of the root is used three times a day to treat painful fallopian tubes (perhaps pelvic inflammatory disease). Root decoctions are used to treat cystitis and venereal disease, including gonorrhoea, in women and men, and powdered root bark is taken for venereal diseases. Root decoctions have been used as a remedy for kidney pain and hydrocoele, and whole plant infusions are taken for constipation. A powder of the root is taken orally in porridge for abdominal pain. A leaf infusion is used as a body wash in measles, and a root decoction is taken orally at the same time.

The lowveld foxglove, *Ceratotheca triloba*, also of the Pedaliaceae family, is used in an infusion to relieve menstrual cramps, and an infusion of the whole plant is taken to cause abortion. See also *Harpagophytum procumbens*, another member of the Pedaliaceae.

Dicoma anomala |Asteraceae| ***HLOENYA*** (Sotho); *maagwortel* (Afrikaans) ■ See Chapter 8. Powdered tuber is inserted into the vagina to treat uterine pain. An infusion mixed with soot and the root of *Aspilia pluriseta* is used to treat a prolonged labour.

Dregea macrantha |Apocynaceae| ***MORARANAKWENALERAJWE*** (Shona) ■ Root decoctions are taken twice a day for abdominal pain in pregnancy. It is also taken for venereal diseases, coughs, chest pain and infections of the mouth.

Eriospermum abyssinicum |Eriospermaceae| **BABOON'S EAR** ■ An infusion of the tuber is taken during the last three months of pregnancy to prevent still-birth.

Ficus sur |Moraceae| **BROOM CLUSTER FIG**; *besemtrosvy* (Afrikaans); *mogo-tshetlo* (Northern Sotho); *umkhiwane* (Xhosa, Swazi, Zulu) ■ A root infusion is taken for uterine pain, to prevent abortion, and by both sexes for infertility, and the latex is taken by mouth as an anti-emetic. A bark infusion is taken to increase lactation, and the powdered root is taken orally in porridge to treat nose bleeds. An infusion of the bark is taken orally for constipation in humans and animals. A root infusion is taken by mouth for sore throat. Latex is dropped directly onto the eye to treat cataracts or painful eyes. Powdered bark is applied to the skin to treat rashes. A cold water infusion of the stem bark of *Ficus sycomorus* (sycamore fig) is taken to stimulate milk production in a nursing mother.

Geranium incanum |Geraniaceae| ***VROUEBOSSIE*** (Afrikaans) ■ Infusions of the plant are said to be useful in treating bladder infections, venereal diseases and menstruation-related ailments.

Gnidia kraussiana |Thymelaeaceae| **YELLOW HEADS** ■ See Chapter 15. The plant is used as an abortifacient (Gelfand *et al.* 1985). Surprisingly, in view of the danger of toxicity, a decoction is taken by pregnant women in South Africa as an *isihlambezo* tonic to ensure healthy foetal growth and a smooth delivery (Veale *et al.* 1992).

Flower of yellow commelina (*Commelina africana*)

Flower of the blue commelina (*Commelina benghalensis*)

Flower of yellow commelina (*Commelina africana*)

Rhizome and roots of the blue commelina (*Commelina benghalensis*)

Lowveld foxglove (*Ceratotheca triloba*)

Leaves and flowers of the *vrouebossie* (*Geranium incanum*)

Gunnera perpensa |Haloragaceae or Gunneraceae| ***UGOBHO*** (Zulu); river pumpkin; *rivier-pampoen* (Afrikaans) ■ This is a vigorous perennial herb that grows in marshy areas and along stream banks. The large, round leaves resemble pumpkin leaves and the tuberous rhizomes are fleshy, soft and pink in cross-section. A decoction of fresh or dry roots is taken for menstrual pain. In larger doses it is a powerful oxytocic, causing the uterus to contract strongly, and is given post-partum to expel a retained placenta (Solomon Mahlaba, pers. comm.). Because of its potency it should never be given during labour to enhance contractions, as deaths have been reported from contraction of the lower segment of the uterus, resulting in necrosis of the tissue. *Ugobho* is also used as an ingredient in *isihlambezo* mixtures, sometimes together with *Rhoicissus digitata*, taken in small doses during pregnancy to tone the uterus. The root is also used to treat female infertility.

Root decoctions are also taken on their own, or with *Acorus calamus*, for male impotence, as they are believed to cleanse the blood and clear the way for an erection (Solomon Mahlaba, pers. comm.). The root decoction was formerly taken for colds and as a tonic for abdominal pain, indigestion, poor appetite, a bleeding stomach, and rheumatic fever, and was also taken internally to treat scabies. Infusions of the root have been used topically and taken orally for psoriasis, while tinctures have been used for urinary stones, and the root has been used as a wound-dressing.

In preliminary tests, crude decoctions of the rhizome showed definite uterotonic activity (Kaido *et al.* 1994). The main active compound responsible for causing contraction of the uterine muscle was isolated and identified as venusol, a phenylpropanoid glycoside (Khan *et al.* 2004).

Haplocarpha scaposa |Asteraceae| ***KGUTSANA***, *lengwako, disebo* (Sotho) ■ The soft, felt-like leaves are used during menstruation, and root decoctions are used in medicines to treat menstrual ailments, venereal diseases and sterility in women (Moffett 2010).

Harpagophytum procumbens |Pedaliaceae| **DEVIL'S CLAW**; *duiwelsklou* (Afrikaans); *sengaparile* (Tswana) ■ See Chapter 8. A root or tuber decoction is taken to treat infertility, and for menstrual cramps. Dried, powdered tuber is taken three times a day during pregnancy and after delivery to relieve pain, and an ointment made of the powdered root is applied topically to the abdomen in women who anticipate a difficult birth (Anderson & Staugård 1986). Interestingly, women from the Molapo community in the Kalahari in Botswana believe that using the plant during pregnancy can cause abortion. The doses used by this community, however, appeared to be considerably higher than doses indicated by Beza (pers. comm.) at Ghanzi. In low doses it can apparently be safely taken during pregnancy. In view of the risk of abortion, however, it is clear that it should not be used during pregnancy.

Holarrhena pubescens |Apocynaceae| **FEVERPOD**; *mukashumukono* (Shona); *koorspeulboom* (Afrikaans) ■ In Zimbabwe, the powdered root is taken in an infusion as an aphrodisiac and for infertility. It is also used as an abortifacient and for asthma, abdominal pain and constipation.

Hermannia depressa |Malvaceae| ***ROOI-OPSLAG*** (Afrikaans); *seretlwane* (Tswana) ■ A root decoction is taken twice a day for abdominal pain in pregnancy. Powdered root is taken with water for nausea and diarrhoea (Anderson & Staugård 1986).

Indigofera arrecta |Fabaceae| **AFRICAN INDIGO** ■ See Chapter 16. The roots of many species of *Indigofera* are used for women's health. When *Indigofera arrecta* is in flower, the roots are cooked with meat and the resulting broth taken orally for infertility. Root infusions are used for menstrual cramps and gonorrhoea, and in Zimbabwe roots of *Indigofera arrecta* or *I. demissa* are inserted into the vagina to induce abortion (Gelfand *et al.* 1985). An infusion of the root of *Indigofera antunesiana* is used for menstrual cramps and an infusion or decoction of *I. rhynchocarpa* is used to treat menstrual cramps. In Namibia, the Damara use a root infusion of *I. rautanenii* to treat venereal diseases.

Flowering plant of *ugobho* or river pumpkin (*Gunnera perpensa*)

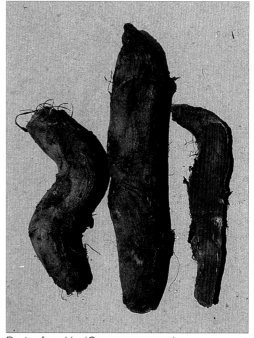

Roots of *ugobho* (*Gunnera perpensa*)

Digging devil's claw roots in the Kalahari

Flowers of devil's claw (*Harpagophytum procumbens*)

Leaves and flower of *seretlwane* (*Hermannia depressa*)

Jatropha zeyheri |Euphorbiaceae| *UGODIDE* ■ See Chapter 11. An infusion of the tuber is taken twice a day for menstrual pain, irregular periods, and during pregnancy to ensure a strong foetus (Anderson & Staugård 1986).

Lannea edulis |Anacardiaceae| **WILD GRAPE** ■ See Chapter 3. A root decoction is taken orally to prevent abortion when it is anticipated, and a root infusion is taken orally for menstrual pain, and to dilate the birth canal in pregnancy. The root of the live-long (*Lannea discolor*) is used for female infertility, excessive menstruation, gonorrhoea and swollen legs. Strong bark decoctions of *Lannea edulis* were taken to treat blackwater fever, diarrhoea and dysentery. Roots cooked with seeds of cowpea (*Vigna unguiculata*) are taken when there is blood in the urine, and for bilharzia. The inner bark of *Lannea discolor* is ground and used for convulsions, diarrhoea, boils and abscesses, and the root to treat whooping cough. The bark fibre is used as a bandage, and twigs as splints for fractures of limbs.

Leonotis nepetifolia |Lamiaceae| *OUSEPAMAWIWIRI* (Herero) ■ The leaves are used by women in Namibia for menstrual problems, as they are antispasmodic and stop bleeding. They are also purgative, and have been used to induce abortion. Decoctions of *L. leonurus* (see Chapter 7) have been used to promote menstruation in amenorrhoea (Watt & Breyer-Brandwijk 1962).

Lessertia frutescens |Fabaceae| **CANCER BUSH** ■ See Chapter 8. The plant has been used as a douche in prolapse of the uterus, and a decoction is taken orally post-delivery on the same day to expel retained blood, treat post-partum pain, and to assist in healing and resolution of the uterus. It is also used to treat cystitis (Dawid Bester, pers. comm.). *Lessertia frutescens* subsp. *microphylla* has been used to treat amenorrhoea (Watt & Breyer-Brandwijk 1962).

Mentha longifolia |Lamiaceae| **WILD MINT** ■ See Chapter 7. An infusion is taken three times a day for cystitis (Dawid Bester, pers. comm.).

Monadenium lugardiae |Euphorbiaceae| *TSHISWOSWO* (Venda) ■ The plant has succulent stems and leaves with irritant milky latex. It has been used as an abortifacient (Gelfand *et al.* 1985).

Myrothamnus flabellifolius |Myrothamnaceae| **RESURRECTION PLANT** ■ See Chapter 6. The whole plant is burnt, and smoke is directed into the vagina to treat uterine pain.

Parinari curatellifolia|Chrysobalanaceae| **MOBOLA PLUM** ■ See Chapter 3. A root infusion made together with *Asparagus* species is taken orally for a painful uterus.

Pavonia senegalensis |Malvaceae| ■ A cold water infusion of the dry roots is taken to induce labour, particularly if the onset has been delayed. A large quantity of root decoction is taken orally if the delivery is difficult (Anderson & Staugård 1986).

Pellaea calomelanos |Adiantaceae| **HARD FERN** ■ See Chapter 7. The whole plant is burned and smoke directed into the vagina for uterine pain (Gelfand *et al.* 1985).

Pouzolzia mixta |Urticaceae| **SOAP-NETTLE** ■ See Chapter 14. The powdered root is inserted into the vagina or taken orally, sometimes in porridge, for infertility, uterine pain and to treat venereal diseases. A root infusion left to stand overnight is taken orally once a day as a contraceptive. Root decoctions and infusions are taken as aphrodisiacs, while the powdered root is inserted into the vagina when an abortion seems imminent. An infusion of the root is instilled into the vagina during labour to dilate the birth canal, and the hand of the midwife is moistened with the soapy infusion. An infusion of the bark or root is instilled directly into the vagina to expel a retained placenta. The roots and bark have been used to treat constipation. A root paste is applied to burns and thin strips of bark fibre have been used to stitch wounds in Zimbabwe (Gelfand *et al.* 1985).

Tubers and leaves of *ugodide* (*Jatropha zeyheri*)

Rhizome and annual branches of
Lannea edulis

Leaves and flowers of *Lannea discolor*

Bark of *Lannea discolor*

Leaves and flowers of *Leonotis nepetifolia*

Flowers of *Lannea discolor*

Rhoicissus tridentata |Vitaceae| ***ISINWAZI*** (Zulu); wild grape (English); *bobbejaantou* (Afrikaans) ■ The plant is a shrubby creeper with glossy green leaves that are divided into three toothed, wedge-shaped leaflets. Inconspicuous yellowish-green flowers are followed by small red berries. The plant is widely distributed in the eastern parts of southern Africa. The tuberous roots, which are blood red when fresh, were known to the San who depicted them in rock paintings.

Infusions and decoctions of the tuber are taken for menstrual cramps and for female infertility. A decoction of the root or tuber is sometimes taken during pregnancy for abdominal distension, and as an ingredient in a pregnancy tonic called *inembe*, which is taken regularly throughout pregnancy to tone the uterus. Leaves crushed in a little water are taken orally as an abortifacient. Cold water infusions are taken orally to initiate labour if the onset is delayed. Decoctions and infusions are taken immediately after delivery to expel a retained placenta (Patrick Ndlovu, pers. comm.). A preparation of the root and leaves of *Cissus cornifolia*, of the same family, is taken a day prior to delivery to induce labour.

The roots or tubers are also taken as infusions and decoctions for colds, bleeding peptic ulcers, kidney and bladder complaints, gonorrhoea, and for backache, epilepsy and insanity. The fruit is edible, and the leaf has been used to wipe babies' bottoms.

The tubers are potentially toxic; pigs are known to have died from eating it. Toxicity has been demonstrated in rabbits, and a human fatality has been ascribed to ingestion of the tubers. Reports are contradictory, as the tubers are recorded as being edible (Palmer & Pitman 1972) and toxic (Fox & Norwood Young 1982). Experiments by Katsoulis *et al.* (2000) showed that an extract of *Rhoicissus tridentata* subsp. *cuneifolia* directly stimulated contractions of the uterus and ileum, most likely due to muscarinic receptors and cyclooxygenase metabolites. In an unpublished thesis, Mshengu (2016) reported that a mixture of asiatic acid and arjunolic acid is responsible for the uterotonic activity.

Sarcostemma viminale |Apocynaceae| ***MELKTOU*** (Afrikaans); *mutungu* (Venda) ■ The plant is given to nursing mothers to stimulate the flow of milk (Watt & Breyer-Brandwijk 1962). This is an example of the concept of the so-called "Doctrine of Signatures", where physical features of a plant are considered to be indicative of the potential uses of the plant.

Schkuhria pinnata |Asteraceae| **DWARF MEXICAN MARIGOLD**; *ruhwahwa* (Shona); *kleinkakiebossie, waaibossie* (Afrikaans) ■ This is an exotic weed with wiry branches and small yellow flower heads. An infusion of the whole plant is used as an abortifacient, and is also taken shortly before intercourse as an oral contraception.

Securidaca longepedunculata |Polygalaceae| **VIOLET-TREE** ■ See Chapter 12. An infusion of the pounded root is drunk for menstrual cramps.

Senna italica |Fabaceae| **WILD SENNA**; *swartstormbossie* (Afrikaans) ■ See Chapter 7. A decoction of fresh or dry roots is used in the treatment of constipation, particularly during pregnancy (Isaac Mayeng, pers. comm.), and sometimes in combination with *Solanum capense*. The root infusion of the sjambok pod (*Cassia abbreviata*), taken orally, is an aphrodisiac and is also used to regulate heavy menstruation and as an abortifacient. The seed is used as a tonic, and the root is taken for toothache. The smoke from smouldering twigs is inhaled to treat headache.

Steganotaenia araliacea |Apiaceae| **CARROT TREE**; *wortelboom* (Afrikaans); *kaab* (Nama); *epondo* (Himba) ■ In Mozambique, an infusion of the roots is taken orally for infertility. A root infusion is taken in Zimbabwe to treat amenorrhoea, and may be abortifacient (Gelfand *et al.* 1985). It is also taken for gonorrhoea and for epilepsy. In Namibia, the roots are used for fever, sore throats and asthma.

Stem tuber of *isinwazi* or wild grape (*Rhoicissus tridentata*)

Flower of *melktou* (*Sarcostemma viminale*)

Broken stem of *melktou* (*Sarcostemma viminale*), showing the copious flow of milky latex

Fruits of the sjambok pod (*Cassia abbreviata*)

Carrot tree (*Steganotaenia araliacea*)

Siphonochilus aethiopicus |Zingiberaceae| **WILD GINGER**, African ginger, *isiphephetho, indungulo* (Zulu); *wilde-gemmer* (Afrikaans) ■ See Chapter 7. An infusion of the rhizome is used for menstrual cramps. In common with other members of the ginger family such as ginger (*Zingiber officinalis*) and turmeric (*Curcuma longa*), the rhizomes and roots contain diarylheptanoids, which are probably responsible for the antispasmodic activity.

Typha capensis |Typhaceae| **BULRUSH**; *papkuil* (Afrikaans); *zaza* (Kung) ■ See Chapter 5. The rhizome, taken in the form of a porridge prepared from the infusion, is taken for menstrual pain, and for any pain in the uterus. An infusion of the rhizome is given to strengthen contractions during labour, and to expel the placenta, in humans as well as animals. Infusions and decoctions of the rhizome are used as male sexual tonics and to improve the circulation (Solomon Mahlaba, pers. comm.). Venereal diseases, dysentery, diarrhoea, enteritis, and kidney and bladder conditions are also treated with the root infusions, and they are believed to be blood-purifying (Gelfand *et al.* 1985; Von Koenen 2001).

Vigna unguiculata |Fabaceae| **COWPEA** ■ See Chapters 2 and 4. A decoction of the seed is taken orally to treat amenorrhoea, and powdered root is eaten with porridge for painful menstruation, epilepsy and chest pain. A root infusion is given to infants for constipation, and a root paste applied to the bitten area as an antidote to snakebite.

Vernonia **species** |Asteraceae| ■ A number of species of *Vernonia* are used in treating women's health problems. An infusion of the root of the bitter leaf (*V. amygdalina*) is taken orally, and is given as a douche for uterine pain. Root infusions are used as an aphrodisiac, and taken for infertility, amenorrhoea, and for treating gonorrhoea. Powdered root of *V. glaberrima* is taken in porridge for menstrual cramps and for venereal diseases. In KwaZulu-Natal, *V. natalensis* is used in *isihlambezo* mixtures to ensure a healthy pregnancy and labour, and leaf and root decoctions are used by the Venda to induce abortion (Mabogo 1990), sometimes with fatal consequences. The genus *Vernonia* is currently under revision and some species have been moved to other genera.

Withania somnifera |Solanaceae| ***UBUVIMBHA*** ■ See Chapter 8. Preparations of this well-known tonic plant have been taken to tone the uterus in women who habitually miscarry (Watt & Breyer-Brandwijk 1962). The plant is used as a general tonic in many African and Asian countries and is one of the most important medicinal plants of Ayurvedic medicine.

Ximenia americana | Olacaceae| **BLUE SOURPLUM**, mountain plum; *blousuurpruim* (Afrikaans); *omuninga* (Herero, Himba); *oshipeke oshikukulu* (Kwanyama) ■ See Chapter 3. Roots are used in Namibia to treat afterbirth pains and the leaves are chewed for venereal disease. An infusion of the leaves is used as an eyewash, and for toothache and constipation (Gelfand *et al.* 1985; Anderson & Staugård 1986).

Ximenia caffra |Olacaceae| **SOURPLUM**; *suurpruim* (Afrikaans); *umthunduluka-obomvu, umthunduluka* (Zulu) ■ See Chapter 3. Powdered root is taken in soup or beer as an aphrodisiac, and root decoctions or leaf powder are taken for infertility. Porridge is made using a decoction of the roots, and eaten once a day for nausea in pregnancy. An infusion of the roots is used for pelvic disease (possibly pelvic inflammatory disease) and venereal disease. Powdered root is applied as a wound-dressing. Root or leaf infusions are taken for abdominal pain and cramps, and root infusions and decoctions for diarrhoea and haematuria, including for bilharzia. Extracts of the bark and roots are used for systemic sepsis and rheumatism. Powdered leaves are taken orally for fever, and extracts of the leaves are used as a gargle for tonsillitis, and as a vermifuge. Cold water leaf infusions are used as an eyewash for painful eye conditions in humans and animals, while powdered leaves are applied to fresh wounds as a styptic.

WOMEN'S HEALTH

Bulrush (*Typha capensis*)

Roots of *Vernonia* species: *innyathelo* (*V. adoense*) with thinner roots and *umhlunguhlungu* (*V. neocorymbosa*) with thicker and longer roots

Xysmalobium undulatum |Apocynaceae| **UZARA** ■ See Chapter 7. Dry powdered root and extracts of the root are an excellent remedy for painful menstrual cramps and have an antispasmodic activity (Pahlow 1979). Uzara has a long history of commercial use in Germany. A comprehensive review was presented by Vermaak *et al.* (2014) and chemical variation and quality control by Kanama *et al.* (2016).

Zantedeschia albomaculata |Araceae| **SPOTTED ARUM LILY** ■ A decoction has been used in South Africa to prevent repeat miscarriages, and to prevent giving birth to small, weak babies (Watt & Breyer-Brandwijk 1962).

REFERENCES AND FURTHER READING: Anderson, S. & Staugård, F. 1986. *Traditional medicine in Botswana. Traditional midwives.* Ipelegeng Publishers, Gabarone, Botswana. **Bruneton, J. 1995.** *Pharmacognosy, phytochemistry, medicinal plants.* Intercept, Hampshire. **Bryant, A.T. 1966.** *Zulu medicine and medicine men,* new ed. Struik, Cape Town. **Cook, P.A.W. 1927.** Customs relating to twins among the Bomvana of the Transkei. *S. Afr. J. Sci.* 24: 516–520. **Cory, H. 1949.** The ingredients of magic medicines. *Africa* 19: 13–32. **Crouch, N.R., Mulholland, D.A., Pohl, T.L. & Ndlovu, E. 2003.** The ethnobotany and chemistry of the genus *Clivia* (Amaryllidaceae). *S. Afr. J. Bot.* 69: 144-147. **Cunningham, A.B. 1988.** *An investigation of the herbal medicine trade in Natal/Kwazulu.* Investigational report no 29, Institute of Natural Resources, University of Natal. **De Almeida, A.G. 1930.** Plantas venenosas e medicinas dos indigenos de Moçambique. *Bolm agric. pecuár. Moçamb.* 1: 9–29. **De Lange, M. 1961.** Dolls for the promotion of fertility as used by some of the Nguni tribes and the Basotho. *Ann. Cape Prov. Mus.* 1: 86–101. **De Wet, H., Nzama, V.N. & Van Vuuren, S.F. 2012.** Medicinal plants used for the treatment of sexually transmitted infections by lay people in northern Maputaland, KwaZulu-Natal Province, South Africa. *S. Afr. J. Bot.* 78: 12–20. **Dornan, S.S. 1932.** Some beliefs and ceremonies connected with the birth and death of twins among the South African natives. *S. Afr. J. Sci.* 29: 690–700. **Duncan, G., Jeppe, B. & Voigt, L. 2016.** *The Amaryllidaceae of southern Africa.* Umdaus Press, Pretoria. **Etkin, N.L. 1986.** *Plants in indigenous medicine and diet. Biobehavioral approaches.* Redgrave, New York. **Fox, F.W. & Norwood Young, M.E. 1982.** *Food from the veld.* Delta Books, Johannesburg. **Gelfand, M. et al. 1985.** *The traditional medical practitioner in Zimbabwe.* Mambo Press, Harare. **Gumede, M.V. 1990.** *Traditional healers. A medical doctor's perspective.* Skotaville Publishers, Braamfontein, Johannesburg. **Hedberg, I. & Staugård, F. 1989.** *Traditional medicinal plants – traditional medicine in Botswana.* Ipelegeng Publishers, Gaborone. **Hutchings, A. et al. 1996.** *Zulu medicinal plants.* Natal University Press, Pietermaritzburg. **Iwu, M.M. 1993.** *Handbook of African medicinal plants.* CRC Press, Boca Raton. **Kaido, T.L. et al. 1994.** The preliminary screening of plants used as traditional herbal remedies during pregnancy and labour. South African Pharmacological Society, 28th Annual Congress, Cape Town, 22–24 September 1994. **Kanama, S., Viljoen, A.M., Enslin, G., Kamatou, G.P.P., Chen, W., Sandasi, M. & Idowu, T. 2016.** Uzara – a quality control perspective of *Xysmalobium undulatum. Pharm. Biol.* 54(7): 1272–1279. **Katsoulis, L.C., Veale, D.J.H. & Havlik, I. 2000.** The pharmacological action of *Rhoicissus tridentata* on isolated rat uterus and ileum. *Phytoth. Res.* 14: 460–462. **Khan, F., Peter, X.K., Mackenzie, R.M., Katsoulis, L., Gehring, R., Munro, O.Q., Van Heerden, F.R. & Drewes, S.E. 2004.** Venusol from *Gunnera perpensa:* structural and activity studies. *Phytochemistry* 65: 1117–1121. **Laidler, P.W. 1928.** The magic medicine of the Hottentots. *S. Afr. J. Sci.* 25: 433–447. **Louw, A., Joubert, E. & Visser, K. 2013.** Phytoestrogenic potential of *Cyclopia* extracts and polyphenols. *Planta Medica* 79(07): 580–590. **Mulaudzi, R.B., Ndhlala, A.R., Kulkarni, M.G., Finnie, J.F. & Van Staden, J. 2011.** Antimicrobial properties and phenolic contents of medicinal plants used by the Venda people for conditions related to venereal diseases. *J. Ethnopharmacol.* 135: 330–337. **Ngubane, H. 1977.** *Body and mind in Zulu medicine. An ethnography of health and disease in Nyuswa-Zulu thought and practice.* Academic Press, London. **Pahlow, M. 1979.** *Das Grosse Buch der Heil Pflanzen. Gesund durch die Heilkraefte der Natur.* Grafe und Unzer, Munchen. **Palmer, E. & Pitman, N. 1972.** *Trees of Southern Africa.* (3 vols). Balkema, Cape Town. **Ponglux, D. et al. (eds) 1987.** *Medicinal plants.* The first Princess Chulabhorn Science Congress, Bangkok, Thailand. **Pujol, J. 1990.** *Naturafrica – the herbalist handbook.* Jean Pujol Natural Healers Foundation, Durban. **Rood, B. 1994.** *Uit die veldapteek.* Tafelberg, Cape Town. **Semenya, S.S., Maroyi, A., Potgieter, M.J. & Erasmus, L.J.C. 2013.** Herbal medicines used by Bapedi traditional healers to treat reproductive ailments in the Limpopo Province, South Africa. *Afr. J. Tradit. Complement. Altern. Med.* 10(2): 331–339. **Smith, A. 1888.** *A contribution to the South African materia medica.* Lovedale, South Africa. **Smith, C.A. 1966.** Common names of South African plants. *Mem. Bot. Surv. S. Afr.* 35. **Steenkamp, V. 2003.** Traditional herbal remedies used by South African women for gynaecological complaints. *J. Ethnopharmacol.* 86: 97–108. **Van Wyk, B.-E., Van Oudtshoorn, B. & Gericke, N. 2009.** *Medicinal plants of South Africa.* Revised and expanded 2nd ed. Briza Publications, Pretoria. **Veale, D.J.H. et al. 1992.** South African traditional herbal medicines used during pregnancy and childbirth. *J. Ethnopharmacol.* 36: 185–191. **Veale, D.J.H. et al. 1999.** Pharmacological effects of *Agapanthus africanus* on the isolated rat uterus. *J. Ethnopharmacol.* 66: 257–262. **Venter, F. 1997.** *Botanical survey of the medicinal plants of the Northern Sotho, Northern Province, South Africa.* Land management and rural development programme, University of the North. **Vermaak, I., Enslin, G., Idowu, T. & Viljoen, A.M. 2014.** *Xysmalobium undulatum* (Uzara) – review of an antidiarrhoeal traditional medicine. *J. Ethnopharmacol.* 156: 135–146. **Von Koenen, E. 2001.** *Medicinal, poisonous and edible plants in Namibia.* Klaus Hess Publishers, Windhoek and Göttingen. **Watt, J.M. & Breyer-Brandwijk, M.G. 1962.** *The medicinal and poisonous plants of southern and eastern Africa,* 2nd ed. Livingstone, London.

WOMEN'S HEALTH

Ulrich Feiter with flowering and fruiting plants of *Xysmalobium undulatum*

Flowering plants of the krantz aloe (*Aloe arborescens*)

Plantation of *Aloe vera* in Harlingen, Texas

The first plantation of *Aloe ferox* (Albertinia, Western Cape)

Leaves and flowers of comfrey (*Symphytum officinale*), a European wound-healing plant

CHAPTER 11

Wounds, burns & skin conditions

LITERALLY HUNDREDS OF different plants are used to treat wounds, burns and skin conditions throughout the southern African region, and a small sample of the most commonly used ones have been described here. Healing in a wound or burn is a complex process, acting on many levels that can be facilitated in a number of ways. The simple process of regular washing followed by occlusion of the wound goes a long way to prevent dirt and exudates from accumulating that may lead to bacterial infection, and healing is enhanced when plants with antiseptic activity are used in the wash or applied topically. Some of the plants used in dressings contain mucilage, which provides a mechanical barrier and also keeps the wound from drying out, and many are likely to have anti-inflammatory, antibacterial and antifungal activities as well. In some cases, plants with significant analgesic activity have been selected for the pain of burns, boils and abscesses. In fresh bleeding wounds, astringent tannins act as styptics by shrinking the tissues and promoting clotting, and may also have specific antimicrobial activities that are important in keeping the wound from getting infected.

One of the most studied wound-healing plants is *Centella asiatica*, and here the wound-healing activity is due to the facilitated development of normal connective tissue. This process includes stimulating an increase in the development of blood vessels in the affected area, an increase in the formation of tissue structural components, and an increase in the keratinisation of the epidermis.

Another famous wound-healing plant is *Aloe vera*, a plant of North African or Arabian origin. It is a sterile cultigen that is propagated by suckers. Aloe was once a material of military strategic importance. An army of foot soldiers needed stomach medicine and a regular purge ("blood cleansing") to keep them in good health because of problems with food quality and hygiene. At the same time, they also needed topical medicine to treat the wounds of battle. Being a long-lasting succulent, *Aloe vera* plants could be carried along for long periods as the perfect two-in-one medicine. It is claimed that Alexander the Great conquered the island of Socotra to ensure a regular supply of aloe. *Aloe ferox* is one of only a few plants depicted in rock art in southern Africa, confirming the traditional importance of aloe as a medicinal plant. Another southern African species, *Aloe arborescens*, has become popular in almost all Asian countries. It is grown as a pot plant so that the leaf gel is available at all times as an emergency treatment for minor bruises, cuts and burns. The gel of *Bulbine frutescens* (burn jelly plant or *balsemkopiva*) is similar to that of *Aloe* species and is traditionally used to treat wounds and burns. The plant has become a popular ornamental succulent and is grown in gardens in all parts of southern Africa.

In recent years there has been considerable research activity, not only to record the plant species that are traditionally used for wound healing and skin care, but also to study the antimicrobial activity of southern African medicinal plants. There are several examples of recent ethnobotanical surveys that documented wound-healing plants (e.g. Grierson & Afolayan 1999a; De Wet *et al.* 2013; Afolayan *et al.* 2014; Lall & Kishore 2014). Studies focusing on the biological mechanisms of action of specific wound-healing plants are quite rare (e.g., Grierson & Afolayan 1999b; Steenkamp *et al.* 2004; Pather *et al.* 2011). General antimicrobial studies reviewed by Van Vuuren (2008) include those of Rabe & Van Staden (1997), Kelmanson *et al.* (2000) and Eloff *et al.* (2008). A review of the role of inflammation and South African medicinal plants with anti-inflammatory activity (Iwalewa *et al.* 2007) included many species that are used in wound healing.

Agathosma betulina |Rutaceae| **ROUND-LEAF BUCHU** ■ See Chapter 8. Vinegar infusions of buchu (*boegoeasyn* in Afrikaans), left to draw in the sun until they reach a syrupy consistency, and hot water infusions are famous early Cape rinses and dressings for fresh and septic wounds, and are still used in some areas to this day.

Aloe arborescens |Asphodelaceae| **KRANTZ ALOE**; *inkalane* (Zulu); *kransaalwyn* (Afrikaans) ■ *Aloe arborescens* is a popular garden subject in many countries in the world. It is especially popular in Japan and is commonly found at nurseries and garden shops under the name "Japan aloe". The split or crushed fresh leaves, and commercial gel extracted from the leaves, have been widely used to treat burns and wounds. The healing value of aloes received attention in the West when nuclear irradiation burn victims from the atomic explosion at Hiroshima were treated with *Aloe arborescens*. Extracts of the leaves have been found to have wound-healing, anti-inflammatory, anti-ulcer, antibacterial, anticancer and antidiabetic effects. These activities are partly ascribed to polysaccharides and glycoproteins.

Aloe ferox |Asphodelaceae| **BITTER ALOE** ■ See Chapters 7 and 8. There are San rock paintings in South Africa depicting *Aloe ferox* as a recognisable species, and early European travellers reported that the Khoi demonstrated its medicinal uses. The tapping of aloes (to obtain the bitter aloe lump) was first demonstrated in the eighteenth century by a slave in the Gouritz River area of the Western Cape, where the South African aloe industry is still centred. Split or crushed fresh leaves are applied directly onto open wounds, sores, burns and ulcers, and have an excellent reputation for healing. They are also used for sores and injuries in livestock. The dry, powdered bitter fraction is sometimes applied as a dusting powder to open wounds, and is also taken orally in small doses as a "blood purifier" in cases of acne. It is also used to dress traditional scarifications and venereal ulcers (Solomon Mahlaba, Ashley Mashigo, pers. comm.). Commercial preparations of the gel have been reported to heal certain chronic leg ulcers and improve some cases of eczema (M.C. Botha, pers. comm.), and give significant relief to acute sunburn.

Aloe vera |Asphodelaceae| ***ALOE VERA*** ■ See Chapter 14. This aloe is planted in large commercial plantations in Central American countries, Mexico and Texas, and nowadays also in China and in the Limpopo Province of South Africa. It produces an abundance of leaf gel. *Aloe vera* has been popularised internationally in a wide range of products for its healing, moisturising and emollient properties. The gel is well researched and is one of the most effective wound- and burn-healing substances.

Boophone disticha |Amaryllidaceae| **BUSHMAN POISON BULB** ■ See Chapter 9. The dry bulb scales, sometimes first soaked in oil, are applied as a dressing to circumcision wounds and to burns to facilitate healing and reduce pain and swelling. They are also applied to infected sores, abscesses and boils, and to skin rashes and painful joints. Analgesic and anti-inflammatory effects can be expected and these are probably due to the rich content of Amaryllidaceae alkaloids (see *Haemanthus coccineus*).

Bulbine frutescens |Asphodelaceae| ***BALSEMKOPIVA***, *geneesbossie* (Afrikaans); burn jelly plant ■ The leaves are filled with a clear gel, similar in appearance and consistency to *Aloe vera* gel. The fresh gel from *Bulbine* species is widely used for burns, wounds, cuts, abrasions, rashes and boils. It is useful for eczema, cracked lips and herpes, and some commercial shampoos include it as a moisturiser. The healing effect is likely to be due to glycoproteins, which are also present in the leaf gel of *Aloe* species. The *in vivo* effects of cutaneous wound healing of *Bulbine frutescens* and *B. natalensis* were studied by Pather *et al.* (2011).

Plantations of *Bulbine frutescens* have been established in the Limpopo Province of South Africa, where innovative commercial skincare products are being produced.

WOUNDS, BURNS & SKIN CONDITIONS

Flowering plant of *Bulbine frutescens*

Leaf gel of *Bulbine frutescens*

Plantation of *Bulbine frutescens* in the Limpopo Province

Cadaba aphylla |Capparaceae| **SWARTSTORM** (Afrikaans) ■ The plant is a robust woody and practically leafless shrub with smooth, greyish green stems and attractive, bright red flowers. The moist powdered plant is applied as a poultice between layers of gauze to draw boils and abscesses. The root is used in small doses as a tonic, and also as a purgative. It is potentially toxic in overdose.

Callilepis laureola |Asteraceae| **IMPILA** (Zulu) ■ This popular Zulu traditional medicine is an erect perennial suffrutex with leafy annual stems developing from a thick, carrot-like, tuberous tap root. Attractive flower heads with dark purple or black disc florets and white ligulate florets appear in the summer months. A paste of the crushed root is applied directly to open wounds, and then covered with a bandage. It is also applied to kill maggots in infested wounds in cattle. Preparations of the root have been used as purgatives and tonics, for tapeworm, infertility, snakebite, coughs, whooping cough, and traditional pregnancy tonics known as *inembe* and *isihlambezo*. Fatalities have occurred from overdose.

Carpobrotus species |Aizoaceae| **SOUR FIG**; *suurvy, vyerank* (Afrikaans) ■ The astringent leaf juice of *Carpobrotus edulis* and other species are used for various skin conditions. Plants often grow along the beaches and are a convenient first aid treatment for bluebottle stings. The protein poison of the bluebottle is probably neutralised by the astringent tannins. The only species which occurs along the subtropical east coast, *Carpobrotus dimidiatus* (eastern Cape to southern Mozambique), is especially well known for this use. The freshly squeezed leaf juice of *Carpobrotus edulis* is a popular application for nappy rash in the Cape and is traditionally gargled as a treatment for sore throat.

Centella asiatica |Apiaceae| **CENTELLA** ■ See Chapter 8. *Centella asiatica* has been applied as fresh pulped herb, and as infusions and ointments to dress sores, wounds, burns, varicose ulcers, and to treat eczema and psoriasis, scleroderma and keloids. Infusions are taken orally at the same time to reinforce the effect. It is a well-known plant in India, where it is used for its wound-healing properties and to treat leprosy. The triterpenoids are believed to be responsible for the healing activity, and proprietary formulas are available in Europe and the USA, standardised to the content of asiaticoside, asiatic acid, madecassic acid and madecassoside. Southern African plants have similar or even higher levels of asiaticoside (Long *et al.* 2012) than the levels reported in commercial raw material.

Cissus quadrangularis |Vitaceae| **CLIMBING CACTUS**, edible-stemmed vine ■ The crushed fresh succulent stems are applied to heal sores and fresh wounds, as well as wounds infested with maggots in humans as well as in livestock. The stem juice is dripped into the ear for earache, and root decoctions are used for swellings and for muscle pain. The crushed stems are put into the goat's vagina to hasten labour.

Erythrina lysistemon |Fabaceae| **COMMON CORAL TREE**; *umsinsi* (Zulu); *nsisimbane* (Tsonga); *muvale* (Tswana); *gewone koraalboom* (Afrikaans) ■ The coral tree is an attractive tree with bright orange-red flowers borne on prickly stems. It can be distinguished from the coastal coral tree (*E. caffra*) by the shape and orientation of the standard petal (straight, narrow and in line with the main axis in *E. lysistemon*; broader and flaring outwards in *E. caffra*). The flowers of the latter appear in the spring in a spectacular display of colour. In the Eastern Cape Province, the appearance of the flowers traditionally indicated the exact time when the crops should be sown. The bark of *E. lysistemon* and that of *E. caffra* is used topically to treat sores, wounds, abscesses and arthritis. Open wounds may be treated with powdered, burnt bark; infusions of the leaves are used as ear drops for earache, and decoctions of the roots are used for sprains. The Vhavenda use the bark for toothache. *Erythrina* alkaloids are known to be highly toxic, but the traditional uses strongly suggest antibacterial, anti-inflammatory and analgesic effects.

Shrub of swartstorm (*Cadaba aphylla*)

Stems and flowers of *swartstorm* (*Cadaba aphylla*)

Stems and leaves of *Cissus quadrangularis*

Tuberous roots of *impila* (*Callilepis laureola*)

Flowers of the common coral tree (*Erythrina lysistemon*)

Bark of the common coral tree (*Erythrina lysistemon*)

Haemanthus coccineus |Amaryllidaceae| **APRIL FOOL**; *rooikwas* (Afrikaans) ■ This attractive bulbous plant has strap-shaped leaves during the winter months that shrivel up and die during the hot summer months. In autumn, the bright red inflorescences (resembling round paintbrushes) emerge from the leafless bulbs. In the Cape, the fresh leaf was applied as a dressing to sores and septic ulcers, and also to the pustules of anthrax. The sliced bulb, boiled in vinegar mixed with honey, was used as a diuretic and for asthma. Recent studies have shown powerful anti-inflammatory activity (Fuchs *et al.* 2015) comparable to commercial anti-inflammatory preparations.

Helichrysum nudifolium |Asteraceae| ***ICHOLOCHOLO*** (Xhosa, Zulu) ■ See page 122. The plant is very similar to *H. pedunculatum* and the leaves are used in the same way to treat septic wounds. The upper leaf surface is rough (scabrid) in *H. nudifolium* and smooth (glabrous) in *H. pedunculatum.*

Helichrysum pedunculatum |Asteraceae| ***ISICWE*** (Xhosa, Zulu) ■ This plant is one of the most important used by the Zulu, Xhosa and Mfengu for treating circumcision wounds (Oswald Macunga, pers. comm.). The leaves are also used to dress septic sores to good effect and the roots to treat coughs and colds.

Jatropha zeyheri |Euphorbiaceae| ***UGODIDE*** (Zulu) ■ The plant is a small perennial herb with distinctive lobed leaves and a thick underground rhizome. The fleshy rhizome is applied fresh as a dressing to wounds and boils, and is also used as a general blood purifier. Pounded tuber is applied to painful feet and legs. A chemical isolated from the plant, jaherin, has been shown to have antibacterial and antifungal activity (Hutchings *et al.* 1996). The fresh tuber is taken orally in porridge in Botswana to treat irregular menstruation and uterine pain.

Kigelia africana |Bignoniaceae| **SAUSAGE TREE**; *muvevha* (Venda); *umfongothi* (Zulu); *worsboom* (Afrikaans) ■ The fresh and dry fruits are pulped or powdered and applied to sores and ulcers. The fruit is known to have antibacterial activity, and there is some evidence to suggest that it may be effective in treating solar keratoses and some skin cancers. It has become popular as an ingredient of cosmetics.

Lobostemon fruticosus |Boraginaceae| ***AGDAEGENEESBOS***, *douwurmbos* (Afrikaans) ■ *Lobostemon fruticosus* is a shrub of up to one metre in height with hairy leaves and attractive pink or blue flowers. Pulped fresh leaves, leaf decoctions and ointments of *Lobostemon* leaves fried in sweet oil or fat are all old Cape remedies for wounds, sores, ulcers, burns and ringworm. The vernacular name *agtdaegeneesbossie* refers to the plant's alleged ability to heal a condition in eight days, and the other Afrikaans vernacular name *douwurmbos*, indicates the use for treating ringworm. The crushed leaves of this plant, and other species of *Lobostemon*, are mucilaginous, and are thus emollient. *Lobostemon laevigatus* is known as *pleisterbos* (Willem Steenkamp, pers. comm.). The leaves are chewed until a slimy mass is formed, which is then applied to a fresh wound. The outer layer dries to form an elastic brown layer over the moist inner part. This "plaster" is left on the wound for more than a week.

According to Willem Steenkamp (pers. comm.), the person who was injured (typically a stab wound) has to chew his or her own plaster. He was adamant that friends or relatives cannot chew someone else's plaster. This bit of information seems unimportant until consideration is given to the fact that pyrrolizidine alkaloids are traditionally considered to be styptics. It may be speculated that the oral dose of pyrrolizidine alkaloids has a styptic effect to slow down the bleeding while the person is chewing the plaster.

Lobostemon is closely related to comfrey, *Symphytum officinale* (see photograph on page 234) and may also contain allantoin, a substance well known for its wound-healing properties.

WOUNDS, BURNS & SKIN CONDITIONS

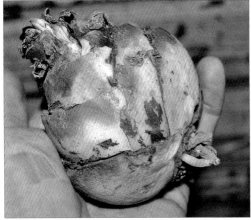

Bulb of the April fool (*Haemanthus coccineus*)

Flowers of the April fool (*Haemanthus coccineus*)

Leaves of *Helichrysum nudifolium*

Fruits of the sausage tree (*Kigelia africana*)

Leaves and flowers of *agdaegeneesbos* (*Lobostemon fruticosus*)

Leaves and flowers of *pleisterbos* (*Lobostemon laevigatus*)

Melianthus comosus |Melianthaceae| ***KRUIDJIE-ROER-MY-NIE*** (Afrikaans) ■ The plant is an attractive shrub with compound leaves and red, nectar-rich, bird-pollinated flowers. The leaves give off a distinctive odour when touched, hence the Afrikaans name. *Melianthus comosus, M. major, M. pectinatus* and *M. elongatus* appear to be used in the same way. They are easily distinguished by the size of the plant and the shape, size and colour of the leaves, inflorescences and flowers. Leaf poultices and decoctions are applied directly to impetigo, septic wounds, sores, ringworm, bruises, backache and rheumatic joints. Dried and powdered leaf is applied directly to sores and open wounds and burns, and is reported to relieve pain, retract the wound, and facilitate healing (Dawid Bester, pers. comm.). A decoction of the leaves or stems of *Melianthus elongatus* is applied topically to bleeding haemorrhoids, and is reputed to be outstanding (Mrs Bester, pers. comm.). *Melianthus pectinatus* is considered to be the most important plant in the Kamiesberg for treating muscular pains (Archer 1990; Nortje & Van Wyk 2015). Fresh leaves are applied to the painful area for a few days. Although weak infusions are sometimes taken, the plants are toxic, and there are cases where internal use has led to fatalities.

Merwilla plumbea (=*Scilla natalensis*) |Hyacinthaceae| ***INGUDUZA*** (Zulu); *blouberglelie, blouslangkop* (Afrikaans) ■ The plant has a large bulb with pale brown papery bulb scales and broad leaves with distinctive veins. Attractive blue flowers are formed in summer on erect stalks. Warmed, fresh bulb scales, slightly burned bulb scales and decoctions of the bulb are applied to wounds, sores, boils, sprains and fractures, and to draw abscesses. Ash from a burnt bulb may be rubbed into scarifications. The plant appears to have significant analgesic and antimicrobial activity (David Matthe, pers. comm.). In spite of potentially fatal poisoning from internal use, the plant is still commonly taken in the form of decoctions and enemas as a purgative, and for treating internal tumours.

Pentanisia prunelloides |Rubiaceae| ***SETIMAMOLLO*** (Sotho); *isimamlilo* (Zulu); wild verbena; *sooibrandbossie* (Afrikaans) ■ See page 154. The roots are boiled and used by Basotho people in preparations to treat festering sores and boils (Moffett 2010). Numerous other uses have been recorded.

Ricinus communis |Euphorbiaceae| ***OLIEBOOM*** (Afrikaans); castor oil plant ■ The large leaves are widely used in the Cape region to treat wounds. A little oil or Vaseline is smeared onto the fresh leaf, after which it is applied to the affected area and secured with bandages.

Rumex lanceolatus |Polygonaceae| ***INDOLOLENKONYANE*** (Xhosa, Zulu); common dock ■ The leaves of this and other species are used in wound treatment, possibly acting as styptics. It is used for internal bleeding and vascular diseases. Leaves or leaf paste is applied to abscesses and boils.

Senecio serratuloides |Asteraceae| ***INSUKUMBILI*** (Zulu); two days ■ The plant is an erect perennial herb of up to two metres in height with prominently toothed leaves and small yellow flower heads. This is an important Zulu wound-healing plant. Fresh leaves are applied directly to septic sores and to draw boils and ripen abscesses. Dry, powdered leaves and powdered charred roots are applied to sores and burns. Although leaf infusions are taken for infections, it may be toxic when taken orally in large doses. In common with wound-healing plants of the Boraginaceae family (*Lobostemon, Symphytum*), *Senecio* species also contain pyrrolizidine alkaloids.

Ximenia caffra |Olacaceae| ***SOURPLUM*** ■ See Chapter 3. The juice from rotten fruits was applied to septic sores, scabies, impetigo and to the pustules of chicken pox. A rationale behind this use is that the fungal growth on the decaying fruits produces antibiotics such as penicillin (Gumede 1990). In Namibia, powdered root is strewn onto slow-healing wounds (Von Koenen 2001).

Common *kruidjie-roer-my-nie* (*Melianthus comosus*)

Namaqualand *kruidjie-roer-my-nie* (*Melianthus pectinatus*)

Large *kruidjie-roer-my-nie* (*Melianthus major*)

Flowering plants of *inguduza* (*Merwillea plumbea*)

Bundle of *insukumbili* or two days (*Senecio serratuloides*) as it is sold on muthi markets

Xysmalobium undulatum |Apocynaceae| *ISHONGWE* (Zulu); *Uzara* (German, English) ▪ The powdered root is used to treat wounds and abscesses.

Zantedeschia aethiopica |Araceae| **ARUM LILY**; *inyabiba* (Xhosa) ▪ The large leaves of the plant are heated and applied as plasters to wounds, sores and boils. Healing is probably promoted through the sealing and moisturising of the wound rather than any chemical reactions.

Ziziphus mucronata |Rhamnaceae| **BUFFALO-THORN** ▪ See Chapter 8. Fresh leaves are chewed or pulped, and applied directly to wounds, boils and sores to reduce pain and inflammation and to promote healing. Dry, powdered leaves are also used. Decoctions of roots may be applied externally, and are taken internally to reinforce the treatment. The roots and leaves are applied to sores, boils and painful swellings to promote healing and to ease the pain.

REFERENCES AND FURTHER READING: Afolayan, A.J., Grierson, D.S. & Mbeng, W.O. 2014. Ethnobotanical survey of medicinal plants used in the management of skin disorders among the Xhosa communities of the Amathole District, Eastern Cape, South Africa. *J. Ethnopharmacol.* 153(1): 220–232. **Anonymous. 1996.** *Centella asiatica* (Gotu kola). *American Journal of Natural Medicine* 3 (6): 22–25. **Archer, F.M. 1990.** Planning with people – ethnobotany and African uses of plants in Namaqualand (South Africa). *Mitt. Inst. Allg. Bot. Hamburg* 23: 959–972. **Bruneton, J. 1995.** *Pharmacognosy, Phytochemistry, Medicinal Plants.* Intercept, Hampshire. **Bryant, A.T. 1966.** *Zulu medicine and medicine men,* new ed. Struik, Cape Town. **De Wet, H., Nciki, S. & Van Vuuren, S.F. 2013.** Medicinal plants used for the treatment of various skin disorders by a rural community in northern Maputaland, South Africa. *J. Ethnobiol. Ethnomed.* 9: 51. **Eloff, J.N., Katerere, D.R. & McGaw, L.J. 2008.** The biological activity and chemistry of the southern African Combretaceae. *J. Ethnopharmacol.* 119(3): 686–699. **Felhaber, T. (ed.) 1997.** *South African traditional healers' primary health care handbook.* Kagiso Publishers, Pretoria. **Fuchs, S., Hsieh, L.T., Saarberg, W., Erdelmeier, C.A.J., Wichelhaus, T.A., Schaefer, L., Koch, E. & Fürst, R. 2015.** *Haemanthus coccineus* extract and its main bioactive component narciclasine display profound anti-inflammatory activities *in vitro* and *in vivo*. *J. Cell. Mol. Med.* 19: 1021–1032. **Gelfand, M. et al. 1985.** *The traditional medical practitioner in Zimbabwe.* Mambo Press, Harare. **Grierson, D.S. & Afolayan, A.J. 1999a.** An ethnobotanical study of plants used for the treatment of wounds in the Eastern Cape, South Africa. *J. Ethnopharmacol.* 67(3): 327–332. **Grierson, D.S. & Afolayan, A.J. 1999b.** Antibacterial activity of some indigenous plants used for the treatment of wounds in the Eastern Cape, South Africa. *J. Ethnopharmacol.* 66(1): 103–106. **Gumede, M.V. 1990.** *Traditional healers. A medical doctor's perspective.* Skotaville Publishers, Braamfontein. **Hedberg, I. & Staugård, F. 1989.** *Traditional medicinal plants – traditional medicine in Botswana.* Ipelegeng Publishers, Gaborone. **Hutchings, A. et al. 1996.** *Zulu medicinal plants.* Natal University Press, Pietermaritzburg. **Iwalewa, E.O., McGaw, L.J., Naidoo, V. & Eloff, J.N. 2007.** Inflammation: The foundation of diseases and disorders. A review of phytomedicines of South African origin used to treat pain and inflammatory conditions. *Afr. J. Biotechnol.* 6: 2868–2885. **Iwu, M.M. 1993.** *Handbook of African medicinal plants.* CRC Press, Boca Raton. **Kelmanson, J.E., Jäger, A.K. & Van Staden, J. 2000.** Zulu medicinal plants with antibacterial activity. *J. Ethnopharmacol.* 69(3): 241–246. **Lall, N. & Kishore, N. 2014.** Are plants used for skin care in South Africa fully explored? *J. Ethnopharmacol.* 153(1): 61–84. **Long, H.S., Stander M.A. & Van Wyk, B.-E. 2012.** Notes on the occurrence and significance of triterpenoids (asiaticoside and related compounds) and caffeoylquinic acids in *Centella* species. *S. Afr. J. Bot.* 82: 53–59. **Moffett, R. 2010.** *Sesotho plant and animal names and plants used by the Basotho.* Sun Media, Stellenbosch. **Nortje, J.M. & Van Wyk, B.-E. 2015.** Medicinal ethnobotany of the Kamiesberg, Namaqualand, South Africa. *J. Ethnopharmacol.* 171: 205–222. **Pappe, L. 1857.** *Florae Capensis Medicae Prodromus,* 2nd ed. W. Britain, Cape Town. **Pappe, L. 1868.** *Florae Capensis Medicae Prodromus,* 3rd ed. W. Britain, Cape Town. **Pather, N., Viljoen, A.M. & Kramer, B. 2011.** A biochemical comparison of the *in vivo* effects of *Bulbine frutescens* and *Bulbine natalensis* on cutaneous wound healing. *J. Ethnopharmacol.* 133: 364–370. **Ponglux, D. et al. (eds) 1987.** *Medicinal plants.* The first Princess Chulabhorn Science Congress, Bangkok, Thailand. **Pujol, J. 1990.** *Naturafrica – the herbalist handbook.* Jean Pujol Natural Healers Foundation, Durban. **Rabe, T. & Van Staden, J. 1997.** Antibacterial activity of South African plants used for medicinal purposes. *J. Ethnopharmacol.* 56(1): 81–87. **Roberts, M. 1990.** *Indigenous healing plants.* Southern Book Publishers, Halfway House. **Roberts, M. & Roberts, S. 2017.** *Indigenous healing plants,* 2nd ed. Briza Publications, Pretoria. **Rood, B. 1994.** *Uit die veldapteek.* Tafelberg, Cape Town. **Smith, A. 1888.** *A contribution to the South African materia medica,* 2nd ed. Lovedale, South Africa. **Steenkamp, V., Mathivha, E., Gouws, M.C. & Van Rensburg, C.E.J. 2004.** Studies on antibacterial, antioxidant and fibroblast growth stimulation of wound healing remedies from South Africa. *J. Ethnopharmacol.* 95: 353–357. **Van Vuuren, S.F. 2008.** Antimicrobial activity of South African medicinal plants. *J. Ethnopharmacol.* 119(3): 462–472. **Van Wyk, B.-E. et al. 2009.** *Medicinal plants of South Africa,* 2nd ed. Briza Publications, Pretoria. **Von Koenen, E. 2001.** *Medicinal, poisonous and edible plants in Namibia.* Klaus Hess Publishers, Windhoek and Göttingen. **Watt, J.M. & Breyer-Brandwijk, M.G. 1962.** *The Medicinal and Poisonous Plants of Southern and Eastern Africa,* 2nd ed. Livingstone, London.

WOUNDS, BURNS & SKIN CONDITIONS

Flowers of the arum lily (*Zantedeschia aethiopica*)

Flowering plant of the arum lily (*Zantedeschia aethiopica*)

Bark of the buffalo-thorn (*Ziziphus mucronata*) as it is sold on muthi markets

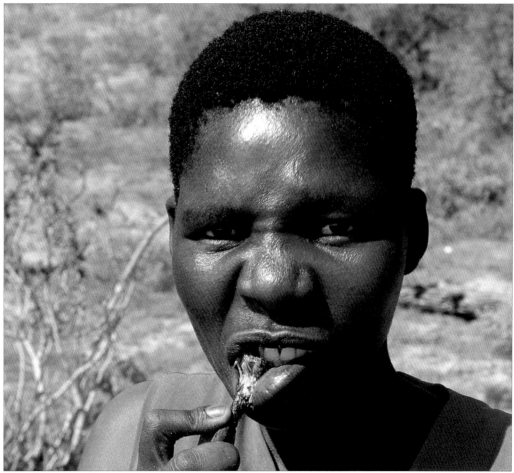

Toothbrush stick made from the root of the bluebush (*Diospyros lycioides*)

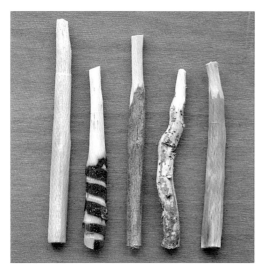

Ethiopian toothbrush sticks

Leaves and fruits of the mustard tree (*Salvadora persica*)

CHAPTER 12

Dental care

VISITORS TO RELATIVELY inaccessible rural areas are often impressed by the good oral health of remote area dwellers. The combination of a high-fibre diet, regular brushing with toothbrush sticks, adequate nutrition and low sugar intake are to a large degree responsible for this. The state of dental health deteriorates markedly as people change from traditional to modern lifestyles, and the poor are most affected. Toothbrushes and toothpaste have to be purchased; refined foods such as sugar and sweets are eaten, and there is an inadequate intake of vitamins, minerals and protein. It is clear that a great deal of traditional knowledge on dental care has been lost, but an impression of the diversity and utility of plants used traditionally for oral health can still be appreciated. Plants have been chosen to illustrate the full spectrum of traditional oral health care, including plants for chewing sticks, dental floss, and to treat gingivitis, aphthous ulcers and toothache, as well as for the pain and bleeding of extraction.

A good chewing stick or toothbrush stick has a fibrous texture, agreeable taste, and some antibacterial or antiplaque activity. Toothbrush sticks are widely used and sold in Africa, and it is widely recognised that scientific investigation of these often reveals significant antimicrobial activity against oral bacteria. In southern Africa, use of toothbrush sticks has declined, but they are still sold in markets in Mozambique, and used in the more remote areas of Namibia and Botswana.

Perhaps the most famous and best-known African toothbrush plant is the mustard tree, *Salvadora persica* (Salvadoraceae). It is a large shrub or small tree of about five metres in height with opposite pairs of pale green somewhat fleshy leaves. The minute yellowish green flowers turn into small round berries of about 10 millimetres in diameter. Both the roots and twigs are commonly sold as toothbrushes in the natural distribution area of the species, especially in Ethiopia (Kassu *et al.* 1999) and other parts of Northeast Africa, as well as the Middle East, Arabia, Pakistan and India. It also occurs in Namibia, where the town of Khorixas is named after the mustard tree. *Khorixas* is the *Khoekhoegowab* (Nama/Damara) name for the tree (Raper *et al.* 2014), which is locally common along the river. Although some medicinal uses have been recorded (e.g. crushed leaves in water are used as an ointment to treat rashes and German measles), there appears to be no unambiguous record of a local traditional use for the roots or stems as toothbrushes.

The tree is common in parts of Arabia, where it is known as *arak*. The small, red fruits are edible and are said to be the "mustard seed" mentioned in the Bible. Pieces of root (ca. 100–200 millimetres long and 10 millimetres in diameter) are sold on local markets in the Arabic world as *miswak* (or *siwak*). The way to use the root as a toothbrush is to remove the bark from the tip (for about 10 millimetres) and then chew the tip until the fibres separate. The teeth are rubbed in vertical strokes, from the cutting edges to the gums.

Root extracts known as "peelu extract" are used as ingredients of commercial toothpaste. The benefits in traditional dental care are ascribed to lignan glycosides, phenolic glycosides such as syringin and especially benzyl glucosinolates. The last-mentioned compounds are enzymatically converted to volatile benzyl isothiocyanate (Al-Bagieh & Weinberg 1988). This mustard oil is active against gram-negative bacteria that are associated with periodontitis (a serious gum infection that destroys the soft and bony tissue surrounding the teeth).

Acokanthera oppositifolia │Apocynaceae│ **COMMON POISON BUSH**; *boesmansgif* (Afrikaans) ■ See Chapter 15. Small doses of the plant are taken orally, and some applied topically for the treatment of toothache.

Albizia adianthifolia │Fabaceae│ **FLATCROWN**; *umgadankawu* (Zulu); *platkroon* (Afrikaans) ■ The leaves and roots are used for toothache (Mabogo 1990).

Anemone vesicatoria (=*Knowltonia vesicatoria*) │Ranunculaceae│ ***BRANDBLARE***, *peper-wortel* (Afrikaans) ■ A small piece of fresh or dry root is inserted into the cavity of a decayed, painful tooth. The root causes a sudden sharp increase in pain, which then subsides. A single treatment is sufficient (Dawid Bester, pers. comm.). The rootlets taste very pungent, and have no local anaesthetic effect. It seems that the activity may be due to the presence of protoanemonin, a toxic irritant oil known to cause skin blistering, which destroys the exposed nerve.

Annona senegalensis │Annonaceae│ **WILD CUSTARD APPLE**; *wildesuikerappel* (Afrikaans); *isiphofu* (Zulu) ■ See Chapter 3. A bark infusion or decoction is taken for toothache (Rood 1994).

Artemisia afra │Asteraceae│ ***UMHLONYANE*** ■ See Chapter 8. The cavity of a painful tooth is packed with fresh leaf, and decoctions may be held in the mouth to relieve pain in gum infections (Roberts 1990; Rood 1994; Palmer 1985). The presence of narcotic and analgesic activity has been found in some tests on *Artemisia afra* (Hutchings 1989).

Azima tetracantha │Salvadoraceae│ **NEEDLE BUSH**; *speldedoring* (Afrikaans); *onyarayongwe* (Herero) ■ The sap of the plant is used against toothache and bleeding gums (Von Koenen 2001).

Barleria prionitis │Acanthaceae│ ■ The plant is used as a mouthwash for toothache, and for treating bleeding gums and aphthous ulcers (Watt & Breyer-Brandwijk 1962).

Berchemia discolor │Rhamnaceae│ **BROWN IVORY** ■ See Chapter 16. The fruit juice is used to treat bleeding gums.

Berula thunbergii │Apiaceae│ ***TANDPYNWORTEL***, *tandpynbossie* (Afrikaans); toothache root; *lehlatso* (Sotho); *libophwani* (Zulu) ■ This perennial herb of wet places is very similar to the water parsnip (*Berula repanda*, previously known as *Sium repandum*) but differs in the marginal teeth of the leaflets: straight and triangular in *B. thunbergii*, incurved and slightly overlapping in *B. repanda* (Van Wyk *et al.* 2013). The plant is widely distributed in Africa and differs from the Eurasian *B. erecta* (with which it has previously been confused) in the smaller, more regular teeth along the leaflet margins. The Afrikaans common name (first recorded in 1830) refers to the use of the rhizomes ("roots") to treat toothache. The rhizomes are either held in the mouth or chewed and have been highly regarded as a toothache remedy. However, the claimed analgesic and local anaesthetic effects (possibly due to polyacetylenes) have not been confirmed experimentally (Durand & Breytenbach 1988). The plant is poisonous to cattle at certain times of the year and should be treated with caution.

Blepharis capensis │Acanthaceae│ ■ A leaf paste is applied as a toothache remedy. Leaves from *Blepharis procumbens* may also be used (Watt & Breyer-Brandwijk 1962).

Carissa bispinosa │Apocynaceae│ **FOREST NUM-NUM**; *bosnoemnoem* (Afrikaans); *murungulu* (Venda) ■ The root is used to treat toothache (Mabogo 1990).

Clematopsis scabiosifolia │Ranunculaceae│ ***PLUIMBOSSIE***, *veerbossie* (Afrikaans) ■ In Zimbabwe, the leaves are applied to the tooth for toothache, while the powdered roots are used as a snuff for headache (Gelfand *et al.* 1985).

Flowering plant of *brandblare* (*Anemone vesicatoria*)

Flowers of *brandblare* (*Anemone vesicatoria*)

Rhizomes of *tandpynwortel* (*Berula thunbergii*)

Flowering plant of *tandpynwortel* (*Berula thunbergii*)

Fruiting plant of the *pluimbossie* (*Clematopsis scabiosifolia*)

Flowers of the *pluimbossie* (*Clematopsis scabiosifolia*)

Colophospermum mopane |Fabaceae| **MOPANE** ■ See Chapter 18. Twigs are used as chewing sticks to clean the teeth. Among the Herero of Namibia it is customary to extract the four lower incisors of children between the ages of 10 and 12, and mopane leaves are applied daily to promote healing of the lower jaw (Malan & Owen-Smith 1974). The leaves are astringent and possibly antiseptic, and chewed leaves are applied to open wounds to stop bleeding (Van den Eynden *et al.* 1992). The extraction of healthy teeth for cultural or cosmetic reasons is an interesting feature unique to southern Africa. Removal of the upper and lower front teeth was once very common in the Cape, and is still practised to some extent.

Commiphora multijuga |Burseraceae| **OMUZUMBA** (Herero) ■ The twigs have a pleasant taste and are used as toothbrushes in Kaokoland. *Commiphora virgata* may also be used.

Cordia sinensis |Boraginaceae| **OMUSEPA** (Herero) ■ The plant, previously known as *Cordia gharaf*, is a small tree with edible fruit. The young branches are used as chewing sticks in northern Namibia (Malan & Owen-Smith 1974).

Cotyledon orbiculata |Crassulaceae| **PLAKKIE** ■ See Chapter 9. Warmed leaf juice is applied as drops for toothache, and as ear drops for earache (Rood 1994).

Croton gratissimus |Euphorbiaceae| **MAQUASSIE** (San); lavender croton ■ See Chapter 13. Bleeding gums are treated by brushing them with the charred and powdered bark (Watt & Breyer-Brandwijk 1962).

Dichrostachys cinerea |Fabaceae| **SICKLE BUSH** ■ See Chapter 7. The plant is used as a remedy for toothache (Watt & Breyer-Brandwijk 1962).

Dicoma anomala |Asteraceae| **HLOENYA** (Sotho); *maagwortel* (Afrikaans) ■ See Chapter 8. Root decoctions are taken for toothache (Hutchings 1989).

Diospyros lycioides|Ebenaceae| **BLUEBUSH** ■ The plant is a shrub or medium-sized tree with small leaves clustered towards the branch ends. Male and female flowers occur on separate plants. The fruit, an oblong or rounded red berry, is edible. The roots are used as chewing sticks and the presence of yellow quinones gives the teeth a yellow colour. They contain antibacterial binaphthalenone glycosides (Li *et al.* 1998) and naphthoquinones such as diospyrin and 7-methyljuglone. Roots and twigs are also used as toothbrushes in Kaokoland (Malan & Owen-Smith 1974). This is perhaps the most important and most widely used of all the chewing stick plants in southern Africa.

Euclea natalensis |Ebenaceae| **NATAL GUARRI**; *umhlangula* (Tsonga) ■ See Chapter 16. The powdered root is taken for toothache, as well as headache (Palgrave 1977), and the root is used as a toothbrush stick in Mozambique (Patrick Ndlovu, pers. comm.). The root bark is peeled from the end of a small root, and the end is chewed to a fibrous brush, which changes in colour from white to yellow as it is chewed, imparting a pungent, refreshing taste to the mouth. The moistened root bark is applied to the lips as a yellow-brown cosmetic (Patrick Ndlovu, pers. comm.). The closely related magic guarri (*Euclea divinorum*, see Chapter 16), apart from its value as dye plant, is also widely used in dental care. People from Kaokoland chew the bark, which serves as a mouthwash and they use the branches as chewing sticks (Malan & Owen-Smith 1974). The sap has a burning taste and is believed to be effective in cleaning the mouth. Twigs are also used as chewing sticks in Mozambique (Patrick Ndlovu, pers. comm.). *Euclea pseudebenus* roots are used as chewing sticks to clean teeth (Van den Eynden *et al.* 1992) and the twigs are used in Kaokoland (Malan & Owen-Smith 1974). *Euclea* species are known to contain naphthoquinones and are chemically similar to *Diospyros lycioides* and related species, so that their use as dye plants and as toothbrush stick plants can be linked to the presence of diospyrin, 7-methyljuglone and other quinones.

DENTAL CARE

Fruiting shrub of the bluebush (*Diospyros lycioides*)

Toothbrush stick made from the root of magic guarri (*Euclea divinorum*)

Fruits of the bluebush (*Diospyros lycioides*)

Flowers of Natal guarri (*Euclea natalensis*)

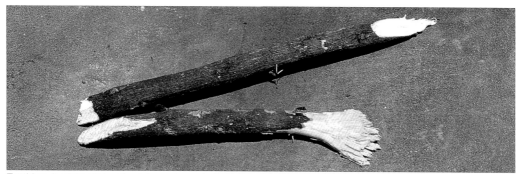

Toothbrush sticks: the yellowish one is made from the root of bluebush (*Diospyros lycioides*) and the other one from a twig of black thorn (*Senegalia mellifera*)

Faidherbia albida |Fabaceae| **ANA TREE**; *anaboom* (Afrikaans); *anas, anahais* (Nama); *omue* (Himba, Herero) ■ Bark strips are used as dental floss by the Topnaar of Namibia (Van den Eynden *et al.* 1992). A decoction of the bark has been used to treat diarrhoea, and the pods have been used as a fish poison.

Galenia africana |Aizoaceae| ***KRAALBOS***, *geelbos* (Afrikaans) ■ The *kraalbos* is a rounded shrub of up to a metre in height. It is a pioneer of disturbed roadsides and overgrazed places where it may form dense stands. The plant is chewed to relieve toothache, although it blisters the mucous membrane of the mouth if used too much (Watt & Breyer-Brandwijk 1962). In the Nieuwoudtville district in the Cape, a leaf infusion is used in the morning and evening as a mouth rinse for toothache (Willem Steenkamp, pers. comm.). Leaf extracts have been used on a small commercial scale as the active ingredient of antiseptic and wound-healing ointments.

Gloriosa superba |Colchicaceae| **FLAME LILY**; *vlamlelie* (Afrikaans); *ihlamvu lasolwandle, isimiselo* (Zulu) ■ This geophyte is well known for its attractive orange (or less often yellow) flowers and is often grown in gardens in tropical and subtropical regions. The seeds have been used as a commercial source of colchicine. Juice from the fleshy, white tuber is dropped onto the painful tooth as an analgesic.

Heteropyxis natalensis |Myrtaceae or Heteropyxidaceae| **LAVENDER TREE** ■ See Chapter 13. A decoction of leaves and twigs is used as a mouthwash for toothache and for mouth and gum infections.

Indigofera cryptantha |Fabaceae| ***ORUKOHATJINYO*** (Herero) ■ The plant is a small shrublet with purple flowers. Malan & Owen-Smith (1974) reported that the twigs are used as toothbrushes and that the sap of the plant is used as a mouthwash. The Herero common name is derived from *koha* (wash) and *otjinyo* (the mouth).

Jasminum fluminense |Oleaceae| ***OKARONDO*** (Herero) ■ The branches of this climber are chewed to clean the teeth (Malan & Owen-Smith 1974).

Leucas **species** |Lamiaceae| ***ORUNWE*** (Herero) ■ The flowering branches of this shrub are used to clean the teeth, and the dry twigs are used as toothbrushes (Malan & Owen-Smith 1974). Many medicinal uses have been recorded for *L. martinicensis* and *L. pechuelii* in Namibia.

Mesembryanthemum tortuosum (=*Sceletium tortuosum*) |Aizoaceae| ***KOUGOED*** ■ See Chapter 9. The plant is used as a local anaesthetic to extract teeth on the lower jaw.

Mundulea sericea |Fabaceae| **CORK-BUSH**; *omukeka* (Herero, Himba); *!gaeb* (Nama); *!ei* (Kung) ■ See Chapter 15. Twigs are reported to be used as toothbrush sticks in Kaokoland (Malan & Owen-Smith 1974).

Myrothamnus flabellifolius |Myrothamnaceae| **RESURRECTION PLANT**; *opstandingsplant* (Afrikaans); *ohanukaze* (Herero, Himba) ■ See Chapter 6. The leaves are chewed to treat gingivitis (Van den Eynden *et al.* 1992).

Parinari curatellifolia |Chrysobalanaceae| **MOBOLA PLUM**; *muchakata* (Shona) ■ See Chapter 3. Teeth are rinsed with a root infusion for toothache (Gelfand *et al.* 1985).

Ricinus communis |Euphorbiaceae| **CASTOR OIL PLANT** ■ See Chapter 7. In cases of toothache, the seeds are ground and boiled, and the oil is rubbed on the affected area of the cheeks. This remedy is also used for mumps. A paste of the roots is applied to the affected tooth to alleviate toothache (Ncindani Maswanganyi, pers. comm.).

DENTAL CARE

Shrub of the *kraalbos* (*Galenia africana*)

Flowers of the *kraalbos* (*Galenia africana*)

Leaves of the *kraalbos* (*Galenia africana*)

Rhizome of the flame lily (*Gloriosa superba*)

Flowers of the flame lily (*Gloriosa superba*)

Salvadora persica |Salvadoraceae| **MUSTARD TREE**, *mosterdboom* (Afrikaans); *khorixas* (Nama) ■ See page 247. Roots (and less often the stems) are used throughout Africa as a source of toothbrush sticks. In Ethiopia, for example, *Salvadora* toothbrush sticks are commonly sold on local markets (Kassu *et al.* 1999). The antibacterial activity has been ascribed to benzyl isothiocyanate (Al-Bagied & Weinberg 1988).

Sansevieria hyacinthoides |Asparagaceae| **BOWSTRING HEMP** ■ See Chapter 19. Juice from a warmed leaf is applied to the painful tooth in toothache, and is dripped into the ear for earache. *Sansevieria pearsonii* (previously known as *S. desertii*) is used similarly.

Securidaca longepedunculata |Polygalaceae| **VIOLET-TREE** ■ The root is chewed for the relief of toothache, and contains methyl salicylate, better known as wintergreen oil. Methyl salicylate penetrates the skin and mucosa to act as an anti-inflammatory, and a number of proprietary oral hygiene products contain it. The roots and bark are taken orally as powdered material or as infusions and decoctions for many conditions, including fever, coughs, tuberculosis, rheumatism, epilepsy, diarrhoea, constipation, backache, venereal disease, worms, infertility, and as an aphrodisiac. Infusions of the roots are used to wash tropical ulcers, while the powdered root is taken as snuff for headache. In Zimbabwe, the roots are placed around the homestead as a snake-repellent. Overdoses are potentially fatal, and suicidal use has been well documented. The plant has been used as an arrow poison in West Africa.

Selaginella dregei |Selaginellaceae| **RESURRECTION FERN** ■ This plant is an unusual fern (pteridophyte) that forms matted layers on rocks. The whole plant is burnt, and the smoke is directed into the mouth for toothache. This plant should not be confused with the resurrection plant, *Myrothamnus flabellifolius* (see above).

Senegalia mellifera (=*Acacia mellifera*) |Fabaceae| **BLACK THORN** ■ The twigs are used as toothbrushes in the D'Kar area in Botswana, but are considered inferior to *Diospyros lycioides* roots. The gum of *Vachellia karroo* has been applied to mouth ulcers, and to treat oral thrush.

Solanum aculeastrum |Solanaceae| ***INTUMA*** (Zulu); poison apple; *gifappel* (Afrikaans) ■ Throughout southern Africa the pulp from the green fruits of many *Solanum* species is applied directly to the tooth and adjacent gum for the effective treatment of toothache. *Solanum supinum* is known as *tandpynbos* in Afrikaans (literally "toothache bush") and is well known in the western and northwestern parts of the Cape as a toothache remedy. In some cases pounded roots are also applied, or the smoke from burning leaves or fruits is directed into the mouth.

In the Kamiesberg, the fruits of *tandpynbossie* (*Solanum tomentosum*) are cut up and inserted into or applied to a painful tooth (Nortje & Van Wyk 2015). In the Still Bay area of the southern Cape, there is an interesting old tradition to treat toothache with *Solanum* fruits (De Vynck & Van Wyk, unpublished). Juice from the unripe fruit is smeared onto a small piece of white cloth tied to the tip of a short stick. A candle is placed in the middle of an enamel bowl filled with water. The cloth with *Solanum* juice is burnt over the candle and the person suffering from toothache holds his or her open mouth above the candle to expose the sore tooth to the smoke. After a while, "the small, white worms with black heads that cause toothache" fall into the water around the candle. All local people firmly believed that these little worms cause toothache. The only logical explanation is that the heat of the flame dries out the cloth so that the small white seeds (now scorched black on the one side) are dislodged and fall into the water while the patient is treated. One can assume that this physical manifestation of the cure for toothache reinforces the chemical part of the treatment.

Solanum species contain toxic steroidal alkaloids such as solanine, solasodine and solanidine, which are used as starting materials in the manufacture of steroidal drugs. It is interesting to note that air-dried ripe fruits of the New World *Solanum carolinense*, which contain solanine and solanidine, are used as sedatives and anticonvulsants.

Mustard tree (*Salvadora persica*) at Khorixas

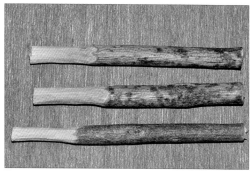

Toothbrush sticks made from mustard tree stems

Leaves and flowers of the violet-tree (*Securidaca longepedunculata*)

Roots of the violet-tree (*Securidaca longepedunculata*)

Flower and fruits of the *tandpynbos* (*Solanum supinum*)

Leaves and flowers of the *tandpynbossie* (*Solanum tomentosum*)

Leaves and ripe fruits of the *tandpynbossie* (*Solanum tomentosum*)

Spirostachys africana |Euphorbiaceae| **TAMBOTI** ■ See Chapters 15 and 17. A drop of the fresh latex is applied to a painful tooth (Mabogo 1990; Von Koenen 1996, 2001). This causes a brief, sharp increase in pain which then subsides. The cytotoxic phorbol esters presumably destroy the exposed nerve in a badly decayed tooth.

Tecomaria capensis |Bignoniaceae| **CAPE HONEYSUCKLE** ■ The powdered bark is rubbed around the teeth for bleeding gums.

Ximenia americana |Olacaceae| **BLUE SOURPLUM** ■ See Chapter 3. Leaf decoctions are taken for toothache.

Zanthoxylum capense |Rutaceae| **SMALL KNOBWOOD**; *umnungamabele* (Zulu); *umlungu-mabele* (Xhosa); *monokwane* (Sotho); *kleinperdepram* (Afrikaans) ■ The plant is a small, much-branched tree, usually about five metres in height but under favourable conditions it may grow to 10 metres. The thick, breast-like thorns on the stems and bole are characteristic, and the common names all refer to this feature.

Bark is removed from the ends of twigs, which are beaten flat to make toothbrushes. The bark and powdered root are applied for toothache, and infusions are used as a mouthwash (Watt & Breyer-Brandwijk 1962; Palmer 1985; Hutchings 1989; Pujol 1990; Roberts 1990). Although *Zanthoxylum capense* has not been well studied, it is likely to contain sanguinarine or related alkaloids (Van Wyk *et al.* 1997, 2009). Sanguinarine is found in many species of *Zanthoxylum*. It has antiplaque and anti-inflammatory activity and is used commercially in toothpastes and oral rinses (Merck 1989; Bruneton 1995). It selectively binds to dental plaque and almost completely inhibits bacterial growth at low concentrations.

REFERENCES AND FURTHER READING: Albagieh, N.H. & Weinberg, E.D. 1988. Benzylisothiocyanate: a possible agent for controlling dental caries. *Micros. Lett.* 39: 143–151. **Bruneton, J. 1995.** *Pharmacognosy, phytochemistry, medicinal plants.* Intercept, Hampshire. **El-Said, F. et al. 1971.** Native cures in Nigeria. II. The antimicrobial properties of the buffered extracts of chewing sticks. *Lloydia* 34: 172–174. **Durand, W.C. & Breytenbach, J.C. 1988.** A pharmacochemical investigation of *Berula erecta. S. Afr. J. Sci.* 84: 297–299. **Gelfand, M. et al. 1985.** *The traditional medical practitioner in Zimbabwe.* Mambo Press, Harare. **Hutchings, A. 1989.** Observations on plant usage in Xhosa and Zulu medicine. *Bothalia* 19: 225–235. **Hutchings, A. et al. 1996.** *Zulu medicinal plants.* Natal University Press, Pietermaritzburg. **Iwu, M.M. 1993.** *Handbook of African medicinal plants.* CRC Press, Boca Raton. **Kassu, A., Dagne, E., Abate, D., De Castro, A. & Van Wyk, B.-E. 1999.** Ethnomedical aspects of the commonly used toothbrush sticks in Ethiopia. *East Afr. Med. J.* 76: 651–653. **Li, X-C., van der Bijl, P. & Wu, C.D. 1998.** Binaphthalenone glycosides from African chewing sticks, *Diospyros lycioides. J. Nat. Prod.* 61(6): 817–820. **Mabogo, D.E.N. 1990.** *The ethnobotany of the Vhavenda.* Unpublished M.Sc. thesis, University of Pretoria. **Malan, J.S. & Owen-Smith, G.L. 1974.** The ethnobotany of Kaokoland. *Cimbebasia* Ser. B 2,5: 131–178. **Merck 1989.** *The Merck Index.* 11th ed. Merck, Rahway. **Ndung, U.F.L et al. 1990.** A comparative study of the efficiency of plaque control by a chewing stick and a toothbrush. *East Afr. Med. J.* 67: 907–911. **Nortje, J.M. & Van Wyk, B.-E. 2015.** Medicinal ethnobotany of the Kamiesberg, Namaqualand, South Africa. *J. Ethnopharmacol.* 171: 205–222. **Palmer, E. 1985.** *The South African herbal.* Tafelberg, Cape Town. **Pujol, J. 1990.** *Naturafrica – the herbalist handbook.* Jean Pujol Natural Healers Foundation, Durban. **Raper, P.E., Möller, L.A. & Du Plessis, L.T. 2014.** *Dictionary of Southern African place names.* Jonathan Ball, Jeppestown, Johannesburg. **Roberts, M. 1990.** *Indigenous healing plants.* Southern Book Publishers, Halfway House. **Rood, B. 1994.** *Uit die veldapteek.* Tafelberg, Cape Town. **Rotimi, V.O. et al. 1988.** Activities of Nigerian chewing stick extracts against *Bacterioides gingivalis* and *B. melaninogenicus. Antimicrob. Agents Chemother.* 32: 598–600. **Smith, C.A. 1966.** Common names of South African plants. *Mem. Bot. Surv. S. Afr.* 35. **Van den Eynden, V. et al. 1992.** *The ethnobotany of the Topnaar.* Universiteit Gent, Gent. **Von Koenen, E. 1996.** *Heil-, Gift- und Essbare Pflanzen in Namibia.* Klaus Hess Verlag, Göttingen. **Von Koenen, E. 2001.** *Medicinal, poisonous and edible plants in Namibia.* Klaus Hess Publishers, Windhoek and Göttingen. **Van Wyk, B.-E. et al. 1997.** *Medicinal plants of South Africa.* Briza Publications, Pretoria. **Van Wyk, B-E., Van Oudtshoorn, B. & Gericke, N. 2009.** *Medicinal plants of South Africa.* Revised and expanded 2nd ed. Briza Publications, Pretoria. **Watt, J.M. & Breyer-Brandwijk, M.G. 1962.** *The medicinal and poisonous plants of southern and eastern Africa,* 2nd ed. Livingstone, London. **Youthed, G. (ed.) no date.** *Dictionary of South African traditional medicinal plants of the Eastern Cape.* Pharmaceutical Society of South Africa, Johannesburg (unpublished).

DENTAL CARE

Leaves of tamboti (*Spirostachys africana*)

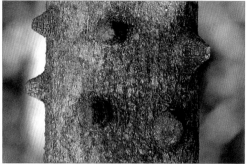

Trees of tamboti (*Spirostachys africana*) showing the characteristic blackish bark

The characteristic woody protuberances on the stem of small knobwood (*Zanthoxylum capense*)

Leaves and fruits of small knobwood (*Zanthoxylum capense*)

Mobile distillation unit for essential oil, designed and fabricated by Grassroots Natural Products

Industrial still for extracting eucalyptus oil

Sab/San from Van der Stel's diary (1685)

Sab/San (*Pteronia onobromoides*)

Beza with a traditional perfume plant, *Syncolostemon bracteosus*

Ocimum filamentosum, a poorly known Kalahari perfume plant

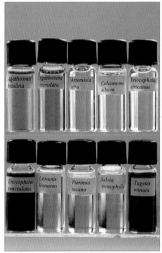

A selection of essential oils from southern African plants

CHAPTER 13

Perfumes & repellents

PERFUMES HAVE ALWAYS played an important part of everyday life in southern Africa. It is claimed that the name of the San people is derived from their use of aromatic shrubs to anoint their bodies (Smith 1966). *San, Son* or *Sab* were the original Khoi names for *Pteronia onobromoides*, an aromatic bush once popular as a perfume, but the name was later applied to any shrub. The names *Sonqua, Sanqua* or *Tanqua* are derived from this term plus the Khoi suffix "*qua*", meaning "men" or "people", as in Namaqua or Outeniqua. *Sanqua* therefore literally means "the people or men who use aromatic bushes to anoint their bodies". This was directly translated to the Dutch "*bosjesman*", which became "*boesman*" in Afrikaans and "bushmen" in English. The practice to rub fat and powdered aromatic plants into the skin has now almost disappeared, but older people of the Karoo still remember when this was an everyday activity around the camp fire. The use of aromatic plants to treat the skin is probably not only for cosmetic reasons but also as an antibiotic protection. The concept of aromatherapy has been popularised as a recent French innovation, but it seems likely that the principle of healing with aromatic plants may have been an ancient African practice.

Essential oils give plants and spices their characteristic scent, flavour and perfume. Sometimes these aromatic oils are present in very large quantities – they literally squirt out when we peel an orange. In contrast, it takes more than a ton of rose petals to produce 300 grams of rose oil. Aromatic oils are volatile (they evaporate easily) and can be found in any plant part, such as the roots, bark, leaves, seeds, flowers, wood or resin. Their function is to attract or repel insects and animals and also to protect the plant from diseases. The attraction and repulsion of essential oils have been used by people since early times for their own benefit and nowadays large industries are based on commercial perfumes and repellents derived from plants. The flavour and fragrance industries use essential oils to give a characteristic and recognisable flavour to end products, such as beverages, confectionery, sweets and chocolates.

Volatile oils can be extracted by steam distillation. Steam is passed through a mixture of crushed plant materials in water. The volatile oils vaporise and mix with the steam, which is then passed through a distillation cooler. The steam condenses to form water, and the essential oils form an oily layer on top of the water, from where they can be recovered as pure oil. A large amount of plant material is required to produce a small yield of oil.

A Frenchman by the name of Piesse devised a system in which fragrances are compared to notes on a musical scale. His basic terminology is still used in perfumery work today. Essential oils are classified into "top", "middle" and "base" notes. The top note has a light, fresh character that is immediately apparent, because of high volatility. Examples are basil, lemon and eucalyptus oils. The middle note is the heart of a fragrance, and forms the bulk of a blend, with the true scent only emerging some time after the top note. Examples include pelargonium and lavender oils. The base note is a rich, heavy scent that emerges slowly and lingers for a long time. It is often used as a fixative to prevent lighter oils from dispersing too rapidly. Examples are myrrh and jasmine oils.

Some aromatic oils are used in commercial insect repellents to repel insects such as mosquitoes and midges. Plants or plant extracts have been used in agriculture since early days as antifeedants to avoid crop damage. The best-known example is the Asian neem tree (*Azadirachta indica*), which contains limonoids. The pepperbark tree (*Warburgia salutaris*) and related species are known to contain powerful antifeedants such as muzigadial and warburganal in the bark (Kubo *et al.* 1977).

The perfumes and repellents of southern Africa are poorly known and many discoveries of scientific and commercial interest remain to be made.

Achyrocline stenoptera |Asteraceae| ***IMPHEPHO*** (Xhosa, Zulu) ■ The plant resembles *Helichrysum* species and is often confused with them. It is commonly sold on muthi markets in KwaZulu-Natal and Maputaland. It is burned as an incense in the same way as *H. odoratissimum*.

Alepidea amatymbica |Apiaceae| ***IKHATHAZO*** (Zulu) ■ See Chapter 8. The plant is used as a bee repellent (Gelfand *et al.* 1985). The dry, powdered rhizome is burnt and the smoke is used to drive out bees from a hive. Anecdotes probably refer to the recently described *Alepidea cordifolia* with which *A. amatymbica* has been confused (the latter does not occur in Zimbabwe).

Aloe species |Asphodelaceae| **ALOE** ■ See Chapter 7. Aloe leaf ash is traditionally used in rural areas to protect winnowed grain against weevils.

Agathosma betulina |Rutaceae| **ROUND-LEAF BUCHU**; *rondeblaarboegoe* (Afrikaans) ■ See Chapter 8. *Agathosma betulina* is a small, multi-stemmed and woody shrub (up to one metre high) that resprouts after fire. It is endemic to the Cederberg region. The small, gland-dotted leaves are typically rounded (less than twice as long as they are broad), hence the vernacular names. The flowers are star-shaped, with five white to pink petals. It is well documented that that *A. betulina* and *A. crenulata* (see below) have been used for cosmetic and medicinal purposes since early days. The early Dutch colonists made extensive use of buchu or *boegoe* in the form of alcoholic tinctures for stomach problems and urinary tract diseases, and in the form of vinegar infusions for washing and treating wounds. Round-leaf buchu contains a valuable essential oil rich in isomenthone and diosphenol. This oil also has minor sulfur-containing compounds which are important in the food industry, because they have a characteristic blackcurrant smell and flavour (Campbell *et al.* 1991; Posthumus *et al.* 1996; Mavimbela *et al.* 2014).

Agathosma crenulata |Rutaceae| **OVAL-LEAF BUCHU**; *ovaalblaarboegoe* (Afrikaans) ■ This species is very similar to *A. betulina* but differs in the erect, single-stemmed and taller growth form (two metres or more) and in the narrower shape of the leaves (more than twice as long as broad). It does not survive fire and regenerates from seeds. The species is endemic to the south-western parts of the Western Cape, as far north as Tulbagh. *Agathosma crenulata* was historically the first buchu to be commercialised and became very popular. However, it yields an essential oil which is less desirable because of the high levels of pulegone, a potentially toxic substance.

Several other species of *Agathosma* have been used to some extent. These include long-leaf buchu (*Agathosma serratifolia*), *basterboegoe* (*A. ovata*) and *muishondboegoe* (*A. pulchella*) (Viljoen *et al.* 2005a). The name "buchu" is sometimes also used for species of *Coleonema* and *Diosma* (see below). All of these fynbos shrubs from the Citrus family are important in the cultural heritage of Cape people.

Artemisia afra |Asteraceae| ***UMHLONYANE*** (Xhosa, Zulu); *lengana* (Sotho, Tswana); *als, wildeals* (Afrikaans); African wormwood ■ The plant is an erect shrub of up to two metres in height, with highly aromatic feathery leaves and small, yellowish flower heads. It occurs over large parts of the eastern half of southern Africa and northwards to tropical east Africa and Ethiopia. It is an important and widely used traditional medicine (see Chapter 8). The plant is rich in essential oils but is remarkably variable, with distinct regional and even local differences in the main compounds of the oil (Viljoen *et al.* 2006b). Some plants produce almost pure eucalyptol, borneol, camphor or thujone, while others may have complex mixtures of monoterpenoids and sesquiterpenoids such as davanone and chrysanthenyl acetate. As a result, suitable clones are being selected and developed for commercial cultivation.

Caesalpinia rubra |Fabaceae| ***AUAUROI*** (Nama) ■ Dried, powdered leaves are used as a perfume (Van den Eynden *et al.* 1992).

Buchu containers: cisticola nest and tortoise shell

Cisticola nest used as a container for buchu powder

Bundle of *imphepho* (*Achyrocline stenoptera*) as it is sold on muthi markets

Plantation of round-leaf buchu (*Agathosma betulina*)

Croton gratissimus |Euphorbiaceae| ***MAQUASSIE*** (San); *korannaboegoe, bergboegoe* (Afrikaans); lavender croton ■ This shrub or small tree of up to 10 metres in height has a rough grey bark and bright green, aromatic leaves which are silver-grey and gland-dotted on the lower surfaces. The distribution extends over large parts of northern South Africa, Zimbabwe, Botswana, Namibia and Angola. For medicinal purposes, the bark is mainly used, but the powdered aromatic leaves are an important traditional perfume, used in much the same way as real buchu (see *Agathosma*). Powdered leaves have been used with oil or fat to anoint the body, and hot water extracts were once made as a substitute for lavender water (Smith 1966). The specific combination of plant parts used in traditional medicine was shown to be important (Van Vuuren & Viljoen 2008).

Coleonema album |Rutaceae| ***AASBOSSIE*** (Afrikaans); Cape may ■ This close relative of real buchu is an aromatic small shrub with yellowish-green, needle-like leaves and small white flowers. The plant occurs in the coastal region of the Cape and is often found close to the sea. Another species, *Coleonema juniperina*, has similar leaves and flowers but is a taller and sparser shrub. It occurs in the northern mountainous parts of the Cape fynbos region.

Coleonema plants contain essential oils with complex mixtures of compounds, including limonene (Berger *et al.* 1990). A study of *C. album* and four other species showed that the oils are dominated by monoterpenoids (Başer *et al.* 2006). These plants have been used as perfumes and diuretic medicines. The vernacular name for *C. album* is derived from its use by fishermen as a perfume for the hands, to hide the foul smell of red bait (*aas* or *rooiaas*).

Coleonema juniperina is known as *koorsbos* (fever bush) in the Nieuwoudtville area and is an important local medicine to treat fever (Willem Steenkamp, pers. comm.). It is used in a mixture with *norraboegoe* (*Pteronia camphorata*) and *sandolien* (*Dodonaea viscosa*). There are many myths and legends around the aromatic buchu relatives of the Cape (such as *Coleonema* and *Diosma*), most of which are now largely forgotten (Smith 1966). *Bokboegoe* (*Diosma hirsuta*), for example, was once widely used as a cosmetic (Forbes 1986) but according to Willem Steenkamp (pers. comm.), men should avoid the plant if they wish to retain their virility!

Further north in Namibia, other buchus of the Rutaceae are also used as perfumes and deodorants. The Himba people use *Thamnosma africana* (known as flea bush or *khanab*) – fragrant powdered roots and flowers – as a scented neck powder, and the Topnaar powder the dried fruits and seeds as a perfume. A decoction of the whole plant is used as an emetic to relieve nausea and stomach pain. The Bergdamara drink a decoction for colds, influenza and infections, and at the same time the body of the afflicted person is covered with the boiled leaves and wrapped to induce sweating (Van den Eynden *et al.* 1992). The Damara also use the plant as a mosquito repellent (Von Koenen 2001). Another aromatic Namibian plant of the Rutaceae, *Zanthoxylum ovatifoliolatum* (*peperhais* in Nama) is used by the Topnaar people. The dry fruits and seeds are powdered as a fragrant body powder or perfume. A decoction of the fruits is taken for sore throats, and the Himba use a similar decoction for abdominal complaints (Van den Eynden *et al.* 1992).

Eriocephalus africanus | Asteraceae| ***KAPOKBOS***, *wilderoosmaryn* (Afrikaans), wild rosemary, Cape snowbush ■ This shrub with its characteristic small leaves, white flower heads and fluffy seeds is a traditional diuretic medicine in South Africa, and has been used to treat oedema and stomach-ache. The essential oil contains α-pinene, β-caryophyllene, γ-terpinene, 1,8-cineole limonene, linalyl acetate and linalool as major compounds. A related species, *Eriocephalus punctulatus*, is known as *boegoekapok*. It is a traditional Griqua medicinal plant (Smith 1966). The essential oil of this species, called "Cape chamomile", is bright blue when fresh due to the presence of azulenic compounds, which are important perfumery constituents. Sandasi *et al.* (2011) showed, on the basis of chemosystematic evidence, that the source of Cape chamomile is probably *Eriocephalus tenuifolius* and not *E. punctulatus*.

Flower of *korannaboegoe* (*Croton gratissimus*)

Leaves and flowers of *korannaboegoe* (*Croton gratissimus*)

Flowering plant of *aasbossie* (*Coleonema album*)

Flowers of the *aasbossie* (*Coleonema album*)

Flowering plant of the *koorsbos* (*Coleonema juniperina*)

Flowers and fluffy fruits of *kapokbos* (*Eriocephalus africanus*)

Eucalyptus globulus |Myrtaceae| **BLUEGUM**; *bloekom* (Afrikaans) ■ Bluegum trees are indigenous to Australia and Tasmania but have become part of the landscape in southern Africa. Of the many species grown in southern Africa, *Eucalyptus globulus* (the real bluegum) is one of the most popular for traditional medicine and the leaves are sometimes sold on muthi markets to treat colds and congestion. *Eucalyptus* species are rich in essential oil, and usually have 1,8-cineole (eucalyptol) as the main component. It is widely used in medicinal preparations (as inhalants and ointments) and in soaps, detergents, food, dentistry and veterinary products.

A related plant from the same family is the famous tea tree (*Melaleuca alternifolia*). The oil is produced mainly in Australia, and has become very popular because it is said to be effective against bacteria, fungi and viruses and is also claimed to have immuno-stimulant properties. Tea tree oil contains terpinene-4-ol, 1,8-cineole, pinene and other minor components.

Foeniculum vulgare |Apiaceae| **FENNEL**; *vinkel, tuinvinkel* (Afrikaans) ■ This carrot-like plant from Europe has become a common roadside weed in South Africa. Fennel fruits contain a valuable essential oil rich in anethole and fenchone, with a distinct anise flavour. Two types of oil are distinguished, depending on the variety of fennel: bitter fennel oil, which should not have less than 60 per cent anethole and 15 per cent fenchone, and sweet fennel oil, which should have more than 80 per cent anethole (Bruneton 1995). Fennel is an industrial source of *E*-anethone, which is used as a flavouring agent in the cosmetics and liquor industries.

Gethyllis **species** |Amaryllidaceae| ***KOEKEMAKRANKA*** (Khoi, Afrikaans); kukumakranka (English) ■ Kukumakranka refers to a group of several bulbous plants from the Cape with often spirally twisted leaves, attractive white or pink flowers and usually fragrant club-shaped berries which emerge in midwinter, long after the flowers and leaves have wilted. The ripe fruits are edible and have a powerful sweet, fruity odour (Kamatou *et al.* 2008). Lita Cole (pers. comm.) once propagated kukumakranka on a small commercial scale in Namaqualand for the fragrant fruits. These berries are not difficult to find, because you simply follow your nose. This is indeed the traditional way in which kukumakranka is gathered, an exciting activity for rural children. The fruits were once popular to perfume rooms and linen. Alcoholic tinctures (*koekemakrankabrandewyn*) used to be a popular medicine to treat stomach ailments (see Chapter 7). *Koekemakranka* is one of only a few Khoi words still in use today. Commonly used species include *G. afra* (*koekemakranka*, *bramakranka*, *ruiker* or *ruikertjie*), *G. britteniana* (*sandman*); *G. ciliaris* (also called *sandman*), *G. oligocephala* (*voëldermpie*) and *G. verticillata* (*bergkoekemakranka, bergmannetjie, bergie, tandratjie*). De Jong and Cecile Van Zyl, Herman Rossouw and Thys Carstens are thanked for providing Afrikaans vernacular names.

Helichrysum odoratissimum |Asteraceae| ***IMPHEPHO*** (Xhosa, Zulu); everlasting; *kooigoed* (Afrikaans) ■ See photograph in Chapter 9. *Helichrysum* species are aromatic perennial herbs or shrublets with hairy leaves and persistent flower heads. Several species are used in traditional medicine but the best known and most widely used perfume and repellent species is *Helichrysum odoratissimum*. It is a popular *imphepho* – a ritual incense. It has been clearly demonstrated that smoke from aromatic plants has therapeutic effects in treating microbial infections (Braithwaite *et al.* 2008). Southern Sotho women make a perfumed ointment from the plant (Watt & Breyer-Brandwijk 1962).

In Namibia, the Topnaar people use the dried, powdered flowering tops of *Helichrysum tomentosulum* subsp. *aromaticum* as a perfume (Van den Eynden *et al.* 1992). The essential oil of *Helichrysum odoratissimum* contains α-pinene and α-humulene as main compounds (Lwande *et al.* 1993; Gundidza & Zwaving 1993). The Afrikaans name *kooigoed* reflects the traditional use as bedding material, known to be effective in repelling parasites and insects and thereby ensuring a good night's rest.

Leaves and flowers of the bluegum (*Eucalyptus globulus*)

Leaves and flowers of the tea tree (*Melaleuca alternifolia*)

Flowers of the *sandman* (*Gethyllis britteniana*)

Leaves of the *bramakranka* or *ruikertjie* (*Gethyllis afra*)

Kukumakranka fruit

Tincture of kukumakranka fruits

Heteromorpha arborescens |Apiaceae| ***UMBANGANDLALA*** (Xhosa, Zulu); *mkatlala* (Sotho); *wildepietersielie* (Afrikaans); parsley tree ■ The parsley tree is a woody shrub or small tree with a characteristic smooth, shiny bark that peels off in horizontal flakes. The leaves are variable: small and simple or large and much divided into smaller leaflets. The roots, bark and leaves are popular traditional medicines. The volatile oil is known to contain α-pinene, germacrene-*D* and sabinene as major constituents (Mwangi *et al.* 1994), and has shown definite antibacterial and antifungal activity (Deans *et al.* 1994).

Heteropyxis natalensis |Myrtaceae or Heteropyxidaceae| **LAVENDER TREE**; *inkunzi, uhuzu, umkhuswa* (Zulu); *laventelboom* (Afrikaans) ■ This aromatic tree of up to 10 metres in height has a flaking, mottled bark and bright green, glossy, aromatic leaves. It occurs in the northeastern parts of South Africa, Mozambique and eastern Zimbabwe. The roots and leaves have been used for numerous medicinal applications, including the treatment of nose bleed, bleeding gums and excessive menstrual flow. A traditional medicinal tea may be prepared from the leaves. The essential oil contains antibacterial monoterpenoids, of which ß-ocimene, 1,8-cineole, limonene, linalool and myrcene are the main ingredients (Weyerstahl *et al.* 1992; Gundidza *et al.* 1993; Van Vuuren *et al.* 2007).

Kyllinga alba |Cyperaceae| ***WITBIESIE*** (Afrikaans) ■ The plant is a hardy small sedge with bright green leaves and erect flowering stems, each of which bears a round, white flower cluster. It occurs over a large part of the interior of southern Africa. The roots are highly aromatic and contain an unknown essential oil, similar to that found in the red nutsedge (*Cyperus rotundus*), which is an ancient perfume plant and medicinal plant from the same family. *Kyllinga* is an important plant in the Kalahari in Botswana, because the roots are traditionally used as a plug (stopper) when ostrich eggs are filled with water. The plug probably has antibacterial properties as a result of the essential oil, so that the water will stay fresh when the eggs are buried in the sand for long periods. An added advantage is that the plant imparts a pleasant fresh taste to the water. The same result can be obtained simply by putting a small piece of *Kyllinga* root in a water container.

Lippia javanica |Verbenaceae| ***MUSUKUDU*** (Tswana); *umsuzwane* (Zulu); fever tea; *koorsbossie* (Afrikaans) ■ This species is an erect woody shrub of up to two metres in height, with highly aromatic leaves which give off a lemon smell when crushed. The plant occurs in large parts of southern Africa and the distribution extends into tropical Africa. It is similar to *Lippia scaberrima* (*musukujane* in Tswana), but the latter has conspicuous leaf-like bracts in the flower heads. Infusions of these plants are used as a tea to treat coughs, colds, fever and chest ailments. The volatile oil of *Lippia javanica* contains myrcene, caryophyllene, linalool, *p*-cymene and ipsdienone (Neidlein & Staehle 1974; Mwangi *et al.* 1991; Viljoen *et al.* 2005; Sandasi *et al.* 2013). The commercial value of the oil as a repellent and its possible use to control bark beetles of the genus *Ips* has been investigated. Lukwa *et al.* (2009) demonstrated that some extract fractions from *Lippia javanica* have mosquito repellent activity of five to eight hours duration, comparing favourably to the repellent activity of DEET (diethyltoluamide), the most common commercial mosquito repellent. Water extracts of *Lippia javanica* have been shown to be effective in Zimbabwe in controlling ticks on cattle, with weekly spraying using a knapsack sprayer. This local innovation provides an effective tick control option for rural folk from readily available wild plants, and peripheral blood samples from the treated cattle confirmed the absence of tick-borne diseases (Madzimure *et al.* 2011).

In rural parts of Sekhukhuneland, the Pedi people use the leaves of *Lippia rehmannii* (*mosunkwane* in Pedi; *laventelbossie* in Afrikaans) to make a tasty tea (Mahlatse Mogale, pers. comm.). They use it as a culinary herb, especially to counteract unpleasant odours when cooking pork. The plant is also used locally as a mosquito repellent.

Leaves and fruits of the lavender tree (*Heteropyxis natalensis*)

The distinctive bark of the lavender tree (*Heteropyxis natalensis*)

Flowering plant of *witbiesie* (*Kyllinga alba*)

The stems and roots of *Kyllinga alba* are traditionally used as plugs for ostrich egg water containers

Leaves and flowers of fever tea or *musukudu* (*Lippia javanica*)

Leaves and flowers of *mosunkwane* or *laventelbossie* (*Lippia rehmannii*)

Lycium cinereum |Solanaceae| **ARIS** (Nama) ■ The Topnaar people dry and powder all parts of the shrub, including roots, for use as a perfume (Van den Eynden *et al.* 1992).

Mentha longifolia |Lamiaceae| **WILD MINT**; *ballerja, kruisement* (Afrikaans), *t'kamma* (Khoi) ■ The plant is commonly found along rivers throughout southern Africa, hence the Khoi (Nama) name *t'kamma*, meaning "at or near water". It has oblong leaves and spikes of white or pale purple flowers. The use of this mint in southern Africa was first recorded by Backhouse (1844), who observed a San family drying the leaves "for tea". The drying process almost certainly indicates that buchu powder was being prepared, rather than tea. The essential oil shows considerable regional variation. The oil of subsp. *capensis* contains mainly menthone, pulegone and 1,8-cineole (Oyedeji & Afolayan 2006) while the subsp. *polyadenia* has one chemotype dominated by menthofuran and another by *cis*-piperitone oxide and piperitenone oxide (Viljoen *et al.* 2006c).

Myrothamnus flabellifolius |Myrothamnaceae| **RESURRECTION PLANT** ■ See Chapter 6. The plant is aromatic and contains an essential oil with very pronounced antimicrobial activity (Viljoen *et al.* 2002). The main compounds are *trans*-pinocarveol, limonene and *trans*- and *cis*-p-mentha-1(7),8-dien-2-ol).

Nymania capensis |Meliaceae| **KLAPPERBOS** (Afrikaans); Chinese lantern tree ■ This attractive plant from the Little Karoo in South Africa has small pink flowers and characteristic inflated fruits, resembling Chinese lanterns. Research by Mark Wright (pers. comm.) has shown that the plant has powerful antifeedant properties, similar to other exotic members of the family, such as the neem tree (*Azadirachta indica*) and the weedy seringa tree (*Melia azedarach*).

Ocimum africanum |Lamiaceae| **BOESMANSBOEGOE** (Afrikaans) ■ This important perfume plant is one of a few aromatic perennial herbs that are traditionally used as perfumes. These plants all have hairy, gland-dotted leaves and white to purple flowers arranged in dense clusters at regular intervals along the flowering stalk. *Ocimum africanum* is widely distributed in South Africa, Botswana, Namibia, Angola, Mozambique and Zimbabwe. The powdered leaves or powdered roots are fragrant and are a traditional body perfume in the Kalahari and in Namibia. The plant is also used in other parts of southern Africa as a cosmetic and an insecticide (Smith 1966). The volatile oil has been studied by Marazanye *et al.* (1988) who found it to be an effective alternative to conventional mosquito repellents. The plant is similar to cultivated basil (*Ocimum basilicum*) and hybrids between the two species are quite common (see photograph). These are more glabrous than true *O. africanum* but show the slender inflorescences and hairy calyces typical of the latter species. They are often cultivated in various parts of Africa and are particularly popular in Ethiopia. *Ocimum filamentosum* (see page 258) is used by San women in the Central Kalahari as a perfume plant. Men avoid contact with the plant as they believe that it may cause them to lose their virility.

Osmitopsis asteriscoides |Asteraceae| **BELS**, *belskruie* (Afrikaans) ■ The plant is an erect shrub with aromatic leaves crowded on the branch ends and attractive white flower heads. *Bels* is a traditional Cape Dutch remedy for numerous ailments. The volatile oil in the leaves is rich in 1,8-cineole (eucalyptol) and camphor as the two main ingredients, with demonstrated synergistic effects in antimicrobial studies (Viljoen *et al.* 2003).

Parmelia hottentotta |Parmeliaceae| **KHAOB** (Nama) ■ This grey-green lichen is powdered and used as a deodorant or perfume by the Topnaar in Namibia (Van den Eynden *et al.* 1992). A decoction is drunk to treat coughs, and to relieve stomach and chest pain. The genus *Parmelia* has been divided into different genera and limited information is available on the species that are used in southern Africa. The correct name for the most commonly utilised *klipblom* (see photograph on page 153) is now *Xanthoparmelia hottentotta*.

PERFUMES & REPELLENTS

Leaves and flowers of wild mint or *ballerja* (*Mentha longifolia*)

Flower and bladdery fruits of the *klapperbos* (*Nymania capensis*)

A commonly cultivated hybrid between wild basil (*Ocimum africanum*) and garden basil (*O. basilicum*)

Flowering plant of *bels* or *belskruie* (*Osmitopsis asteriscoides*)

Pelargonium capitatum x _P. radens_ │Geraniaceae│ **ROSE-SCENTED PELARGONIUM** ■
This pelargonium hybrid is a shrubby, hairy plant with lobed leaves and attractive pink flowers. It is one of several species grown for essential oil and forms part of the group of shrubby pelargoniums known as the section _Pelargonium_ (Van der Walt 1985). Other aromatic species of this group include _P. radens_ (rasp-leaved pelargonium), _P. odoratissimum_ (sweet-scented pelargonium), _P. graveolens_ (rose-scented pelargonium), _P. capitatum_ (also rose-scented pelargonium – see Demarne _et al._ 1993), _P. crispum_ (lemon-scented pelargonium) and _P. tomentosum_ (peppermint-scented pelargonium – see Demarne & Van der Walt 1990; Lalli _et al._ 2006). These plants are commonly grown in herb gardens in South Africa and Europe, not only for their attractive flowers and aromatic foliage but also for use as culinary herbs.

One of the most famous perfume pelargoniums is the so-called cultivar Rosé, which is grown on Réunion Island as a source of an essential oil known commercially as Bourbon oil. It is used to replace the valuable "attar of rose", the essential oil derived from the damask rose (_Rosa_ ×_damascena_), of which the Bulgarian type is considered to be superior for use in perfumes. The cultivar Rosé was originally thought to be derived from _P. graveolens_, but it was later found that it originated as a hybrid between _P. capitatum_ and _P. radens_ (Demarne & Van der Walt 1989).

The components which give the characteristic rose scent to geranium oil (citronellol, geraniol, linalool and nerol) occur at best in trace quantities in _P. graveolens_ and _P. radens_.

Some species were traditionally used as perfumes in southern Africa. For example, the dried and powdered leaves of _Pelargonium ramosissimum_ (_dassiepoeier_ or _dassieboegoe_ in Afrikaans) were used as a fragrant deodorant powder.

Pteronia onobromoides │Asteraceae│ **_SAB_**, _san_ (Khoi) ■ _Pteronia_ species are aromatic shrubs with a wide distribution in the western and dry central parts of southern Africa. The name of the San people is thought to be derived from the original Khoi name for _Pteronia onobromoides_ (Smith 1966; Hulley _et al._ 2010a). It is interesting to note that the species was beautifully illustrated in the diary of the Cape Governor Simon van der Stel, who encountered the plant on his expedition to Namaqualand in 1685 (see photograph on page 258). Unfortunately, he did not describe any uses. Several species of _Pteronia_ are known as _boegoebossie_, _boegoekaroo_ or _laventelbossie_, all reflecting their similarity to buchu and lavender, and their traditional use in cosmetics and skin care. See also notes under _Coleonema album_.

A second species of special interest is _Pteronia divaricata_, a traditional medicine that was only recorded in recent years (Hulley _et al._ 2011). This woody shrub has several vernacular names in the Cape, including _flip-se-bos_, _inflammasiebos_, _pylbos_ and s_palkpenbos_ (see Chapter 16, photographs on page 309). It is one of the most important of all traditional medicines in the Cederberg region of the Western Cape. The leaves have antibacterial activity, with sabinene, myrcene, β-caryophyllene and bicyclogermacrene as main volatile constituents.

Another example is _norraboegoe_ (_Pteronia camphorata_) which has remained scientifically poorly known, despite its important role in San and Nama medicine (Hulley _et al._ 2016). Laidler (1928) called it "_D/nhora_", and described it as one of the important types of buchu used by the Nama people. The botanical identity has remained unknown until recently. The main oil compounds are sabinene, limonene, 1,8-cineole, _p_-cymene and terpinene-4-ol (Hulley _et al._ 2016).

The essential oil of _laventelbossie_ (_Pteronia incana_) contains α-pinene, ß-pinene, sabinene and myrcene as main components (Hulley _et al._ 2010b). This widely distributed Karoo shrub (_karoobossie_) has numerous vernacular names, including _asbossie_, _perdebossie_, _vaalbossie_, _kraakbossie_ and _skieterbossie_. The last two names refer to the crackling effect (like crackers or fireworks) when the oily stems are burnt in a fire.

Leaves and flowers of rose-scented pelargonium (*Pelargonium* cultivar Rosé)

Leaves and flowers of *Pelargonium capitatum*

Peppermint scented pelargonium (*Pelargonium tomentosum*)

Plant of the *sab* or *san* (*Pteronia onobromoides*)

Flower heads of *norraboegoe* (*Pteronia camphorata*)

Salvia stenophylla |Lamiaceae| ***FYNBLAARSALIE*** (Afrikaans); blue mountain sage ■ The plant is an erect herb with narrow leaves, wavy leaf margins and small blue flowers. This species may easily be confused with *Salvia runcinata*, but the latter has markedly hairy stems and broader leaves. *Salvia stenophylla* occurs mainly in grasslands (often as a roadside weed) and is found in many parts of South Africa, Botswana and Namibia (Codd 1985). About one-third of the essential oil of this species comprises α-bisabolol [the (+)-epi-α-isomers] (Viljoen *et al.* 2006d). Similar compounds [(−)-α-isomers] occur in German chamomile oil (from *Matricaria chamomilla*). The valuable inky blue oil of German chamomile is popular in aromatherapy.

Spirostachys africana |Euphorbiaceae| **TAMBOTI** ■ See Chapter 17. Pieces of the wood are put in clothing as insect repellents. In Namibia, perfumed beads made from the wood are worn as fragrant necklaces by the Herero, and have a sweetish scent similar to sandalwood. Powdered leaves and twigs are burnt so that clothing can be perfumed with the smoke (Von Koenen 2001).

Tagetes minuta |Asteraceae| **TALL KHAKI BUSH**; *lang kakiebos* (Afrikaans) ■ This South American plant is an erect, highly aromatic annual with compound, glandular leaves and small, yellow, cylindrical flower heads. It is a troublesome weed of old lands and disturbed places throughout southern Africa. The repellent properties of the essential oil has been known for a long time and it was found many years ago to be effective in preventing sheep from becoming infected with blowfly larvae (Smith 1966). Many gardeners use warm water extracts of the fresh plant (often with a little soap added) to keep roses and other garden plants free from insects (especially aphids) and fungal diseases. The essential oil (known commercially as *tagette* or *taget*) is used in perfumery and as a flavourant in food, beverages and tobacco. Characteristic components of tagetes oil include ocimene, dihydrotagetone and ocimenone (Tankeu *et al.* 2013). Innovative pioneering work was done by Prof Earle Graven, who designed and commissioned a mobile steam distillation unit (see photograph on page 258) for the extraction of tagetes oil on farms in South Africa.

Turraea obtusifolia |Meliaceae| **WILD HONEYSUCKLE** ■ This shrub has glossy green leaves and attractive white flowers. It is said to have powerful antifeedant effects against leaf-eating insects. The wild honeysuckle tree (*Turraea floribunda*) has the same effect, which is probably due to the presence of limonoids. Limonoids with antifeedant effects are known from other members of the family (see *Nymania capensis*).

Vachellia erioloba (=*Acacia erioloba*) |Fabaceae| **CAMEL THORN** ■ (See Chapter 18.) A powder made from the inner bark is applied in quantity to the body as a perfume by the Topnaar of Namibia, and is also used to scent the home (Van den Eynden *et al.* 1992).

REFERENCES AND FURTHER READING: Backhouse, J. 1844. *A narrative of a visit to the Mauritius and South Africa.* Hamilton, Adams and Co., London. **Başer, K.H.C., Demirci, B., Özek, T., Khusal, P., Viljoen, A.M. & Victor, J.** 2006. Composition of the essential oils of five *Coleonema* species from South Africa. *J. Essent. Oil Res.* 18: 26–29. **Bello, H.** *et al.* **2017.** A taxonomic revision of the *Pteronia camphorata* group (Astereae, Asteraceae). *S. Afr. J. Bot.* 113: 277–287. **Berger, R.G.** *et al.* **1990.** The essential oil of *Coleonema album* (Rutaceae) and of a photomixotrophic cell culture derived thereof. *Z. Naturforsch.* 45(3&4): 187–195. **Braithwaite, M., Van Vuuren, S.F. & Viljoen, A.M. 2008.** Validation of smoke inhalation therapy to treat microbial infections. *J. Ethnopharmacol.* 119: 501–506. **Bruneton, J. 1995.** *Pharmacognosy, phytochemistry, medicinal plants.* Intercept, Hampshire. **Campbell, W.E.** *et al.* **1991.** Sulphur-containing essential oils from the Diosmeae. *Flavour Fragrance J.* 6(2): 113–116. **Codd, L.E. 1985.** Lamiaceae. *Flora of Southern Africa* 28(4): 1–247. **Deans, S.G.** *et al.* **1994.** Antimicrobial activities of the volatile oil of *Heteromorpha trifoliata* (Wendl.) Eckl. & Zeyh. (Apiaceae). *Flavour Fragrance J.* 9: 245–248. **Demarne, F. & Van der Walt, J.J.A. 1989.** Origin of the rose-scented *Pelargonium* cultivar grown on Réunion Island. *S.Afr. J. Bot.* 55(2): 184–191. **Demarne, F.** *et al.* **1993.** A study of the variation in the essential oil and morphology of *Pelargonium capitatum* (L.) L'Herit. (Geraniaceae). Part I. The composition of the oil. *J. Essent. Oil Res.* 5: 493–499. **Forbes, V.S. (ed.) 1986.** *Carl Peter Thunberg Travels at the Cape of Good Hope* 1772–1775. Van Riebeeck Society, Cape Town. **Gelfand, M.** *et al.* **1985.** *The traditional medical practitioner in Zimbabwe.* Mambo Press, Harare. **Graven, E.H.** *et al.* **1992.** Antimicrobial and antioxidative properties of the volatile (essential) oil of *Artemisia afra* Jacq. *Flavour Fragrance J.* 7: 121–123. **Gundidza, M & Zwaving, J.H. 1993.**

Flowering stem of *fynblaarsalie* (*Salvia stenophylla*)

German chamomile (*Matricaria chamomilla*)

Plants of the tall khaki bush (*Tagetes minuta*)

Flower heads of the tall khaki bush (*Tagetes minuta*)

The chemical composition of the essential leaf oil of *Helichrysum odoratissimum* from Zimbabwe. *J. Essent. Oil Res.* 5: 341–343. **Gundidza, M.** *et al.* **1993.** The essential oil from *Heteropyxis natalensis* Harv.: Its antimicrobial activities and phytoconstituents. *J. Sci. Food Agric.* 63: 361–364. **Hodge, W.H. 1953.** The drug aloes of commerce, with special reference to the Cape species. *Econ. Bot.* 7: 99–129. **Hulley, I.M., Viljoen, A.M., Tilney, P.M., Van Vuuren, S.F., Kamatou, G.P.P. & Van Wyk, B.-E. 2010a.** Ethnobotany, leaf anatomy, essential oil composition and antibacterial activity of *Pteronia onobromoides* (Asteraceae). *S. Afr. J. Bot.* 76: 43–48. **Hulley, I.M., Viljoen, A.M., Tilney, P.M., Van Vuuren, S.F., Kamatou, G.P.P. & Van Wyk, B.-E. 2010b.** The ethnobotany, leaf anatomy, essential oil variation and biological activity of *Pteronia incana* (Asteraceae). *S. Afr. J. Bot.* 76: 668–675. **Hulley, I.M., Viljoen, A.M., Tilney, P.M., Van Vuuren, S.F., Kamatou, G.P.P. & Van Wyk, B.-E. 2011.** *Pteronia divaricata* (Asteraceae): a newly recorded Cape herbal medicine. *S. Afr. J. Bot.* 77: 66–74. **Hulley, I.M., Tilney, P.M., Van Vuuren, S.F., Kamatou, G.P.P., Viljoen, A.M. & Van Wyk, B.-E. 2016.** San and Nama indigenous knowledge: the case of !nhora (*Pteronia camphorata*) and its medicinal use. *S. Afr. J. Sci.* 112 (9/10) Art. #2016-0044, 9 pages. **Kaiser, R.** *et al.* **1975.** Analysis of buchu leaf oil. *J. Agric. Food Chem.* 23: 943–950. **Kamatou, G.P.P., Viljoen, A.M., Özek, T. Başer. K.H.C. 2008.** Headspace volatiles of *Gethyllis afra* and *G. ciliaris* fruits ("kukumakranka"). *S. Afr. J. Bot.* 74, 768–770. **Kubo, I.** *et al.* **1977.** Muzigadial and warburganal, potent anti-fungal, anti-yeast, and African army worm antifeedant agents. *Tetrahedron Lett.* 52: 4553–4556. **Laidler, P.W. 1928.** The magic medicine of the Hottentots. *S. Afr. J. Sci.* 25: 433–447. **Lalli, J., Viljoen, A.M., Başer, K.H.C., Demirci, B. & Özek, T. 2006.** The essential oil composition and chemotaxonomical appraisal of South African *Pelargoniums* (Geraniaceae). *J. Essent. Oil Res.* 18: 89–105. **Lukwa, N., Molgaard, P., Furu, P. & Bogh, C. 2009.** *Lippia javanica* (Burm.f.) Spreng: its general constituents and bioactivity on mosquitoes. *Tropical Biomedicine* 26(1): 85–91. **Lwande, W.** *et al.* **1993.** Constituents of the essential oil of *Helichrysum odoratissimum* (L.) Less. *J. Essent. Oil Res* 5: 93–95. **Madzimure, J.** *et al.* **2011.** Acaricidal efficacy against cattle ticks and acute oral toxicity of *Lippia javanica* (Burm.) Spreng. *Tropical Animal Health and Production* 43(2): 481–489. **Marazanye, T.** *et al.* **1988.** Wild local plant derivatives as alternative to conventional mosquito repellent. *Central African Journal of Medicine* 34(4): 91. **Mavimbela, T., Vermaak, I. & Viljoen, A.M. 2014.** Differentiating between *Agathosma betulina* and *Agathosma crenulata* – A quality control perspective. *Journal of Applied Research on Medicinal and Aromatic Plants* 1: e8–e14. **Mwangi, J.W.** *et al.* **1991.** Essential oils of Kenyan *Lippia* species. Part III. *Flavour Fragrance J.* 6(3): 221–224. **Mwangi, J.W.** *et al.* **1994.** Volatile components of *Heteromorpha trifoliata* (Wendl.) Eckl. & Zeyh. *Flavour Fragrance J.* 9: 241–243. **Neidlein, R. & Staehle, R. 1974.** Constituents of *Lippia javanica*. III. *Deut. Apoth. Ztg.* 114(40): 1588–1592; 114(49): 1941. **Oyedeji, A.O. & Afolayan, A.J. 2006.** Chemical composition and antimicrobial activity of the essential oil isolated from South African *Mentha longifolia* (L.) L. subsp. *capensis* (Thunb.) Briq. *J. Essent. Oil Res.* 18: 57–59. **Posthumus, M.A.** *et al.* **1996.** Chemical composition of the essential oils of *Agathosma betulina*, *A. crenulata* and an *A. betulina × A. crenulata* hybrid (buchu). *J. Essent. Oil Res.* 8: 223–228. **Sandasi, M., Kamatou, G.P.P. & Viljoen, A.M. 2011.** Chemotaxonomic evidence suggests that *Eriocephalus tenuifolius* is the source of Cape chamomile oil and not *E. punctulatus*. *Biochem. Syst. Ecol.* 39: 328–338. **Sandasi, M., Kamatou, G.P.P., Combrinck, S. & Viljoen, A.M. 2013.** A chemotaxonomic assessment of four indigenous South African *Lippia* species using GCMS and vibrational spectroscopy of the essential oils. *Biochem. Syst. Ecol.* 51: 142–152. **Smith, C.A. 1966.** Common names of South African plants. *Mem. Bot. Surv. S. Afr.* 35. **Spreeth, A.D. 1950.** A revision of the commercially important *Agathosma* species. *Jl S. Afr. Bot.* 42: 109–119. **Tankeu, S., Vermaak, I., Viljoen, A.M., Sandasi, M. & Kamatou, G.P.P. 2013.** Essential oil variation of *Tagetes minuta* in South Africa – a chemometric approach. *Biochem. Syst. Ecol.* 51: 320–327. **Van den Eynden, V.** *et al.* **1992.** *The ethnobotany of the Topnaar.* Universiteit Gent, Gent. **Van der Walt, J.J.A. 1977.** *Pelargoniums of Southern Africa.* Purnell, Cape Town. **Van der Walt, J.J.A. 1985.** A taxonomic revision of the type section of *Pelargonium* L'Herit. *Bothalia* 15(3&4): 113–121. **Van Vuuren, S.F., Viljoen, A.M., Özek, T., Demirci, B. & Başer, K.H.C. 2007.** Seasonal and geographical variation of *Heteropyxis natalensis* essential oil and the effect thereof on the antimicrobial activity. *S. Afr. J. Bot.* 73: 441–448. **Van Vuuren, S.F. & Viljoen, A.M. 2008.** *In vitro* evidence of phyto-synergy for plant part combinations of *Croton gratissimus* (Euphorbiaceae) used in African traditional healing. *J. Ethnopharmacol.* 119, 700–704. **Viljoen, A.M., Klepser, M.E., Ernst, E.J., Keele, D., Roling, E., Van Vuuren, S., Demirci, B., Başer, K.H.C. & Van Wyk, B.-E. 2002.** The composition and antimicrobial activity of the essential oil of the resurrection plant, *Myrothamnus flabellifolius*. *S. Afr. J. Bot.* 68: 100–105. **Viljoen, A.M., Van Vuuren, S., Ernst, E.J., Klepser, M.E., Demirci, B., Başer, K.H.C. & Van Wyk, B.-E. 2003.** *Osmitopsis asteriscoides* (Asteraceae) – the antimicrobial activity and essential oil composition of a Cape-Dutch remedy. *J. Ethnopharmacol.* 88: 137–143. **Viljoen, A.M., Subramoney, S., Van Vuuren, S.F., Başer, K.H.C. & Demirci, B. 2005.** The composition, geographical variation and antimicrobial activity of *Lippia javanica* (Verbenaceae) leaf essential oils. *J. Ethnopharmacol.* 96: 271–277. **Viljoen, A.M., Moolla, A., Van Vuuren, S.F., Başer, K.H.C., Demirci, B. & Özek, T. 2006a.** A seasonal variation study of the chemical composition and antimicrobial activity of the essential oil of *Agathosma ovata* (Thunb.) Pillans (Rutaceae). *J. Essent. Oil Res.* 18: 30–36. **Viljoen, A.M., Van Vuuren, S.F., Gwebu, L., Demirci, B. & Başer, K.H.C. 2006b.** The geographical variation and antimicrobial activity of African wormwood (*Artemisia afra* Jacq.) essential oil. *J. Essent. Oil Res.* 18: 19–25. **Viljoen, A.M., Petkar, S., Van Vuuren, S.F., Figueiredo, A.C., Pedro, L.G. & Barroso, J.G. 2006c.** The chemo-geographical variation in essential oil composition and the antimicrobial properties of "wild mint" – *Mentha longifolia* subsp. *polyadena* (Lamiaceae) in southern Africa. *J. Essent. Oil Res.* 18: 60–65. **Viljoen, A.M., Gono-Bwalya, A., Kamatou, G., Başer, K.H.C. & Demirci, B. 2006d.** The essential oil composition and chemotaxonomy of *Salvia stenophylla* and its allies *S. repens* and *S. runcinata*. *J. Essent. Oil Res.* 18: 37–45. **Von Koenen, E. 2001.** *Medicinal, poisonous and edible plants in Namibia.* Klaus Hess Publishers, Windhoek and Göttingen. **Watt, J.M. & Breyer-Brandwijk, M.G. 1962.** *The medicinal and poisonous plants of southern and eastern Africa,* 2nd ed. Livingstone, London. **Weyerstahl, P.** *et al.* **1992.** Constituents of the essential oil of *Heteropyxis natalensis*. *J. Essent. Oil Res.* 4: 439–445.

Flowers and fruit of the wild honeysuckle (*Turraea obtusifolia*)

Flower and fruits of the wild honeysuckle tree (*Turraea floribunda*)

Camel thorn tree (*Vachellia erioloba*)

Frieda Bastian with bars of homemade soap (Kleinplasie Farm Museum, Worcester)

CHAPTER 14
Soaps & cosmetics

SEVERAL PLANTS ARE traditionally used as natural sources of soap. Soap plants contain large amounts of saponins that have the ability to dissolve fat and oily substances and are at the same time soluble in water. They have therefore been widely used as detergents (cleansing agents) for washing clothes and for bathing. The presence of saponins in plant material can easily be demonstrated by the large quantity of foam that is formed when crushed plant material is shaken vigorously in water. Soap bushes such as *Helinus integrifolius* and *Noltea africana* are examples of soap substitutes which were once commonly used.

Traditional methods of soap making are still encountered in rural areas of southern Africa. The main ingredients are animal fat and the lye (*loog* in Afrikaans) which is used to convert the fat or oil into soap. This chemical process is known as saponification. What happens is that the fat is hydrolysed by a caustic alkali. The fat plus the alkali give soap plus glycerol. The soap which is formed is actually the sodium or potassium salt of the fatty acids. In former times, the alkali was obtained by lixiviating ash from various plants with water to yield lye. A once flourishing trade in lye ash from plants like *seepganna* (*Salsola aphylla*) and *asbos* (*Mesembryanthemum junceum*, previously known as *Psilocaulon junceum*) gradually came to a halt as industrial caustic soda (sodium hydroxide; NaOH; *bytsoda* in Afrikaans) became more readily available. A typical recipe for farm-soap or homemade soap (*boerseep* in Afrikaans) is given by Dykman (1891). One bucket of ash and half a bucket of lime in five buckets of water are boiled for two hours. The resultant lye is filtered, about nine kilograms of molten fat are added and the mixture is boiled (with stirring) for 12 hours. The soap is then poured into the moulds and left to cool and solidify. Dyes and perfumes are often incorporated into the soap as additives to achieve the desired colour and fragrance.

Vegetable oils or other ointments are commonly used as cosmetics and moisturisers to protect the skin against the harsh African sun. In recent years there has been a keen interest in novel seed oils from indigenous plants such as baobab (*Adansonia digitata*), marula (*Sclerocarya birrea*), blue sourplum (*Ximenia americana*), tsamma (*Citrillus lanatus*), mongongo (*Schinziophyton rautanenii*) and bushveld Natal-mahogany (*Trichilia emetica*) (Van der Vossen & Mkamilo 2007; Grace *et al.* 2008; Vermaak *et al.* 2011).

Face masks, known as *umemezis*, are widely used in southern Africa and are particularly popular in the Eastern Cape Province. The use of cosmetics (mainly of mineral origin – ochre and clay) in this part of southern Africa is linked to social customs such as the initiation rites of boys and girls (De Lange 1963; Dold & Cocks 2012). White kaolin clay, for example, is used by initiates into manhood (*abakhwetha*) to cover the whole of their bodies during the period of isolation. *Umemezis* are used not only as moisturisers and sun screens but also as skin lighteners and simply as cosmetics. The way in which natural *umemezis* act as skin lighteners is well known; most of these ointments and creams contain hydroquinone, either as an additive or as a natural product of the plant that was used to prepare the ointment. Hydroquinone is an inhibitor of melanin synthesis in the skin, so that it is often incorporated in commercial cosmetic preparations, at concentrations of up to two per cent (Bruneton 1995). Prolonged or repeated use should be avoided, because dark skin blemishes or skin marbling may occur. Hydroquinone-containing products as over-the-counter cosmetics were banned in South Africa in 1990 (Khan 1996; Daniels 1997) but it seems that the use of natural, plant-derived *umemezis* has remained popular as decorative cosmetics.

Adansonia digitata |Malvaceae| **BAOBAB** ■ See Chapter 3. The seed oil is nowadays used in various cosmetic products and applications (Vermaak *et al.* 2011; Komane *et al.* 2017).

Aloe ferox |Asphodelaceae| **BITTER ALOE** ■ See Chapter 7. The leaf gel of the bitter aloe is used in a range of hair and skin care products, similar to the way in which *Aloe vera* gel is used. The pharmaceutical product known as Cape aloes is traditionally used as a laxative medicine but is also a rich source of aloesin and other chromone derivatives that are being developed as ingredients of skin-lightening creams. It is interesting to note that a mixture of aloe ash and soap was once popular amongst young Swazi men as hair bleach (Coertze 1930). In earlier times, Cape aloe bitters was powdered and rubbed onto the face as a skin lightener (Solomon Mahlaba, Ashley Mashigo, pers. comm.).

Aloe vera |Asphodelaceae| ***ALOE VERA*** ■ This is a famous succulent plant of North African or Arabian origin which has become one of the most important commercial crop plants of the world. The plant has thick, fleshy leaves and erect flower stalks with usually yellow but occasionally red flowers. The leaves are harvested in such a way that the cut surfaces remain sealed to prevent deterioration. The leaves are "filleted" to remove the outer layer with its bitter yellow juice, so that only the fleshy inner leaf pulp remains. Further processing removes all traces of the bitter fraction, so that only the valuable, tasteless gel (white juice) remains. The gel contains polysaccharides, sugars, pectins, amino acids and various ingredients claimed to be biologically active, such as enzymes and glycoproteins. It forms the basis of a very large *Aloe vera* cosmetics industry and is also extensively used in health drinks and tonics.

Bulbine frutescens |Asphodelaceae| ***BALSEMKOPIVA*** (Afrikaans) ■ See Chapter 11. *Bulbine* species are easily recognised by the aloe-like growth form, succulent leaves, yellow flowers and particularly by their hairy stamens. The leaf gel is widely used for treating wounds, burns and skin conditions. The wound-healing properties are probably due to glycoproteins such as aloctin A and aloctin B, which are known from the leaf gel of *Aloe arborescens*.

Calodendrum capense |Rutaceae| ***WHITE UMEMEZI***; *umemezi-omhlope* (Zulu); Cape chestnut ■ This plant is a large forest tree with gland-dotted leaves and attractive pink flowers. The bark is commonly sold on street markets as white *umemezi* but the value and uses of the product in cosmetics and skin treatment are poorly recorded.

Cassipourea malosana (=*Cassipourea gerrardii*) |Rhizophoraceae| **ONIONWOOD**, common onionwood; *umemezi-obomvu* (Zulu) ■ It is a shrub or small forest tree with dark green leathery leaves, small greenish flowers and thinly fleshy orange capsules. Freshly cut timber has a distinctive smell like onions, hence the common name. The bark has many medicinal and magical properties but it is widely used as a skin lightener, particularly in KwaZulu-Natal. Concern has been expressed about the way in which trees have been eradicated in many parts as a result of bark harvesting. To prepare the skin mask, finely ground bark is mixed with sodium carbonate and milk. Onionwood contains dimeric anthocyanins which produce hydroquinone as an intermediate compound when treated with sodium carbonate (Drewes *et al.*1996). According to Mr Mutwa (pers. comm.), the fresh or dry bark is used as a skin lightener, for pimples in post-adolescent years, and for acute sunburn. It is generally only used by females, and only on the face. It must not be used during lightning, as it is believed to attract lightning. As a skin lightener, about a teaspoonful of powdered bark is mixed with a little water and applied directly to the face. It is left on the face and not rinsed off. This is done daily. A lightening effect will be noticeable after three to four weeks. To treat pimples, it is not applied topically but is only used to steam the face, and as a *phalaza* (emetic). To alleviate the discomfort of acute sunburn on the face, the powdered bark is mixed with water and applied directly as a paste, in the same way as calamine lotion.

Flowers of white *umemezi* (*Calodendrum capense*)

Bark of white *umemezi* (*Calodendrum capense*)

Women with decorative *umemezis*

Citrillus lanatus |Cucurbitaceae| **TSAMMA** ■ See Chapter 3. The roasted seeds are ground to a coarse white meal. This meal is chewed and moistened with saliva, and is then smeared over the body and rubbed in thoroughly. The treatment is used mainly by women in the same way as skin creams are used nowadays. The skin becomes smooth and takes on a healthy reddish colour (MacCrone 1937).

Commiphora pyracanthoides |Burseraceae| **COMMON CORKWOOD** ■ See Chapter 18. The gum is boiled in water to form a lather for washing clothes, and resin from the stem bark is used as a hair straightener (Malan & Owen-Smith 1974).

Dicerocaryum eriocarpum |Pedaliaceae| ***SEEPBOS***, *elandsdoring, beesdubbeltjie* (Afrikaans); boot-protector, devil's thorn, stud thorn; *tshêtlhô-êtonanyana* (Tswana) ■ See Chapter 10. The *seepbos* is a prostrate creeping plant with small, greyish leaves and attractive pink flowers. The fruits are characteristic. They are flat and have two erect thorns. All parts of the plant contain saponins and are markedly soapy and slimy. If crushed plants are left in water overnight, the resultant mucilage is a useful substitute for soap and shampoo. The plant has been used to treat bovine parabotulism (*lamsiekte*). In recent years, commercial cosmetics have been developed from this species.

Harpephyllum caffrum |Anacardiaceae| **WILD PLUM** ■ See Chapter 3. The bark, known as *umgwenya* in Xhosa and Zulu, is important for cosmetic purposes. It is used to treat acne and eczema (Pujol 1990) and is usually applied in the form of facial saunas and skin washes. According to Mr Mutwa (pers. comm.), the bark is primarily used to purify the blood in a person with "bad blood", which manifests as pimples on the face. It is usually used on people older than 18, but can also be used for the acne of puberty. For the same patient, it is given firstly as a facial steaming, then as a *phalaza*, and then orally as an *imbiza* daily. The bark is used fresh and can be collected in any season. It is typically sold on muthi markets as finely chopped material and not in the more usual form as pieces of bark.

Helinus integrifolius |Rhamnaceae| **SOAP PLANT**; *ubhubhubhu* (Zulu); *seepplant, seepbos* (Afrikaans); *mampehlele* (Northern Sotho) ■ The plant is a shrubby creeper with heart-shaped leaves, small, yellowish flowers and distinctive coiled tendrils with which it climbs onto other plants. The roots and stems are stirred in cold water and the frothy liquid is drunk as an emetic to treat hysteria. The leaves are used against sandworm and gonorrhoea (Watt & Breyer-Brandwijk 1962; Hedberg & Staugård 1989; Venter 1997). Crushed leaves, which contain slime cells and saponins, have been used as soap substitutes. Decoctions are said to be traditionally used as prophylactic medicine and remedy for black quarter (black-leg or *sponssiekte*) in cattle (Smith 1966). It is possible that plants rich in saponins, such as *Helinus integrifolius,* are used in medicinal mixtures not only for their own biological activities but also to enhance the absorption of compounds in the mixture that would normally not be absorbed (or that would be absorbed very slowly).

Kigelia africana | Bignoniaceae| **SAUSAGE TREE**; *worsboom* (Afrikaans); *modukguhlu* (Northern Sotho); *moporota* (Tswana); *muvevha* (Venda); *umvongothi* (Zulu) ■ This typical bushveld tree has large compound leaves, striking maroon flowers and large, pendulous, gourd-like fruits. Dried, pulverised fruits have been traditionally used to treat syphilis, ulcers and sores. Claims have been made that it is beneficial against some forms of skin cancer. Fruit extracts are nowadays becoming popular as ingredients of cosmetics and skin lotions. Quinones and coumarins are likely to be responsible for the antimicrobial and skin-healing effects. Verminoside (an iridoid compound) is a major constituent, and in a laboratory study showed significant anti-inflammatory activity (Picerno *et al.* 2005).

Flowers and fruits of the seepbos (*Dicerocaryum eriocarpum*)

Chopped bark of *Harpephyllum caffrum* as it is sold on muthi markets

Leaves and flowers of the soap plant (*Helinus integrifolius*)

Manochlamys albicans |Amaranthaceae| ***BOESMANSEEP***, *seepbos, bergsoutbos, spanspek-bos* (Afrikaans) ■ This shrubby plant grows up to one metre in height and has distinctive diamond-shaped leaves, inconspicuous flowers and green berries. It occurs over a wide area in the Cape and southern Namibia. The whole plant is traditionally used as a soap substitute to wash hands and clothes (Willem Steenkamp, pers. comm.).

Mesembryanthemum junceum (=*Psilocaulon junceum*) |Aizoaceae| ***ASBOS***, *loogbos* (Afri-kaans) ■ *Asbos* is a succulent shrub with fleshy, seemingly leafless stems, small purple or pink flowers and conical fruit capsules. The plant is exceptionally common in the dry interior of South Africa and Namibia. In the treeless parts of Namaqualand, the stems are stacked in a semi-circle to form the traditional *kookskerm* or *asbosskerm* around the fire. Plants of *Mesembryanthemum junceum*, *M. coriarium* and other species were incinerated in large quantities as a valuable source of alkali ash used in soap making. They are said to have replaced *seepganna* (*Salsola aphylla*) as the main source of ash after 1772 (Smith 1966) and became an important commercial commodity in the Karoo.

Noltea africana |Rhamnaceae| **SOAP BUSH**, soap dogwood; *seepblinkblaar, seepbos* (Afrikaans); *umkhuthuhla* (Xhosa) ■ The soap bush is a shrub or small tree with oblong, dark green glossy leaves, inconspicuous flowers and small, three-lobed capsules. It is restricted to the southern coastal parts of South Africa (Western and Eastern Cape provinces only). The leaves are crushed in water and are commonly used as a soap substitute. It is also said to be of value in treating black quarter in cattle.

Pouzolzia mixta |Urticaceae| **SOAP-NETTLE**; *seepnetel* (Afrikaans); *dekane* (Sotho) ■ See Chapter 10. This shrub or small tree occurs in bushveld areas from Malawi to KwaZulu-Natal in South Africa. The leaves are dark green above and densely white-hairy below, and may be cooked as a green vegetable. The bark is fibrous and is used for rope and string. Crushed leaves are soapy and have been used as a soap substitute to wash hands and clothes.

Salsola aphylla |Amaranthaceae| ***SEEPGANNA***, *gannabos, ganna-asbos* (Afrikaans) ■ See photographs on page 285. This plant is an untidy and somewhat woody shrub with minute greyish green leaves compressed along the stems. The flowers and fruits are minute and inconspicuous, but the plant is easily recognised by the cypress-like branches. The inhabitants of the dry interior of southern Africa used the bush to produce lye ash (*loogas* in Afrikaans) which was boiled in water to form the lye required for soap making. When piling up *asbos* (*Mesembryanthemum junceum*) to produce lye ash, a layer of *seepganna* (*Salsola aphylla*) was placed at regular intervals in the stack to ensure that the ash binds into lumps or cakes for easier handling (André Brits, pers comm.).

Schinziophyton rautanenii |Euphorbiaceae| **MANKETTI, MONGONGO** ■ See Chapter 2. The seed oil – manketti nut oil – is used in modern cosmetics. It is not only a very nutritious source of fatty acids (mainly linoleic, oleic, palmitic, linolenic and erucic acids) but is also rich in vitamin E. It has been used as a hair lotion and body rub to clean and moisturise the skin. It is non-viscous and easily absorbed into the skin, making it ideal as carrier oil for cosmetics and for use in aromatherapy (Van der Vossen & Mkamilo 2007; Vermaak *et al.* 2011).

Sclerocarya birrea |Anacardiaceae| **MARULA** ■ See Chapter 6. Marula seed oil is edible but also has medical and cosmetic uses (Komane *et al.* 2015). The oil is traditionally used as a body lotion and to treat dry and cracking skin. It has also been used as a shampoo to restore dry and damaged hair and can be used to make specialised liquid soaps. Marula oil is rich in oleic acid and is therefore similar to olive oil, with similar potential applications in cosmetics (Van der Vossen & Mkamilo 2007; Grace *et al.* 2008; Vermaak *et al.* 2011).

SOAPS & COSMETICS

Leaves and fruits of *boesmanseep* (*Monochlamys albicans*)

Flowering stems of the *asbos* (*Mesembryanthemum junceum*)

Flowers of the soap bush (*Noltea africana*)

Leaves and flowers of the soap-nettle (*Pouzolzia mixta*)

Sideroxylon inerme |Sapotaceae| **WHITE MILKWOOD**; *amasethole* (Zulu); *witmelkhout* (Afrikaans) ■ The white milkwood is a shrub or small tree, often with a gnarled appearance. It is an evergreen with dark green, leathery, glossy leaves that contain a milky latex. The small flowers are followed by dark purple to black berries. The bark is a traditional Zulu medicine but it is possibly also used nowadays for *umemezi*. There are some famous white milkwood trees, such as the "Treaty Tree" in Cape Town, the "Post Office Tree" at Mossel Bay and the "Fingo Milkwood Tree" near Peddie, all of which have been declared national monuments.

Trichilia emetica |Meliaceae| **BUSHVELD NATAL-MAHOGANY** ■ See Chapter 17. The seeds yield about 32 per cent of an odourless oil which was considered to be suitable for soap making (Jamieson 1916). Two types of oil can be produced: mafura oil from the fleshy seed arils and mafura butter from the seed kernels (Van der Vossen & Mkamilo 2007). The oil is rich in palmitic and oleic acids, indicating that it should have good skin permeation enhancing activity. It has a wide range of traditional and modern applications (Grace *et al.* 2008; Komane *at al.* 2011; Vermaak *et al.* 2011). These include the treatment of skin ailments, and nourishing and emollient uses for the skin and hair. It can be used to manufacture lip balms, natural soaps and candles.

REFERENCES AND FURTHER READING: Arkhipov, A., Sirdaarta, J., Rayan, P., McDonnell, P.A. & Cock, I.E. 2014. An examination of the antibacterial, antifungal, anti-giardial and anti-cancer properties of *Kigelia africana* fruit extracts. *Pharmacognosy Communications,* 4(3): 62–76. **Bruneton, J. 1995.** *Pharmacognosy, phytochemistry, medicinal plants.* Intercept, Hampshire. **Chenia, H.Y. 2013.** Anti-quorum sensing potential of crude *Kigelia africana* fruit extracts. *Sensors* 13(3): 2802–2817. **Coertze, P.J. 1930.** Volkekundige studies in Swaziland. *Tydskr. Wet. Kuns* 9: 10–20. **Cunningham, A.B. 1988.** *An investigation of the herbal medicine trade in Natal/Kwazulu.* Investigational report no 29, Institute of Natural Resources, University of Natal. **Daniels, G. 1997.** Skin-deep beauty remains elusive for many SA women. *The Star,* 19 June 1997, p. 13. **De Lange, M. 1963.** Some traditional cosmetic practices of the Xhosa. *Ann. Cape Prov. Mus.* 3: 85–95. **Dold, T. & Cocks, M. 2012.** *Voices from the forest.* Jacana Media, Johannesburg. **Dykman, E.J. 1891.** *Kook-, koek- en resepteboek.* Paarlse Drukpers Maatskappy, Paarl. **Drewes, S.E. et al. 1996.** Constituents of muthi plants of Southern Africa: magical and molluscicidal properties. Proceedings of the First International IOCD-Symposium, Victoria Falls, Zimbabwe, February 25–28, 1996, pp. 261–265. **Grace, O.M., Borus, D.J. & Bosch, C.H. (eds) 2008.** *Vegetable oils of tropical Africa. Conclusions and recommendations based on PROTA 14: Vegetable oils.* PROTA Foundation, Nairobi. **Hedberg, I. & Staugård, F. 1989.** *Traditional medicinal plants – traditional medicine in Botswana.* Ipelegeng Publishers, Gaborone. **Hutchings, A. et al. 1996.** *Zulu medicinal plants.* Natal University Press, Pietermaritzburg. **Iwu, M.M. 1993.** *Handbook of African medicinal plants.* CRC Press, Boca Raton. **Jamieson, J.S. 1916.** Examination of the bark and seed oil of *Trichilia emetica. S. Afr. J. Sc.* 13: 496–498. **Khan, F. 1996.** Black beauty, white mask. *Veld & Flora,* March 1996: 15. **Komane, B.M., Olivier, E. & Viljoen, A.M. 2011.** *Trichilia emetica* (Meliaceae) – A review of traditional uses, biological activities and phytochemistry. *Phytochemistry Letters* 4: 1–9. **Komane, B., Vermaak, I., Summers, B. & Viljoen, A.M. 2015.** Safety and efficacy of *Sclerocarya birrea* (A.Rich.) Hochst (Marula) oil: A clinical perspective. *J. Ethnopharmacol.* 176: 327–335. **Komane, B., Vermaak, I., Kamatou, G.P.P., Summers, B. & Viljoen, A.M. 2017.** Beauty in Baobab: A pilot study of the safety and efficacy of *Adansonia digitata* seed oil. *Revista Brasileira de Farmacognosia* 27: 1–8. **MacCrone, I.D. 1937.** A note on the Tsamma and its uses among the Bushmen. *Bantu Stud.* 11: 251–252. **Picerno, P., Autore, G., Marzocco, S., Meloni, M., Sanogo, R. & Aquino, R.P. 2005.** Anti-inflammatory activity of verminoside from *Kigelia africana* and evaluation of cutaneous irritation in cell cultures and reconstituted human epidermis. *J. Nat. Prod.* 68(11): 1610–1614. **Pujol, J. 1990.** *Naturafrica – the herbalist handbook.* Jean Pujol Natural Healers Foundation, Durban. **Smith, C.A. 1966.** Common names of South African plants. *Mem. Bot. Surv. S. Afr.* 35. **Van der Vossen H.A.M. & Mkamilo, G.S. (eds) 2007.** *Plant Resources of Tropical Africa. 14. Vegetable oils.* PROTA Foundation, Wageningen / Backhuys Publishers, Leiden. **Venter, F. 1997.** *Botanical survey of the medicinal plants of the Northern Sotho, Northern Province, South Africa.* Land management and rural development programme, University of the North. **Vermaak, I., Kamatou, G.P.P., Komane-Mofokeng, B.M., Viljoen, A. & Beckett, K. 2011.** African seed oils of commercial importance – cosmetic applications. *S. Afr. J. Bot.* 77: 920– 933. **Watt, J.M. & Breyer-Brandwijk, M.G. 1962.** *The medicinal and poisonous plants of southern and eastern Africa,* 2nd ed. Livingstone, London. **Youthed, G. (ed.) no date.** *Dictionary of South African traditional medicinal plants of the Eastern Cape.* Pharmaceutical Society of South Africa, Johannesburg (unpublished).

SOAPS & COSMETICS

Plant of *seepganna* (*Salsola aphylla*)

Stems of *seepganna* (*Salsola aphylla*)

Leaves and fruits of the white milkwood tree (*Sideroxylon inerme*)

Fish kraals at Kosi Bay

Gaukwalelo, "the last hunter of the Kalahari"

Springhare hunters with springhare hooks

CHAPTER 15

Hunting & fishing

AS THE COUNTRIES of southern Africa have become more developed and populous, the once abundant game and fish resources have dwindled, and are now mainly to be found in public and private game reserves and other controlled areas. Regional conflicts have resulted in an oversupply of cheap black-market military rifles which have contributed to severe overhunting and poaching of wild game. Knowledge of the use of hunting poisons is now fragmentary, with hunting by bow and spear mainly taking place in remote parts of Mozambique, the Kalahari and the Zambezi Valley.

The hunting bow is made from flexible branches, mainly from *Grewia flava*, but sometimes *Dichrostachys cinerea*. Quivers for carrying the arrows are often made from the roots of *Vachellia luederitzii*. A straight piece of thick root is chosen and the bark is neatly trimmed away at both ends. After heating the root in hot ash, the root is held firmly and pounded against a rock, so that the cylinder of bark is separated from the woody part of the root. The ends are covered with skin, preferably skin from the knee of a large antelope. Stems of the well-known quiver tree (*Aloe dichotoma*) were also once hollowed out and used as quivers. Arrows are made from straight stems taken from *Grewia flava*, *Catophractes alexandri*, *Searsia* species or even the common reed (*Phragmites australis*). The metal or bone arrowhead is attached to a short wooden foreshaft which is linked to the 35 to 50 centimetre shaft by a grass or reed linkshaft. To prevent accidents, the arrow poison is applied to the shaft of the arrow head and not to the tip.

Spears are not used for hunting, but are used to finish off an animal that has been weakened by poison. Wooden clubs may also be used, especially for killing smaller animals. Hunting success often depends not only on the skill of the hunter but on the skill of the hunting dogs. Springhare hooks are used in the Kalahari to hook springhares in their burrows. These poles of up to five metres long are made from slender *Grewia flava* branches that are tied together end to end with sinew. A small metal barb is attached to one end. When an animal is hooked, it is held firmly in place while the hunters dig down in the sand to reach it. Rope snares are also a popular method of catching birds and small game. Snares are made from the leaf fibres of *Sansevieria* species (see Chapter 19), usually coloured to make them less visible and rubbed with grass to make them smooth so that they function properly.

The main hunting poisons are fast-acting cardiac glycosides from the widely distributed genera *Acokanthera*, *Boophone*, *Strophanthus* and *Adenium*. Poison beetle larvae (*Diamphidia*) that feed on *Commiphora* species are the favoured poison of the San in the Kalahari. The arrow poisons have complex plant chemistry, so it is not surprising that many of them are also used medicinally, administered in low doses, or applied topically. Several plants are also used in a spiritual context related to hunting (Leffers 2003), mainly to bring success to the hunt and the hunter.

Sophisticated technologies have developed to capture and trap freshwater fish in southern Africa, including permanent structures such as kraals, as well as fishing baskets which are used in fish drives (McLaren 1958; Tinley 1964). These methods are mostly used in flood plains and estuaries, where the water is quite shallow.

In rivers and streams, fish poisons have been used, although this method of fishing is no longer very popular. Standing water or a pool with slow-flowing water is needed for fish poisons to be effective. Rotenone, extracted as the main ingredient from derris roots (*Derris* species, Fabaceae) is the best-known fish poison. Rotenone is highly selective and kills fish through the powerful inhibition of mitochondrial electron transport, without affecting other animals such as crabs.

Acokanthera oppositifolia |Apocynaceae| **COMMON POISON BUSH**; *boesmansgif* (Afrikaans); *mothoko-nyepe* (Northern Sotho); *inhlungunyembe* (Zulu) ■ The plant is a shrub or small tree with white latex, thick leathery leaves, attractive white flowers and red berries that turn dark purple when they ripen. The latex, fruit and decoctions of the wood were widely used as a source of arrow poison in southern Africa, sometimes in combination with *Euphorbia* latex, the sap of *Senegalia mellifera* and the venom from the poison glands of snakes. In the northern Cape of South Africa, arrows poisoned with *Acokanthera* and snake venom were used to kill antelope and buffalo, and against enemies. The plant has also been used as an arrow poison in Zambia, and the root bark was used to poison spears and to destroy hyenas and stray dogs in South Africa. The wood and roots of *Acokanthera oblongifolia* were used as sources of arrow poisons and to destroy dogs, and the bark and wood are reported to have caused fatalities through suicide, murder and by accident.

Acokanthera oppositifolia is extremely toxic. It contains several cardiac glycosides of which acovenoside A is the major compound, with smaller amounts of acolongifloroside K and several other minor constituents. Among the minor constituents is ouabain, also found in *Acokanthera schimperi*, the classic hunting poison of East Africa. Acovenoside A is highly toxic in exceedingly small doses, which first cause apathy, then restlessness, followed by convulsions and death, with the heart stopping in asystole (Neuwinger 1994, 1996). Fatalities have followed use of the wood as a meat-skewer. The toxicity of the fruit appears to be variable, with ripe fruit sometimes safely eaten raw or made into jam. Reports of abdominal pain, excessive salivation and vomiting from eating the fruit, indicate that there are toxic varieties, so the fruits are best avoided altogether. The fruits of *Acokanthera oblongifolia* (dune poison bush) have caused fatalities in children.

Acokanthera oppositifolia leaves are used in the form of a snuff to treat headaches and in infusions for abdominal pains and convulsions (Phillip Kubukhele, pers. comm.) and septicaemia. Powdered roots are administered orally or as a snuff to treat pain and snakebite and root decoctions are taken for anthrax and tapeworm.

Adenium boehmianum |Apocynaceae| *OUZUWO* (Herero); *pylgif, boesmangif* (Afrikaans); Kaoko impala lily ■ The plant is a thick-stemmed succulent shrub with a swollen base, large glossy green leaves and purplish flowers with a darker throat. It occurs in northern Namibia and southern Angola. The latex of the plant has been commonly used in northern Namibia as the sole ingredient in a potent arrow poison. The common name *ouzuwo* is the Herero word for poison. The thickest branches and roots are heated over fire until a sticky sap exudes, and this is collected by winding it onto a piece of wood. The poison is smeared directly onto the shaft of the arrow head, or onto the connection piece between the iron arrow head and the wooden shaft. The concentrated poison has been an item of trade. Large antelope generally die within a few hours of being struck, and sometimes within 100 metres of where they were hit by the arrow, while springbok usually die within an hour (Neuwinger 1996). On occasion the latex of *Euphorbia virosa, E. subsala* or *E. kaokoensis* is added to increase the efficacy of the poison (Malan & Owen-Smith 1974). *Adenium oleifolium* was used in earlier times as an arrow poison in southern Namibia. The latex of *Adenium multiflorum* has been used as an arrow poison, and is used as a fish poison in Mozambique and parts of South Africa. *Adenium* (Apocynaceae) is sometimes confused with *Adenia* (Passifloraceae). The best-known *Adenia* species is *A. gummifera* (called greenstem; *impinda* in Zulu; *slangklimop* in Afrikaans). This distinctive woody climber has bright green stems and lobed leaves. Pieces of the characteristic green stems are usually available for sale on muthi markets in South Africa. Infusions are used as emetics and are said to help with some forms of depression. The plant is highly toxic.

Asclepias stellifera |Apocynaceae| *MELKBOS* (Afrikaans) ■ The latex of this shrub has reportedly been used as an arrow poison, probably on the basis of cardiac glycosides (Watt & Breyer-Brandwijk 1962).

Flowers of the common poison bush (*Acokanthera oppositifolia*)

Fruits of the common poison bush (*Acokanthera oppositifolia*)

Flowering plant of the *ouzuwo* (*Adenium boehmianum*)

Flowers of the impala lily (*Adenium multiflorum*)

Stem, leaf and fruits of *impinda* (*Adenia gummifera*)

Stems of *impinda* as they are sold on muthi markets

Bobgunnia madagascariensis (=*Swartzia madagascariensis*) |Fabaceae| **SNAKE BEAN**; *slangboon* (Afrikaans) ■ The tree occurs in the tropical part of southern Africa (Caprivi to Mozambique) and has been used as a fish poison.

Boophone disticha |Amaryllidaceae| **BUSHMAN POISON BULB**; *gifbol* (Afrikaans); *incwadi* (Xhosa); *leshoma* (Sotho, Tswana); *incotha* (Zulu) ■ See Chapter 9. Preparations of the bulb were used in earlier times as the main arrow poison in southern Africa, primarily for small game. It was used alone, or was added to *Euphorbia* latex, and sometimes the venom of poisonous snakes. The bulbs were cut transversely around the time the leaves were sprouting from the bulb, and the thick fluid that exuded was dried in the sun until it reached a gum-like consistency (Neuwinger 1996). After animals have been wounded by the poisoned arrow, they reportedly run for quite a distance, sometimes only being found by the hunters the following day.

Commiphora africana |Burseraceae| **HAIRY CORKWOOD**, hairy poison-grub corkwood; *harige kanniedood* (Afrikaans); *n/'hodi* (Kung) ■ This is a deciduous shrub or small tree with thick stems, papery bark and velvety leaves. Resin from the plant is used against termites. The commonest arrow poison in Namibia and Botswana is the fluid squeezed from the larvae of *Diamphidia* beetles. The body fluids of the larvae are squeezed fresh onto the shaft behind the arrow head, or they are dried and powdered for storage. In the dry form they are liquefied by the addition of plant juices before being applied. The larvae are herbivores and are specific to a particular host tree, with *Diamphidia nigroornata* being found in the sand near the roots of *Commiphora africana*, and the larvae of *D. vittatipennis* being found in the roots of *C. angolensis* (Neuwinger 1996). Digging for the larvae is only undertaken if there are signs of leaves having been eaten. Toxic proteins are thought to cause death through massive haemolysis of the blood and neurotoxicity, leading to weakness and generalised paralysis.

Croton megalobotrys |Euphorbiaceae| **LARGE FEVER-BERRY**; *grootkoorsbessie* (Afrikaans); *murongo* (Kwanyama); *motsibi* (Northern Sotho); *motsêbê* (Tswana); *muruthu* (Venda) ■ The tree is small to medium-sized with grey bark and watery latex. The leaves have two glands where the leaf stalk is attached to the leaf blade. Small, yellowish flowers are followed by woody, three-locular capsules. The bark and fruit are used as a fish poison in South Africa and in Botswana, and the seeds, bark and root have been taken as a purgative. The bark has been used as an abortifacient, and the seeds and the bark are reported to have been effective in treating malaria.

Dicerocaryum eriocarpum |Pedaliaceae| ***BEESDUBBELTJIE*** (Afrikaans); devil's thorn, boot protector, stud thorn; *tshêtlhô-êtonanyana* (Tswana) ■ See Chapter 10. The root is peeled, dried, and powdered, together with the dried fruit of *Bobgunnia madagascariensis*. The mixture is applied to the arrow (presumably with a plant sap adhesive).

Drimia brachystachys (=*Urginea brachystachys*) |Hyacinthaceae| ■ The bulb has been used as an arrow poison, and a man died three hours after being hit by a poisoned arrow (Gelfand *et al.* 1985).

Euphorbia ingens |Euphorbiaceae| ***NABOOM*** (Afrikaans); common tree euphorbia; *mohlohlo-kgomo* (Northern Sotho); *nkondze* (Tsonga); *mukonde* (Venda); *umhlonhlo* (Zulu) ■ The plant is a spiny succulent tree with a single main stem and a large crown of numerous erect stems. The branches thrown into the water are used to poison fish in South Africa and Zimbabwe. The wood is light and tough, and is used for boats, planks and doors. Before cutting, the trunk is burned to coagulate the latex to prevent it from splashing, as it is toxic and can cause blindness if it gets in the eye. Grass soaked in the latex of the bushveld candelabra tree (*E. cooperi*) is thrown into pools as a fish poison. *Euphorbia virosa* and *E. subsala* are popular arrow poisons in Namibia and southern Angola.

Plant of the bushman poison bulb or *gifbol* (*Boophone disticha*)

Fruit of the large fever-berry (*Croton megalobotrys*)

Fruiting stems of the *naboom* (*Euphorbia ingens*)

Thorny stems of *boesmansgif* (*Euphorbia virosa*)

Gnidia kraussiana |Thymelaeaceae| **YELLOW HEADS**; *harige gifbossie* (Afrikaans) ■ This is a small shrublet with hairy leaves, yellow flower heads and thick, fleshy rhizomes. The crushed rhizome has been used as a fish poison in Zimbabwe, Malawi and further north. In Malawi, it is believed to be the most effective of all fishing poisons. In other parts of Africa, the root is combined with *Strophanthus hispidus* for use as an arrow poison. *Gnidia* species contain very toxic diterpene esters, and coumarins are also present. The roots are used medicinally for many conditions, including constipation, boils, coughs, insanity and poor appetite. A leaf infusion is used as ear drops for earache.

Hyaenanche globosa |Euphorbiaceae| **HYAENA POISON**; *gifboom, wolwegif, boesmangif* (Afrikaans) ■ Hyena poison is the only species in the genus. It is a small, rounded tree with dark green leathery leaves characteristically arranged in fours along the stems. Male and female flowers are both small and occur on separate trees. The fruits are large, rounded capsules with several segments. The name *Hyaenanche* is Greek, meaning "hyena poison", and was given because the fruits were used to poison carcasses to destroy hyenas, jackals and vermin. The mountains near Van Rhynsdorp are called the Gifberg ("Poison Mountain") because of the presence of this tree, which is found only here and nowhere else. The crushed and finely ground seeds (perhaps rather the fruits?) are said to have been used as an arrow poison by the San. The toxicity is due to the presence of tutin (previously known as hyaenanchin) and related compounds – extremely toxic substances, known to cause coma, delirium and convulsions in humans. It may be interesting to reinvestigate the toxicity of various parts of the tree.

Milletia grandis |Fabaceae| **UMZIMBEET** ■ See Chapter 17. The roots of the tree have been used as a fish poison, and also apparently as an arrow poison. Several *Milletia* species are used as fish poisons in Central and West Africa, and rotenone, the well-known insecticide and fish poison, has been isolated from various *Milletia* species.

Mundulea sericea |Fabaceae| **CORK-BUSH**; *kurkbos, visgif* (Afrikaans); *omukeka* (Herero); *mošita-tlou* (Northern Sotho); *umsindandlovu* (Zulu) ■ This shrub or small tree has a thick, corky bark, silvery leaflets, dark purple or rarely white flowers and narrow, velvety pods. It is very common in the northern parts of southern Africa. In South Africa, Mozambique and Zimbabwe, and also in tropical Africa, India and Sri Lanka, the leaves, pods, bark and roots have been used for poisoning fish. The pounded material is thrown into the water, and the fish are killed rather than stupefied. Surprisingly, the leaves are safely browsed by cattle and game. It is used medicinally and ritually as a purifying emetic, and root infusions are taken for infertility. Rotenone, deguelin, tephrosin, munduserone and mundulone are some of the compounds that have been found in the bark.

Neorautanenia ficifolia |Fabaceae| ***BLOUERTJIE*** (Afrikaans); *eona* (Herero) ■ The small genus *Neorautanenia* has three closely related species, all of which are rather similar. They have enormous underground tubers with creeping annual flowering branches bearing large, hairy, lobed leaves. The attractive bright blue flowers develop into large, woody pods. Perhaps the best-known species is the *gemsbokboontjie* or *blouboontjie* (*Neorautanenia amboensis*), a plant of the Kalahari, which is said to be the favourite food of gemsbok, hence the common name. Another species of tropical bushveld areas, *N. ficifolia*, is known to be poisonous to fish and insects, and there has been an unconfirmed report of it actually being used as a fish poison (Smith 1966). This seems quite likely, as the closely related tropical African species, *N. mitis*, has been used as a fish poison in Zimbabwe (Gelfand *et al.* 1985).

Pachypodium lealii |Apocynaceae| **BOTTLE TREE**; *bottelboom* (Afrikaans) ■ This large succulent tree has spiny branches and attractive white flowers. The species is found only in the northern part of Namibia. Latex from the plant has been used as an arrow poison in Namibia.

Flowering plant of the yellow heads (*Gnidia kraussiana*)

Fruits of the hyena poison or *gifboom* (*Hyaenanche globosa*)

Flowers and pods of the cork-bush (*Mundulea sericea*)

Flowers of the *blouertjie* (*Neorautanenia ficifolia*)

Sphenostylis marginata |Fabaceae| ***WILDE-ERTJIE*** (Afrikaans) ■ The plant is a small shrub with leaves characteristically divided into three smaller leaflets. The flowers are bright yellow and soon develop into long, narrow seed pods. It is easy to cultivate and has been evaluated as a possible fodder crop. Unspecified parts have been used as a fish poison (Gelfand *et al.* 1985).

Spirostachys africana |Euphorbiaceae| **TAMBOTI** ■ See Chapters 12 and 17. The tamboti is used in Namibia as an arrow and fish poison (Von Koenen 1996, 2001), and in Zimbabwe as a fish poison (Watt & Breyer-Brandwijk 1962). Although weak infusions of the bark and root have been used as purgatives, all parts of the tree are toxic and fatalities have occurred from its use. The latex is extremely irritant to the skin, and the sap may cause blindness if it gets into the eye. The wood has been kept with clothing as an insect repellent.

Strophanthus kombe |Apocynaceae| **POISON-ROPE**, kombe poison-rope; g*iftou* (Afrikaans); *ntsulu* (Tsonga) ■ The crushed seeds have been used as arrow poisons in Mozambique and Zimbabwe, and the fruit as a spear poison. In Mozambique, the seeds are crushed, mixed into a paste with saliva, and exposed to strong sunlight for several hours. The poison is extremely potent and is reported to bring down large game within a distance of around 100 metres (Neuwinger 1996). Cardiac glycosides are responsible for the activity. The common poison-rope (*Strophanthus speciosus*) from South Africa, has been reported to be poisonous, and was possibly used as an arrow poison in the past. The seeds of *S. gratus* from equatorial Africa are a source of the cardiac glycoside ouabain (strophanthin-*G*) which has been used in the past in the medical treatment of congestive heart failure.

Trichilia dregeana |Meliaceae| **FOREST NATAL-MAHOGANY** ■ See Chapter 17. Both this tree and the bushveld Natal-mahogany (*T. emetica*) have been used as fish poison.

REFERENCES AND FURTHER READING: Anon. no date. *Poisonous plants used by the Becwana for medicine, charms and poisons.* Botswana National Archives S24/11. **Coates Palgrave, K. 1977.** *Trees of Southern Africa.* Struik, Cape Town. **Codd, L.E.W. 1951.** Trees and shrubs of the Kruger National Park. *Mem. Bot. Surv. S. Afr.* 26. Botanical Research Institute, Pretoria. **Gelfand, M.** *et al.* **1985.** *The traditional medical practitioner in Zimbabwe.* Mambo Press, Harare. **Gerstner, J. 1949.** The arrow-poison *Strophanthus* in Southern Africa. *S. Afr. Med. J.* 23,20: 390. **Gordon, I. 1947.** A case of fatal Buphanine poisoning. *Clin. Proc.,* Cape Town 6: 90–93. **Heinz, H.J. & Maguire, B. 1974.** The ethnobiology of the !Ko Bushmen – their botanical knowledge and plant lore. *Occasional Paper* No 1, Botswana Society, Gaborone. **Helly, K. 1906.** Die wirkungsweise des Pachypodiins, eines Africanischen pfeilgifte. *Z. exp. Path. Ther.* 2: 247–251. **Juritz, C.F. 1915.** South African plant poisons and their investigation *S. Afr. J. Sci.* 11: 109–145. **Leffers, A. 2003.** *Gemsbok bean and Kalahari truffle. Traditional plant use by Jul'hoansi in north-eastern Namibia.* Gamsberg Macmillan, Windhoek. **Lewin, L. 1923.** *Die pfeilgifte.* J.A. Barth, Leipzig. **Liengme, C.A. 1983.** A survey of ethnobotanical research in southern Africa. *Bothalia* 14, 3&4: 621–629. **Malan, J.S. & Owen-Smith, G.L. 1974.** The ethnobotany of Kaokoland. *Cimbebasia* Ser. B 2,5: 131–178. **McLaren, P.I.R. 1958.** Fishing devices of Central and Southern Africa. *Rhodes-Livingstone Museum Occasional Paper* 12: 1–48. **Neuwinger, H.D. 1994.** *Afrikanische Arzneipflanzen und Jagdgifte.* Wissenschaftliche Verlagsgesellschaft, Stuttgart. **Neuwinger, H.D. 1996.** *African ethnobotany: poisons and drugs: chemistry, pharmacology, toxicology.* Chapman & Hall, Germany. **Palmer, E. & Pitman, N. 1972.** *Trees of Southern Africa.* (3 vols). Balkema, Cape Town. **Schapera, I. 1925.** Bushmen arrow poisons. *Bantu Stud.* 2: 190–214. **Shaw, E.M. et al. 1963.** Bushmen arrow poisons. *Cimbebasia* 7: 2–41. **Smith, C.A. 1966.** Common names of South African plants. *Mem. Bot. Surv. S. Afr.* 35. **Steyn, H.P. 1981.** Nharo Plant Utilization. An Overview. *Khoisis* 1. **Tanaka, J. 1980.** *The San hunter-gatherers of the Kalahari. A study in ecological anthropology.* Tokyo University Press, Tokyo. **Tinley, K.G. 1964.** Fishing methods of the Thonga tribe in north-eastern Zululand and southern Moçambique. *Lammergeyer* 3,1: 9–39. **Vahrmeijer, J. 1981.** *Poisonous plants of southern Africa that cause stock losses.* Tafelberg, Cape Town. **Van Wyk, B.-E., Van Heerden, F.R. & Van Oudtshoorn, B. 2002.** *Poisonous plants of South Africa.* Briza Publications, Pretoria. **Von Koenen, E. 1996.** *Heil-, Gift- und Essbare Pflanzen in Namibia.* Klaus Hess Verlag, Göttingen. **Von Koenen, E. 2001.** *Medicinal, poisonous and edible plants in Namibia.* Klaus Hess Publishers, Windhoek and Göttingen. **Watt, J.M. & Breyer-Brandwijk, M.G. 1962.** *The medicinal and poisonous plants of southern and eastern Africa,* 2nd ed. Livingstone, London. **Wink, M. & Van Wyk, B.-E. 2008.** *Mind-altering and poisonous plants of the world.* Timber Press, USA and Briza Publications, Pretoria.

Leaves and flowers of the poison-rope (*Strophanthus kombe*)

Leaves and flower of the common poison-rope
(*Strophanthus speciosus*)

Flowering and fruiting plant of the common poison-rope (*Strophanthus speciosus*)

Flowers of the tropical African *Strophanthus gratus*

Karos (skin blanket) tanned with elandsbean
(*Elephantorrhiza elephantina*)

Traditional leather clothing

Basket from dyed mokola palm leaves

Small Bayei basket showing all the natural
Ngamiland dye colours

CHAPTER 16
Dyes & tans

TRADITIONAL DYES ARE mainly associated with two major basket-weaving areas, corresponding to the distribution of *Hyphaene* palms: Ngamiland in northern Botswana and the Maputaland coastal plain (northern KwaZulu-Natal and southern Mozambique). Basotho baskets are characterised by a complete absence of design, and thus no need for dyeing. Dyes are used to change the natural cream colour of palm leaves (or other weaving fibres) into shades of brown, yellow, red and purple. A list of common dye sources is given by Cunningham & Terry (2006).

The main sources of dye in Ngamiland are the roots of *Euclea divinorum* (rich dark brown), *Berchemia discolor* roots or bark (various shades of reddish brown), *Indigofera tinctoria* or *I. arrecta* leaves (light purple or mauve), *Diospyros lycioides* roots (yellowish brown) and *Aloe zebrina* roots (yellow). All the classical Ngamiland dye colours are visible in the small open Bayei basket shown on the opposite page.

In Zululand and Maputaland, roots of *Euclea divinorum* and *E. natalensis* (both dark brown) are the most popular dye sources, with leaves or roots of *Indigofera arrecta* (purplish to dark brown or grey), bark of *Syzygium cordatum* (orange or red-brown) and *Sclerocarya birrea* (mauve, pink, brown or red) of lesser importance.

The use of metals as mordants is usually associated with the dyeing of wool and other textile fibres. Alum (potassium aluminium sulphate, *aluin* in Afrikaans) is the best-known mordant, but others include chrome, iron, copper, tin, ammonia, cream of tartar and vinegar. The fibres are pretreated by boiling in the mordant (*beitmiddel*), which creates a chemical bond between the fibre and the pigment, so that the colour is more permanent. The practice of dyeing palm leaves in silty mud, followed by boiling (to obtain a colour-fast dark grey) is possibly based on this principle. According to Gumede (1990), salt was often used as a mordant. In the early years, mordants and dyes were introduced into the Cape, along with the establishment of the wool industry. Examples are onion skins (bright yellow), cochineal (purplish red), walnut shells (brown) and also lichens (*klipblomme*). A large number of natural dyes from indigenous plants are now in use, but many of these are undoubtedly of recent origin. The paucity of early records of dye plants in the Karoo seems obvious. Traditional clothing was mostly made from leather and required tanning, not dyeing.

Tannins are traditionally important for their tanning ability, transforming fresh animal hides into leather. Tanning causes the formation of chemical bonds between the collagen fibres in the raw hide, which makes it resistant to water, heat and abrasion. In the past, a large-scale tannin-producing operation was located at Beira in Mozambique, where bark of the white mangrove (*Avicennia marina*) was commercially utilised (Tony de Castro, pers. comm.). In South Africa, black wattle (*Acacia mearnsii*) forms the basis of a large industry that produces tannin. One of the most widely used traditional sources of tannin is the root (rhizome) of *Elephantorrhiza elephantina*, which gives leather a characteristic reddish-brown colour. In the Western Cape, *kliphout* (*Heeria argentea*) was once a commercial source of bark for tanning. The bark and leaves of *pruimbas* or *blaarbas* (*Osyris compressa*, also known as *Colpoon compressum*) is another traditional source of material for tanning.

The intricate traditional technology used for hide dressing in KwaZulu-Natal has been described in detail (Vaughan-Kirby 1918). Seed oil of sourplum (*Ximenia caffra*) was the oil of choice for hide softening because of its purity and lack of odour. A thorny aloe leaf (probably *Aloe marlothii*) was used to laboriously raise a nap on the inside of the hide. Various sources of tanning agents are listed below.

Alectra sessiliflora |Scrophulariaceae| ***VERFBLOMMETJIE*** (Afrikaans); *sono* (Swazi) ■ The flowers or roots of this plant and several others have traditionally been used as dye sources. *Alectra* is a partial parasite with bright yellow to orange-yellow underground stems, which have been used by rural people in South Africa to dye cloths and other textile materials.

Aloe zebrina |Asphodelaceae| **SPOTTED ALOE**, zebra aloe; *bontaalwyn* (Afrikaans); *kgope* (Tswana) ■ There are many different aloes in the group of so-called spotted or maculate aloes, which are all characterised by their relatively small, usually stemless rosettes, spotted (blotched) leaves and swollen flower bases. Other summer-flowering spotted aloes such as *Aloe transvaalensis* are sometimes not distinguished from *Aloe zebrina*. Since they are all similar it seems likely that the roots of almost any species would be suitable as a source of dye. In the Pongola floodplain area, for example, the roots of another spotted aloe (*Aloe parvibracteata*) are used as dye source. In the same area, the roots of the mountain aloe or *umhlaba* (*A. marlothii*) seem equally suitable. *Aloe cryptopoda* has been used as a dye for wool and gives a reddish-brown to purplish-red colour, depending on the mordant that is used. *Aloe speciosa* leaves give a beautiful delicate pink colour to wool, even without mordants. In the Cape, *Aloe succotrina* leaves are said to give a royal purple colour.

Aloe zebrina has an extensive distribution, not only in Ngamiland (where it is a well-known source of dye), but also in Namibia, Angola, Zimbabwe, South Africa and Mozambique. *Aloe parvibracteata* is more or less restricted to Maputaland (northern KwaZulu-Natal to southern Mozambique).

For dyeing, the roots are harvested from the wild on a small scale but no details about marketing, if this indeed occurs, have been documented. Unlike some other dye sources, aloe roots can easily be utilised on a sustainable basis, provided the plants are left to grow again (they readily form new roots when replanted). Spotted aloes are plentiful in the main basketry areas of southern Africa. The roots are boiled with the weaving material and give a golden yellow colour.

Aloe roots and leaves both contain yellow sap, but the chemical constituents are actually quite different. The yellow leaf sap of most aloes contain anthrone *C*-glycosides such as aloin and homonataloin, while the roots have yellow anthranoid aglycones such as chrysophanol and asphodeline, which are chemically unrelated to the leaf anthrones. The roots of both *Aloe parvibracteata* and *A. zebrina* contain chrysophanol, asphodeline, aloesaponarin, aloesaponol and related compounds of the 1-methyl-8-hydroxyanthraquinone pathway. Isoeleutherol is a unique chemical compound in the roots of spotted aloes.

Berchemia discolor |Rhamnaceae| **BROWN IVORY**, bird plum; *bruinivoor* (Afrikaans); *motsentsila* (Tswana) ■ See Chapter 3. This is a medium-sized to large tree of low-altitude bushveld. It is evergreen or deciduous and the leaves are shiny and dark green, with raised veins on the lower side. The fruits are greenish yellow to pale orange when ripe. The tree has a wide distribution, from northern Zululand to Mpumalanga in South Africa, and in Mozambique, Zimbabwe, northern Botswana, northern Namibia and Angola. It is an attractive garden tree but grows slowly and is sensitive to frost.

The tree has become a scarce resource in Botswana, where it is locally over-exploited as a dye source for commercial basketry (Cunningham & Milton 1987). Synthetic dyes to replace the indigenous ones were suggested as a possible solution. The stem and root bark give a beautiful red-brown colour to palm leaves. In Namibia, the fruit is boiled with weaving material to give an orange dye (Van den Eynden *et al.* 1992).

It is interesting that this popular dye plant of Ngamiland does not appear to be used for dyeing in Zululand and Maputaland. The fruits are rich in vitamin C, are delicious to eat and are sometimes used to make beer. The timber is hard, pale brown to yellowish brown and is quite useful for furniture, sticks and as firewood. Leaves and bark are popular in traditional medicine and are used to make poultices for wound treatment and various other purposes.

Leaves of the spotted aloe or zebra aloe (*Aloe zebrina*)

Flowers of *Aloe parvibracteata*

Roots of spotted aloe or zebra aloe (*Aloe zebrina*) give a yellow dye

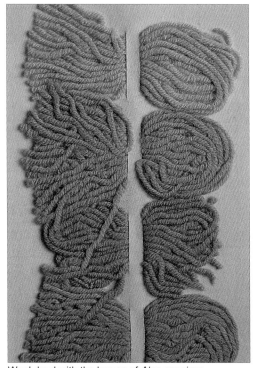

Wool dyed with the leaves of *Aloe speciosa* (unmordanted colour at the top)

Bidens sulphureus |Asteraceae| **ORANGE COSMOS**; *oranje kosmos* (Afrikaans) ■ The flower heads of this exotic ornamental plant give bright yellow and orange colours to wool.

Bulbinella latifolia |Asphodelaceae| ***GEELDIRK*** (Afrikaans) ■ The rhizome is said to give a useful red dye. *Bulbinella* roots are known to contain anthraquinones similar to those of aloes and these provide a logical explanation for the colour effects in dyeing.

Carissa macrocarpa |Apocynaceae| **AMATHUNGULU** ■ See Chapter 3. The fruits give a pink dye (Gumede 1990).

Combretum erythrophyllum |Combretaceae| **RIVER BUSHWILLOW**; *riviervaderlandswilg* (Afrikaans); *moduba-noka* (Northern Sotho); *modubu* (Tswana); *umdubu wehlanze* (Zulu) ■ The tree occurs along river banks over large parts of southern Africa and produce beautiful autumn colours before the leaves drop. It is a popular garden tree because it grows quickly and is resistant to frost. The timber is sometimes used for furniture and for carving. When damaged, the stems exude a gum which is said to be useful as a varnish. Roots give a much richer dark brown colour than is obtained from *Elephantorrhiza* (Gumede 1990).

Diospyros lycioides |Ebenaceae| **BLUEBUSH** ■ See Chapter 12. The roots yield a popular yellowish-brown dye. Naphthoquinones such as diospyrin and 7-methyljuglone in the roots are undoubtedly responsible for the colour reaction.

Elaeodendron croceum |Celastraceae| **COMMON SAFFRON**; *gewone saffraan* (Afrikaans); *umbomvane* (Xhosa, Zulu) ■ The bark has been used for dyeing and tanning. *Elaeodendron zeyheri* (small-leaved saffron; previously known as *Cassine crocea*) is also known as *umbomvane* in Xhosa and was widely used in former times, particularly in KwaZulu-Natal, for dyeing and tanning. These trees are commonly referred to as saffron trees because of the saffron-like properties of the bright orange bark. The bark of *Elaeodendron transvaalense* (Transvaal saffron; *ingwavuma* in Zulu) is used in Kaokoland for tanning leather and in many parts it is an important general medicine (see Chapter 7).

Elephantorrhiza elephantina |Fabaceae| **ELANDSBEAN**; *elandsboontjie, baswortel, leerbossie, looiersboontjie* (Afrikaans); *intolwane* (Xhosa, Zulu); *mositsane* (Sotho, Tswana); *mupangara* (Shona); *g//ariba, n//ami* (San) ■ This plant has large, thick underground stems (rhizomes) of up to eight metres long, with thin annual flowering and fruiting branches of less than a metre in height, which are characteristically unbranched. The oblong clusters of small, cream-coloured flowers are followed by large, woody pods. A related species, *Elephantorrhiza burkei*, is a minor source of tannin and dye (it gives a pale brown dye). It is a more woody plant of rocky areas with thick, branched, perennial stems and larger leaflets.

Elephantorrhiza elephantina occurs in grassland areas over large parts of southern Africa, including South Africa, Lesotho, Swaziland, Botswana, Namibia, Mozambique and Zimbabwe. It is common locally and it seems unlikely that harvesting has had any significant impact.

The underground rhizomes, commonly referred to as roots, are dug up and are used in rural areas for dyeing and tanning. In the Kalahari, the bark is removed and pounded to pulp (a little water may be added). The paste is then applied to hides, not only to dye them but also to soften them. It is likely that a similar tanning procedure is followed in other parts of southern Africa. To dye grass for weaving, the pounded rhizomes are boiled with the grass for several hours, giving a brown or reddish-brown colour.

The Afrikaans common names such as *leerbossie* ("leather bush") and *looiersboontjie* ("tanner's bean") reflect the popularity of this plant for tanning. Numerous medicinal uses are also known and the roots (rhizomes) are commonly sold on muthi markets in South Africa.

Hide tanned with the rhizome of elandsbean (*Elephantorrhiza elephantina*)

Flowering plant of elandsbean (*Elephantorrhiza elephantina*)

Plant of the large elandsbean (*Elephantorrhiza burkei*)

Euclea divinorum |Ebenaceae| **MAGIC GUARRI**; *towerghwarrie* (Afrikaans); *metlhakola* (Tswana); *mushitondo* (Hambukushu); *umhlangula* (Zulu) ■ This is a bushveld shrub or small tree with separate male and female plants. The long, narrow leaves are papery in texture and have wavy margins. The small, white or cream-coloured flowers are followed by round, single-seeded, black berries. The magic guarri is indigenous to southern Africa and occurs in the eastern parts of South Africa, Swaziland, Mozambique, Zimbabwe, eastern and northern Botswana and Namibia. The related *Euclea natalensis* with its tough leathery leaves has a more restricted distribution in the eastern parts of southern Africa. Both species are harvested in the wild and are not cultivated.

The roots are dug up, beaten to bruise the bark and are then boiled. More or less equal quantities of palm leaves and fresh roots are required. The roots of *Euclea divinorum* are one of the most popular sources of colour-fast dye in southern Africa and are commonly used both in Ngamiland (where it is said to be overexploited) and in Maputaland. The colour is dark brown to black, depending on how long the boiling is allowed to continue. A related plant, *Euclea natalensis* (hairy guarri; *idungamuzi* in Zulu), is also popular as a source of dye in Zululand. The roots yield a dark brown to black dye similar to that of *E. divinorum*. When used to dye wool, the roots give a wide range of brown colours, ranging from burnt sienna to pure black. *Euclea* species are known to contain naphthoquinones, and these compounds or their derivatives most likely act as pigments when the plants are used for dyeing.

The frayed ends of the roots of both *Euclea divinorum* and *E. natalensis* are used as toothbrushes. Guarri species (*Euclea*) belong to the same family as bluebush (*Diospyros lycioides*), which is one of the favourite sources of toothbrush sticks in southern Africa. Toothbrush sticks and dental care are dealt with in Chapter 12 (see *Diospyros lycioides*). The latter is also an important dye plant in Ngamiland. The roots give a yellowish-brown dye. The name *Euclea divinorum* (and magic guarri) refers to the use of the plant in divination. The wood of both *Euclea divinorum* and *E. natalensis* is avoided and is not used for firewood.

Ficus glumosa |Moraceae| **MOUNTAIN FIG**; *harige rotsvy* (Afrikaans); *omumbaha* (Herero) ■ The bark is said to be the most important tanning agent for leather in Kaokoland. The bark is finely chopped and soaked in water. It gives leather a desirable red colour, particularly favoured by the Himba people. The bark of *Ficus cordata* and *F. guerichiana* is also used for the tanning and dyeing of hides, while that of *F. sycomorus* is considered to be a poor alternative.

Galium capensis |Rubiaceae| ***KATTEKLOU*** (Afrikaans) ■ The roots give bright orange to brown colours to wool, depending on the type of mordant used.

Gnidia deserticola |Thymelaeaceae| ***HOTNOTSVERFBOSSIE*** (Afrikaans) ■ The dry flowers of this plant were used by the Khoi people for dyeing leather (Burchell 1822–24).

Guibourtia coleosperma |Fabaceae| **COPALWOOD**; *bastermopanie* (Afrikaans); *motsaodi* (Tswana) ■ The red aril of the seed contains a red dye that has been used to stain furniture.

Harpephyllum caffrum |Anacardiaceae| **SOURPLUM**; *wildepruim, suurpruim* (Afrikaans); *umgwenye* (Xhosa); *umgwenya* (Zulu) ■ The bark is used for dyeing and gives a mauve or pink colour.

Heeria argentea |Anacardiaceae| ***KLIPHOUT*** (Afrikaans); rockwood ■ The bark used to be an important source of tannin to treat leather at the Cape. It was once harvested in the Cederberg as an item of trade.

Hypoxis hemerocallidea |Hypoxidaceae| ***INKOMFE*** (Zulu); star-flower, "African potato"; *sterblom* (Afrikaans) ■ The leaves are used as dye and give a black colour.

Leaves and fruits of the magic guarri (*Euclea divinorum*)

Leaves and fruits of Natal guarri (*Euclea natalensis*)

Leaves and fruits of the *kliphout* (*Heeria argentea*)

Wool dyed with the roots of *Euclea natalensis* (unmordanted colour at the top)

Indigofera arrecta |Fabaceae| **AFRICAN INDIGO**; *verfbossie* (Afrikaans), *mohetsola* (Tswana); *umphekambedu* (Zulu) ■ African indigo is a woody herb, usually one to two metres high, but sometimes up to three metres. The stems are somewhat ridged and densely covered with white or reddish-brown hairs. The compound leaves have seven to 17 leaflets, which are usually hairless on the upper sides. The pinkish flowers are followed by straight brown pods of 12 to 17 millimetres in length, each with four to six seeds.

Real indigo (*Indigofera tinctoria*) is also found in southern Africa. It is closely related and very similar to African indigo but can be distinguished mainly by the slightly smaller plant size (0.5 to 1.7 metres tall) and the longer and often somewhat curved fruits of up to 35 millimetres long, which have eight to 12 seeds each. Southern African forms of real indigo usually have distinctly curved pods (not completely straight as in African indigo).

Both species of indigo are indigenous to eastern and southern Africa. African indigo is found from the eastern and northern parts of South Africa northwards throughout tropical Africa to Madagascar and Arabia. Real indigo is widely distributed in Botswana, Angola, Zimbabwe, Mozambique and Zambia and also northwards to east Africa and Asia. Both plants are commonly cultivated for indigo, so that their distribution areas have been extended in recent years. In southern Africa, these plants are rarely cultivated and are mainly harvested from the wild. They are often found in old lands and disturbed places.

The leaves are the main source of indigo, but the roots are sometimes also used for dyeing. In Ngamiland, *Indigofera* leaves are increasing in popularity for dyeing palm leaves used for basketry. It gives a light purple to mauve colour, or sometimes dark brown or grey, depending on the dyeing time.

Indigo is one of the oldest colouring matters known to man. Natural indigo was first discovered in *Indigofera* species, but nowadays it is made artificially for textile dyeing. Indigo is a nitrogen-containing pigment (indole alkaloid) also known as indigotin or indigo blue. It occurs in plants as a water-soluble, colourless glucoside but it is commercially used in aglycone form as a dark blue powder. Natural indigo was originally produced through a complicated process of aerobic fermentation and agitation, followed by heating of the precipitated sludge, which is then formed into cakes for shipment.

Jamesbrittenia atropurpurea |Scrophulariaceae| *SAFFRAANBOSSIE*, *verfbossie* (Afrikaans) ■ The plant is a Karoo shrublet with small leaves and unusual brown flowers. It was previously known as *Sutera atropurpurea*. This and several other species of *Jamesbrittenia* have been used in former times to dye linen, wool and veldskoens.

Kigelia africana |Bignoniaceae| **SAUSAGE TREE**; *worsboom* (Afrikaans); *umvongothi* (Zulu) ■ See Chapter 14. The roots are said to give a bright yellow dye. Naphthoquinones (such as lapachol) have been isolated from the roots and bark and it is likely that these compounds are responsible for the colouring effects.

Lannea schweinfurthii* var. *stuhlmannii |Anacardiaceae| **FALSE MARULA**; *valsmaroela* (Afrikaans); *ximombonkanye* (Tsonga); *mulivhadza* (Venda) ■ The bark is used by the Tsonga people to dye basket material a purplish-brown colour (Liengme 1981). Roots are sometimes used to form the rims of baskets and the bark may be used as cord.

Lawsonia inermis |Lythraceae| **HENNA** ■ This famous dye plant is an evergreen shrub with a natural distribution area in South Asia, the Middle East and the Mediterranean region. The powdered leaf is commonly used to colour hair and nails but is best known for traditional Indian body art. Intricate reddish-brown patterns and decorations are made on hands and feet. The colour is due to lawsone, a naphthoquinone (Jansen & Cardon 2005; Van Wyk & Wink 2015).

African indigo plant (*Indigofera arrecta*)

Fruits of African indigo (*Indigofera arrecta*)

Flowers of African indigo (*Indigofera arrecta*)

Leaves and flowers of real indigo (*Indigofera tinctoria*)

Leaves and flowers of the *saffraanbossie* (*Jamesbrittenia atropurpurea*)

Leonotis ocymifolia |Lamiaceae| **WILD DAGGA**; *klipdagga* (Afrikaans); *utshwale benyoni* (Zulu) ■ Stalks and bark impart a pink colour (Gumede 1990).

Mesembryanthemum crystallinum |Aizoaceae| **ICE PLANT** ■ The plant is a robust annual with large, succulent leaves dotted with numerous water cells which give a shiny appearance (hence the name ice plant). Both the juice expressed from the leaf and the dry leaf were used from the earliest times in South Africa to remove hair from animal hides in preparation for tanning and softening. A common method was to apply a thick layer of crushed leaves and stems onto the outer (hairy) side of the hide, after which it is rolled into a tight bundle and buried underground for seven or eight days. The hairs are then easily removed. The leaves of *M. barkleyi* are also used in Namaqualand for this purpose.

Osyris compressa or *Colpoon compressum* |Santalaceae| **CAPE SUMACH**; *pruimbas, wildepruim, basbessie, blaarbas* (Afrikaans) ■ [According to Manning & Goldbatt (2012) *Colpoon compressum* is the correct name for this species.] The Cape sumach is a shrub or small tree which grows as a partial parasite on the roots of other plants. It is restricted to coastal dunes along the South African coast, from the Cape to Kosi Bay. The leathery leaves are blue-grey in colour and are borne in opposite pairs. Small, yellowish-green flowers occur in clusters on the tips of the branches. The tree is closely related to an inland species, *Osyris lanceolata* (known as *bergbas* or rock tannin-bush), but the latter can easily be recognised by the alternate leaves and the axillary flowers. The fresh leaves of Cape sumach were used to tan leather a light brown colour, while the bark was used to tan leather dark brown. A layer of crushed leaves or bark, depending on colour preference, was put into the bottom of a trough, and the hide, with hair removed (see *Mesembryanthemum crystallinum*) was placed on top of the plant material. Successive layers of plant material and hides were made, and the wet mass was pressed flat with weights and left to tan for two weeks before removing and drying (Dawid Bester, pers. comm.). A decoction of fresh leaves was used to tan cotton fishing lines and nets to make them more durable in the days before nylon lines (Mrs Bester, pers. comm.).

Parmelia **species** |Parmeliaceae| **LICHENS**; *klipblomme* (Afrikaans) ■ A range of different dyes can be obtained, producing shades of orange, rust or brown. When dyeing wool with lichens, there is no need for a mordant. The genus *Parmelia* has been split into several genera and it is not clear which genera and species have been used (or are suitable) for dyeing.

Pelargonium triste |Geraniaceae| *KANEELTJIES*, *rasmusbas* (Afrikaans); *wit n/eitjie* (Khoi) ■ The plant has tannin-rich tubers which are used in Namaqualand for tanning leather, producing a reddish colour.

Physalis peruviana |Solanaceae| **CAPE GOOSEBERRY** ■ See Chapter 3. Leaves give a green colour.

Protea nitida |Proteaceae| *WABOOM* (Afrikaans) ■ Thunberg noted the use of bark for tanning. A useful ink was made from *waboom* leaves. Dry or fresh leaves are boiled with a rusty nail and a piece of sugar is added. This bluish-black liquid appears to be quite a good black ink that can also be used for dyeing. The timber was traditionally used as brake blocks for wagons (hence *waboom*) and is today still used to carve butter bowls and ornaments. The leaves of some *Protea* species are said to yield a gold dye.

Pterocarpus angolensis |Fabaceae| **KIAAT** ■ The powdered roots yield a red dye that is used in basket-making to colour palm leaves (Jansen & Cardon 2005).

Pterocelastrus tricuspidatus |Celastraceae| **CANDLEWOOD** ■ The bark and leaf were used for tanning hides.

Ice plant (*Mesembryanthemum crystallinum*)

Flower of the ice plant (*Mesembryanthemum crystallinum*)

Tree of the *bergbas* or rock tannin-bush (*Osyris lanceolata*)

Leaves and berries of the Cape sumach (*Osyris compressa*)

Rasmusbas flowers (*Pelargonium triste*)

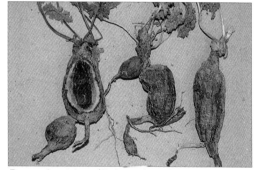

Rasmusbas tubers (*Pelargonium triste*)

Waboom (*Protea nitida*)

Leaves and flower head of the *waboom* (*Protea nitida*)

Pteronia divaricata |Asteraceae| **SPALKPENBOS**, *pennebos, pylbos, inflammasiebos, flip-se-bos* (Afrikaans) ■ The woody stems are exceptionally strong and were traditionally used to make wooden pegs (*spalkpenne* or *spalke*) for stretching a hide. The plant is also an important traditional medicine in the Western Cape (Hulley *et al.* 2011).

Rhoicissus tridentata* subsp. *cuneifolia |Vitaceae| **BUSHMAN'S GRAPE**; *boesmansdruif* (Afrikaans); *isinwazi, thluze* (Zulu) ■ The roots produce a red dye.

Rubia cordifolia |Rubiaceae| **ROOIHOUTJIE**, *kleefgras, vaskloubossie* (Afrikaans); sticky-leaved rubia; *mahlatsoa-meno* (Sotho); *impundisa* (Zulu) ■ The plant is a slender scrambler or creeper (vine) with bright red roots, hence the scientific name *Rubia* and also the vernacular name *rooihoutjie* (directly translated, "red little stick"). Small, heart-shaped leaves are typically borne in groups (whorls) of four at the nodes. A distinctive feature (also found in *Galium* species) is the tiny recurved hooks on the stems and leaves, making them adhere (*kleef*) to clothing, hair and wool. *Rubia* species are very similar to *Galium* species (*rooistorm, rooivergeet* or *rooihoutjie*), with which they share not only red roots but also this remarkable "Velcro" effect. In southern Africa, *Rubia* species can easily be distinguished by their stalked leaves and fleshy fruits (in *Galium*, the leaves are sessile and the small fruits are dry).

    Rubia cordifolia roots are occasionally used for dye, giving an orange or reddish-brown colour. Different mordants have a pronounced influence on the final colour, which may be brick red, coral pink or dark brown. In Europe, *Rubia tinctoria* yields a red dye called "madder".

Schotia brachypetala |Fabaceae| **WEEPING BOER-BEAN**; *huilboerboon* (Afrikaans); *mulubi* (Venda); *ihluze, umgxamu* (Zulu) ■ The bark is used for dyeing, giving a red-brown or red colour. It is used to colour the sangoma's cloak (Corrigan *et al.* 2011).

Sclerocarya birrea |Anacardiaceae| **MARULA** ■ See Chapter 6. The bark yields a brown, pink, mauve or red dye, depending on the method used.

Searsia lancea |Anacardiaceae| **KAREE**; *umhlakotshane* (Xhosa); *mushakaladza* (Venda) ■ The bark gives a brown dye. *Searsia undulata* bark is a traditional source of tannin in Namaqualand. The bark of *S. viminalis* gives a reddish-brown colour (Gumede 1990). The root of *S. ciliata*, the wood of *S. lancea*, the bark and wood of *S. lucida* and the root bark and wood of *S. tomentosa* have been used for tanning according to Watt & Breyer-Brandwijk (1962).

Senegalia caffra (=*Acacia caffra*) |Fabaceae| **COMMON HOOK THORN**; *wag-'n-bietjiedoring* (Afrikaans); *motholo* (Northern Sotho); *umtholo* (Zulu) ■ The bark gives a light brown colour (Gumede 1990).

Solanum nigrum |Solanaceae| **UMSOBA**, black nightshade ■ See Chapter 3. The berries give a light to dark blue dye. The depth of colour is increased by adding more berries, and the leaves are used for a green colour (Gumede 1990).

Sorghum bicolor |Poaceae| **SORGHUM**; *mabele* (Sotho); *amazimba* (Xhosa) ■ The stalks and leaf sheaths give a brick red dye.

Steganotaenia araliacea |Apiaceae| **CARROT TREE**; *wortelboom* (Afrikaans); *omutiwonyoka* (Herero); *epondo* (Himba); *kaab* (Nama) ■ The root bark gives a pinkish-brown dye (Cunningham & Terry 2006).

Syzygium cordatum |Myrtaceae| **UMDONI** (Zulu); waterberry; *waterbessie* (Afrikaans) ■ The bark is used for dyeing; it yields red-brown or orange colours. The edible berries are used as a purple dye.

DYES & TANS

Leaves and flower heads of *Pteronia divaricata*

Spalkpenbos or *pennebos* (*Pteronia divaricata*)

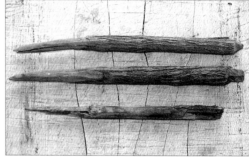

Spalke (pegs) made from *Pteronia divaricata* stems

Rooihoutjie plant (*Rubia cordifolia*)

Flowers of the weeping boer-bean (*Schotia brachypetala*)

Flowers and fruits of madder (*Rubia tinctoria*)

Bark harvesting of the weeping boer-bean (*Schotia brachypetala*)

Tagetes minuta |Asteraceae| **KHAKI BUSH**, tall khaki bush; *lang kakiebos* (Afrikaans) ■ The flower heads make an excellent dye, giving bright, rich colours to wool. Depending on the mordant, the colours vary from old gold, olive, sienna, green-grey, lemon yellow, maroon or brick red.

Tylosema fassoglense |Fabaceae| ***NTHAMULA*** (Tsonga); creeping bauhinia; *rankboerboon* (Afrikaans); *khubakhulu* (Swazi) ■ The Tsonga people use the roots for a brown dye (Liengme 1981).

Vachellia karroo (=*Acacia karroo*) |Fabaceae| **SWEET THORN**; *soetdoring* (Afrikaans) ■ Bark is used for dyeing and tanning leather. It is said to give leather an acceptable reddish colour but unpleasant smell. The bark of *Vachellia luederitzii* (kalahari thorn, *kalaharidoring*) is also used for tanning. Extracts of the pods of *Vachellia nilotica* (scented thorn, *lekkerruikpeul*) give various bright shades of brown to wool, depending on the choice of metal salt used as mordant. The bark of *Vachellia sieberiana* var. *woodii* (paperbark thorn, *papierbasdoring*) gives a grey colour (Gumede 1990).

Xysmalobium undulatum |Apocynaceae| ***ISHONGWE***; milkwort; *bitterwortel, bitterhoutwortel* (Afrikaans); *Uzara* (German) ■ See Chapters 7 to 10. The powdered root is sprinkled on skins and hides to prevent dogs gnawing on them.

Zantedeschia aethiopica |Araceae| **ARUM LILY**; *aronskelk, varklelie* (Afrikaans) ■ The leaves are said to impart various shades of yellow to wool.

REFERENCES AND FURTHER READING: Archer, F.M. 1990. Planning with people – ethnobotany and African uses of plants in Namaqualand (South Africa). *Mitt. Inst. Allg. Bot. Hamburg* 23: 959–972. **Burchell, W.J. 1822–1824.** *Travels in the interior of southern Africa.* 2 vols. Longman, Hurst, Rees, Orme and Brown, London. **Coates Palgrave, K. 1977.** *Trees of Southern Africa.* Struik, Cape Town. **Corrigan, B.M., Van Wyk, B.-E., Geldenhuys, C.J. & Jardine, J.M. 2011.** Ethnobotanical plant uses in the KwaNibela Peninsula, St Lucia, South Africa. *S. Afr. J. Bot.* 77: 346–359. **Cunningham, A.B. 1987.** Commercial craftwork: Balancing out human needs and resources. *S. Afr. J. Bot.* 53: 259–266. **Cunningham, A.B. & Milton, A.S. 1987.** Effects of the basket weaving industry on mokola palm, *Hyphaene petersiana,* and on dye plants in northwestern Botswana. *Econ. Bot.* 41(3): 386–402. **Cunningham, A.B. & Terry, M.E. 2006.** *African basketry.* Fernwood Press, Cape Town. **Gillett, J.B. 1958.** *Indigofera* (*Microcharis*) in Tropical Africa. *Kew Bull.* Add. Ser. 1: 5–166. **Gillett, J.B. et al. 1971.** Leguminosae subfamily Papilionoideae. *Flora of Tropical East Africa.* Royal Botanic Gardens, Kew. **Gumede, M.V. 1990.** *Traditional healers. A medical doctor's perspective.* Skotaville Publishers, Braamfontein. **Heinz, H.J. & Maguire, B. 1974.** The ethnobiology of the !Ko Bushmen – their botanical knowledge and plant lore. *Occasional Paper* No 1, Botswana Society, Gaberone. **Hulley, I.M., Viljoen, A.M., Tilney, P.M., Van Vuuren, S., Komatou, G.P. & Van Wyk, B.-E. 2011.** *Pteronia divaricata* (Asteraceae): A newly recorded Cape herbal medicine. *S. Afr. J. Bot.* 77(1): 66–74. **Jansen P.C.M. & Cardon, P. (eds) 2005.** *Plant resources of tropical Africa. 3. Dyes and tannins.* PROTA Foundation, Wageningen / Backhuys Publishers, Leiden. **Levinsohn, R. 1984.** *Art and craft of southern Africa. Treasures in transition.* Delta Books, Johannesburg. **Liengme, C.A. 1981.** Plants used by the Tsonga people of Gazankulu. *Bothalia* 13, 3&4: 501–518. **Malan, J.S. & Owen-Smith, G.L. 1974.** The ethnobotany of Kaokoland. *Cimbebasia* Ser. B 2,5: 131–178. **Manning, J. & Goldblatt, P. 2012.** Plants of the Greater Cape Floristic Region 1: the Core Cape flora. *Strelitzia* 29. South African National Biodiversity Institute, Pretoria. **Marincowitz, H. 1985.** *Kleur van wol en bokhaar met natuur-kleurstowwe.* Unpublished notes. **Mtshali, J.H. 1927.** Indigenous and vegetable dyes. *Native Teachers' Journal* 6: 245. **Nixon, J. 1942.** Home dyeing with natural dyes in native schools. *Native Teachers' Journal* 22: 20–24. **Palmer, E. & Pitman, N. 1972.** *Trees of Southern Africa.* (3 vols). Balkema, Cape Town. **Pooley, E. 1993.** *Trees of Natal.* Natal Flora Publications Trust, Durban. **Pooley, E. 1998.** *A field guide to wild flowers. KwaZulu-Natal and the Eastern Region.* Natal Flora Publications Trust, Durban. **Smith, C.A. 1966.** Common names of South African plants. *Mem. Bot. Surv. S. Afr.* 35. **Steyn, H.P. 1981.** Nharo plant utilization. An overview. *Khoisis* 1: 1–30. **Terry, M.E. 1987.** The anatomy of an Ngamiland basket. *Botswana Notes and Records* 19: 151–155. **Van Wyk, B.-E. & Wink, M. 2015.** *Phytomedicines, herbal drugs and poisons.* Kew Publishers, Kew / University of Chicago Press, Chicago / Briza Publications, Pretoria. **Van Wyk, B.-E. et al. 1995.** Chemotaxonomic survey of anthraquinones and pre-anthraquinones in roots of *Aloe* species. *Biochem. Syst. Ecol.* 23: 267–275. **Van Wyk, B. & Van Wyk, P. 1997.** *Field guide to trees of southern Africa.* Struik, Cape Town. **Vaughan-Kirby, F. 1918.** Skin dressing: a description of the process of converting the raw hides of game or domestic cattle into articles of native wearing apparel. *Man* 18,23: 36–40. **Venter, F. & Venter, J.-A. 1996.** *Making the most of indigenous trees.* Briza Publications, Pretoria. **Watt, J.M. & Breyer-Brandwijk, M.G. 1962.** *The medicinal and poisonous plants of southern and eastern Africa,* 2nd ed. Livingstone, London. **Xaba, E.A. 1923.** Some native dyes. *Native Teachers' Journal* 4: 41–42.

Samples of wool boiled for 1hr in a 40%
extract of flower heads of _Tagetes minuta_ and then
mordanted with the following salts.

Ridgway's Color Standard.

Zinc sulphate.	Old gold.
Ammonium vanadate.	Brownish olive.
Chromium chloride.	Raw sienna.
Ferrous sulphate.	Dusky green gray.
Stannous chloride.	Cadium yellow.
Sodium tungstate.	Lemon yellow.
Uranium acetate.	Maroon.
Nickel sulphate	Olive yellow.
Ammonium molybdate.	Morocco red.
Unmordanted.	Pinard yellow.

Wool dyed with the flower heads of tall khaki bush (*Tagetes minuta*) using various mordants

Hut under construction, using mopane poles

Forest guard with logs of stinkwood (*Ocotea bullata*)

Woodcarver using the root of saligna gum (*Eucalyptus grandis*)

CHAPTER 17
Utility timbers

ALTHOUGH SOUTHERN AFRICA is relatively poorly endowed with natural forests, there is a remarkable diversity of useful timber trees. It is almost as if nature provided this astounding diversity to compensate for the rather meagre quantity. The effect is that different timbers contribute substantially to interesting diversity in the material cultures of the people of southern Africa. This richness is being eroded by the inevitable process of standardisation. Furniture, carvery and musical instruments no longer reflect the beauty of diversity and individuality, but are mass produced, using standard cheap timbers and engineered uniformity. Commercial forestry is based on the cultivation of relatively few species of exotic trees, mostly pines, eucalypts (gums) and to a lesser extent acacias and poplars. Some of the exotic timbers are only briefly mentioned, but most of the well-known and interesting indigenous timbers are highlighted below. Woodworkers and wood enthusiasts are referred to the beautiful full-colour book entitled *Southern African Wood*, authored by Dyer *et al.* (2016) that features the wood properties of 134 indigenous and six popular exotic timbers.

The identification of timber is a relatively difficult process requiring practical experience and at least some basic knowledge of wood anatomy. Colour and weight (density) are useful to some extent, but there is much variation even within a single tree. Some timbers have distinctive odours, making them relatively easy to identify (cedar wood, camphor wood and sneezewood, for example). Many timbers do not have any recognisable odour, so that a study of the wood structure, as seen in cross section with a 10× hand lens, is called for. The surface of a fresh cut made with a very sharp knife reveals interesting and distinctive features. Keys for the identification of southern African timbers (Kromhout 1975; Dyer 1988) rely mainly on the distinctive appearance of the end grain of wood. Various features such as the size and distribution patterns of growth rings, tracheids, parenchyma, resin canals, wood vessels (pores), rays and fibres can be used for identification.

The presence or absence of wood vessels (minute pores which are visible as grooves on the surface of most timbers) is a first clue to the identity of the wood as a so-called softwood or hardwood (*naaldhout* or *loofhout* in Afrikaans, *Nadelholz* or *Laubholz* in German). These terms are often misunderstood – they have nothing to do with the softness or hardness of the timber. Softwoods are from coniferous trees such as yellowwoods, pines, cypresses and cedars. They completely lack any wood vessels, and are often resinous, uniform in microscopic structure but usually have distinct growth rings, where there is an abrupt transition between wood formed in the active growing season (broad bands of soft and pale wood) and wood formed in the cold or dry season (narrow bands of hard, darker wood). Hardwoods, in contrast, have wood vessels (the wood is distinctly porous, at least when viewed with a 10× lens). The size of the wood vessels is one of several important characters to distinguish between hardwoods. Pores range in size (diameter) from very large – larger than 200 micrometres (μm) as in *Erythrina lysistemon*, to medium – 100 to 150 μm as in *Ocotea bullata*, to very small – less than 50 μm as in *Ochna arborea* (see Dyer *et al.* 2016). Pale-coloured, thin-walled cells, known as parenchyma, are sometimes present in groups around the vessels and/or in tangential lines. Most hardwoods have visible rays (rows of cells radiating from the central core of the trunk to the bark) and they often have a layer of pale outer wood contrasting with a darker inner core. This creates the beautiful flames characteristic of timbers such as tamboti and kiaat.

There are many excellent books on the trees of southern Africa, details of which are given in the reference list at the end of this chapter. Many of these books include notes on timber properties and a diversity of traditional uses. Particularly valuable is the *Dictionary of names for southern African trees* (Van Wyk *et al.* 2011) that includes more than 14 000 tree names in 30 languages.

Acacia melanoxylon |Fabaceae| **AUSTRALIAN BLACKWOOD**; *swarthout, Australiese swart-hout* (Afrikaans); *umtfolo, ingulukane* (Sotho) ■ This exotic acacia is an erect tree with an oval crown and somewhat sickle-shaped, leaf-like phyllodes. The rounded, fluffy flower heads are pale yellow and trees are quite attractive when in full flower. The species originates from Tasmania and southeastern Australia, but has become an invader in parts of southern Africa, especially in the forests of the George–Knysna area where it was once planted in gaps created by windfalls. For obvious ecological reasons, this practice is no longer followed, but the tree has become locally important as a plantation tree, yielding excellent timber, not unlike stinkwood. Good quality Australian blackwood is indeed difficult to distinguish from stinkwood without resorting to finer details of the wood anatomy (the wood vessels in stinkwood are usually single or arranged in small radial groups of up to five, while the vessels in Australian blackwood have a tendency to form irregular tangential groups). Stinkwood is predominantly brown – pale to dark brown – never pinkish or reddish as in blackwood (see photographic comparison of the timbers under *Ocotea* on page 327). Australian blackwood is a popular and valuable furniture timber, and contribute substantially to the flourishing furniture trade along the Cape Garden Route.

Acalypha glabrata |Euphorbiaceae| **FOREST FALSE-NETTLE**; *bosvalsnetel* (Afrikaans); *nyokana* (Tsonga); *uthovothi* (Zulu) ■ The flexible stems are the most important material for making the traditional fishing basket (*isiFonyo*) in Maputaland (Cunningham 1987). Other species used for this purpose include *Canthium setiflorum* (rough turkeyberry, *skurwedoringklipels* or *umbhangwe* in Zulu) and *Dalbergia obovata* (climbing flatbean, *rankplatboontjie* or *umzungulu* in Zulu).

Afrocarpus falcatus (=*Podocarpus falcatus*) |Podocarpaceae| **OUTENIQUA YELLOWWOOD**; *Outeniekwa geelhout, kalander* (Afrikaans); *mogôbagôba* (Northern Sotho); *mufhanza* (Venda); *umkhoba* (Xhosa); *umsonti* (Zulu) ■ The tree is a distinctive forest giant with an erect, unbranched bole and a wide crown, characteristically clothed with lichens (*Usnea* species). It usually emerges far above the forest canopy. The bark is pale grey, with angular flakes and the small leaves are somewhat sickle-shaped. The cones are modified to round, fleshy structures, resembling small apricots when ripe. The distribution extends from the southern parts of the Cape in South Africa northwards into tropical East Africa.

This yellowwood is the well-known "big tree" of the Knysna and Tsitsikamma forests in South Africa, sometimes reaching more than 60 metres in height. The tree yields a valuable, finely grained, non-resinous timber, with a uniform pale yellow colour and indistinct annual rings. It is relatively light, yet fairly hard in relation to the low density. This popular furniture timber is widely used for high-quality furniture and is particularly popular for table tops. It combines well with the structurally superior stinkwood, giving an attractive contrast to the dark lustre of the latter.

A second important species of yellowwood is *Podocarpus latifolius* (see below).

Afzelia quanzensis |Fabaceae| **CHAMFUTI**, pod-mahogany; *peulmahonie* (Afrikaans); *nxenhe* (Tsonga); *muṭokoṭa* (Venda); *inkehli* (Zulu) ■ This is a medium-sized to large tree with a characteristic flaky, patchy bark and a spreading, umbrella-shaped crown. The leaves are compound, with four to six pairs of opposite leathery leaflets. Small yellow flowers are followed by a large, flat, woody pod of up to 150 millimetres long. The seeds are dark brown or black, with one-third of the surface enveloped by a bright red or orange-red aril. These attractive seeds are popular for necklaces and ornaments. The wood is light, brown to reddish brown and of good quality, so that it is widely used for furniture, panelling, plywood and floor blocks. Trunks are used to make dugout canoes and grain stamping mortars (Cunningham 1987, 2016). The timber is similar to that of kiaat, but it lacks the coarse texture, variable colour and characteristic odour of the latter. In cross-section, it is easy to see the large bands of parenchyma, which form eye-shaped groups around the very large vessels, together with occasional narrow bands. The rays are clearly visible with a hand lens.

UTILITY TIMBERS

Traditional fishing basket made from the flexible stems of *uthovothi* (*Acalypha glabrata*)

The Knysna "big tree", a large specimen of Outeniqua yellowwood (*Afrocarpus falcatus*)

Chamfutı tree (*Afzelia quanzensis*)

Comparison of Outeniqua yellowwood (*Afrocarpus falcatus*) and real yellowwood (*Podocarpus latifolius*)

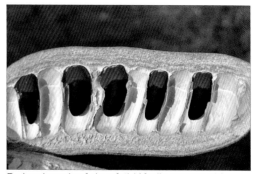

Pod and seeds of chamfuti (*Afzelia quanzensis*)

Albizzia versicolor |Fabaceae| **TANGA-TANGA** ■ The tree has a wide spreading crown and may reach 18 metres in height. The bark is greyish brown and rough and the leaves are twice compound, with rusty hairs on the lower surfaces. Numerous fluffy flowers are arranged in rounded heads, followed by large, reddish-brown pods. The seeds are poisonous and often lead to stock losses. Trees occur in open woodland over large parts of the subtropical part of southern Africa, and are particularly common in Zimbabwe and Mozambique, where it is considered to be a first-class timber tree. It is used for grain stamping mortars. The wood is brown to dark brown or reddish brown and closely resembles that of kiaat (*Pterocarpus angolensis*) but it often has a coarse figure (resulting from irregular groups of vessels associated with numerous parenchyma cells). It also lacks the characteristic smell. The most accurate way to distinguish tanga-tanga is to study the parenchyma in cross-section. It is not arranged in tangential bands as in kiaat.

Androstachys johnsonii |Euphorbiaceae| **LEBOMBO IRONWOOD**; *lebombo-ysterhout* (Afrikaans); *ubukhunku* (Zulu) ■ This is an erect tree, often forming dense stands on slopes and hillsides. The wood is extremely hard, heavy and durable. It is very popular for use as fence poles or hut poles because it is indestructible and will withstand termite attacks almost indefinitely.

Baikiaea plurijuga |Fabaceae| **ZAMBEZI TEAK**, Rhodesian teak; *zambezikiaat* (Afrikaans) ■ The tree is deciduous and has a large, dense, spreading crown. The leaves are divided into several leaflets with notched tips. Attractive pink or purple flowers are borne in long clusters, followed by flat, woody, velvety pods. This is one of the most important timber trees of southern Africa. It occurs in open woodlands in the deep Kalahari sands of northern Namibia, northern Botswana and eastern Zimbabwe. The wood is hard, heavy and durable, with an attractive dark red to dark reddish-brown colour. Considerable quantities have been exported from southern Africa as "Rhodesian teak". It has been used for furniture, flooring and railway sleepers. The wood is known for its ability to withstand abrasion without splintering and is easily identified by its heaviness, hardness and reddish-brown colour, as well as the minute vessels (they are hardly visible, even with a hand lens).

Balanites maughamii |Balanitaceae or Zygophyllaceae| **TORCHWOOD** ■ The wood is used to make the traditional meat dish (*uGqoko*) in Maputaland (Cunningham 1987).

Berchemia zeyheri |Rhamnaceae| **RED IVORY**; *rooi-ivoor* (Afrikaans); *monee* (Northern Sotho); *moye* (Tswana); *umncaka* (Zulu) ■ Red ivory is a shrub or small tree of up to 10 metres in height with distinctive, prominently veined leaves that are slightly paler on the lower surfaces. Small, greenish flowers are followed by sweet and tasty, berry-like fruits (see Chapter 3). Trees occur in open woodlands in the eastern and central parts of southern Africa. It is considered to be a precious timber (known as *pau-rosa*) in Mozambique. The strong and heavy wood is easily recognised by the bright red colour. It is often used for craftwork and ornaments, and the striking red colour is a common sight at formal and informal curio markets in southern Africa.

Breonadia salicina |Rubiaceae| **MATUMI**; *mingerhout* (Afrikaans); *muthuma* (Tsonga); *mutulume* (Venda); *umfula* (Zulu) ■ Matumi is usually a large tree of up to 40 metres tall with an erect trunk, narrow crown and distinctive bright green leaves, arranged in clusters of four along the stems. The yellowish flowers and the tiny fruit capsules are borne in dense, rounded clusters. The tree may easily be confused with the quinine tree (*Rauvolfia caffra*) but the latter has milky latex. Matumi occurs along rivers and streams in the northeastern parts of southern Africa (from Swaziland northwards through South Africa and Mozambique to eastern Zimbabwe. The valuable, heavy wood is easily recognised by the oily texture and the characteristic smell, reminiscent of linseed oil. It is usually dark brown with irregular paler patterns, but may also be uniformly yellowish brown. As a durable timber it has few equals in southern Africa for furniture, floor boards and boat building. Dugout canoes are made from it in Malawi.

Colour and surface pattern of the wood of zambezi teak (*Baikiaea plurijuga*)

Tree of torchwood (*Balanites maughamii*)

Colour and surface pattern of red ivory wood (*Berchemia zeyheri*)

Colour and surface pattern of matumi wood (*Breonadia salicina*)

Bridelia micrantha |Phyllanthaceae| **MITZEERI**; *mitserie, bruinstinkhout* (Afrikaans); *munzere* (Venda); *umhlalamgwababa* (Zulu) ■ The tree is small to medium-sized, about 12 metres tall, and usually has at least a few bright red leaves, even before the autumn colours appear. The small, yellowish flowers occur in small clusters, followed by blackish, edible berries. The attractive and durable wood may be identified by the pale to dark brown colour, the natural lustre and particularly the rays, which are paler than the rest of the wood. It is much in demand for furniture and ornaments.

Burkea africana |Fabaceae| **WILD-SERINGA, WILD SYRINGA**; *witsering* (Afrikaans); *monatô* (Northern Sotho, Tswana); *mufhulu* (Venda) ■ The reddish-brown timber is moderately heavy and has been used to make high quality furniture.

Calodendrum capense |Rutaceae| **CAPE CHESTNUT**; *Kaapse kastaiing* (Afrikaans); *umbhaba* (Swazi, Xhosa, Zulu) ■ The yellowish to straw-coloured, even-grained timber is very popular amongst woodworkers and woodturners (Dyer *et al.* 2016).

Cassine peragua |Celastraceae| **CAPE SAFFRON**; *boslepelhout* (Afrikaans); *ikhukhuzi* (Xhosa); *umkhukhuze* (Zulu) ■ The pale reddish-brown timber is of excellent quality and has been used for furniture, turning and veneer. It was once popular for making ladles.

Celtis africana |Celtidaceae| **WHITE STINKWOOD**; *witstinkhout* (Afrikaans); *mothibadifate* (Northern Sotho); *lesika* (Sotho); *umvumvu* (Swazi, Xhosa, Zulu) ■ The timber has an unpleasant smell when freshly cut, hence the common name. It is somewhat coarse in texture but has been widely used for ox yokes, floors, furniture and bentwood articles (Dyer *et al.* 2016).

Chaetacme aristata |Ulmaceae| **THORNY ELM**; *doringolm* (Afrikaans); *pumbulu* (Tsonga); *muṭhavhalunzhi* (Venda); *umkhovothi* (Xhosa, Zulu) ■ The wood is yellowish brown but heavy and tough. It has been used for making tool handles and small ornaments.

Cinnamomum camphora |Lauraceae| **CAMPHOR TREE**; *kanferhout* (Afrikaans) ■ It is a large tree with heavy branches and coarse, fissured bark. The leaves have three veins arising from the base and smell strongly of camphor when crushed. Inconspicuous white flowers are followed by small, round, purple berries. Camphor trees originate in China and Japan, but were introduced to southern Africa as ornamental trees many years ago. Essential oil (gum camphor) is distilled from the wood and is used for medicinal purposes (see Chapter 7). In former times, the wood was frequently used to make linen cupboards, because the camphor smell was believed to repel moths.

***Combretum* species** |Combretaceae| ■ See Chapter 18. The trunks of *Combretum imberbe* and *C. molle* are used to make traditional grain stamping mortars.

***Commiphora* species** |Burseraceae| ■ See Chapter 18. The soft wood of several species is used for carving spoons and other household items (Mannheimer & Curtis 2009).

Cunonia capensis |Cunoniaceae| **RED ALDER**; *rooi-els* (Afrikaans); *umqwashube* (Xhosa); *umaphethu* (Zulu) ■ The wood is an attractive reddish-brown colour and has been used for furniture, carving and turning, despite the fact that it tends to warp if not carefully dried.

Dalbergia melanoxylon |Fabaceae| **ZEBRAWOOD**; blackwood dalbergia, African blackwood; *sebrahout* (Afrikaans); *pau-preto* (Portuguese) ■ The timber of this shrub or small, much-branched tree is considered a precious timber in Mozambique despite the small size. It is much in demand for ornaments, walking sticks and musical instruments. The wood is very attractive because the purplish-black heartwood is in strong contrast to the yellowish-white sapwood. It is a dense, very hard and durable timber. The high prices that can be obtained in Europe and elsewhere result in over-exploitation, which is a serious concern (Cunningham 2016).

UTILITY TIMBERS

Colour and surface pattern of mitzeeri wood (*Bridelia micrantha*)

Colour and surface pattern of camphor wood (*Cinnamomum camphora*)

Camphor tree (*Cinnamomum camphora*) at Kirstenbosch

The dark-coloured heartwood of zebrawood (*Dalbergia melanoxylon*)

Diospyros kirkii |Ebenaceae| **AFRICAN EBONY**, pink jackalberry, pink diospyros; *ebano africano* (Portuguese); *pienkjakkalsbessie* (Afrikaans); *mushenje* (Shona) ■ This plant produces much sought-after, edible berries and also yields a hard, black wood which is considered to be a precious timber in Mozambique. It is much in demand for carvery.

Diospyros mespiliformis |Ebenaceae| **JACKALBERRY**, African ebony; *jakkalsbessie* (Afrikaans); *mutšhenje* (Tswana); *musuma* (Shona, Venda) ■ The pinkish-brown wood is suitable for a wide diversity of uses but is rarely available. It is traditionally used to make dugout canoes.

Diospyros whyteana |Ebenaceae| **BLADDERNUT**; *swartbas* (Afrikaans); *umanzimane* (Zulu) ■ The timber is moderately heavy and suitable for tool handles and implements.

Dombeya rotundifolia |Pentapetaceae| **WILD PEAR**; *blompeer, dralpeer* (Afrikaans); *mokgoba* (Northern Sotho); *unhliziyonkulu* (Zulu) ■ The timber is tough and strong and was traditionally used in wagon building.

Ekebergia capensis |Meliaceae| **CAPE ASH**; *essenhout* (Afrikaans); *nyamarhu* (Tsonga); *muṯovuma* (Venda); *umnyamathi* (Zulu) ■ This is a large tree with a rounded crown and compound leaves of four to six leaflet pairs. The small, white flowers are followed by round, fleshy, red fruits. The roots and bark are widely used in traditional medicine. The timber resembles true mahogany but it lacks the white deposits and dark resinous substances visible with a hand lens in the vessels of the latter. It is pale brown, usually pinkish grey in colour, with many regularly spaced bands of parenchyma visible in cross-section. The annual rings are often visible as dark lines on the tangential surface. The wood is soft and easy to work, and makes a fine furniture timber.

Entandrophragma caudatum |Meliaceae| **MOUNTAIN MAHOGANY**, wooden banana; *bergmahonie* (Afrikaans); *mophumêna* (Tswana); *munzhounzhou* (Venda) ■ This large tree has a long and straight bole, and compound leaves with five to eight pairs of leaflets and no terminal leaflet. The inconspicuous green flowers occur in clusters, followed by a characteristic large, woody, cigar-like capsule which splits open to give the appearance of a partly peeled wooden banana. The trees are characteristic for the Zimbabwean woodlands on Kalahari sands. The valuable and durable wood is much in demand for furniture and cabinet work. It is a light pinkish brown to reddish brown, with a beautiful streaky surface pattern. In cross-section, pale layers of cells (parenchyma) are present in irregularly spaced but clearly defined layers or bands.

Eucalyptus grandis |Myrtaceae| **SALIGNA GUM**; *salignabloekom* (Afrikaans) ■ Saligna gum is by far the most important commercial gum tree in southern Africa, with a total plantation area of nearly half a million hectares. Other gums are relatively unimportant by comparison. They include karri (*Eucalyptus diversicolor*), tallowwood (*E. microcorys*), spotted gum (*E. maculata*) and many others. The Australian gum trees have become an integral part of the southern African landscape, ever since the early introduction of the true bluegum (*E. globulus*). The Afrikaans word *bloekom* is a corruption through phonetic abrasion of the English name bluegum.

The timber of gum trees can be distinguished by the vessels (as seen in cross-section), which are not grouped in radial or tangential groups but rather in diagonal groups, forming a zigzag pattern (echelon formation). The very large vessels are unevenly arranged in areas of high and areas of low vessel density. *Eucalyptus grandis* yields a pinkish- to reddish-brown timber of medium strength and density. Logs and planks have a tendency to split (crack) when sawn. The timber is used for a wide range of products, including furniture, panelling, floor boards, telephone poles, mine props, fibre board and rayon pulp. In parts of KwaZulu-Natal, it is nowadays commonly used as a replacement for *umkhuhlu* (*Trichilia emetica*) in the local carving industry where the latter has become scarce.

Jackalberry trees (*Diospyros mespiliformis*)

The streaky surface pattern of mountain mahogany wood (*Entandrophragma caudatum*)

Colour and surface pattern of Cape ash wood (*Ekebergia capensis*)

Colour and surface pattern of wood from the saligna gum (*Eucalyptus grandis*)

Faurea saligna |Proteaceae| **BOEKENHOUT**, red beech; *boekenhout* (Afrikaans); *mohlakô* (Northern Sotho); *mugarahungwe* (Shona); *monyena* (Tswana) ■ Red beech or boekenhout is an erect tree of bushveld areas, with a narrow crown, dark, deeply fissured bark and drooping, slightly sickle-shaped leaves. The cream-coloured flowers occur in dense pendulous spikes and are followed by small, hairy nuts. The trees are very common in Zimbabwe and in the northeastern parts of South Africa. The wood is reddish brown and has a very distinctive net-like pattern, resulting from large rays that are clearly visible as boat-shaped spots on the tangential surface, and as thick lines in a cross-section of the wood. Despite a tendency to be cross-grained, the wood is used to make attractive furniture and ornaments. It is very popular amongst woodturners (Dyer *et al.* 2016). Broad-leaved beech (*Faurea rochetiana*, previously known as *F. speciosa*) is known as a valuable timber tree in Mozambique.

Gonioma kamassi |Apocynaceae| **KAMASSI**, Knysna boxwood; *kamassie* (Afrikaans); *igala-gala* (Xhosa) ■ The wood is exceptionally fine-textured and has been widely used for carving, turnery and engraving blocks. It is recommended for making small items, as it tends to be unstable in use (Dyer *et al.* 2016). It closely resembles European boxwood (*Buxus sempervirens*) and was exported in former times for making spools and shuttles for the textile industry.

Guibourtia coleosperma |Fabaceae| **COPALWOOD**, African rosewood; *grootvalsmopanie* (Afrikaans); *motsaodi* (Tswana) ■ This tree is well known as an important food source in northern Botswana (see Chapter 2). The soft, pinkish-brown timber is useful but not readily available. It is similar to kiaat but heavier.

Guibourtia conjugata |Fabaceae| **SMALL COPALWOOD**, small false mopane; *chacatepreto* (Portuguese); *kleinvalsmopanie* (Afrikaans); *ntsotso* (Tsonga) ■ The tree is small to medium-sized and deciduous, with paired leaflets similar to those of mopane (but they lack the small appendage between the two leaflets). The leaflets are almost sessile and have rounded tips, unlike those of *Guibourtia coleosperma*, which are shortly stalked and pointed. The flowers are small and white and the pods are short, flat and leathery. The species occurs mainly in Mozambique and Zimbabwe, where it is found on deep sands or along rivers in dry bushveld. The wood is classified as a precious timber in Mozambique. It is hard, heavy and dark brown.

Inhambanella henriquesii |Sapotaceae| **INHAMBANELLA**, milkpear; *mepiao* (Portuguese); *melkpeer* (Afrikaans); *mpiao* (Shona); *umbenkela* (Zulu) ■ The tree has a rather localised distribution in northern Zululand, southeastern Zimbabwe and Mozambique, where it is considered to be a valuable timber species.

Khaya anthotheca |Meliaceae| **RED MAHOGANY**, Portuguese mahogany; *umbaua* (Portuguese); *rooimahonie* (Afrikaans); *mururu* (Shona) ■ As one of the largest forest trees in southern Africa, the red mahogany often reaches a height of more than 50 metres. The trunk is usually buttressed in old specimens and the bark on the tall boles is greyish brown and somewhat flaky. The large glossy green leaves have two to seven pairs of leaflets. The inconspicuous white flowers are followed by large woody capsules that split into four or five valves to release the winged seeds. There is a famous "big tree" in the Chirinda forest near Mount Selinda in eastern Zimbabwe. This specimen is more than 60 metres tall and has a girth of nearly 16 metres at breast height. Red mahogany is one of the most important timber trees of Malawi, Zimbabwe and Mozambique, and is used not only for furniture and carpentry, but also for ornaments, carving and dugout canoes. The wood is an attractive pinkish-brown colour and has an attractive even grain and figure. The timber superficially resembles that of marula, but the rays are paler than the rest of the wood (not darker as in marula) and the vessels are usually single, without the tendency to occur in groups of two to four as in marula.

Daryl Koutnik with a fine specimen of red beech (*Faurea saligna*)

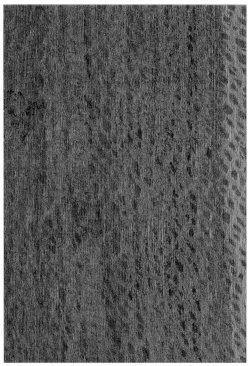

Colour and surface pattern of the wood of red beech (*Faurea saligna*)

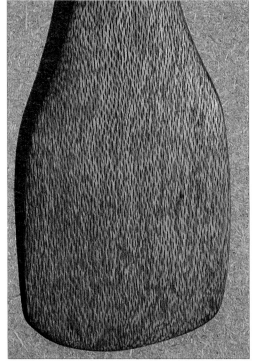

Kitchen utensil made from red beech (*Faurea saligna*)

Colour and surface pattern of red mahogany wood (*Khaya anthotheca*)

Kigelia africana |Bignoniaceae| **SAUSAGE TREE**; *worsboom* (Afrikaans); *umvongothi* (Zulu) ■ The timber tends to be coarse and of uneven texture but has been used in the past for making dugout canoes, household utensils and grain stamping mortars (Dyer *et al.* 2016).

Kiggelaria africana |Kiggelariaceae| **WILD PEACH**, spokewood; *vaderlandsrooihout, speek-hout, wildeperske* (Afrikaans); *umkhokhokho* (Xhosa); *isiklalu* (Zulu) ■ The tree is widely distributed (from Table Mountain to eastern Zimbabwe) and is commonly grown in gardens. It is the host plant of the garden red butterfly (*Acraea horta*), and garden trees are sometimes completely defoliated by the larvae. The wood is durable and has a fine texture and even grain, so that it is suitable for a wide range of uses (Dyer *et al.* 2016). It has been used in the past for making spokes of wagon wheels, tool handles, implements and rafters.

Milicia excelsa (=*Chlorophora excelsa*) |Moraceae| **IROKO**; *mvule* (Swahili) ■ Iroko is a large tree of more than 50 metres in height, with large leaves and small, white, male and female flowers that are borne on different trees. Trees occur in lowland forests of Mozambique and southeastern Zimbabwe. The attractive, heavy timber is much in demand for building timber and for furniture. It is coarsely textured and may be identified by the distinct, irregular, tangential bands of parenchyma, visible on the surface of the wood as pale blotches on the yellow to dark brown surface.

Milletia grandis |Fabaceae| **UMZIMBEET**; *umzimbeet* (Afrikaans); *umsimbithi* (Xhosa, Zulu) ■ The tree is a coastal species and grows to a height of about 10 metres. The attractive purple flowers are followed by brown, velvety pods. The timber is of excellent quality and is particularly popular for domestic implements and especially for walking sticks. The closely related *Milletia sutherlandii* (bastard umzimbeet) is a larger tree with smaller leaflets but the wood is of an inferior quality.

Milletia stuhlmannii |Fabaceae| **PANGA-PANGA**; *patryshout* (Afrikaans); *moada* (Tsonga); *muangaila* (Venda) ■ This beautiful tree is variable in size but may become a large forest tree of up to 20 metres tall, with a large, spreading crown. The leaflets are large and broad, and the large, showy, lilac flowers are similar to those of the other species. The tree grows over large parts of southern Mozambique and eastern Zimbabwe. The durable wood (known commercially as panga-panga) is dark brown to almost black, finely grained and very attractive (Dyer *et al.* 2016). It tends to splinter easily but has been widely used for flooring, furniture and sleepers.

Mimusops caffra |Sapotaceae| **COASTAL RED-MILKWOOD**; *kusrooimelkhout* (Afrikaans); *umtunzi* (Xhosa); *umkhakhayi* (Zulu) ■ The timber is regarded as a royal wood in Zululand (Dyer *et al.* 2016) and has been used for house building, fish traps, household utensils and knobkieries.

Mimusops zeyheri |Sapotaceae| **MOEPEL** ■ See Chapter 3. The timber is sometimes used for furniture (Smith 1966), but the tree is better known for its edible fruits.

Morus mesozygia |Moraceae| **AFRICAN MULBERRY** ■ This is a large tree of evergreen forests in Maputaland and Mozambique, with leaves resembling those of the cultivated mulberry (*Morus alba*), but smaller. In Mozambique, the tree is a source of first-class timber.

Nuxia floribunda |Buddlejaceae| **FOREST ELDER**; *vlier* (Afrikaans); *isikhali* (Xhosa) ■ The timber is durable, stable and easy to work, so that it is popular amongst carpenters and woodworkers for making furniture (Dyer *et al.* 2016). It was used in the past for implements and wagon felloes.

Ochna arborea |Ochnaceae| **CAPE PLANE**, African boxwood; *Kaapse rooihout* (Afrikaans); *umthentsema* (Xhosa); *umthelelo* (Zulu) ■ The smooth and mottled bark is attractive and distinctive (and cold to the touch), making it easy to identify this tree in a high forest, where leaves are not readily visible. The very strong and fine-textured timber is suitable for tool handles, carving and turnery (Dyer *et al.* 2016). It was traditionally used for wagon wheel spokes and fence posts.

UTILITY TIMBERS

Wild peach tree (*Kiggelaria africana*) at Kirstenbosch

Leaves and fruits of wild peach (*Kiggelaria africana*)

Colour and surface pattern of the wood of wild peach

Fruits of umzimbeet (*Milletia grandis*)

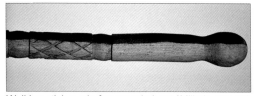

Flowers of umzimbeet (*Milletia grandis*)

Walking stick made from umzimbeet (*Milletia grandis*)

Ocotea bullata |Lauraceae| **STINKWOOD**, black stinkwood; *stinkhout* (Afrikaans); *umnukane* (Xhosa, Zulu) ■ The tree is evergreen and of medium size, with a relatively straight bole, and a narrow, much-branched crown. The bark is smooth and greyish, but may become dark brown, coarse and flaky in old trees. The relatively large, glossy green leaves are easily distinguished by the round, warty blisters (bullae or *domatia*) at their bases. The inconspicuous yellow flowers are followed by small, egg-shaped, purple fruits, partially enclosed at their bases in cup-like structures, so that the fruits resemble tiny purple acorns.

Stinkwood has a typical Afromontane distribution, but is restricted to the southern and eastern parts of South Africa. Trees occur only in moist evergreen forest. They are particularly common in the Knysna forests. Unlike most other forest trees, the stinkwood does not die when felled, but produces coppice shoots from the stump. Each coppice shoot may become a tree in its own right, so that a small ring of stems is often seen where a large stinkwood specimen was felled many years ago. The common name is derived from the unpleasant smell of freshly sawn wood. Stinkwood bark is commonly used in traditional African medicine, although no clear rationale has yet been found for its popularity (see Chapter 7).

Few timbers can equal the natural lustre and beautiful figure of stinkwood, and it is no wonder that it has been the most highly prized of all indigenous timbers. Top-quality stinkwood logs are amongst the most expensive in the world. The main use nowadays is for fine furniture, turnery and small ornaments.

The wood varies from yellowish grey to dark brown and it is hard and strong, has a medium density and a relatively fine grain, but is not particularly durable. It is somewhat similar to good-quality dark Australian blackwood, so that unsuspecting people can easily be deceived by unscrupulous dealers. Stinkwood varies from greyish brown to almost black, but does not have the pink or red tinge characteristic of Australian blackwood. Dark brown or black stinkwood is often used in combination with yellowwood.

Olea capensis |Oleaceae| **IRONWOOD**; *ysterhout* (Afrikaans); *sitimane* (Swazi); *musiri* (Venda); *umzimane* (Zulu) ■ The ironwood is an attractive evergreen shrub or tree, usually with an erect bole and a spreading, rounded crown. The bark is smooth, greyish and mottled. Glossy green leaves are arranged in opposite pairs on the twigs, which have the scattered white spots (lenticels) so characteristic of the olive family. Small, white flowers are followed by oblong, olive-like, purple berries. The tree is widely distributed in the eastern parts of southern Africa (Cape to Zimbabwe) but is particularly common in the southern Cape forests, where it often forms the main component of the forest canopy. The exceptionally attractive wood is unfortunately very hard and heavy, so that it is usually avoided by sawmillers because it dramatically shortens the lifespan of any saw blade. It has nevertheless been used for railway sleepers, floors and to a limited extent also for furniture.

Olea europaea* subsp. *africana |Oleaceae| **WILD OLIVE**, African olive; *olienhout* (Afrikaans); *mohlware* (Northern Sotho); *mohloaare* (Sotho); *motlhware* (Tswana); *umnqumo* (Zulu) ■ This tree is a close relative of the real olive tree (*Olea europaea* subsp. *europaea*). Trees are often too small to yield useful furniture timber. The wood has a golden brown colour with black lines and markings. It is sometimes used to make small pieces of furniture, but the basal part of the bole and the roots are popular for turning and for making small ornaments. Few timbers can compare with the beauty of the figure in a carefully selected piece of wild olive root. It is not unlike burred walnut.

Olinia emarginata |Oliniaceae| **MOUNTAIN HARD PEAR**; *berghardepeer* (Afrikaans); *umngonalahlo* (Xhosa); *unquthu* (Zulu) ■ The mountain hard pear is similar to the well-known hard pear (*Olinia ventosa*) but has a characteristic mottled bark and the leaves are notched at their tips. The timber is heavy, hard and tough, similar to hard pear (see below) but very rarely available.

Colour and surface pattern of stinkwood (*Ocotea bullata*)

Colour and surface pattern of Australian blackwood (*Acacia melanoxylon*, see page 314)

Ornaments made from stinkwood (front) and wild olive (back)

Colour and surface pattern of ironwood (*Olea capensis*)

Olinia ventosa |Oliniaceae| **HARD PEAR**; *hardepeer* (Afrikaans); *umngenalahla* (Xhosa) ■ The hard pear is an erect, medium-sized to tall forest tree. The bark is pale and smooth but becomes dark and fissured with age. The small oval leaves occur in opposite pairs on distinctly four-angled twigs and emit a strong smell of almonds when crushed. Attractive clusters of small, white to pinkish flowers are followed by spherical red berries, each with a distinctive ring-like scar at the tip. The tree occurs along the southern and eastern coastal regions of South Africa, from the Cape Peninsula to southern KwaZulu-Natal. The hard and heavy wood is dark yellowish brown, has a beautiful wavy figure and takes a fine finish. It has become very popular in the southern Cape, where selected logs are skilfully converted into high-quality furniture, comparable to the best walnut.

Pinus patula |Pinaceae| **PATULA PINE**; *treurden* (Afrikaans) ■ This is the most important commercial tree species in southern Africa. The tree is easily recognised by the heavy crown and long, drooping needles. The timber is white and soft, with distinct wide annual rings and conspicuous resin ducts (visible as dark spots in cross-section). It is used for structural timber and particularly for pulp and to manufacture paper. *Pinus radiata* (radiata pine) is also a valuable exotic plantation tree, producing a good-quality timber – pale yellowish brown, often with a slight reddish tinge to the heartwood. The timber is heavier than that of *P. patula*. Several other *Pinus* species are grown commercially in southern Africa, particularly loblolly pine (*P. taeda*), slash pine (*P. elliottii*) and cluster pine (*P. pinaster*).

Podocarpus latifolius |Podocarpaceae| **REAL YELLOWWOOD**; *opregte geelhout* (Afrikaans); *mogôbagôba* (Northern Sotho); *muhovho-hovho* (Venda); *umcheya* (Xhosa); *umkhoba* (Zulu) ■ This yellowwood is a typical tree of Afromontane forests and is widely distributed in southern Africa and further north in Africa. It is a tall, erect tree with reddish-brown and longitudinally fissured bark. The leaves are oblong and much broader than those of *Afrocarpus falcatus*. The small round cones turn reddish purple when ripe and are borne on a thick, fleshy base which also turns purple as the cone ripens. The wood tends to be slightly darker than that of *Afrocarpus falcatus*, but it is so closely similar that even the experts have difficulty distinguishing between them. No other indigenous timber has been more frequently used for furniture, and it is often combined with dark stinkwood. It also provided the broad floor boards for the traditional yellowwood floors of old Cape Dutch homesteads.

Populus deltoides |Salicaceae| **MATCH POPLAR**, cottonwood ■ Poplars are all exotic and several species are grown as ornamental trees in southern Africa. The two best-known ones are the North American match poplar, which found its way to southern Africa via France; and the grey poplar (*Populus canescens*) which appears to be a commercial hybrid between *P. tremula* and *P. alba*. The grey poplar is troublesome because it has a tendency to multiply through suckering, forming dense stands. It is an important source of poles in rural areas. As the name implies, the match poplar is grown mainly for the production of matches; the grey poplar proved to be somewhat less suitable for this purpose. Timber from both species is used on a small scale as furniture timber, known locally as cottonwood. The wood is a pale yellowish colour. It is easy to work with and takes a fine polish, so that it is sometimes mistaken for more precious timber, such as yellowwood. In cross-section, poplar wood can easily be distinguished from yellowwood by the presence of widely spaced, very narrow parenchyma bands and the presence of numerous tiny vessels (easily visible with a hand lens) that are characteristically somewhat oval and not round in outline.

Pseudobersama mossambicensis |Meliaceae| **FALSE WHITE ASH**; *tonduè, minhe-minhe* (Portuguese); *valswitessenhout* (Afrikaans); *umopho* (Zulu) ■ This tree is a characteristic element of coastal forest and is widely distributed along the east coast of Africa, from Maputaland to Kenya. In Mozambique, where the tree is common, it yields a light but durable timber.

UTILITY TIMBERS

Colour and surface pattern of hard pear wood (*Olinia ventosa*)

Comparison of patula pine (*Pinus patula*, top) and radiata pine (*Pinus radiata*, bottom)

Coffee table made from cottonwood (*Populus canescens*)

Chess set made from yellowwood (*Podocarpus latifolius*)

Colour and surface pattern of cottonwood (*Populus deltoides*)

Ptaeroxylon obliquum |Rutaceae| **SNEEZEWOOD**; *umthathi* (Xhosa); *umthathe* (Zulu); *nieshout* (Afrikaans); *molaka* (Northern Sotho) ■ The plant varies from a shrub to a large tree and occurs in a wide range of habitats. The bark becomes grey and flaky in old trees. The compound leaves have several pairs of leaflets which are distinctly angular and minutely gland-dotted. Sweetly scented, white to pale yellow flowers are borne in profusion, often resulting in a spectacular display of colour just before the new leaves appear. The fruit is an oblong capsule, which splits down the middle into valves to release the two-winged seeds. The old capsules often remain on the tree for several months. Sneezewood is widely distributed along the eastern parts of southern Africa and also occurs in northern Namibia, Angola and further north into tropical Africa.

The plant has many uses in rural areas, not only as a source of general purpose timber and poles but also in human and veterinary medicine. The wood is an attractive golden brown, quite heavy and easily recognised by the distinctive peppery smell. The vessels are minute and difficult to see, even with a hand lens. Sneezewood has been used for railway sleepers, but makes a fine furniture timber. It is said to be an important traditional source of hut poles. The irritant terpenoids in the wood are presumably responsible for the fact that sneezewood poles are very durable and will last for many years. The sawdust is highly irritant and causes sneezing, hence the common name.

The Chopi people of Mozambique have a great reputation of *timbila* – xylophone making – and sneezewood is their most important timber for making the keys (MacGillivray 1999). In earlier times, the wooden keys were heated over coals in a pit, but they are nowadays baked in an oven at high temperatures for a few hours. On removal from the heat, the wood is almost flexible, but it soon hardens with an almost metallic resonance. The longer it is baked the better the sound, up to a point of no return, and each key is worked independently with great skill. The wood was heavily over-exploited in the past, but because of its resistance to fungal and insect attack, old sneezewood fence posts can be made into keys.

Pterocarpus angolensis |Fabaceae| **KIAAT**, bloodwood; *greinhout, dolf* (Afrikaans); *omuhuva* (Herero); *mbira* (Shona); *mokwa* (Tswana); *mutondo* (Venda); *umvangazi* (Zulu) ■ Kiaat is a medium-sized to large tree with a wide umbrella-shaped crown. The bark of mature trees is brownish grey, fissured and somewhat corky. The large leaves are compound, with about 20 egg-shaped and conspicuously veined leaflets. The attractive orange-yellow flowers are borne in short clusters, followed by peculiar and characteristic round pods. The central part of the pod has numerous long bristles and is surrounded by a wide, papery wing. These fruits tend to remain on the tree after the leaves are shed in early winter, making it very easy to recognise the trees.

Kiaat is an excellent timber, probably second only to stinkwood in terms of quality and popularity. The heartwood has an attractive reddish-brown colour, contrasting strongly with the yellow sapwood. The wood is stable, strong, elastic, hard and durable. It is slightly coarse-grained but can easily be worked and finished, and takes a fine polish. Distinctive features by which this timber can be recognised include the characteristic smell, coarse texture and variability of colour. The few but exceptionally large vessels can be seen in cross-section, as well as the narrow but clearly defined wavy lines of parenchyma.

Although not always readily available, the timber is popular for furniture, carpentry, panelling, turnery and carvery. According to a recent study (Cunningham 2016), current levels of harvesting are not sustainable. The exceptional stability, even under wet conditions, makes it ideally suited for window frames, outer doors and boat building. It is considered to be one of the best woods for canoes, canoe paddles and fish spears and may also be used for mortars and drums. The excellent quality and stability makes this one of the most popular timbers for general carving and for a wide range of household items. The characteristic dishes made from kiaat are nowadays freely available at roadside craft stalls, craft markets and curio shops. They are easily recognised by the contrasting colours of the reddish brown heartwood and yellowish sapwood.

UTILITY TIMBERS

Colour and surface pattern of sneezewood
(*Ptaeroxylon obliquum*)

Colour and surface pattern of kiaat (*Pterocarpus angolensis*)

Bowls of kiaat (*Pterocarpus angolensis*) at a roadside stall

Pterocarpus rotundifolius |Fabaceae| **ROUND-LEAVED KIAAT**; *dopperkiaat* (Afrikaans); *mohwahlapa* (Northern Sotho); *mumungu* (Shona); *muaṭaha* (Venda); *indlandlovu* (Zulu) ■ The timber is also used to some extent, but is considered inferior to real kiaat because it is less stable. Kiaat is derived from "Kajate", the name for the true *kiaathout* (Burmese or Indian teak, *Tectona grandis*). In earlier years, the latter was imported to the Cape to alleviate the local shortage of timber. The name *kajatenhout* or kiaat was later applied to various timbers and is now used almost exclusively for *Pterocarpus angolensis*.

Sclerocarya birrea |Anacardiaceae| **MARULA** ■ See Chapter 6. The tree provides a useful, splinter-free and easily workable wood which is the source of household items (wooden platters, spoons, stamping blocks, milk pails and drums), carved ornaments and woodroses. The wood varies from pale brown to brown or pink, with the rays clearly visible (with the naked eye); in cross-section it appears more reddish than the background. The vessels are arranged in groups of two to four, and are visible with a hand lens as short lines on the tangential surface. Trees are rarely felled for timber because of their valuable fruit, which is used in beer making. To use the marula tree, special permission is needed from the local chief or headman (Krige 1937), and then care is taken to fell only male trees. Woodroses have been the subject of detailed study (Dzerefos & Witkowski 1997). Most of those used in the curio trade are derived from two mistletoes, *Erianthemum dregei* (previously known as *Loranthus dregei*) and *Pedistylis galpinii* (previously *L. galpinii*). Woodroses are flower-like, intricate, "cancerous" outgrowths of the wood of the host tree, which was formed in response to the mistletoe. The branch of the host tree (with the woodrose) is cut off, and the woodrose is cleaned by carefully removing the non-durable remains of the mistletoe. The woodrose is usually mounted on a wooden stand, or it is cut in such a way that a piece of host stem (or three stems) remains to form a stand. Woodrose-producing mistletoes are most often found on marula trees, but they also grow on *Combretum collinum* and various other trees.

Spirostachys africana |Euphorbiaceae| **TAMBOTI**, sandalwood; *sandalo* (Portuguese); *tambotie* (Afrikaans); *omupapa* (Herero); *morekuri* (Northern Sotho); *morukuru* (Tswana); *muonze* (Venda); *umthombothi* (Xhosa, Zulu) ■ See Chapters 12, 13 and 15. The well-known tamboti is a medium-sized deciduous tree with a rounded crown and characteristic greyish to blackish, flaky bark. The very toxic latex can cause skin irritations and has been used as hunting poison. Tamboti trees are widely distributed in low-lying bushveld areas in all the southern African countries except Lesotho. The wood has an attractive natural lustre and is highly sought after for furniture and cabinet work. It is classified as one of the precious timbers of Mozambique. The contrast between the dark brown heartwood and pale yellow, less durable sapwood is very striking, and can create beautiful flame-like patterns when cleverly exploited by skilful carpenters. The hard, heavy and durable wood is extremely toxic and sawdust causes extreme eye irritation. Tamboti is never used as firewood, because even the smoke is poisonous, and may cause headache and nausea. The timber is easily identified by the beautiful brown to dark brown colour, flame-like surface pattern and the very distinctive sweet, spicy smell. The wood vessels are extremely small and are hardly visible in cross-section, even with a hand lens.

Trichilia dregeana |Meliaceae| **FOREST NATAL-MAHOGANY**; *nkuhlu* (Tsonga); *umkhuhlu* (Xhosa, Zulu); *bosrooiessenhout* (Afrikaans) ■ The soft wood of this species and that of the closely related *Trichilia emetica* (bushveld Natal-mahogany) are important sources of timber for the rural carving industry in southern Africa. In Maputaland, several traditional items are carved from *T. emetica* wood, including bowls (*iziMbenge*), meat dishes (*uGqoko*), spoons (*iziNkhezo*) and head rests (*iziGqiki*) (Cunningham 1987). Most of the carved birds and animals sold along roadsides in northern KwaZulu-Natal are made from *umkhuhlu*. The timber is pale pinkish grey to very pale brown (never dark brown) and not very durable. It can be identified in cross-section by the numerous minute parenchyma bands which are visible only with a hand lens.

Two woodroses from a marula tree (the one at the back was caused by the mistletoe *Pedistylis galpinii*)

Colour and surface pattern of tamboti wood (*Spirostachys africana*)

Colour and surface pattern of bushveld Natal-mahogany (*Trichilia emetica*)

Roadside carver with large birds carved from forest Natal-mahogany or *umkhuhlu* (*Trichilia dregeana*)

Widdringtonia cedarbergensis |Cupressaceae| **CLANWILLIAM CEDAR**; *sederhout, Clanwilliam-seder* (Afrikaans) ■ This interesting tree is highly localised and occurs only in the Cederberg mountains near Clanwilliam in the southwestern Cape. Young specimens are single-stemmed and upright in habit, superficially similar to cultivated cypresses. Old specimens are often forked and gnarled, have massive trunks, and can be up to 20 metres high when protected from fire. Nowadays, it is rare to find trees of more than eight metres in height. The strange beauty of the tree is enhanced by the rugged sandstone mountains of their natural habitat. The bark is reddish grey and peels off in small, angular flakes. The leaves are minute and scale-like. Male cones are only a few millimetres long and short-lived, but the female cones become rounded, woody, tuberculate and resinous at maturity.

Clanwilliam cedars have dwindled rapidly in number due to over-exploitation in the past, as well as some devastating veld fires. Only a few isolated patches on high mountain peaks still remain, but efforts to propagate the tree have been quite successful. In the past, the trees were the only available source of timber in the dry western parts of the Cape. Only trees older than 200 years were considered suitable for cutting. The excellent timber quality resulted in over-exploitation for furniture, doors, window frames, panelling, fence posts and even telephone poles. One of the most popular uses of the timber to this day is for coffins.

The wood is exceptionally beautiful and durable. It has a yellowish to rich, pale brown colour and a pleasant aromatic smell due to the presence of a resinous oil. This resin seems to contribute to the durability and borer-resistance of the timber. Fence posts and beehives have lasted for more than a century without any preservatives. Cedarwood was used in many of the old public buildings in Clanwilliam. It is easy to recognise by the strong, distinctive smell, the yellowish brown colour, the indistinct annual rings and the dark brown rays.

The term cedar is used for a wide range of unrelated timbers, the only common feature being the resinous smell. The true cedars, such as the "cedar of the Libanon" (*Cedrus libani*) and the closely related deodar cedar (*Cedrus deodara*) are popular ornamental trees in southern Africa. The only other indigenous southern African "cedar" besides *Widdringtonia* is the African pencil cedar (*Juniperus procera*). It has been recorded from a single locality in eastern Zimbabwe, but is common further north on the highlands of Kenya and Ethiopia, where it is an important timber tree.

Widdringtonia whytei |Cupressaceae| **MULANJE CEDAR** ■ This species has a narrow distribution range in Malawi and occurs only on Mount Mulanje. It is the most important timber tree of Malawi, but has become severely threatened as a result of over-exploitation. For many years the mulanje cedar was considered to be merely a large form of the generally more shrubby mountain cedar (*Widdringtonia nodiflora*) but it is now generally accepted as a distinct species (Pauw & Linder 1997). It resembles the Clanwilliam cedar in that it does not survive fire and only re-establishes from seed. In contrast, the common mountain cedar (*Widdringtonia nodiflora*) is not killed by fire but resprouts from the base. It is known as *lerokwana* in Northern Sotho and *thaululo* in Venda.

REFERENCES AND FURTHER READING: Archer, F.M. 1990. Planning with people – ethnobotany and African uses of plants in Namaqualand (South Africa). *Mitt. Inst. Allg. Bot. Hamburg* 23: 959–972. **Bandeira, S.O. 1994.** The ethnobotany of non-medicinal plants of Inhaca Island, Mozambique. In: Seyani, J.H. & Chikuni, A.C. (eds), Proceedings of the 13th plenary meeting of AETFAT, Zomba, Malawi, 2–11 April 1991, Vol. 1, pp. 39–46. National Herbarium and Botanic Gardens of Malawi, Zomba, Malawi. **Bandeira, S.O.** *et al.* **1994.** The ecology and conservation status of plant resources in Mozambique. *Strelitzia* 1: 105–115. **Boon, R. 2010.** *Pooley's trees of eastern South Africa.* Flora and Fauna Publications Trust, Durban. **Burrows, J. & Burrows, S. 2003.** *Figs of Southern and South-Central Africa.* Umdaus Press, Hatfield. **Campbell, B.M. & Du Toit, R.F. 1988.** Relationships between wood resources and use of species for construction and fuel in the communal lands of Zimbabwe. *Monogr. Syst. Bot. Missouri Bot. Gard.* 25: 331–341. **Coates Palgrave, K. 1977.** *Trees of Southern Africa.* Struik, Cape Town. **Coates Palgrave, M. 2002.** *Keith Coates Palgrave trees of Southern Africa.* 3rd ed. Struik Publishers, Cape Town. **Codd, L.E.W. 1951.** Trees and shrubs of the Kruger National Park. *Mem. Bot. Surv. S. Afr.* 26. Botanical Research Institute, Pretoria. **Cunningham, A.B.**

UTILITY TIMBERS

Young tree of Clanwilliam cedar (*Widdringtonia cedarbergensis*)

Mature tree of Clanwilliam cedar (*Widdringtonia cedarbergensis*)

African pencil cedar (*Juniperus procera*)

Ben Zimri with a gnarled specimen of Clanwilliam cedar

Ripe cone of Clanwilliam cedar (*Widdringtonia cedarbergensis*)

& Gwala, B.R. 1986. Plant species and building methods used in Thembe Thonga hut construction. *Ann. Natal Mus.* 27: 491–511. **Cunningham, A.B. 1987.** Commercial craftwork: Balancing out human needs and resources. *S. Afr. J. Bot.* 53: 259–266. **Cunningham, A.B. 2016.** *Trade study of selected east African timber production species.* BfNSkripten 445. Bundesamt für Naturschutz, Bonn (www.dnl-online.de). **Curtis, B.A. & Mannheimer, C.A. 2005.** *Tree atlas of Namibia.* The National Botanical Research Institute, Windhoek. **Dyer, S.T. 1988.** *A description of the macroscopic characteristics of a number of well-known indigenous and exotic timber species in South Africa and a key to their identification.* Bulletin 62. Forestry Branch, Department of Environmental Affairs, Pretoria. **Dyer, S., James, B. & James, D. 2016.** *Guide to the properties and uses of southern African wood.* Briza Publications, Pretoria [also in Afrikaans]. **Dzerefos, C.M. & Witkowski, E.T.F.** 1997. Development and anatomy of the attachment structure of woodrose-producing mistletoes. *S. Afr. J. Bot.* 63(6): 416–420. **Esterhuyse, N., Van der Merwe, I., Von Breitenbach, J. & Söhnge, H. 2016.** *Remarkable trees of South Africa.* Briza Publications, Pretoria. **Ferreira, F.H. 1928.** Setlhapin nomenclature and uses of indigenous trees of Griqualand West. *Bantu Stud.* 3: 349–355. **Galpin, E.E. 1925.** Native timber trees of the Springbok flats. *Mem. Bot. Surv. S. Afr.* 7. **Godfrey, R. 1932.** The umsimbili walking-stick. *Blythswood Review* 9, 98: 24. **Hoffman, A.C. 1952.** Venda dug-out canoe. *National Museum Researches, Bloemfontein* 1: 23–28 **Kirby, P.R. 1932.** The music and musical instruments of the Korana. *Bantu Stud.* 6: 182–204. **Kirby, P.R. 1934.** *The musical instruments of the native races of South Africa.* Oxford University Press, London. **Kirby, P.R. 1943.** South African native drums, particularly the great Ngoma of the Venda. *Bull. S. Afr. Mus. Ass.* 3,2: 42–48. **Knuffel, W.E. 1973.** *The construction of the Bantu grass hut.* Akademische Druck, Austria. **Krige, E.J. 1937.** Note on the Phalaborwa and their morula complex. *Bantu Stud.* 11: 357–366. **Kromhout, C.P. 1975.** *'n Sleutel tot die uitkenning van die vernaamste inheemse houtsoorte van Suid-Afrika.* Bulletin 50. Departement van Bosbou, Pretoria. **Larson, T.J. 1975.** Craftwork of the Hambukushu of Botswana. *Botswana Notes and Records* 7: 109–120. **Lawes, M.J., Eely, H.A.C., Shackleton, C.M. & Geach, B.G.S. (eds) 2004.** *Indigenous forests and woodlands in South Africa. Part. 3. Wood and timber use.* University of KwaZulu-Natal Press, Scottsville. **Lawes, M.J., Eely, H.A.C., Shackleton, C.M. & Geach, B.G.S. (eds) 2004.** *Indigenous forests and woodlands in South Africa. Part. 4. Woodcarving and the craft industry.* University of KwaZulu-Natal Press, Scottsville. **Lemmens, R.H.M.J., Louppe, D. & Oteng-Amoako, A.A. (eds) 2012.** *Plant resources of tropical Africa 7(2). Timbers 2.* PROTA Foundation, Wageningen / Backhuys Publishers, Leiden. **Liengme, C.A. 1981.** Plants used by the Tsonga people of Gazankulu. *Bothalia* 13, 3&4: 501–518. **Liengme, C.A. 1983.** A study of wood use for fuel and building in an area of Gazankulu. *Bothalia* 14,2: 245–257. **Louppe, D., Oteng-Amoako, A.A. & Brink, M. (eds) 2008.** *Plant resources of tropical Africa 7(1). Timbers 1.* PROTA Foundation, Wageningen / Backhuys Publishers, Leiden. **MacGillivray, S. 1999.** *Making music from science.* Supplement to *Mail and Guardian,* 12–18 March 1999. **Malan, J.S. & Owen-Smith, G.L. 1974.** The ethnobotany of Kaokoland. *Cimbebasia* Ser. B 2,5: 131–178. **Mannheimer, C.A. & Curtis, B.A. (eds) 2009.** *Le Roux and Müller's field guide to the trees and shrubs of Namibia.* Macmillan Education Namibia, Windhoek. **McLaren, P.I.R. 1958.** Fishing devices of Central and Southern Africa. *Rhodes-Livingstone Museum Occasional Paper* 12: 1–48. **Miller, O.B. 1940.** The Bantu as forest botanist. *Jl S. Afr. For. Ass.* 4: 21–23. **Moll, E. 1992.** *Trees of Natal.* University of Cape Town, Eco-lab Trust Fund, Cape Town. **Nurse, G.J. 1972.** Musical instrumentation among the San of the Central Kalahari. *African Music* 5, 2: 23–27. **Palmer, E. & Pitman, N. 1972.** *Trees of Southern Africa.* (3 vols). Balkema, Cape Town. **Pauw, C.A. & Linder, H.P. 1997.** Tropical African cedars (*Widdringtonia,* Cupressaceae): systematics, ecology and conservation status. *Bot. J. Linn. Soc.* 123: 297–319. **Peters, C.R. 1988.** Notes on the distribution and relative abundance of *Sclerocarya birrea* (A.Rich.) Hochst. (Anacardiaceae). *Monogr. Syst. Bot., Missouri Bot. Gard.* 25: 403–410. **Pooley, E. 1993.** *The complete field guide to trees of Natal, Zululand & Transkei.* Natal Flora Trust, Durban. **Poynton, R.J. 1975.** *Suid-Afrikaanse boomgids.* Tafelberg, Cape Town. **Poynton, R.J. 1977.** *Tree planting in Southern Africa, Vol. 1. Pines.* Department of Forestry, Pretoria. **Poynton, R.J. 1979.** *Tree planting in Southern Africa, Vol. 2. Eucalypts.* Department of Forestry, Pretoria. **Poynton, R.J. 2009.** *Tree planting in Southern Africa, Vol. 3. Other Genera.* Department of Agriculture, Forestry and Fisheries, Pretoria. **Schmidt, E., Lötter, M. & McCleland, W. 2007.** *Trees and shrubs of Mpumalanga and Kruger National Park.* 2nd. ed. Jacana, Johannesburg. **Sim, T.R. 1921.** *The forest and forest-flora of the colony of Cape of Good Hope.* Taylor & Henderson, Aberdeen. **Sim, T.R. 1921.** Native timbers of South Africa. *Mem. Dep. Mines Inds. Un. S. Afr.* 3. **Smit, N. 1999**. *Guide to the Acacias of South Africa.* Briza Publications, Pretoria. **Smith, C.A. 1966.** Common names of South African plants. *Mem. Bot. Surv. S. Afr.* 35. **Steyn, H.P. 1981**. Nharo Plant Utilization. An Overview. *Khoisis* 1. **Thomas, V. & Grant, R. 1998.** *Sappi tree spotting guide: Highveld and Drakensberg.* Jacana, Johannesburg. **Tinley, K.G. 1964.** Fishing methods of the Thonga tribe in north-eastern Zululand and southern Moçambique. *Lammergeyer* 3,1: 9–39. **Van der Merwe, I.J. 2002.** *The Knysna and Tsitsikamma forests: Their history, ecology and management.* 2nd. ed. Department of Water Affairs and Forestry, Pretoria. **Van der Waal, C.S. 1977.** *Die woning en woonwyse onder die Venda.* M.A. thesis, University of Pretoria. **Van Voorthuizen, E.G. 1976.** The mopane tree. *Botswana Notes and Records* 8: 223–230. **Van Vuuren, N.J.J., Banks, C.H. & Stöhr, H.P. 1978.** *Shrinkage and density of timbers used in the Republic of South Africa.* Bulletin 57. Department of Forestry, Pretoria. **Van Wyk, B. & Van Wyk, P. 1997.** *Field guide to trees of southern Africa.* Struik, Cape Town. **Van Wyk, P. 1995**. *Field guide to the trees of the Kruger National Park.* Struik, Cape Town. **Van Wyk, B., Van Wyk, P. & Van Wyk, B.-E. 2008.** *Photo guide to trees of southern Africa.* 2nd ed. Briza Publications, Pretoria [also in Afrikaans]. **Van Wyk, A.E., Van den Berg, E., Coates Palgrave, M., Jordaan, M. 2011.** *Dictionary of names for southern African trees.* Briza Publications, Pretoria. **Venter, E. 2011.** *Trees of the Garden Route: Mossel Bay to Storms River.* Briza Publications, Pretoria. **Venter, F. & Venter, J.-A. 1996.** *Making the most of indigenous trees.* Briza Publications, Pretoria. **Von Breitenbach, F. 1974.** *Suid-Kaapse Bosse en Bome.* Government Printer, Pretoria. **Von Breitenbach, F. 1986.** *National List of Indigenous Trees.* Dendrological Foundation, Pretoria. **Walton, J. 1948.** South African peasant architecture. Southern Sotho folk building. *Afr. Stud.* 7,4: 139–145. **Weiss, E.A. 1979.** Some indigenous plants used domestically by East African coastal fisherman. *Econ. Bot.* 31(1): 35–55. **Willoughby, W.C. 1905.** Notes on the totemism of the Becwana. *S. Afr. J. Sci.* 3: 263–293. **Wood, E.N. 1976.** A study of the traditional music of Mochudi. *Botswana Notes and Records* 8: 165–174.

A multi-stemmed specimen of Clanwilliam cedar (*Widdringtonia cedarbergensis*)

Colour and surface pattern of cedarwood
(*Widdringtonia cedarbergensis*)

Old cupboard door made from cedarwood
(*Widdringtonia cedarbergensis*)

Children in Namaqualand gathering firewood

Corn cobs (*mieliestronke*) used as firewood

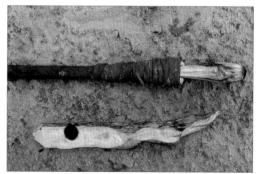

Used fire-sticks from the common corkwood (*Commiphora pyracanthoides*)

Making fire with friction using dry donkey dung

CHAPTER 18

Fire making & firewood

TRADITIONAL METHODS OF fire making have been relatively well recorded. Fire making by friction is a common method and is still used in some rural areas. Apart from the choice of timber species to use, the basic method is similar for the whole of southern Africa (see *Commiphora pyracanthoides*, where the use of fire-sticks is described and illustrated). Various types of tinder are used, including specific types of dry grass or dry donkey manure. Before matches and firelighters became available, a tinderbox was commonly used to light the fire. Examples of tinder (*tontel* in Afrikaans) that were used include the leaf hairs of *tontelblaar* (*Hermas gigantea*) and seed hairs of *tontelbos* (*Gomphocarpus fruticosus*).

Firewood is by far the most important plant use, if measured in terms of volumes alone. More than half of the energy needs of South Africa are met by firewood harvested from natural areas and plantations (Basson 1987). The fuel supply for cooking and heating is often not sustainable and may lead to serious deforestation and environmental degradation. The supply of cheap electricity is an important priority in southern Africa but even in areas with a reliable supply of electricity, firewood is still used in large quantities. Studies in Namaqualand showed that a family uses about 15 kilograms of firewood per day (Archer 1990). This consumption is almost exactly the same as the 14.9 kilograms found by Liengme (1983) in Gazankulu. Estimates of the requirement per family vary from 1.5 to 7.7 tons per year (Liengme 1983). Based on a *per capita* firewood consumption of 0.6 cubic metres per year, Le Roux (1981) estimated that 7.23 million cubic metres are required in the rural parts of South Africa. Surveys in Zimbabwe (Banks 1981; Furness 1981a, 1981b) and Malawi (Nkaonja 1981) have generally shown an imbalance between supply and demand and several projects are now underway to establish woodlots for firewood. Fast-growing eucalypts and other exotic species such as *Leucaenia leucocephala* have become popular for this purpose. Since trees with a small diameter (less than 50 millimetres in diameter) are mostly used for firewood in rural areas, these trees are grown on highly productive short rotations where coppice material can be harvested at regular intervals. Naturalised exotic tree species such as black wattle (*Acacia mearnsii*), rooikrans (*A. cyclops*) and Port Jackson (*A. saligna*) are also important in supplementing the rather meagre indigenous firewood resources in some regions.

The mopane (*Colophospermum mopane*), sweet thorn (*Vachellia karroo*), camel thorn (*Vachellia erioloba*), sickle bush (*Dichrostachys cinerea*), rooibos (*Combretum apiculatum*) and *hardekool* (*Combretum imberbe*) are important sources of indigenous firewood, but there are obviously many other species of regional value. These firewoods are often sold in urban areas in southern Africa as fuelwood or as charcoal, mainly for cooking and for the famous southern African tradition of *braaivleis* or barbecue (meat cooked on a grid-iron over an open fire or over coals). The stumps of grape vines (*wingerdstompies*), when they are removed to rejuvenate old vineyards, are an important fuel source in the Cape. Corn cobs (*mieliestronke* in Afrikaans) are especially important in the treeless landscape of the grasslands.

Firewoods are typically heavy and hard, and differ from utility timbers in their high energy values, their ability to form coals rather than ash and their slow burnout time. They should also be free from poisonous substances (see tamboti), the smoke should not impart unpleasant odours or flavours to the food and the smoke should not cause irritation or discomfort. An example is the bluegum tree (*Eucalyptus* species) which is not popular because of the pungent smell of the smoke and the fact that it affects the taste of food (Archer 1990). High-quality firewood is often in short supply, so that availability is often a far more important consideration than fuel properties.

Acacia cyclops |Fabaceae| **ROOIKRANS** (Afrikaans); Cape coast wattle, red eye ■ *Rooikrans* is a rounded shrub or small tree with oblong, leaf-like phyllodes, each with three to five veins. The flower heads are dull yellow and the curled pods are borne in clusters, each with several black seeds surrounded by a bright red aril (hence the Afrikaans name *rooikrans*). The closely related Port Jackson wattle or Port Jackson (*Acacia saligna*, see below) is a more erect tree. The phyllodes are larger with a single midrib, and the flowers are bright yellow and showy. Both species were introduced from Australia to stabilise the sand dunes around the Cape coast. The species have adapted so exceptionally well that they have become serious invaders, threatening the integrity of natural systems, particularly the Cape fynbos. The trees are undesirable from an ecological point of view, yet they are very important sources of fuelwood in the Cape. It was estimated that the value of the fuelwood industry in the Cape alone is worth nearly R30 million a year.

An important ecological distinction can be made between *rooikrans* (*Acacia cyclops*) and Port Jackson (*A. saligna*). Rooikrans is killed when it is felled for fuelwood, and it will not regrow except from seeds. Port Jackson, on the other hand, resprouts vigorously from the base after it has been cut down. This difference should be kept in mind when clearing alien vegetation from stream banks and natural areas, as Port Jackson requires additional control measures. In the Cape, axes and saws are traditionally used to cut *rooikrans* trees and to remove the smaller branches. Thick pieces produced in this way are cleft (split) so that the end result is a piece of relatively uniform size. *Rooikrans* firewood was traditionally sold by the piece (*stukkie* in Afrikaans) in cities and town, a practice dating back to the days of the wood and coal stove.

Acacia dealbata |Fabaceae| **SILVER WATTLE**; *silwerwattel* (Afrikaans) ■ This species is often confused with black wattle but can easily be distinguished by the silvery stems and leaves. The bright yellow flowers are fragrant. Silver wattle is the most common woody invader in Gauteng, forming dense stands along rivers. The flowering branches are used in the florist trade, especially in southern Europe. The timber is an important informal source of firewood on the highveld of South Africa.

Acacia decurrens |Fabaceae| **GREEN WATTLE**; *groenwattel* (Afrikaans) ■ Green wattle is similar to black wattle but the ultimate leaflets are longer and narrower, and the flowers are bright canary yellow. It was formerly cultivated on a large scale for tannin production but the bark gives an undesirable reddish colour to leather. It is an excellent firewood.

Acacia mearnsii |Fabaceae| **BLACK WATTLE**; *swartwattel* (Afrikaans) ■ The black wattle is extensively used in commercial forestry in South Africa and occurs as a troublesome woody invader throughout the eastern parts of southern Africa, from the Cape Peninsula to Mozambique and Zimbabwe. It is the main source of tannin for the leather industry but the timber is also important, especially for the production of laminated board products. The wood is widely used as an excellent firewood.

Acacia saligna |Fabaceae| **PORT JACKSON**, Port Jackson wattle ■ This woody invader is an erect tree with a rounded or somewhat weeping crown. It bears large phyllodes with a single midrib, bright yellow, showy flower heads and slender, straight pods. Unlike *Acacia cyclops*, it is not killed by fire or clearcutting but rapidly sprouts, forming coppice shoots. In order to stop the spread of Port Jackson, biological control became necessary, and a gall-forming rust fungus (*Uromycladium tepperianum*) was introduced. The fungus reduces the formation of flowers and fruits by producing large brown galls on the inflorescences. The stress caused by gall formation all over the tree eventually contributes towards killing it. As a firewood, Port Jackson is inferior to *rooikrans* but it is nevertheless an important fuel source and many people (especially in the Cape region of South Africa) rely on it for their daily energy needs.

FIRE MAKING & FIREWOOD

Cutting firewood from *rooikrans* (*Acacia cyclops*) near Cape Town

Silver wattle (*Acacia dealbata*)

Rooikrans (*Acacia cyclops*)

Black wattle (*Acacia mearnsii*)

Port Jackson (*Acacia saligna*)

Colophospermum mopane |Fabaceae| **MOPANE**; *mupani* (Venda); *mopanie* (Afrikaans); *omupungu* (Herero); *mohlanare* (Northern Sotho); *mupane* (Shona); *muphane* (Tswana) ■ See Chapter 12. The mopane is usually a shrub or small tree, but old specimens may reach 18 metres under favourable conditions. Plants are deciduous and occur in large, dense stands in hot low-lying areas; the term mopane woodland is used to describe this veld type. The bark is dark grey and strongly fissured. A characteristic feature of mopane is the leaf, which has two symmetrical halves with a tiny appendage (a vestige of a reduced third leaflet) in between, and a distinct turpentine smell. In hot, dry weather, the two halves fold onto one another to reduce transpiration, so that the trees provide little shade. The small, inconspicuous, greenish flowers are followed by leathery pods, each with a single, flat, resinous seed. Mopane is indigenous to the northern parts of southern Africa, and occurs in a broad band from Namibia and Angola to Botswana, Zimbabwe, Mozambique and the extreme northern parts of South Africa. The trees can be grown from seeds, which should be planted pod and all, but growth is very slow and the seedlings are prone to fungal infections.

Mopane trees are an important natural resource in southern Africa and few other trees can match its versatility. The special cultural and religious significance of mopane to the Herero-speaking people of Namibia, for example, is reflected in various customs and ceremonies (Malan & Owen-Smith 1974). Only mopane wood is used for the sacred fire, and for the ceremonial removal of teeth. It is by far the most important source of poles as building material in Kaokoland and in many other parts of southern Africa. The popularity is due to the hardness and durability of the timber, which is reddish brown to almost black in colour and highly resistant to termite damage. Mopane often accounts for more than 90 per cent of the timber used for huts. Strong poles are required to support the roof of a hut, particularly when it is heavy after rain. The walls of huts are not designed to carry this weight. The timber is hard and heavy but is sometimes used to make ornaments, musical instruments and furniture.

As a firewood, mopane has few equals. It burns readily even when green, and gives off a sweet smell and an intense heat. Coals may last for several hours. No wonder that the mopane is the tree of choice for firewood, collected and traded on a large scale in many rural parts of southern Africa. The inner bark is sometimes used for cordage, particularly to tie poles and withes together in hut construction. The leaves are nutritious and have a high crude protein content (about 13 per cent). Despite their turpentine smell, they do not appear to taint milk or meat, although the breath of an animal browsing on green mopane leaves is said to smell strongly of onions (Van Voorthuizen 1976). The bark is used as a drench for diarrhoea in cattle.

The mopane tree is the host of the mopane worm, an important and popular source of protein for the human diet in rural areas. The worms are called *mashonja* in Sotho and Tsonga. Mopane worms are the larvae (caterpillars) of the mopane moth or anomalous emperor moth (*Imbrasia belina*) and they occur in very large numbers on mopane trees, from December to April and May. The large caterpillars are squeezed to remove their intestines and they are then sun-dried for transport and storage. The dried caterpillars are exceptionally rich in proteins and can be eaten directly as a snack, or fried, roasted or cooked with vegetables as a stew. There is a small but lucrative local trade in dried mopane worm, but the occurrence of the caterpillars is unpredictable and the outbreaks are often localised. Mopane worms are sometimes confused with another edible caterpillar, the larva of the pallid emperor moth (*Cirina forda*), which feeds mainly on the wild-seringa tree (*Burkea africana*).

Small stingless bees use hollows in mopane trees as hives that have a trumpet-shaped wax entrance. The blackish honey is a local delicacy in mopane woodland.

Bark decoctions are taken for diarrhoea; leaf infusions are used for constipation and the chewed leaves are applied to fresh wounds to stop bleeding.

A load of mopane firewood

A large mopane tree (*Colophospermum mopane*)

Leaves and flowers of mopane (*Colophospermum mopane*)

Dried mopane worms (*mashonja*), a much sought after delicacy in parts of southern Africa

The mopane moth (*Imbrasia belina*)

Combretum apiculatum |Combretaceae| **RED BUSHWILLOW**; *rooiboswilg, rooibos* (Afrikaans); *omumbute* (Herero); *mohwelere* (Northern Sotho); *mpotsa, mugavi* (Tsonga); *mofudiri* (Tswana); *musingidzi* (Venda); *ombondwe* (Zulu) ■ The tree is small to medium-sized, with a rounded crown and a grey to brownish smooth bark that becomes rough with age. The leaves are large, broadly oblong and narrow to slender, with twisted tips. Minute scales are present on the leaf surface, which is sticky and shiny in young leaves. Oblong clusters of fragrant cream-coloured flowers are followed by four-winged, reddish-brown fruits. The tree is common in dry bushveld in the northern parts of Namibia, Botswana, South Africa and large parts of Mozambique and Zimbabwe.

The red bushwillow is an important fodder tree for browsing animals. Poles are sometimes cut for fencing and hut building because they are resistant to termites. The timber is highly prized as firewood. It is perhaps second only to mopane in terms of its popularity as a firewood in rural areas, where small pieces have to be collected by hand. The wood is sold commercially as firewood in the northern parts of South Africa and the coals are reputed to last for a whole day. A refreshing tea may be brewed from the leaves.

Combretum imberbe |Combretaceae| **LEADWOOD**; *hardekool* (Afrikaans); *mbimba, mondzo* (Tsonga); *omumborombonga* (Herero); *!haab, !has* (Nama); *mohwelere-tšipi* (Northern Sotho); *motswiri* (Tswana); *mundzwiri* (Venda); *impondondlovu* (Zulu) ■ The leadwood is a small to large tree with a characteristic fissured bark, which has deep furrows and transverse cracks, forming rectangular flakes. The small leaves are leathery and distinctly greyish green and give the tree its characteristic greyish appearance. Cream-coloured flowers are followed by small, four-winged, yellow-green fruits. Leadwood trees are found in all the bushveld regions of southern Africa and usually grow in mixed woodland along rivers and in pans. The tree is rarely cultivated but it makes a fine shade tree and becomes very old. Large specimens are thought to be over 1 000 years old. The tree has numerous uses. Smoke from burning leaves is inhaled to treat coughs and colds. An edible gum sometimes exudes from the tree in early summer.

Leadwood is exceptionally hard, heavy, strong and durable. Stumps of trees felled during road construction are known to have remained intact for many years without the slightest deterioration. The wood is so hard that it is almost impossible to work without blunting and damaging tools. Nevertheless, it is becoming increasingly popular for making heavy, almost indestructible furniture. Ornaments and sculptures are sometimes made from it and according to Coates Palgrave (1977), leadwood hoes were used before metal became available. It has also been used to a limited extent for railway sleepers, mine props and quite frequently for fence posts.

There are few trees more popular for firewood than the legendary leadwood. No bushveld experience is complete without a leadwood camp fire and a *braai* or barbeque over leadwood coals. The slow burnout time of leadwood contributes to its great reputation as an excellent firewood. Large stumps may take several days to burn out completely, so that the water for the morning coffee may be boiled without the need to rekindle the fire. In lion country, it is important to have a firewood that will burn throughout the night. The ash is said to have a high lime content and is used for toothpaste and as a substitute for whitewash (Coates Palgrave 1977). The tree has special cultural and religious significance in Namibia (Malan & Owen-Smith 1974).

Combretum hereroense |Combretaceae| **RUSSET BUSHWILLLOW**; *kierieklapper* (Afrikaans); *omutapati* (Herero); *mokabi* (Northern Sotho); *mpotsa* (Tsonga); *mokabi* (Tswana); *mugavhi* (Venda); *umhlalavane* (Zulu) ■ See Chapter 6. The tree is easily recognised by the velvety brown hairs on the lower surfaces of young leaves and the clusters of reddish-brown fruits. The wood makes an excellent firewood with long-lasting coals. The Afrikaans common name is derived from the use of the wood to make knobkieries. The wood of several species of *Combretum* is occasionally used as firewood but the three included here are the most popular and best-known sources of firewood.

Leadwood trees (*Combretum imberbe*)

Grain mortar carved from leadwood (the pestle is made of mopane)

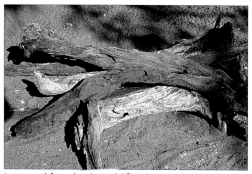

Firewood from leadwood (*Combretum imberbe*)

Leaves and fruits of the russet bushwillow (*Combretum hereroense*)

Commiphora glaucescens |Burseraceae| **BLUE-LEAVED CORKWOOD**; *tsaura* (Khoi); *bloublaarkanniedood* (Afrikaans); *omutungi* (Herero) ■ The wood is quite soft but is nevertheless used as firewood in the northwestern parts of Namibia. It is one of several *Commiphora* species that are used in Namibia as a source of soft timber to carve household utensils and containers (Mannheimer & Curtis 2009). These include *C. africana*, *C. anacardiifolia*, *C. angolensis*, *C. discolor*, *C. glandulosa*, *C. mollis* and *C. mossambicensis*.

Commiphora pyracanthoides |Burseraceae| **COMMON CORKWOOD**; *gewone kanniedood* (Afrikaans); *omboo* (Herero); */inîb* (Nama); *liminyela* (Swazi); *xifati* (Tsonga); *morôka* (Tswana); *muṭalu* (Venda); *iminyela* (Zulu) ■ The plant is a spiny shrub or small tree and is usually multi-stemmed. The bark is yellowish green and peels off in yellow papery flakes. The hairless leaves are simple and occur in clusters on short, spine-tipped branches. Small yellow to reddish flowers are followed by small, round, fleshy fruits. This plant is widely distributed in the subtropical parts of southern Africa and often occurs in dry areas on sand. The roots are eaten, raw or cooked, and the bark is used in Himba traditional medicine (Von Koenen 2001).

Commiphora wood is traditionally popular for carving household utensils such as spoons and stirring sticks, but the wood of this species is considered too soft. It does, however, have an important traditional use as one of the most popular sources of fire-sticks in southern Africa. It is used for both the "female stick" (*otjiya* slab – see Malan & Owen-Smith 1974) and the "male stick" (pers. obs. – see below). The powdered wood has been used as tinder for flint lighters. It is perhaps the ease with which wood powder ignites that makes this such a popular fire-stick plant. Twigs of other *Commiphora* species such as *C. giessii* are also used as fire-sticks (Van den Eynden *et al.* 1992).

Traditional fire making by friction requires two fire-sticks – a slender male stick ("bull-stick") of about 500 millimetres long and about as thick as a finger, and a short, thick "female stick" of about 200 millimetres or less. The male stick is often made up of two parts, the actual friction tip and a longer twirl stick, into which the former is wedged and firmly tied with bark. The friction tip and the female stick are often from the same timber, but the twirl stick is chosen for its mechanical properties (straight, flexible). Only certain types of wood are used for fire-sticks and there are strong regional differences. Twigs of the wild custard apple (*Annona chrysophylla*) have been used for fire-sticks, specifically for the sacred fire (Ferreira 1948). The soft wood of wild figs such as *Ficus petersiana*, *F. natalensis* and *F. thonningii* are also popular. Other known sources of fire-sticks are *Mimusops zeyheri*, *Brachylaena discolor* and other *Brachylaena* species.

The traditional process has been described in detail by Friede (1979). It takes between 45 seconds and several minutes to make fire by friction. Considerable skill is required to perform this seemingly easy task. In the central Kalahari (see photographs) the procedure we witnessed took approximately two minutes, using *Commiphora pyracanthoides* wood as both female stick and friction tip, the latter inserted in a straight *Grewia flava* stem to serve as twirl stick. In this case, the female stick was flattened above and below and a small slot or groove was cut on the one side, close to a small hole on the upper surface, into which a pinch of sand was placed to increase the friction. The female stick was then held firmly on top of a hunting knife and the sharpened friction tip inserted into the tiny hole to begin the twirling process.

After perhaps four or five rapid drilling motions, fine black wood dust started sifting along the narrow groove in the female stick onto the blade of the knife below. More and more of this hot dust or ash accumulated to form a tiny smouldering ember. The chief took the knife from the man who performed the drilling operation, and used the little coal (perhaps symbolically) to first light his cigarette, after which it was handed to another man. This was Tilo, who used a special fine grass as tinder and skilfully blew life into the ember by carefully regulating the air flow with his lips and tongue. Smoke soon arose, and after a little more blowing, flames miraculously appeared from the small bundle of grass.

FIRE MAKING & FIREWOOD

Tying the friction tip to the twirl stick, using a piece of *Grewia flava* bark

Female stick (note the notch on the side and the small hole on the upper surface)

Twirling the male stick (note the sawdust trickling down the notch in the female stick)

Blowing the ember, using fine grass as tinder

Dichrostachys cinerea |Fabaceae| **SICKLE BUSH**; *sekelbos* (Afrikaans); *omutjete* (Herero, Himba); */goes, /gowes* (Nama); *morêtšê* (Northern Sotho); *motsêlêsêlê* (Tswana); *murenzhe* (Venda); *ugagane* (Zulu) ■ See Chapter 7. Large parts of the bushveld regions of southern Africa have become overgrazed and are subject to bush encroachment by this species. Overgrazing results in a removal of grasses, so that the annual veld fires in winter are not sufficiently intense to kill the seedlings of woody plants as they normally would. Lack of fire is detrimental to the grasses and leads to an increase in woody and especially thorny plants. These woody plants tend to shade out the grasses, thus further contributing to the cycle of bush encroachment.

The sickle bush is a robust shrub or small tree with an untidy growth form and thorny branches. The feathery leaves resemble those of *Senegalia* and *Vachellia* species. The unusual and attractive flower clusters hang down from the branches, and make it easy to identify the tree. Bright yellow, fertile flowers occur in the upper half of the cluster (or the lower part in the hanging cluster). Sterile flowers, in sharp contrast, are bright pink and are arranged at the bottom end of the cluster (uppermost in the hanging cluster). The pods are borne in clusters on long stalks, and are curled and twisted. Despite the undesirable ecological impact, sickle bush is nevertheless a valuable plant. Numerous medicinal uses are known (see Chapter 7). The bark yields a tough fibre used for rope and tying. Straight branches are used as durable fence posts. Sickle bush has also become a valuable source of high-quality firewood and is nowadays sold commercially in South Africa. The harvesting of sickle bush for firewood and charcoal is an excellent example of turning liabilities into assets, and at the same time contributing to the restoration of degraded habitats.

Diospyros austro-africana |Ebenaceae| **FIRE BUSH**, firesticks; *kraaibos* (Afrikaans); *kritikom* (Khoi); *matjhitje, senokonoko* (Sotho); *umbongisa* (Xhosa) ■ This widely distributed plant is a large, woody shrub or small tree with a rounded crown and very small silvery leaves. The characteristic fruits are topped by prominent and persistent calyx lobes and are said to be fit only as food for crows, hence the Afrikaans common name. The roots and leaves are widely used in traditional medicine in the Karoo and Namaqualand. The wood and stems were formerly much used as fire-sticks to make fire by friction.

Euclea pseudebenus |Ebenaceae| **EBONY GUARRI**; *ebbeboom, ebbehoutghwarrie* (Afrikaans); *omuthema* (Herero); *tsabis, tsawis* (Nama) ■ This small tree occurs over large parts of Namibia and the adjacent parts of South Africa. It has characteristic drooping branches, long, narrow leaves and round, black berries. The wood is pitch black and valuable as a general timber for building and carving but pieces are usually small. It is an important firewood in Namibia and Namaqualand (Smith 1966; Archer 1990). In contrast, the wood of the magic guarri (*Euclea divinorum*) is considered to be unsuitable for firewood. *Euclea undulata* (guarri) and *Pappea capensis* (*wildepruim*) were once amongst the most popular firewoods in the Little Karoo but the supply is too small to be sustainably utilised. The true ebony is an Indian species, *Diospyros ebenus*, the tree that produces the much sought after black timber used for carvery, ornaments, inlay work and carpentry. However, *Dalbergia melanoxylon* (zebrawood) is used in the same way and has long been a much sought after timber in Europe, especially to make musical instruments such as the clarinet, oboe and bagpipes (see Chapter 17). The scientific name "*pseudebenus*" means "false ebony" and the vernacular names all refer to the resemblance to ebony.

Ficus sur |Moraceae| **WILD FIG**; *wildevyeboom* (Afrikaans); *umkhiwane* (Xhosa, Zulu) ■ Pieces of wood of this tree were once popular fire-sticks, used to produce fire by friction (Smith 1966).

Hermas gigantea |Apiaceae| ***TONTELBLAAR*** (Afrikaans) ■ The use of the dense layer of leaf hairs as tinder (*tontel*) for the tinderbox was first recorded by Thunberg in 1772. Seed hairs of *Gomphocarpus fruticosus* (milkweed, *tontelbos*) were used in the same way.

FIRE MAKING & FIREWOOD

Firewood from the ebony guarri (*Euclea pseudebenus*)

Leaves and fruits of the ebony guarri (*Euclea pseudebenus*)

Fruits of the fire bush (*Diospyros austro-africana*)

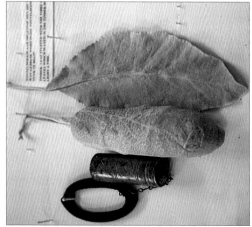

Hermas leaf hairs were used in former times to stuff the tinderbox

Monsonia crassicaule (=*Sarcocaulon crassicaule*) |Geraniaceae| **BUSHMAN'S CANDLE**; *boesman(s)kers* (Afrikaans); *norap* (Khoi) ■ The plant is a thick-stemmed succulent with compound leaves that persist as thorns, and attractive delicate flowers. The stem bark has a waxy texture and is flammable, so that even wet stems can be used as a kindling to light fires. The same applies to other *Monsonia* species such as *M. patersonii* (candle bush, *kersbossie*). The waxy part of the stem remains intact for many years and can be used to start a fire.

Morella cordifolia (=*Myrica cordifolia*) |Myricaceae| **WAXBERRY**, candle berry; *wasbessie* (Afrikaans) ■ This shrub grows on sand dunes in the southwestern Cape. It has small, shiny, heart-shaped leaves with finely serrated margins. The separate male and female flowers are inconspicuous. The plants tend to grow in fairly dense communities that may cover extensive areas of coastal sand dune. They send long runners to colonise and bind exposed areas of sand.

The small fruit is covered in a visible layer of "berry wax", which is technically a fat, not a wax. Berry wax used to be produced in January by placing the berries, or branches laden with the berries, into a large container of boiling water. The fat melts and floats to the surface so that it can be decanted off and cooled until it solidifies. The wax was then reheated to liquefy it so that it could be filtered through a cloth and allowed to cool again. This method of obtaining berry wax, described by Dawid Bester (pers. comm.), coincides with the earliest written description by Thunberg in 1772.

Berry wax was once eaten as a food by the Khoi, and it was also a valuable item of trade in the early days of the Cape Colony. Early records indicate that berry wax was a greenish colour and was sometimes bleached white, although the authors found that white wax results from simply boiling fruits stripped from the branches for half an hour. The wax is friable, and burns rapidly, so the colonists used to add tallow to the raw product. Dawid Bester (pers. comm.) reports that his mother used to make candles from berry wax by melting together equal quantities of berry wax and animal fat, adding a pinch of salt, and pouring the melted wax into moulds. Mrs. Bester made floor polish by melting together berry wax, paraffin and candle wax. Berry wax was used as a base for ointments used in dressing wounds, and to make soap. The root and stem bark was used medicinally for its astringent properties, and was also used to tan hides. This species is easy to propagate, and should be investigated for commercial production of berry wax, which can be used in the production of natural cosmetics, soaps, candles and medicinal ointments.

Muraltia spinosa (=*Nylandtia spinosa*) |Polygalaceae| **TORTOISE BERRY**; *skilpadbessie* (Afrikaans); *cargoe* (Khoi) ■ This spiny plant has small pink flowers and attractive red edible fruits. The stems are highly flammable, even when green, and are traditionally used as kindle to start a fire.

Passerina filiformis |Thymelaeaceae| **BAKER'S GONNA**; *bakkerbos, windmakerbos, bruin-gonna, bakkersgonna* (Afrikaans) ■ The *bakkerbos* is a shrub with long, slender branches and short, needle-shaped leaves that have a waxy secretion on their surfaces. The plant has been used to heat up ovens (Smith 1966) and the name *windmakerbos* is said to be derived from the tremendous blaze which is produced when the bush is set alight. The name baker's gonna and *bakkerbos* (baker's bush") commemorates an era at the Cape when the official licenced bakers used this plant. It is now quite scarce around Cape Town, so that the commercial use of the plant may have had an impact on this once abundant resource. In many parts of the interior, *Passerina corymbosa* (=*P. vulgaris*) is also known as *bakkerbos* and was used for the same purpose, namely to rapidly heat up the outside oven. The name *bakkerbos* is also applied to several other woody shrubs which could be used to produce rapid heat. *Bakbossie*, on the other hand, is used for *Conyza scabrida*, a small shrub with leafy branches that is used to make a hand broom for sweeping out ovens.

Passerina montana |Thymelaeaceae| **MOUNTAIN GONNA**; *berggonna* (Afrikaans); *dithaba, lehlaku, phuukgu* (Sotho) ■ This is a favourite fuel of the Basotho people (Moffett 2010) and is used fresh or dried.

Inflammable stems of the bushman's candle or candle bush (*Monsonia patersonii*)

Bushman's candle, the dry waxy stems of *Monsonia* species

Waxberry (*Morella cordifolia*) grows in sand dunes

Leaves and fruits of the waxberry (*Morella cordifolia*)

Wax from the waxberry floating to the surface

Leaves and flowers of the *bakkerbos* (*Passerina corymbosa*), one of several *Passerina* species used to heat up ovens

Baking bread in the *buite-oond* (outside oven)

Searsia undulata (=*Rhus undulata*) |Anacardiaceae| **T'KUNIE BUSH** ■ The wood is considered to be one of the most important and best-quality firewoods in Namaqaland (Archer 1990). *Searsia incisa*, *Calobota sericea* and *Tamarix usneoides* are alternatives. In Namibia, bees are smoked out by smouldering twigs of *Searsia tenuinervis* so that honey can be collected from their hives. The crushed leaves are applied to stings to reduce pain and swelling (Von Koenen 1996, 2001). Several *Searsia* species are occasionally used as firewood, but the choice depends on local availability, rather than good fuel characteristics.

Vachellia erioloba (=*Acacia erioloba*) |Fabaceae| **CAMEL THORN**; *kameeldoring* (Afrikaans) ■ The camel thorn is one of the most important sources of firewood of southern Africa, particularly because it grows in sparsely treed bushveld areas. The tree is umbrella-shaped and old specimens can be very picturesque, often with large nests build by sociable weavers. An infusion of the gum is taken for coughs, colds and tuberculosis, and a bark decoction is taken for diarrhoea. A root decoction is taken for coughs, and is used for nose bleeds. In times of famine, the Topnaar eat the pulp of the pods. The roasted seeds are used as a coffee substitute (Van den Eynden *et al.* 1992). The timber is hard and heavy; and the heartwood is a dark red to reddish-brown colour, surrounded by a pale yellow layer of sapwood. As a high-quality firewood, the camel thorn certainly has few equals. Increasing quantities of firewood and charcoal are imported into South Africa from Namibia with a potential danger of over-exploiting the resource.

Vachellia karroo (=*Acacia karroo*) |Fabaceae| **SWEET THORN**; *soetdoring* (Afrikaans) ■ This is one of the most widely distributed of all thorn trees. The wood is popular as a firewood in many dry parts of southern Africa. It is particularly valuable in the Karoo region, where there are practically no other trees available. Apart from the useful wood, the tree also produces an edible gum that has been marketed and sold as Cape gum. It is traditionally used for various ailments, including haemorrhage and oral thrush. Cape gum is similar to gum arabic, and has in the past found uses in the pharmaceutical industry. Leaves and bark are used in traditional medicine, mainly to treat diarrhoea and dysentery. Bark has been used to tan leather and it also serves as a cordage.

REFERENCES AND FURTHER READING: Archer, F.M. 1990. Planning with people – ethnobotany and African uses of plants in Namaqualand (South Africa). *Mitt. Inst. Allg. Bot. Hamburg* 23: 959–972. **Banks, P.F. 1981.** The planting of woodlots for the fuelwood requirements of Tribal Trust land populations in Zimbabwe/Rhodesia: a review of past and future development. *S. Afr. For. J.* 117: 13–15. **Basson, J.A. 1987.** Energy implications of accelerated urbanisation. *S. Afr. J. Sc.* 83: 284–290. **Best, M. 1979.** *The consumption of fuel for domestic purposes in three African villages.* M.Sc. thesis, University of Cape Town. **Campbell, A.C. 1976.** The traditional utilization of the Okavango Delta. In: Proceedings of the symposium on the Okavango Delta and its future utilization. Botswana Society, Gaborone. pp. 163–173. **Campbell, B.M. & Du Toit, R.F. 1988.** Relationships between wood resources and use of species for construction and fuel in the communal lands of Zimbabwe. *Monogr. Syst. Bot. Missouri Bot. Gard.* 25: 331–341. **Coates Palgrave, K. 1977.** *Trees of Southern Africa.* Struik, Cape Town. **Cunningham, A.B. 1989.** Indigenous plant use: balancing human needs and resources. In: Huntley, B.J. (ed.), *Biotic diversity in southern Africa*, Oxford University Press, pp. 93–106. **De Vaal, I.B. 1942.** Ysterbewerking deur die Bawenda en die Balemba in die Soutpansberg. *Tydskr. Wet. Kuns.* 3,1: 45–50. **Ferreira, F.H. 1948.** The apple of forgetfulness. *Afr. WildLife* 1,4: 69. **Friede, H.M. 1979.** Methods of traditional fire-making in pre-industrial South Africa. *Trees S. Afr.* 31,3: 58–63. **Furness, C.K. 1981a.** Estimating indigenous resources of fuelwood and poles and plantation requirements in the Tribal Trust lands of Zimbabwe/Rhodesia. *S. Afr. For. J.* 117: 6–9. **Furness, C.K. 1981b.** Some aspects of fuel-wood usage and consumption in African rural and urban areas in Zimbabwe/Rhodesia. *S. Afr. For. J.* 117: 10–12. **Le Roux, P.J. 1981.** Supply of fuel-wood for rural populations in South Africa. *S. Afr. For. J.* 117: 10–12. **Liengme, C.A. 1981.** Plants used by the Tsonga people of Gazankulu. *Bothalia* 13, 3&4: 501–518. **Liengme, C.A. 1983.** A study of wood use for fuel and building in an area of Gazankulu. *Bothalia* 14,2: 245–257. **Malan, J.S. & Owen-Smith, G.L. 1974.** The ethnobotany of Kaokoland. *Cimbebasia* Ser. B 2,5: 131–178. **Mannheimer, C.A. & Curtis, B.A. (eds) 2009.** *Le Roux and Müller's field guide to the trees and shrubs of Namibia.* Macmillan Education Namibia, Windhoek. **Moffett, R.O. 1979.** The genus *Sarcocaulon*. *Bothalia* 12: 581–613. **Nkaonja, R.S.W. 1981.** Rural fuel-wood and poles research project in Malawi: a general account. *S. Afr. For. J.* 117: 19–21. **Palmer, E. & Pitman, N. 1972.** *Trees of Southern Africa.* (3 vols). Balkema, Cape Town. **Poynton, R.J. 1975.** *Suid-Afrikaanse boomgids.* Tafelberg, Cape Town. **Shackleton, C.M., Grundy, I.M. & Williams, A. 2004.** Use of South Africa's woodlands for energy and construction. Chapter 11 in Lawes, M.J. *et al.* (eds), *Indigenous forests and woodlands in South Africa.* University of KwaZulu-Natal Press, Scottsville. **Smith, C.A. 1966.** Common names of South African Plants. *Mem. Bot. Surv. S. Afr.* 35. **Van Voorthuizen, E.G. 1976.** The mopane tree. *Botswana Notes and Records* 8: 223–230. **Von Koenen, E. 1996.** *Heil-, Gift- und Essbare Pflanzen in Namibia.* Klaus Hess Verlag, Göttingen. **Von Koenen, E. 2001.** *Medicinal, poisonous and edible plants in Namibia.* Klaus Hess Publishers, Windhoek and Göttingen.

FIRE MAKING & FIREWOOD

Flower heads of the sweet thorn tree (*Vachellia karroo*)

Fruits of the sweet thorn (*Vachellia karroo*)

Gum exuding from the bark of sweet thorn (*Vachellia karroo*)

Eating gum gathered from blue thorn (*Senegalia erubescens*)

Firewood from camel thorn (*Vachellia erioloba*)

Firewood from sweet thorn (*Vachellia karroo*)

Detail of a well-woven Venda *mufaro* basket made from the split stems of *Senegalia ataxacantha*

Large Bayei storage basket with a "forehead of the zebra" design

Bridle made from the leaves of the mokola palm (*Hyphaene petersiana*)

The tough bark of the wild cotton tree (*Hibiscus tiliaceus*) is often used for cord and rope

CHAPTER 19

Basketry, weaving & ropes

MANY DIFFERENT ITEMS made from fibres, fibrous stems or bark are used by rural people in their daily lives, such as rope or cord for tying, baskets for carrying and storing food and for catching fish, beer strainers, sitting mats and sleeping mats, hand brooms for sweeping and even items of clothing such as grass hats. The main fibre-yielding plants and their traditional uses are described below. Plants used for thatching are dealt with in Chapter 20 and fishing baskets are included in Chapter 15.

It is not generally known that a pre-colonial textile industry based on wild cotton (*Gossypium herbaceum*) existed in southern Africa in the thirteenth century and perhaps also earlier. Evidence came from hundreds of spinning weights excavated at Great Zimbabwe (Ellert 1984). This Iron Age technology continued up until as late as 1940.

Four cultures in southern Africa are particularly famous for their basketry: the Zulu, Hambukushu, Bayei and Basotho (Levinson 1984; Terry 1987; Cunningham & Terry 2006). Few people realise how sophisticated the basket-making process actually is. The basket types (Levinson 1984; Terry 1987; Lamprecht 1976; Cunningham 1987; Cunningham & Terry 2006) are quite similar but differ markedly in design (ornamentation). Zulu baskets have distinctly symmetrical designs. Hambukushu and Bayei baskets have both asymmetrical and symmetrical designs, with the Hambukushu often having a unique overstitch which is not seen in the baskets of other cultures (Levinson 1987). Bayei baskets have symbolic "standard" patterns, such as the "forehead (face) of the zebra" (*phatla ya pitsa*), "tail of the swallow" (*sentiia ya pelwana*), "knees of the tortoise" (*manole a khudu*), "tears of the giraffe" (*dikelede ya thutlwa*), "urine of the bull" (*moroto wa makaba*) and shield (*thebe*) designs (Levinson 1987). An example of a large Bayei storage basket with a "forehead of the zebra" design is shown here. The process of weaving palm leaves (from *Hyphaene coriacea* and *H. petersiana*) is described below. Basotho baskets are easily recognisable because they are not made from palm leaves, but from grass (Moffett 1997; Cunningham & Terry 2006). Traditionally, they do not have any surface designs either (Levinson 1987). In addition to baskets for household use, there are numerous other basket-like items required for daily life, such as fishing baskets (Cunningham 1987; McLaren 1958; Tinley 1964), beer strainers and grain stores (Lamprecht 1976; Cunningham 1987; Moffett 1997; Cunningham & Terry 2006).

Weaving materials for baskets do not come only from palm leaves, but from numerous grasses and grass-like plants as well (Gerstner 1938; Liengme 1981; Malan & Owen-Smith 1974; Jacot-Guillarmod 1971; Cawe & Ntloko 1997; Moffett 1997; Heinsohn & Cunningham 1991; Cunningham & Terry 2006). These include the stems of true grasses such as *Digitaria eriantha* (*isikhonko* in Zulu) and the non-grass stems of forest climbers (kanoti grass, *Flagellaria guineensis*; and *motsoketsane*, *Cocculus hirsutus*). Kanoti grass or *ugonothi* forms the basis of a small basketry industry at Port St Johns and Lusikisiki in the Eastern Cape Province.

Some items of clothing have traditionally been made from grass, such as grass skirts and the well-known traditional Basotho hat (*mokorotlo*) which is worn by men only (the women wore a smaller sun hat called a *mosetla*, see page 114). In former times, hats were made mainly from two grasses, *moseha* (*Merxmuellera macowanii*) or *mosua* (*M. drakensbergensis*). Other materials are sometimes used nowadays (Moffett 1997).

Adansonia digitata |Malvaceae| **BAOBAB** ■ See Chapter 3. The baobab is an iconic African tree with numerous myths and legends associated with it. With their impressive size and appearance, these trees leave a lasting impression on visitors from near and far. They also inspire photographers and authors, as can be seen from the numerous books that have been written about them. The massive stems are often hollow and may store water for use in the dry season, as well as provide shelter for animals and humans. In addition, the diversity of medicinal and non-medicinal uses captures the imagination (Wickens 1982).

The dry fruit pulp is not only very nutritious but has a delicious sour taste. It has become an important international food product that is incorporated into health drinks and energy bars (see Chapter 3). The bark, roots, leaves and fruit pulp are all of value in traditional medicine. Dry fruits are fashioned into containers and rattles for making music.

One of the most important parts of the tree is the smooth, fibrous bark that is used as a source of fibres for weaving. A flourishing trade has developed and beautiful handcrafted items such as mats, handbags and hats are freely available at roadside craft markets and curio shops. A remarkable feature of the baobab is its ability to survive even complete ringbarking. New bark is generated from the parenchyma-rich soft wood where the bark has been stripped off by elephants or humans.

Agave sisalana |Agavaceae| **SISAL**; *xikwenga* (Tsonga); *garingboom* (Afrikaans) ■ This exotic aloe-like plant was introduced as a fibre crop and is now widely distributed in southern Africa. The long, firm-textured leaves are bright green in colour, not greyish green as in the related *Agave americana*, which is also commonly encountered in southern Africa.

Agave plants flower only once and then die, but there are usually numerous suckers produced from the base of the plant to ensure regeneration. The thick flowering stems are sometimes used as fence poles in Gazankulu (Liengme 1981) and to make strong, lightweight ladders in the Karoo. After removal of the leaves, the stems (trunks) of *A. americana* are hollowed out, painted and sold as innovative flower pots (Jan September, pers. comm.; see photograph on page 6).

The leaves of *Agave sisalana* contain exceptionally strong fibres and the plant is produced on a commercial scale in tropical countries of the world for extraction of the fibres, to manufacture rope, mats and other fibre products. Commercial plantations were also established in southern Africa, but many of these have since been abandoned. In rural areas, leaf fibres are still extracted from the leaves of *Agave sisalana* for ropes and for weaving, and it seems that *A. sisalana* has partly replaced *Sansevieria* species in some rural areas as the main source of strong fibres for string, rope, table mats and floor mats.

Brachystegia boehmii |Fabaceae| **MUFUTI**; *mapfuti* (Shona) ■ This tree is widely distributed in Zimbabwe (and further north) and is one of two main sources of bark fibre used for *gudza* cloth that is particularly prevalent amongst the Shona-speaking people of the Masvingo Province of Zimbabwe (Ellert 1984). The other is also from the legume family: *Julbernardia globifera* (*munhondo* in Shona). Bark fibre was obtained from these trees by cutting away large sections of bark from mature trees. The large piece of bark was buried in the ground to loosen the corky outer layer. This outer layer was gradually loosened with special tools, so that only a "sheet" of fibres remained. This was used as a blanket after stretching and softening. A more common practice was to weave or knot the soft inner bark to produce *gudza* cloth and *nhova* bags. Bark *gudza* cloth is warm and pliable and has been used for many different household items (storage bags, beer strainers) and clothing (garments and dresses with geometric patterns).

Another bark fibre came from the bark of the horn-pod tree (*Diplorhynchus condylocarpon*, *mutowa* in Shona), which belongs to the Apocynaceae family. In Zimbabwe, the cloth was woven or knotted into pieces as large as blankets but unfortunately the methods were never recorded (Ellert 1984). The material, known as *gupo*, was worn by women.

Baobab trees (*Adansonia digitata*)

Bag woven from the bark fibres of the baobab (*Adansonia digitata*)

Sisal plant (*Agave sisalana*) in a rural area, used locally as a source of fibre

Cannabis sativa |Cannabinaceae| **HEMP** ■ See also Chapter 9. The hemp plant is a robust erect annual similar to *dagga* but with no psychoactive effects. This tall form of the species was specifically selected over millennia for the production of fibres and seed oil and is known botanically as *Cannabis sativa* subsp. *sativa*. Subsp. *indica* is the source of medicine and mood-altering drugs – see Chapter 9. Hemp should be treated as a separate entity to *dagga*, as it has very low yields of the intoxicating cannabinoids.

The hemp plant is sensitive to day length and will flower before the required duration of vegetative growth, resulting in short stems. This is one of the main obstacles for cultivating the crop in tropical or subtropical areas, but the development of cultivars that are not sensitive to day length is currently receiving attention. The crop can be manipulated to produce either seed or fibre, depending on market demand. After harvesting, a retting process is required to extract the fibres.

Hemp fibres are exceptionally strong and clothing made from it can withstand washing and wearing much better than linen or cotton. The plant was used to make rope in ancient Egypt (Manniche 1989). In the days of the sailing ship, hemp fibres for sails and ropes were of strategic, commercial and military importance. During the late 1800s and early 1900s, hemp was an important commercial commodity, which contributed substantially to agricultural development in North America. Nowadays, it is rapidly gaining ground as a source of high-quality raw materials for industrial applications.

Products from this hardy plant include superior paper, fibre board, insulation, recyclable vehicle parts (hemp is used to replace glass fibres in fibre glass), textiles, carpets, horse bedding, veterinary products, cosmetics, soaps, paints, animal feed, foods and beverages. Innovative product development is one of the features of the modern hemp industry. Hemp clothing and other hemp products are becoming increasingly popular worldwide as the advantages of this ecologically friendly crop become known, and about 30 countries are rapidly scaling up hemp production. Since hemp fibre board is much stronger and more elastic than wood composites, forestry companies are also showing a strong interest in hemp production.

The development of a viable hemp industry in southern Africa is lagging behind initiatives elsewhere, but investment in the development of suitable local strains of plants has begun. A major problem has been the red tape that had to be negotiated because of the confusion between hemp and *dagga*: "Its rope not dope, say hemp farmers" (Haffajee 1998).

Cocculus hirsutus |Menispermaceae| ***RISOTSE*** (Tsonga); *lexhi* (Seyei); *motsoketsane* (Thimbu-kushu) ■ This plant is a woody vine (creeper) with slender stems. It occurs in the tropical parts of southern Africa and is commonly used in basketry. The thin stems may form the central core or coil of the Ngamiland baskets, particularly when the overstitch Hambukushu method is used. The Tsonga people of South Africa make conical baskets (*xirundzu*) from the stems (Liengme 1981). Venda people sometimes use the stems on their own as weaving material.

Cyperus textilis |Cyperaceae| **MAT SEDGE**; *matjiesgoed* (Afrikaans); *imisi grass* (Xhosa) ■ The stems or culms of various species of *Cyperus* are used in southern Africa to make mats (see Chapter 20) but are also used for weaving, including *C. textilis*, *C. natalensis* and *C. sexangularis*. The former species has rounded stems like *C. textilis*, while *C. sexangularis* has very characteristic angled stems. Traditional articles made from *Cyperus* species in the Ingwavuma district of KwaZulu-Natal are listed by Cunningham (1987). In addition to sleeping mats, the traditional collecting basket (*umthaba*), winnowing basket (*inhlelo*), grinding mat (*isithebe*) and rolled twine (*phota inthambo*) are all made from the *Cyperus* species listed above. Intricate weaving with *Cyperus* stems or leaves is frequently seen in southern Africa. Examples shown here are the traditional round-bottomed harvesting basket (*ingobozi* in Xhosa), which is balanced on the head for carrying and the traditional cutting board (*isiteli* in Xhosa).

BASKETRY, WEAVING & ROPES

Plantation of hemp (*Cannabis sativa* subsp. *sativa*)

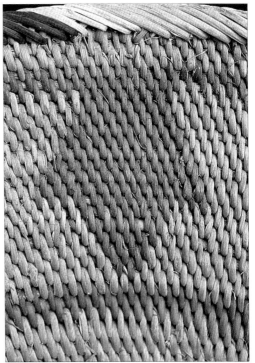

Detail of a Venda basket, woven from stems of *Cocculus hirsutus*

Traditional harvesting basket and cutting board, woven from stems of *imisi* grass (*Cyperus textilis*)

Dais cotonifolia |Thymelaeaceae| ***BASBOOM***, *kannabas* (Afrikaans); pompon tree; *intolzane* (Xhosa); *intolzwane emnyama* (Zulu) ■ This popular garden tree with its attractive heads of pink flowers occurs naturally from the Eastern Cape Province of South Africa to Zimbabwe and Mozambique. The strong, fibrous bark has been used for weaving (Smith 1966) and for tying bundles of firewood. When plaited, it makes a very strong rope.

Eragrostis plana |Poaceae| ***UMTSHIKI*** (Xhosa, Zulu); *modula* (Sotho); tough love-grass; *taaipoleragrostis* (Afrikaans) ■ This tough grass is widely distributed in southern and central Africa. It is characteristically difficult to pull out of the ground. The leaves are popular for weaving baskets, hats and bangles (Moffett 1997; Cunningham & Terry 2006).

Flagellaria guineensis |Flagellariaceae| **KANOTI GRASS**; *ugonothi* (Xhosa) ■ This is a bamboo-like forest climber with stems and leaves closely resembling those of a grass. The leaves taper to slender tips which curl and form tendrils. These tendrils cling firmly to leaves and twigs, helping the kanoti plant to climb towards the light. Small, yellow flowers are followed by bright red berries (Cawe & Ntloko 1997). The fruits are edible and known to be eaten in Mozambique.

Kanoti grass occurs all along the eastern coastal parts of southern Africa, but is only used for weaving and basketry in the Pondoland region (Cawe & Ntloko 1997). In this region, the plants are very common along the beach and on forest margins, where they sometimes form dense masses. New stems develop where plants have been cut, so that it is possible to harvest this resource on a sustainable basis. The stems, which may be as thick as a finger, are split into strips (up to four or more strips if it is a thick stem) and these are used in basketry. Beautiful and exceptionally strong baskets are distributed from the Port St Johns and Lusikisiki areas to many parts of southern Africa for sale in the large centres. The intact stems are traditionally used to weave the railings on ox sledges (Gordon Sink, pers. comm.). A suitable forked tree is used, and kanoti stems are woven between pegs driven into the sledge.

Gossypium herbaceum* subsp. *africanum |Malvaceae| **WILD COTTON** ■ Wild cotton is a shrub of up to one and a half metres tall with hairy stems and large, lobed leaves. Each of the yellow flowers has three large bracts with toothed margins, forming a so-called epicalyx around the real calyx. The smooth fruit capsule splits open to release several densely hairy seeds. Wild cotton is indigenous and endemic to southern Africa and is widely distributed in the subtropical region, from Namibia and Angola through Botswana to Zimbabwe, Mozambique and South Africa.

No attempts seem to have been made to cultivate wild cotton in southern Africa, so that harvesting was done from wild plants (Ellert 1984). It has been suggested that the cultivated form of cotton (*Gossypium herbaceum* var. *herbaceum*) was developed from the southern African wild cotton, after early traders introduced it from Zimbabwe to North Africa (Hutchinson 1962). However, the exact origin of cultivated cotton is shrouded in mystery and we may never know with certainty if southern Africa (Zimbabwe) was indeed the origin of cultivated cotton before *Gossypium* species from the New World (*G. hirsutum* and *G. barbadense*) were introduced and re-introduced into Africa. It is generally accepted that two African cotton species, *G. herbaceum* and *G. arboretum*, are ancestral not only to Old World diploid cottons, but also to the New World tetraploid cottons before they were domesticated (Wendel 1995).

The spinning and weaving of wild cotton was practised in Zimbabwe up until 1940, using Iron Age techniques. Traditional cotton weaving seems to have completely died out in Zimbabwe, but fortunately the salient points were documented (Ellert 1984). Wild cotton was collected from wild plants and the bolls (of which some had red fibres) were cleaned of plant debris. The lint was placed into a small gourd (*dembe*) from which it was spun onto a spindle (*chivhinga*). Spinning and weaving were exclusively done by men (Ellert 1984), who wove the spun yarn on low looms.

Baskets made from kanoti grass (*Flagellaria guineensis*)

Kanoti grass, showing the bamboo-like stems and leaves

Detail of a basket woven from kanoti grass (*Flagellaria guineensis*)

Flowers and berries of kanoti grass (*Flagellaria guineensis*)

Wild cotton (*Gossypium herbaceum* subsp. *africanum*)

Grewia flava |Malvaceae| **VELVET RAISIN** ■ See Chapter 3. The tough, fibrous bark is commonly used in central and western Botswana for tying (see photograph on page 347 of fire making for example, where the fire-drill is tied with *Grewia* bark). It is also used in weaving (Terry 1994). The bark is wrapped around the grass coils in coil-constructed baskets (used in the same way as palm leaves elsewhere) and the elastic branches may form the rims of winnowing baskets.

Hibiscus tiliaceus |Malvaceae| **WILD COTTON TREE**; *lihlombe* (Ronga/Tsonga); *wildekatoenboom* (Afrikaans) ■ The plant is a shrub or small tree with large rounded leaves and large yellow flowers with purple centres. The distribution area of the species is a narrow coastal strip from the Eastern Cape Province in South Africa northwards to the Mozambique coast. Plants occur along the edges of lagoons and along river banks. The tough fibrous bark is widely used as rope and twine in building, sewing mats and generally to bind things together.

Hyphaene coriacea |Arecaceae or Palmae| **ILALA PALM**; *ilala* (Zulu) ■ (Also see *Hyphaene petersiana* – *mokola* or *mokolwane* – in Chapter 6). This palm is closely related to the mokola palm (*H. petersiana*) and the two trees are practically identical in the appearance of the stem and leaves. The only clear difference lies in the fruits: pear-shaped in this species, and rounded in the case of *H. petersiana*. The wild date palm (*Phoenix reclinata*, see Chapter 3) and the borassus palm (*Borassus aethiopum*) are both also used as fibre and food sources and for making palm wine. The latter is a graceful, erect palm, similar to the ilala palm, but it has a distinct swelling in the middle of the stem and the fruit is much larger, with three seeds instead of the single seed as in *Hyphaene* species.

The ilala palm is a coastal species and is restricted to the east coastal region of southern Africa, from KwaZulu-Natal and the Mpumalanga Province in South Africa to southern Mozambique and the adjoining parts of eastern Zimbabwe. The palm belt in South Africa alone was estimated to occupy an area of 156 000 hectares with 10.5 million trees producing about 33 million leaves per year (Moll 1972). Cunningham (1988) estimated that about 2.5 million leaves can be harvested sustainably in this area. The mokola palm (*H. petersiana*) occurs in the far north of Namibia, northern Botswana, northern Zimbabwe, Mozambique, Angola, Zambia and Malawi. In contrast to the ilala palm, it was found to be locally over-exploited in Botswana (Cunningham & Milton 1987). Neither of the two *Hyphaene* species is cultivated. The seeds do not germinate readily and the plants grow very slowly. Since they develop a strong tap root, it is not easy to transplant these palms, so that they are rarely seen in gardens and parks.

The methods of harvesting, preparing for weaving and the actual weaving process itself are described in clear detail by Terry (1994). Similar methods are used for both palm species (i.e. in Botswana and in Maputaland). Pliable young leaves are harvested before the folded leaf segments unfold. Only about one-third of the young leaf is removed (a length of 40 to 100 centimetres), so that the same leaf can develop further and be harvested again. The leaf ends are prepared for weaving by boiling them in water for half an hour and then drying them in the sun. They may also be boiled in one of the natural dyes (see Chapter 16) for one or two hours, depending on the desired colour. According to Terry (1994) some weavers prefer to remove the tougher outer edges of the leaf segments before boiling, to ensure that the material remains its natural creamy white colour. In any case, only the inner part of the leaf segments is actually used for weaving. The outer edges (called *ditsitsiri*) may be used to form the central coil for coil-built baskets. Weavers may also use grass such as *Eragrostis pallens* or creepers such as *Cocculus hirsutus* to form the coils (Terry 1994). A strip of palm leaf soaked in rain water is then wrapped around the coil by weaving it through small holes made with an awl at regular intervals along the previously wrapped coil row. The work continues in a spiral until the basket reaches the required size, when the last piece of the coil is reduced in thickness to gradually merge with the last coil row. An overstitch of one stitch over two coils can be woven with dyed leaf to create design or texture (texture was originally functional, to

Trees of the ilala palm (*Hyphaene coriacea*)

The young palm fronds are harvested for weaving before they unfold

Example of a Zulu basket woven from ilala palm leaves

"catch" the cereal grains during the winnowing process). According to Terry (1987) it takes about 25 hours of actual weaving to produce a small basket 30 centimetres in diameter. This does not include harvesting of materials, dyeing and other preparations.

The basket-weaving industries of Ngamiland and Maputaland are important as a source of income for rural women. The many different types (shapes) of baskets produced in Ngamiland are described by Lamprecht (1976). These include the winnowing tray (*leselo*), the open carrying basket (*setego*), and the more or less bottle-shaped storage basket (*setutwane*). Around Hluhluwe in KwaZulu-Natal, the decorated beer basket is the most popular tourist item (Sutton 1994) but several other products are also made. Although basket weaving is hard work, it provides an opportunity to alleviate poverty in rural areas and to preserve traditional knowledge and artistic skills.

Juncus kraussii │Juncaceae│ **SALTMARSH RUSH**, matting-rush; *uduli* (Xhosa); *incema* (Zulu); *soutmoerasbiesie* (Afrikaans) ■ See Chapter 20. The stems are one of the favourite weaving materials in parts of KwaZulu-Natal, especially for making the traditional sleeping mat or *icansi*.

Phoenix reclinata │Arecaceae or Palmae│ **WILD DATE PALM**; *wildedadelpalm* (Afrikaans); *mutshevho* (Venda); *isundu* (Xhosa, Zulu) ■ The leaves of the wild date palm are widely used in southern Africa for weaving, although they are less popular than those of the ilala palm. Hand brooms are made by pounding the end of a suitable length of stem so that the fibres separate.

Phragmites australis │Poaceae│ **COMMON REED**; *fluitjiesriet* (Afrikaans); *umhlanga* (Zulu) ■ See Chapter 20. The hollow stems are sometimes used to construct winnowing baskets and, in Botswana, it is the traditional material for the large grain storage baskets (Terry 1994).

Sansevieria aethiopica │Asparagaceae│ **BOWSTRING HEMP**, piles root; *kai, ghaiwortel* (Khoi); *xikwenga* (Tsonga); *aambeiwortel* (Afrikaans); *isikholokotho* (Xhosa) ■ The plant is a tough semi-succulent with erect, hard, mottled leaves arising from thick, fleshy rhizomes. Attractive cream-coloured flower clusters are followed by fleshy orange berries. There are three common species of *Sansevieria* in southern Africa (Obermeyer 1992), all of which are used for their tough leaf fibres. *Sansevieria aethiopica* has numerous half-folded (v-shaped) leaves with a coarse surface, while *S. hyacinthoides* has two to eight flat, smooth leaves; *S. pearsonii* has long cylindrical leaves with narrow longitudinal grooves. *Sansevieria aethiopica* and *S. pearsonii* are widely distributed, while *S. hyacinthoides* is confined to the eastern parts of the region. The plants grow easily and are commonly used as pot plants and garden ornamentals.

The leaves are cut during the growing season, as the fibres are said to be weaker in the dry season. The traditional way to extract the fibres from the leaves is to scrape the leaf on the leg or thigh with the tip of the digging stick or other wooden instrument. If a hard surface is used to support the leaf during the scraping operation, the fibres are broken. All green leaf material is carefully scraped away, so that only the white fibres remain. These are divided into three equal bundles and are converted to rope or twine by rolling them on the thigh with the palm of the hand. The forward stroke of the hand results in the fibres within each individual bundle being rolled up, while the backstroke rolls the three bundles around each other in the opposite direction. In this way, an incredibly strong twine or rope is produced. In some parts of southern Africa, the exotic sisal (*Agave sisalana*) has replaced *Sansevieria* as the main source of rope.

The rhizomes and leaves of *Sansevieria* species are important traditional medicines. Juice from a heated leaf is squeezed into the ear or mouth to treat ear infections, earache or toothache. Fresh or boiled rhizomes are eaten to treat haemorrhoids, ulcers and intestinal parasites. The medicinal value in treating haemorrhoids can clearly be linked to the presence of ruscogenin and related sapogenins, which are used commercially as anti-inflammatory agents and venotonics.

BASKETRY, WEAVING & ROPES

The common bowstring hemp (*Sansevieria aethiopica*)

Flowering plant of the eastern bowstring hemp (*Sansevieria hyacinthoides*)

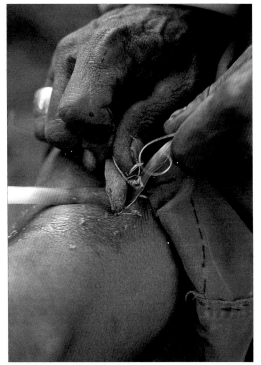

Traditional method of scraping the leaf of bowstring hemp to extract the fibres

Strong rope made in the traditional way from bowstring hemp (*Sansevieria aethiopica*)

Senegalia ataxacantha (=*Acacia ataxacantha*) |Fabaceae| **MULUWA** (Tsonga, Venda); flame thorn; *vlamdoring* (Afrikaans) ■ The plant is a scraggly shrub or tree with scattered thorns on the branches, elongated spikes of fluffy flowers and attractive bright red pods. It is an important source of craft material in the northern parts of South Africa (especially in the Mpumalanga Province – Liengme 1981, and in Limpopo Province – Mabogo, pers. comm.), where strips of wood are commonly used to make several types of baskets (Liengme 1981), including a shallow winnowing basket (*rihlelo*). An example of a well-made *mufaro* basket is shown at the introduction of this chapter. The *mufaro* or traditional Venda basket is associated with guests, who traditionally bring a *mufaro* full of gifts or niceties (*zwidyangudyangu*) when they visit a family. The hosts in turn fill the same *mufaro* with gifts for the visitor to take back home.

Sparrmannia africana |Sparrmanniaceae or Malvaceae| **AFRICAN HEMP**; *wilde stokroos* (Afrikaans) ■ The plant is a shrub or small tree with very large, hairy, lobed leaves and attractive white flowers with yellow and purple stamens. African hemp is indigenous to a relatively small area on the southeastern coast of South Africa. The plant grows easily in cultivation and has been popular as a greenhouse plant in Europe. It is occasionally seen in gardens in southern Africa, but deserves to be planted more often. The traditional uses of the stem fibres appear to be unrecorded, but they were tested in Europe and found to be of excellent quality. About 100 years ago, commercial harvesting was started at Storm's River by the Khama Fibre Syndicate, but the industry never gained momentum. With a renewed interest in natural bast fibres, this plant may once again prove to be of commercial value.

Sporobolus africanus |Poaceae| **RAT'S TAIL DROPSEED**; *umtshiki* (Xhosa, Zulu); *umsingizane* (Xhosa); *taaipol* (Afrikaans); *motolo a maholo* (Sotho); *moshanje* (Tswana) ■ This tough grass is similar to *Eragrostis plana* and has the same common name in several languages. Both species are very difficult to uproot and have strong leaves that are popular material used in weaving and basketry. Even when not in flower, *Sporobolus africanus* can easily be distinguished from *Eragrostis plana* by the rounded leaf sheaths (they are distinctly flattened in *Eragrostis plana*). Both species are commonly used to weave traditional bangles in the Eastern Cape, KwaZulu-Natal and Swaziland (Cunningham & Terry 2006). Weaving is done in late summer or early autumn while the grass is still green but mature. The bangles are initially green but turn yellow when they dry out. Several traditional bangle weave patterns have been recorded and illustrated by Cunningham & Terry (2006) and earlier authors. Numerous names exist for the various designs, often based on comparisons with snakes and snake parts. Necklaces and bangles are more often made from other materials such as palm leaves, *Sansevieria* fibres, sedges, animal hairs and copper, brass or aluminium wire.

Sterculia africana |Malvaceae| **AFRICAN STAR-CHESTNUT**; *bosluisboom* (Afrikaans); *omuhako* (Herero) ■ The strong, fibrous bark is used in Namibia for making hats, mats and ropes (Mannheimer & Curtis 2009).

Sterculia rogersii |Malvaceae| **STAR-CHESTNUT**; *sterkastaiing* (Afrikaans); *lumbu* (Swazi); *samani* (Tsonga) ■ The bark fibres are used to make strong rope and twine. It has been used to weave fishing nets (Coates Palgrave 2002).

Strelitzia nicolai |Strelitziaceae| **NATAL WILD BANANA**; *kuswildepiesang* (Afrikaans); *ikhamanga* (Xhosa); *isigude* (Zulu) ■ See Chapter 2. Fibres from the leaf petioles are used as strong rope in the construction of houses and fish kraal fences (Cunningham & Terry 2006). The fence is constructed by tying together the leaf petioles of wild date palm (*Phoenix reclinata*) which are used as poles. *Strelitzia* petiole fibres are also used for decorative weaving in the construction of Tembe-Thonga houses, of which it is a special feature.

BASKETRY, WEAVING & ROPES

Flame thorn or *muluwa* (*Senegalia ataxacantha*)

Flowers of flame thorn (*Senegalia ataxacantha*)

Flowering plant of African hemp (*Sparrmannia africana*)

Flowers of African hemp (*Sparrmannia africana*)

Rat's tail dropseed or *taaipol* (*Sporobolus africanus*)

Tough love-grass or *osgras* (*Eragrostis plana*)

Terminalia sericea |Combretaceae| **SILVER CLUSTER-LEAF**; *mogonono* (Tswana); *moxonono* (Northern Sotho); *mususu* (Shona, Venda); *amangwe* (Zulu); *vaalboom* (Afrikaans) ■ This is a small to medium-sized tree with an erect trunk and widespreading crown. The leaves are silver hairy and crowded near the branch tips and the cream-coloured flowers, which have an unpleasant smell, are followed by winged fruits. The species is characteristic of sandy savanna areas over a very large part of southern Africa. The roots or stem bark are used in traditional medicine to treat stomach disorders, diarrhoea and several other complaints. Roots yield a yellow-brown dye but are seldom used for dyeing. The hard yellow wood is used for implement handles, yokes for oxen, and furniture. Bark is stripped from young trees and is commonly used as a strong cord or rope.

Xerophyta retinervis |Velloziaceae| **MONKEY'S TAIL**; *bobbejaanstert* (Afrikaans); *tshikundandazi* (Venda) ■ The tough leaves are used by the Lobedu people in the Limpopo Province to weave beer strainers called *lethodo* (Cunningham & Terry 2006). Stems of *Triumfetta* species and the leaf midribs of wild banana (*Ensete ventricosa*) are used for the same purpose.

REFERENCES AND FURTHER READING: Brink, M. & Achigan-Dako, E.G. (eds) 2012. *Plant resources of tropical Africa 16. Fibres.* PROTA Foundation, Wageningen / Backhuys Publishers, Leiden. **Cawe, S.G. & Ntloko, S.S.T. 1997.** Distribution, uses and exploitation patterns of *Flagellaria guineensis* Schumach. with particular reference to Port St Johns, South Africa. *S. Afr. J. Bot.* 63: 233–238. **Coates Palgrave, K. 1977.** *Trees of Southern Africa.* Struik, Cape Town. **Coates Palgrave, M. 2002.** *Keith Coates Palgrave trees of Southern Africa.* 3rd ed. Struik Publishers, Cape Town. **Cunningham, A.B. 1987.** Commercial craftwork: Balancing out human needs and resources. *S. Afr. J. Bot.* 53: 259–266. **Cunningham, A.B. 1988.** Leaf production and utilization in *Hyphaene coriacea*: Management guidelines for commercial harvesting. *S. Afr. J. Bot.* 54: 189–195. **Cunningham, A.B. & Milton, A.S. 1987.** Effects of the basket weaving industry on mokola palm, *Hyphaene petersiana*, and on dye plants in N.W. Botswana. *Econ. Bot.* 41(3): 386–402. **Cunningham, A.B. & Terry, M.E. 2006.** *African basketry.* Fernwood Press, Cape Town. **Ellert, H. 1984.** *The material culture of Zimbabwe.* Longman, Zimbabwe. **Fanshawe, D.B. 1967.** The vegetable ivory palm – *Hyphaene ventricosa* Kirk – its ecology, silviculture & utilisation. *Kirkia* 6: 105–116. **Gibbs-Russell, G.E. et al. 1990.** *Grasses of southern Africa.* National Botanical Institute, Pretoria. **Haffajee, F. 1998.** It's rope not dope, say hemp farmers. *Mail & Guardian.* Vol. 14, No. 26. July 3 to 9, 1998. **Heinsohn, R.-D. & Cunningham, A.B. 1991.** Utilization and potential cultivation of the saltmarsh rush, *Juncus kraussii.* *S. Afr. J. Bot.* 57: 1–5. **Hutchinson, J.B. 1962.** The history and relationships of the world's cotton. *Endeavour* 21: 5–15. **Jacot-Guillarmod, A. 1971.** *Flora of Lesotho.* J. Cramer, Lehre. **Jurgens, R. 1999.** Archaic laws hinder hemp's crop potential. *Reconstruct.* Supplement to the *Sunday Independent*, February 28, 1999. **Kingwill, H. 1998.** Coming out of the closet. *The Big Issue*, Cape Town. Issue 14, Vol. 2. September 1998. **Lamprecht, D. 1976.** Basketry in Ngamiland. *Botswana Notes and Records* 8: 179–187. **Larson, T.J. 1975.** Craftwork of the Hambukushu of Botswana. *Botswana Notes and Records* 7: 109–120. **Levinsohn, R. 1984.** *Art and craft of southern Africa. Treasures in transition.* Delta Books, Johannesburg. **Liengme, C.A. 1981.** Plants used by the Tsonga people of Gazankulu. *Bothalia* 13, 3&4: 501–518. **Obermeyer, A.A. 1992.** *Sansevieria. Flora of Southern Africa* 5: 5–9. National Botanical Institute, Pretoria. **Malan, J.S. & Owen-Smith, G.L. 1974.** The ethnobotany of Kaokoland. *Cimbebasia* Ser. B 2,5: 131–178. **Mannheimer, C.A. & Curtis, B.A. (eds) 2009.** *Le Roux and Müller's Field Guide to the trees and shrubs of Namibia.* Macmillan Education Namibia, Windhoek. **Manniche, L. 1989.** *An ancient Egyptian herbal.* British Museum Press, London. **McLaren, P.I.R. 1958.** Fishing devices of Central and Southern Africa. *Rhodes-Livingstone Museum Occasional Paper* 12: 1–48. **Moffett, R.O. 1997.** *Grasses of the eastern Free State. Their description and uses.* Uniqwa, Phuthaditjaba. **Moll, E.J. 1972.** The distribution, abundance and utilization of the lala palm, *Hyphaene natalensis*, in Tongaland, Natal. *Bothalia* 10: 627–636. **Palmer, E. & Pitman, N. 1972.** *Trees of Southern Africa.* (3 vols). Balkema, Cape Town. **Robinson, R. 1996.** *The great book of hemp.* Park Street Press, Vermont. **Shackleton, S.E. 1990.** Socio-economic importance of *Cymbopogon validus* in Mkambati Game Reserve, Transkei. *S. Afr. J. Bot.* 56(6): 675–682. **Shaw, E.M. & Van Warmelo, N.J. 1974.** Material culture of the Cape Nguni. 2. Technology. *Ann. S. Afr. Mus.* 58,2: 103–214. **Small, E. & Cronquist, A. 1976.** A practical and natural taxonomy for *Cannabis. Taxon* 25: 405–435. **Small, E. 1995.** Hemp. Chapter 9 in: Smartt, J. & Simmonds, N.W. (eds), *Evolution of crop plants,* 2nd ed., pp. 28–32. Longman, London. **Smith, C.A. 1966.** Common names of South African plants. *Mem. Bot. Surv. S. Afr.* 35. **Steyn, H.P. 1981.** Nharo plant utilization. An overview. *Khoisis* 1. **Sutton, M. 1994.** ... from Ilala Weavers. *The Indigenous Plant Use Newsletter* 2(2): 4. **Terry, M.E. 1987.** The anatomy of an Ngamiland basket. *Botswana Notes and Records* 19: 151–155. **Terry, M.E. 1994.** Made in Botswana – crafts from indigenous plants. *The Indigenous Plant Use Newsletter* 2(2): 1,3. **Tinley, K.G. 1964.** Fishing methods of the Thonga tribe in north-eastern Zululand and southern Moçambique. *Lammergeyer* 3: 9–39. **Van Oudtshoorn, F. 2012.** *Guide to grasses of southern Africa.* 3rd ed. Briza Publications, Pretoria. **Wickens, G.E. 1982.** The baobab – Africa's upside-down tree. *Kew Bull.* 37(2): 173–209. **Wendel, J.F. 1995.** Cotton. In: Smartt, J. & Simmonds, N.W. (eds), *Evolution of crop plants,* 2nd ed., pp. 1358–366. Longman, London. **Zeven, A.C. & De Wet, J.M.J. 1982.** *Dictionary of cultivated plants and their regions of diversity.* Centre for Agricultural Publishing and Documentation, Wageningen. **Zohary, D. & Hopf, M. 1994.** *Domestication of plants in the Old World,* 2nd ed. Clarendon Press, Oxford.

BASKETRY, WEAVING & ROPES

Leaves and fruits of the silver cluster-leaf (*Terminalia sericea*)

Tree of the silver cluster-leaf (*Terminalia sericea*)

Flowering plant of the monkey's tail (*Xerophyta retinervis*)

Flowering plant of the wild banana (*Ensete ventricosa*)

Zulu sleeping mat and traditional beehive hut (*qhugwane* hut)

Roof being thatched with Albertinia thatching reed (*Thamnochortus insignis*)

Restio brooms (*rietbesems*) for sale

Hand brooms made from the fibrous stems of wild date palm (*Phoenix reclinata*)

A supply of common reed (*Phragmites australis*)

CHAPTER 20

Thatching, mats & brooms

THATCHING IS A universal and age-old art, passed on from one generation to the next. Unfortunately, the traditional methods are gradually being replaced by modern methods and materials. The use of natural building materials such as poles, reeds and grass are still commonly encountered in rural areas and has several advantages. They are renewable resources and their use is labour-intensive, thereby offering job opportunities while at the same time preserving the traditional knowledge of building and thatching.

Any grass or fibrous material can serve as thatch, but the species mentioned below are the most popular and widely used. Some of these species have considerable commercial value in the thatching industry nowadays. In the central Kalahari, the huts and shelters are not systematically thatched but simply covered with tufts of silky bushman grass (*Stipagrostis uniplumis*) to form a more or less waterproof layer. In contrast, there are the intricately and decoratively woven roofs of the Tembe-Thonga huts (Cunningham & Gwala 1986) or the carefully insulated and long-lasting roof of a modern thatch house (Long 1978). Popular thatching grasses include *umgunga* or *tamboekie* grass (*Cymbopogon nardus*), *idobo* or common thatch grass (mainly *Hyparrhenia hirta* but also *H. dregeana, H. anamesa* and *H. filipendula*), *nduli* grass or cottonwool grass (*Imperata cylindrica*) and yellow thatching grass (*Hyperthelia dissoluta*). Thatching reed or *dekriet* is not derived from true grass but from restios. It comes from the Cape and include Albertinia thatching reed (*Thamnochortus insignis*, the main commercial source) and Cape thatching reed (*Elegia tectorum*). The common reed or *umhlanga* (*Phragmites australis*) is widely used for walls and bomas, though rarely for thatching. The methods of harvesting, preparing and bundling thatching grass and thatching reed are described below.

There are interesting regional and cultural differences in the architectural styles and building methods used in southern Africa. These have been recorded by Walton (1948), Knuffel (1973), Malan & Owen-Smith (1974), Van Voorthuizen & Odell (1976), Johnson (1982), Liengme (1981, 1983), Cunningham & Gwala (1986) and Cunningham & Terry (2006). Only the basic principles of building and thatching are summarised here. Detailed technical information and modern methods of thatching can be found in Long (1978). The traditional dwelling or hut is usually of a circular design, and is started with a circular row of strong upright poles to support the roof. The walls are formed by a lattice of flexible poles, woven or tied onto the support poles, filled in with mud and cow-dung and plastered inside and outside. The roof framework is usually partly constructed on the ground and is then lifted onto the walls before they are plastered. The rafters are sturdy poles, with flexible saplings or stems curved and tied to the rafters with bark cord or rope to act as thatching battens or withes. Thatching starts at the verge of the roof and successive rows of thatch bundles are tied down onto the battens at regular intervals. Each successive layer conceals the pole, rope or wire that was used to tie down the previous layer. Instead of thatch bundles, pre-prepared thatching mats are sometimes used in traditional hut construction. This method is described by Liengme (1981) and in detail by Cunningham & Gwala (1986). In Namaqualand, the entire house is built from reed mats (see *Pseudoschoenus inanis, Juncus acutus* and *Cyperus marginatus*).

Various types of mats are made to serve different purposes, of which thatching mats used for house construction have already been mentioned. The art of making traditional sleeping mats and sitting mats has fortunately been kept alive, partly as a result of the income generated by craft markets. The soft, spongy stems or culms of sedges (*Cyperus* species) and the saltmarsh rush or *incema* (*Juncus kraussii*) are particularly popular for sitting and sleeping mats (see below).

Hand brooms are needed to sweep meal from the grinding stone, and to sweep inside and outside the house. A wide range of grasses and sedges are suitable for making brooms and hand brooms, and there are interesting regional differences in the style and choice of materials. Stems used for thatching are often also suitable for broom making. In the Cape, thatching reeds or restios (*riete*) are traditionally used for brooms, known as the *rietbesem* or *werfbesem* in Afrikaans. In Lesotho, several grasses are suitable for this purpose and the brooms vary in style and use. Some are for outside the hut and others for use inside. In Maputaland, small hand brooms are made from the stems of the wild date palm (*Phoenix reclinata*) and larger brooms from the leaves of the ilala palm (*Hyphaene coriacea*). In South Africa's Limpopo Province and in Zimbabwe, hand brooms are made from bulrush leaves and larger brooms from the leafy stems of *Athrixia* species.

Aristida congesta |Poaceae| **TASSEL THREE-AWN**; *phuthadikgoba* (Sotho); *seloka* (Tswana); *ingongoni* (Zulu) ■ This is a hardy, short-lived perennial grass that typically occurs on roadsides and other disturbed places throughout all parts of southern Africa. It is sometimes used for thatching. Sotho people commonly use it to make brooms (Moffett 2010) but they also use *Aristida adscensionis*, *A. diffusa* and *A. junciformis* for soft brooms, and *A. bipartita* for outside brooms.

Aristida junciformis |Poaceae| **WIREGRASS**, gongoni three-awn; *umgongoni* (Zulu); *phuthadi-kgoba* (Sotho) ■ Wiregrass forms dense tufts of thin culms, up to 750 millimetres long. The grass is unpalatable and increases with overgrazing. It nevertheless has considerable value as a thatching grass, and good-quality brooms are also made from this species.

Arundinella nepalensis |Poaceae| ***LEHLAKAMANE*** (Sotho) ■ This grass is sometimes used as thatching by Basotho people (Moffett 2010).

Athrixia phylicoides |Asteraceae| **MOUNTAIN TEA** ■ See Chapter 6. In the Limpopo Province of South Africa, whole plants (or leafy stems tied in bundles) are commonly traded as popular brooms. The plant is also an important source of traditional tea, the details of which are given under beverages in Chapter 6.

Cymbopogon excavatus |Poaceae| **BROAD-LEAVED TURPENTINE GRASS**; *mosagasolo* (Tswana) ■ This robust grass is easily confused with other *Cymbopogon* species, but it has a characteristic erect growth form, with leaves high up on the culms and the leaf bases broader than the culms (Van Oudtshoorn 2012). The grass makes an aromatic and durable thatch and is particularly popular in Botswana.

Cymbopogon nardus (=*Cymbopogon validus*) |Poaceae| **TAMBUKI GRASS**, giant turpentine grass; *umqunga* (Xhosa); *reuse terpentyngras, tamboekiegras* (Afrikaans) ■ Tambuki grass is a robust perennial that grows to a height of more than two metres. It is similar to *Hyparrhenia* species but can easily be distinguished by the bitter taste of the leaves and the turpentine-like smell. This grass is unpalatable but is one of the most popular thatch grasses of southern Africa (Johnson 1982; Shackleton 1990), perhaps because of its large size, local abundance and agreeable smell. The grass is often very thick, with culms of more than four millimetres in diameter, which is considered too coarse for commercial use (Long 1978). Xhosa huts are said to last for up to 25 years (Johnson 1982). The grass is an important resource, providing cheap building material and has the potential to supplement the income of people in rural areas.

The name "tambuki grass" is sometimes used as a synonym for "thatching grass". It is actually also a common name for several species of *Cymbopogon*, *Hyparrhenia* and *Miscanthidium* and includes almost all of the most important traditional thatching grasses (Smith 1966; Van Oudtshoorn 2012). According to Smith (1966), the name "tambuki" refers to a group of San people who were absorbed into the Bovana people (later called the Amathembu) who inhabited Tambukiland (later Tembuland) in the present-day Queenstown district of the Eastern Cape Province.

Hut thatched with broad-leaved turpentine grass (*Cymbopogon excavatus*)

Hand brooms made from *Athrixia phylicoides* (top) and *Aristida junciformis* (below)

Harvested tambuki grass (*Cymbopogon nardus*)

Cleaning and sorting broad-leaved turpentine grass (*Cymbopogon excavatus*)

Cyperus fastigiatus |Cyperaceae| **MOTHOTO** (Sotho) ■ The stems are used as temporary thatch in fields to protect crops and are also used for ropes and plaited mats (Moffett 2010). It is used in traditional medicine and ethnoveterinary medicine. Sotho people also use *Cyperus congestus*, *C. haematocephalus*, *C. marginatus* and *C. obtusiflorus* to make baskets, ropes and necklets.

Cyperus marginatus |Cyperaceae| **MATJIESGOED** (Afrikaans); |*harab* (Khoi) ■ The famous *matjieshuis* or beehive house, the traditional Nama desert dwelling, is made from mats of *Cyperus marginatus* or from some other reeds such as *hardebiesies* (see *Pseudoschoenus inanus* or *Juncus acutus*). *Cyperus marginatus* is widely distributed in the dry parts of southern Africa (Snijman 2013). It is also used as a thatch in Namibia (Van den Eynden *et al.* 1992) and in Lesotho to weave mats, beer strainers, baskets and hats, including the well-known Basotho hat known as the *mokorotlo* (Moffett 2010). In former times, dried animal gut (mostly from goats) was used to sew the culms together to form the mats. Nowadays, machine-made rope is often used. To make a house, the mats are neatly wrapped over curved poles and tied down. The entrance is covered with a vertical mat, which is rolled up and tied in a roll when the house is occupied. Visitors can therefore tell from a far distance if someone is at home or not.

There are interesting reasons why the *matjieshuis* is such an effective desert dwelling. In dry weather, the culms shrink, leaving small gaps between them and allowing for air movement through the house. In wet weather (a rare occurrence in Namaqualand) the culms swell out and become watertight, thereby offering protection from the rain and cold winds. When the nomadic lifestyle demands a trek to better grazing, the lightweight mats are simply rolled up and carried along.

Until recently, the *matjieshuis* often functioned as a tent when Karoo, Bushmanland and Namaqualand farmers came to town for the annual religious gathering (*Oktobernagmaal*), which usually lasted for ten days or longer. During this period, babies were baptised, sons and daughters were married and important commodities were traded. An example from the small town of Nieuwoudtville in the Northern Cape Province of South Africa is shown here.

The cultural prominence of the *Cyperus marginatus* resource (*matjiesgoed*) in former times is reflected in the numerous farms and other places bearing the Afrikaans name *Matjiesfontein* ("fountain where mat material can be found"). In the dry semi-desert region of southern Africa, these fountains were not only crucial sources of water, but they had commercial value and are therefore said to have been places of strategic and political importance in bygone days.

Cyperus textilis |Cyperaceae| **UMBRELLA SEDGE**; mat sedge; *matjiesgoed, matjiestou* (Afrikaans); *umzi, imisi* grass (Xhosa); *imusi* (Zulu) ■ The stems (culms) of various *Cyperus* species are used in southern Africa to make the traditional sleeping mat (*makhuku* in Xhosa, *icansi* in Zulu, *matjies* in Afrikaans). These include *C. textilis*, *C. natalensis*, *C. latifolius* and *C. sexangularis*.

Cyperus textilis is a robust sedge found in wet places from Piketberg to Cape Town and from there to the Eastern Cape and southern KwaZulu-Natal. The plant has erect stems or culms with a tuft of long, flat leaves at the tips. According to Dold & Cocks (2012) this species is known as *umzi* and is a popular source of material for making mats and baskets in the Eastern Cape. It is similar to *Cyperus natalensis* and *C. latifolius*, both of which are also used for mats. The latter is known as *ikhwane* in Zulu and is traditionally used for making sleeping mats in the Mbongolwane wetland near Eshowe in KwaZulu-Natal. The angular stems make it easy to distinguish *C. sexangularis*, which is also commonly used for sleeping mats. In the Ingwavuma district of KwaZulu-Natal, non-traditional floor mats are made from the leaves of *C. latifolius* (Cunningham 1987).

To make the traditional sleeping mat, the stems are cut, dried in the shade, punctured at regular intervals and then sewn together. *Cyperus papyrus*, the well-known papyrus with its thick, triangular culms and rounded tufts, is used in northern Botswana for sleeping mats (Terry 1994). The split stems are sewn together with rope rolled from the *mokotsi* plant (*Sansevieria pearsonii*).

THATCHING, MATS & BROOMS

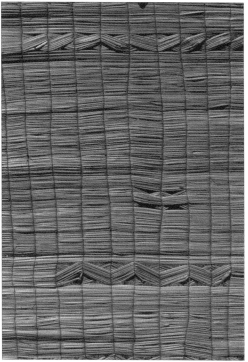

Sleeping mat (*makhuku* in Xhosa) made from *imisi* grass (*Cyperus textilis*)

The method of making sleeping mats from *imisi* grass (*Cyperus textilis*)

Plants of *imisi* grass or *matjiesgoed* (*Cyperus textilis*)

Temporary *matjiesgoed* shelter on Nieuwoudtville Church Square, October 1984

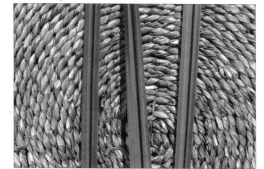

Non-traditional floor mat made from the fibrous leaves of *ikhwani* grass (*Cyperus immensus*)

Deverra denudata |Apiaceae| ***VEEBOS*** (Afrikaans) ■ The plant is a robust virgate shrub with many leafless stems arising from a woody rootstock. Small yellow flowers are borne in typical umbels, followed by small hairy fruits. The stems are used in the Agter-Hantam region of South Africa to make brooms (*vee* means "to sweep").

Elegia tectorum (=*Chondropetalum tectorum*) |Restionaceae| **CAPE THATCHING REED**; *Kaapse dekriet* (Afrikaans) ■ The plant is a decorative reed which forms attractive clumps of dark green culms, up to one and a half metres in height. Male and female plants differ considerably in appearance when in flower. Cape thatching reed is widely distributed in the regions around Cape Town and was once an important and popular thatch, but nowadays the Albertinia thatching reed (*Thamnochortus insignis*) has become the main commercial species. *Elegia tectorum* is, however, often seen in gardens as an ornamental plant and has become very popular in landscape gardening in all parts of southern Africa. It may be distinguished by the deciduous leaves (represented by dry, bract-like structures) which fall off early to leave a dark brown or black ring at each node. In *Thamnochortus*, the bract-like leaves remain on the culms indefinitely. Cape thatching reed is often used along the southern Cape coast as a thatch for fishermen's houses. It is also popular for making brooms. On the Cape west coast, *Thamnochortus spicigerus* (*duine dekriet*) is traditionally used for thatching.

Other Cape restios (family Restionaceae) used for broom making include *Thamnochortus fruticosus* (*besemriet*), *Elegia intermedia* (*besemriet*), *E. juncea* (*besemriet, duineriet*), *Cannamois virgata* (*bergbamboes, besemriet, olifantsriet*), *Restio leptoclados* (=*Ischyrolepis leptoclados*), *R. sieberi* (=*Ischyrolepis sieberi*) and *Restio triticeus*. *Restio sieberi* (also called *besemriet*) is especially popular in Namaqualand and the Cederberg for making brooms. The stems or culms are tied together in a rounded or flat bunch at the end of a sturdy stick. The ends are then neatly trimmed. These restio brooms or *rietbesems* have been popular at the Cape since early times, particularly for outside use (*werfbesem* in Afrikaans). Making and selling restio brooms is an important source of income for some Cape people.

Enneapogon scoparius |Poaceae| ***LEFIELO***, *jwang ba mafika* (Sotho); *dasgras* (Afrikaans) ■ This widely distributed grass is used by Sotho people to make brooms (Moffett 2010).

Eragrostis pallens |Poaceae| **BROOM LOVE-GRASS**; *muhonyi* (Thimbukushu); *gemsbokgras, olifantsgras* (Afrikaans) ■ This grass is commonly used in northern Botswana for thatching and for making brooms. According to Terry (1984) it is also popular for forming the interior of the coils in basketry.

Eragrostis gummiflua |Poaceae| **GUM GRASS**; *gomgras* (Afrikaans); *kgitapoho, dikonono* (Sotho) ■ The grass is easily recognised by its hard, perennial, tufted growth form and the presence of sticky glands on the leaf sheaths and nodes (Van Oudtshoorn 2012). According to Moffett (2010) it is used by Sotho people to make strong and long-lasting brooms.

Erica simii |Ericaceae| ***WASSOURA*** (Portuguese) ■ This plant is a shrub and occurs in small, dense stands on sandy coastal plains in the Beira area of Mozambique. According to Tony de Castro (pers. comm.) the branches are cut and sold for use as brooms.

Helichrysum tomentosulum |Asteraceae| ***ONGWAMBUNDU*** (Herero); *!uruheb* (Nama) ■ The plant is a spiny shrub from rocky areas in the Kunene Region (formerly Kaokoland). The branches are used as thatch for huts and shelters in dry areas where no grass is available (Malan & Owen-Smith 1974). Several medicinal uses have been recorded in Namibia (Von Koenen 2001). Thatching grasses used in this region include *ondorozu* (*Oryzidium barnardii*) and *orwandjandja* (*Sorghum verticilliflorum*).

Cape thatching reed (*Elegia tectorum*)

Albertinia thatching reed (*Thamnochortus insignis*)

Plant of *veebos* (*Deverra denudata*)

Mrs Zimri with a hand broom made from *besemriet* (*Restio sieberi*)

Hyparrhenia hirta |Poaceae| **COMMON THATCHING GRASS**; *dekgras* (Afrikaans); *leqokwana, mookwana wa tsephe* (Sotho) ■ The plant is a dense and erect tuft that often forms extensive stands along roadsides and disturbed places. Several species of *Hyparrhenia* are used as thatching and are all superficially very similar. This species can be distinguished by the four to seven hairy brown thorns on each flower cluster. The latter are borne in pairs and the two clusters are erect and close together in this species. The related *Hyparrhenia filipendula* and *H. anamesa* are both used as thatch and are often confused with *H. hirta*. Both these grasses usually have fewer than four awns per flower cluster and the two clusters or racemes point away from one another in these species, often downwards in *H. anamesa* (Van Oudtshoorn 2012). *Hyparrhenia hirta* is widely distributed over most parts of southern Africa, while *H. filipendula* is restricted to bushveld regions along the eastern part of southern Africa. Other popular thatching grasses include *nduli* grass or cottonwool grass (*Imperata cylindrica*) and yellow thatching grass (*Hyperthelia dissoluta*).

Thatching grass is cut in autumn or winter (March to August), after the first frost has killed the leaves. Harvesting is usually done with a sickle, but mechanical cutters are sometimes used. Hand cutting will produce about 50 to 100 bundles a day, and a mechanical cutter and binder about 6 000 bundles per day. Bundle sizes vary from region to region. In Botswana, most bundles are about two hands (37 to 41 centimetres) in circumference, while in South Africa they are usually one and a half hands (about 30 centimetres) in circumference (Van Voorthuizen & Odell, 1976). Commercial bundles are 75 to 100 millimetres in diameter in South Africa (Long 1978).

The grass is prepared by shaking each bundle vigorously to remove all loose material. The lower two-thirds of the stems are cleaned from leaves by repeatedly passing a sickle between them and working towards the thick ends. If high-quality thatch is required, the bundles are combed to remove all leaves. This operation is usually performed at the construction site but it may also be done in the field, immediately after harvesting. A comb is made by driving a row of nails into a horizontal pole, leaving even gaps of about 10 millimetres wide. Combed thatch is required for the bottom layer or *spreilaag* on a roof, immediately above the thatching battens.

The tools needed for thatching include a homemade thatching spade (*dekspaan* in Afrikaans), as well as a straight needle of about 300 millimetres long or a curved needle of about 600 millimetres long. The thatching spade is used to push the thatch into position to create an even surface. The needles are used to tie or "stitch" the bundles of thatch onto the thatching battens below – the short one is used if two persons do the stitching simultaneously (from above and below the roof); and the long, curved one if one person does the thatching from above. Bundles are butted against a level surface to make sure that the bottom ends are even. They are then thrown up to the thatcher, who unties the bundles and arranges them neatly in a row on the roof, butt end lowermost. Each bundle is tied (stitched) to the batten below, sometimes by using poles or thick wire along the length of each row to make sure that even pressure is applied, thus ensuring an even thatched surface. The next row is placed in such a way that it hides the poles or wire, thus forming a two-bundle thick layer of at least 150 millimetres thickness. Sometimes a laminated aluminium foil and building paper reinforced with fibreglass is placed between the *spreilaag* and the main thatch layer as protection against fire (Long 1878). The apex of the hut or ridge (if the roof is rectangular) is the most vulnerable part of the room and great care is taken to seal it completely. This is traditionally done with a thick layer of clay and cow-dung or a woven thatch cap. Nowadays, a manufactured galvanised metal cap is used, or cement reinforced with chicken wire. This cap, sealed and painted when dry, may form the capping. Expert thatchers also make the capping from bent thatch, which is carefully tied down to make it waterproof.

If properly laid with mature, high-quality grass, a roof will last about 25 to 30 years. A thatched roof has excellent insulation properties – usually better than most modern roof materials (Long 1978) – and ensures that the hut or house is cool in summer and warm in winter.

Roof being thatched with common thatching grass or *dekgras* (*Hyparrhenia hirta*)

Cutting yellow tambuki grass (*Hyperthelia dissoluta*)

Harvested thatch grass (*Hyparrhenia hirta*)

A truckload of good quality thatching grass (*Hyparrhenia hirta*)

Juncus acutus │Juncaceae│ ***BIESIE***, *hardebiesie, soutmoerasbiesie* (Afrikaans) ■ This species usually grows in brackish marshes or along dry river beds. It is a hard, tufted perennial of up to two metres in height. The leaves are round in cross-section and end in sharp, thorny tips. They are one of the most important sources of *matjiesgoed* in Namaqualand, which is used to produce the mats for making the traditional Nama *matjieshuis* (beehive house).

There is considerable confusion between the various grass-like plants that are traditionally used for thatching and for making mats, including true grasses, sedges (*biesies* in Afrikaans), rushes (*moerasbiesies* or *hardebiesies* in Afrikaans) and restios (*riete* in Afrikaans).

True grasses belong to the grass family or Poaceae (also called Gramineae) and can be recognised by the generally hollow stems and the open leaf sheaths. They are commonly used for thatching and weaving (and for brooms) but rarely for making mats.

The genera *Cyperus*, *Pseudoschoenus* and *Schoenoplectus* belong to the sedge family (Cyperaceae), typically with solid but spongy stems that are often triangular or at least somewhat angular in cross-section, and closed leaf sheaths (the leaves are often partially or completely fused to the stems). These plants are rarely used for thatching but they are very popular for weaving and especially for mat making.

The rush family (Juncaceae) is represented by a single genus, *Juncus*. Although quite variable, the plants closely resemble some sedges (species of Cyperaceae) but it is usually not the stems but rather the stem-like leaves (round in cross-section and typically hard, not spongy) that are used for making mats. The leaf tips are often spiny and extend beyond the inflorescences.

The restios (family Restionaceae) are easily recognised by their round (terete), solid and practically leafless stems (leaves are represented by small brown bracts) and their dioecious habit (male and female flowers occur on separate plants). The species are notoriously difficult to identify because it is often difficult to see which male and female plants belong together. Restios typically occur in fynbos vegetation and are used for thatching and brooms, but not for weaving.

Juncus kraussii │Juncaceae│ **SALTMARSH RUSH**, matting-rush; *uduli* (Xhosa); *incema* (Zulu); *soutmoerasbiesie* (Afrikaans) ■ The plant grows in shallow water and has long, slender, stem-like leaves arising from a rhizome which grows in the mud. It can be distinguished from the similar *Juncus rigidus* (Obermeyer 1985) by the more compact flower cluster, the dense groups of flowers, the capsules which are as long as the petals (not longer) and the coastal distribution (*J. rigidus* is an inland species of salt pans and brackish places).

Juncus kraussii has a very wide distribution in the southern hemisphere and occurs in South America, Australia and Africa. In southern Africa, it is relatively rare and occurs mainly in the estuaries along the northeastern coast of southern Africa, particularly the Kosi Bay and St Lucia systems. Intense harvesting pressure has resulted in concern about the sustainability of the resource and conservation measures (controlled harvesting) have been developed to ensure sustainability. Heinsohn & Cunningham (1991) have shown that the plant can easily be cultivated in freshwater paddy fields. Since the stems are one of the favourite weaving materials in parts of KwaZulu-Natal (especially for making the traditional sleeping mat or *icansi*) it is an important source of income for rural people. Sleeping mats made from the thin, strong *incema* stems are of a high quality and they last much longer than similar mats from *Cyperus* and *Schoenoplectus* species. These high-quality mats are sold at a much higher price and can easily be recognised by the thin stems and contrasting yellow and brown colours.

Stems of the plant (split lengthwise, then rolled and twisted) are also the favourite material for making the traditional beer strainers called *iintluzo* in Xhosa (Dold & Cocks 2012). The flexible beer strainer, traditionally used to strain fermented home-brewed beer, is one of the best examples that demonstrates the remarkable skill associated with indigenous arts and crafts.

THATCHING, MATS & BROOMS

Plant of *biesie* or *hardebiesie* (*Juncus acutus*)

Flowering stems of the *hardebiesie* (*Juncus acutus*)

A flowering plant of the saltmarsh rush or *incema* (*Juncus kraussii*)

Traditional Zulu *icansi* (sleeping mat) made from the stems of *incema* grass (*Juncus kraussii*)

Miscanthus capensis |Poaceae| **DABA GRASS**, east coast broom grass; *mothala* (Sotho); *umtala* (Zulu) ■ The plant is a tall, robust grass of up to 2.4 metres in height. It is endemic to southern Africa and is distributed mainly along the eastern parts, from the Eastern Cape to the Free State, Lesotho and KwaZulu-Natal. According to Moffett (2010), the culms are used by Sotho people when constructing a hut. The grains are used as a famine food and children chew on the sweet rhizomes.

Miscanthus junceus |Poaceae| **WIRELEAF DABA GRASS**; *moxa* (Tswana) ■ The grass grows in wet places such as river banks, vleis and marshes. The leaves are round and solid in transverse section and the flowers are borne in a feathery clusters. It is endemic to southern Africa and is the most common grass in the Okavango Delta, where it is harvested for thatching. The thick, hollow stems are used for fencing in the same way as those of the common reed (*Phragmites australis*).

Phragmites australis |Poaceae| **COMMON REED**; *umhlanga* (Zulu); *lehlaka* (Sotho, Tswana); *fluitjiesriet, vaderlandsriet* (Afrikaans); *hanta(m)* (Khoi) ■ The plant is a large bamboo-like grass with erect, unbranched stems. When the leaves fall off, the leaf sheaths surrounding the stems are left behind. The flowers are hairy and are borne in large tufts at the tips of the stems. This truly cosmopolitan grass is found in all parts of the world and is very common in southern Africa. It occurs not only in high rainfall regions but also in seasonally wet places and along temporary rivers in the Karoo and other arid regions. The plants often form vast stands (called reed beds). A second species, the lowveld reed (*Phragmites mauritianus*) also occurs in southern Africa. It may be distinguished from the common reed by the sharp-tipped leaves (Van Oudtshoorn 2012).

The thick, hollow stems are an important building material in the subtropical parts of southern Africa. They are widely used for walls and bomas though rarely for thatching. Neat fencing around huts, houses, fireplaces and swimming pools is made by tying the reeds close together onto horizontal support poles. These fences are a distinctive feature of the bushveld regions of southern Africa. In Botswana, traditional sitting mats are made from these reeds and they are occasionally used in basketry (split stems are woven to make large winnowing baskets). Stems are also used for arrow shafts, tobacco pipes and musical instruments. According to Smith (1966), it was used to make toy whistles (*fluitjies* in Afrikaans) but children in Namaqualand make a whistling sound by blowing on a piece of leaf stretched between the thumbs. In Lesotho, the stems are used in hut building and the rhizomes are chewed as a famine food (Moffett 2010). Women use it to make a musical instrument known as *lekoope*.

The common reed is often confused with the non-indigenous and invasive Spanish reed (*Arundo donax*). Spanish reed (*spaansriet* in Afrikaans) has also been traditionally used in the Cape to make the reed ceiling (*rietplafon* in Afrikaans) that is still commonly seen in Cape Dutch style rural houses. The plant is native to the Mediterranean region and the Middle East but has been cultivated in South Africa since early colonial times. It has become highly invasive and does not necessarily grow in or near water as is the case with the common reed. Spanish reed is a taller plant with broad lobes at the base of the leaf blade (there are no leaf lobes in the common reed). The inflorescences are erect and dense (not sparse and directed to the side as in the common reed). Another difference is the ligule (situated where the leaf blade is attached to the sheath): it is inconspicuously hairy in Spanish reed but has long, thin, soft hairs in the common reed.

According to Raper *et al.* (2014), the Hantam River in the Western Karoo in South Africa was once known as *Vaderlandsrietrivier*, which was apparently a direct translation of the original Khoi name for the river. The name was derived from the Khoi words *han* (fathers, *ha* means father) and *t'a* (reed). The name *Hantam* therefore seems to have originated from the Khoi word *hanta* ("the reed of our forefathers", i.e., *P. australis*) and not from *heyntame* (the Nama word for red-rooted species of *Pelargonium*), as was previously suggested by Smith (1966).

Bundles of the coarse thatching grass known as wire-leaf daba grass (*Miscanthus junceus*)

Fence in northern Botswana made from common reed (*Phragmites australis*)

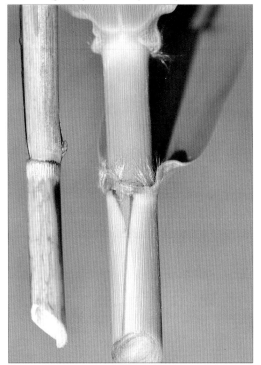

Stems of common reed (*Phragmites australis*)

Stems of the Spanish reed or *spaansriet* (*Arundo donax*)

Traditional *rietplafon* (reed ceiling) made from *Phragmites australis* or *Arundo donax*

Pseudoschoenus inanus |Cyperaceae| ***MATJIESGOED***, *matjiesriet, hardebiesie* (Afrikaans); mat sedge ■ The plant is an erect tuft with smooth stems or culms, sometimes about a metre in length but often more than two and a half metres long. The stems are hairless, round in cross-section, firm in texture and without nodes. Small reddish-brown flowers are produced in clusters of about 150 millimetres long and the female flowers form small dark brown nuts.

Pseudoschoenus inanis (previously known as *Scirpus inanus* or *S. spathaceus*) occurs over large parts of southern Africa (Snijman 2013). It is particularly abundant in the western parts, where it was commonly used by the Nama people, together with *Afroscirpoides dioicus* (=*Scirpus dioicus*) and *Juncus acutus*, to produce mats for building the traditional Nama beehive huts (see also *Cyperus marginatus* and *Juncus acutus*). Unlike *Cyperus marginatus*, which is naturally soft and spongy in texture, the much firmer *hardebiesie* has to be softened before it can be threaded into a mat. The stems are moistened and left under a wet blanket until needed for threading. In the old days, a sharp bone needle and dried animal gut was used, but later metal needles and machine-made rope replaced the traditional materials. In the dry climate of Namaqualand, a *hardebiesie* mat, if well made, will last for several decades.

A traditional Nama house is shown here. As explained under *C. marginatus*, the house is well ventilated in hot weather, because the culms shrink under hot, dry conditions, but seals quite tightly in cold, wet weather when the culms take up moisture and expand to fill the gaps. Note that the door mat is rolled up, thus signalling potential visitors from afar that the occupants are home.

Details of the construction method are summarised by Geldenhuys (1991). Poles or laths were cut, debarked with a pocket knife, bent into a curve and then tied together while still wet (green). After a few days of drying, the poles are untied and they are now permanently bent. A round clay floor is prepared. Material from crushed anthills is often compressed to give the desired floor covering. About 40 or 50 bent poles are now implanted around the floor, and the top ends of opposite poles are tied together with thongs. Thinner, bent poles tied to the uprights are cross-laths, and the whole structure is covered with mats in such a way that the upper mats overlap the lower ones. As a result, rainwater will run down along the mats and there will be no leakage. The size of the house depends on the size of the family, but a second house is usually constructed if the family increases in number. Cooking is not done inside the house, but in a separate cooking shelter some distance away from the house.

The cooking shelter or *skerm* is usually constructed by piling up layers of plant material. *Asbos* (*Mesembryanthemum* species, formerly *Psilocaulon* species) is often used, but sometimes also other species of mesembs or euphorbias). Soil may be added between the layers to firm the structure down and to make it more effective against the cold night winds. As protection against rain, a dome-shaped shelter may be constructed from mats at the one edge of the *skerm*. This shelter is similar to the beehive house but it is completely open on the one side.

Pseudoschoenus and *Juncus* species were also used by early colonists as thatch for a very specific type of pioneer dwelling known as a *hartebeeshuis* or wattle-and-daub hut (Geldenhuys 1991). These houses were rectangular in shape and were once a common sight in the dry interior of South Africa, where *Pseudoschoenus* or *Juncus* stems were available for tying down onto the cross-laths as thatch. Geldenhuys (1991) describes the construction method. The Voortrekkers apparently built the *hartebeeshuis* before more permanent buildings were erected, but several other types of pioneer houses are known, including *kapstyl* houses, corbelled houses, square houses, clay houses, sod houses and brack-roofed houses (Geldenhuys 1991). The name *hartebees* house is a corruption derived from the word *hardebiesie* ("tough rush") and has no connection with the hartebeest antelope (Smith 1966).

Pseudoschoenus and *Juncus* species are generally poorly known and their uses have not been systematically recorded, so that precious cultural knowledge may be lost already.

Typical beehive hut or *matjieshuis* in Namaqualand

Plants of *matjiesgoed* or *hardebiesies*
(*Pseudoschoenus inanus*)

Matjiesgoed being softened under a wet blanket

Raphia australis |Arecaceae or Palmae| **KOSI PALM**, raphia palm; *umvuma* (Zulu) ■ The Kosi palm is a tall, erect, single-stemmed tree with enormous leaves more than nine metres in length. The leaves are thought to be amongst the largest of all plants. The stems are covered with old leaf bases and numerous small breathing roots are present at the base of the stems (these also grow up out of the mud around the stem). The large flower cluster has male flowers towards the tip and female flowers lower down. The fruits are attractive cone-like structures with numerous glossy brown overlapping scales. Inside is a single seed surrounded by a thin layer of sweet flesh (the food of the famous palm-nut vulture, *Gypohierax angolensis*).

This large and graceful palm occurs only in the freshwater swamps in the extreme northeastern corner of South Africa. It is one of a few species of raphia palms, of which the tropical African ones are well known as a source of fibre known as raffia. The South African species was for a long time thought to be the same as the tropical African *Raphia vinifera*, but the latter has pendulous flower plumes, while those of the Kosi palm are erect and stand out above the leaves. Another species with drooping flower heads is the raphia palm (*R. farinifera*). It is called *muware* in Shona and has a limited distribution in Zimbabwe and Mozambique. The leaf stalks and midribs have been used to make furniture. *Raphia* species are short-lived and die after flowering.

The enormous leaves of *R. australis* are sometimes used for thatching, but they are not as widely used for this purpose as other raphia palms. The palm leaves are actually harvested mainly for the thick and strong leaf stalks and midribs, which are used for house construction and for rafts. These rafts are well known and have been used, probably since ancient times, as a means of transport across the swamps.

Schoenoplectus brachyceras |Cyperaceae| **NXOBOZI** (Zulu); *matjiesgoed* (Afrikaans); mat sedge ■ This plant was previously known as *Scirpus corymbosus* (Smith 1966). It is a tall sedge of up to three metres in height with bright green culms or stems and small clusters of inconspicuous brown flowers.

Schoenoplectus brachyceras occurs in the eastern parts of southern Africa and is found in wet places such as marshes and rivers. The plant is traditionally harvested for making mats, and it is particularly popular for the traditional Zulu sleeping mat or *icansi*. Along the coastal parts of KwaZulu-Natal, the thick spongy culms of a saline water sedge, *Schoenoplectus scirpoideus* (*uqumbu* in Zulu), are also used to make mats. The length of the culms and their spongy texture are given as the main reasons why *Schoenoplectus* species are favoured for making sleeping mats. However, they are considered to be inferior to *incema* (*Juncus kraussii*) and will not last as long as mats made from the thin, durable stems of the latter species.

Schoenoplectus species and their uses are poorly recorded, probably because the various genera and species of the family Cyperaceae are so difficult to identify, and are often mistaken for one another. When processed into a sleeping mat, it would be almost impossible to distinguish between *Schoenoplectus* and various other genera and species. In many cases, only a study of the anatomical structure of the culms would show which species had been used.

As with many natural resources, it is often the local availability that is important, rather than the actual physical features. When the populations of the favoured plant become depleted, substitutes may be found to replace the scarce resource. In recent years, plants traditionally used for mats have come under considerable pressure from craft workers, and conservation authorities had to start regulating harvesting activities in reserve areas. At St Lucia, for example, the harvesting of *incema* reeds (*Juncus kraussii*) in the estuary is nowadays only allowed in May. The long-term solution may be to cultivate *Juncus, Cyperus, Schoenoplectus* and other suitable sedges and rushes on a commercial basis in paddy fields, as is done in other parts of the world. Research work by the Institute for Natural Resources of the University of Natal (Heinsohn & Cunningham 1991) has shown that this may indeed be feasible.

THATCHING, MATS & BROOMS

Forest of Kosi palms (*Raphia australis*) at Kosi Bay

Stems of *nxobozi* (*Schoenoplectus brachyceras*) are used for making mats

Stems and flowers of *nxobozi* (*Schoenoplectus brachyceras*)

Sleeping mat made from the spongy stems of *uqumbu* (*Schoenoplectus scirpoideus*)

Stipagrostis uniplumis |Poaceae| **SILKY BUSHMAN GRASS**; *blinkaarboesmangras, witbees-gras, gemsbokgras, gemsboktwa, twaagras, toagras* (Afrikaans) ■ The grass is an erect, almost shrubby tuft with hard culms, tough rolled leaves and sparse, feathery flower clusters. Each flower has a distinctive feathery awn, which gives a silky appearance to the grass when it occurs in dense stands. Three varieties of silky bushman grass have been described, of which the variety *uniplumis* is the most common and widely distributed. There are 27 different species of the genus *Stipagrostis* in southern Africa, and several of them contribute to the unique texture and character of the Bushmanland and Kalahari landscapes. The vernacular name "bushman grass" applies to most species, with some qualifying word to distinguish between the species. The original San name is *toa, twaa* or *twa*, and this is perhaps a more appropriate name to use. Patterson first recorded in September 1778 that the San people in Bushmanland and Namaqualand used to collect the seeds of *Stipagrostis brevifolia* (*langbeentwagras*) from ant or termite nests (Smith 1966). The seeds were winnowed, stamped, mixed with water to make a dough and then cooked on the fire. Several explorers who visited the Gariep area confirmed this interesting early form of cereal use.

Stipagrostis uniplumis var. *uniplumis* is one of the most widely distributed of all African grasses and can be found in all dry savanna and desert regions from South Africa to Uganda, Somalia and Senegal. In southern Africa, it occurs over the whole of the dry interior and western parts, but the species is noticeably absent from the southern and eastern coastal regions. It is important as a dune stabiliser because the shrubby growth form reduces the impact of wind on the sand. In many parts, it is the dominant grass and therefore of importance in grazing. In the Kunene Region (formerly Kaokoland), for example, it is considered to be an important grazing for cattle, even though it appears to be mainly palatable in the young stage.

The grass is the most important thatching used for shelters and huts in the Kalahari. Being tough and fibrous, it may last for many years. It is the dominant grass over most of the region, so that the thatch is easily replenished when the need arises. In the short rainy season, which rarely lasts for more than three months, large parts of the Kalahari are transformed into a waving grassland, with occasional deep-rooted trees such as camel thorn (*Vachellia erioloba*) and the Kalahari apple-leaf (*Lonchocarpus nelsii*) that survive on subsurface water during the dry season. The vegetation of the Kalahari is classified as dry savanna and not true desert. The fact that no surface water is available for at least nine months of the year is perhaps the main reason for the popular perception that the Kalahari is a desert.

Poles of *Terminalia sericea* (*za'o* in the Kung language) are the preferred building material of the San people in the Kalahari for the upright poles of the hut, but *Senegalia mellifera* (*g!âu* in Kung) is also sometimes used. The poles are planted in a circle and the ends are tied together with *Terminalia sericea* bark. The flexible roots of the latter are used as cross-laths, tied firmly with bark. Two large poles are placed close together to form a narrow gap for an entrance. As protection against wild animals, the entrance is closed off at night by inserting a thick log as "door" between the two "doorposts".

Stipagrostis uniplumis is the main source of thatch grass, with *Schmidtia bulbosa* and *Eragrostis lehmanniana* having been recorded as minor sources. The tufts are not cut, but are simply pulled out of the ground for use, roots and all. The thatch is not neatly arranged – the tufts are simply packed onto the wooden framework of the shelter without tying them down. Loose poles may be placed against the outside to help keep the thatch in position.

It is generally believed that the San people of the Kalahari are nomadic and never stay in one place for any length of time. This idea may be questioned if one considers the distinctive and interesting architecture of the typical San huts, which are remarkably uniform in design over most parts of the Kalahari. These shelters, rough and unsophisticated as they may be, have a unique style and character.

Stands of silky bushman grass (*Stipagrostis uniplumis*) in the central Kalahari

The typical San hut, thatched with silky bushman grass (*Stipagrostis uniplumis*)

Thamnochortus insignis |Restionaceae| **ALBERTINIA THATCHING REED**; *Albertinia dekriet, dekriet* (Afrikaans) ■ The plant is a tall tuft up to two and a half metres high. Male and female flowers occur on separate plants and differ markedly in appearance. The plant was originally restricted to the Albertinia district, but seeds fallen from loads of thatch in transit have resulted in a much wider distribution, from the Cape Peninsula to Port Elizabeth (Linder 1990). A thriving industry has developed in Albertinia, and the railway siding near the town has the name "Dekriet siding". It is said that 10 000 bundles can be loaded on the standard 39-ton open railway wagon (Long 1978).

Thatching reed has to be cut after the end of the growing season after the culms have hardened "ripened" sufficiently, but before the new growth is five centimetres long (Linder 1990). This is to avoid the thatch breaking at the nodes and pieces of thatch falling out of the roof (Hannes Conradie, pers. comm.). Cutting is traditionally done by sickle, with a leather glove to protect the hands from the sharp stubble. The culms are actually broken over the blade rather than cut (Long 1978). Portable brush cutters are sometimes used. The green culms are spread out until they change to a rich golden yellow colour and are then gathered and tied into bunches of about 75 millimetres in diameter (traditionally "as thick as a bottle"). *Cyperus textilis* culms were formerly used for tying, but nowadays sisal string is used. Bundles are stacked into large heaps until they are transported.

The skill of thatching is passed on from generation to generation. The increasing popularity of thatch-roofed houses has ensured that the traditional know-how is preserved. *Dekriet* roofs often last a little longer than grass, perhaps 30 to 35 years, but in dry regions up to 70 years (Linder 1990). Old timers in the thatching industry maintain that thatching reed tends to go mouldy in the summer rainfall regions, so that it is mainly used for the bottom layer or *spreilaag*, thus eliminating the need to clean (comb) the thatching grass.

Typha capensis |Typhaceae| **BULRUSH** ■ See Chapter 5. The leaves are stitched together to make traditional sitting mats, used to receive women visitors (McDonald 1940). Bulrushes are widely used in southern Africa for weaving and for making hand brooms.

REFERENCES AND FURTHER READING: Brink, M. & Achigan-Dako, E.G. (eds) 2012. *Plant resources of tropical Africa 16. Fibres.* PROTA Foundation, Wageningen / Backhuys Publishers, Leiden. **Cunningham, A.B. & Gwala, B.R. 1986.** Plant species and building methods used in Thembe Thonga hut construction. *Ann. Natal Mus.* 27: 491–511. **Cunningham, A.B. & Terry, M.E. 2006.** *African basketry.* Fernwood Press, Cape Town. **Dold, T. & Cocks, M. 2012.** *Voices from the forest.* Jacana Media, Johannesburg. **Dorrat-Haaksma, E. & Linder, H.P. 2012.** *Restios of the Fynbos.* Struik Nature, Cape Town. **Geldenhuys, H. 1991.** *Home construction and furniture of the pioneer trek farmers.* Unpublished notes, Worcester Museum. **Haacke, W.H.G. 1982.** Traditional hut-building technique of the Nama (with some related terminology). *Cimbebasia* Ser. B 3: 77–98. **Heinsohn, R.-D. & Cunningham, A.B. 1991.** Utilization and potential cultivation of the saltmarsh rush, *Juncus kraussii. S. Afr. J. Bot.* 57: 1–5. **Johnson, C.T. 1982.** The living art of hut building in Transkei. *Veld & Flora* 68: 109–110. **Knuffel, W.E. 1973.** *The construction of the Bantu grass hut.* Akademische Druck, Austria. **Liengme, C.A. 1981.** Plants used by the Tsonga people of Gazankulu. *Bothalia* 13, 3&4: 501–518. **Liengme, C.A. 1983.** A study of wood use for fuel and building in an area of Gazankulu. *Bothalia* 14,2: 245–257. **Linder, H.P. 1991.** The thatching reed of Albertinia. *Veld & Flora* 76: 86–89. **Long, K. 1978.** *Introductory guide to thatching.* National Building Research Institute, CSIR, Pretoria. **McDonald, C.A. 1940.** *The material culture of the Kwena tribe of the Tswana.* M.A. thesis, University of South Africa. **Malan, J.S. & Owen-Smith, G.L. 1974.** The ethnobotany of Kaokoland. *Cimbebasia* Ser. B 2,5: 131–178. **Moffett, R. 2010.** *Sesotho plant and animal names and plants used by the Basotho.* Sun Media, Stellenbosch. **Obermeyer, A.A. 1985.** Juncaceae. *Flora of Southern Africa* 4(2): 73–90. **Raper, P.E. 2014.** *New dictionary of South African place names.* Jonathan Ball, Johannesburg. **Shackleton, S.E. 1990.** Socio-economic importance of *Cymbopogon validus* in Mkambati Game Reserve, Transkei. *S. Afr. J. Bot.* 56(6): 675–682. **Shaw, E.M. & Van Warmelo, N.J. 1972.** Material culture of the Cape Nguni. 1. Settlement. *Ann. S. Afr. Mus.* 58,1: 1–101. **Smith, C.A. 1966.** Common names of South African plants. *Mem. Bot. Surv. S. Afr.* 35. **Snijman, D.A. 2013.** *Plants of the Greater Cape Floristic Region 2: The Extra Cape Flora.* South African National Biodiversity Institute, Pretoria. **Steyn, H.P. 1981.** Nharo plant utilization. An overview. *Khoisis* 1. **Van der Waal, C.S. 1977.** *Die woning en woonwyse onder die Venda.* M.A. thesis, University of Pretoria. **Van Oudtshoorn, F. 2012.** *Guide to grasses of southern Africa.* 3rd ed. Briza Publications, Pretoria. **Van Voorthuizen, E.G. 1976.** The mopane tree. *Botswana Notes and Records* 8: 223– 230. **Van Voorthuizen, E.G. & Odell, M. 1976.** Thatching in Botswana: the social-ecology of traditional construction. *Botswana Notes and Records* 8: 165–174. **Walton, J. 1948.** South African peasant architecture. Southern Sotho folk building. *Afr. Stud.* 7,4: 139–145. **Weiss, E.A. 1979.** Some indigenous plants used domestically by East African coastal fisherman. *Econ. Bot.* 31(1): 35–55.

THATCHING, MATS & BROOMS

Typical fisherman's house, thatched with Albertinia thatching reed (*Thamnochortus insignis*)

Loading Albertinia thatching reed (*Thamnochortus insignis*); note some plants in the foreground

Acknowledgements

This book has a very wide scope and many people contributed information, literature and photographic material. The publisher and authors would like to thank the following institutions and individuals:

The Department of Science and Technology and the National Research Foundation for funding the National Research Chair in Indigenous Plant Use (NRF Grant Number 8442). The University of Johannesburg for logistic and financial support over many years. The National Biodiversity Institute of South Africa for the use of its herbarium and library facilities (PRE and NBG) – A special word of thanks to Estelle Potgieter and Anne-Lise Fourie of the Library in Pretoria. Staff and students of the University of Johannesburg and the library staff of the University of the Witwatersrand. Staff of the Kleinplasie Farm Museum, Worcester, including Frieda Bastian, Johannes Malgas, Vyver van Aardt and especially Matty Malherbe of the library. A very special thanks to Veronica Roodt and Lenyatso July for unforgettable moments in the field. We would also like to thank the San community of Molapo for spontaneously sharing their rich knowledge of plant use. Thanks to the informants of D'Kar, Braam le Roux and Maude Brown of the Kuru Development Trust, Botswana and to the staff of the D'Kar library, for literature on San plant use. Lorella Ambrosano is thanked for translating Portuguese texts into English. The American Botanical Council provided HerbClip summaries.

Although based primarily on published literature, the information presented was substantially enriched and reinforced by numerous anecdotes provide by many people over a long period. All sources of verbal information are acknowledged in the text as personal communications.

Our sincere thanks and appreciation to the following persons, who shared information and anecdotes, and provided logistic support with fieldwork, photography and literature searches, or agreed to be photographed: Lukas Abrahams, Niklaas and Katrina Adams, Carl Albrecht, James Alleman, Claire Archer, Fiona Archer, Cynthia Arendse, Christina Baadjies, Jan Baadjies, Johanna Baardman, Sophie Basson, Dawid Bester, Mrs Bester, M.C. Botha, Linda Brady, André Brits, Gael Campbell, Sizwe Cawe, Jac Conradie, Johan Cloete, Stephanus Cloete, Alta and Erwin Coetzee, Louw Coetzer, Lita Cole, Maxie Compion, Bridget Corrigan, Anna Damara, Bettie de Beer, Josef de Beer, Michelle de Beer, Ben Dekker, Tony de Castro, Jan de Vynck, Chris de Wet, Gert Dirkse, Ken Dodds, Rosemary du Preez, Graham Duncan, Cathy Dzerefos, Joyce and Esmé Edgecome, Ulrich Feiter, Merissa Fillies, Lynn Fish, T.G. (Bird) Fourie, Coert Geldenhuys, Boris Gorelik, Earle Graven, Cathy Greever, Willem Hanekom, Patricia Hans, Dianne Hardien, Johannes Hekter, Manton Hirst, Margaret Hulley, Meraai Isaacs, Caroline Jacquet, Janavi Jardine, Louis Jordaan, Lenyatso July, Gift Kafundo, Lynn Katsoulis, Henok Kinfe, Japjap Klaase, Marinda Koekemoer, Rupert Koopman, Andries Kotze, Phillip Kubukele, Hein and Susan Lange, Peter Linder, Kolie and Ina Louw, Edward Mabogo, Oswald Macunga, Anthony Magee, Khathutselo Magwede, Solomon Mahlaba, Sylvia Malinga, John Manning, Coleen Mannheimer, Pat Marincowitz, Ashley Mashingo, Ncindani Maswanganyi, Matambo, Million Matonsi, David Matthe, Patricia Mawongo, Isaac Mayeng, Greg McCarthy, Mahlatse Mogale, Lodewyk Morries, Dineo Moshe, Annah Moteetee, Jan Muller, Tr. Dr. Mutwa, Vernie Naidoo, Mrs Ndlovu, Patrick Ndlovu, Geoff Nichols, the Nieuwoudts of Dwarsrivier, Nathaniel Nondyei, Janneke Nortje, Caroline Ntilashe, Chris Pattinson, Koos Paulse, Cassim Petker, Antoinette Pienaar, Patrick Pule, Domitilla Raimondo, Gail Reeves, Emmy Reinten, Veronica Roodt, Herman Rossouw, Ashton Ruiters, Colin Ruiters, Kobus and Elsa Schonken, AnneLise Schutte-Vlok, John Molefi Sekaji, Seth Seroka, Gordon Sink, Christo Smit, Ernst Smit, Gideon Smith, Marietjie Stander, Roger Stewart, Anna Stewe, Nico Steenkamp, Willem Steenkamp, Haffie Strauss, Jas Strauss, Livet Taferaai, Peter Takelo, Patricia Tilney, Jakop Tromp, Erika van den Heever, Ernst van Jaarsveld, Bosch van Oudtshoorn, Frits van Oudtshoorn, Sandy van Vuuren, Braam van Wyk, Herman van Wyk, Mariana van Wyk, Piet van Wyk, Teodor van Wyk, De Jong and Cecile van Zyl, Alvaro Viljoen, Deon Viljoen, Jan Vlok, Fanie Wagenaar, Buys Wiese, Johannes Willemse, Pieter Winter, Benjamin Zimri, Mrs Zimri and Menzizwa Zitoti.

Photographic contributions

All photographs are by Ben-Erik van Wyk and Nigel Gericke, except those listed below. These are arranged alphabetically from top to bottom and left to right according to photographer and page number: CSIR (Stellenbosch) 335a,b; David Brazier 25abcd; Sizwe Cawe 361e; Roger Culos (Wikimedia Commons) 47e; Josef de Beer 351b; Earle Graven 258a; Marinda Koekemoer 221d, 240c; John Manning 107a; Geoff Nichols 39c; Johann Pretorius 49h, 255c; Ton Rulkens (Wikimedia Commons) 65a; Patrick van Damme 37abce; Ryan van Huyssteen 65b; Frits van Oudtshoorn 23b,c; Braam van Wyk 61b; Eben van Wyk 33b, 89b, 338b, 367ef; Piet van Wyk 23e, 53d, 63d, 295a; Pieter Winter 141d.

Index

Names and page numbers in **bold** indicate main entries; page numbers in *italics* indicate photographs.